THE BLUE PULLMAN STORY

Fully Revised and Unabridged

Kevin Robertson and Mike Smith

crecy.co.uk

This book is dedicated to Ron Smith, father of co-author Mike Smith, who inspired his love of the Blue Pullman. 'Dad – thanks for the bath-time stories of your trips on the "beautiful Midland Pullman" and how you struggled to eat your soup!'

First published 2020 by Crécy Publishing Ltd

All rights reserved. No part of this book may be reproduced or transmitted in any form or by any means, electronic or mechanical, including photocopying, recording, scanning or by any information storage without permission from the Publisher in writing. All enquiries should be directed to the Publisher.

© Kevin Robertson and Mike Smith 2020

A CIP record for this book is available from the British Library

Publisher's Note: Every effort has been made to identify and correctly attribute photographic credits. Any error that may have occurred is entirely unintentional.

Printed in Bulgaria by Multiprint

ISBN 978 086093 688 6

Crécy Publishing Limited
1a Ringway Trading Estate, Shadowmoss Road, Manchester M22 5LH
www.crecy.co.uk

FRONT COVER Blue Pullman at St Pancras. Next stop Manchester, maybe Leicester/Nottingham? Note the single windscreen wiper only on the driver's side' this is believed to have been unique to this (unidentified) power car but was retro-fitted later. *Lawrence Hassall/Author's collection*

REAR COVER INSET FROM TOP Works drawings for the trains were still being passed from the builders to BR at least as late as September 1963.

Artwork by Stephen Millership. Available from https://www.redbubble.com/people/smillership/works/27563089-the-blue-pullman?p=poster

REAR COVER MAIN London Midland Region set again in standard formation: Motor First – Kitchen First – Parlour First – Parlour First – Kitchen First – Motor First. The leading vehicle M60093 shows a small blemish to the bodywork on the left-hand corner above the marker light. The location is almost certainly believed to be near Kimbolton on the former Midland Railway line from Bedford to Huntingdon.

FRONTISPIECE 'Midland Pullman' set at Bletchley on 2 May 1964 on a charter special for the Cup Final. It is believed the BP set operated from Sheffield Midland to St Pancras and return. (The match was between Preston North End – so no doubt who chartered the train – and West Ham United. West Ham won 3-2.) *Colour Rail/ Malcolm Thompson DE1625*

CONTENTS

Introduction to the 2020 edition 4
Bibliography 7
    Social media, books and magazines 7
    Films (DVDs and VHS) 8
    Internet sources 9
    References at national and local archives and museums 9
    A note on photographs and other sources 9
Acknowledgements 11
    Co-Author's note 11
Abbreviations and Glossary 12
    Description of Blue Pullman cars 13
Preface – One special day in 1960 14
Chapter 1. Blue Pullman – In the Modernisation Plan 16
Chapter 2. Blue Pullman – From a concept to a design (a difficult period) 41
Chapter 3. Blue Pullman – A testing time allied to publicity and an introduction to the public 61
Chapter 4. Blue Pullman – From aesthetics to engineering 96
Chapter 5. Blue Pullman – Are you being served – or not? The trials and tribulations of catering on the Blue Pullman 123
Chapter 6. Blue Pullman – Timeline 1. Pullman on the London Midland Region 1960-1966 134
Chapter 7. Blue Pullman – Timeline 2. Pullman on the Western Region 1960-1966 190
Chapter 8. Blue Pullman – Timeline 3. The years 1966-1973: 'Just *too many* trains!' 248
Chapter 9. Blue Pullman – Timeline 4. Progress and the end of the dream 301
Chapter 10. Blue Pullman – Artefacts, merchandise, collectibles and a new build? 324
Appendix 1. Bibliographies of the principal players 330
Appendix 2. Sample logs of runs and comments thereon 332
Appendix 3. Operating instructions WR: 'Working of Diesel Pullman Trains' 338
Appendix 4. Extracts from BR (WR): 'Multiple Unit Diesel Pullman Trains' 343
Appendix 5. Excerpt from BR North Eastern Region Sectional Appendix, 9–22 April 1966 345
Appendix 6. WR train reporting numbers 1960 to 1967 348
Appendix 7. Interior finish and paint schemes 349
Appendix 8. The 'Wells Fargo' workings. Extracts from Pullman Car Services Archive
    'The Blue Pullman Standby Pullman Sets' by Terry Bye 352
Appendix 9. British Railways Board, Operational Research Department. Blue Pullmans (Western Region) May 1965,
    Report No O.77. Blue Pullmans Western Region 359
Appendix 10. Charters, special runs and BR open days 367
Appendix 11. Pullman dates to traffic, withdrawal and disposal 374
Appendix 12: The official photo lists 378
Index 383

INTRODUCTION TO THE 2020 EDITION

Kevin Robertson:
'Welcome to this, the definitive story of the Blue Pullmans. If you are wondering why I have written another book on these charismatic trains it is because I wanted not to just consolidate the information that I had produced in the past, but also to take advantage of the many new sources of information and also images that have come to light since the publication of my 2005 hardback Blue Pullman, 2009 Blue Pullman Supplement *and* 2012 Blue Pullman Pictorial. Mike Smith and I met in consequence of my research and I quickly established Mike had a huge knowledge of the trains and via Philippa Dudek-Mason's social networking skills had access to information and people I was totally unaware of.

Conjoining efforts was the logical progression and I genuinely believe OUR book is all the richer as a result. Mike, thank you, as I could not have done this without you and of course Pip who deserves a special mention too!'

Mike Smith:
'My Dad Ron Smith was lucky enough to have six rides (more detail in Chapter 6) on the "Midland Pullman" and one of the many stories he would tell this little boy in the mid seventies was the detail of those trips. As the youngest child I poured through worn copies of my elder siblings book's such as TRAINS by Nelson and the Deans Gold Medal Book of World Travel *and* feasted on their marvellous illustrations of the Blue Pullman albeit with inaccurate captions about the 'Midland Pullman' going to Birmingham!

'We lived in Chorlton Cum Hardy in the suburbs of Manchester, and Dad told me the Blue Pullman went through Chorlton station. Of course this station had been closed years earlier and to me Central Station was a fairly scary old shack where we sometimes parked the car! Occasionally after school I could hear a slow noisy diesel Class 40 diesel freight train on the now single track in Chorlton and I watched from the bridge just hoping somehow a Blue Pullman would appear. Manchester Piccadilly was now the mainline station for the London route and I did see the reverse livery Mk2 electric loco hauled Manchester Pullman and later the newer style BR Executive livery on the Mk2s and newer Mk3s. None seemed as good looking as the Blue Pullman pictures I'd seen!

'By now though I was smitten with the Inter City 125 (and the APT-P) as the newest most exciting trains. I went to look for a Blue Pullman in the various museums and thought I had found one at York when I saw the HST prototype from the rear side view. Eventually I found out they were all scrapped and was also told they had an uncomfortable ride, which Dad had unwittingly told me years ago when laughing about his soup leaving the bowl on his trips. Given they now had Unicorn status I tried to find out everything I could about the Blue Pullmans so of course when Kevin's books came out I was very excited

'Would Sir care for a drink before we set off?' Pullman service seen from platform level. The vehicle is a first-class car – identified by the split glass and therefore two separate Venetian blinds. Also seen is one of 'those' table-lamps...

and I eagerly bought all three books, yet was still hungry for more information.

'I also collected what I could, including a working 1st class seat, a 2nd class seat from W60096 speedometer from M60090, builder's plates, blind winder, silver tea sets, ashtrays, books, models, etc and watched as many film clips as I could find. I love the sound they made, from the recordings we have; a beautiful rumble and under acceleration a bit of a supercharger whine. Even on the last day in service there was that nice low growl at speed, almost as if all those lions from the Pullman crests were purring.

'I had information myself that I provided the lovely Philippa (Pip!) with and loved seeing the input from others in The Blue Pullman group on Facebook. To hear from those who worked on, travelled on and watched the Blue Pullmans was a dream for me and the stories just get better and better.

'Terry Bye in his excellent Pullman newsletters uses the phrase "Information is for sharing, not gathering dust", so I started to share information with him and when told Kevin was doing a new book I started to send Kevin and Terry any information I had. Kevin's response was terrific and very kind.

'He appreciated any new information and was delighted to receive information, whether it added to his own research or even corrected his earlier writings. I couldn't quite believe it when Kevin, after three years of his own work writing the book, asked me to be co-author and to add in my own information and that from Pip's collection of personal recollections via The Blue Pullman Facebook group. I feel honoured and privileged to have been given this opportunity by Kevin and he has kindly allowed me to include my Dad's story. I can honestly say every conversation with Kevin is enjoyable be it about trains, our pet dogs or police cars etc etc…I have made a good friend and what can be better about a hobby than that!'

Kevin continues:

In addition to this, having been responsible for the original hardback of 2005 (is it really 15 years ago..?), and with this book, along with the 'Supplement', being out of print collector's items for some time now, and very few copies of the 'Pictorial' remaining, I wanted to combine their information into one cohesive volume. More importantly was to specifically include new information on the politics, design stages, operation, and difficulties in running that has only recently been accessed.

'Going back to 2005 I really thought, naively, there was little else to uncover. How wrong that turned out to be, for as with most research when a new fact is discovered it invariably leads to further questions being thrown up which were not considered before. Consequently in what follows there are any number of new revelations from both our investigations which might even appear trivial today but at the time I wrote the first book appeared as almost insurmountable. The number of "names" that also became involved both in the design/construction of the original train, and more recently who have so willingly given their time and information, is similarly amazing and so despite having referred to now being able to disclose plenty of "new information" in what follows, I will also say that in 2018 prior to Mike coming on board I had justifiable reason to believe there still remained a number of unanswered question which I felt would also probably remain unanswered.

'Fantastically, when Mike arrived on the scene many of these questions have now been answered not only through his persistent quest for accurate facts and the relationships built by and with Pip.'

Jointly:

What does come to be realised is that the 'modern' era of railway history can sometimes have greater gaps in its reporting when compared with years past. Why this should be is open to speculation, but it is possible that once an era has passed records were deliberately cast aside on the basis of space rather than malice. At the time it would have been defined as 'no longer relevant' and so never likely to be referred to again. Two of these relate to gaps in the era of the Modernisation Plan and the design of the actual train and are referenced in the early chapters of this work.

So far as the former is concerned we can only state what we have repeated within the text, and that is the scholarly work of David Clough in describing the Modernisation Plan is his own book – see bibliography – has saved the present authors countless hours of research. Indeed, without access to and permission from the publisher to quote from this work it is unlikely this new work would have been possible. Similarly, whilst fortunate to gain access to a newly available file on the design of the trains – together with all the trials and tribulations associated therewith – we had not realised how much of a one-sided approach that was, until reading David Lawrence's masterful *British Rail Designed 1948-97*. Naturally Blue Pullman forms just a very small part of both of these books, but we can honestly say that without the assistance of the two gentlemen in producing their own work it would have been foolhardy to commit to paper what – I can say with absolute certainly – will be Kevin's final involvement with the Blue Pullman story – although I cannot speak for Mike of course!

The story of the Blue Pullman sets must then be akin to a jigsaw, with what follows in the next pages and chapters an attempt to place the pieces in order and so produce a true picture of events. Within the text it is often convenient to refer to all five trains under the generic heading of 'Blue Pullman' which will be the case unless we need to refer to the specific region (or individual LMR or WR trains). In the early chapters we have deliberately concentrated as much on the politics and behind the scenes manoeuvring that went on as the technical aspects – most readers will we suspect know of the trains anyway. After the passage of time we think we have at least recognised where many of the pieces of the story actually fit; the trouble is, and as stated at the start we suspect, there are some pieces of our jigsaw which remain missing.

When writing about the Blue Pullmans a blinkered view can directly lead to one of two specific pitfalls of concentrated opinion, focusing firstly on the poor riding qualities of the

LMR (six-car) and WR (eight-car) Blue Pullman sets in revenue earning service. Quoting from the late O. S. Nock in his book *British Railways in Transition*, 'Jack Howe styled the vehicles in partnership with manufacturers Metro-Cammell. Howe later became known for designing the first British ATM machine, and he brought his understanding of form and material to the exterior and interior appearance of these trains. With George Williams he visited several European railways to study express trains. As a sophisticated, high-speed application of the diesel multiple-unit idea, the sets had driving cabs in the motor coaches at each end of the six- or eight-car formations. Jack Howe succeeded in combining the crisp aesthetic of the Great Western railcars (*see illustration on page 20*) with a unique form based on triangular panels joined by precise curved creases. Great Western influence is further evidenced by the crease carried up into the cab roof dome, shown in early artist's impressions as a definite ridge, but softened in production. The trapezoid windows set in their recessed panel around the cab fronts also suggested the inspiration of contemporary jet airliners such as the de Havilland Comet. Continuing the appearance of flat planes, the motor coaches and trailer carriages had near-straight sides, a form that would be taken forward for subsequent British Railways standard passenger coach designs. Howe kept the unit ends free from all unnecessary detail and placed the ventilation louvres in an ordered pattern – considering the initial overheating of the engine compartment did he in fact alter what had been proposed? Cab fronts were carried down around the buffer stocks, concealing the drawgear behind hinged doors. Three lamp units arranged across the front served as tail and head lights by the fitting of red or opaque covers. A redrawn version of the Pullman coat of arms, lavishly decorated in gold, replaced the initial plan for a four-character headcode box in the lower part of the cab fronts.' (The original design for the coloured coat of arms also had to be altered as the arms of Wales were produced incorrectly.) *Bill Chapman and Adrian Vaughan*

train, and secondly on the fact it has in recent years been described as the forerunner to the later HST. Both of these statements could be said to be true in part, but both are dependent totally upon the perspective presented and consequently neither avenue is pursued 'in-toto' in what follows and instead we have attempted to build a succinct picture of the lead up to the development, building, testing and operation of the sets where each of the earlier statements has its place but does not overshadow the complete picture. Having Mike on board has been very useful in getting a second opinion from someone fascinated by the Blue Pullman for all of his life and consequently he often presents an interesting insight.

You may disagree with our opinions, as indeed is your prerogative, and we have certainly not set out to be intentionally obdurate. Blue Pullman was, we would suggest, in many ways an enigma and as mentioned earlier, somehow we doubt we will ever know all that went on!

Kevin Robertson, Berkshire 2020 and Mike Smith, Cheshire 2020

Note: The authors have no known connection with other individuals having the same surnames mentioned in the text either at British Railways or Metropolitan-Cammell.

BIBLIOGRAPHY

Social media, books and magazines
This Facebook group is free to join where Mike Smith and Simon Altham will make you most welcome. Many photographs and Blue Pullman discussions https://www.facebook.com/groups/thebluepullman/

A Pictorial Record of British Railways Diesel Multiple Units, Brian Golding, Cheona Publications, 1995

Backtrack, various issues.

'Blue for You!' Article by Adrian Curtis in July 2002 issue of *Traction* Magazine.

Blue Pullman, Kevin Robertson, Kestrel Railway Books 2005.

Blue Pullman Supplement, Kevin Robertson, Noodle Books 2009.

Blue Pullman Pictorial, Kevin Robertson, Noodle Books 2012.

Bristol Railway Panorama, Colin Maggs, Millstream Books, 1990.

British Rail 1948–1978 A Journey by Design, Brian Haresnape, Ian Allan, 1979.

British Rail DMUs & Diesel Railcars, Brian Morrison, Ian Allan, 1998.

British Rail Designed 1948–97, David Lawrence, Ian Allan, 2016, reprinted Crecy Publishing 2017.

British Rail Mark 2 Coaches Michael Harris, Mallard/Venture Publications, 1999.

British Railways 1948–73. A Business History, T. R. Gourvish, Cambridge University Press 1986.

British Railways Engineering 1948–80, John Johnson and Robert A. Long, Mechanical Engineering Publications Ltd, 1981.

British Railways Illustrated, various issues of magazines and annuals, Irwell Press.

British Railways in Transition, O. S. Nock. Thomas Nelson & Sons, 1963.

British Railways Magazine – London Midland Region, various issues. Published by British Railways.

British Railways Magazine – Western Region, various issues. Published by British Railways.

British Railways Mark 1 Coaches, Keith Parkin. Published by the HMRS, 2006 edition.

British Trains of Tomorrow, G. Freeman Allen, Ian Allan (c1960).

Design No 171 March 1963 (Special issue on British Railways), The Council of Industrial Design.

Diesel Railway Traction; issues for 1960.

Disconnected – Broken Links in Britain's Rail Policy, Chris Austin and Richard Faulkner, Ian Allan 2015.

Do You Know About Railways?, Collins 1964.

Hydraulic vs Electric, The Battle for the BR Diesel Fleet. David N. Clough, Ian Allan 2011.

Locospotters Annual 1962, G. Freeman Allen, Ian Allan, 1962.

Locospotters Annual 1971, G. Freeman Allen, Ian Allan, 1971.

Looking Back at DMUs II, Kevin Derrick, Strathwood, 2019.

Metro-Cammell, 150 years of Craftsmanship, Keith Beddoes et al, Runpast, 1999.

Modelling Railways in O Gauge, John Emerson, The Crowood Press, 2016.

Modern Railways, various issues.

Modern Railways Profile No 10, Colin Marsden, Ian Allan.

On and Off the Rails, Sir John Elliot, George Allen and Unwin, 1982.

Pullman, Julian Morel, David & Charles, 1983.

Pullman in Europe, George Behrend, Ian Allan, 1962.

Pullman Trains in Britain, R. W. Kidner, Oakwood Press, 1998 'Signalling the Blue Pullmans' by Adrian Vaughan.

Railways on the Screen, John Huntley, Ian Allan, 1993.

Railway World Annual 1979, Published by Ian Allan, specifically pages 76-79 *The Changing Face of British Railways.* Bruce Peter, Lily Publications 2018.

The Golden Way, published by the Pullman Society – various issues but particularly Nos 62-64 Autumn 2001–Spring 2002 article(s) by Charles Long.

The GWR Exposed: Swindon in the days of Collett and Hawksworth by Jeremy Clements. Published OPC, 2015.

The GWR Gas Turbines – a myth exposed, Kevin Robertson, Alan Sutton 1989.

The Modernisation Plan: British Railways: Blueprint for the Future, David Clough, Ian Allan, 2014.

The Railway Gazette, particularly June 1960.
The Railway Magazine, various issues.
The Railway Observer (various issues, 1959–1973), The Railway, Correspondence and Travel Society.
The Railwaymen (Volume 2): The History of the National Union of Railwaymen, Philip S. Bagwell, Harper Collins, 1982.
The Western Since 1948, G. Freeman Allen, Ian Allan, 1979.
Traction Magazine, various issues including Nov 1997 and July 2002.
Trains Illustrated and its successor *Modern Railways,* (various issues) Published Ian Allan.
Two miles a minute, O. S. Nock, Patrick Stephens, 1980
Other references are mentioned in the text.

Films (DVDs and VHS)

British Pathe First Diesel Pullman *The Best of British Transport Films (70th anniversary)* contains a Blu-Ray HD version of BTF's 'Blue Pullman' ASIN B07NBP8JZY.
Blue Pullman by Kingfisher Productions contains: The Metro-Cammell construction films BFT's Blue Pullman.
Let's go to Birmingham/London to Birmingham in four minutes – a speeded up view taken from the cab of a WR set depicting a complete run over the WR Birmingham main line. (Sadly the driver is Ernie Morris who later died in the 1963 Knowle and Dorridge crash using 'Wells Fargo' stand-in Pullman stock).
On and Off the Rails produced as part of the British Transport Films collection series also contains the BTF Blue Pullman films.
In 2019 *Blue Pullman* was shown on the satellite channel 'Talking Pictures' in High Definition. See http://www.britishtransportfilms.co.uk/productions/films/BT0429/BT429.html.
Buster Keaton: The Genius Crushed By Hollywood also uses clips of the BTF Blue Pullman film to portray the exterior of a train Keaton is travelling on in the USA!
Men of Steam from 1962 with Sir John Betjeman has some great footage of the 'Bristol Pullman' including sounds.
A WR set appears twice in the 1963 British Transport Film *Snow* in both a panoramic view and seen in a passing shot from an adjacent track at slow speed plus inside shots.
A Blue Pullman set also featured in the 1965 film *Be My Guest* starring David Hemmings and various musicians.

A Nanking Blue Western unit appears in the 1965 comedy Norman Wisdom film *The Early Bird* where Norman plays the part of a milkman. Given the early white staff uniforms of the Western Region crews, this would seem quite fitting. The Pullman appears to demolish Norman's hand cart (with the help of some special effects miniatures depicting the handcart on a level crossing) and Norman gets covered in eggs, yoghurt and cream!
Modern Traction Classic Archive The Vintage years Vol 5 by Telerail ref MTRCT5 features the units.
Diesel and Electric Archives by Transport Video Publishing.
Diesel and Electric on 35mm with John Huntley (Vol 1 to 3).
London Railways in the 1960s Timereel London on Film. Incredible colour film of the Nanking Blue Blue Pullman.
Cab Compendium. The Western Way by Globe Video has some brief but great footage inclusive of engine sounds and even shows the last run.
Look at Life Series 2 Episode 5 'Transport' has some lovely 'Midland Pullman' footage.
A small mention and two clips of the Blue Pullman are in Vol 1 of the excellent *Power of The HSTs Vol 1 and Vol 2* by Transport Video Publishing with the 125 Group https://www.125group.org.uk/
Blue Pullman interest firms on You Tube films at time of writing (subject to deletion) are:
An early shot of a Western Pullman entering Paddington here https://www.youtube.com/watch?v=PSDLo9ovhAo
Jeremy Turner's amazing childhood footage of units awaiting scrapping/burnt and cut frames plus lots of Briton Ferry loco action https://www.youtube.com/watch?v=RrQwU7bGWTY&t=115s
Unknown origin footage of the 'Birmingham Pullman' sounding like a jet at Hatton Hill https://www.youtube.com/watch?v=56MSgkR7esk
1962 Blue Pullman passing Taplow https://www.youtube.com/watch?v=qsUvJ2BxFcg
1964 'Midland Pullman' at Nottingham Midland Station https://www.youtube.com/watch?v=cJhxz8aU5BA_
1964 'Midland Pullman' in Nottingham https://www.youtube.com/watch?v=srr5vX0xuAQ
The advert for the short lived 2006 HRT Charter Blue Pullman using Mk2s https://www.youtube.com/watch?v=KQrR0N7rqMs&t=204s.
Railway Roundabout Revisited.

In addition there are many films showing all makes and sizes of model Blue Pullman (Hornby Triang/Graham Farish/Bachmann/Kitmaster/Various O gauge/Mardyke Ride on) and the 2006 Blue Pullman in action.

Readers may also wish to explore 'Flickr' and other similar sites where it seems a regular amount of Blue Pullman images appear.

The making of the 'Blue Pullman' film and Captain Crewdson's Westland Widgeon helicopter used in the shoot as seen from the train.

Internet sources
Stuart Mackay's excellent DMU website has comprehensive Blue Pullman information and there was a good information exchange between Stuart and the authors. https://railcar.co.uk/type/blue-pullman/summary

For details of the dining staff strike see: https://www.marxists.org/history/etol/newspape/lr/vol05/no01/arundel.htm

References at national and local archives and museums
(Additional and/or specific sources are referenced within the text.)

At the National Archives (Public Record Office) Kew:
  AN5/5 (repeats Rail 420/422) also AN 5/3
  AN7/185
  AN13/1523
  AN43/23
  AN90/56
  AN92/291
  AN97/291, 296 and 297
  AN109/956 and 1122
  AN139/285 and 294
  AN142/89
  AN143/23
  AN156/754
  AN160/70 (noted as a 'Secret file' – *see comment on p47*), 71, 559 and 560
  AN167/848, 849, 851 and 852
  AN172/1, 2, 3, 294, 295 and 296
  AN173/19
  AN 174/1731
  AN185/119
  Rail 420/422 (repeats AN5/3)
  ZSPC 11/567/41

At the Wiltshire and Swindon History Centre Ref:
  2515/410/1173

Various files held at also the National Railway Museum, York, in particular NRM Blue Pullman Technical Files: Tech/MC/1 and 2

A note on photographs and other sources
Notwithstanding the existence in 2005 of the world wide web, at that time the amount of photographic material available was limited. Even so a number of archives and collections, both public and private were 'trawled' in an attempt to find material suitable for inclusion and which would reflect the salient points referred to in the text.

It was the burgeoning amount of new photographic material that was one of the reasons for the subsequent 'Supplement' and 'Pictorial' volumes that were published post 2005.

Some years on now in 2020, new material continues to appear, much on the internet and which in itself poses an issue. Does one attempt to source a copy of literally every new view that has appeared, replacing everything with new images, or stick with the original material? After all it is very likely the reader will already know what a Blue Pullman set looked like.

The result has to be a compromise. Physical books may be regarded by some as perhaps belonging to the dark ages, and yet new titles in their thousands (not all of course on railways) are on the shelves of bookshops and available to purchase from various internet sites.

By comparison 'e-books' on railway topics remain in the minority, not because they have not been attempted but because the majority of the target audience for a book of this type still appear to want the tangible product in their hands. That is not to say the reader will not use the internet but simply prefers to use this resource for other purposes.

The 'net' has given the opportunity for a proliferation of material on Blue Pullman and other subjects which would likely never had otherwise reached a wider audience. I have to say that on some internet sites original sources are not quoted and in consequence some statements on web sites should, we respectfully suggest, be regarded with caution. It is for this reason that references to the principal sources used do appear in this work.

But to return to the subject of images contained on these pages. We do hope the reader will find a large proportion of the views that follow are indeed new to the eye. Every reasonable effort has been made to secure as many as possible in this category but there are also going to be somewhere the phrase 'I have seen that one before' can indeed be justifiably said. Under such circumstances we would respond by stating one of two reasons for this:

1 It is still the only located view showing a specific, and important, aspect of the train.
2 It was the only one that is was practical to use, possibly due to cost or access.

Invariably what will of course happen is that the day subsequent to publication a new source will appear, or a few days later someone will kindly write in, with the words, 'I have Blue Pullman pictures...'.

Under these circumstances the response has to be, 'Sir or Madam, thank you very much, sadly until today we did not know of you.' We are not of course complaining at such a kind offer but there comes a time when any research has to be concluded and the manuscript 'put to bed'.

However if you do have new information it would make sense to share it on Facebook in The Blue Pullman group.

In order to avoid unnecessary duplication we have deliberately not attempted to access all of the various photo sites where images of the train appear although we would still recommend the reader put 'Blue Pullman' and or permutations thereof into an online search engine such as Google – you may well be surprised what turns up!

Mike suggests you try 'Diesel Pullman', 'Midland Pullman', 'Bristol Pullman', 'Birmingham Pullman', 'South Wales Pullman',

'Swansea Pullman' and 'Metro-Cammell Pullman' as these all bring results. Similarly I (Kevin) am personally not particularly into the trend for social media so you would certainly have found fewer than expected images from these sources until Mike Smith and Pip plus others in the Acknowledgements started to contribute. Again, check out the BP group on Facebook named The Blue Pullman.

We have been able to include some fantastic photographs in this book but even so what can be especially frustrating during research is that it is not always possible to get back to an original photo that we know existed in the past from references in the official files such as 'I return the images of the train…'. This is probably the most galling, as what *did* happen to these views afterwards?

Indeed the very presence of the Blue Pullman created much contemporary media hype including an enthusiast interest, and which meant in the latter category a considerable number of books, magazines, and even at least one colouring book from the time featured views or drawings of the trains. Sometimes where a very special view appeared it is possible to scan this for re-use, but more often the printing techniques of the day result in a muddy image, albeit then a tantalising glimpse of an original we are now unlikely ever to locate.

The compromise is thus to use something different wherever possible but only if it is both feasible and cost-effective. I regret the budget simply does not run to the £500+ for a single image which is what one specific photograph library expected in response to our enquiry.

Most importantly of all, we must thank all those who have so willingly assisted in the search for images and who have also allowed their views and information to be used. Names and sources are referenced both in the Acknowledgements and also at the end of the captions – where known. This can also raise difficulty when ownership and possibly also the copyright of an image has changed hands or the same view is sourced from more than one collection; individual views and collections are a commodity which are sold from time to time. Should an error in accreditation have occurred we apologise to the parties concerned.

Despite the preparation and hype surrounding the introduction of the new trains to the media at Marylebone in June 1959, other than textual reports – reported later in this book – images of the press day appear to be very thin on the ground with even official BR views appearing conspicuous by their absence. We 'believe' this to have been one of a series of similar interior photographs taken on one of the trial runs. No names or other information as to the travellers are reported although we can say for certain it was taken in a first class vehicle.

Turning now to sources and references, the basic facts, dates and figures relating to Blue Pullman are well known and are included in the text. What links all these together is the entwined history and on top of this the personal reminiscences and folklore. Imagine then the dates, facts and figures as the bricks of a wall, the entwined history as the mortar holding those bricks together and the personal stories and folklore the moss that has grown on the wall over time. Using that analogy, in some places a brick may be missing, mortar likewise might have fallen out, whilst in other places there will be a considerable amount of moss perhaps in the process overshadowing the bricks and mortar and elsewhere there is none at all.

In this book we have taken the research on Blue Pullman to what we hope is a new level. Unlike in the earlier hardback volume, specific sources are, where it is considered necessary, quoted within the text and identified as footnotes often with additional explanation or clarification at the end of the specific chapter. Where a source has been identified we have deliberately tried not to go off at too many tangents; to do so would only add more confusion. In a work of this type it is all too easy to digress too far. There is no doubt somebody could make a cogent case to link Blue Pullman to almost any other subject if they had the time and force of will to do so. Consequently we have tried to stick to the obvious and limit our 'tangents' as necessary to 'one part' removed.

The trouble with any research (and we make no excuses for repeating ourselves here) is that the more one discovers, the more unanswered questions emerge. To use a particular metaphor, if you turn over enough stones it is very likely at least one will have something underneath. Identifying where that something may fit into the scheme of things can also be difficult. Where folklore has been used again it is acknowledged where possible.

Finally we must thank all of those who through Mike and Philippa have so kindly forwarded images, ephemera and the like of their own. Some is included within these pages and others not, but simply because of space constraints. It matters not whether the picture was taken by a professional or perhaps a quick snapshot with a 'Box Brownie' or similar. It is all a contribution to history and none can be repeated today. Each is also unique in its own way.

Where no photographic credit is given then confirmation as to ownership has not been possible to ascertain – or one of us has had a genuine 'senior moment'.

ACKNOWLEDGEMENTS

Between myself, Mike and Terry Bye the decision was made to include the contribution of various people where their own personal memories could appear in the main text.

What is especially interesting about many of these recollections is how the aura of the train often made good for any apparent deficiencies in the ride. We should not criticise this as BR and Metropolitan-Cammell had in many ways achieved what they had set out to do: to build a rather 'special' train, so different to anything else that it was the memories of the positives that shine through – and continue to do so more than half a century later.

In addition the authors owe profound thanks to: The 125 Group especially Alex Woods, also to Peter Abraham, Mark Alden, Simon Altham, Graham Anderson, Elaine Arthurs at 'STEAM' Museum, Swindon, the staff at Messrs Bachmann, David Bailey, the late Audie Baker at the Kidderminster Railway Museum, Nigel Barnes-Evans – with grateful thanks for his foot-slogging on our behalf, Val Berni, G. J. M. (Malcolm) Botham CEng FIMechE, Neville Bridger, Kevin Brigginshaw, Steve Brocklebank, Peter Brumby, Ashley Butlin, Terry Bye – what would the lovers of Pullman do without him, David Canning, Ian Chancellor, Bill Chapman, David Clough, Paul Cooper, , Neil Couzens, Philip Crook, Amyas Crump – a true friend, Adrian Curtis, Alan Davis, John Dedman, David Direktor, John Dickson, Peter Dobson, Michael Downes, Philippa Dudek-Mason ('Pip') – an invaluable help, Jim Eades, Stephen Ellingham, Jeremy English, Iain Fanthom, Michael Farr, Colin Finch, Mike Floate, Antony Ford – again a true Pullman lover, John Ford, Bernard Fox, Simeon Gaskell, Ray Gomm, Nick Grant, the Great Western Trust at Didcot and in particular Peter Rance, Paul Green, Tony Hagon, Paul Harold, Dave Harris, Tony Harris, Christopher H. Head and the Head Forward Consulting Ltd., Ian Heath, Buster Hewitt, Richard Hildebrand, Richard Himson, Peter Hotchkiss, Chris Hopper, Jerry Howlett, David Hyde, Lyn Jones, Chris Lade Jnr, Danielle Lade, Nick Lade, Andrew Lance, Andrew Lane, Simon Lee, David Lewis, Tony Llewellyn, Keith Long, Sue Long, Paul Ludbrook, Stuart Mackay of Railcar.co.uk, Colin Marsden, Wayne Marshall, Greg Maxwell-Collett, the late Michael Mensing, Bernard Mills, Stephen Millership, Simon Mold, Peter James Morris, Richard H. F. Moore, Michael Narduzzo, Gerry Nichols and the library of the Stephenson Locomotive Society, David Lawrence, Chris Sayers-Leavy, Charles Long, Paul Metcalfe, Peter O'Brien, Doug Parfitt, Julian Peters, David Phillips, Jon Porter, Steve Povey, Chris Price, The Pullman Society, Dave Postle at the Kidderminster Railway Museum, Nigel Ratledge, Dave Redfern of Kidderminster Railway Musuem, Alison Reilly of Great Western Railway, Keith Riley, Brian Rolley, Neil Ruffles, Gary Seamarks, Dave Sharp and the late Mick Hayes of www.peakrail.co.uk/sheffieldbranch , Ian Shawyer – a special thank you, Paul Sheppard, Mike Smith who graduated to co-author after giving so much help, the late Ron and Sheila Smith, Richard Sparks, Howard and Clare Sprenger – for their trust and encouragement with the original book, Paul Strathdee, Susan Sutton, Peter H. Swift, Andrew Timms, M. F. Thorley, Andrew Timms, Nick Tozer, Jeremy Turner, Dominic Turner, staff at the Tyseley Railway Museum, Adrian Vaughan, Peter Waller and the library of the On-Line Transport Archive, Glynn Waite, Pete Waterman, Lester Watts, the late Chris Webb, Brian Wharton, Nick Wheat, Adrian Willats, Alan Williams, Gerald Williams, Stuart Williams, Mike Woodhouse, Gerry Worth and with sincere apologies to anyone else unintentionally omitted. We should also mention our publisher Messrs Crecy, especially Jeremy and Charlotte for having faith in the project and accepting that delays do happen.

Co-Author's note: As has been referred to previously, this will probably be Kevin's final book on the Blue Pullman subject. We have tried to bring together every little fact and detail it has been possible to uncover and in consequence we have drawn on literally hundreds of sources. Human frailty (ours) means that somewhere along the line we have probably incorrectly attributed, or failed to attribute, a quote, comment or illustration to the correct individual or organisation. For that we are sorry, mistakes happen and notwithstanding the advantages of technology these things still do sometimes unintentionally occur. In a work approaching 180,000 words it was perhaps inevitable and we again apologise unreservedly for any such occasion.

ABBREVIATIONS AND GLOSSARY

Throughout the text the term 'BP' may be taken to refer to the train sets in general terms. If discussing the specific LMR or WR, six- and eight-coach trains, these are specifically identified.

ASLEF – Associated Society of Locomotive Engineers and Firemen
ATC – Automatic Train Control
AWS – Automatic Warning System
BP – Blue Pullman
BR – British Railways
BRCW – Birmingham Railway Carriage Works
BTC – British Transport Commission
BTHCS – British Transport Hotels & Catering Services
CCS – Chief of Commercial Services, BR
CM&EE – Chief Mechanical and Electrical Engineer
DRT – Diesel Railway Traction
DMU – Diesel Multiple Unit
ECML – East Coast Main Line – that from King's Cross north
ecs – empty carriage stock
ER – Eastern Region (British Railways)
GCR – Great Central Railway
GM/AGM – General Manager/Assistant General Manager
GWR – Great Western Railway (the original GWR which ceased to exist at the end of 1947, not the modern day train operating company)
(G)WR – British Railways Western Region but dating back to the Great Western Railway era
LMR – London Midland Region (British Railways)
LMS – London Midland & Scottish Railway
LNER – London & North Eastern Railway
LNWR – London & North Western Railway
MBF – Motor Brake First
MBS – Motor Brake Second
MC – Metropolitan-Cammell
MP – The 1955 Railway Modernisation Plan
MU – Multiple Unit
NER – North Eastern Region (British Railways)
NUR – National Union of Railwaymen
OOC – Old Oak Common
PR – Public Relations Department
PRO – Public Relations Officer
RM – *Railway Magazine*
RO – *Railway Observer*
RR – Rolls-Royce
ScR – Scottish Region (British Railways)
SR – Southern Region (British Railways)
SWP – 'South Wales Pullman'
TEE – Trans Europe Express
'The Kremlin' – British Railways Headquarters, 222 Marylebone Road
TSG – Transport Survey Group
TSSA – Transport & Salaried Staff Association
WR – Western Region (British Railways)

Western Region set in standard formation comprising: Motor Second – Parlour Second – Kitchen First – Parlour First – Parlour First – Kitchen First – Parlour Second – Motor Second. The location is on the Birmingham service near the summit of Hatton bank. Unlike 'traditional' Pullman cars up to that time, the BP trains departed from convention in that none of the vehicles ever carried names.

Abbreviations and Glossary

London Midland Region set again in standard formation: Motor First – Kitchen First – Parlour First – Parlour First – Kitchen First – Motor First. The leading vehicle M60093 shows a small blemish to the bodywork on the left-hand corner above the marker light. Note too the kitchen cars have yet to have the white banding painted. Clearly the set has run a number of trials as the underframe is decidedly grubby. The view was taken by the LMR photographer on 20 April 1960 two months before the press day and entry to service. The location is almost certainly believed to be near Kimbolton on the former Midland Railway line from Bedford to Huntingdon.

DESCRIPTION OF BLUE PULLMAN CARS			
At several points during the text reference is made to the cars making up the Blue Pullman train sets. To allow for clarification, their description, BR 'TOPS' designation, type, and running numbers are shown here.			
M60090-3 (BR 251/1) Motor Brake First	67.5 tons	12 seats	Type 1
W60094-9 (BR 251/2) Motor Brake Second	67.5 tons	18 seats	Type 2
W60644-9 (BR 261/1) Parlour Second	45.5 tons	42 seats	Type 3
M60730-3 (BR 261/1) Kitchen First	49 tons	18 seats	Type 4
W60734-9 (BR 261/2) Kitchen First	36 tons	18 seats	Type 5
M60740-3 (BR 261/2) Parlour First	33 tons	36 seats	Type 6
W60744-9 (BR 261/2) Parlour First	33 tons	36 seats	Type 6
Prefix 'M' refers to sets allocated to the London Midland Region. Prefix 'W' refers to trains allocated to the Western Region. Type numbers are the official designations assigned by the builder to differentiate the vehicle types. In normal public service, the formations were always LMR (six-car): Motor Brake First – Kitchen First – Parlour First – Parlour First – Kitchen First – Motor Brake First. WR (eight-car): Motor Brake Second – Parlour Second – Kitchen First – Parlour First – Parlour First – Kitchen First – Parlour Second – Motor Brake Second. Set numbers were not carried.			

It may also be convenient to have early reference available to the following table where the differing types of Pullman Car that would make up the Blue Pullman trains are identified and also giving an official reference (by type – not running number). These designations are taken from the formal descriptions of the vehicles by BR.

Type	Vehicle Designation and code	Seats	Bogie Designation and Type	Subsequent Distribution No. of Cars		
				WR	LMR	Total
1	Motor Second – MS	18	A B (power)	6	-	6
2	Parlour Second	42	C (power) D	6	-	6
3	Kitchen First	18	Trailer Trailer	6	-	6
4	Parlour First	36	Trailer Trailer	6	4	10
5	Kitchen First	18	C (power) Trailer	-	4	4
6	Motor First – MF	12	A B (power)	-	4	4
Under 'TOPS' coding the trains were given the designation of Class 251 for the motor cars and Class 261 for the kitchen and parlour cars.						

13

PREFACE
One special day in 1960

'Following an extensive period of service trials, British Railways will shortly introduce the first of a batch of de-luxe diesel-electric Pullman trains designed for high-speed travel, with superior standards of comfort and a personal service of meals and refreshments for all travellers. These trains, which have been supplied to British Railways by the Metropolitan-Cammell Carriage & Wagon Co Ltd, are powered by two 1,000bhp NBL/MAN diesel engines, each direct-coupled to a GEC main generator. The complete order is for five trains, two of which are six-car trains for first class passengers only, and three are of eight cars with first and second class accommodation. The six-car train will run in the London Midland Region, on the main line between Manchester Central, London St Pancras and Leicester, and the eight-car trains in the Western Region between Bristol, London Paddington, and Wolverhampton, Birmingham and Paddington. Passenger accommodation is in enclosed saloons, and all seats on the de-luxe trains are reserved.' (*The remainder of the article may be found on p84.*)

So stated the *Railway Gazette* for 24 June 1960, published just one day after the pomp and exuberance which had accompanied the introduction of the new trains to an enthusiastic audience of press and VIPS at Marylebone. Taken at face value, both the launch and published article presented proof of the latest offering by British Railways and with it a giant leap forward in luxury travel.

In summary Blue Pullman had been conceived in the 1950s, the first full decade of peace after World War 2 and a time when the nation was rebuilding both economically and socially. To this new generation the past was seen as anything built before 1939 and the few years of peace in the 1940s remained a time of austerity to be forgotten as quickly as possible. Consequently it was no wonder the country wanted something tangible and new and in Blue Pullman this was certainly provided.

As just stated in an earlier caption, photographs of the Press Day at Marylebone are distinctly thin on the ground. Indeed, we have found two, this one and another, on the website of a commercial photo source showing a train leaving on a demonstration run – this image also shows the terrible weather associated with the day, 'Flaming June' but not quite in the literal sense. Instead we have this single image which is probably more interesting anyway as through the front cab windows of this LMR set – identified as such for there is no ATC cancelling plunger – notice the 9ft x 6ft display board set up by BR near to what was the end of Platform 3. Different colour lapel badges were issued to visitors according to their origins whilst technical guides were provided by the LMR and WR. (A reproduction of an invitation brochure for 24 June 1960 together with copies of other Blue Pullman paperwork may be found in the original Blue Pullman hardback book.) *MC Times Newspapers.*

Preface – One Special Day in 1960

A gleaming LMR set at St Pancras with a trial run on Friday 1 July 1960, public services would commenced the following Monday 4 July. The station clock shows 12.15pm so it could well be this was a full dress rehearsal with the set being made ready for its first 'fill-in' turn to Leicester (the public schedule for this was a 12.45pm departure). The vehicles used formed 'Set 2' with power car M60092 at the terminal end (the other vehicles in order were: [M60092], M60732, M60742, M60743, M60733 and M60093). The red flag attached to the driver's door indicates the train must not be moved as there may be staff working trackside but this gives at least two youthful spotters the opportunity to peer into the cab – considering this was a Friday, shouldn't they really be at school? Understandably BP seems to be centre of attention for nearly all, although it is a pity staff had not been available to clear the detritus from between the platforms, hopefully this was done over the weekend. On the first day of public service and no doubt specially orchestrated, the train had arrived from Manchester seven minutes early on the first up run and arrived back from Leicester at 4.00pm to be prepared for what will be a degree of pomp and ceremony (see later images) on the first public down return to Manchester at 6.10pm. *I. S. Carr/ARPT Treasury*

Naturally in the summer of 1960 the proof would come when the trains entered full service over the next few weeks and whilst we now know that behind the scenes there were serious engineering concerns, obviously these were not conveyed to press and public alike.

With hindsight the short life of Blue Pullman was really little different to the appalling waste spent on any number of 'first generation' diesel locomotives ordered as a result of the Modernisation Plan. To effect a rapid replacement for steam locomotives, designs were being ordered in bulk without proper consideration and several would have an even shorter life than the Blue Pullman.

It is, though, easy to look back, far easier than looking forward, and those men, designers, engineers, and operators from the 1950s, had every reason to believe in their new train and with it, hopefully, future orders, certainly a lifespan way beyond what would actually transpire – to the first few years of the 1970s.

The consensus from the enthusiast seems to be that Blue Pullman was the forerunner of the later 'Inter City 125' (the HST), although for reasons later described in the text this statement is not totally true but even if it were and taking the longevity of the HST as the benchmark, then the Blue Pullman sets should have been in use until well into the present century instead of being dismantled or physically buried (yes – buried) as was actually the situation in one case. (Aside from some remaining 'short sets', the HST as we know it will likely have disappeared from all but the Midland main line by the end of 2020.)

Thursday 23 June 1960 though was outwardly intended as a day of celebration. Unfortunately the gods of the weather had other ideas and a 'flaming June' might well have been referred to more in the colloquial than the factual. Indeed the clouds that ranged across the sky that day were in reality little more than an accurate forecast of what lay in store for the actual train and the operators in the years ahead.

15

1
BLUE PULLMAN
In the Modernisation Plan

In the original hardback book on Blue Pullman (it is convenient here to refer to the trains in the generic 'Blue Pullman' term), the first chapter commenced in the year 1960, with the public launch of the trains. This was at a time when modernisation had, in reality, only made a limited impact upon much of the network and trains. In many quarters the network had changed little in the preceding decade, steam engines still worked quiet branch lines albeit in some places, particularly within the metropolitan combines, these had been replaced by diesel multiple units, whilst pick up goods services shuffled to and fro invariably behind steam. Steam also remained the dominant motive power on most of the principal main line services even allowing for the introduction of the 'first generation' of main line diesel locomotives. The time of Dr Beeching was also still to come.

But something was about to change, for in July 1960 from Manchester and St Pancras and then in September 1960 from Wolverhampton, Birmingham, Bristol and Paddington, sleek new multiple unit diesel Pullman trains in a blazing 'Nanking Blue' livery began to run in regular service.

Compared with what had gone before this was a revolution. Up to now it mattered little whether there was a steam or diesel locomotive at the front of the train. The timings were similar, the coaches similar and the service provided was again similar. Blue Pullman would change all that and at the same time, if those watching the first arrivals and departures had realised, point the way towards a future when multiple unit services would come to dominate almost totally the passenger-carrying railway.

At the time of the original book, published in 2005, the year 1960 appeared to be a logical place to start, after which we would backtrack with subsequent chapters to retrace the history and then to explain how this new train had come about. This was followed by its mechanical concept, a description of the trains in service and finally concluding with the run down and withdrawal of the sets just 13 years later.

For this revised and expanded volume we have rewritten probably in excess of 95% of the original narrative to reflect the new information available. Part of this new information includes much more on the politics of the design including the BR Modernisation Plan, plus the British Railway's Design Panel, its members and consultants. There is also more on the trains themselves plus various aspects of their operation, although we will also be the first to admit that in outline

The typical express passenger train of the mid 1950s: steam engine and rolling stock and, in this case, the latter definitely pre-nationalisation. For the purposes of this work it matters not what it is, where or when (for the record 'A1' No 60162 *St Johnstoun* at Inverkeithing in August 1958), the point being that this *was* the typical express train of the period – steam engine and all. The railway needed to modernise, to cast aside an image that had in reality changed little since pre-war days, a 'modern' railway was required. Blue Pullman was in the forefront of that intended revolution. It looked different: it was of course different and in style and colour it was glamorous. The fact that only a very select few were able to avail themselves of its features really did not matter; it was the promise of the future which the passenger could anticipate would one day be available to all.
Roger Holmes

and design Blue Pullman was a unique product and as such whilst some of the images seen within this work are new, others will naturally be familiar to the reader.

We include a detailed resume of what the legacy of Blue Pullman might be said to be. A legacy that in some – but certainly *not* in all ways – could be said to be the HST. But it is also a legacy that might not even have existed at all, had a certain well known senior railwayman of 1962 – and yes we WILL be naming names – had his way and contrived the sale of the trains to Peru in 1962. To find out more you will just have to read on!

So we go back initially to the railway Modernisation Plan of 1955. Many aspects of this plan, namely the intention to revolutionise rail infrastructure, traffic movement and rolling stock plus motive power, must for the sake of space but also relevance be left out of this work – the MP was certainly not just concerned with the elimination of steam as has been popularly portrayed in the past. (Arguably the lead source for a detailed synopsis of all aspects of the Modernisation Plan is the David Clough book, *The Modernisation Plan: British Railways' Blueprint for the Future* published by Ian Allan in 2014.)

In his book Clough refers to the Blue Pullman as having been a 'white elephant', (blue might perhaps be more appropriate) and certainly with hindsight that might well be a reasonable assessment. However, before reaching the hindsight stage we should first set the scene so far as the Blue Pullman train, as it came to be known, was concerned. It is important also to recall that, (quoting from Clough), 'In June 1954 the BTC *(British Transport Commission)* acquired total control of the Pullman Car Co. Despite this, the Commission decided to leave it as a self-contained, semi-autonomous entity but it was viewed with suspicion by the railway unions even though Pullman employees were union members.' Indeed the issue of staff relations and union difficulties over the operation of the BP trains would come back to haunt management both before and during the early years of operational service, so much so that it would ultimately lead to disquiet and the withdrawal of labour on the Nottingham BP services operating out of St Pancras – see Chapter 5.

Before this, and this time from Clough in his work *Hydraulic vs Electric: The Battle for the BR Diesel Fleet* (Ian Allan 2011), the author asks the question where exactly did the idea for a self-powered Pullman train originate? In response we think we can safely say the answer is probably from more than one source although from the concept of recorded history we may credit one man, H. P. Barker, whose influence will be explained very shortly.

Three months following the acquisition of Pullman by the BTC in September 1954 we see the first sounding for an extension of Pullman on BR with a brief reference to the addition of two Pullman cars to be added to London–Liverpool services (AN172/1). Nothing further is subsequently mentioned so we may assume this did not actually occur although the idea of Pullman on ordinary trains would certainly come up again soon after.

Then six months after the acquisition and at its meeting of 20 January 1955, the British Transport Commission debated how they might secure the best advantage from their new acquisition. Before outlining the discussion at that meeting, the views of one part-time member of the BTC had (if it had been known) set the scene of the future. This was the same H. P. Barker[1], who in a memo to the Commission dated 11 October 1954 set out what he saw as the potential for exploiting the Pullman brand:

'I think there is a need to establish as quickly as possible and perhaps in advance of the main re-equipment programme, a new type of "prestige" inter-city service, characterised by the highest passenger comfort and reasonable though not excessive speed. His specific comments are shown below as '1' and '2' and he continued on the theme of the development of what was already a recognised phrase 'Inter-City' diesel multiple units and also the Pullman brand (but not specifically to a Blue Pullman type of train – yet). Here was the opportunity '… to catch the imagination of the public and give a viable demonstration of the new potential of rail travel.' (This was indeed a visionary statement and one which would continue to be accurate for some years to come. Indeed in September 1960 when the first stage of what would eventually become the 25Kv AC West Coast Electrification – between Crewe and Manchester – was inaugurated, there were opposing remarks ranging between '… how wonderful …' and '… yes, but it should have been ten years earlier …'. That same electrification scheme would also be the first stage of the eventual Euston to Manchester electrification that would eventually oust Blue Pullman from its role as the premier train between the two cities.

Consider too that at the time the Crewe to Manchester line was energised at 25Kv the timescale was also only three months since BP had entered service and so to some the 'stop-gap' perception of the train was possibly already in mind. Perhaps it was the BP *concept* that was really intended to project modernisation, a propaganda tool, with the physical train really little more than a vehicle to hold the interest of the public and so both retain and hopefully attract rail clientele. These thoughts appear to have also occurred to Barker for he continued:

'1 – British Railways need to do something that will catch the imagination of the public and give a visible demonstration of the new potentialities of rail travel.

'2 – It may be commercially desirable to show our air competitors that they stand little chance of attracting inter-city passengers from us, at least below 200 miles. The attitude of the public towards internal air travel remains in the formative stage and could be warped away from it as in France. *(It is interesting too how the words 'inter-city' are used here, although it would not be until 1966 that the term was adopted by BR as a general phrase when referring to longer distance express passenger workings. A named express passenger train, the 'Inter City', was also in operation on the WR from 1950 to 1965 between Paddington to Wolverhampton Low Level.)*

Two of the 'Belle' named trains to run on the Southern Region of BR at differing period: others were the 'Brighton Belle', and the 'Thanet Belle'. The name 'Belle' derived from the meaning 'beautiful' and was really associated with a perception of beauty, in both organic and inorganic terms. Despite an individual's personal liking for a type or design of steam engine, one could hardly say a Bulleid Pacific was a thing of beauty. However, the destinations of the trains concerned might be: the beaches and scenery of North Devon, likewise the 'bathing belles' to be seen on the sands at Bournemouth. Again, the locomotives are inconsequential to the purpose of this narrative but we may say they are an original 'Merchant Navy' on the 'Devon Belle' and a 'Battle of Britain', No 34055 *Fighter Pilot* on the 'Bournemouth Belle'. The suffix was very much of its time and whilst H. P. Barker used the term in his examples for prestige services we may perhaps be thankful that we did not in the end have a 'Leicester Belle', 'Wolverhampton Belle' or Bristol Belle' – with absolutely no disrespect intended to any person! The name had its hey-day in pre-World War 2 times, it was now necessary to move on when it came to naming trains.

'Two instruments have been placed in our hands recently, these are:

'The possibility of using the Pullman name, which I believe has great sales value, and also the arrival of the multiple-unit diesel train and consequent upon the above, the possibility of reversing trains, maintaining a shuttle-like service thereby achieving an intensive use of the equipment.

'I suggest that the Commission staff and the Regional Managers should examine the possibility of introducing a series of named Pullman trains, eg the "Birmingham Belle", the "Manchester Belle", the "Leeds Belle", operating once or twice per day in each direction. The trains would be two-class probably with a supplementary charge and to modern Pullman standards.

'Mechanically, I suggest that the trains should be of the multiple-unit diesel-type, with maximum running speeds of say 85mph and sufficient power reserve to be able to make up reasonable lost time. [This figure was based upon a six-car DMU which would need a power output of 1,600hp. The comparative figure for a loco hauled six-car train – needing of course extra power to compensate for the weight of the locomotive – was 1,800hp.] The train would be reversible and I envisage would be serviced after each round trip; that is to say, if such a train ran on the Midland route to Birmingham, it would depart from the same Euston platform at which it arrived, and perhaps not more than half an hour afterwards. This would mean, I suppose, some new organisation for servicing the train on arrival but this cannot be a mighty problem; if the airlines can do it, so can we!

'From the staffing point of view, I picture that the train would be run by the Pullman Co staffs.

'We are preparing at Swindon to build the inter-city trains for Glasgow to Edinburgh and Birmingham to Swansea. I do not know if the mechanical design of these trains [ie the chassis] would be suitable for the purpose envisaged but it might be that the design and construction of these trains could be a joint enterprise between Swindon and the Pullman Car Co.

'I know that there is some prejudice in railway circles against the Pullman Co as such. If the Commission seriously intends to develop the Pullman principle, this may be the way to go.'

Clearly too Barker had gauged the mood perfectly, for his recommendation on the development of prestige services were approved by the BTC just a week later on 27 January 1955 – minute '8/38'. The stage was thus set for what would eventually lead to BP.

However, before jumping headlong into the development of BP as a train, we need to look further at both Barker and the potential for development of Pullman. Without doubt Barker was the visionary, indeed the genus of his idea on train operating would be the norm just a few short decades later. We should not criticise him either for the fact that both BP and indeed Pullman generally would fade from the scene in later years. This was a decision taken by the contemporary operators although it may be noted that in the 21st century GWR as an operator have resurrected 'Pullman Dining' on a limited number of their services.

Consequently Barker's quote, '…the possibility of reversing trains, maintaining a shuttle-like service and thereby

'Midland Pullman' set passing Bedford in 1965. Calculations submitted by Major-General Llewelyn Wansborough Jones showed that a maximum speed of 90mph would reduce the journey time (between where and where?) by just 1½ minutes – presumably when compared with then current schedules. But we may suspect this did not take into account the improved performance of a diesel train in maintaining high speeds on up gradients and also faster acceleration. Perceptively, on 19 March 1956 (in AN97/296) he also spoke of the express passenger train of the future travelling at an average speed of 75mph with a maximum of 120 according to the route. BR themselves in 1956 through the Derby Research Department had considered a fast London to Nottingham service running via Oakham with consideration for this to be operated either by a six-coach diesel or a 2,300hp Sulzer diesel with the equivalent load. *Rail Online ZF-5438-95371-1-005*

achieving an intensive use of the equipment …' is exactly what is the standard operating procedure on 99% of passenger services running today. (Although we doubt even he could have seen how his idea would have developed.) It may have been some other members of the Commission shared the same views, yet it is Barker alone who is credited as such. Interesting also as per footnote 1, Barker was not a full time member of the BTC nor a career railwayman. Instead he was an industrialist and which then begs the comment that by bringing in an outsider unconstrained by tradition and able to 'think outside the box', the railways were being shown perhaps for the first time (and possibly rudely shaken up as well) the potential for the future even if perhaps it was not totally recognised as such at the time. Indeed in *Disconnected – Broken links in Britain's Rail Policy* by Chris Austin and Richard Faulkner (Ian Allan 2015), the two authors describe Blue Pullman as '. . . providing the inspiration for the Inter City diesel train of the future – the HST . . .'. But old concepts can also be deeply ingrained, for seven years after Barker's statement in October 1962 John Ratter[2] who had been appointed to the BTC in 1958 wrote to the LMR General Manager at Euston as follows, '. . . I think you would probably agree that there is no case to build more of them [meaning the Blue Pullman trains.] If we wanted more de-luxe trains [the word 'de-luxe' is from the French meaning 'of luxury' – particularly elegant, sumptuous, elaborate, superior quality or refinement and many similar synonyms], a conventional locomotive-hauled Pullman would be a more flexible and economic solution. (The above quote is accurate even if taken slightly out of context; reference the complete draft of Ratter's memo to the GM of the LMR. *See page 175* for the full draft.)

Meanwhile Clough (*The Modernisation Plan: British Railways' Blueprint for the Future,* David Clough, Ian Allan 2014.) continues with what is undoubtedly the best summary of the politics and discussion within the higher echelons of the BTC, covering the early days and approval for the trains, the design parameters and constraints, and the reasoning as to why certain of the regions were loath to embrace the concept. With the kind permission of Messrs Crecy Publishing (successor to Ian Allan Publishing Ltd.), sections of the relevant text (with a limited number of changes and additions to suit the present work) are included within the present chapter.

In practical terms the (Inter-City) DMUs to which Barker had referred as under construction at Swindon were unsuitable for several reasons, not least because their maximum design speed was only 70mph. Nevertheless his memo provided a springboard for thoughts within both BR headquarters and the Regions, which would turn out to be completely polarised.

A copy of Barker's memo on expanding Pullman (as a train/service/brand) was sent to the regions for comment. The Eastern Region view was that it couldn't recommend any additional Pullman services, although the possibility would be kept in mind. (It certainly did, because it introduced a loco-hauled 'Sheffield Pullman' from King's Cross in Autumn 1958 when Regional boundary changes effectively transferred the Marylebone to Sheffield route to the LMR from the start of the year.) However, the ER did note that it would soon be necessary to replace the existing hauled Pullman coaches and the possibility of a Pullman train in DMU format should be considered. What was never mentioned by the ER was any mention of Pullman service heading east from London in the direction of Norwich or Cambridge.

At this stage it is particularly interesting to report that, 'No more of a favourable response came from the LMR, which saw operating problems on the Euston to Birmingham route. In fact the Region had no plans at all for Pullman services and wished to see the performance of the inter-city DMUs being designed at Swindon before committing itself further.'

Further north, the North Eastern Region thought there might be a case for Pullman services between Hull, Leeds and Liverpool, although it doubted their viability – a contradiction in terms if ever there was one. This was because of the lower seating capacity and the deterrent effect of supplementary fares. The Region thus concluded that the best prospect was for services into, and out of, London. So without knowing if there had been un-minuted discussions between the BRB (Barker perhaps) and the regions, it appears three of the regions had come up with basically the same as what Barker had proposed, viz a 'Manchester Belle', 'Birmingham Belle' or 'Leeds Belle' which would certainly appear to refer to a 'London to. . . (wherever)' service. Ironically it was also exactly the same as would be indicated in later BR conclusions from the mid-1960s onwards at a time when a search was being made as to how to utilise all five BP trains sets profitably. In fact the only thing that was out of step were the names, 'Belle' being a distinct throwback to the 1920s and 1930s and so hardly conducive to the idea of a modern train.

Elsewhere the Scottish Region also gave Barker's idea a 'thumbs down' because it judged the services from Glasgow to Edinburgh and from these cities to Aberdeen to be unsuitable. It also ruled out a service between Glasgow, Edinburgh and England, conveniently having overlooked the existing 'Queen of Scots' Pullman that linked Leeds with Edinburgh and Glasgow!

Further south the Southern Region drew attention to its already expansive use of Pullman trains with one running in each of its three divisions – Western, Central, and Eastern – which it did not propose to expand. It was also of the opinion that there were no suitable cross-country services existing on which Pullman might be introduced. Indeed the reaction of the Southern Region is not altogether surprising. They already operated the 'Bournemouth Belle', Brighton Belle' and 'Thanet Belle', but had singularly failed to attract sufficient clientele to make the 'Devon Belle' viable, hence this latter service had been withdrawn. (The reader is also referred to extracts from the Charles Long article on the 'Devon Belle' as appear in Chapter 5.) We may discern the reason for the commercial failure of the 'Devon Belle' a little later, when a clue is given in the limited survey of Pullman passengers carried out by BR in the 1960s – subject to appreciating the rapid changes that had taken place in society between the withdrawal of the 'Devon Belle' and the time of the actual survey – see page 248.)

Similarly at this time, the WR expressed no comment at all on the introduction of Pullman services. It merely confirmed the views of the LMR and went on to vent chapter and verse as to the unsuitability of the new inter-city DMUs being designed at Swindon for adaptation to Pullman sets. From this alone we may gather the independent attitude of Swindon still prevailed, something that would continue to be apparent even during the operation of the BP sets on the Region when it came to pooling resources with the LMR.

Just why the Regions were so disinterested is unclear, especially because the Chief of Operating Services on the British Railways Central Staff (this may have been Edward Wilcox Ireland Arkle) was also quite positive. He saw Pullman trains as a further weapon in the fight against the private car

GWR 'Streamline' railcar in BR livery. This was the design which O S Nock referred to as having '. . . crisp aesthetic . . .' lines and which he compared in parallel with Blue Pullman. Known by some rather cruelly as 'Flying bananas' they spurned a later design with sharper edges, the latter referred to as being of the 'razor edge' type. Intended to provide a fast modern service between certain cities, these early vehicles did not work in multiple and were not of the Pullman type. In some cases they were a victim of their own success and a locomotive-hauled train had to be substituted due to excess loadings.

and suggested the regions be asked to prepare schemes for the trains, which would also have to be additional to services already running because of the issue of lower seating capacity; London to Manchester being the main route identified. (Might it have been that Arkle was viewing the greater picture and was attempting to secure some return for the investment in acquiring Pullman? At this stage we are also not told what the other routes might have been although some – perhaps all – are mentioned later.)

So far as the Chief of Commercial Services (was this the same position as occupied by Arkle but with a slightly changed role name? Contemporary records in respective National Archive files are not totally clear on this point) was concerned, the running of high-speed trains with special accommodation would have distinct commercial advantages, provided they were not to the detriment of ordinary services. Even so the CCS was concerned that running additional services might not generate sufficient additional revenue to cover the new total costs. Like his headquarters' colleague, he suggested the Regions should work up one or two proposals. But this in itself was not an easy situation to resolve. The success of such a prestige working would depend greatly on the ability of the operators to ensure a clear pathway: as perhaps on a lightly trafficked route or when running a 'one-off', but on the routes where Pullman traffic was most likely to succeed, i.e. in and out of London, traffic levels and in consequence the likely chance of congestion were already high. It was one thing to arrange a special path for a single one-off working, but a habitual daily train was a different matter. Regular delays would also quickly negate any prestige value any such new service might otherwise have gained. What was now being proposed was a 'high-speed' (sic) train, and as such this would be even more difficult to slot into a timetable of slower running services.

Returning to the January 1955 meeting, the Commission Members were of the view that the first objective of any change (it is not clear if this should be taken to mean 'Pullman' or 'Modernisation') would be to use altered/new services to develop railway passenger traffic which could be carried (naturally) at a profit. It appeared that any development policy would also have to follow two stages. The first and short term period would consist of testing the possibilities by the traffic/operating development in running additional services, particularly over routes not associated with Pullman services. The second stage, and the longer term one, would largely be governed by the results of the first experiment and might involve substantial new construction of Pullman stock.

Stage 1 then would be by conducting an experiment with existing Pullman stock over a new route or routes. Despite their earlier lacklustre responses. the SR, ER and NER regions already operated a number of regular Pullman services, whilst the 'Queen of Scots' ran into the Scottish Region. With no Pullman services on the LMR or WR, it was considered that the possibility of a new Pullman experiment on one or both of these regions was the most desirable. In some ways this might appear a logical

Pullman on the Eastern Region, this example being the 'Queen of Scots' seen here behind 'A3' No 60100 *Spearmint*. At varying times the ER also had trains with the name 'Pullman' including the 'Yorkshire Pullman' and the 'Hull Pullman'. One thing that comes through time and time again is how British Railways suffered from chronic under-funding in the years following nationalisation. The cost of producing 999 new standard steam locomotives between 1951 and 1960 was a proverbial drop in the ocean (some pre-nationalisation steam designs were also still being built up to 1956) compared with the rebuilding and electrification of the main routes that went on in mainland Europe post World War 2. Modern diesel and electric inter-city services were operating in Europe in the 1950s; it took us until 1960 to witness the start of anything similar. Even then funding for modernisation had to come from cost savings elsewhere, hence it was no real surprise to see the run down and closure of lines during this time, Dr Beeching merely continuing the same policy. A discussion on the rationale and behaviour of Government during this time is out of place here although suffice to say the railways, and with it their available budgets, were under continual scrutiny, small wonder that managers could sometimes obtain promotion based as much on how many savings they could make (in realising assets and by cutting services) as they could on actual ability. As an aside the name 'Spearmint' may seem an unlikely choice for a steam locomotive but was in fact one of a number of the class the LNER named after famous race horses, 'Spearmint' being the winner of the Derby in 1906. *E. R. Wethersett*

conclusion but in other ways the idea that the LMR and WR should be at the vanguard of experiments was slightly strange. The opposite argument was that as the ER/NER and SR had current experience of Pullman it was to them that any experimental service should be aimed. But against this was the continuing difficulty of finding a new route for the successful operation of Pullman on these regions. Historically the predecessors to the LMR and WR, respectively the LMS and GWR, had achieved little success with Pullman in previous times. It was indeed a leap of faith to believe the opposite might now be true.

(We might even draw the conclusion that Headquarters recognised there was no place for additional Pullman workings on the already Pullman populated regions mentioned, and to act otherwise would effectively 'over Pullman' one particular area. Strange then that just a decade later in 1966/7 this fact was conveniently ignored when the decision was made to concentrate all of the train on the WR. It just goes to show that in almost every facet of life/business we fail to recall/react to the lessons of history over and over again.)

The running of additional Pullman services, no matter how successful in attracting new traffic, was almost certain to have an effect on the patronage of the existing railway restaurant cars. This would also impact on the interests of the Commission's Hotel and Catering services in two ways. First it would reduce their gross takings, perhaps necessitating a curtailment of the service which they provided, and secondly, it raised the potential for those difficult staff questions, more of which anon.

Basically, railway restaurant car staff tended to regard the extension of Pullman services with some antagonism. This was particularly marked after nationalisation when the Pullman Car Co. was still in private hands. It was still likely to be a significant factor, partly because notwithstanding the Pullman Car Co. charging a premium to its passengers, pay rates and conditions of service were rather less favourable to their staff compared with British Railways restaurant car staff, and partly because there was a fear that the extension of Pullman services would affect some of the most remunerative of the existing railway catering services, leading to loss of earnings by senior staff and some risk of redundancy. The fact that pay for Pullman staff was less is a contradiction when considering that the passenger had to pay more to travel by this means.

With these general considerations as a background, there were two possible ways of making the experiment, the first being to run Pullman cars on established services for an experimental period. In this connection, the Regional Managers suggested that one first and one third class (Pullman – the term 'third class' was still a throwback to earlier times although 'third' on normal services was in effect 'second') car be run on each of the following routes:

WR:
Wolverhampton to Paddington;
Cheltenham to Paddington;

LMR:
Manchester to Euston via Wilmslow and Crewe,
 returning from Euston to Manchester via Stoke;
Manchester to Euston via Stoke, and back to
 Manchester via Crewe and Wilmslow.[3]

Passengers in these (Pullman) cars attached to existing services would retain their seats throughout the journey and be served meals/refreshments in conventional Pullman style 'at their seats'. On ordinary trains the passenger had to move to a separate restaurant car to partake of refreshment. (One might argue – *very* gently – that a modern day Pullman service exists on many trains in 2020 where a trolley moves up and down the aisles serving drinks and refreshments to seated passengers.) British Railways restaurant car facilities would, for the period of the experiment, remain on substantially the same scale as at present, and the Pullman staff would not canvass the remainder of the train for the custom of any passengers wishing to be served with meals or drinks. (So what type of Pullman car was envisaged – one with its own separate catering provision? Probably most likely as we can only imagine the industrial relations conflict should a Pullman conductor request a BR chef to prepare refreshments for his own Pullman passenger!)

This was also the principal difference between Pullman and the contemporary dining/refreshment services then available. As we know, on Pullman trains meals and drinks were served to the passenger at his seat. On an ordinary train, a separate restaurant (later a Buffet or mini-Buffet/Griddle) car was provided to which passengers would venture to partake of meals (or purchase refreshments to take back to their seat) although on some services light snacks might well be served throughout the train. The design of the restaurant car, in particular the seating, was also such that it needed to encourage the passenger to take a meal but was not such so as to encourage him to linger and thus prevent further 'sittings'. The observation car of the short-lived 'Devon Belle' service was purposely designed in this form with seats that were much firmer than on the rest of the train. The other disadvantage of having a separate restaurant dining car(s) was the deadweight of the vehicle together with its investment, running and staffing costs. These factors had to be considered when setting the tariff for the refreshments available.

A 'part-Pullman' experiment conducted on these lines was seen to have three main advantages. First, it could be made without incurring additional passenger train mileage. Secondly, it would enable the Pullman Car Co to 'feel its way' over new routes and gradually to build up staff based on the provincial centres served. Finally, it could be introduced without delay.

Against this was the principal disadvantage that it would be necessary to make some curtailment of the existing restaurant car facilities available on the same train and would invariably lead to an intensification of the staff objection to the introduction of the new services.

The second possible method was to run a new all-Pullman train with the ideal being that this should really be one of the two proposed experiments, either on the Western or on the London Midland regions. Whilst either, or indeed both, might well be a good assessment ground, we now come up with the practical aspect, as unfortunately the only coaching stock that could be made available for this experiment – without disruption of established services – was limited to the Pullman cars previously employed on the former 'Devon Belle', hence in reality there was a choice: just one region and just one train. It is worth mentioning at this point is that the two observation cars formerly used on the 'Devon Belle' were already earmarked for future use on the scenic railway of North Wales and Scotland. Perhaps it is indeed a pity they were never tried on other locomotive-hauled Pullman trains; we will never know if they might have been a success regardless. (It may have been that the idea was mooted to use the same redundant Pullman stock first on one region and then the next, although to do so could well have created a backlash against a new service which was introduced and then withdrawn.) A curious note now appears in the National Archives file 'AN172/1', undated other than the year, 1955, which refers to a proposal for converting the vehicles from the electric 'Brighton Belle' to locomotive-hauled stock and/or providing a through corridor between sets! This note does not correspond to any other paperwork in the file and it is therefore inappropriate to attempt to consider further without additional information. One final point on this specific topic: Pullman cars were owned by the Pullman car company, so presumably then the 'Brighton Belle' stock was railway and not Pullman owned, and as such BR were – no doubt subject to whatever notice the operating agreement stated – able to do with it as they wished?

Further discussion now took place, but what exactly, when and involving whom is not clear, but we do have a later note, of 12 December 1955, worth bringing in at this point sourced from the same 'AN172/1' file when it is made very clear the Pullman company themselves were pushing for a 12-car Pullman train to be operated between London and Manchester. What this rationale was based on is not reported but clearly it had something to do with the loss of revenue resulting from the withdrawal of the 'Devon Belle' and an obvious attempt to make up the shortfall. The LMR were totally against this proposal, basing it on future electrification work which would invariably disrupt the service. As an aside, whilst many facts are available and are so reported, some detail, but vital to the individuals concerned such as the fate of the Pullman staff displaced by the withdrawal of the 'Devon Belle', is not mentioned.

What discussion took place we do not know, but a decision was made and a complete new all-Pullman train would be trialled on the Western Region. Suffice to say it was to operate between South Wales and London and was timetabled to leave Swansea at 7.45am for Paddington, calling at Port Talbot, Cardiff and Newport and thence non-stop though to London. The service would return later in the day from Paddington. The likely reason for choosing this route was that existing trains were already well loaded general-purpose services, and a Pullman train with its limited accommodation was therefore not intended to be a substitute but instead meant to be seen as an additional service.

There were other advantages of this trial: it would not affect the composition of the existing services in the early stages of the experiment; it would not therefore have any marked effect on railway catering services; and finally the impact to the public of the running of a new full Pullman service was likely to be far greater than that of Pullman cars being added to an existing service. (Pullman vehicles are always known as 'cars', never carriages, a throwback to the importation of the Pullman ideal from America in the 19th century and where all passenger carriages were then and indeed still are referred to as 'cars'.)

But there were also disadvantages: additional train mileage and it would also only test the feasibility of Pullman operation on one route. There would also be an unavoidable lead time for the Pullman Car Co to prepare the necessary staff and rolling stock arrangements for the running of a full train. What transpired was that it showed the 'railway' could move relatively quickly when required, for with a decision made in January as to the 'where' and also the 'when', progress was quickly established, the intention being to commence the service around Easter (10 April) 1955. Time would then tell as to whether the introduction of a 'luxury' service or an existing route would add to the existing passenger numbers. (Of course this was still using Pullman cars that were on average 20+ years old, but in reality so were all the other Pullman vehicles then operating whilst the latest ordinary passenger stock on the regions, Mk1 stock, was still being supplemented by pre-war designs on most of the principal trains.)

Notwithstanding the trial nature of the new train, standard conditions of carriage would apply, hence Pullman supplements would accord with those already in force on other routes. In view of the staff aspect referred to previously, early consultation with the National Union of Railwaymen (NUR) was also started.

The Commission judged that, as a commercial venture, there was little to choose between the two alternatives (additional Pullman cars/a new train), but the operation of a new Pullman train was likely to have the least disturbing effects on the business and staff of the BTC catering services, hence it was this alternative that was preferred. As it turned out April 1955 was a somewhat optimistic date whilst further delay was occasioned due to the (unrelated) ASLEF strike of footplate staff from 28 May to 14 June. Consequently the new locomotive-hauled 'South Wales Pullman' was finally inaugurated on 27 June 1955, formed from eight umber and cream coaches (Pullman, not GWR/WR traditional liveried vehicles), and was worked by a Swansea, Landore, based 'Castle' class steam locomotive in each direction. (At least they did not follow Barker's original idea and name the train the 'Swansea Belle' – *with due respect to those who may wish to sunbath on the beaches around the Gower or elsewhere!*) As an aside, the 'South Wales Pullman' remained virtually (possibly totally) steam-hauled throughout its life, that is until it was superseded in 1961 by using the spare WR Blue Pullman set, as is described later. (The original suggested idea of withdrawing the service a year later and perhaps transferring the stock to an LMR route for a similar trial is not mentioned again. But even if this had been considered at some time it was clearly discounted as the new 'South Wales Pullman' was destined to be resounding commercial success.)

The Blue Pullman Story

Beyond the experiment described above, the Commission turned its attention to the second stage suggested in Barker's original memo, where it had been proposed there should be a greater series of named Pullman trains between major cities. Two separate ideas emerged, the first being Barker's suggestion for high-speed DMUs between destinations. These would be additional to existing services and also be expressly designed to meet competition from other forms of transport. The second possibility came as a sea-change by the Regional Managers of the Eastern and North Eastern, and which was to replace existing steam-hauled Pullman trains by diesel Pullman vehicles. (One is tempted to be slightly cynical here and suggest perhaps the respective managers saw this as a prime opportunity to secure more modern rolling stock rather than a true desire to embrace the high-speed dmu which with hindsight can now be seen as progressing towards the dmu-pullman concept. Bear in mind also the Swindon inter-city DMU was originally built for a maximum of 70mph [later revised to 80] and that the former figure was regarded as representing high-speed at the time. Ironically in later years the Swindon intercity design m/u stock would [as with BP] be affected by complaints of bad riding resulting in modifications being made to BR single bolster bogie.)

The Commission thus reviewed these two approaches. If the first were developed, it would mean the potential use of a train identical to or similar to that being designed at Swindon. For the second it would be desirable for one or more Regions, in consultation with the Pullman Car Co and the Commission's hotel and catering services, to prepare 'pilot' schemes for consideration, but it was still judged prudent to defer the preparation of such pilot schemes until results of the experiment with the new 'South Wales Pullman' were available.

Progressing the ER/NER plan would require the Pullman Car Co and the regions concerned to prepare a joint report. This could proceed immediately, as it related to existing Pullman services and would not be substantially affected by the outcome of the 'South Wales Pullman'. The meeting resolved to go forward with both these options, as well as continuing the experimental 'South Wales Pullman' working. Even so, for the present the

The steam-hauled 'South Wales Pullman' which commenced operations on 27 June 1955, *not* 13 June as per the advertising poster previously seen. The reason for the delay was an ASLEF strike which ended on 14 June although presumably it took a little time to get normal services recommenced before starting a completely new working. The 'Castle'-hauled train is seen here at Cardiff almost ready for departure to Paddington but with the fireman taking the opportunity to push some choice coal forward. The only intermediate stop between Cardiff and Paddington was at Newport; 6.19pm, later changed to 6.20pm. in the down direction.

LEFT Complete with headboard and train reporting number and also in superb external condition, 'Castle' No 5016 *Montgomery Castle* awaits departure from Paddington with the down 'South Wales Pullman'. Although the train would change to a BP set in September 1961 locomotive haulage returned on occasions owing to non-availability of the booked Pullman set. Invariably this was with diesel-hydraulic haulage but we cannot say for certain steam was never used again after that time.

ABOVE Bar service on board the loco-hauled 'South Wales Pullman'. This was old-style Pullman service, where in addition to a 'meals at your seat' provision there was also the opportunity to wander to the bar area at leisure, something that was not replicated on BP. Prices were high for the time but understandably so when it is considered the staff and vehicle running costs had to be taken into consideration. *Antony Ford collection*

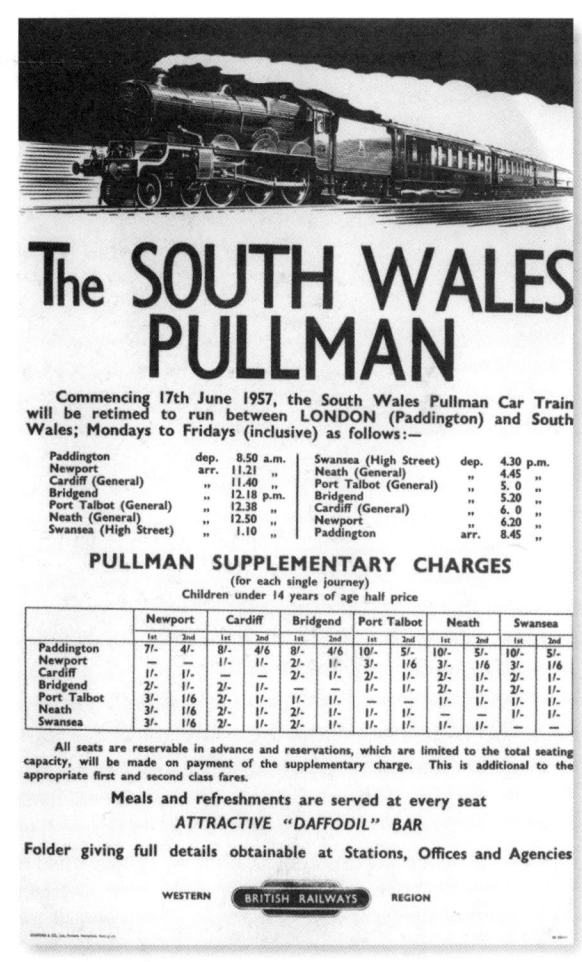

concept of an all-Pullman dmu was seemingly still far from settled.

On the same day, 14 June 1955, that 'normal service' had been resumed following the ASLEF industrial action, a BTC committee was set up, the 'Diesel Multiple-Unit Mainline Express Services Committee'[4], under the Chairmanship of H. H. Phillips, the Assistant Regional Manager of the WR, who had also chaired the 'Forms of Motive Power Sub-Committee' in 1954. Against a remit of a self-powered train-set, the Committee gave consideration to a wide range of aspects, including the desirability of air conditioning and also that no standing passengers be allowed (the no-standing concept is not defined so we are not made aware if this should be taken as referring to a particular train or perhaps even all trains). The Committee made a partial report in July 1956 whilst in the interim members had ventured across the channel to study practice on other railways, particular reference being paid to the 'TEE' proposals then under way in Europe. 'TEE' were the initials for 'Trans Europe Express', defined as a network of connected inter-city routes intended to serve the principal cities of Europe. The TEE trains themselves varied according to their country of origin and not surprisingly for the period included locomotive hauled sets. According to Clough they were first class only and were aimed at the business traveller and likewise intended to compete with air travel. Due to variations in the electric catenary supply (some countries then being DC and others AC) electric power was not used and instead diesel locomotive were used to haul coaches but there were also some 'high-speed' fixed formation diesel trains. Those with the latter were of German, Swiss and Dutch origin. The point to note was that all the trains were first class only whilst initially there was no 'meal at each seat' service.

Examples of European TEE trains which were the subject of study by the 'Diesel Multiple-Unit Mainline Express Services Committee' and personal inspection by George Williams and Jack Howe. As a sophisticated, high-speed application of the diesel multiple-unit idea, the sets had driving cabs in the motor coaches at each end of the six- or eight-car formations. Based on their findings the Minutes of the BTC Technical Committee refer to Den Hollander being invited to comment on the use of multiple units in place of loco-hauled trains. DH had been a leading figure in the introduction of such trains on the continent in the form of TEE sets. These were first class only and aimed at the business traveller competing with air travel and fitted with a power car at each end. Backtracking slightly, as an aside the BR Meeting of 10 March 1955 was supportive of multiple unit diesel trains for important runs between London and the North. A few months later on 9 February 1956 the Committee decided that for publicity purposes the word 'multiple' would be dropped. Here we see two TEE trains, the first at Amsterdam (and upon which the interior of BP was based) and the second at Saignelégier, Switzerland. *https://commons.wikimedia.org/w/index.php?curid=12950280 and httpscommons.wikimedia.orgwindex.phpcurid=2989397*

In his earlier book *Hydraulic vs Electric* (referenced previously) Clough asks the same question as now as to exactly where did the idea for a self-powered Pullman train actually originate? Clough contends that the minutes of the BTC Technical Committee then refer to a new name/organisation, that of Den Hollander, being invited to comment on the use of multiple unit sets in place of loco-hauled trains, Den Hollander having been a leading figure in the introduction of such trains on the continent in the form of the European TEE fixed-formation sets.

For the present though let us content ourselves with returning to fact and report that the Phillips' 'Diesel Multiple-Unit Mainline Express Services Committee' likely met slightly earlier than is officially stated, on 10 March 1955, and quickly came out as supportive of multiple unit diesel or diesel-electric trains for '. . . important runs between London and the North.' This was followed by a full report issued on 23 August 1955 – although we are not told how many times in the interim the committee had sat. This report stated, '. . . it would be necessary to formulate one or two pilot schemes to enable the practical advantages, particularly as to utilisation, to be assessed, and the London Midland and Western regions are now exploring the possibility of running trains of the type envisaged. Services between London and Manchester, Birmingham and Bristol are being considered.' No doubt there had been much manoeuvring behind the scenes by the respective committee members before reaching these actual conclusions. Similarly we can take it there would have been attempts by those representing the likely regional recipients of the new trains to ensure their own wishes and advantages were included, or even made paramount, but this did not prevent the consensus stated.

What is strange is the reference to two regions running pilot trains, as we know already there was only enough spare Pullman stock available for one train and that had already been agreed to operate as the (experimental) 'South Wales Pullman'. It is not clear then what other type of service might have been operated simultaneously on the LMR – unless at this stage there was still a belief a second Pullman trial of some sort might be tried.

Frustratingly now there is little else reported so far as dates – and the progression of ideas relative to these. But, and this is a big BUT, around this time Phillips (& Co.) emerged with a very detailed provisional specification and correspondingly close to what eventually transpired – *allowing for a few deviations en-route!*

How and why Phillips and the Committee settled on just two options for train formations – a six-coach set for first class only and an eight-coach set with accommodation equally divided between first and second class – is not clear. But this decision was made and seemingly also with the regions if not the actual routes totally set, consequently now the traffic departments of the LMR and WR regions became involved.

We are assuming of course that this timeline is correct but questions will certainly be raised when we note that the second formal meeting of the committee was held on 3 November 1955 although again prior to this and no doubt in anticipation of this meeting, each region had submitted its view on the Committee's ideas. So does the term 'formal' have any particular significance here and in which case does the proposal for six- and eight-coach trains relate to an actual 'Diesel Pullman' or should we read this as simply a suggested train make-up? In the light of what follows it is probably safer to say the latter.

At the November 1955 meeting the Western Region view (could this have been Phillips but this time wearing his Assistant GM's hat?) claimed that better utilisation of stock could be achieved with a conventional locomotive-hauled train, while the Midland proclaimed an interest in any number of services, which included Euston to Glasgow, and St Pancras to Leicester, Nottingham and Derby. At the same time, one member of the Committee (who that was is not stated) requested that the LMR look into the possibility of an early morning Leeds to St Pancras train. It almost gives the impression the LM region would agree to anything if they felt this was a way of modernising their services more rapidly than might otherwise be possible under the existing modernisation plan.

These representations to the Committee are worthy of further exploration as they indicate a distinctly independent stance by both regions concerned, each definitely attempting to promote their individual advantage. The WR also seems to have conveniently ignored one of the main criteria for the proposed new trains – 'multiple unit operation'. The response of the LMR is also surprising as it appears not to have fully considered the specific business class ambition as well with the need to ensure routes were chosen where the suggested maximum and average speeds could be achieved. (A Glasgow service was impossible at the time if the desired speeds were to be achieved, but did the London–Glasgow proposal have any bearing on the later introduction of the 1957 lightweight steam-hauled 'Caledonian' service?) Leeds was subsequently discounted as a destination due to operational difficulties which included severe speed restrictions in the area caused by mining subsidence, whilst around the same time a separate proposal to base any new trains at Sheffield was ruled out for similar reasons. The reader will also recall Barker's suggestion for high-speed services only on existing routes – meaning between destinations where traffic flows were already proven. It was for this reason any new services between two points that had never previously had a fast through service were viewed with suspicion. From the traffic/operators' perspective the idea of a new train to hopefully stimulate a demand where one had never existed before made perfect sense, although such a move was also a gamble. Barker it will be recalled, was all in favour of attempting to attract new traffic with his various 'Belle' proposals although one thing Barker does fail to grasp is what we have also mentioned before and that was ensuring there was line capacity for a new fast service to operate on a regular basis.

A further meeting of the Committee of 9 February 1956 decided that for publicity purposes the word 'multiple' would be dropped, although in reality this was never really fully achieved.

Meanwhile the committee had now got down to practical details with a consensus that the new train should be '… of similar design to the proposed "Hastings" line sets'. For the sake of completeness, these were six-car fixed formation trains then under construction at Eastleigh comprising a power-car at either end containing a floor mounted diesel-electric power unit but which also contained passenger accommodation in a separate saloon. The trains were gangwayed within set only (meaning between each carriage) and included buffet accommodation.

At this point we now need to both step back slightly and analyse in slightly more detail the decision reached. Firstly, the Hastings sets, the first of which did not actually enter service until 1957, were hardly a massive leap forward in technology. In fact the concept was already 25 years old: a fixed formation diesel-electric set having the same basic plan based on one of the ideas that had been under discussion by the GWR in the early 1930s and seen then as a means of modernising the Paddington suburban workings. Likely because it was too radical a step for the 'conservative' GWR at this time, steam would prevail but it is interesting to again recall that the committee Chairman, H. H. Phillips was a WR man – is it too tenuous a link to suggest he still recalled the GWR scheme from two decades earlier? (See Ch 8, and in particular p128, of *The GWR Exposed*.)

The GWR's own version of the six-car DMU proposal dating from the early 1930s. Multiple unit trains were not of course new at this time anyway; several of the pre-nationalisation companies had them and the LMS, LNER and SR also had all-electric multiple units. But this would have been the first time anything like a six-car fixed formation diesel had been contemplated although it should be made clear, the GWR design was for a suburban service not a fast inter-city service as was now being proposed by BR. In concept the Southern Region Hasting's line sets of the late 1950s showed little real imagination beyond what is seen here.

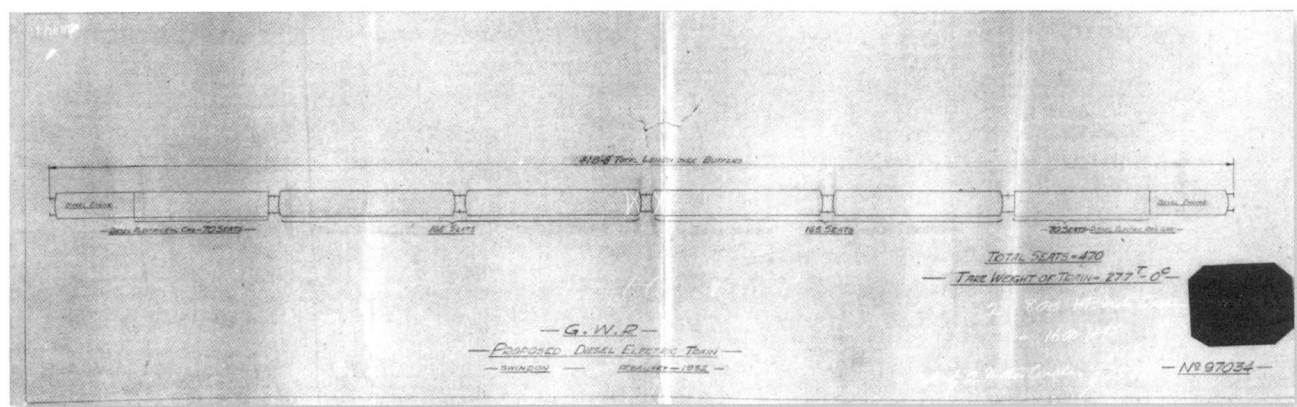

Again we know there was much manoeuvring behind the scenes but a consensus was reached for a report to form part of the BTC Chairman's conference on the Modernisation Plan in September 1956 and where it was made public the first reference to a proposed diesel Pullman service but notably without going into much detail. How the matter had morphed into a diesel Pullman is not clear, but without information to the contrary it would seem as if the views of H. P. Barker had resonated even if as we know he was initially at least not a member of the Diesel Multiple Unit Main line Express Committee – reference footnote 4.

No doubt this may have in part resulted from the involvement of the operating/commercial departments of the regions as for its part the London Midland Region would deploy a first-class-only train between Manchester Central and St Pancras whilst the Western Region would have a pair of first/second class sets working from Birmingham Snow Hill, and Bristol Temple Meads to Paddington. Meanwhile the Eastern Region had also been invited to draw up a proposal for a Marylebone to Sheffield Victoria Pullman service operating over the former Great Central route.

We now need to briefly 'fast-forward' (temporarily) to 4 July 1960 and an article that appeared in *The Guardian*. As will be recounted later, this was the start date for the new 'Midland Pullman' service from Manchester, the newspaper naturally reporting this fact but, more relevant to this time, also looking back to the politics of how the concept had evolved. As such we are afforded information that does not appear to exist from other sources and is now reported probably for the first time in a historic railway context.

With the newspaper (in 1960) having first described the new trains the article continues, 'In the Metropolitan-Cammell contract was the stipulation that the company should appoint a consultant designer *[we know this to be Jack Howe]* approved by the BR Design Panel and the Pullman company.' (We are not told what his actual remit was although we perhaps come close to the truth in the *Railway Gazette* for 24 June 1960 when in referencing the new trains it states Howe as having been, '. . . design consultant to Metropolitan-Cammell for passenger amenities and décor.) The newspaper report continued with a slightly strange phrase, for it commented that the task of Jack Howe, was not just to make the train look beautiful for he is stated, '. . . as one of those responsible for introducing the Schlieren bogie.' (This is surely strange as Howe was a designer and not an engineer.)

To return though to 1956 and something that was subject to an embargo at the time, indeed it was 'Closed' at the National Archives until 1986, and that is the financial situation of the British Transport Commission. This report which runs to 55 pages, 104 paragraphs, plus four Appendices (http://filestore.nationalarchives.gov.uk/pdfs/small/cab-129-83-cp-56-211-11.pdf) covers not only the financial position of the railways together with rates, charges and expenditure, but describes in its Chapter IV much detail on the proposals for modernisation. Although it is extremely tempting to digress, we must confine ourselves to Paragraphs 30 and 31. Starting then with paragraph 30: 'Plans are also well advanced for the introduction of a small diesel rail car especially suited to branch lines and other stopping services in rural areas, where if traffic by rail is to continue the highest degree of operating economy must be practised,' *(if it had been known at the time, an oblique reference to what would come later: namely Dr Beeching).* Then in Paragraph 31: 'A third type of diesel train is envisaged, offering high speed and special amenities. Accordingly plans are being developed for the introduction of de-luxe multiple unit diesel expresses to operate at high speed on selected services between important cities. These will incorporate all that is best in modern design for the comfort and convenience of the traveller.' The paper was discussed by the Cabinet on 21 September 1956. (It is not exactly clear if the 'small diesel rail car' was the 'first' type of diesel train. Similarly was the 'second' the 'conventional' dmu or an ordinary diesel locomotive hauling passenger stock? For the sake of this narrative the answers are really irrelevant.)

Thus we learn of the concept of the high speed diesel train – the word Pullman is not mentioned anywhere in the report but would of course result in the plans for what would later emerge as the 'Blue Pullman'. *The Guardian* also refers to the MC contract for the trains and the remit of the Design Panel: 'The panel is concerned with equipment of all kinds used by passengers, customers and staff, or which is prominently visible to them or to the general public. The BTC believes that if the Panel achieves its purpose one increased result will be an enlarged sense of pride among the staff and a new confidence in the future of the service on the part of both staff and public. The work of the new panel would be much easier if it acted as a dictatorship. In designing a new type of train, it was intended that the 'Midland Pullman' should not be tied to any previous ideas of train design and the panel knew there would be many conflicting views. But these conflicts had to be reconciled by agreement and not arbitrary ruling.' The word 'dictatorship' is certainly strange, indeed one can almost imagine the resultant cartoon – an engineer being told where to put his bogies by a design expert!

With reference again to the BR Design Panel, this may be the appropriate point to mention that this was set up by Sir Brian Robertson (General Brian Hubert Robertson) in his position as Chairman of the BTC in June 1956. It held its first meeting in August of the same year.

We should also make the point that what follows later is not intended to imply failure or ineptitude on the part of the Design Panel or indeed any of their members. Indeed the impact of the Design Panel and its various members was influential in both locomotive and multiple unit design, locomotive, and multiple unit colour and paint schemes as well as in architecture and general styling. (The reader is strongly advised to seek out *British Rail Designed 1948-97* by David Lawrence, for a readable and factual account of the design process undertaken by BR in the period now under discussion in this work.)

Reverting back to 1956 vis-à-vis the article in *The Guardian* in 1960, it is interesting to consider for a moment why it appears to have only been this newspaper which had picked up this particular reference. Was there perhaps a press embargo on part of the detail at the time, or possibly more likely it arrived on a day of more newsworthy text and with the result it was eventually forgotten – until 1960 that is? (There was indeed a press embargo of sorts consequent upon an edict by Sir Brian Robertson – *see page 59*.) What is most interesting however, is that from all these loose pieces of information we are able to glean more and more of the politics and machinations that took place and which gradually come together to form this fuller picture. If those first passengers in 1960 had only known how their train might not have arrived at all!)

So away from 1960 and a return to 1955 when the concept was really only starting to take shape. It has been popular (and at times, truthful) to deride the Western Region for its independent stance following Nationalisation, so much so that it was sometimes referred to as the 'Great Western Region'. The most obvious departure from the norm being the retention of its pre-nationalisation locomotive numbering and the widespread use of a pseudo-GWR livery on its locomotives and rolling stock. However, in the case of the Blue Pullman, it is the London Midland that is more deserving of criticism. Contemporary LMR management appears to have totally ignored the full potential offered by their available alternative lines in and out of London. LMR management was seemingly content to consider Pullman aspirations as only suitable to the former LNWR line in and out of Euston with scant regard paid to the opportunity presented by the Midland line from St Pancras. This is especially strange as there had been a regular prestige passenger service between St Pancras and Manchester Central for many years including at least one named train, 'The Palatine'. Indeed the LMR, despite recognising Manchester as a likely source of potential revenue for the new service, was of the opinion that the trains could not run from Manchester to Euston due to 'operational difficulties'. When pushed, they insisted that this was due to the lack of available paths, hence the scheme put forward for the multiple unit to cover a four-leg circuit based on Derby and comprising Derby to St Pancras, St Pancras to Nottingham, Nottingham to St Pancras and St Pancras to Derby. The fact that no consideration had been given by the LMR to the use of the Midland line north of Derby to Manchester for a new service was similarly commented on by the late Michael Bonavia in his book *British Rail: The First 25 Years* as something that, '…outraged common sense'. (Bonavia was a former LNER man, and a serving member of the Phillips Committee.) The fact that the trains did eventually serve Manchester was due in no small part to the efforts of the Committee's secretary, Peter Keen (a future Chief Passenger Manager on BR), who, having carefully studied the working timetables, was able to demonstrate that it was perfectly feasible to find paths for the new service over the Midland line between Manchester and St Pancras at the required times. One might hope that this 'lack of memory' over the suitability or even existence of the route from Derby to Manchester through the Peak District was not to be taken as an indication that traffic over the line was already to be discouraged? 'Closing the circle' at this point means we should mention that the through route between Derby and Manchester via Millers Dale was indeed eventually closed by British Railways in 1968 but this was of course after the 'Midland Pullman' had been withdrawn.

Behind the scenes there may have been an additional reason why LMR management was reluctant to consider Manchester as a potential customer target for the new units at that time, and this was their fear that if Manchester were chosen, major industrial relations problems could lie ahead. Charles Long (a former Pullman man and recognised authority on the Company) recalls the north-west as having, '. . . the presence of a hard-knot of militant members of the NUR among Manchester-based restaurant-car staff.' He is also of the opinion that it was the threat of strike action that later forced the indefinite postponement of the planned service launch from January 1960. (This may not quite be the truth for as will be seen later there were also significant mechanical problems that needed to be resolved.) It was certainly far from 'out of the factory and into the platform ready for service'.

So why this now lukewarm response from the LMR? It would be tempting to suggest the lack of thought over routing, or the fears of union hostility by the LMR, were respectively an oversight and an over-reaction, but both views must be questioned. Some of the best brains on the railway were serving on, or accessible to, the Committee, and one inevitable conclusion to be reached is that factions within the LMR were starting to turn away from the idea of a prestige service in favour of concentrating resources on the electrification of the LNWR route which was to be in the vanguard of modernisation, and planned to be completed around the same time as the East Coast Main Line scheme. (Electrification of the ECML was eventually put-back [until the 1970s] and instead the ER opted for a fleet of 22 twin-engine 'Deltic' diesel locomotives intended to replace 55 steam locomotives and at the same time provide for regular 100mph running on locomotive-hauled trains.) The reader will have gathered there were several committees forming part of the BTC and consequently several schemes running which would eventual conjoin to affect almost every aspect of the railway, all part of this overall 'Modernisation Plan'.

But regardless of the support or otherwise of the respective regions at this time the most important result of the November 1955 meeting was a set of outline drawings giving various options for projected six- and eight-coach sets, having either under-floor, bogie-mounted or frame-mounted above-floor engines.[5] To date (1955), multiple unit diesel trains in Britain had only been equipped with bus-type under-floor engines that provided sufficient power only for secondary and branch

Concurrent with the discussions that would eventually culminate in Blue Pullman was the development of Inter-City type units. Construction of these was not restricted to the area in which they would operate either hence this six-car set (later designated Class 124) intended for the Trans Pennine route between Liverpool and Hull was built at Swindon. It is seen here on 20 July 1960 on a trial run at Earlestown. Eight six-car sets were built together with three spare cars. The trains entered service in 1960/61 and lasted until 1984. *Arthur Gray*

line use. Similarly there was discussion on whether each vehicle should be individually powered or power concentrated in just a few vehicles. Everything it seemed was open to question with little practical experience either at home or oversees available to afford guidance. Regardless of type, the example was given of fitting twin engines per vehicle (bus type?) each of 150hp installed in a seven-car formation so as to achieve a total of 2,100hp, or, five of the seven vehicles powered this time again with twin motors but now rated at 200hp each so totalling 2,000hp. Knowing also that the Committee had, it appeared, almost certainly settled on six- and eight-car trains it is strange to relate that they now used the example of a seven-car (compromise?) formation.

Frame-mounted power units had been used before in Italy but here the actual rail vehicles were 80ft long, (as we are speaking of mainland Europe we suppose we should really quote this number in metres and so for those who want the metric equivalent the figure is 24.384m). British vehicles were an average of 63ft 6in – 'BP' would later come out at a maximum of 68ft over gangways. Vehicle weights for various configurations were also carefully calculated. Consequently frame mounting was, at this stage, ruled out but it is again interesting to comment that contemporary designs had frame-mounted power units and generators which were intended to be, and indeed were, installed in the SR Hastings (and later 'Hampshire', 'Berkshire' and 'Sussex' demu sets). I think it once again proves the point that in some ways each separate BR committee dealing with modernisation was in effect working in its own little bubble and there was simply little or no cohesive strategy, knowledge or indeed awareness of what one's neighbours in the next-door committee room were dealing with. When considering the whole aspect of attempting to modernise an industry so vast, so far reaching and so fragmented as British Railways as a whole, as quickly as was desired, such behaviour was probably not really surprising.

So we return to the consideration being given to the power plant and in light of home-grown experience with under-floor engines judged to be liable to generate vibration and intrusive noise, the preference emerged for 1,000hp floor-mounted engines installed at each end of the LMR trainsets coupled to an electric generator and traction motors. In the last statement we appear to have the first piece of the BP settled – the power units. But before moving on the WR now managed to have their say (and independence). How this was achieved is not reported – likely behind the scenes discussion – but somehow it was also stated that the WR sets would, despite having the same engine, be instead coupled to hydraulic transmission, using either a MAN/Voith or Maybach/Mekydro powertrain.[6] In both cases auxiliary diesels of 354bhp would provide power for the train equipment.[7] (The vibration issue associated with under-floor engines attached to each vehicle is still so true with the current 'Voyager' units operated by 'Cross Country', but then for years we passengers had to put up with 'first generation' diesel-mechanical units with all the inherent noise and vibration referred to.)

Exactly where and by what route the search for suitable engines took the Committee overseas is not recorded, but it did eventually settled on German-designed MAN 1,000hp engines, which were planned to be built in the UK under licence by the North British Locomotive Company. Regardless of the number of coaches, the two power cars would have an engine of the same power so giving each set a combined power output of 2,000hp. It is likely that at this stage, R. C. Bond, as one of the engineering members of the Committee, was able to calculate the likely power-to-weight ratio of the new trains, and so relate them to the speeds required. No paperwork has been found to substantiate this, but it is also likely that the various strategic decisions were made at this time, for example, that the trains be equipped with the 354hp auxiliary engines to supply power for catering and air-conditioning (although, exactly when this latter feature was decided upon is not recorded), and also of course the important question of scheduling.

It is in this area and including TEE where the assumption is made on how continental practice influenced the Blue Pullman trains; for up to now the only true comparison related to the chosen manufacturer of the power units. The new service with (a now proposed) 100mph (maximum) and 60mph (average) speeds would demand significantly more output, and an engine able to produce this type of necessary output was just not available locally at that time (why the existing English Electric

1,600/1750hp/2,000hp power unit was not mentioned is not explained; perhaps physical size/weight was an issue) hence the search overseas for inspiration. (Surviving files at The National Archive include within the BP files a brochure on the contemporary American 'Aero-Train', but whether this was an attempted sales drive by the manufacturers, or simply the result of a trawl by the BTC through the latest railway technology is not clear; probably more the latter.) We also cannot know when the desirability for 100mph running was mentioned but straight away this would have run into conflict with the average speed of other trains over the same route and consequently pathing conflicts.

Now at this time, and we are still mainly in 1955, there were only a few diesel units operating (but with many others in the process of design/building) on BR and this fact seems to have been conveniently ignored. What we end up with is a comment that frame mounting was ruled out; it appears simply because the only example of such practice mentioned as having been considered was from Italy but where the vehicles were 80ft long. The proposed British vehicles were then to be restricted to 63ft 6in with vehicle weights for various configurations also carefully calculated. In addition it was stated that any form of power unit placed under a passenger-carrying vehicle was less than ideal as it was judged to be liable to generate vibration and intrusive noise hence the continued preference for 1,000hp at each end of the trainset.

Using the two (LMR/WR) options, the respective power configurations were calculated to result in a total engine/transmission weight of 49 tons for the diesel-electric variant and 28½ tons for the diesel-hydraulic at respective costs of £71,000 and £61,300, a clear advantage in all respects for the latter type. Not surprisingly the Committee made a strong recommendation in favour of diesel-hydraulic, not least because some Trans-Europe Express sets on the Continent were similarly powered. Additionally, the saving of 20 tons would assist the WR eight-car sets in attaining better timings, although with less trailing weight this would not be an issue on the LMR's six-car formations.

Regardless of available paths and even with the reduced weight available from a hydraulic variant, the power output was considered insufficient for the hoped for maximum of 100mph, so hereafter a 90mph maxima was settled upon. Even so, there were still fears that 2,000hp would not be sufficient for an eight-coach set, and it was even suggested that all the sets be restricted to a maximum of six-cars. (Similar NBL/MAN engines were installed in the 1958 'Warship' class diesels, and also in Nos D833-D865 of the 1960 'Warship' class: might this have already been considered and it was thus an attempt at achieving some form of standardisation?) The same plans show passenger seating that both revolved and reclined, and included clip-on trays for meal service – the latter definitely as per continental practice. Each train, regardless of whether it was formed with six or eight cars, was (at the time) shown as fitted with centre doors, and was symmetrical in the layout of its accommodation. (Each half was actually a 'mirror' of the other, since the kitchen, toilets and double seats were all on the same side.)

As stated, unfortunately we do not have access to these original layout plans although contemporary notes and reports have survived and so afford a verbal if not illustrative description of the proposed layout. In the six-car train, the first three cars were respectively: motor first, kitchen first and open first, with the second set of three being (in mirror/reverse order) open first, kitchen first and finally, motor first. The eight-car sets had a motor second followed by an open second, with the last two cars of each four-car half-set being identical to vehicles two and three in the six-car formation. At this stage the length of each vehicle had also increased slightly to 64ft 6in, but in practice this would increase further by some two feet. In other areas there were close similarities with the vehicles as actually built, although some variations in the seating accommodation were introduced. On-train catering now moves centre-stage; with the reader forewarned he will now have to sit through several 'courses' but it is still equally fascinating.

Up to now we still have nothing to confirm that the 'Pullman' designation/criteria would apply to the new units. Pullman branding is of course the assumption as this was the eventual development but it must be stated this had not been settled at the start. By later defining the train as Pullman it immediately becomes an up-market DMU aimed at the business traveller. However, at some stage it did of course change to a Pullman concept. This could very well have been as the results, and likely to have been consistent results as well, started to appear from the new 'South Wales Pullman' service. This is even more surprising when it is recalled this was a totally new train on a route which had never operated Pullman in the past and using cars which were at the very least 'aged'. Even better was that the new service had not adversely affected loadings on other services; it was all new business for the railway.

But now this begs the question, did the new train have to be Pullman? The fact there was no such thing as a 'Pullman Airline' had not put off the air traveller. Where air travel scored, apart from the obvious time factor, was in catering (not specifically in the literal sense) for the business classes and then in the 'meals and refreshments at seat' service although there was of course no reason why such a service could not be provided on any suitable train without having to give it a specific brand, hence Pullman marketing may have been a factor. At the time it must also be recalled that then, unlike now, within Britain the name Pullman was already embedded in the mind as representing luxury. Barker was right, if you have a prestige brand at your finger tips it should be used – exploited may be a better term. The only problem was that the image of Pullman was seen as representing tradition, and with a need to transform the image of the railway through modernisation we can quickly see how it was but a small step for a new Pullman train to also represent a new design. Thinking ahead briefly, try and imagine how the new train must have appeared to press

1961 comparisons. First we have the old-fashioned interior of a locomotive-hauled car on the 'South Wales Pullman' as it appeared in 1961, before this service was replaced by the third WR Blue Pullman set. (Seen is second class Car No 55.) This is followed by the interior of a first class saloon on a Western Region BP – to be fair the comparison is not helped by the dark interior of Car No 55. Similarities are hard to find and so with perhaps such a great contrast one can begin to imagine the later push by Sir John Elliot to step back somewhat from the 'modernism' displayed. Conversely Jack Howe had designed a train for the (then) present day, unhindered by tradition or sentimentality. Notwithstanding the aged interior of the loco-hauled SWP, it was due to the very success of this service that the Pullman concept of service was decided upon for the new trains – we might otherwise have simply been writing the history of an express DMU. (The cardboard on the floor was no doubt to keep the carpet pristine in what is likely a pre-service view.) *Antony Ford collection and Bruce Jenkins*

and public alike in 1960? With its Pullman branding and fresh colour scheme and up to the minute interior, 'revolutionary' is probably the most accurate word with which to describe it. Indeed, half a century later when looking at photographs of the actual cars (possibly excluding the power cars) each could still be said to look modern, whilst other than a change of fabric within, the interiors would also surely pass the same test.

Thus we can only say that somewhere along the line the Pullman designation starts to appear and we can state with certainty the word is first mentioned when the subject of on-board catering starts to be considered (meals at seats etc etc). After all and being deliberately cruel, if this inter-city service was intended to compete with air travel between cities it was the passenger (in this case 'customer' would appear appropriate) service that counted as much as the train.

Around this time, Herbert Phillips as Chairman of the Committee contacted Colonel Frank Harding, the General Manager of the Pullman Car Co, and also E. K. Portman-Dixon, the Chief of Restaurant Cars at the BTC. The reason becomes clear when it appears that the BTC Committee was concurrently investigating a totally radical approach to catering on future trains regardless of type. This would involve the use of pre-packaged frozen foods that just need to be reheated – as with airline catering. (It is not known whether this would have involved pre-packed set meals, or whether a varied menu would still have been provided.) It appears that the aim of these discussions was to establish whether or not this form of catering might save kitchen space which could then be given over to additional seating. *(Fast forward again to the 21st century!)* Related to this same topic, although not explicitly mentioned anywhere, is the decision that not only was some form of catering desirable, but that it should be the 'at-your-seat' service, which again immediately implies Pullman, and with it so much more than the conventional kitchen/restaurant car service then available on most principal services where the desire for a meal meant leaving your seat and walking to the restaurant car.

The 'at your seat' service was of course exactly the Pullman style, whilst the involvement of Col Harding once more implies that the decision had now been made that the new trains should be Pullman-based; so it is strange that this important issue is not more explicitly referred to within the various Committee minutes. Another advantage of having pre-prepared food that only needed to be heated was a weight saving and a smaller kitchen/pantry being required. In the event pre-packed frozen meals were not used and the proportion of seating space against kitchen and 'engine' requirements meant that pro-rata to seating the Blue Pullman trains operating on the LMR were exactly the opposite, viz: half the power car for seating, one complete parlour car with seats for passengers, and half a kitchen car also available, dependent upon the way one may wish to portray it, 50% of the train length without 'bums on seats'. (The mirror image set-up of the sets could not alter this fact.) On the WR eight-car sets the proportion was slightly better, but it would become worst of all in the last years when the two ex LMR sets ran in multiple from and to Bristol. Four kitchens in twelve cars … ! An awful lot of (expensive) eating – and consequent bills had to be (consumed) achieved to cover the costs.

As a contemporary comparison and when dealing with a normal service, consider a train of, say, ten vehicles comprising eight first or composite vehicles plus a restaurant car for seating and a kitchen car. The last-named might be the most weighty at perhaps 40 tons and the rest perhaps 30 to 35 tons apiece, giving a total net weight of perhaps 320 tons. Two of those vehicles (the kitchen and restaurant cars), perhaps amounting to 75 tons together, would be devoted solely to occasional use. Revenue from on-train catering thus has to cover the wear, tear and depreciation of these vehicles, catering staff wages, and naturally the wholesale cost of the food and drink, whilst a proportion would also have to go towards infrastructure financing. It is this reason why train catering has inevitably been regarded by the travelling passenger as expensive. Little wonder that the railway looked for a means of guaranteeing a greater return on vehicle and running costs than that provided by the vagaries of catering. A later (but fairly obvious) 1960s comment, probably equally applicable in the 1950s, stated that the proportion of passengers on Pullman services partaking of all kinds of refreshments was greater than on services where the travelling public had the option of visiting the restaurant/buffet car, compared with being served at their seat. Pullman passengers were a captive audience – once seated (aside from the occasional foray to the toilet) they remained where they were, and were regularly assailed by attendants seeking to supply refreshments. Small wonder the 1960s survey (referred to earlier) commented that it was hard to resist such attention.

Returning to the suggestion to serve frozen meals, a response from the Pullman Car Company has not come to light, but the General Manager of the BTC Hotels and Catering service, Frank Hole (to whom Portman-Dixon reported), was known to be enthusiastic. He did however express the opinion that Pullman might not want to be associated with what would be seen as a lessening in standards (again here is the inference that the decision had already been made to make the new trains Pullman-based). Nevertheless, Portman-Dixon was tasked with investigating the practical issues involved, and he subsequently reported that he could not guarantee any significant savings by using frozen food, the comparative figures being 15s 6d (77.5p) per head for a meal based on conventional cooking and £1 for a frozen meal. Although it is not mentioned, he no doubt based his results on the fact that a conventional oven would still be needed to reheat the frozen food, and would therefore occupy the same space. Today that may be a little difficult to understand, but the magnetron based microwave oven, whose technical origins can be traced back to the development of 'RADAR' in World War 2, had only been commercially available since 1954, and even then at a size and price that was only suited to very large commercial catering institutions. It would be the early 1970s before what is now almost seen as an essential domestic appliance became widely available and affordable. The recent reduction in the number of restaurant/kitchen cars and their replacement by trolleys on today's trains owes as much to changes in lifestyle as it does to the space savings of the microwave cooker.

Away from the aroma of cooking, the next major report from the Committee to have been located was presented to the BTC on 25 July 1956 (later recorded as BTC Minute 9/384). This included a number of interesting proposals, one of which had originated from an LMR suggestion of 30 December 1955, that saw the new LMR trains being based at Derby and operating the four-trip itinerary referred to previously. The same report also vetoed the suggested London to Leeds route, due to the fact that this was being given priority for electrification in the 1955 Modernisation Plan. (Proposed Leeds electrification in 1955 . . ?) We shall, though, return to the proposal for a suggested Leeds service later. To be fair, whichever locations and times were eventually chosen, there would inevitably be a compromise. A conventional morning start from Manchester arriving in London mid- to late-morning was not considered suitable for all, and it was recognised that there would be those who would find alternative means to reach the Capital in time for an early-morning appointment. However, by setting the return departure time from St Pancras (as was later accomplished) at just after 6.00pm, most business meetings would be concluded by then, and the train could be expected to be well patronised with the potential for many passengers willing to partake of dinner in comfort.

This same July 1956 report, consisting of more than 30 paragraphs, covered a variety of topics, some duplicating previous presumed decisions, including thoughts on the number of cars that were considered desirable, the proportion of first to second class accommodation (third class had been officially designated as second class in May 1956) and the types and methods of propulsion. As would be expected, the subject of on-board catering was again discussed, and while this might perhaps appear to be a bilious-inducing amount of narrative on a dietary subject, it is worth continuing the story as for a while at least the emphasis now appeared to be moving away from any Pullman involvement.

This arrived in a bombshell, a note from Col Harding (Pullman) that was included in the July 1956 report. Here it was noted that, 'The General Manager of the Pullman Car Co (Col Harding), has been consulted, and has agreed that the catering accommodation proposed is adequate.' It continued, 'The possibility that the Pullman Car Co. might provide the catering on these services has been considered, and while it would be possible for this to be done, the General Manager of the Pullman Car Co. does not consider it desirable that his company should undertake the work, since it does not maintain establishments at any of the points on which the service will be based. It is therefore recommended that catering should be undertaken by the Restaurant Car Service. The Chief of Restaurant Cars and Refreshment Rooms is in agreement with this recommendation. Since it is not recommended that the Pullman Car Co. should provide catering on these services, it would not be appropriate to apply the name "Pullman" to them. It is (still) felt that the service will be sufficiently distinctive if the trains are not named.' Clearly there was still a long way to go before the Committee reached any decision that the trains would appear in the form in which they were later remembered.

We now move away from reporting contemporary fact and instead allow comment on the same, especially pertaining to Col Harding. This is from the words of Pullman historian Charles Long in his article, 'Fact, Fiction, and Pullman Folklore' which appeared in the 'Pullman Society' journal. 'As set out here, Col Harding's reasoning seems odd. Equally, of course, the (Pullman) company did "not maintain establishments" in Newcastle, Bradford, Harrogate, Hull or Sheffield, but it had no problem in supplying the "Tees-Tyne", "Yorkshire" and (later) "Master Cutler" Pullman trains on arrival at King's Cross by a van service from its commissary depot in Battersea – as, indeed, was to happen also at St Pancras and Paddington when the Blue Pullmans were eventually introduced in 1960. *(It must also have operated the same way since the introduction of the SWP in 1955.)* Could it be that Pullman's General Manager had simply misunderstood what he had originally been told about the routing of the new trains, and he thought that it was proposed to run them between Manchester, Birmingham and Bristol (or some other provincial centre)? It has been said that the good Colonel managed to get hold of the wrong end of the stick on at least two occasions that I can clearly recall. There was the time, when, returning from a visit to King's Cross, he burst into the Traffic Superintendent's Office at Victoria, plainly much agitated, and announced that he had just seen *Topaz* in the 'Queen of Scots' when it should be in the Transport Museum (then at Clapham). I'm still not quite sure whether he really believed an assurance that one of the 1960-built cars had taken the same name as the preserved 1914 vehicle. On another occasion, having been told that (bearing in mind the low seat capacity of "classic" first class Pullmans) the provision of a special train for upwards of 350 passengers would be quite impractical, he came in with a copy of L. T. C. Rolt's book *Red for Danger*, and triumphantly pointed out that the West Coast express which had derailed at Wigan in August 1873 had 25 coaches in all. "If the railways could run such long trains then they can surely do it now". It had evidently not occurred to him that main-line trains were at that point in the 19th century formed exclusively of lightweight and often very flimsy four- and six-wheel coaches.'

It might appear reasonable to the reader that the subject of catering was being given paramount importance compared with the actual selection of routes, design of stock and mechanical matters, but the success of the proposed new service was totally dependent upon attracting the right clientele, and so the catering arrangements had to be just right. However, the conclusions of the Committee on catering was only one of the ideas that the BTC had to consider as it had also requested a feasibility report from its own Traffic Survey Group (TSG) in the form of what would today be termed as 'market research'. Little appears in the minutes pertaining to the establishment or make-up of the TSG, so it could be that this was a permanently running section, with the identification of potential new markets for its services as just one of its allotted tasks.

Taking a more general view, the TSG had submitted a report to the BTC some time prior to 26 July 1956 in which it concluded that the railway should provide three distinct types of express passenger service in future. Foremost of these was a Pullman de-luxe service, intended for the business traveller, for which a supplementary fare would be charged. Next were special express services, limited in capacity, and again with the possibility of a supplementary charge. Finally there were the ordinary express services. Pullman services were deemed to be strictly limited to the first category. Interestingly, three individuals who were involved in the subsequent discussion on the points raised by the TSG also sat on the Phillips Committee. Indeed it could be argued that the BTC had set its own agenda as to the conclusions it wished to see reached, and (purely the opinion of the present writers) seems to have adopted the principle that, 'if you don't like the result, move the goal-posts' – nothing new there! (Surviving paperwork also reveals the general decline in passenger journeys that was occurring at the time. From a peak of 1,295 million passenger journeys in 1937, numbers had shrunk to 1,001 million in 1951 and to 991 million by 1954. National Archives file AN172/1 quotes the number of Pullman passengers on the Southern Region in 1952 as 1,036,210 but this cannot be said to be good or bad as there are no other yearly figures to gauge it against. (As a comparison in 2018 the total number of passengers carried on franchised rail services was stated to be 1.750 billion, and represents an increase of 51 million on the previous year. Even so a massive increase against 1937 and on a network today having perhaps only two-thirds of the route mileage.) In 1954, the number of vehicles on the roads had also doubled against 1937. One rather hard to believe statistic for the time was that in 1954 there had been just over one million domestic air passengers in the UK as well.)

We now return to the choice of Leeds as a potential terminus for the new service, and it is appropriate to state that the reluctance of the Committee to recommend the Yorkshire city for the new trains was based on potentially sound logic. As mentioned, the 1955 Modernisation Plan had envisaged early electrification of the East Coast Main Line, which implied a major engineering upheaval which would have roughly coincided with the introduction of the new trains. Even at this stage the BTC was very conscious of its public image, and wisely felt that a prestige new service being affected by major delay was far from advisable. (Recounting what was reported earlier, electrification of the ECML was delayed, and steam was eventually superseded by the 'Deltic' diesels; then by HST operation, with the route not being electrified until the 1970s.)

The proverbial 'thorn in the operator's side' of the Western Region almost from the time of the introduction of the BP services between Paddington and Bristol. This was the existing 'Bristolian' service which covered the same ground as the Pullman train to a very similar time but without the need to pay a supplementary fare. So what did Blue Pullman offer that the ordinary train could not? The answer was modernism, air-conditioning and an 'at your seat service', but against this was the supplementary fare whether the passenger travelled first or second class Pullman. For the regular service train it was cheaper and sometimes over the years faster as well. 'You pays your money and takes your choice', but many did and we know that for a time in the late 1960s the Bristol up morning and down evening trains were running as 12 cars – but with four kitchens in the paired LMR trains it was an awful lot of overhead to carry. Seen here in August 1957 in the days before the Pullman competitor, 'Castle' No 7014 *Caerhays Castle* blasts its way north past Dr Day's Bridge Junction towards Filton and the Badminton line ready for its fast dash to Paddington. Locomotives of the 'King' and 'Britannia' classes were also known to work the service on occasions. The renowned photographer and painter George Heiron used the same view for a painting based on the same scene. *George Heiron*

Again according to Charles Long, the BTC made the final decision to market the new trains as Pullman services in July 1956, and although no specific date is known for this, the decision it is safe to say was subsequent to, but fairly soon after, the submission of the reports outlined above.

From the Phillips Committee, the BTC had by now distilled the recommended technical details and the make-up of the trains, while it was the views of the Traffic Survey Group that determined the standard of service to be provided. Perhaps this proves that the criteria the Committee had been working to had indeed been altered at some stage, but the BTC's decision to go for Pullman was to have far-reaching consequences, and would also lead to a difficult relationship between its own catering arm and the BTC's more recently acquired Pullman company.

Charles Long again makes an interesting comment on the Pullman concept for the new trains which is contained in his article within *The Golden Way* (Issue 64). '...the fact remains that the committee [the Diesel Multiple-Unit Main-Line Express Services Committee] had largely settled the general layout of the trains before Pullman was, after all, designated as the favoured catering supplier, and one can only speculate what changes might have been made had the company's representatives been more closely involved in the project earlier.'

As mentioned previously, the Committee had set out its idea of the proposed train formation and layout (six- and eight-car) which, while it included two kitchen cars, adopted a '2+1' seating arrangement for first class. Possibly some of the die-hards of the Pullman Car Co regretted this break from the traditional '1+1' seating in first class, but had this original standard been adopted in the new trains, the total accommodation in a six-car set would then have been no more than 88 passengers. (It would also have increased the passenger ticket price by a proportionate amount whih remember was still intended to be comparable with the equivalent cost of a single air ticket between Manchester and London.)

Vehicle width was another issue to be considered as the WR loading gauge was more generous than the LMR's; here the Commission wisely insisted on a standard width for these five 'experimental units' – the first time also that the word 'experimental' had been used. Phillips as Chairman had submitted his own (bias) view separate to the committee that the new trains should be built to take full advantage of the generous (GWR) loading gauge and so be 9ft 7ins wide – the independence, some might say arrogance, of Paddington again. This he argued would allow for '2+2' seating in second class and so accommodate more passengers. He was overruled on this point on the very sensible basis that as the trains were 'experimental' they may later be required to work over other routes and so such a restriction was not feasible. (The way though was left open for wider trains for the WR at a later stage provided spares were standardised, but as we of course know, this would never occur.) Even so the trains as supplied were still '2+1' seating in both first and second class, the only difference being that an additional six seats were provided in the second class saloon so reducing the leg-room slightly: 42 passengers in second class against 36 in first class.)

An added complication was the cramped layout at Manchester Central and this dictated adoption of the 'C1' loading gauge. The same excuse as to the experimental nature of the project also caused the BTC to conclude that hydraulic transmission should not be used, perhaps surprising in view of the saving in both weight and cost that would have been achieved. At least the decision to standardise the loading gauge and transmission type between the sets was prudent.

With the choice made to produce the new trains to the Pullman standard, the Committee made the understandable recommendation to the BTC that the work should be entrusted to the Wolverton Carriage Works, excepting that is the power cars where, to avoid any delay caused by tendering, '...a suitable firm should be selected in conjunction with the Carriage & Wagon Builders Association ... subject to adequate financial safeguards and which together would ensure the quickest delivery time.' Wolverton was to be supplied with the necessary mechanical parts by an outside contractor. Presumably invitation to tender forms were sent to various builders – who these were and whether they responded is not reported – but we do know that on 11 November 1956 Metropolitan-Cammell were awarded the contract to build the mechanical parts. (Another source within the same archive refers to a date of 29 November.) Regardless of date the price for the contract was £1.215 million consisting of 36 vehicles making up the five train sets: 2 x 6-car LMR (12 vehicles), and 3 x 8-car WR (24 vehicles).

But now came another problem, for as the vehicles were to carry the Pullman name, BR workshops could not legally produce them, as Pullman was still deemed to be an outside company! Accordingly all the work now had to be entrusted to a contractor. Thus on 29 November 1956, the BR Works Committee gave its recommendation to the Commission and on the same day approval was given to the awarding of the complete contract to Metropolitan-Cammell (MC) for 36 vehicles to form five trainsets, two for the LMR and three for the WR, the contract sum again stated as being £1.215 million. (Without doubt Metro-Cammell were at the vanguard of rolling stock design at this time, so their success in securing the contract is not altogether surprising.) The estimate quoted included the necessary sub-contractor work that would cover the supply of the power units and other ancillary equipment. The formal contract between the parties was signed on 14 December of the same year. What we do not know is any timescale that may have been quoted. We know MC would not have accepted the work without assessing the cost and having some drawings already prepared so it is likely a timescale would have been fixed as well. From what will be reported later it is reasonable to suppose this may well have been in the order of two years, perhaps slightly more. Thus with the first of the new trains ready for trials in the autumn of 1959, two and three-quarter years after being awarded the contract, it was still a remarkable achievement, the more so that this was a totally new design – the builder literally starting from the wheels up.

By now it had also been confirmed that the two six-car sets would operate on the LMR between Manchester and London; David Blee, the General Manager of the region, confirmed this in a memorandum to the BTC on 22 October 1956. His note stated that, '. . . the decision to serve Manchester has been influenced by the concern at the growing increase in air travel between the city and London, and it is considered most desirable to provide a competitive alternative ... by the introduction of a high-speed service with exceptional standards of comfort, catering and service'.

Even so, Blee voiced what would later be an oft-quoted criticism that in achieving this aim it would be necessary to maintain one train as a spare, but that, ' . . the practicalities of obtaining additional mileage by running an intermediate service between London and Leicester is being examined'. Presumably there would also have been a similar announcement by the management of the Western Region around the same time, but evidence for this has not been located. (In 1956, there was a brief discussion about making all the trains consist of eight cars but nothing more is heard of this or the cost – and other – implications that would have been involved.)

The point about the spare train-set is interesting. The Committee had identified a need for one in its July 1956 report, with paragraphs 4.4 and 4.5 accepting that, the requirement for '...one spare train set for each region is high ... if further sets are introduced then this will reduce.' No doubt due to confidence placed in the presence of the new design in general and with the back-up of the spare set there was no mention of the necessity to maintain any locomotive-hauled cars as stand-bys, as was indeed done later on *both* regions. Nowhere either (as it later turned out perhaps fortuitously) does it appear to have been considered that perhaps just a single 'half-set' would have sufficed as a spare as was the arrangement with the TEE trains. An important point to make and to be emphasized again, is that each train consisted of two identical halves – each half a mirror of the other. Although an involved process, it was later an occasional practice to split the trains in two when necessary for maintenance or repair. Out of the five sets there would then be two complete trains spare, hardly the most economic proposition but surprisingly financial constraints do not appear to have been the driving influence at this stage. But documents can also contradict each other for when in another comment from the BTC it referred to the quoted cost (we are not told what this figure was) for the inclusion of air conditioning as being too high, there was therefore a definite risk that this feature might be omitted. Fortunately that was not to be the case and the provision of air-conditioning was later to become one of the strongest selling points of the new service.

The general concept was announced to the public with some speed almost as soon as the agreement for construction had been arranged: 'As part of the Modernisation Plan announced last year, British Railways are to introduce a new high-speed Diesel Multiple Unit built to operate between important cities, and to contain all that is the best to offer for the comfort and amenity of the passenger. Public reaction to the new trains will be carefully watched before increasing the fleet.' The only comment to confirm here is that we are believing this mention refers to the Pullman sets and not the Inter-City diesel trains. No doubt to keep matters in the public eye, a further announcement was made in March 1957, in which it was stated that it was hoped to introduce the trains in March 1958, even if it must have been obvious to the hierarchy of BR at that time that this date was hopelessly optimistic.

Notwithstanding also the Chairman's comments back in 1956, it appears up to now much of the foregoing and indeed later details of the order were carefully (and no doubt deliberately) kept 'under wraps'. But then at the start of 1958 the Birmingham Railway & Carriage Works (BRCW) – a totally separate company to Metropolitan-Cammell although based in the same city – offered an alternative trainset. It is likely news of the order to Metro-Cammell had leaked across Birmingham and as their alternative BRCW proposed using a single 2,150hp Sulzer engine. The BTC decided to await the outcome of the trials with the sets already on order before giving this new proposal any further consideration.[8]

Behind the scenes there were still hurdles to overcome and it was recognised at Marylebone Road that staff/union consultation needed to be carried out quickly. This was especially so as Pullman developments were not confined to the 'Blue Pullmans' for in September 1957 the Commission sanctioned the replacement of 44 locomotive-hauled Pullman carriages by a like number of new ones, 'to be of the most modern design'. During the same month, the Commission accepted that a realistic date for commencement of the new diesel (Pullman) services on the LMR would now be the spring 1959, but allowing for a degree of contingency, '. . . if more convenient, the summer 1959 timetable', the latter due to commence in June.

Conscious of the need to also portray a sharp new title for the trains, the original title 'Diesel Multiple-Unit Main-Line De Luxe Express' was shortened to 'Blue Pullman' indicative of the choice having been made as to the external livery of Nanking Blue. (Colin Marsden in his excellent publication *Modern Railways Profile No 10*, refers to tenders being sought in 1958/9 but this clearly contradicts the 1956 timeline referred to earlier. In reality it has to be the earlier date as otherwise it would have been impossible to have the trains operating when they did.)

From 1956 onwards design work progressed, slowly at times, rapidly at others (some of the reasons for which are discussed in the next chapter). A flavour of the fact that the project was soon reported as considerably behind schedule emerges from the BTC minutes of July 1959 – by which time the LMR sets should already have entered service – but at which date the Works Committee had only just finalised details of the vehicles. Not surprisingly costs had also escalated and the Commission now called for a reassessment of the financial consequences, both actual and projected, for the programme, and at regional and Pullman Car Co. level. The subject of finance was discussed again by the Commission in March 1960 although clearly there must have been a (reasonably) blank-cheque provided as there is no indication that work, or aspects thereof, was ever curtailed or slowed. What though does emerge is that when the Design Panel/Consultant(s) made certain suggestions that might have resulted in additional cost, J. F. Harrison (who in 1959 had taken over as the CME of BRB in 1959) refused – again see the next chapter. At the same March 1959 meeting, the Commission noted that trial running was under way and timetabled operation were planned to start on the LMR in June. (This was clearly incorrect information or incorrect reporting, for trials did not in fact start until the autumn of 1959.) But even at this late stage, with trials soon to start, these were subject to an agreement being reached with the NUR on the staffing of the trains, notably catering personnel. The reader will clearly note that already three years had elapsed since the project had been sanctioned but staffing was still the issue that remained unresolved. On this specific topic we are left with two possible conclusions, either one or both sides had deliberately placed the whole topic in the 'too difficult' tray, or discussions had indeed been taking place but had dragged on since 1956 still with no consensus being achieved.

Of course one of the issues outside of the control of both BR and the builders was that society generally and with it the expectations of the travelling public were also moving on at an ever-accelerating pace, particularly as the end of the (1950s) decade approached. Had the new trains arrived earlier, they might have had a greater acceptance, but although it was expected that there would be a book life for them of 30 years in which to recoup the investment, no-one could have foreseen the

'That view'. This photograph appeared in the December 1959 issue of *Trains Illustrated* accompanied by the following text presumably written by the Editor G. Freeman Allen. 'The controversial "Midland Pullman"...'

The term was explained in a written piece which makes the point concerning under-utilisation with the prophetic statement, 'It is difficult to imagine substantial first-class custom for the afternoon trip the "Midland Pullman" is to make from St Pancras to Leicester and back ... so that the economics of operating two luxury six-car sets may well depend on about seven hours' each day weekday use of one of them between Manchester and London.' The piece goes on the say that with a 9.00am departure from Manchester utilisation of the two kitchens in the up direction is likely to be very light. 'The second problem is the future of both this and the prospective Paddington–Birmingham–Wolverhampton diesel Pullman service when the LMR electrified operations begin between Euston, Birmingham and Manchester.' Comment was also made over the inflexibility of multiple-unit long-distance luxury trains. '... Most US railroads abandoned this method years ago; the Germans are having second thoughts and it is perhaps significant that the crack lightweight services on the newly electrified Paris–Lille line of the SNCF, roughly comparable with the route between London and Manchester, are locomotive hauled; and in our country the Eastern Region has opted for locomotive haulage of its Sheffield Pullman trains.' The caption to the uncredited image went on to say that the supplementary fare from Manchester to St Pancras would be 18s and between London and Leicester 10s. A separate piece in the same issue also referred to staffing issues affecting the trains' introduction into service. As we know this was partly true but not mentioned were the riding issues that had shown up almost immediately; it was almost as if Mr Freeman Allen was being 'fed' information. Was there even perhaps a mole...?

changes in lifestyle and expectations that would occur within only a third of that time

Again though we are now jumping ahead somewhat but it is still worth completing Clough's analysis of the train before moving on to the detail design parameters and other issues. Clough comments, 'The "Midland Pullman" began running on 4 July 1960 and (initially at least) achieved both very high standards of punctuality and much favourable comment from the travelling public. The trains were air-conditioned throughout, a feature that would not be provided in standard coaching stock until 1971, with first class passengers having reclining seats and a full "at-seat" service. WR "Blue Pullman" sets running between Wolverhampton/Birmingham and Bristol and Paddington were put into service slightly later on 12 September. On the Midland Line, timings were sharp. The morning up service took just under 3¼ hours and was even quicker heading north in the evening. Passing Bedford, the 49.6 miles up to town were timed for 84mph, which included an uphill section at 1 in 200. The WR was less adventurous. For example, with one stop the down "Bristol Pullman" was 15 minutes slower than the best non-stop steam. (The route of the 'Bristol Pullman', originally via Badminton, was also quickly changed to include a stop at Bath in both the up and down directions amid protestations from the Berger's resident of Bath.)

'Sadly, the ride of the trainsets deteriorated rapidly, despite the Swiss design of bogie performing admirably on the Continent. This was the second instance of a good-riding Continental bogie design proving unsuitable on British Railways track and spoke much about the state of the permanent way here. [Clough does not elaborate on which other bogie type had been found wanting.] Urgent work was put in hand on bogie suspension to resolve the issue and some improvements were indeed made but the issue was never totally satisfactorily resolved.

'By the end of 1961 the WR had arranged Pullman workings so that all three sets had daily diagrams. Not so on the LMR, where there was only one daily diagram, giving an uneconomic 50% utilisation. Even deploying the one set in use on a mid-day fill-in turn to Nottingham was eventually abandoned due to trade union [and loading] restrictions. Completion of electrification to Euston brought the sensible [?] move to transfer the whole fleet to the WR but the experiment was never extended, though the LMR did get 29 hauled Pullman carriages for their new services along the electrified West Coast line to Liverpool Lime Street as well as Manchester Piccadilly.'

Thus ends the politics of the train, its planning, the hopes pinned upon it and the belief that somehow this new train would almost be the saviour of first class. What it actually had to offer in attempting to fill this wide-ranging and as it turned out, almost impossible, role will be discussed in the next chapter.

Notes

(1) Hugh P. Barker was principally an industrialist (the Managing Director of Parkinson-Cowen Ltd, later its Chairman) and part-time member of the British Transport Commission. For his foresight it is he who may be said to be the true progenitor of the Blue Pullman trains.

(2) John Ratter was Chief Officer, Civil Engineering at the BRB. One of several individuals designated 'Chief Officer' each with responsibility for a particular discipline. As such it might appear a little strange that a Civil Engineer would be passing comment about the working of passenger services. Mr Ratter was also elected as President of the UIC (International Union of Railways) for the period 1961/2.

(3) In June 1955, the Committee that had been established to report on the proposed introduction of DMU express trains had anticipated their introduction,'…within, say, the next five years for operation on services such as the following: London–Leeds, London–Manchester, London–Birmingham, and London–Bristol.'

(4) Quoting from the original *Blue Pullman* work, 'Ten members comprised what was officially known as the Diesel Multiple Unit Main line Express Committee, the participants having been proposed by Arthur J. Pearson, Chief of General Duties on the BTC, and whose own career had started on the Cheshire Lines Committee. It appears that Pearson was astute enough to arrange for a cross-section of individuals who would bring varying experience with them, as well as being 'broadly' (a slightly tongue-in-cheek use of the word but appropriate considering some of the comments made at times by Mr Phillips of the Western Region) of similar character. Chaired by Herbert Phillips, Assistant General Manager of the Western Region, the group was sometimes referred to as the 'Phillips Committee'. Other members included W. P. Allen, David Blee, Michael Bonavia, Roland C. Bond – who was CME at the time but was superseded by J. F. Harrison in 1959, J. R. Pike, and S. B. Warder. Peter A. Keen acted as secretary, and in addition, E. K. Portman-Dixon was involved as catering consultant, when necessary. (Consultant for the on-train catering that is, *not* refreshments for the Committee!)' At the time of publication of the 2005 book I stated, 'Presumably it was Pearson, on behalf of the BTC, who set out the terms of reference within which the committee would work', but in the light of the new information already quoted it would appear more likely that Barker may well have been the guiding influence. Whatever, the set criteria was:

'Economic operation would require an extremely rapid turn-round, and new and accelerated methods of servicing, fuelling and maintenance at terminals. (The committee inferred that to achieve this requirement stock and shunting moves should be abolished. It was then a small step to recognise that multiple-unit operation was the ideal.)

'The trains will only succeed if they offer great strides forward in speed, comfort and convenience, and punctuality must be taken for granted.' (Here this same statement might well have been aimed at the design and introduction of the first production HST sets put into service in 1976, and as we know, they certainly did provide 'what was said on the tin'.)

'There should be a maximum speed of 100mph, and a start to stop average of not less than 60mph.' (A big ask and which, as stated, could well have resulted in certain routes being deliberately ruled out.)

'Comfort, with which is associated personal service to passengers, must vie with airline standards. Appearance and décor must be ultra-modern. They should run at times suitable to businessmen. The public will be prepared to pay for this service, but this should not exceed Pullman charges.'

(5) This mention of 'plans' is most interesting and the question must immediately be asked, 'Who was it that prepared them?' So, might these have been the plans for the Hasting sets and variants thereon, or could we even suppose it was a dusted off version from the 1932 GWR multiple unit scheme? Bear in mind we are talking at this stage of November 1955 and the formal contract to build the trains was not signed with Metropolitan-Cammell until a year later in November 1956 – so where *did* these drawings come from? There is no factual evidence of any sort to give a clue here and it can only be surmised that informal discussions had already taken place with a builder – presumably Metropolitan-Cammell – and that this showed an initial idea. Another option was that the said drawing(s) had been prepared by one of the BR workshops to indicate an 'outline' of what the railway expected for the make-up/layout/design of the trains after which this 'rough' would be shown to the proposed contractor for them to turn into a feasibility study and eventually a contract drawing – and contract price. We know Swindon operated in a similar, but not identical fashion, in the 1930s at a time when the idea of a diesel multiple-unit service was being considered for the commuter services around Paddington and Bristol.

(6) The 'hydraulic-versus-electric' debate so far as transmission types is concerned has been aired elsewhere and so need not be dwelled upon to excess here. Suffice to say the (G)WR already had experience of both mechanical and electrical transmission in the area of motive power: mechanical in their fleet of railcars together with a solitary 0-4-0 Fowler built in 1933 but disposed of to the Ministry of Supply in 1940. The diesel-mechanical railcars gave sterling service on both branch and main lines even if at times the driver might return with a 'box of bits' that had been dropped or come adrift en-route! (The latter folklore refer to the use of the GW railcars on the Lambourn branch.) Electrical transmission had been experienced from 1936 onwards in a 0-6-0 diesel-electric shunter supplied by Hawthorn Leslie in 1936. This was similar (but not identical) to several 'early generation' shunters supplied to the various pre-nationalisation companies, most of which shared electric transmission. More pointedly was the experience the Western Region gained from 1950 with their gas turbine-electric locomotives, Nos 18000 and 18100. All that need be said

here was that several of the failures in service attributable to this pairing were indeed down to the electrical transmission hence it is small wonder the WR were pressing for a more robust option. (The fact servicing conditions were partly to blame for these failures was evidently not considered.) What was also considered was the weight saving possible with hydraulic; even so the eventual decision by BR to standardise with the same transmission type to be used on both the LMR and WR sets was perfectly logical. (The full story of the Gas Turbines is told in the author's *The GWR Gas Turbines – a myth exposed* – see bibliography for more details.)

(7) This is the first time there is mention of an 'auxiliary engine'. At the stated 354hp it was also considerable higher than the 150/200hp engines previously considered for placing under each vehicle. There would also seem to be some 'double-standards' here, for this 354hp would indeed be located UNDER the floor although to be fair when in service vibration does not seem to have been mentioned much if at all in the later criticism of the trains. *(Perhaps the riding was just so bad nobody noticed!)* The purpose of this auxiliary engine, which was not in any way electrically connected to the drive units but was in turn coupled to its own generator, was to supply electrical power for the on-board services, notably the air-conditioning, although the more accurate term and which is nowadays in common use might be to say 'climate control' – because this is what it was. As will be seen later, the conclusion would also be that this separate engine probably ran at an almost constant output, excepting in conditions of extreme temperature. Two such auxiliary engines were provided for each complete train-set, one on each mirrored half. If output were an issue then it is perhaps surprising the proven English Electric power unit was not used which had already been developed to produce 2,000hp – as per the SR Loco No 10203.

(8) The BRCW proposal with the 2,150hp Sulzer engine might at first glance have seemed to almost satisfy the need for a power unit and auxiliary engine in one go. But on close examination this was a 'single' power unit, and according to National Archives file AN92/291 which is the BTC Technical Division Committee, it was also an *underfloor* power unit! If the reported minute is accurate and because it is such a high output power unit the idea of being placed underfloor the accuracy has to be questioned. If correct it is certainly a radical proposal. With due reference to the record, with hindsight the truth is more like it was an 'above-floor' power unit. Might it even have been a 'locomotive' that was being referred to? Even so, the thought of having a single high-output prime-mover at one end of a multiple unit train which would in effect then be push-pull operation was probably a bit too drastic for the railway at that time although such things did of course come along later – albeit totally unrelated to the Blue Pullman story.

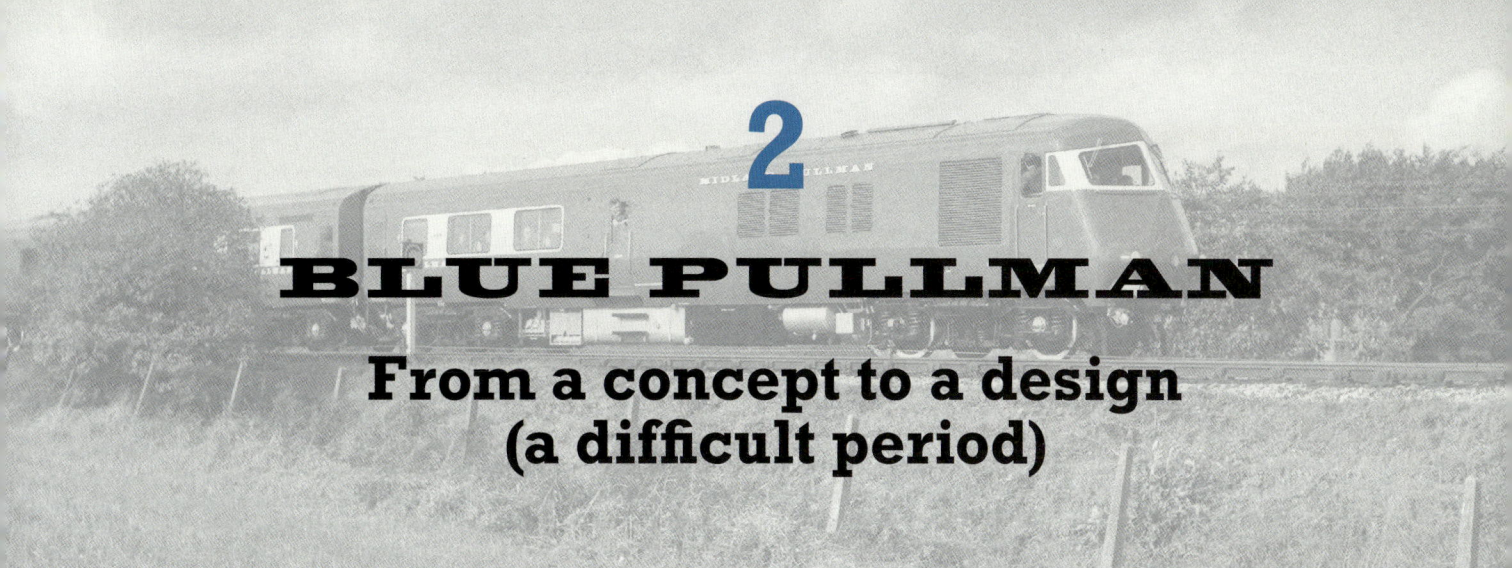

2
BLUE PULLMAN
From a concept to a design (a difficult period)

Although certainly not intended to take as long, the design and subsequent construction of the Blue Pullman trains was to occupy almost three years – from December 1956 when the contract between British Railways and Metropolitan-Cammell had been signed through to the trial runs of the first sets in late 1959. We do not of course know for certain how much preparatory work had been undertaken prior to December 1956 but as mentioned in the previous chapter, at the very least there would certainly have been a crucial outline drawing. Thus with the central criteria set, all that was left (!) was to produce detail design drawings and turn the whole into a working example – simple really! (But of course no C.A.D. available in those days.)

As it emerged Blue Pullman was unlike anything that had ever been seen. Externally different, an interior again

The Metropolitan-Cammell factory at Saltley with direct access to the main BR system. Construction of the BP trains was concentrated here although a number of individual components were of necessity sourced from outside contractors. Saltley should almost be regarded as both a construction and assembly point as well. Due to space constraints only limited test running was possible on the site, especially for a fixed formation six-/eight-train set.

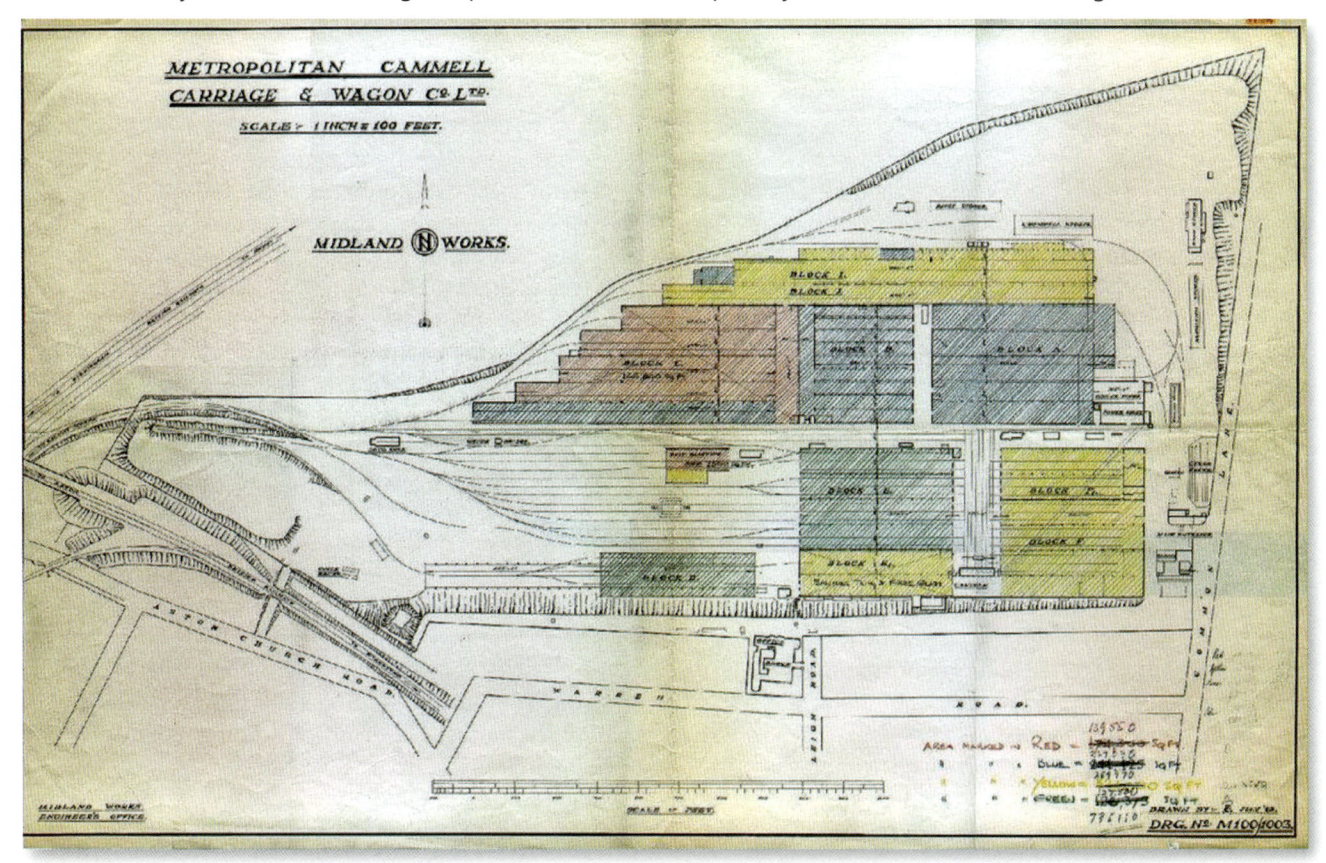

41

THE BLUE PULLMAN STORY

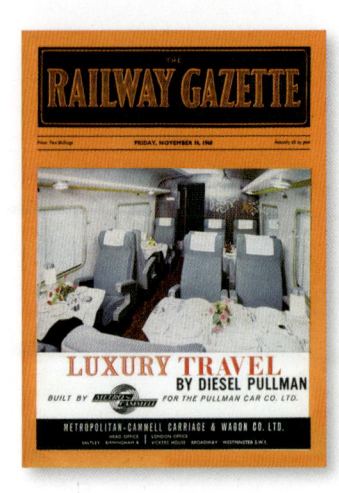

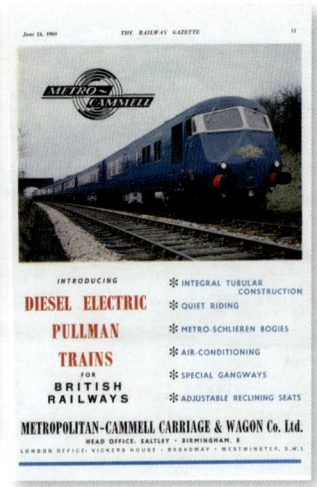

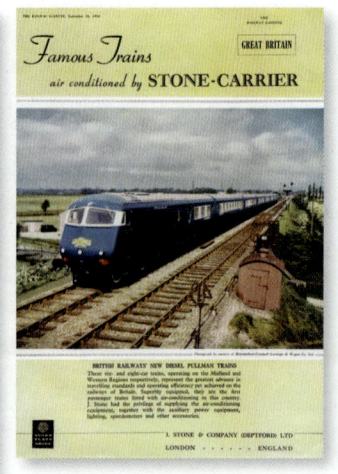

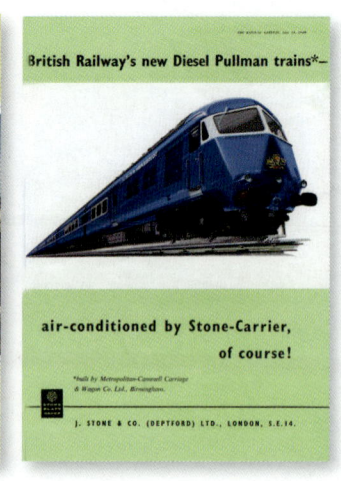

Metropolitan-Cammell were justifiably proud of their achievement with the new trains. Notwithstanding the issues later identified, they continued – as did various component manufacturers – to use the BP sets as the mainstay of their multiple unit train advertising until the mid-1960s. Many of these adverts appeared within the *Railway Gazette* whose readership reached far beyond UK shores. Whether they might have considered these 'in your face' reminders might eventually have had a negative effect is not known; after all if a potential overseas buyer noticed that it was still just the original five trains that were in service and the fleet had not been increased, might this very fact have sounded a warning in itself? We will never know what, if any, further serious enquiries were received from BR or overseas although as intimated in the final chapter the railways of Greece may have made an early request for information. Even allowing for the design weaknesses subsequently discovered, MC were justifiably proud of their design and no doubt a 'Version 2' would have been better. This pride can be understood as nothing else like it had been seen before or indeed was to be seen for over a decade – until the advent of the HST that is. Indeed up to at least 1970 the train was still being referred to at the factory as the 'High Speed'. Some if not all of the colour images used in the advertising were from MC themselves and with similar views referred to several times in the correspondence files now held (and consulted for this work) at the National Archive. Sadly they also appear to be views that have just not survived; now we may only speculate how many are lost for ever.

like nothing from the past, and most important of all, a mechanical design which was unique. It may be slightly cruel but with hindsight was this too much untried engineering at one time? To partially answer the same question the power unit and generator were well proven but the concept of a second diesel engine for auxiliary purposes rather than drawing power for auxiliaries from the former source was new; even so we now know the auxiliary engine was similarly proven to be subsequently reliable. In general terms this left the bogies, couplings and interior. The latter would be the subject of much discussion and scrutiny as time passed and was destined to take up what appears to have been a disproportionate amount of time and effort as the whole concept moved towards completion. This left the bogies and couplings. Little is mentioned about the physical connections between the vehicles although these were again unique to the train, similarly the bogies, referred to in many sources as the Achilles-heel of the whole design: their selection was based on perfectly sound consideration at the time, but then both in engineering and personal terms have we not all placed our faith in an item at some stage only to be subsequently let down?

So to achieve a revolutionary and complete working train from a standing start in the timescales must still be held to be an excellent achievement, especially when it is considered that a mock-up, and then of the interior of at least one saloon, was only available from around mid 1958 onwards. It was also only after this that a production line system for the building of all the trains would actually commence, the first two complete units (six-car sets) being ready in 12-14 months and the remaining three WR sets following on in fairly quick succession.

As was mentioned in the original book, one thing that is missing are records in the form of both paperwork and some of the many photographs from Metropolitan-Cammell appertaining to this time. BR documents about building progress are similarly limited in their coverage. Hence we do not have sight of the original 'Heads of Agreement' or 'Contract' for the building of the trains, so we do not know, for example, if there was in fact a set contract time – might there even have been a penalty clause over non-completion by a specified date? Certainly as time passed there appeared to have been some pressure exerted by J. F. Harrison at the British Railways Board to have the trains operational.

In times past, the awarding of a contract by a railway company to an outside manufacturer would invariably only see the two specific players involved. Blue Pullman would be an exception for in addition to the builder, BR had established a Design Panel[1] whilst in addition the Pullman Car Company, notwithstanding having been vested within

42

British Railways since 1954, was still being operated as an independent organisation.[2] In addition Metropolitan-Cammell had a considerable number of outside suppliers (sub-contractors) to deal with, some supplying major items – engines, generators etc - others with what might be deemed trifling – toilet fittings, carpets etc – but all essential components to be incorporated into the complete train. Each supplier would also need consulting in their specific area; it was a true case of 'juggling', most of the time successfully, although, as we shall see, occasionally things did come crashing down to earth.

Then there was the involvement of Jack Howe[3], a renowned and capable industrial designer who it appears was contracted to Metropolitan-Cammell with the full knowledge and consent of British Railways, and with the remit (put here in the simplest of terms) to produce a 'modern' train. The involvement of Mr Howe will feature heavily in what follows.

Having at the end of 1956 placed the contract with the builder there was perhaps some hope that the trains would in fact be operational sooner rather than later. Indeed there was an ongoing fear over the potential threat from the proposed motorway network, allied to the ongoing development of internal air services, principally operated by British European Airways (BEA). Although not specifically mentioned, it is likely both of these would no doubt have been considered by and likely part of the decision making process which had been enough to convince the BTC, not only of the need for the new trains, but also for as much haste as possible in design and development. (One aspect of the Modernisation Plan that was not proceeded with but which also related to air travel, was the proposal to install helicopter terminals at a number of main-line stations.[4])

It is relevant at this stage to look into the rationale behind the setting up of the Design Panel, which was intended to portray a modern and progressive railway image to the public. Part of this justification was a considered fear that modern (non-steam) locomotives and multiple units could otherwise present a bland, perhaps even stark 'box-like' appearance, and with the future success of the railway generally perceived to be related as much to image as to financial matters, steps were considered necessary so as to present an appropriate face to the world. The Design Panel can also be considered as the first real step towards the evolution of BR's (corporate) Modern Image. (Post 1948 the only real progress towards a corporate image was literally in the term 'British Railways' and in the standard steam designs and Mk1 coaching stock. Otherwise the new 'regions' had continued much as before maintaining their individual identity and equipment, nearly all of which dated back to private company days.) Recall too that at this time much of the external design work especially on new non-steam locomotives and multiple unit stock was being contracted out of BR's hands, the amount of new locomotives and rolling stock needed in consequence of the Modernisation Plan was far in excess of the new-build capacity (and in some cases expertise) in BR workshops where it was still necessary to maintain the steam fleet as existing rolling stock. Consequently there was a fear that this re-equipping could result in some manufacturers together with their own in-house designers having too much of a free rein. Of course the opposite perspective was to risk the stifling of new ideas, hence the remit of the Design Panel to find 'centre ground' and which as might be expected was tuned more towards aesthetics than engineering. 'Beauty is in the eye of the beholder' of course, and while this is not the time to discuss the relative aesthetics of the first fleet of diesels (for which the reader is referred to Brian Haresnape's *British Rail 1948-1978, a Journey by Design* and its more recent successor *British Rail Designed 1948-97* by David Lawrence), it cannot be disputed that the appearance of some of the first-generation locomotives and multiple units was, frankly, appalling. All credit, therefore, to BR for identifying this need at an early stage, but it must also be said that the Design Panel was hampered by limited staff resources, as well as reluctance, nay sometimes even hostility, from individual manufacturers to effect change.

Haresnape expounds on this well in his book, and the result was that machines introduced after 1956 did not always benefit from aesthetic advantages that might otherwise have been gained. (In the subjective opinion of some, the classic example from the negative end of the spectrum is the 'Metro-Vick' Co-Bo design of 1958 – even though Howe had attempted to improve this – while at the opposite end of the spectrum, the 'Western' class from 1961 was one of the best looking diesel types ever.) For the Blue Pullman project, BR (or was it Metropolitan-Cammell?) appointed Jack Howe FRIBA, FSIA as a design consultant. The aesthetic theme was given added importance by the BTC's appointment of George Williams as Design Officer for the Panel[5]. Unfortunately, Jack Howe's enthusiasm to create a modern approach was not universally shared by all of the Pullman Car Company's senior managers as indeed is commented upon later in a reported 'spat' between Howe and the then Pullman Company Chairman, Sir John Elliot, in early 1959.

Design Consultant Jack Howe. Howe's insistence on clean lines for BP was, in the main, followed in the production design, although what his thoughts might have been on the later years' modifications with the fitting of jumper cables to the front ends of the former LMR power cars are perhaps best left to the imagination.

THE BLUE PULLMAN STORY

LEFT A redrawn version of the Pullman coat of arms, lavishly decorated in gold, replaced the initial plan for a four-character headcode box in the lower part of the cab front and on the side of the intermediate cars. Although we speak of six- and eight-car formation trains, it had originally been commented that by adding/removing vehicles, any required length of train could be achieved to suit traffic demands. (So far as BP was concerned anything more than an eight-car train might have severely taxed the available power when it came to maintaining schedules, hence one of the advantages of a design where an engine exists under each carriage and the power available is thus proportionate to the train length.) Clearly this was before the railway had really grasped the concept of the fixed-formation m/u train but it still does lead to some interesting conjecture. (We are not told where the 'crossover' connections existed to ensure when one unit was 'pulling', the other was 'pushing'. Unless this was achieved independently by electrical means, likely this was on one of the actual intermediate vehicles and we suspect the kitchen car.) Even so, other than when the occasional half set or when two power cars ran paired together in connection with maintenance, the odd occasion when a five- or seven-car train operated was very rare indeed. In the case of the former this was when a five-car set appeared as an early demonstration at Marylebone and in the case of the latter during the time when the two former LMR sets had been modified to operate in multiple on the WR. Worth mentioning is that on 22 September 1960, and no doubt in consequence of the wealth of publicity surrounding their introduction, the LMR were approached with a request to run a special BP service from London to Tyneside for 200 guests for the launch of a new vessel, the SS Northern Star built for the Shaw, Savill & Albion Line. The request was refused by the LMR for the simple reason the LMR sets only accommodated 132 passengers. The WR were similarly approached, or perhaps the same request had been passed on to Paddington from Euston, but the request was greeted with the same negative response, with Paddington commenting, 'Well before that we expect to have all three sets in operation'. This was a slightly optimistic response as at that time only two of the WR sets were working, one each on the Bristol and Birmingham routes, the South Wales diesel Pullman service not starting until the end of the summer the following year, 1961. Whether the shipping company subsequently travelled by ordinary Pullman cars, a special train or even by rail at all is not reported. Clearly there was no intention then of attempting the 'any length of train' scenario once discussed. (The SS Northern Star was in service as a tourist ship until 1975 when she was scrapped, see https://en.wikipedia.org/wiki/SS_Northern_Star_(1962) .)
Colour Rail 103364

ABOVE Jack Howe's design for Blue Pullman was based on the latest design trends, a concept that commenced at the front, continued throughout all the vehicles and missed nothing down to the smallest detail. The result was a design icon and probably why amongst the enthusiast fraternity the trains still create such a degree of nostalgia.
Martin Brown

In essence Jack Howe brought his understanding of form and material to the exterior and interior appearance of the Blue Pullman trains. For example, the trapezoid windows set in their recessed panel around the cab fronts suggested inspiration from contemporary jet airliners such as the de Havilland Comet. Continuing the appearance of flat planes, the motor coaches and trailer carriages had near-straight sides, a form that would be taken forward for subsequent British Railways standard passenger coach designs. Howe also kept the unit ends free from all unnecessary detail and placed the ventilation louvres in an ordered pattern. Cab fronts were carried down around the buffer stocks, concealing the drawgear behind hinged doors. As the trains would only ever work as an express passenger service (or running ecs) it was only necessary to fit three headlamps which could also serve as tail lamps by the fitting of a red cover.

Charles Long comments that the non-traditional approach that Howe brought with him was unwelcome and would be resisted from the start. But to be fair, much of this existing opposition was based on tradition – a change from pre-war Pullman ideals and service levels into what would nowadays be called 'blue-sky thinking',

RIGHT Artist's impression (believed to date from July 1958) of the proposed design complete with headcode box. Written on the side is the wording 'Midland Pullman'. A second not dissimilar front end mock-up appeared on page 10 of the original *Blue Pullman* book with the wording 'Western Pullman' – see also page 19 of *Blue Pullman Supplement*. A colour rendition of this same drawing, possibly from a slightly later date, shows the train in the standard 'blue/white' livery. David Lawrence in correspondence with Colin Marsden suggests a green/black version of the same model may have existed at some time. *BR/LMR Public Relations and Press Office*

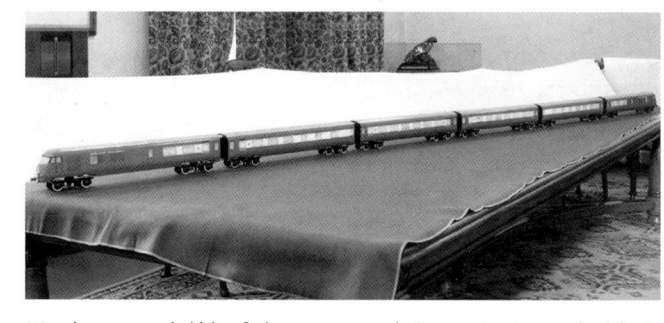

Mock up model(s) of the proposed six-car train probably in a rest/club room at MC and photographed on 28 October 1957. Assuming these dates to be correct then it indicates the exterior appearance of the trains had basically been decided two years into the project. Howe was clearly right in his final design – the addition of a headcode box completely destroyed the aesthetics. We also know a half-inch to the foot model was made which totalled 16 feet – perhaps this was indeed the one seen here. Folklore has it that at one stage this model was on display at a public school, either Repton or Rugby, although the reason for either of these strange resting places is not known.

where nothing was sacrosanct. An example was the insistence by Sir John Elliot that traditional table lamps be provided in the new trains. In reality these were totally unnecessary, as the diffused lighting in the new vehicles was more than sufficient. However, Pullman had always had separate lamps for each table, and it was their (more accurately, Sir John Elliot's) will that eventually prevailed. (The term 'table-lamp' is used for simplicity, but is not strictly accurate in this context, as the lamps were permanently attached by a swan-neck stem to the interior waist panelling of the vehicle, rather than being placed free-standing to the tables as had been Pullman practice in the past.)

Indeed Jack Howe was so incensed over their inclusion that on 17 June 1959, he wrote to George Williams on the subject: 'I am enclosing for your information a copy of a drawing number 134/40 showing details of the proposed Pullman table lamp. You are, I know, aware that I have produced this design under protest because I consider it entirely unnecessary, and in my opinion it detracts from the overall design of the coaches. I take a very poor view indeed of (the Chairman of Pullman) Sir John Elliot's action in demanding these lamps at a time when all the details of the train interior had been approved by the Design Panel and the Pullman Car Company. As you know,

One of series of 'mock-ups' of the cab design produced at MC and seen here as a 'screen capture'. Similar mock-ups of part of the intermediate cars were also made for the purpose of gauging reaction by senior railway staff. It is likely that upon viewing one of these came the request for separate table lamps. Regretfully the mock-ups were most likely destroyed later.

'Those' table lamps and some idea of the frustration clearly felt by Mr Howe.

structural changes had to be made and wiring rerouted in order to accommodate them, and I would say that this change alone has unnecessarily added at least £5,000 to the cost of the job. In view of (the CME of BR) Mr Harrison's' urgent plea for economy, I think this is a shocking waste of money. As Mr Summerson was present when the final prototype interiors were approved, and he himself came out strongly against table lamps, I would like him to know my views on the matter.'

Strong words indeed, and Howe's argument was one that could hardly be disputed on financial grounds. Perhaps with hindsight, Elliot[6] can be seen to have been correct, but only on the basis of aesthetics, and all of the BP trains were ultimately equipped with table lamps. But in other areas it was the ideas of the designers, Howe perhaps and so not necessarily the Design Panel, which were found to be too radical. One was the naïve belief that the addition of air-conditioning would remove the need to segregate smoking and non-smoking passengers; in practice of course this did not work. An amusing but absolutely serious sideline was the perfectly logical suggestion that toilets should be segregated for ladies and gentlemen. Accordingly, the panelling in those intended for female use was pink, and that for males blue, although the fittings in each cubicle were identical. While, in theory, this was a perfectly sound suggestion, the percentage of female passengers could not be guaranteed to be very high, so to avoid a potentially long walk to find an unoccupied cubicle, the idea was abandoned before the trains entered service, although the colour of the panelling, blue or pink, confirmed the original intention. In a fleeting image within the BTF film of the train under test, the exterior of a toilet door bearing the distinct sign 'Ladies' may be seen.

Away from interior detail and on to a more serious note, Metropolitan-Cammell and British Railways had decided on a new type of bogie for the train and although it is not stated why, the likely reasons must have been for weight saving and ride quality.

Writing this in 2019, it has been popular both nowadays and indeed for several decades past to deride the Blue Pullman trains over the issue of ride-quality, and indeed this issue cannot and should not be ignored nor glossed over. But what is often conveniently forgotten is that before the final bogie design was selected an extensive evaluation of the Schlieren bogie *HAD* been given under three standard Mark I vehicles operating on the LMR from 1957 onwards. (Three pairs of Schlieren bogies had arrived on 22 March 1957, the intention being to compare these against Wegmann bogies. A cost for all of not exceeding £107,000 is mentioned in the official paperwork.)

All were fitted underneath Mk1 corridor second coaches (coincidentally also built by MC), the Schlieren fitted vehicles originally carrying the running numbers Nos M25280-2 where they apparently gave excellent results. We know that tests were also made with other types of bogie (the Wegmann type?) under various Mark 1 coaches around this period, although it is likely these were unrelated tests

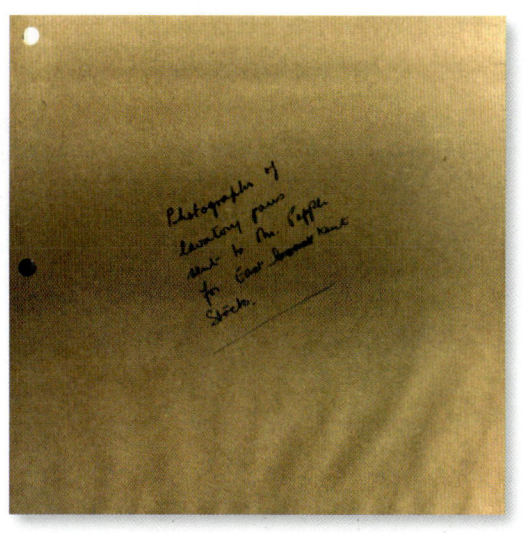

The only photograph within the Kew files of the Blue Pullman trains is one of a pair of toilet bowls, this is not withstanding almost continuous mention along the lines of, '… I enclose …' or '…herewith returned …'. For sartorial purposes only it is reproduced here. We do of course know the original intention had been to have separate 'Ladies' and 'Gentlemen's' toilets on the trains, indeed in one scene on the BTF film with a unit clearly on test, there is a view of the exterior door of the Ladies Toilet attached to which is a temporary paper label 'Darkroom'. (So were they developing photographs of the train en-route or some other product which required a darkroom? It might seem strange there was such urgency for photographic attention whilst on test.) The laudable idea of affording separate lavatory accommodation was dismissed when it was pointed out the proportions of the sexes who were likely to be passengers – business 'men' very much still the by-word at the time. Had the segregation gone ahead as planned the idea was also for the 'Gentlemen's facilities to have incorporated a urinal, but with separate toilets at either end of each car and a predominance of male travellers another result could well have been far more persons wanting to move through the train in an effort to locate an unoccupied cubicle. (Incidentally it was this file at the National Archives, AN160/70, that when requested to view Kevin was politely informed [the staff at the National Archives are almost without exception most helpful] that he would have to be supervised as the whole was marked 'Secret'. Consequently, he was shown into a separate room with ceiling-mounted cameras no doubt recording his every move and indeed on the outside of what was a single bulky file there was a sticker 'SECRET'. Despite this photography of the contents was allowed. So why secret? Was Blue Pullman somehow likely to have a destabilising influence on the Western world, was there fear we might suddenly see a fleet of Blue Pullman copies built under clandestine conditions in . . . wherever. Were there even potential spies tasked with finding out every detail on the livery of a 60-year train? Away from flippancy the truth is probably much closer to home, simply that it is most likely the original file cover was destroyed and the papers placed in a replacement outer sleeve that just happened to bear a 'Secret' label. But do consider one other point: with the one exception seen here, all the photographs referred to within the correspondence – and that is a considerable number including some specifically referred as in colour – were missing. For whatever reason these images were likely removed before the file ever reached Kew – this is not the only example the author has found when researching unrelated subjects. Unless of course the 'Secret' classification applied because of the image of the toilet bowl … perhaps equipped with a listening device to record the thoughts of the businessman on his way to London! We will never likely know…)

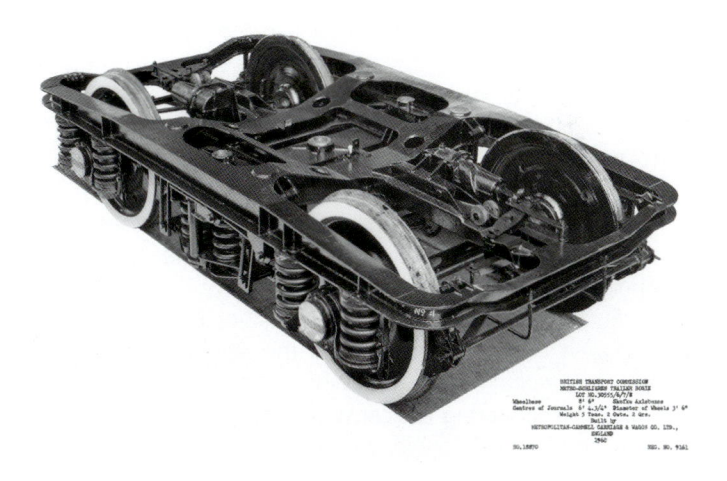

The Metro Schlieren bogie, this example being of a trailer type, which worked so well in Europe and similarly when on trial under standard BR Mk1 vehicles. Regretfully the same results were not obtained under BP. It should be mentioned that no evidence has ever been located to suggest replacement bogies might be fitted to the trains to cure the riding issues.

intended to source a replacement for the standard BR 'Mk1' bogie and which eventually led to the 'Commonwealth' type bogie – the latter giving a very good ride but at the disadvantage of increased weight. It is not thought these other tests were in any way seeking an alternative for the Metro-Schlieren type which by now were a fixed part of the design for the new Pullman trains.

Moving forward in time but concluding the tests of other bogies we might mention that three National Archives documents – AN143/14 of September 1958, AN143/23 of June 1959, and AN143/27 of June 1959 – refer to the tests, comparisons and modifications to the general suspension of the vehicles fitted with these bogies. Despite the fact the design was not subsequently chosen as the future BR Standard, it should not be taken to mean it was considered inferior. Indeed at least one of these Schlieren-fitted vehicles was running in 'The Palatine' express between St Pancras and Manchester Central (and return) in 1959 – exactly the same route that would be taken by the 'Midland Pullman' train after 1960. One of the BR coaches fitted with Schlieren bogies, the original No M25282, also remained in use until 1982 but possibly receiving a bogie change to a more conventional product sometime during its final 12 months of service. Back in 1958/9 there appeared to be no reason why the 'Metro-Schlieren' type might not be deemed perfectly suitable for use on the new trains.

Despite the fact MC were now tasked with supplying the new trains, it is surprising to relate that no specific information has come to light covering developments between the signing of the contract for the new trains at the end of 1956 and the period through to July 1957. Possibly information may have been recorded in various MC official documents but as reported elsewhere, these appear not to have survived. What little we do know is that in July 1957 was held the first of three special meetings intended to bring together the management of three of the four parties involved in the new trains: namely the London Midland Region, Western Region, and Pullman. (The fourth was of course the builder.) The three attendees were represented by David Blee (LMR), Kenneth Grand (WR) and Stanley Adams (Pullman). (Adams retired in 1959 and was succeeded as Chairman of the Pullman Car Co. by Sir John Elliot – on which again more later.) Further meetings were held in October 1957 and then April 1958 – whilst there may of course have been others. Apart from the April 1958 meeting, see below, we are not told where these meetings took place.

For the April meeting, the participants together with at least one other individual, Mr N. Johnson, the CME of the Pullman Car Co., (from what follows, others likely attended as well) visited the Birmingham factory of Metropolitan-Cammell where there was an inspection of the mock-ups at the works*, but even this visit for senior staff to view for the first time the mock-ups of the new train was not easy to arrange especially in attempting to find a time and date that were mutually convenient to both the LMR and WR. In the event David Blee sent George Dow to represent the LMR, but the WR were conspicuous in not sending anyone! (*Although not reported in detail at the time we later discover that these 'mock-ups' were parts of both first and second class saloons.) [footnote]

We learn from the same papers at the National Archive (AN 109/956), that some suggestions (we are not told what) had been made apropos the existing design, by presumably the April visitors. Whatever they were, these changes had been made by August and undoubtedly would have involved detail rather than concept.

Despite being unable to arrange a mutually suitable date for the aforementioned visit there was certainly no breakdown in communication between the respective regional GMs at Paddington and Euston (or even a breakdown in the keeping of records) for on 11 December 1958, a joint letter from Paddington and Euston was sent to the Secretary General of the BTC at Marylebone Road, (Major General Wansbrough-Jones). The letter was headed, 'Diesel Multiple Unit Mainline De-Luxe Express Services. Consultation on Design.' The GMs stated that despite being involved in all discussions on '. . . appearance, styling, seating layout, passenger décor and passenger amenities . . .' the CME (R. C. Bond) has now approved recommendations from the April meeting '. . . the minutes from which were not received until three months later . . .'. It was noted also that CMEs of the two regions were also requesting a further inspection of the mock-up.

The letter was passed by Wansbrough-Jones to T. H. Summerson, Chairman of the Design Panel. Summerson in turn sent a private note to Christian Barman[7] asking how he should respond.

There is no paper response in the file from Barman but we know the two men were also in contact by telephone so this is likely to have been how matters were progressed.

Accordingly Summerson replied to Major General Wansbrough Jones with two typed pages of foolscap. After repeating what we already know as regards to the 1957 meetings, matters then turned to the inspection visit of April 1958. Summerson repeats that, 'Grand sent no one . . . however, a full note of the inspection was sent to him and acknowledged by him on the 14 May.' This straight away is a direct contradiction of the information Grand had stated.

Summerson then states that, '. . . being told that time was pressing, I gave on the spot decisions as to the final recommendations which should be made concerning a very few items of minor detail including two items relating to the Pullman Company's preference for folding tables and hooks on walls which appeared to lie within that Company's province.' Note – neither separate coat hooks or folding (or part folding) tables were a feature of the final production trains.

Summerson defends himself further by advising that two days later he had reported the April meeting to the Design Panel at a gathering where the Chief Carriage and Wagon Engineering Officer was also present. Summerson states he gave six copies of his notes to this BR man for distribution including for the regional General Managers. '. . . If he failed, as is implicit in their letter . . . to inform the General Managers accordingly, that can hardly be laid at the Panel's door.' (The file contains several copies/drafts of what was actually sent but the above is a reasonable précis of the salient points from all.)

Matters now move back to Jack Howe and an undated (but certainly late 1958) letter sent by Howe to George Williams advising that Gordon Cullen who had been intended to produce a design for the end walls of the train had let them down due to a forthcoming trip to India. Howe states, 'I am rather cross about it as I had put in a lot of work and we now seem to be back where we started. I cannot think of anyone suitable to do the job and time is now uncomfortably short . . . My only fear is that the Pullman car Co. may come along afterwards and put something rather tatty in this space but I feel we must take a chance on that.' (A design did subsequently appear on the end walls of the first class saloons but in the same place in the second class Western Region trains the area was left blank. This 'replacement' design was the work of George Mitchell who was paid 25 guineas 'for initial work' in early 1959 followed by a further £25.00 each for a total of 36 'decorative panels' in the first class saloons. From the copy correspondence this was also not the only occasion when Jack Howe was incensed over detail and took his frustration out in a letter to another party. Sixty years later it all seems to be somewhat pathetic.)

Jack Howe was in touch with George Williams again on 16 October 1958, this time requesting that Williams make contact with Christopher Ironside asking him to produce another, bolder design for the Pullman crest. The heraldic – Pullman – colours to be of Williams choice. Why it should be that Howe made this request through a third-party is not explained but from comment made later in the *Design* magazine article, it is possible Howe and Ironside were to some extent at odds around this time. Howe appears to have had definite ideas about how he wished others to proceed and if they failed to meet his criteria he was ruthless in his condemnation. Nowadays one might describe him as someone who behaved a bit like a martinet but one who also appears to give his subordinates a totally free-hand although the result must be exactly what was in the remit with no room for variation or innovation. (It was later reported that the revised crest had been produced jointly by both Christopher and his brother Robin Ironside.)

Two days before Christmas 1958 a note appears in the files which almost sums up the difficulties experienced in 1958. Although unsigned it is likely to have been the work of Christian Barman. No recipient is shown either but the overwhelming evidence points to this having been sent to Jack Howe, 'I think it is true to say that the Panel has done more about consultation over these trains than it has over any other job . . . our normal practice is to employ consultants who initiate designs through the Panel. In this case the Commission stipulated that the contractors should employ the consultant *[meaning*

The end wall design within the first class saloons. *Roger Carpenter*

Metropolitan-Cammell employed Jack Howe.] This meant in effect that the contractors were required to submit designs to Robson[8], and that the Panel was merely one of the parties to be consulted by him.'

Clearly there was some difference of opinion as to defined design responsibility as this same un-named individual (Barman?) continues 'I agree it might be useful if we could have a word about this problem generally. But first let me remind you that responsibility for consultations rests – as I think it should – with Officers having primary and overall design responsibility . . . People like Harrison and Harrington would resent any attempt to attach specific responsibility for consultation to the Panel and I personally would agree with them'.

But even if Jack Howe had supposedly been chastened he had time over Christmas to 're-group and come out fighting' for he was at the forefront over the next discussion to take place, this time over the destination blinds to be carried on the side of the power-cars on the Western Region sets.

This starts on 1 January 1959 with a set of correspondence on the proposed destination blinds for the WR sets which were intended to show all place names served – so obviously these locations had been fixed prior to this date. The 'Train Name' ie 'Birmingham Pullman' or 'Bristol Pullman' would also be shown in colour so as not to cause any confusion with the list of stopping places names. Again looking back, surely something as

Much discussion also ensued on the destination blinds to be fitted to side of the 'Type 2' power cars (builder's description running on the Western Region). Again Jack Howe was seemingly incensed over what in reality was a trivial matter, even to the inclusion of the word 'Pullman'. This display of resentment was also spread far and wide amongst the individuals he was working with. All, though, were too professional to commit what thoughts they may have had to paper. Seen here is the side of a 'Type 2' power car.

straightforward as a list of names could leave little for debate but this time Jack Howe objected to the requirement that the word 'Pullman' be included and, '. . . will in my opinion, be more confusing than my design and therefore less satisfactory from a practical working point of view.' One can almost feel Mr Howe becoming more and more irritated as he continues, 'I feel very strongly about this change which I consider to be for the worse, particularly as it had been made such a very long time after precise instructions were received and worked to.' The letter was sent to a Mr Large at Metropolitan-Cammell, with copies to Christian Barman and George Williams. The final outcome was eight different WR blinds. Unfortunately we are not given further details as it would certainly be interesting to know what these eight were. 'Paddington–Birmingham' and 'Paddington–Bristol' certainly but what were the others? Unless of course both the services mentioned were shown with alternative stopping places? (The mention of separate blinds would also imply that this was not therefore one continuous 'roller blind' but separate rollers which the guard would affix accordingly.)

Perhaps in an attempt to bring the various parties together, Wansbrough Jones wrote to Summerson on 2 January 1959, with copies to J. F. (Freddie) Harrison, Blee and Barman, confirming there should be a further inspection of the mock-ups and that this time '. . . the "GMs" will do their best to attend'. Interestingly Kenneth Grand was not on the circulation list but is clearly referred to (David Blee was included in his capacity as Chairman of the General Manager's conference), but then neither was Jack Howe included, perhaps in the latter case as he was by now considered to be a 'loose cannon' and was being given time to cool down. But again might it also be that Harrison, who was by now in overall charge of the combined Locomotive, Carriage and Wagon departments, had decided to take overall control into the hands of British Railways? (R. C. Bond had retired from the role of CME in 1958.) Before however writing off Jack Howe we should also repeat we only have one (perhaps 'one and a bit') sides of the story and we should consider for a moment the frustration Howe must have felt as changes were made or previously confirmed ideas altered, all of which were pushing the launch of the trains further and further into the distance.

As an example of how in some ways progress was proceeding at the rate of two steps forward and one back, we can do no better than refer to correspondence of 7 January 1959 concerning the interior panelling it was proposed to use. This was of the 'Lanide' type, and with a problem identified as to whether the foam backing of the Lanide product would adhere sufficiently to flameproof hardboard if attached using 'Evostik'. Whilst the results of flame tests carried out by the 'British Railways Research Department – Chemical Services', then based at 28 Euston Square, were perfectly satisfactory, it was the adhesive characteristics that were being brought into question. Although only a minor episode in the history of the building of the trains it is yet another example where the papers do not provide any clue as to what conclusions and action was subsequently taken. (The checking of the fire-resistance of the proposed panelling might appear obvious, but it should not be forgotten that this was only a few years since the Penmanshiel Tunnel train fire of June 1949, the cause of which was traced to the flammable carriage wall covering then being used.) Jumping ahead somewhat, it would later be reported that delay in the trains entering service was in fact down to 'outside suppliers', especially those involved in supplying various internal fitting. As such no blame should be inferred as being apportioned to one particular outside contractor in what follows.

Meanwhile a visit to Metropolitan-Cammell was being arranged for the afternoon of 26 January. The proposed attendees being: Messrs Summerson (Design Panel), Blee

(LMR), Grand (WR), Adams (Pullman), Harrison (BR), Barman (BR), Williams (Design Officer BR), Harding (Pullman), Johnson (Pullman), Howe (Consultant and obviously back in favour) and Edwards (LMR).

All were men in senior positions and as such attempting to co-ordinate them so each would be available at the appointed time turned out to be a logistical nightmare. First one stated he wanted an earlier inspection so as to be able to return home on a more suitable train, then another wanted a car to pick him up from the station . . ; the file of correspondence on arranging this one meeting was considerable.

To give an example of the 'two steps forward one step back' scenario, the subject of the tables inside the cars came up again for discussion on 15 January. Somebody, no name was mentioned in the paperwork, was still in favour of 'telescopic tables', apparently then in use on T.E.E. services operated by the French SNCF company. Likely this may have been originated by an individual from Pullman who was concerned over passenger access and egress to the window seats when there was otherwise a fixed table for four. The matter was addressed to Harrison who in turn passed it to Barman, who in turn placed in squarely in the lap of the builders. In view of what had gone on in the past perhaps it was not altogether surprising Jack Howe was not copied in.

Metropolitan-Cammell than took a hand in the above with mention that as the Pullman Co. wished passengers to be welcomed on board and directed to their seat where a pre-laid table complete with cutlery and glassware would waiting, such a folding or telescopic table system was just not possible.

Meanwhile the countdown to the 26 January inspection was taking place – the original 3.00pm time being retained as Messrs Blee and Grand were unable to alter their own schedules to accommodate any earlier proposed time. (It was later mentioned that Messrs Blee and Grand were at the Austin Works at Longbridge until 2.30pm. One may wonder what might have involved them there?) All the participants would also be arriving by train (today no doubt it would be 'all would be arriving by car!') whilst the return would see eight of the party travelling back to London on the 5.00pm from Birmingham Snow Hill to which (Special) saloon No 9004 was to be attached for their use. (A note attached to the itinerary for the day concerning this aspect of travel stated, 'Mr Grand has invited everyone to accompany him back to London in his own coach (!) which will be attached to the 5.00pm train, and is writing to everyone concerned.' Clearly the spirit of the 'Great Western' was still alive and well and would remain so basically until the time of Stanley Raymond [1962] who '. . . was sent to Paddington as General Manager with an instruction to flush out the old [GWR] guard' – quoted from *British Railways 1948-73: A Business History* by T. R. Gourvish and N. Blake. Concluding on the theme of the [Great] Western Region and its stubbornly independent streak, we may even wonder how and why Paddington had agreed to accept the Blue Pullman trains in the first place? Possibly they were simply instructed to do so, in the same way that 'Standard' type steam engines had been foisted upon Swindon to build with several of the standard designs being used on the Western Region as well. 'Blue Pullman' would also be the first main line power units to run on the WR having a diesel engine AND *electric* transmission since the days of the Gas Turbines – or did Paddington still have the vain hope they might end up with a hydraulic version!!!

One slightly amusing aspect of the pending visit appears in a note to Christian Barman from an un-named (but clearly very frustrated) individual, as said person notes: 'The above arrangements have involved about 50 telephone calls, whilst every secretary has found it necessary to telephone me two or three times, everyone confirming everyone else's arrangements. It might be simpler if the time of the meeting were fixed by one person (myself where Design Panel affairs are concerned) with the various secretaries and details of transport left to the latter.'

As intimated previously, Jack Howe would, it appears, finally meet his match over design detail when Sir John Elliot took over from Stanley Adams as Chairman of the Pullman Co. from early 1959. Elliot would make his mark in several ways, one being his insistence that colour be incorporated within the shields contained in the Pullman crest and scroll rather than using just gold, again a detail not to the liking of Howe. Neither was Howe particularly discreet over his thoughts, for in a letter to Christopher Ironside (with whom Howe appears to have resolved his differences) dated 6 March 1959 on the subject of the design of the crest, he comments, 'I know we [meaning Howe and Ironside] had discussed this together and I was for leaving it out . . . had there not been a change in chairmanship I think we would have got away with it, but the retirement of Stanley Adams and the appointment of Sir John Elliot was something we had not foreseen.' Attempting to analyse as complex an individual as Howe, we get the impression that he seems to seek out allies amongst his peers no doubt feeling more comfortable in his outward criticism when believing others shared his own (Howe's) views. In reality it was probable that in most cases those who Howe consulted were just as likely to want to continue with their own tasks and simply not get involved in such spats.

As the Pullman Co.'s new Chairman, Sir John Elliot had by reputation been both a forceful and efficient manager. Following a military career he held senior leadership positions on the Southern Railway, Railway Executive, and London Transport Executive, thus it is not surprising then that he asked to see for himself the new trains then under construction in Birmingham. This was arranged for 23 April 1959. Even before this though Elliot was starting to make specific requests, such as mentioned above when he insisted the Pullman arms should be reproduced in colour, even though the Panel had unanimously preferred a plain gilt finish. Elliot would get his way, and the design of the coat of arms that was subsequently featured on the front of the trains was indeed in full colour – notwithstanding much 'muttering' in memo form from the Panel! (Somewhat late in the day, Summerson as Chairman of the Design Panel made a point of asking if the arms were heraldically correct? The answer – although from whom it is not stated – was to the effect that although 'unauthorised' by the College of Heraldry, they had been used by the Pullman Car Company for many years!)

One very interesting point over the design of the new trains comes in a note from Jack Howe of 4 May 1959 to George Williams and for which we may now clearly have sympathy with Howe. It is a short missive, but certainly worth repeating in full. A copy was also sent to Christian Barman, 'Dear George, I am indeed grateful for the trouble you are taking over the table furnishing of the Pullman trains. I must confess that after the meeting with Sir John Elliot in Birmingham, I was a little depressed and rather felt that he had inserted the thin end of the wedge and that they [the Pullman Company] would strive at all costs to make the trains as Edwardian as possible. I am quite sure that I shall not object to the designs that you have in mind and I only hope we shall, together, succeed in persuading the Pullman Car Company to adopt them.' Was this even Howe starting to feel himself 'out on a limb', and so needing again to find an ally?

At some stage also it was not surprising that consultant and design detail cost came under scrutiny. This came (but possibly of course not for the first time) on 13 May 1959 with a note from Harrison to Summerson in which the CME comments, 'I would like to have a talk about the possible effect of Design Panel recommendations upon the cost and delivery dates.' As it happened the two LMR trains came first in September and October 1959 and it is believed the WR sets followed one a month thereafter. Of equal importance was an additional sentence, '. . . I would like to look into the statement that the Panel has recommended a departure from British Railways quality standards for certain materials.' Unfortunately in both these areas this is another example of questions raised that cannot be answered. This is the only piece of paper on the topic within the file and to discuss further would amount to mere speculation. Even so, and on the basis of information already to hand, it would appear Harrison was likely correct on both counts. (It was Harrison who also vetoed Howe's later idea of rubber bellows – as per the pre-war LNER 'Coronation' train – to hide the 'plumbing' between coaches. This refusal was on the basis of cost although Harrison did leave the door open for a further look at the issue once the trains were in service. As we now know, it never was considered subsequently whilst the impression is also gained that Harrison may even have been getting a little fed-up with delays caused by trifling detail. Indeed, apart from various modifications to the bogies and other mechanics of the trains, aesthetically only one change can possibly be confirmed to have taken place up to the time the LMR sets were transferred to the WR – see footnote 6 to Chapter 4.)

Mention has already been made of the influence Sir John Elliot brought to the latter stages of the design, and the comments of others to these. What occurs though from approximately 25 May 1959 was to be perhaps the major issue raised by the new Chairman of the Pullman Car Co. It commences with a letter from (we think) Williams to Summerson referencing the visit made by Sir John Elliot to the factory on 23 April. Williams notes that Sir John is requiring the tables be fitted with lamps and also small 'making-up' mirrors on the walls. The latter was apparently a totally new requirement which Sir John had not mentioned before. So far as the provision of table lamps was concerned, Williams comments, 'Metropolitan-Cammell originally advised against this idea; their recommendation was accepted at the time by the Pullman Co. and the two Regions as well as the Panel.' So was this Sir John Elliot attempting to continue Pullman 'tradition' in the new trains where his predecessor was perhaps disposed to embrace a more modern image, or was it more a 'control' issue – the new man wishing to establish himself in his new role? In the opinion of the present author I would suggest the odds are likely in favour of the former. This is based on two precepts: firstly the opinion voiced earlier by Howe that given the chance he (Elliot) would strive to make the train as Edwardian as possible, and also that Sir John Elliot had already proven his business acumen many times over with his other positions. There would simply be no need for him to do so again.

Meanwhile the ramifications of this latest round of changes/additions was starting to be commented upon by others. Summerson writes to Barman on 26 May thus: 'Dear Barman. . I had already heard from Sir John Elliot regarding the proposed mirrors but not the table lamps. Personally, I am more in favour of having mirrors than the contrary. My wife always makes a frightful row when there are not plenty of mirrors available for her to tinker with her hair and face; and I imagine the bulk of other women think likewise. If, in the light of experience, it is found that neither the table lamps or mirrors, or both, detract seriously from the appearance and convenience of these carriages, we shall have plenty of scope for learning by our mistakes.'

Jack Howe was charged with producing the drawing for the table lamps, which he did but clearly under protest as seen in the letter shown a few pages ago to George Williams. Howe was obviously still annoyed as a few days later after the table lamps letter on 19 June 1959 and now in response to a criticism of his design for the actual lamp (which incorporated a magazine rack at its base) he adds, 'I agree entirely the magazine tray is not as deep as I would like but unfortunately it has to conform to the shape of the brackets which are already made.' He continues, 'It is just another one of those unsatisfactory compromises which have to be made when dealing with afterthoughts.'

Unfortunately this is another case where questions are raised and the answers are not available. Firstly we do not have the drawing referred to, secondly the cost of the trains is only ever given in broad (a final cost of the project rather than individual items) terms and we do not know for certain if the figures quoted are estimates or actual costs – lastly there is no record of a reply of comment from Summerson in response to Jack Howe.

The exterior area between the cars (coaches) carrying necessary pipe and cable works, together with on certain vehicles the vertical exhaust pipes of the auxiliary engines, was also the subject of comment by Jack Howe. As mentioned, he had originally proposed a flexible rubber sleeve to cover what he describes as, '…a pretty unhealthy crop of ironmongery beginning to appear…'. He added that the builders were rather unwilling to do anything about it. Howe's suggestion was for a form of rubber sleeve extending beyond each coach for a distance of about eight inches, '…a form of camouflage without completely closing the gap.' It was not acted upon. (Howe had originally proposed rubber bellows be fitted to cover the whole gap.)

Moving away from what might appear to be a preoccupation with detail, 24 June 1959 saw a letter from George Williams to Jack Howe. Much of this two-page note dealt with furnishing and fittings but in his second paragraph Williams states, 'Now that these trains are to be Pullman property it is perhaps understandable that they are a bit chary about having too much assistance from the Commission, but Christian and I are quite convinced that Frank Harding will continue to listen to us on this particular subject.'

The next subject to come under discussion was the antimacassars with questions such as should these be full width or just central, the logo or slogan to be used, and also the material: linen or 'Terylene'? Overall (pardon the pun), the impression given is one where every last detail was being considered, reconsidered, discussed, planned, and then sometimes modified. Six decades plus later, it is difficult to form a consistent opinion over such discussions. Was it really necessary to spend so much time (and with it cost) on minor detail? Were British Railways by this time losing interest? Was the appointment of Sir John Elliot a good or a bad thing so far as the new trains were concerned, and perhaps most obvious at the time, was the influence of Jack Howe having a good or bad effect? For the present the reader is left to form his own view with such questions being discussed in greater detail in the final chapter.

Meanwhile on 10 September 1959, Jack Howe made a visit to the builders which prompted the following letter to George Williams just one week later.

'I do not normally send you copies of my notes on visits to Metropolitan-Cammell but for convenience I am enclosing a copy of my meeting there on the 10 September.

'I think the attention of the Design Panel should be drawn to the items which I have marked in red as it is an indication of the complete lack of co-operation between B.T.C. Engineers and Industrial Designers. In the present case, it could, of course, be argued that as I am Consultant to Metropolitan-Cammell there is no need for B.T.C. to consult me on questions of this kind but in such cases surely the Design Panel should be informed.

Vehicle connections were necessary but hardly in keeping with the overall appearance Howe was attempting to achieve. His alternative was some form of bellows to hide the various items but it was here that form came up against function and practicality won through, although cost may well have also been a factor. Notice the inward opening doors of the cars and just a glimpse of the slot into which the car letter has been inserted – another thing Jack Howe was strongly opposed to. We might also mention the white wall tyres; whether all the sets commenced their life with this embellishment is not clear.

He then reverted back to one of his seemingly favourite gripes, 'In regard to lavatories I think it is an error in the case of these prestige trains that at this late stage they should decide to revert to common toilet accommodation. I fully appreciate the argument that there might be occasions when trains would run with a preponderance of male passengers, but I still think the prestige value is more important. [Six weeks later on 26 October, Howe wrote to Mr N. Johnson., the Chief Engineer of the Pullman Car Co, with a suggestion that an indicator be provided within each car to show the location of the nearest vacant toilet. Metropolitan-Cammell quickly pointed out this was impossible to install on the two LMR sets and the matter was left for a decision by Harrison so far as the WR trains were concerned.]

'It was quite by chance on this occasion that my visit coincided with that of Mr Rhodes (BTC) who was there for the sole purpose of deciding on the type and position of lettering to go on the outside of the coaches. Fortunately I was able to be there and make the right decisions.'
Howe's notes are references below with the items he referred to as marked in red now shown in italics:

1. Mr Howe reported that a request had been made to exhibit the two mock-ups at the forthcoming Furniture

Exhibition (commencing 20 January, 1960) and Mr Christian Barman had written to Mr Powell indicating that the British Transport Commission would back this project. The opinion was expressed that the first class mock-up particularly was very much out of date and would need very considerable refurbishing, furthermore, Metropolitan-Cammell were reluctant to divert labour for such work during the last stages of the actual train construction. It was agreed, however, that Mr Powell (Metropolitan-Cammell) would reply to Mr Barman stating the position and giving an approximate estimate of the cost of bringing the mock-ups up to date. *(This comment that the first class mock-ups were considerably out of date is most interesting and implies other changes, not seemingly referred to in the located files, took place. Oh for some of those missing images . . ! Also, did this exhibiting actually take place?*

2. Mr Howe mentioned that *Design Magazine* were proposing to devote a large portion of the magazine to the Pullman trains early in the New Year. This proposal had the approval of the Design Panel and Mr Robert Spark, who will be responsible for the main descriptive articles, would like to visit Saltley when the first train is complete and later pay a second visit with a photographer in order to take a series of black and white and colour photographs.

3. Mr Barnes (Metropolitan-Cammell) reported that Stones' proposed method of obscuring the surface of the perspex lighting panels had not proved successful and it was proposed to do this work at Saltley by hand. Mr Howe did not consider that the sample panels were satisfactory but it appeared that there was no alternative.

4. It was reported that two of the decorative panels had shown signs of cracking where large areas of resin occurred and Mr Howe agreed to get in touch with Mr George Mitchell suggesting he should visit Saltley in order to see the panels for himself and give any advice or assurance necessary.

5. It was agreed that the approved colour blue for the outside of the coaches was B.S.2660 No. 0/013.[10]

6. Mr Howe mentioned that a number of notices and labels were required, by the Pullman Car Company and it was agreed that he would combine these where possible resetting in type appropriate to the design of the train. These will be produced in self-adhesive anodised aluminium or printed on paper sandwiched and sealed between transparent plastic sheets.

7. It was reported that Mr Harding had received transfers of the new Pullman crest and was dissatisfied with the rendering of part of the right-hand lion. It was not possible to check this as no transfers had yet been applied at Saltley but it was agreed that the original drawing would be required from the transfer makers so that this position can be checked.

8. Mr Finch was disturbed that Carters had let them down over the mosaic floors to the lavatories. It appears that these had been held up for three weeks and promises to make a start had not been kept. Mr Howe agreed to contact Mr Inns, a Director of Carters, in order to make sure that there was no further delay.

9. Mr Howe learnt that B.T.C. had given instructions that no ladies lavatories were to be provided on any of these new trains and expressed his disappointment that the decision had been delayed until now. In spite of the fact that great care had been taken to incorporate the inscription on the lavatory doors these would now have to be covered by applied labels. It was agreed that these would be of the self-adhesive type as used for 'First-Class' and 'No Smoking'.

10. It was noted that the alarm signal plates were still in position with the engraved lettering which had been condemned some time ago. This lettering was not Gill Sans as specified and had been appallingly carried out. It is essential that these be taken down and properly engraved.

11. Mr Howe expressed disappointment that he had not been consulted regarding the coupling hook cover on the front of the trains which has now been perforated to provide an air inlet grille. In his opinion this detracts from the appearance and the air inlet could have been equally well provided by a scoop under the front cowling.

12. It was noted that attendant's lamps in the coaches were in polished chromium plate whereas all other metalwork was satin finished. This has been mentioned previously and it was thought that the correct finish would be provided.

13. It was agreed with Mr Rhodes that all lettering and instructions which had to be inscribed on the skirt of the coaches could be standard Gill bold, ¾ inch-high, white. These inscriptions should be kept to an absolute minimum and should retain a level bottom line 2in up from the lower edge of the skirt. Mr Howe promised to send Metropolitan-Cammell type sheets of this lettering of the correct size.

14. Mr Howe pointed out that the metal key plates on the edge of the Perspex lighting panels were crude and unnecessarily obtrusive. Mr Finch agreed to reduce these in size and provide a concealed fixing in the manner discussed, the plates to be satin chrome not painted.

15. It was noted that the fixing of the wash basins in the lavatories was unsatisfactory. Mr Howe agreed to get in touch with Twyfords (Mr Ellis) and ask them to get someone along to Saltley to investigate.

16. Mr Howe was extremely disappointed to learn that B.T.C. had given instructions to omit the [rubber] screens at the ends of the coaches after details had been worked out and a mock-up agreed. Now that the equipment at the coach ends is accumulating (including exhaust pipes and silencers) it is clear that these spaces will be eyesores. It is regretted that B.T.C. do not consider this important.

17. Mr Howe noted that the exterior lettering transfers reading PULLMAN and MIDLAND PULLMAN had been made as separate letters. It was pointed out that when applying the transfers the spaces between letter, must be exactly as drawing 134/32 and 33.

Members of the Design Panel were back at the Saltley works in early October on the same occasion as a visit by the Pullman, LMR and WR general managers. (Others may well have been included; we know for example Sir John Elliot was also present.) We learn this in a note Howe sent to George Williams on 9 October with the latter clearly attempting to include himself in the visit. At first it seems he was not invited but later he did manage to 'wangle' himself along – as will be seen shortly!

It is very likely the VIPs who attended on this visit were able to see the first (or possibly even the second) six-car set well on the way to completion, certainly with the external painting complete. We learn this from a note to George Williams from E. S. Cox dated 15 October, who enquires of the Design Panel about their view on applying an extra coat of varnish to those already specified (two coats extra pale varnish on the blue and one coat of similar on the white) in order to achieve greater durability. This recommendation had been made by the builders but who also pointed out the addition of the extra coat would have the effect of darkening the shades of both the blue and the white. The suggestion to apply the additional, third coat, was in the end taken up but with the final result that when unveiled to the press and public the livery was indeed slightly darker than had originally been intended.

By 6 November 1959, Howe was yet again in a fit of frustration. This time we might also have some sympathy for the beleaguered consultant in a letter he sent to George Williams, 'When we met the other day I mentioned to you the fact that the white band on the side of the trains had not been extended along the length of the kitchen cars in the same manner as the other coaches. I have now asked Metropolitan-Cammell if they would be good enough to do this and I have had a reply to say that it is impossible as far as the Midland Region trains are concerned but that they will carry out my design on the Western Region.

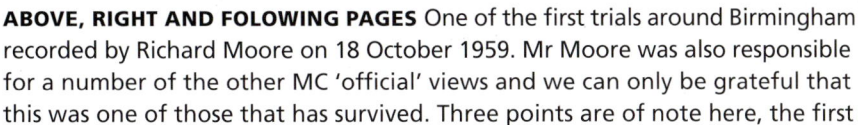

ABOVE, RIGHT AND FOLOWING PAGES One of the first trials around Birmingham recorded by Richard Moore on 18 October 1959. Mr Moore was also responsible for a number of the other MC 'official' views and we can only be grateful that this was one of those that has survived. Three points are of note here, the first being the lack of continuity of the white banding on the non-passenger portions of the kitchen cars; next note the transfer Pullman crest is missing from the front of the train although it is present on the car sides; finally the apparent white paint on the axle box covers was in fact a light yellow with a red horizontal bar across the centre – to signify that roller bearings were fitted. From certain angles the front end design of BP, especially the trapezoidal window styling, was said to resemble the rear of the pre-war Gresley beaver-tail observation car. This was a trial run from the works at Saltley via Castle Bromwich and Aldridge as far as Lichfield Road Junction near Walsall, a gentle round trip of 31 miles. A cropped version of the first view seen was also used as the cover for the April 1960 issue of *Trains Illustrated*. Although recorded in October, preliminary driving instructions for both the LMR and WR units had been issued as early as July 1959, running to some 18 pages of foolscap.

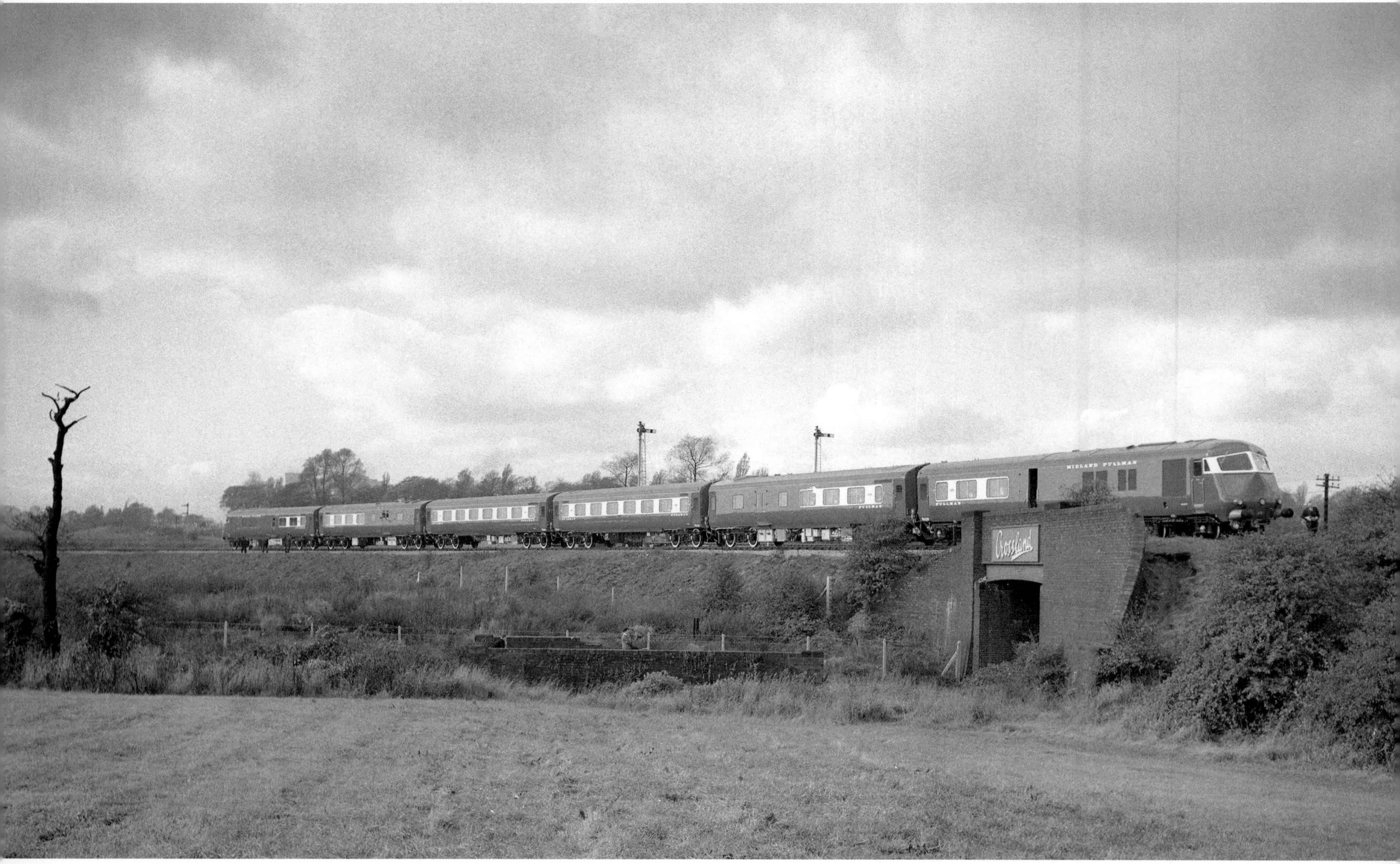
MIDLAND PULLMAN
PULLMAN
Crossland

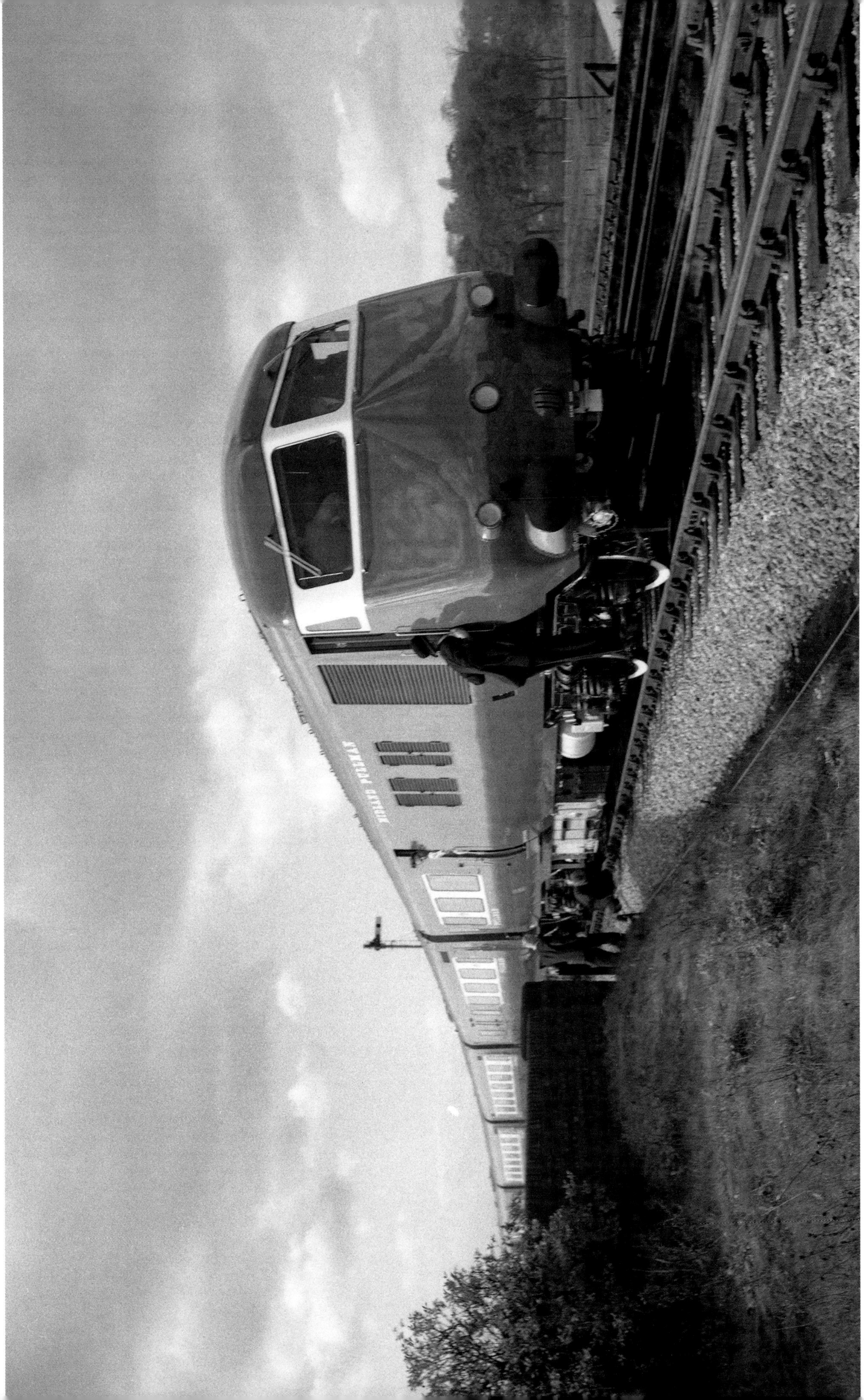

The Blue Pullman Story

'Although we are all agreed that these trains are pretty good, quite a number of mistakes like this have been made. The other blatant example was in connection with the Perspex lighting diffusers which have all been made with the flutes uppermost against the specific instructions of the Design Panel at their inspection on the 12 August, 1958, the minute of which states: "The Perspex ceiling diffuser panels should be fitted as in the 2nd class mock-up which was approved for both classes." The mock-up referred to had the flutes on the underside.

'During the last few months the standard reply has been used to any request or complaint on my part for work to be carried out properly, that under pressure from B.T.C. there is no time. As I have already told you, there is no co-operation between Mr Harrison's department and myself. Instructions are issued to Metropolitan-Cammell without any reference to me, in fact I doubt if Mr Harrison knows that I exist. I am only saying this so that the Design Panel will be aware of the position, and in regard to the exterior painting, will understand why the Midland Region trains will appear different from Western Region.' (In the end of course they did not, and the painting was altered on the two LMR sets. Interestingly, in a letter from Williams to Metropolitan-Cammell on 19 November, we hear Williams referring to the sets as 'High Speed trains'.)

Now we hear of a further, and this time more significant issue, compared with complaints over paint styles and other sundry matters. It involved the possibility of industrial action by BR staff over the manning of the new trains and which the unions felt might then have an adverse effect on existing services and with it the jobs of some catering staff. Consequently we learn in a letter of response from Williams to Howe, dated 13 January 1960, that the embargo on all photographs being seen outside a very small circle in the 'need to know' category had come from the very top; Sir Brian Robertson direct to Metropolitan-Cammell, '…nothing must be divulged until the strike danger is over.' Co-incidentally in the same note we learn that 'Train No 3' – for the Western Region – was also now complete.[11] Clearly the 'man at the top' was not totally informed as in the previous month Wansborough Jones had become aware that publicity and at least one picture has already appeared in the railway press – *Trains Illustrated*, for December 1959, as was mentioned, and depicted, earlier.

From snippets within the files we can also gather that trials with the two Midland trainsets did finally commence in late 1959 whilst the first WR train was similarly tested from early 1960 onwards. How then BR hoped to keep the existence of the sets secret when they would have been seen in public by this time is a mystery – not least because of the striking livery and appearance.

As will have been gathered much of the new material to hand concerns design detail but there is already a hint at something slightly more serious in a note which initially appears to refer solely to the livery of the LMR trains. This comes in a letter from Harrison to the builders dated 25 February 1960, in which he comments, 'There is still a little time left before these vehicles go into service, during which

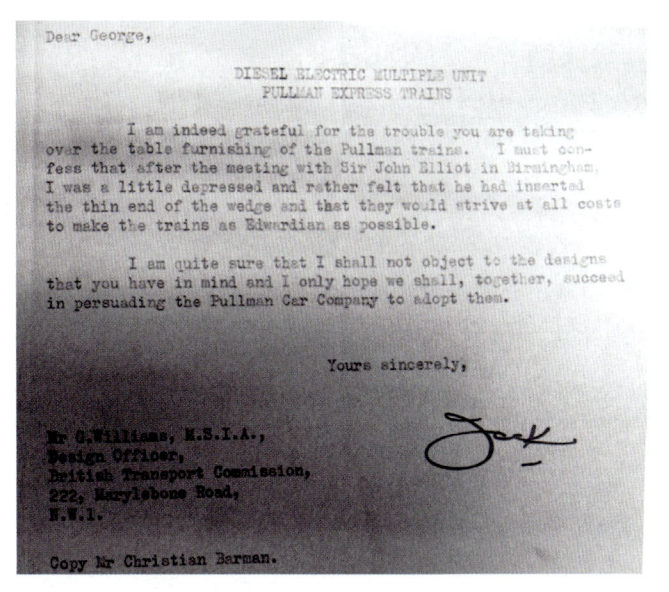

What else might we have missed?

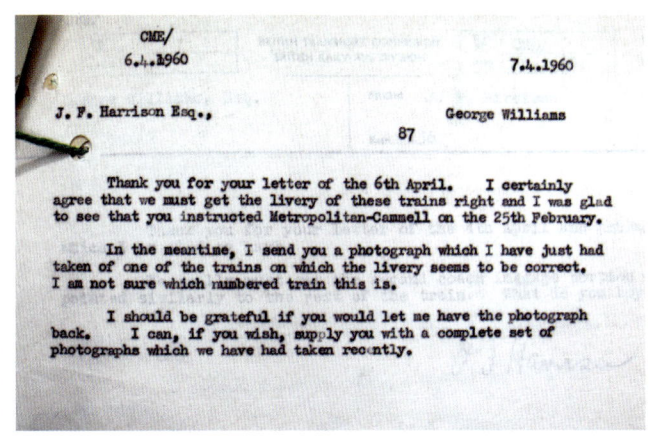

The researcher's frustration!

they will be back in your works for either bogie attention (springing) or braking, and you would have an opportunity to complete the livery finish as required.' Harrison was clearly already aware of 'issues' and we will of course cover these as the text progresses.

It would be fascinating to know more on the mechanics of the trains during the design period, the decisions made with reference to the bogies being the obvious gap. However, we must also be grateful for the large amount of new material now available but like any new source whilst it certainly answers some questions it similarly poses others that had not been considered before. Fortunately the same National Archives file also affords new information on other areas of these trains and which has been deliberately omitted from this section as having more relevance in the next and subsequent chapters.

Notes

(1) The British Railways Design Panel had been established following the 1955 Modernisation Plan. Its remit was not to undertake design itself but to oversee the work of outside consultants who would be contracted for particular jobs. This new approach to design was seen as essential in creating a visual change to the railways as modernisation progressed. There was thus much liaison with the Council of Industrial Design and whereas aesthetics may not always have been the greatest priority for the railway in the past, it was now to be given a degree of importance with a more modern appearance in everything from locomotive and carriage design, through to station infrastructure, lettering and publicity. The Design Panel was later (and out of the time span of the BP design) superseded by the independent Design Research Unit and it was from this source that the well known, and still extant 'double-arrow' symbol was born. (Two private companies would later come to dominate outside design used by British Railways, the Wilkes and Ashmore partnership, and the Design Research Unit – despite its name the latter being a private consultancy started in 1943 by a number of designers including Misha Black.)

(2) The British Transport Commission had acquired total control over the Pullman Car Company in June 1954. Despite this, the Commission decided to leave it as a self-contained, semi-autonomous entity – see Chapter 1.

(3) Jack Howe and Partners of Edgeware Road, London, were an independent practice of Chartered Architects and Industrial Designers.

(4) From British Railways Engineering 1948-80 by John Johnson and Robert A. Long, published by Mechanical Engineering Publications Ltd 1981. This is a learned and scholarly work the contents of which also reflect exactly 'what it says on the tin'. Even so, owing to the vast subject in general to be covered, the number of references to 'Blue Pullman' are limited. Another equally scholarly work is British Railways 1948-73 – a Business History by T. R. Gourish published by Cambridge University Press. The rear cover 'blurb' refers to this volume (780 sides) as having been 'Commissioned by the British Railways Board and based on the Board's extensive archives'. Consequently it is slightly strange that this book does not appear to make a single reference to 'Pullman' in any way whatsoever, indeed the words 'Design Panel' appear only once in the index and then as little more than a passing reference within the text.

(5) See portrait and potted biography of George Williams in Appendix 1.

(6) See portrait and potted biography of Sir John Elliot in Appendix 1.

(7) Christian Barman (1898-1980) held the role of Chief Publicity Officer of the British Transport Commission (1947-62). He was also an Executive Member of the BTC Design Panel from 1956-62. To the enthusiast fraternity he is probably best known as the author of Next Station, published by the GWR in 1947 and reprinted in 1972 as The Great Western Railway's last look forward. Barman commenced his transport career as the Publicity Officer for the London Transport Passenger Board in 1935 where he was generally responsible for the visual presentation of the undertaking to the public. Between 1941 and 1945 he was with the Ministry of Works before joining the GWR. He authored several books on various topics including architecture, as well as a biography of Frank Pick (The Man who built London Transport: a biography of Frank Pick, David & Charles, 1979), as well as two books under the pseudonym Christian Mawson. (See also Appendix 1.)

(8) This is A. E. Robson, a former LMS man who had taken the post of Carriage and Wagon Engineer with the British Railways Board.

(9) Like the references to photographs that are made in the file, neither these nor the drawings quoted appear to have survived.

(10) Early drawn impressions by Peter Ashmore of consultants Wilkes & Ashmore suggest an overall green livery having black window surrounds and a grey roof, in some respects similar – although not identical – to the dark green chosen for DMU units generally. But in keeping with the 'leap into modernity' the new trains suggested, a radical new colour was chosen; all-over Nanking Blue (hence the name 'Blue Pullman'), with white panels along the line of the windows and Pullman crests complementing the white panels. It might be assumed that the blue was selected by Jack Howe; but it is important also to note the presence of Misha Black as another consultant to the British Transport Commission Design Panel. He had a distinct preference for Nanking Blue, adapting it for British Railways electric locomotives, and securing it as the hue to denote London Underground's Victoria line on which he was lead design consultant. 'Pale Nanking', sometimes spelt as 'Nankin', Blue was originally identified in glazes for Chinese porcelain items produced during the Kangxi period of the early 18th century. (Taken from British Rail Designed 1948-97, David Lawrence, Ian Allan 2016.)

(11) 'Trains 1 and 2' were by definition the two sets intended for the London Midland Region, Nos 3, 4 and 5, were the Western Regions sets. Note that although each 'train' was in fact made up of two identical 'mirror' units, it was only when two paired units were coupled together that they were ever referred to as a complete 'train/set'. In this way the term 'half-set' will also thus be easier to understand as it is used.

3

BLUE PULLMAN

A testing time allied to publicity and an introduction to the public

As was mentioned in the first chapter some information on the new trains appears to have been deliberately 'leaked' in 1957 and again also in the following year; this included an anticipated start date for the new service 'sometime in 1958' although it must have been obvious to all that concerned it was a totally optimistic ideal for an absolutely new and untried venture. Even so the subsequent fact that all 36 vehicles was eventually completed in less than 42 months could it itself be stated a remarkable achievement.

But some months before the first train was ready for testing (see two paragraphs down), the *Manchester Guardian* carried a short article in its edition of 28 April 1959, entitled, 'Non-stop Pullman train postponed'. The paper continued, 'The non-stop train of six first-class Pullman coaches which was to have started running between Manchester (Central) and London (St Pancras) in the autumn has been postponed until early next year. The reason given for the postponement is that the rolling-stock will not be ready in time. The Manchester district council of the National Union of Railwaymen was opposed to the running of the train because the catering on it was to have been 'done by an outside firm.' A British Railways official said last night that he understood there would be no alteration in the time-table until the new train begins running next year.'

A further expose, this time from *The Guardian* appeared in print on 11 March 1960 and although perhaps slightly out of time-context at this point, it is convenient to record its text as a continuation of the above; it was accompanied by a photograph of the train crossing Monsal Dale viaduct on one of the test runs. The title of the piece was also somewhat prophetic as it was called, 'Seeking perfection for new Pullman. Last word in rail travel', again perhaps an unofficial leak or perhaps even the same journalist as before with in interest in railways for whatever reason. (We might even be tempted to suggest a 'third party' with a vested interest was the leak but there is no evidence to support this theory.) To return then to the newspaper: 'The non-stop train of six first-class Pullman coaches which was originally supposed to start running between Manchester and London last autumn may not be in service before next autumn. This is the train which was largely responsible for the national strike of dining-car attendants which began in Manchester last October and lasted two weeks. The dispute was about whether British Railways employees should man the Pullman coaches, but the difficulty now is technical. It has been decided that British Railways men shall work on the coaches, but Mr J. Royston, Divisional Traffic Manager for the London Midland Region, said at Manchester yesterday that he would not accept the train until it was "100 per cent perfect." There had been "certain difficulties in regard to design and running of the vehicles", which he described as being constructed by private enterprise. Mr Royston was speaking at the showing of a film on the modernisation of the railways to an audience of newspapermen and perhaps (in)appropriately called, "Coffee unspilt". One of the railway officials present said that the Pullman service between Manchester and London would probably start "by the end of the year." He said that all the individual units of the train were perfect but when running together they were less than perfect. The difficulty was to get the engine and the coaches to work in cohesion. He said that last week one set of engine and coaches had run so well together at 90mph that cups full of coffee in the coaches had not spilt a drop. Mr Royston said that the Pullman train would travel between Manchester (Central) and London (St Pancras) in 3hr 5min, and continued, "in spite of all the brickbats thrown at the railways, the delay in bringing that service into operation is not the fault of British Railways. The units are being constructed by private enterprise and the plain fact was that while they have turned out a very fine job indeed we require perfection before we feel able to go to our public and say this is the last word." He said that before 1964 there would be other electric services between Manchester and London with "very comparable journey times" to the Pullman service. Another film, *Report on Modernisation*, which was introduced by Mr Royston, was made for British Railways employees with the idea of letting the right hand

THE BLUE PULLMAN STORY

LEFT Having failed to locate the Monsal Dale photograph that appeared in *The Guardian*, we hope the reader will accept an alternative from slightly later in October 1960 and from a different location. Following its introduction into service in 1960 Blue Pullman remained at the forefront of publicity both official and enthusiast for some considerable time. It might even be described as a prolonged honeymoon during which time images would appear, posters and pamphlets were produced, general media advertising took place and of course information, albeit of a less technical nature, was written for the enthusiast market. In the latter category we might include the cover of the October 1960 *Meccano Magazine* depicting a WR set, 'colourised' we are told from a photograph by A. F. Wright. There was no separate article in the issue as might perhaps have been expected but the regular 'Railway Notes' section compiled by R. A. H. Weight did include a summary of the train.

BELOW These 'cut-aways' were one of a number relating to technology that appeared in the weekly *Eagle* comic aimed at encouraging youthful interest in engineering, science and technology. They appeared in consecutive weeks, 22 and 29 October 1960. Under each was a more typical comic feature, 'Luck of the Legion – The Shield of Saladin', produced in contemporary comic style.

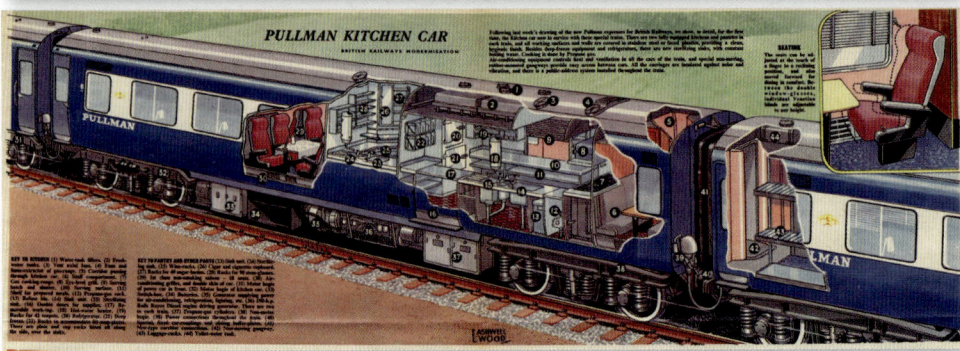

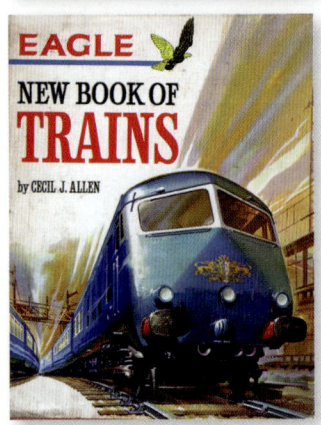

ABOVE The enduring appeal of the trains to the younger market is underlined in the cover of this 1963 book. Artistically the low angle of the image emphasized the design and even in more 'serious' periodicals (including *Design*) the same angle was often used.

of the railway, know what the left hand was doing, but it is now being shown to a wider public. An audience of Conservatives at the recent Blackpool conference were said yesterday to have been so impressed with the film that over a dozen people queued up afterwards to apologise to a railway official for the harsh things they had been saying about train services. A film unit is at present working in the Manchester area to bring the film entirely up to date.'

We immediately have questions raised. Where and how did this information come from? Certainly what we can say this is what we would nowadays refer to as a 'leak' but as is mentioned elsewhere in the text, BR had been very wary about announcing anything, almost insisting on a total embargo on news. Likely the most reasonable answer is in several parts: a reporter looking for a story; a follow-up from a promise of a new modern train probably made by some BR official in the past; and a link to a complaint or incident relative to the existing service. Within the article itself the comment about the 'outside firm' is of course a reference to Metropolitan-Cammell, whilst perhaps most surprising of all is that the piece was not picked up and expanded upon by another newspaper elsewhere. We may also question the wisdom of publicly admitting the teething troubles; perhaps it was a question of giving the newshounds something to chew on and so prevent rather more awkward questions.

In the event, the first complete six-car train-set (at this stage referred to as Nos 60091, 60731, 60741, 60740, 60730, and 60090, although Mxxxx series numbers were used later), was out-shopped from Saltley in September 1959, although prior to this it is believed that the first two motor coaches (Nos 60090 and 60091) had been tested separately within the works area. (British Transport

Commission minutes for March 1959 refer to trial running having already commenced, but this should be read with caution and could simply be a slight exaggeration of the truth to perhaps imply the power units at least had been started! No doubt such 'economy of truth' was intended to assure that progress was being made but it would then backfire later when questions were subsequently asked as to why the trains had not yet entered service.)

Instead we return to fact and report the movement of the first full LMR set (vehicles numbers reported above) took place on BR metals on 18 October 1959. Prior to this, and between September and October, static tests and low-speed movements were made within the Metropolitan-Cammell yard and sidings.

The public's first view of the new train would have been from the Saltley works on a test to Lichfield Road Junction near Walsall. This took the set north of Birmingham through Castle Bromwich and Aldridge, a distance of almost 31 miles. It is believed trials with all the subsequent sets followed a similar pattern after which they would venture further afield. With the second six-car set completed by the builders in October 1959 it too would soon be using the same route.[1]

Neither were the trials confined to weekdays, for available line occupancy resulted in a number of runs being made at weekends, with at least one on a Sunday during the autumn. At this stage whilst a BR driver, 'fireman' and no doubt a locomotive inspector (the term 'Traction Inspector' would appear more appropriate but did not come into general usage until a few years later) were in charge, the testing was under the auspices of the builders. What we also know is that at this stage all the runs made were undertaken at low speeds, hence the need to ensure line availability – not to delay scheduled traffic – whilst more importantly any issues over ride quality would not have been apparent at slow speed.

With the builders evidently satisfied (?) the first set was transferred to Derby sometime later in October and officially handed over from the builders to BR for 'testing, staff-training and familiarisation' on 16 November 1959. Whether this was in effect little more than a 'paper' transfer or whether there was in fact some form of formal ceremony or 'signing of documents' is not reported. The second (LMR) set arrived in similar fashion at Derby in November.[2]

We now need to backtrack slightly for as a precursor to the anticipated scheduling of the trains, at least two steam trials took place, in date order one on the WR and then on the LMR. That on the Western Region took place on 24 October 1957 between Paddington and Birmingham and involved 'Castle' No 5082 *Swordfish* with five coaches and the track-recording car (the latter better known as the 'Whitewash coach'). The down run was scheduled for 110 minutes to Birmingham and 135 minutes to Wolverhampton. In the event the train was 1 minute late reaching Birmingham and according to the December issue of *Trains Illustrated* due to engineering work in the area of Banbury. The return, 'up', working fared better, and arrived at Paddington five minutes early, presumably on the same 110-minute schedule. If so then this was a whole 15 minutes better than the standard two-hour steam service then in operation. No mention is made of a high speed steam trial on the WR to either Bristol or Swansea.

On the LMR the steam trial took place between Manchester and St. Pancras. This was on Tuesday 25 August 1959, and involved a 'Jubilee' and just three coaches, one of which was the track-recording car.[3] The run was completed in 3 hours 15 minutes, but that did include a severe loss of time due to a permanent way slack. (The Pullman service would later be scheduled at 3 hours 10 minutes.) It is possible that this trial was to establish whether a substitute steam service might be viable if required but in the event it is not thought steam was ever used as a substitute on the LMR workings. An interesting and important operational procedure for the test was the use of double-block working; where a train could not be accepted by a signalman unless, not only was his block clear to the next box, but also that of the box ahead. In this way faster speeds could be maintained, although the trade-off was the difficulty in keeping other traffic out of the way. Double-block working had also been used by the LNER in pre-war days for its streamlined express workings. Whether this double-block working on the LMR applied to just the high-speed steam trial mentioned, the test runs of the Blue Pullman, or eventually the normal public service (and if so, for how long), is not clear. The Midland line between St. Pancras and Manchester was not fitted with Automatic Train Control (ATC), so the trains destined for the LMR were similarly not equipped with the necessary cab equipment (although brackets for the later addition of this equipment were provided). The omission of ATC from the new LMR trains, together with the intention to run a regular fast service over a part-congested route, is perhaps slightly curious. True, the equipping of the whole route between St Pancras and Manchester with ATC would have been very expensive, but it also seems that certain elements within BR had short memories after the terrible collision at Harrow and Wealdstone, just a few years earlier in 1952. Here, the provision of ATC might well have prevented a dreadful loss of life whilst in the immediate aftermath BR publicly announced that they intended to equip all main lines with train protection as soon as possible. Yet just eight years later, a faster service than had ever existed before on the Midland main line was scheduled to commence where ATC was conspicuous by its absence. Readers must form their own opinions on the decisions made at the time. By contrast, on the WR, the lines out of Paddington to both Bristol, Birmingham, Wolverhampton and Swansea, had long been fitted with the GWR-style ATC contact ramps, and the WR Blue Pullman sets were suitably equipped with this type of cab-signalling from the outset.

Returning to the LMR, from Derby test running took place over the Midland main line commencing on the day of the official handover, 16 November 1959, and involved a test between Leicester and Luton. The first six-car set to be completed ran in a 'Q' path (these were spare paths available in the timetable for extra or special workings, which could then be slotted in without interfering with other traffic), departing ironically from Derby after the 8.55am Manchester Central to St Pancras, and returning from Luton behind the 12.25pm St Pancras to Manchester Central. Unfortunately it was from this very first day, of course the first occasion when anything other than low-speed runs had been attempted, that issues over the riding quality were noticed. (This information is again contradicted elsewhere for in official paperwork it is mentioned that the trials were 'suspended' in October 1959 [ostensibly then before they even started!] and so as not to exasperate the ongoing staffing discussions. Such contradictions can make research all the more interesting but also all the more frustrating.)

In the slightly naive belief that everything would work well 'out of the box', a 'Press Day' had been scheduled for 25–27 November 1959 (who this was organised by is not reported, nor whether it was for just the LMR trains or those destined for the WR as well. Whatever, somebody had evidently not been anticipating any problems as there were of course only two weeks left in the month of November after the formal handover at Derby). At the time the intention was to introduce the new service from 4 January 1960 – although other reports refer to 11 January. The date was then put back to 1 February but still somewhat optimistically as there is reference in surviving paperwork to 'teething difficulties' and even more poignantly, 'technical difficulties'. We may conclude from this that the respective PRO of the regions were not always kept up to date with progress. It was also fortunate that press invitations had not been sent out for as time passed the dates were put back further first to March then June and finally to July 1960 – when things did actually take place. Indeed between these times, in March 1960, the subject of the train's entry into service was discussed at the very top – Commission level. The results minuted that those present were informed trial running was under way with timetabled operation planned to start on the LMR in June, but as we of course know this was still a month on the optimistic side. The other point recorded from the same meeting was that these arrangements were subject to an agreement with the NUR on the staffing of the trains, notably concerning catering personnel. Indeed three years had elapsed since the project had been sanctioned but the staffing issue remained unresolved.

Even though the Commission may have been satisfied progress was being made and no doubt such dates passed down the line to respective departments, it was still dependent upon the Chief Mechanical Engineer being prepared to release the trains to traffic and it may well be that any of the dates quoted were 'targets' only. One useful excuse from earlier was that January was a bad month in which to introduce any new service as weather delays were more likely to occur at that time of year.

The main-line trials with the new trains involved various tests including emergency brake tests, which showed that on a falling gradient of 1 in 200, a six-car train could come to a stop from 90mph in 1,202 yards in a time of 53.8 seconds. At 45mph, the time was just 16.5 seconds in a distance of 206 yards. The weather and rail conditions during the trials were not reported, but the information gained assisted the calculation of accurate scheduling and permissible maximum speeds over varying sections of line. Due allowance also had to be made for braking distances (signal placings) in what was almost entirely a mechanically signalled area. General high-speed running tests were also undertaken around this time.

It was between October 1959 and July 1960 and with both LMR sets in operation that the famed British Transport Film *Blue Pullman* was made.

Whilst the (Midland) sets were based at Derby, a number of publicity (stills) photographs were taken on the Wirksworth branch, a favourite location for such events. Moving ahead slightly, it is appropriate to mention that similar photographic shoots are known to have taken place in March 1960 on the Bedford–Hitchin branch. In addition, the former Midland Railway line from Kettering towards Cambridge was used for slow speed stop-start testing.

Back in time now to the start of 1959 and publicity was another topic that comes up for regular discussion in the National Archives files (AN 109/956), the more so as time passed. Charged with producing the original colour drawings was artist Peter Ashmore, these based on elevations prepared by Jack Howe. Howe was eager to point out the external detail differences between the power cars for the different regions whilst also by this time, 29 January 1959, the decision had been made not to proceed with a box for a train reporting number on the front and instead traditional marker lights were to be used. Whether Ashmore's work was eventually ever used for publicity is not confirmed as another name, A. N. Wolstenholme, is credited with at least one of the first posters. (Wolstenholme is certainly known for a number of his iconic railway posters of the era, see: http://collectionsonline.nmsi.ac.uk/detail.php?type=related&kv=20247&t=people .)

Following the October 1959 inspection of the first six-car set, by then externally painted and almost complete, Sir John Elliot was again attempting to enforce change, this time with the words 'Midland Pullman' or 'Midland' and 'Pullman' (in the case of the WR sets just 'Pullman') included in white on the exterior of the power cars underneath the front windows of the driver's cab. Howe writes to Metropolitan-Cammell to object to the idea on 16 October, which had emanated from discussion amongst the VIPs on their return train journey to London following inspection of a complete train set. Howe comments on this return journey in a note to Christian Barman, in which he says, 'The General Managers were like kids with a new toy . . .' There was a lot of talk about publicity and the impression I got was that all were going to charge off and produce posters etc., which I feel is not a good thing. I know nothing of the publicity arrangements which you or the BTC Publicity Department have made and no doubt everything is being properly buttoned up but I think the arrangements should be known to, say, the General Managers and the

ABOVE LEFT AND RIGHT Again from the BFT film, this time we see more serious promotional material being printed. Posters for what was in this case the 'Midland Pullman' appeared at principal stations on the proposed route and also at various London termini. They were deliberately not placed throughout the country based on the reasoning that not all at the far reaches of the kingdom would be the target audience. The opinion of the Press department at BR was to the effect that a regular two months of continuing publicity was required to attract potential clientele prior to the trains entering public service.

ABOVE In similar fashion menus were printed for the forthcoming service. These consisted of a stiff outer cover to which could be added the specific choices available on a daily basis.

Pullman Car Co so that everyone is aware of what is happening.' (Despite his misgivings, Howe did his best to accede to the requirement for lettering to appear on the front of the LMR trains. Visual experiments carried out quickly showed that the only version that had satisfactory ocular acceptance was when the single word 'Pullman' was used. A drawing was also produced showing the words in place but after that nothing is mentioned in the paperwork and it is perhaps fortunate that the trains eventually appeared without this suggested embellishment. No images of this addition appear to have survived but even using just imagination it is hard to think how this would have improved the overall appearance,)

Much correspondence also ensued on the size of the lettering on the coaches together with the size of the vehicle numbers. The end result was a reduction in size from 4 inches to 2 inches although on the WR trains the wording to designate 'first class' was also increased (the change in size is not given).

Meanwhile the saga over the release of photographs rumbled on. In January 1960 Jack Howe wrote to George Williams complaining that he could not obtain photographic material out of the builders. Howe appeared to be in his usual prickly form concluding that, '. . . I also discovered two very good colour exteriors [photographs] which Metro-Cammell will not let me have at any price . . . this all seems a stupid situation when one considers that BTC is the customer.' Behind the scenes it is perhaps a little more clear, BR were still awaiting to arrange the formal press release so who could blame them for not wishing any risk of someone (unintentionally even) 'usurping the party', whilst Jack Howe concludes his letter to George Williams by stating he was off to Moscow for 10 days on 17 January. The risk of (accidental) advance release of detail information was probably simply just too great.

With more of the story available to us now compared with what was known by Jack Howe at the time, it is likely the negative (no pun intended) attitude of Metropolitan-Cammell and BR had more to do with increasing mechanical difficulties that were starting to manifest themselves during the trials rather than a desire to ensure there was no advance leak of publicity.

This conclusion is drawn from a from a report by A. E. Robson, the Chief Mechanical Engineer of the LMR, who had in a report dated as early as the 27 November 1959, highlighted no less than, '. . . 21 mechanical and other problems that would have to be rectified before the BR Commissioning Engineer would be satisfied that the trains could enter service.' These included:

• Poor riding of the driving motor coaches, in which 'the public could not be expected to sit'.

• Intermittent loss of power from the Rolls-Royce auxiliary engines. This is not commented upon subsequently, so we can be assumed to have been resolved satisfactorily.

• Oil leaks from the Brown-Boveri gear-cases, which were reported to be still noisy after 1,550 miles. The manufacturer's comment that the noise would disappear after the mechanics had fully bedded-in, and that this should occur after 4,500 miles. There was no further comment on the oil leaks.

• Severe overheating of brake blocks causing distortion and cracking, attributed to the brake-block keys working loose on the motor and kitchen cars, when braking from above 40mph. The eventual cure was twofold; firstly, there was a change to a thicker type of brake block throughout, and secondly, the air-brake pressure was varied according to the vehicle and direction of travel. No doubt these changes involved considerable trial and error, but they eventually came down to reducing the pressure from 65psi to 55psi on the leading power bogies, while on the non-powered bogies the pressure was increased to 80psi. *(On the BTF film referred to above there is a brief scene where a set is seen moving slowly out of its shed with wires attached to the brake gear, possibly this was in connection with the overheating issue.)* It is not clear from the paperwork whether a similar 80psi was applied to the rear-most power bogies when they were trailing and a similar question hangs over the effect that these changes might have made to the overall braking distances. Presumably, there must have been several high-speed braking tests, although it is not known what pressures were involved with reference to the earlier speeds/times/distances braking trials. (There is a second reference to braking issues in another memorandum of 21 December 1959. Again it speaks of distortion of the brake blocks when braking from speed and this time also the loss of a block that was actually lost on the trials as well as unspecified 'fractures'. A suggestion made at this time was to fit two brake blocks or even clasp brakes, both of which solutions would have assisted in dissipating heat better. In the event it was the earlier, simpler and no doubt cheaper option that was adopted, that of reducing the maximum brake pressure and providing thicker blocks on the leading bogie of the power cars.)

- Overheating of gas supply pipes in the kitchens, and ventilation problems in the kitchen cars, causing some burners to be extinguished at speeds above 60mph. Both of these were, presumably, cured.

- Overheating of floor-level heating grills in the passenger saloons, causing discomfort and the risk of setting fire to the fabric of the coach. There is no doubt that these matters were resolved, but again, no subsequent details are given.

- Ingress of rainwater through the kitchen doors, and of soot through the door ventilation grills when passing through tunnels. This was resolved, but what modifications were required to address this (and the next three items) is once more not reported.

- Floor-level draughts throughout the train, and excessive draughts through the door seals in the entrance vestibules at speeds of more than 40mph.

- Problems with the continuity of the hot-water supply in the toilets. Tests showed that the warm water in toilets took eight minutes to be replenished after use.

- Toilet vents too large, leading to the toilet cubicles being cold.

- The pressure required to operate the passenger communication equipment (emergency brake) varied between 26 and 36psi from vehicle to vehicle. It is not certain whether any changes were made, but there is an inordinate amount of surviving paperwork relating to the actual pressure required at each of the emergency communication cord points. Again, no final conclusions are to hand, but it might be that some changes took place subsequently, related perhaps to the variations in brake pressure.

- An engine compartment temperature of 180°F, despite there being vents provided in the floor and in the roof. This is perhaps one of the more interesting comments, as a note in the files refers to a circulating fan being fitted to the second train. The inference is that the now familiar roof fan fitted on all above-floor mounted railway engines was not initially thought necessary and so was a new innovation at this time.

- Flashover on No 4 traction motor. This was both an unfortunate and expensive failure, and as is usual with this type of defect was caused by a breakdown in the insulation. The only cure was a partial or complete strip-down and rewind of the commutator, depending on the degree of burning that had occurred.

So much then for the 'straight out of the box' hoped for success!

The day following the report, David Blee sent a letter marked 'Personal' to Wansborough Jones. The letter was couched in friendly enough terms but was depressive in its content: 'Midland Pullman'. 'I think I should let you know that we appear to be running into trouble during the trials of the "Midland Pullman". Subjoined is an extract from a report I have received, together with photostat of report which Randle has sent to Robson, and of which copy has also been forwarded to Harrison.' The following paragraph was added below in quotes, 'At the Diesel Committee this morning, Mr Randle gave a gloomy report about the new trains. A lot of faults have been found, including a serious one about the rough riding in the motor compartment. According to Randle the public could not be expected to sit in this compartment as it is now.'

Blee's attachment adds more to the detail to the above Robson report and as such is included in full:

'No 1 High Speed de-luxe Pullman Train.
As a result of the inspection and running tests with the above train, comprising the following vehicles:

M60090, 60730, 60740, 60741, 60731 and 60091

I give below details of items which will require to be followed up before the train accepted:

1 Propane Gas Equipment. It will be necessary for an investigation to be carried out into the design of the compartment roof ventilators and burners as several burners were extinguished at speeds in excess of 60mph. A suitable notice should be displayed near the main gas cook inside the car, as if this is left "off" the roof fan is continuously working. The propane gas supply pipes and regulators are becoming overheated. The cylinder box doors are difficult to remove. It will be necessary to refit these and replace the rubber gaskets with gaskets having more positive adhesion.

2 Kitchen compartment outside double doors. The design of the door checks on these doors is unsatisfactory as considerable water ingress is being experienced inside the kitchen compartment during inclement weather. In addition the ventilator slats are too wide apart and after the first trial run on 16 November the whole of the interior of the compartment was covered in soot as a result of passing through tunnels.

3 Brakework. a) Excessive temperatures at brake blocks causing distortion and cracking. b) Brake block keys loose and becoming displaced, particularly on the motor cars and kitchen cars as a result of high pressure braking (over 40mph).

4 Outside inwards opening doors (lobby ends). The design of the draught excluder requires investigation as excessive draughts are being experienced in this portion of the car at speeds in excess of 40mph.

5 Seats. These are extremely cold when first used, and at speed excessive rolling motion is experienced to the passengers' discomfort.

6 Lavatory Compartments. The top ventilator grill is too large and as a result the lavatories are very cold when travelling at speed.

7 Buffer heights. During preliminary trials the lifting brackets on the underframe of the motor cars fouled the plugs on the top of the Westinghouse cylinder, and although the design of this plug was altered to give increased clearance, it was found necessary to fit ½-inch steel packings between the bogie bolster and the underframe and additional packings under the bolster springs to give further clearance. This has resulted in the buffer heights of the motor cars being increased from 3 feet 5½ drawing height to 3 feet 6¼ and 3 feet 6½ inches. Particulars of the lead tests will be forwarded to you in due course.

8 Passenger Communication Equipment. The design of this equipment is not ideal, and although every effort has been made to obtain a working pressure of 20lbs to pull the chain, the linkage in this equipment has resulted in increased pressure being required as follows:

Vehicle No	Pressure	Point of Test
60090	33lbs	Saloon
60730	26lbs	Saloon
60740	26lbs	Saloon
"	28lbs	Toilet
"	34lbs	Lobby
60741	24lbs	Saloon
"	28lbs	Toilet
"	36lbs	Lobby
60731	30lbs	Saloon
60791	34lbs	Saloon

9 Car Reservation Identification. The letters A B C etc. have been transferred on to the side of the cars, and if as envisaged, are sent into works for overhaul, in certain circumstances a full train may comprise two half trains A B C C B A. This of course would completely confuse the seat reservation arrangements. The question therefore of providing detachable tablets fitted into slots on the outside of the car is raised. I understand the Western Region have already arranged this with the builders so far as their trains are concerned.

10 Heating and Ventilation Equipment. Although the thermostats were set static by the builder's Works during the first day's trial it was found that the adjustment was not satisfactory and it will be necessary for heating tests etc. to be carried out under running conditions in two sections, ie: with one auxiliary motor running and with two auxiliary motors running, so that final adjustment can be made and the performance of the equipment proved. It was also noticed during the first test run that draughts were being created at floor level throughout the train which can cause discomfort to the passengers. Part of this trouble is due to the fact that the saloon doors have no catch to retain them in a closed position when the brake is applied and the builders are looking into the question of what can be done in this direction.

11 Attendant's Bell Communication, cancelling buttons (located on the table leg). The Bakelite plungers are not strong enough to stand normal use and are failing at the pin hole.

12 Table Lamps. The table lamp shades are too close to the table and two have already failed through fracturing.

13 Hot Water Supply in Toilet compartments. The supply of warm water is such that after one person has used the facility, then a further supply of warm water is not available for eight minutes.

14 Securing of Bogies to underframe for re-railing in case of derailment. Provision for above to be made on all bogies – provision is already made on motor cars, but it is not considered entirely satisfactory.

15 Indicator lights panels on Kitchen Cars. Modification of terminal blocks to ensure more positive connections.

16 Floor heating grill. These grills are becoming excessively hot and constitute a danger to passengers and coach fabric.

17 SLYDLOCK fuses. Re checking of fuse loadings will be necessary, as difficulty has been experienced due to blown fuses.

18 Auxiliary engines. Intermittent loss of revs on Rolls Royce engines, cause unknown, will require further investigation. It may ultimately be found that this trouble is due to a design weakness in other equipment, and ensuing tests will prove this. A further report will be forwarded to you in due course when the actual trouble has been isolated.

19 Steriliser Immersion heaters in Kitchen Cars. A protective cover is required to this equipment.

20 Traction Equipment. In general terms the traction equipment on this train has so far provided a satisfactory performance, slightly better than the designed speed curve for the Derby–Luton portion of the revenue earning route. The most serious failure has been a flashover on No 4 traction motor. This has been changed and a report is awaited from GEC. It is possible that the cause was due to an earth fault developing on either the armature or one of the main field coils. One Brown-Boveri drive is noisy and would have been rejected but for an assurance from the contractors that the gears would bed in after about 4,000 miles. There is no improvement so far (1,500 miles). The Brown-Boveri gear cases are leaking. There is a drain hole provided in the outer wall of the case to act as a tell-tale for leakage past the seals, but upon examining the case, removed when No 4 traction motor was changed, it became evident there had been a manufacturing fault which allowed oil to drain from an internal baffle in addition. The attention of the contractors has been drawn to this feature. The fuel and lubricating oil system on the main and auxiliary engines have been free from leakage. One leak did develop on the high pressure pipe from the fan motor to the fan oil pump. This was soon rectified. The main air compressor was fitted with a glass bottle for anti-freeze solution. This was obviously undesirable and a metal container is to be provided. Meanwhile, no anti freeze is being used. Dirty filters in the fuel supply line to both the main and auxiliary engines have caused fuel starvation on two occasions and daily attention is being given to these filters until the system is clear. The provision of a slot at floor level in the engine compartment has not had much effect on engine room temperature. The maximum reading so far reached 138°. With the prevailing ambient this is too high and vents will have to be provided in the roof or body sides, although I understand that a circulating fan is being fitted into the second train.

21 Riding. The riding over the power bogies, particularly on the power car, is not good. Vertical accelerations are fair except when negotiating crossovers, but there is a harshness in the lateral vibrations which may be accounted for by incorrect damping.

Given the amount of what was little more than 'trial and error' associated with the test runs, it is interesting to observe that it was not until some while after 1962 that the use of mathematical models was developed at BR's Derby research laboratories to study and predict the behaviour of wheels and running gear at speed. But it was still the riding problems that were the main concern, the report commenting that, 'traction motors had never been fitted to the design of bogie beforehand'. Even so, no cure was mentioned at this stage, and it again appears that trial and error prevailed rather than a considered engineering solution. Modifications included the use of different strength springs; longer, 24-inch, swing-links mounted on rocking washers; and the installation of transverse hydraulic dampers (shock-absorbers). Of particular note is that it was the symptoms rather than the cause that was being treated, and it was in this form that the trains would enter service.

Every Christmas the Metro-Cammell workers were allowed to take their children to the Christmas Party and Greg Maxwell Collett, whose father Howard Collett worked in the body shop from 1933 to 1974, recalls seeing the unpainted 'Western' units in build in the huge erecting shops.

Paul Sankey had a nice surprise when he had a lift from his cousin. 'The idea was to visit Aston shed, Saltley Shed and Tyseley Shed so I was armed with film and camera. On the way my cousin had stopped off to do an errand at Water Orton near the station and I could see a photographer on the grass verge with a tripod. I thought something interesting must be coming through like a Clan or a Pacific, then slowly this blue vision came into view, absolutely brand new from Saltley Works and as it crawled for the photographer I was able to get a good look and take some of my own photos. I believe from Philippa of The Blue Pullman group on Facebook this was the last Western set built with W60099 nearest the camera.'

Colin Page observed the eight-car WR sets a few times making their way from Saltley and Washwood Heath heading through Small Heath via Tyseley to the Henley on Arden. They would return through Tyseley at around 4.30pm.

It is believed that some of the necessary modifications were first applied to the WR sets which were also then on trial, and when found to be successful the work was similarly undertaken on the Midland line trains.(5) More detailed testing was destined to take place in 1961, and this is dealt with in subsequent chapters. With hindsight, it is surely nothing short of incredible that the sets were introduced to the Press and the public in the sure knowledge that the riding was not up to the standard expected for a prestige luxury train. Even so it would not be right after all these years to apportion blame to any particular organisation or individual and it should be

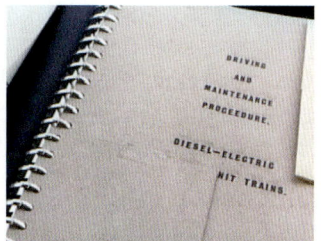

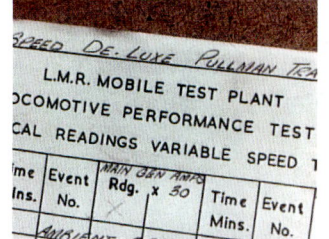

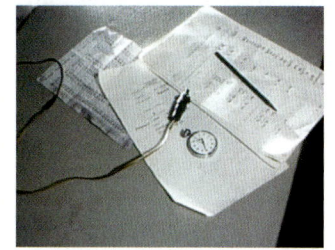

The commencement of trials and a screen capture of images of mobile testing en-route. Some of the views are clearly taken in the engine compartment, which it will be recalled registered 138°, necessitating the installation of an additional fan in the roof of the second built train – presumably the initial set was retro-fitted.

remembered that the pressures of modern business applied to all involved, the manufacturers, BR and the Pullman Car Co, as well as the engineers involved in the testing. So despite the trains' known shortcomings, there was a huge desire to see the sets enter revenue-earning service. It is unlikely that anyone involved considered the situation to be in any way dangerous – just that the ride was less than what was hoped for: nay had been expected. The difference can be likened to paying for a prestige luxury motor car, but finding comfort levels more akin to a sports car with hardened suspension.

So with matters not resolved but also no doubt with mounting pressure from various quarters to place the trains in service as soon as possible, we may quote an extract from the 'Technical Committee'(?) of 8 June 1960: 'The Chief Mechanical Engineer gave an assurance that the riding of the Diesel Pullman de-luxe trains would be sufficiently acceptable when the service began in July, but further detail modifications would be required and were in hand'.

It was originally intended to assign a painted letter to each car 'A to F' (or 'A to H' for the WR sets), but as each train would be maintained as two half-sets, it was, as mentioned, realised that a situation could potentially arise

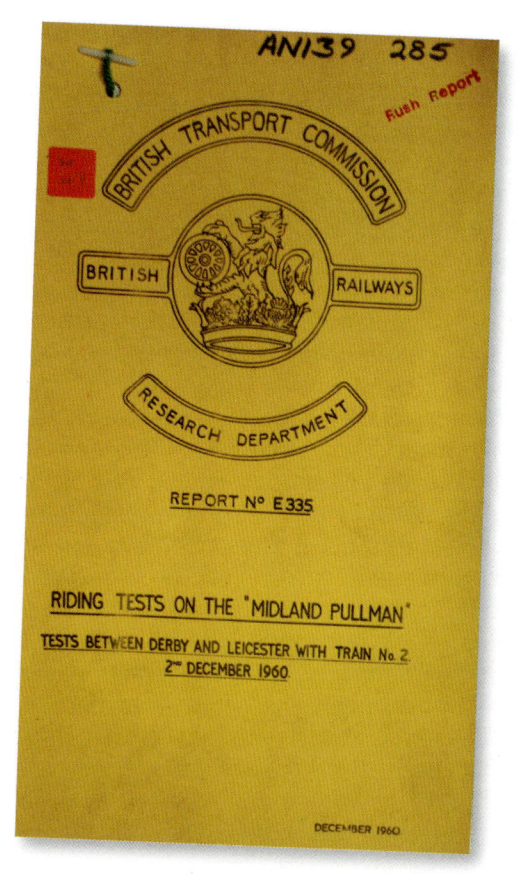

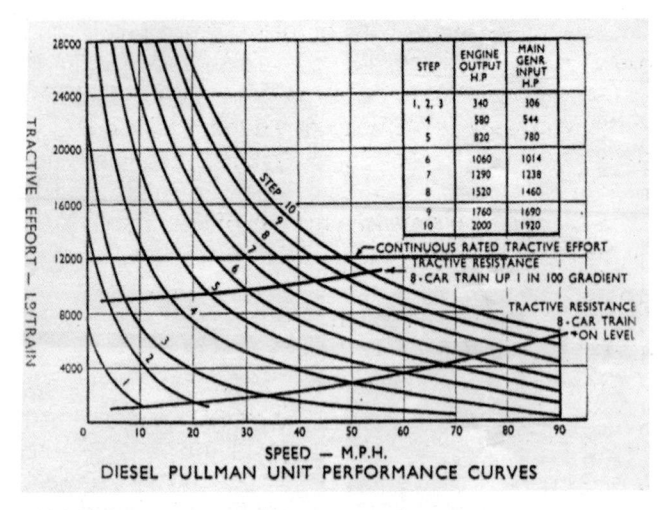

Speed/performance curves.

where a complete train could be formed of two half-sets each with the motor-coach lettered 'A'. ('A to C' or 'A to D' or half-sets lettered 'D to F' or 'E to H'). The resulting 'A-B-C-(D)-(D)-C-B-A' was not acceptable. The solution was the WR one, simple removable plates made up for each letter and which could be slotted into holders on the side of each car. In this way, the 'A to F' or 'A to H' lettering could be maintained, regardless of how the half-sets were marshalled together.

An obvious a straightforward answer we might think, but then this did not take into account a certain Jack Howe.

On 29 June 1959, the WR sent a request to Metropolitan-Cammell (via Harrison) for the removable carriage letters in the form of metal plates be added to their trains. The metal plates would also be reversible, thus with the car lettering on the WR sets intended to run from 'A' though to 'H', the 'A' plate if reversed would show 'H', 'B' would show 'G' etc. Through whom Jack Howe heard of this change is not known but it brought forth a stinging reaction, 'It seems to me that the frequency with which it would be necessary to substitute a half-train would not be very great and for both halves to be required at the same time very remote indeed. It is therefore my considered opinion that the need for this kind of reversible plate on all the trains hardly arises.' [Howe was in favour of the painted/transfer letter]. He would lose the argument and the WR trains would enter service with small metal carriage letter identification plates as described, painted to match the carriage sides. These were affixed at eye level adjacent to each carriage end door. Beneath the plate were seat numbers applicable to that particular vehicle. These metal plates were only fitted to the WR trains and it not believed they were retrospectively fitted to the Midland Region train sets upon later transfer to the WR. A further argument put forward by the Western Region, although not surprisingly by the Midland, was that the carriages would be interchanged at least once a month during servicing deliberately intended to meet a programme which had been laid down for maintenance on diesel-electric equipment. At this point Jack Howe raised the same question, indeed he was like the terrier that just would not let go! His solution was the use of a 'temporary' stick-on label should the occasion arise. (In all of this another aspect shows through, Howe was a designer – and an extremely capable one – but he was also no engineer and no operator. He had little concept that sometimes, just sometimes, machinery does not always perform as predicted.)

Meanwhile time was marching on and the decision was finally taken on 4 June 1960 by the Board of British Railways that the LMR Manchester–St Pancras (and return) service, running via the former Midland Railway 'Peak District route', would commence exactly one month later on Monday 4 July 1960. In this last statement we may also appear to have jumped ahead in time somewhat and so far as documented paperwork that is correct. Instead it appears the file content suddenly jumps to almost 100% publicity and launch considerations with no further mention for now at least of the riding and other issues that had certainly not gone away overnight. Whilst Kew (the National Archives) does provide a separate file concerning defects, this in the main relates to subsequent test runs a year or more after entering service and we are left then with the unfortunate conclusion that there must have once been another set of paperwork on the test runs and remedies attempted, this covering the period from the start of 1960 through to 'launch' date, but that it may well not have survived. As if to confirm this omission we have a record in the main file, dated 2 June 1960, when it was reported that on a test run the Blue Pullman set passed a steam train whilst traversing Dove Holes Tunnel. The consequent air turbulence caused diesel fumes to be sucked back into the train with, according to the travelling staff, a rapidly 'polluted' atmosphere. To address the issue the technicians on board immediately switched off the air-conditioning which prevented the situation getting any worse. Having learnt this valuable lesson, a similar instruction was issued to Pullman staff to do likewise when the train was in service. The point is that accompanying this note there was a reference to a 'corresponding report' but again it is missing from the accessed file.

This particular difficulty also raises other questions, obvious perhaps but even just 50+ years ago now difficult if not impossible to answer. Did this 'switch off' take place just in the 2,984yd Dove Holes Tunnel or did it also apply elsewhere on the LMR journey – there is a handwritten note on the piece of paper referred to that implies it may have been Disley Tunnel where the problem occurred – or was it even both? Similarly were there such issues on the WR, through the tunnels at Box, Alderton, Chipping Sodbury, under the Severn and on the route to Birmingham? (As a total aside one of your authors recalls having several authorised trips in the front of an HST along the Badminton line some years ago. At the time it was noted that the speed limit for these trains was 110mph through the short Alderton tunnel and yet 120mph through the much longer Chipping Sodbury tunnel. When enquiring as to the reason, the accompanying Inspector replied, 'Simple really, the shorter tunnel is not ventilated, and if two of these trains met at speed the air pressure could result in the contents of the toilet being pushed in the wrong direction . . .'.)

Backtracking from this date very slightly, it was now that the publicity machine swung into gear with a lavish Press launch arranged for Thursday 23 June 1960. The finalised timing was also fortuitous for on 2 June 1960, Sir Brian Robertson as Chairman of the British Transport Commission had been called before a Parliamentary Committee with one of the questions levelled at him being when would the new trains enter service? National Archives paperwork refers to Sir Brian 'fending off' the questions raised and no doubt also able to report the launch as having been arranged for three weeks hence.

The terminus at Marylebone was chosen as the venue for the Press day, partly because as it was close to the BRB Headquarters at 222 Marylebone Road (unkindly referred to in some quarters as 'The Kremlin' but today the luxurious Landmark Hotel), but also because there was spare capacity at the station. Marylebone also had a long history as a location where new products were unveiled, previously in LNER times and continuing into BR days. As a precursor to the launch, a five-car (not the normal six-car) train made what was a trial visit to Marylebone on 29 May, with what would later become LMR Set 2, consisting of vehicles M60092, M60732, M60742, M60743 and M60093 (absent from the rake was TKFL, M60733). After photographs and inspections, the set departed, possibly for High Wycombe.

There will undoubtedly have been a flurry of activity behind the scenes at both Euston and Paddington prior to launch day for the event covered not only the LMR set but also an eight-car WR train. The schedule stated the Midland set would be at Platform 3 between 10.00am and 3.30pm, and the WR set present (no platform number given) from 11.30am to 3.30pm. Viewing by members of the BTC – together with General Managers and Chief Officers – was to take place between 12.45pm and 1.30pm. (The formal memorandum sent out by the BTC was dated 14 June and invited Chief Officers '. . . and staff as you may consider feasible . . .', to visit between 2.30pm and 3.30pm. The railway VIPs invited included the Assistant Secretary General, Principal Officer Administration, Principal Works and Equipment Officer, Chief Railway Accountant, Chief Officer Parliamentary, Chief Estate and Rating Surveyor, Chief Constable, Chief of Research, Chief Contracts Officer, Chief Supplies Officer, Chief Publicity Officer, Design Officer, Architect, Chief Traffic Officer, Chief Mechanical Engineer, Chief Electrical Engineer, Chief Civil Engineer, and the Chief Signal Engineer. It is not known how many actually attended whilst it is interesting to note that the official invitations were seemingly not extended to the General Managers of the Eastern or Southern regions – probably one of the reasons why later on some of these worthies sought a free ride themselves!

Perhaps even as a precursor of things to come, 23 June was a day of thundery showers. Even so it did little to dampen the enthusiasm of the day for in addition to the 'great and the good' there were Ambassadors and High Commissioners as well as journalists from Britain and overseas. No doubt foreign orders were hoped for but in correspondence with the author in 2006, Malcolm Botham formerly of MC when asked the specific question stated he was not aware of any 'serious enquiries'. But there had certainly been hopes, for as early as 27 July 1960 eight visiting American railroad officers travelled on BP (we are not told which train or service), and gave it, 'The laurel for the best train in Europe'. Likely the chance of an order from 'across the pond' was too great an ambition but nearer to home on 13 October 1960 there was a visit by two delegates from the Italian State Railways who travelled from Paddington to Birmingham by Pullman and went on to a visit at MC. Probably there were other similar sales efforts. It is sad but understandable to relate that in the end no similar trains were ever built and Blue Pullman remains unique in being the sole diesel-multiple Pullman train ever to have been built anywhere in the world. Even so both MC, and Rolls Royce, the supplier of the auxiliary engines, were still using a background view of the train to advertise their respective businesses in *Modern Railways* magazine at least as late as 1965.

BR made every effort to ensure that the press day passed without incident, a veritable tome of paper orders distributed to ensure that the inspections, seating and actual train trips on which the attendees would travel would pass off with military precision. At least one return trip was made to High Wycombe, possibly using the WR set, the only difficulty encountered being with the windscreen wipers, which were reported as being continually blown back over the cab roof. This had already been noted during the trials, and was simply due to the effect of the slipstream at speed, accentuated no doubt by passing other trains, cuttings, bridges, and so on. It was later quickly and effectively remedied. (One may wonder if this had been experienced previously why it was not also similarly rectified before?)

According to *British Railways Illustrated*, 'One of the foremost railway commentators of the period, G. Freeman Allen, was on the first press trip to High Wycombe and back, during which the Western unit attained 90mph' The 'BRILL' article continued, 'Allen had been on the German TEE only the day before ("the most relaxing rail ride in Europe") but thought the Pullman rode noticeably harder over rail joints than the German trains, resulting in rattling crockery and "visual evidence of vibration in the empty seats" – the fact there were any empty seats is a little surprising considering the clamour that had been expressed before.' Freeman Allen though trod a conciliatory path and took the view that this was a reflection of there being better welded track in Germany compared with the '. . . neglected old GC stuff out of Marylebone'. He then states the obvious, 'If the state of the track on the old Great Central was known to BR engineers (as it most certainly would have been) one wonders why Marylebone to High Wycombe was selected in the first place? Probably, and as stated, this was simply the only route out of London with spare capacity at the time, although this could be challenged

Brand new WR eight-car set prior to entering service and, from the upper quadrant signal in the background, probably taken in the Birmingham area. In preparation for the press launch a series of meetings were held to provide for the necessary setting out of the launch day. Unfortunately for the second arranged date in June 1960 records do not appear to have survived but we do have a copy of the arrangements proposed for the originally intended three-day 25-27 November 1959 launch which was probably broadly similar. Interestingly this document only refers to a press day for the six-car LMR set. The circulation list included names and roles but, on the basis the same person may not have been in the same job some months later, for this example it is only roles that are given. Records show that a preparatory meeting was held at the 'BTC/HQ' (222 Marylebone Road – aka 'The Kremlin') on Monday 19 October 1959. Present were: Chief Public Relations Officer, Press Officer and Assistant, Design Engineer BTC, Publications Officer, representative of the PRO for the LMR, representative for the LMR Divisional Traffic Manager, two representatives of the LMR CM&EE, the Marylebone Station Master and the Assistant DOS (District Operating Superintendent) GC (Great Central) LMR. The first day envisaged a preview for the BBC, ITV and Cinematic Newsreels in the morning. A similar period was set aside for 'press' on the second day. Nothing else is shown as applicable for the first day but on 'day-2' a half-hour cleaning period was scheduled after the press visits following which came a one-hour inspection by the BTC. The day concluded with a 1½-hour visit by 'Trade' invitees and other invited officers of BRCS(?) and BR regions. For the third day the whole time, 10.30am to 3.30pm, was open to 'Other BTC, BRCS, and BR regional staff'. In all cases Platform 4 was to be used with instructions for this to be specially cleaned and the edge whitened. Of particular interest is that there is no reference to an actual 'demonstration run' on any of three days. Instructions were issued that the set was to arrive from Derby two days earlier and be stored 'under cover' (the latter term underlined and in capitals) in the carriage sheds at Marylebone with the passenger accommodation locked. All main items in the power cars and on the train were to be labelled describing their purpose. Tables were to be laid with cutlery and china during the inspection periods and the train lights switched on. Interestingly a temporary division is spoken of: dividing the train into its two respective halves for 'administrative purposes' and labelled sections 'A' and 'B'. (We may take this as meaning the placing of a barrier in the centre corridor rather than a physical uncoupling.) Cleaners were to be available with the underside cleaned after its journey from Derby by CM&EE staff. Drivers, and stewards were to be present, the latter representing the builders, equipment suppliers and Pullman. Steps would also be available at both ends to allow visitors access to the track. At Marylebone direction signs would be suspended from the girders of the station roof, red-roped barriers, a reception desk, press desk, and a large display board provided, the latter showing photographs and a large outline drawing of the train indicating its main equipment. So far as the photograph display was concerned there were even instructions as to what would be required to be displayed: 'Perspective photographs of the train moving and at rest, on a slight curve in a cutting with gently sloping embankments, are needed for the display board. [Also desired] … The train to be in open country on a twin-track route to simulate the surroundings of a main line journey.' A note added that the BTC Publications Officer will arrange for the photographer.

given that the runs took place outside peak hours. It is also suggested (in the *Railway Observer*) that a further Press trip was made – see table – the following day, 24 June, from Marylebone to High Wycombe but this cannot be confirmed. What is known is that an additional Press run, this time for the benefit of the Manchester community, was made on 1 July 1960 (again, a prelude had taken place with a full six-car set making a quiet visit to Manchester on 30 June – see also Chapter 4 page 81). The 1 July train was ceremoniously signalled away by the Lord Mayor John Balmer of Manchester, and included in its complement of VIP passengers, Sir John Elliot (Chairman of the Pullman Car Co) and Sir Reginald Wilson (Chairman of the LMR Board). On arrival at St Pancras, the train was quickly made ready for a round trip to Leicester to convey a number of businessmen, who were treated to luncheon en-route.

The Blue Pullman also had probably the best promotional film ever made for a train. The blurb for the award winning British Transport Film *Blue Pullman* stated 'A new luxury express is put through its paces. This film looks over the shoulders of a select band of craftsmen, technicians and operators, whose combined skills ensure that a train journey becomes a delightful experience.' Produced by Edgar Anstey and directed and written by James Ritchie, with Hugh Raggett as Editor, this impressive film has a memorable and mysterious score by Clifton Parker.

Nick Wheat has some of the original film clips that didn't make it in the film and gives this précis of the film: 'Far from being a utilitarian presentation of the steps needed to test this new train, the film is an elaboration of surface and designed style, set at the beginning as a sort of murder mystery complete with headless body on the floor. Clifton Parker's music is a set of variations on Bartok's Concerto for Orchestra, an ominous backing to technical equipment swaying in the motion of the carriage, with wires, string, cables, and an abandoned set of headphones on a seat. Both lavatories are in use, one as a Dark Room, the other to house testing equipment. Throughout the film, incidentally, we are spared the Narrator's voice. The silky flow of the camera through the unoccupied carriages adds to the sense of unease. Suddenly the train goes into a tunnel and, reflected in the darkened window, are two technicians in shirtsleeves. A magical moment. Slowly the viewer pieces together the function of this journey, a series of still lives, shots of documents, the paraphernalia of catering, the mechanics of the trajectory. The point of view switches to the Driver's Cab, and then the tracks leading into the Engine Shed. The doors close. At this journey's end we see the assessment of the train's performance through a montage of documentation and earnest brows. We then cut to a still life of machine parts in action, but this time, it is the printing of posters advertising the new de-luxe Pullman service, and the printing of the dedicated menus. In the third section, we see the Completion of Trials certificate and glimpses of staff being trained in the use of the apparatus of luxury – air conditioning, lighting, blinds. The fourth section of the film is devoted to the first working journey of the train,

David Watkin filming the Midland Pullman from John Crewdson's Westland Widgeon helicopter. *David Watkin*

non-stop from Manchester Central to London St. Pancras. The service was aimed at the business classes and it shows. The middle aged men with briefcases take their seats. Only a flirtatious glance from one young buck through the seats to a token bimbo disturbs the atmosphere of the *Financial Times* and self importance. One later section of a close-up of a passenger's face and out of focus shots of the attendant's jacket clearly implies a sleepy haze induced by the combination of alcohol and travel by rail. The last minutes of the film show the train catching up time, hurtling through the landscape, filmed from on-board, from the point of view of track workers, from a station platform, and, memorably, from a helicopter, edited with gusto by Hugh Raggett. It is no surprise by now that the Blue Pullman is on time arriving at 1a.m. by the Hotel Clock at St. Pancras, to the enormous satisfaction of all involved.'

Hugh Raggett wrote to Nick and recalls: 'Blue Pullman was a big production for BTF that gathered several awards and ran for three weeks at the Odeon Marble Arch, looking far better than it does on DVD! The film is not a good transfer from the 35mm original . . . a shame because the colour is far too bright and harsh, the original show copies had more fine detail and were softer. As an editor looking at it again after nearly fifty years I see all my mistakes – for instance, the soundtrack is too thin and needs far more life with sound effects and conversation. The whole film was shot silent and all dialogue was added at the editing stage – i.e. I recognise my own voice explaining the air-conditioning!'

Hopefully the new Blu-Ray version for the 70th anniversary of the BTF is more acceptable; it certainly looks fantastic to these authors!

The photography and camera work were by David Watkin and Jack West who hired in the pilot Captain John Crewdson of Film Aviation Services who worked on many blockbuster films such as the Steve McQueen film *The War Lover* and no less than four James Bond films. Crewdson was experienced in flying helicopters as well as planes and indeed with his wife, stunt performer Gillian Aldam, would demonstrate a sling harness in which Gill would be carried at speed underneath the helicopter; later this was used on the Bond movie with Johnny Jordan in the sling.

Crewdson used his Westland Widgeon, converted from a Military Dragonfly (G-ANLW), for filming the Pullman. David Watkin recalled in his book: 'There was something of an education on the next film Ritchie directed, about a new high-speed diesel-electric Pullman service, in as much as it involved a helicopter sequence. The pilot, John Crewdson, had the machine on a landing pad in his nicely tended garden in Surrey, and we took off from there to fly up to Derbyshire, stopping at Elstree airfield to refuel. John walked me round the hangar there and showed me an autogyro, the safest plane there is (and banned accordingly). The NC Mitchell was on a Moy head, mounted on a dexian platform outboard the aircraft. On the start line, attired in one of those leather flying helmets with a throat mike and earphones, I was more than a little anxious – that is until first assistant, David McKeand, jollied things up. "You look like Amy Johnson." It was exactly what was needed. The moment I unlocked the Moy it became a different world. It is how people do hazardous jobs – once you're working, that is where you're focussed. John's comments were a delight, especially when he referred to the train as a "snail" when it had to slow down for engineering works. But he then adds, "However when the snail got going we were pushed to keep up with it. At one point, with the train on an embankment, we were below it tilted up – and the hedge-hopping was literal. After one hedge a 'Whoops' from John led me to enquire what had happened. "There was an old so and so on a tractor I hadn't spotted 'cos of the hedge." …' Hugh Raggett writes, 'The last sequence of the train at speed was shot and intercut between the helicopter and another train on a convenient piece of rail track that ran near the Blue Pullman line for a mile or so.'

The film should be viewed carefully as this is not a single film but an amalgam of several films of the 'Midland Pullman' sets conjoined. For example, on the what is supposed to be the inaugural journey the lead power car changes a few times and Marylebone becomes Manchester Central and St Pancras!

Even some of the dates on the tests appear to be after the film was released. Here is a shot where both 'Midland Pullman' sets pass each other for probably the only time on film. Nick Lade and his school friend Tony Hagon remember Nick's Dad, Chris Lade (Pullman Conductor), telling them he had to go to Brighton (?) to film on a new Pullman train. Looking at his Dad's old diaries, Nick can confirm his Dad stayed at 'good digs' which were the Derby Midland Hotel and they filmed on 5 to 8 April with Chris modestly noting 'Tiring shooting all day, don't think they go much on my mug'! Chris was filming again on the train from 24 to 28 April. Filming switched to Marylebone on 22 May and 29 May and on 22 and 23 June it was back to Marylebone for filming for the BFT unit, the manufacturers and hosting press including BBC and ITV. Metro-Cammell staff were hosted on 24 June at Marylebone.

Steward Chris Lade was the elite of the Pullman staff and has had the honour of attending the Queen and Prince Philip plus various other Royals including those from abroad. He was also aboard the Pullman funeral train for Sir Winston Churchill. Chris pops up a lot as the poster boy for Pullman services and Nick, along with his daughter Danielle, have made sure that Chris's achievements were recorded firstly by Terry Bye of the Pullman Car Society and then with Terry's help by creating a 'Christopher Lade Archive' at the National Railway Museum.

Chris was famous for swimming in the sea at Brighton each day before his normal work on the 'Brighton Belle' and he continued to swim into his old age. The Queen would always make a point of asking Chris about his swimming and his keep fit regime. When Chris passed away in 2007 the Lade family was touched to receive a letter from Buckingham Palace expressing Her Majesty's sympathies. Chris Lade was obviously a special man working on special trains and the special Blue Pullman Attendant teddy bears are in his honour.

Also starring in the film are more real Pullman staff. The conductor is T. N. Peart and the other steward is Maurice Haffenden. Driver Edwards of Kentish Town is at the controls and we also see Manchester Central's Station Master John Balmer. A note within the sleeve of the BTF collection refers to the making of the film, 'This was a troublesome film in terms of production, as it was only in October 1959 that the unit learnt that a film would be required and that it would be needed quickly for screening at the launch of the service in January 1960. Shooting began immediately although production was hampered by the persistent development faults that dogged the new train. Shooting halted while the faults were put right and the launch was postponed until the summer giving the BTF the opportunity to go back and develop the script further. With stunning aerial footage taken before the introduction of the low-flying embargo and wearing a shining coat of Technicolor, the film achieved the distinction of opening at the Odeon Marble Arch on the same morning as the Pullman service began in July 1960. Blue Pullman ran at the Odeon for three weeks and won numerous awards on the festival circuit.'

The following review appeared in *Monthly Film Bulletin* of August 1960: 'It is difficult for a railway enthusiast to view the subject matter of this fascinating account of the new Manchester–St Pancras diesel Pullman train dispassionately. It opens with some intriguingly presented sequences of the train's trials, with boffins aboard and all manner of testing going on. Then, after scenes of the amenities and services provided by this business man's first class express, comes the lengthy, beautifully photographed and exciting final sequence of the train in action with many excellent shots from the air and from the driver's cab. It is a pity that the producers, for some inexplicable reason, appear reluctant to show the train starting and stopping properly: the arrival at St Pancras in particular is sadly botched and comes as a let down after the vivid presentation of the Blue Pullman in motion. A very nicely made score by Clifton Parker, stylish editing and a commendable inclination to let the visuals speak for themselves: how pleasant indeed not to have an incessantly chattering commentator and, indeed, to have descriptive comments kept to a minimum.' The film would go on to win a silver cup in Genoa, Italy.

With publicity now very much to the fore, an illustration of the front of the new trains appeared in *Design Magazine* for August 1960[6]. Moving ahead in time, further publicity was obtained with another Press run sometime in October/November 1960, this time in the presence of news cameras from the BBC, ITV and cinema newsreels.[7]

Meanwhile on 12 May 1960 and following on from a recent press conference on Railway Modernisation, *Design Magazine* informed the BR Design Panel it was their intention to publish a promised article on the trains in the August issue.

Unfortunately all did not go well with the eventual article. For whilst chronologically we may again be jumping ahead slightly at present, it is worth dealing with this topic in one go. A proof of the piece was sent to George Williams by John Blake, the editor of *Design Magazine* in late June 1960, and which elucidated the following précised, but forceful response, 'I must first deal with the things in the Pullman article to which we strongly object. The most important is the reference to imported ideas. It seems that DESIGN has gone out of its way in referring to the various main components so as to give adverse publicity to the Commission when as you know it can well do with the opposite at this time. The mention of the German diesel engines, the Swiss traction motor driver, bodies and corridor connections have nothing at all to do with the kind of design criticism which is made elsewhere in the article. It is significant that no mention whatsoever was made of the origin of these components in the Commission's press hand-out and I should be very grateful if you could delete the references to them. In fact, your information is by no means correct, as the bogies, for instance were designed basically and manufactured by Metropolitan-Cammell, only certain features of them were made under licence. The same certainly applies to the corridor connections.' Williams continues, 'Your criticism of the blue livery is solely concerned with the suitability of the paint for practical purposes. We were trying to help you when we advised you not to mention this particular colour. The colour is guaranteed first not only by the manufacturers but by the British Transport Commission's Director of Chemical Research, who has the final say on practical grounds on the selection of any colour treatment used in the railways.

'We are also anxious that your readers should not be led astray when you speak of the way in which this train has been planned, and when you say it could have been planned in a quite different and presumably more efficient way, what your article is really saying is that one should design a restaurant first and produce a type of service to suit the design and we presume you mean tray meals. The Pullman service is not one which uses this kind of catering technique, neither is it ever likely to do so. This is a Pullman train in the true sense and the service is designed to match it.

The cover of *Design* for August 1960 which contained the article on BP.

'The seat spacing is based entirely on known traffic requirements and is dictated by the need to make these luxury trains as comfortable as possible consistent with the BR operating restrictions and economy. To support your criticisms in a proper way, it would be necessary to show an alternative seating plan in the article and describe how you would cope with the serving of the normal Pullman service, by which great store is set by the businessmen who will use the trains.

'I do not want to labour the nose design, but I must say that you have chosen a conveniently bad photograph on page 38 *[of the magazine]* in an attempt to illustrate your point. The highlights and shadows do not appear here and the whole front is distorted. I think any reader seeing the alternative illustration on page 41 *[again in Design magazine]* is likely to disprove your comments.' (The published page numbering of the final magazine did not totally follow the draft numbering referred to here.)

The article in *Design* penned by one Robert Spark (of whom we know nothing) described the train primarily, and understandably, from a design perspective with the relevant text as under: 'Pullman Express. The introduction of the first of a new series of diesel electric Pullman Express trains for the London–Manchester service was announced last month.' In this article the author (Robert Spark) discusses their design, which he compares with similar Continental express trains. 'There can be no doubt that the new Pullman sets are some of the best rolling stock in Britain today and

The Blue Pullman Story

here they are critically assessed from the aspects of passenger comfort and amenity.

'It is plain to anyone who has travelled by rail in Britain over the past few years that the new diesel-electric Pullman trains are a considerable advance over existing equipment in practically every aspect. Put simply, they are the first really modern trains to run on British Railways since before the war. They incorporate the work of a design team consisting of engineers, technicians, and an industrial designer, working in association with the British Transport Commission's Design Panel . . . The general engineering design was the responsibility of the contractor while the mechanical requirements were laid down by the BTC. A condition of the contract was that the builder should retain the services of a designer who was acceptable to the commission's Design Panel. With the approval of the latter, Metropolitan-Cammell appointed Jack Howe to be responsible for the treatment of the exterior and interior, working in close collaboration with the manufacturer's engineers . . . Certain features of the train, including the fact that meals would be served to passengers at their seats, and that both reclining seats and air-conditioning would be utilised, were laid down in the specification."

There was then a sub-heading: 'Design problems produces compromise. The fact that the design team had to satisfy the BTC, the operating region and the Pullman Car Co added to the design problem. The development of the trains was marked by two major meetings. At the first, the proposed layout for the coaches was agreed and no major alterations were called for. The second meeting was to examine the proposed design of the interior and exterior. This was done with the aid of mock-ups which were the scene of many lengthy discussions. One of the biggest problems for example, was the seat design as it had to combine the twin functions of an armchair and a dining chair . . . The result is an unhappy compromise. The chair has two movements: the first alters the position of the back to either an upright or slightly reclining position. The second moves the chair forwards or backwards. With the chair forward and the back upright the position is good for eating at the table. It is in the reclining position that the chair seems unsatisfactory. Although the basic proportions conform to anthropometrical requirements, its width seems restricted and the headrest uncomfortable. It could probably be improved by having a small loose cushion in the headrest attached by straps to the rear of the seat. Space seems restricted, and while it is appreciated that additional space could only be obtained with this type of layout by reducing the number of passengers accommodated, it is possible that alternative layouts would increase comfort while maintaining the required passenger density. This might mean a reconsideration of the catering facilities provided.

'Some doubts must have been expressed on the wisdom of including passenger accommodation in the leading coach which also includes a 1,000hp diesel engine, and in the kitchen car, which has a 190hp diesel engine below the floor for generating current for the auxiliary services. The former is, however, quite satisfactory, while the latter is noisy enough to be noticeable, but free from vibration. In conception, the new Pullmans are so close to the Trans-Europe Express trains that comparisons are inevitable. For example the difficult problem of frontal treatment is dealt with variously from the aggressive German example to the much more imaginative Italian treatment. On the other hand the British diesel Pullman suffers from a weak, unimpressive nose. The faceted shape, when seen from a three quarter view has the effect of reducing the apparent width at the front, making the train look strangely tall and narrow.

'Imported ideas. But internally the Pullman trains are better than some of the TEE trains, although the basic design appears to owe much to the Swiss-Dutch example. The diesel Pullmans also use other Continental ideas, and this is sensible since this country has lagged behind the Continent in the design of passenger coaches during the last 20 years, and there is no tradition of steady development from which new equipment could be evolved. There are for example German diesel engines, Swiss traction motor drives, and also bogies and corridor connections which have been developed from certain Swiss principles, and French inter-coach electrical connectors. Most of these items have been made under licence in Britain. On one major point the Pullmans score over many similar trains overseas. This is in the matter of detailing. Many of the smaller fittings are very well integrated with the overall design. There has obviously been considerable care in the selection of existing equipment as well as in the design of new. On the whole, the new Pullmans are certainly in advance of existing British rolling stock, and are up to the best standards in other countries. The trains are in the luxury class.'

A view of the interior was complimentary and concluded with the words, '. . . all emphasize a comfort-in-silence there'. There was also a page devoted to small images of the internal fittings (each image was identified by a number), mostly complimentary and including the words, 'Nearly all items . . . show a high standard of workmanship'. The same page comes with two points of criticism, 'In 11 can be seen a lamp, mounted from the bodyside, which was a later addition demanded by Pullman to perpetuate its tradition of a table lamp. It is superfluous and is liable to get in the way particularly at the single seat tables'. The captions continue, 'All the lavatory fittings are uniformly neat, but the appearance of the lavatory is marred by the use of crude colours for the mosaic floor.' On the following page where further detailed images were shown the gangways come in for criticism, 'The same type of gangway

LEFT Sam Lambert's striking view of the LMR train; whilst sparkling in the sunshine above the solebar the underframe shows clear signs of workaday dirt. In *Design* it was trimmed to present a portrait view. Notwithstanding the comments in the text about this image presenting 'visual distortion', to the present writers this is not apparent. The photograph was taken on Gorsey bank on the Wirksworth branch line from Duffield north of Derby.

The Blue Pullman Story

Extracts from the *Design* magazine article.

has been used in the Swiss-Dutch TEE trains but they have been offset to one side to provide more spacious vestibules. This technique might well have been applied to the British trains as it is not intended to divide the sets in the event of mechanical failure. The nose of the diesel Pullmans is commendably clean being clear of pipes, couplings, jumper cables and air-blast horns. On the other hand it lacks character and is not integrated with the rest of the design.' The roofs also came in for criticism, '. . . the roofs of the power and kitchen cars are blemished by crude, bolted-down hatches. These are of course a necessity to allow access for periodic servicing, though the treatment could be improved. British Railways insistence on maximum accessibility has led to two further unfortunate features in the external appearance: the ugly gap between coaches with the exposed connections and cables, and the use of only a narrow valance or skirt to conceal under-slung equipment. The body panelling is of high quality, as is the finish. However, the choice of a blue and white colour scheme, while attractive and distinctive, is debatable. Such colours have a poor wearing reputation in railway service, although it is claimed that there will be no colour deterioration with the paint used on Pullman. The lettering on the coaches is good, in keeping with Pullman's previous style, but the crest, which has been redrawn by Christopher Ironside, does not provide a forward looking symbol appropriate for such a modern train.'

Evidently some pre-publications changes were made but not enough to placate either George Williams or Jack

ABOVE Another of 'those' lamps. Robert Spark had also condemned these as '…superfluous…' but in view of the information uncovered we have to ask was this Mr Sparks' independent assessment? Certainly no complaints appear to have been made as to their presence by the travelling public. Note alongside, the respective 'call' buttons to summon the steward. The only subsequent reference to said lamps appears to be in *Trains Illustrated* for April when the commentator and railway author Brian Haresnape writes, 'Internally the Pullmans set new BR standards. The fussy little table-lamps … are the one superfluous feature, incorporated merely on traditional grounds.' A definite swipe at Sir John Elliot. Still on the subject of '*TI*', and although slightly ahead of ourselves in some way, reference to the riding behaviour of the trains was made several times in the various magazines including in August 1960, October 1960, April 1961 and subsequently in *Modern Railways* in July 1963. Again Brian Haresnape, for example, in '*TI*' for April 1961 stated, '…one worrying feature is that when the train is in motion, empty seats tend to vibrate incessantly.' Hopefully there were not too many of these! (Excepting on the Leicester and Nottingham trips of course.)

Howe. Accordingly it went to print and was released in the August issue of *Design* no doubt to the chagrin of at least the two named individuals.

The author Robert Spark certainly appears to have agreed with the criticisms levelled by Howe plus others we have here mentioned for the first time. But in the light of Howe's previous outbursts it is strange to relate he does not appear to have taken issue (publicly at least) with *Design*. It all leads to ever more speculation: was *Design* given the lead by Howe?

Jack Howe, who was mentioned by name as being the 'Industrial design consultant responsible for general exterior and interior design together with detailing and finishing', was curiously silent over the whole episode, especially as it was he who had first spoken about the builders providing facilities to a photographer etc. from the magazine in his report of the previous 10 September. It thus remains puzzling why it appears there should have been so much

79

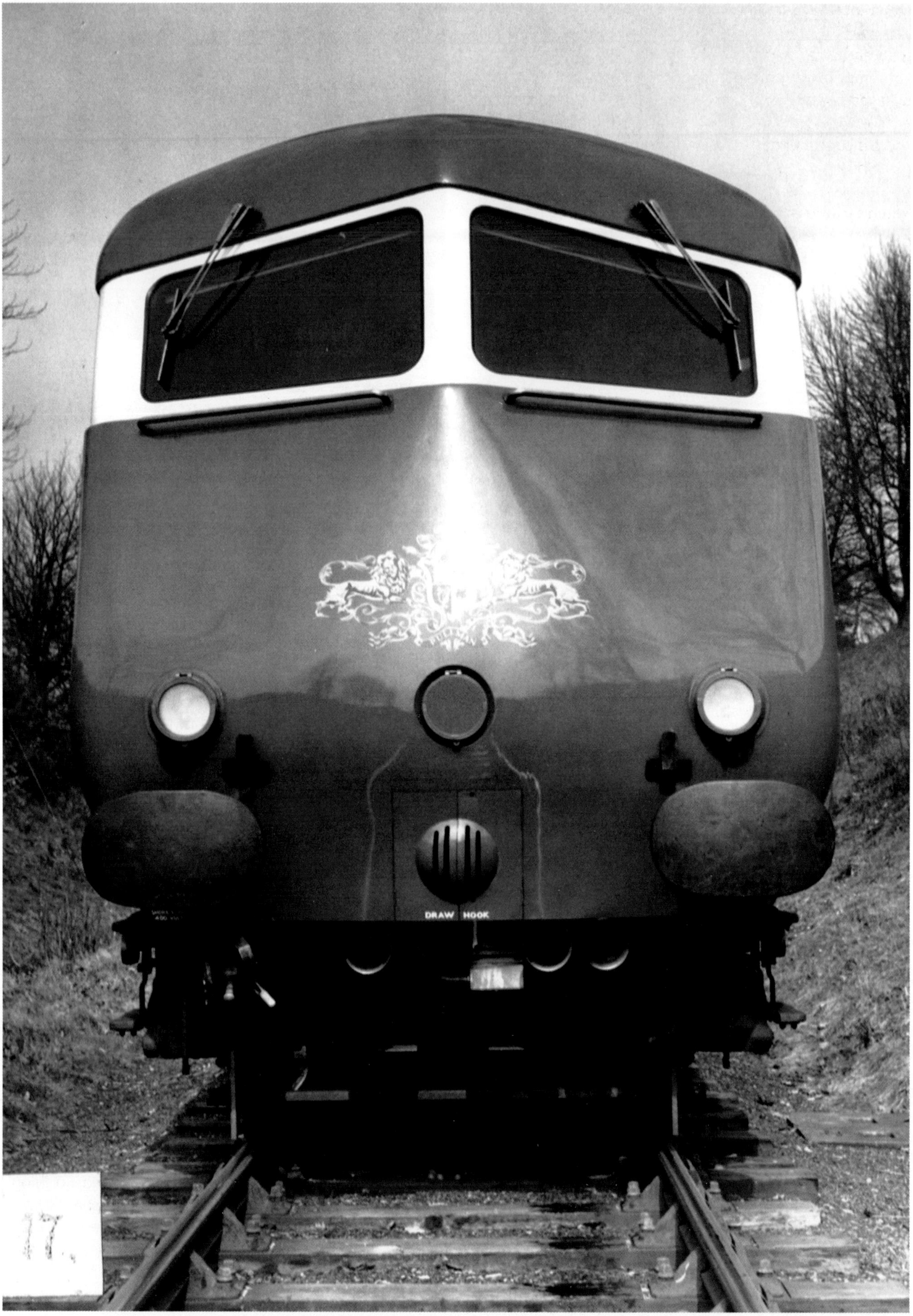
DRAW HOOK

LEFT Another 'Sam Lambert type' image, possibly taken on the Wirksworth branch at the same time as the view seen earlier. Lambert was a commercial photographer contemporary with the introduction of the train and was charged (by whom we do not know) with taking images for publicity purposes. In National Archives file AN160/71 there is correspondence from Jack Howe criticising Lambert's work but without apparent justification. It would appear that in general the publicity images for the train were taken by at least five individuals/concerns. These were the builders Metropolitan-Cammell, British Railways, London Midland Region and also the Western Region, and Lambert. It is also likely some of the advertising material used from mid 1960 onwards was recorded by Fleet Street photographers although recourse may also have been made to one of the aforementioned sources as it has been noted that an identical view could well appear in different publications and brochures. Notwithstanding some of the negative comments within *Design Magazine*, George Williams received a note from Jack Howe suggesting the trains be nominated for the 1960 Design medal. We do not know if this was proceeded with.

criticism in the magazine article. Was Williams being ultra-sensitive; was the article truly the work and opinion of a single journalist at *Design* magazine; or was there even someone feeding material in the background with 'an axe to grind' over aspects of the design they felt should have been different? Was this person even Howe?

Whatever, it must be recalled that a specialist magazine aimed at a specific professional audience will usually have far less impact than more mass market publicity; certainly who amongst the travelling public would care much for the criticism of the bolt-down panels on the roof? More pointedly it was noted that in both the *Guardian* and the *Times* – the likely read for the kind of traveller the train was intended to attract – the reaction to the new LMR trains was positive. Indeed Jack Howe briefly wrote to George Williams on this very point on 4 July 1960, 'I think the *Guardian* has done us proud and apart from one or two inaccuracies I was very heartened and refreshed to read a grown-up account of the Pullman after the adolescent rubbish that *Design* magazine produced.'

From *The Times*, Friday 24 June 1960, which also refers to an illustration which accompanied the article:

'One of the diesel-electric Pullman trains on a trial run. The British Transport Commission are paying about £2m. for five diesel-electric Pullman trains, and a ride on one yesterday showed that luxury has been achieved. There are Venetian blinds, adjustable seats for first-class passengers, and separate arm-rests for everyone. At 90mph it is possible to talk without raising the voice and to drink coffee without spilling it. Windows are double glazed and the floors fully insulated. "Notice the air-conditioning", said a loudspeaker message. An engineer dabbing his perspiring forehead was able to turn down the temperature – each carriage has its own control. To travel so smoothly and without the familiar din from tracks and stations is to be reminded of the detachment of air travel. The B.T.C. see in their new acquisitions a chance to rival the best that an airline can offer in services between cities. Altogether five luxurious expresses will soon be running

ABOVE Marylebone display for the Press Days in June 1960.

KNOWN DEMONSTRATION RUNS (NOT TEST RUNS)	
23 June 1960	Marylebone; one each LMR and WR sets. Press and PR trips.
24 June 1960	Believed Marylebone to High Wycombe. Stock involved not known. Metropolitan-Cammell demonstration.
28 June 1960	St Pancras–Leicester return. Demonstration run for Ticket Agents. LMR set.
30 June 1960	LMR sets on static view at St Pancras and Manchester Central.
1 July 1960	Believed two LMR sets: one St Pancras–Leicester return, the other Manchester–Derby return. No other details.
8 September 1960	Paddington–Swindon.
6 September 1961	'South Wales Pullman' demonstration run.

It is possible this particular image from the MC collection may have been on the actual Press day: a six-car LMR set seen passing Wembley Hill on the GCR main line. Whilst those invited to participate received a complimentary meal on the train this did not run to free drinks all round as the records show the Pullman Co. billed British Railways a total of £410 14s 2d for the press runs. (This figure is again taken from the official file where all the photographs are missing and yet tantalisingly refers again to 'enclosed photos and press cuttings'.) Other press trips indicated an equally thirsty clientele: the 1 July run to between St Pancras and Leicester revealed those travelling spent £185 10s 6d on drinks, the breakdown being 85 measures of brandy at 3s each, together with a similar amount of gin and 50 cigars. No cost is given for meals – assuming these were served. On the Derby demonstration of the same day we know meal costs (chargeable to BR) were £475 1s which seems an almost excessive amount compared with the two trains that operated from Marylebone where the figure was less. On the Derby run the drinks figure was £112 19s 8d, the vast majority of this, £102, on gin alone! One guest on the Derby trip asked the steward if the drinks were complimentary, no doubt hoping for a little more than just a free ticket for the trip. Overall, though, the Press day was a success with several letters of thanks and congratulations received by David Blee after the event. Those on the train on this occasion were in fact the lucky ones as there had been much discussion over the allocation of seats for the inaugural runs. In the end, of the 132 seats on the LMR trains, 80 were allocated to the LMR/Met Cam/Pullman, 22 to the Press, three to representatives of the railway unions, the NUR. ASLEF and TSSA, and the remainder apparently 'fought over' by BTC. Later on such was the interest in the trains that requests for complimentary seats were being received from a considerable number of senior staff on other regions – and no doubt others from elsewhere. This resulted in the General Manager of the LMR GM dictating that in future only he would authorise such complimentary journeys. (These requests from the GMs of the other regions does beg the question, were they now seriously looking at a BP type train for their own routes or was it really just an excuse for a 'jolly'.) Finally, notice the very small dent on the front bodyside corner; this identifies the vehicle as No 60091. How it was caused and at such an early stage is not known. WR Power car 60096 also had a similar indentation.

between London and the provinces, two trains for first-class passengers only and three for both classes. The first services to Manchester and Leicester will begin on July, and the other soon afterwards. In looks as well as service – 18 staff and one conductor will provide for 228 passengers on an eight-car train – the intention of British Railways to set a new standard is obvious. The exterior colour is Nanking Blue. The Western Region driver is a white-collar worker in a snowy coat, and he has his own small cooker in the cab to provide a meal during breaks. But "There is nothing like eggs and bacon done on a nice clean shovel", said Driver Tom Stevenson, who drove on yesterday's test run."(A later report in *The Times* was also praised as they managed to get right the difference between a heraldic crest and the Pullman coat of arms.)

But the Press day might not have gone quite as well as it did. For a few weeks beforehand on 23 May 1960 an aesthetic bombshell had been dropped with a note from Christian Barman to T. H. Summerson over the Western

Region trains. In this we learn that at least two (possibly all three) of the allotted trains were now on the region where they were undergoing trials and crew familiarisation training. But what is most interesting within the note is what Barman advises he has heard from the WR General Manager, Mr Grand, '. . . they are finding it terribly difficult to keep the new Diesel Pullmans clean.' Barman continues, 'I was very definite, in my reply to him, that ways and means must be found of getting over this difficulty. Nevertheless, it is possible that we may be required to select an alternative livery or liveries; and I think that, so as to ensure that we are not caught napping, you should give some thought to this subject in the future.

'If the worst comes to the worst, I feel sure that the Western Region will bring pressure to bear on us to revert to their own traditional livery. This might not be so bad if the chocolate and cream were the best available colours falling within these descriptions. The present shades could be hardly worse.' The livery/cleanliness issue had obviously been resolved before the June press day (with both the LMR and WR trains appearing in blue and white) whilst it is interesting that no such complaint was recorded reference the LMR sets. Was one region cleaning their trains by hand and the other via a carriage washer perhaps? Even so the thought of a Diesel Pullman in chocolate and cream is still slightly mind-blowing![8]

The Times in their report may also have been slightly incorrect in relation to their assessment of the costs, for against their £2m quoted, BR were stating a figure of £1.662m, even so a 37% increase in the original estimate which does not account for inflation. A six-car train was reported as costing £285,000 and an eight-car set, £341,500. Spares accounted for a further £57,500, and there is also an entry for 'Special Design' costs amounting to £10,000, half of which was possibly attributable to those table lamps! These figures do not appear to include any allowance for the provision of the necessary fixed installations, such as maintenance sheds and shore supplies. (These items are discussed in detail within the chapters dealing with the running and operation of the trains on the LMR and WR.)

Continuing with the praise lavished on the trains both on press day and thereafter, for completeness we may quote further from some of the newsprint of the time. Worth bearing in mind is the comparison (in time scales only) with the coming into office of a new government or 'over the pond' a new president. Invariably such an incumbent will benefit from a 'honeymoon' period during which any failings and shortfalls are ignored or glossed over. It was exactly the same for the Blue Pullman trains. Initially their shortcomings were simply overlooked, such misgivings instead swamped by praise for the design,

A standard publicity image of a WR set deliberately colorized for the present authors by Tom Marshall. This should not be seen as a '1 April' view but is instead one which might just have had a more serious meaning. Within the paperwork at the National Archives readers will recall the euphoria that greeted the late 1959 inspection by the respective General Managers – '… kids in a sweetshop … ' was how Jack Howe described the trip back from Birmingham. Up to that point Kenneth Grand, the WR General Manager, appears to have somehow failed to grasp the fact that the new trains for the WR would be painted in Nanking Blue and white, hence this rendition of what might have been with a pseudo 'chocolate and cream' livery. It is perhaps surprising that Sir John Elliot in his attempt to recreate an 'Edwardian dining room' had not similarly attempted to change the livery to the Pullman 'umber and cream' colours.

LEFT AND RIGHT The manufacturers Metro-Cammell produced their own brochure incorporating a correct livery for the image shown previously, examples from which are shown. (There is slight confusion that MC may have produced a second brochure at some time as well. Possibly they ran out of the first and a reprint or revised second edition was produced. Presumably a copy of 'a brochure' was given out to all on the June 1960 Press day and subsequently on the various demonstration runs, in which case the required number for these alone would have exceeded 1,000.) Blue must have been the in-vogue colour for the time as in the same year as the BP sets were introduced the Glasgow 'blue trains' commenced work, although carrying a different hue to that seen on BP.

service and modern styling. It also interesting to note that, especially in the *Guardian* articles accuracy appears to be the order of the day even to the point that comment is made in areas which the present authors do not feel qualified to pass judgement upon and certainly not to contradict. Each is therefore reproduced 'integrum' without further remark.

We may start with the professional perspective from the *Railway Gazette* of 24 June 1960. 'Luxury Trains – the term "de-luxe" applied by the British Transport Commission to the new diesel-electric Pullman multiple-unit trains which begin operation shortly in the London Midland and Western Regions of British Railways suggests an over-abundance of rare but desirable qualities which are not necessary for life. While this would be true if applied to the average man, "life" for the business executive, whose travelling needs the new trains are designed primarily to serve, brings particular problems not the least of which is the need for both comfort and safety at much higher rail speeds than have been common in this country hitherto. The passenger who has no alternative but to devote the maximum time between successive appointments in different cities to either discussion of business matters or the concentrated study of paper work uninterrupted by telephone calls and visitors, or who is responsible for the entertainment of guests, perhaps potential customers from overseas, is deserving of just those special facilities during transit which, until recently, only a sea voyage or a long aeroplane flight could offer. Yet both ships and aircraft are subject to many more unpredictable conditions than those which apply to rail transport. Commercial flying problems have only been solved by the application of intensive scientific research, whereas, for rail travel, the best standards of comfort and convenience achieved early in the century have since been widely accepted in this country as satisfactory and the same empirical basic design formulae appear to have continued in general use until the present day for much of the main-line and some suburban rolling stock currently being placed in service.

'With the de-luxe Pullmans, despite advanced suspension design and the extensive use of rubber pivots and mountings, little advantage appears to have been taken of the opportunity to gain improved train performance for given power by strictly enforcing a low weight limitation. This should have received a higher priority in the comprehensive scheme of unconventional design adopted in relation to passenger comfort. Steel remains the predominant material of construction resulting in a six-car train, weighing nearly 300 tons, having a total installed power of only 8bhp per ton, about 37 per cent less favourable than the heaviest of the air-conditioned first class Trans-Europ Express trains introduced some three years ago. Nevertheless, experience of riding in the diesel-locomotive-hauled but otherwise-conventional British Pullmans of recent years with their swift acceleration and excellent timekeeping can give only a small impression of the degree of luxury achieved by the new de-luxe Pullman trains.

The reasons are not far to seek in the illustrated description given elsewhere in this issue. So successful is the Metro-Schlieran design of helically-sprung frictionless bogie suspension with hydraulic damping, in combination with heavy insulation to bodysides and suspended flooring in passenger compartments, wide air-sealed gangways between cars, and double glazing, that a new conception of the possibilities of railway travel becomes obvious to the passenger during the earliest stages of a journey. In fact there is a most welcome isolation from all fatiguing sensations of unpleasant sound and harsh vibration. Full air-conditioning is used for the first time in Britain, with controlled temperature and humidity. Armchair seats are deeply padded with foam rubber and those in the first class saloons can be adjusted easily to give a reclining position. Table service will include specially selected menus and wine list. A smooth pick-up on starting and stable riding at high speeds are ensured by a new type of permanent coupling which absorbs both buffing and drawing loads. The ability to stop quickly and safely from speeds of up to 90mph is essential. For this reason Westinghouse automatic air brakes have been adopted with special electro-pneumatic two-stage operation and automatic slack adjustment. A characteristic of the conventional cast-iron brake blocks is that their coefficient of friction increases considerably as they reduce the speed of the train. If the limit on braking force, necessary at low speeds to prevent skidding, is effective also at high speeds then the stopping distance is greater than the minimum

Metropolitan-Cammell was nominated by the British Transport Commission to design and construct five special diesel electric de-luxe express trains for service with The Pullman Car Company Ltd., on selected routes. Many new features have been incorporated on passenger rolling stock for the first time in U.K., including full air-conditioning.

This photograph illustrates the interior of a first-class saloon.

Page 2

After eighteen months in service the following extract appeared in "The Railway Gazette" on 15th December, 1961, and is reproduced by kind permission of the Tothill Press Limited:-

SUCCESS OF MIDLAND PULLMAN. The London Midland Region of British Railways has announced that the Midland Pullman is attracting an average loading of 95 per cent capacity and has a record of 95 per cent punctuality.

BRITAIN GIVEN LAURELS FOR NEW TRAIN

FROM OUR OWN CORRESPONDENTS
NEW YORK, Tuesday.

BRITAIN was given the laurels for the best train in Europe by a delegation of eight leading American railway executives who returned to-day in the Queen Elizabeth after travelling through Britain, Russia, France, West Germany, Holland, Switzerland and Italy.

They agreed that the finest train they had seen abroad was the new Pullman which is to be placed in service between London and Manchester. "We were particularly impressed by the interior decoration and the speed," said the delegation leader, Mr. Curtis Buford, vice-president of the Association of American Railroads.

"The seating was comfortable, the lighting excellent and the air-conditioning good. We found the kitchens very well planned and we had good food on our trial run."

The delegation was the first industrial party from the United States to visit Russia under a new State Department exchange programme. Mr. Buford said they had found standards of comfort on Russian trains "very mediocre."

Reproduced by kind permission of "The Daily Telegraph"

85

possible achieved with the two-stage system. The increased brake force can be used when needed most without increasing excessively the general wear-rate of tyres and blocks.'

The Guardian devoted no less than three separate articles in its London and Manchester editions around the same date, 4 July 1960, the first having the heading, 'New Look in luxury', accompanied by a view of a coach interior. The text reads; 'If the design of the "Midland Pullman" was the work of many people. Metro-Cammell were chiefly responsible, but the Transport Commission's design panel, which has a hand in the entire railway modernisation programme, was at work on the project from the beginning.

'It was in Metro-Cammell's contract that the company should appoint a consultant designer-architect approved by the design panel and the Pullman company. Mr Jack Howe was selected, and it is an indication of the fact that his job was not simply to make the train look beautiful that he was one of the people responsible for introducing the Schlieren bogie from the Continent. The Schlieren design was developed under licence by Metro-Cammell, whose product is the Metro-Schlieren bogie. *[This is surely a very strange statement to make for as we have stated Jack Howe was a designer, not an engineer.]*

'The design panel was appointed by the BTC. in October, 1956, the same month that the Minister of Transport announced "high speed luxury diesel electric trains running between large cities" which would "contain all that is best to offer for the comfort and amenity of the passenger." The panel is concerned with equipment of all kinds used by passengers, customers, and staff, or which is prominently visible to them or to the general public. One of the chief purposes of the panel is to make the most effective use of professional designers and consultants outside the transport industry as well as the Commission's own staff designers. The Commission has said that new equipment should be "in line with the best current standards in industrial design while preserving the dignity and simplicity appropriate to a great public service."

'Priority is given to the railway modernisation plan. The Commission believes that if the panel achieves its purpose, one important result will be an increased sense of pride among the staff and a new confidence in the future of the service on the part of both staff and public. The work of the panel would be much easier if it acted as a dictatorship. In designing a new type of train – and it was intended that the "Midland Pullman" should not be tied to any previous ideas of train design – the panel knew there would be many conflicting points of view. But these conflicts had to be reconciled by agreement, not by an arbitrary ruling. Some of the people, for example, who had spent their working life in the Pullman service took time to adjust themselves to the idea of a blue-and-white train. The customary chocolate and cream meant as much to them as regimental colours. The number of seats on each side of the gangway was another problem. The Pullman fashion has been to put only one seat on each side, and there are still members of the Pullman staff who believe that having two seats together (even on only one side of the gangway) takes away from the idea of treating the customer as an 'individual'. On the other hand, there was a suggestion by some officials of the Western Region, where similar trains are to be run, that there should be two seats on each side of the gangway. This scheme was obviously attractive from the money-making point of view, but it would have broken several Pullman hearts. An example of compromise in a comparatively minor detail is the tableware. Some would have liked all of it to be of an entirely new design, but as it turns out the glasses are newly designed, the metal containers such as coffee-pots and sugar basins were selected by Mr Howe from a new design in the shops, and Pullman has adapted its own standard crockery and cutlery. This combination is to be put into all Pullman cars throughout the service. Adaptation like this was not always possible. Usually one idea had to prevail over several. The designers were working for a clean modern look without unnecessary applied decoration or over-emphasised shapes. The colour scheme was chosen to emphasise this clean look, and in fact was possible only because in recent years blues that will not fade have been developed by the paint industry. It would also be wrong to give the impression that the Pullman influence was opposed to people who were forward-thinking. The train must be modern in function as well as name and developments were suggested at various times which the company felt would detract from the Pullman Character. Many features of the Pullman, such as inward opening doors, were welcomed by all the designers. In a number of small ways, also, Mr Howe took advantage of Pullman ideas. He redesigned the coat of arms so that, as one member of the design panel has said, "it belongs to a speedy object." It is elongated and in other ways streamlined. On the outside of the carriages Mr Howe has used another Pullman colour effect by enfolding the windows in a cream band. People who know the Pullman style more by repute than by experience may think that the "Midland Pullman" has taken it in one bound from the nineteenth century to the twentieth. This suggestion is resented by Pullman officials who point to the new style of the coaches introduced in the past ten years. But there is one test of the Pullman style which people can themselves apply to the "Midland Pullman". "Pullman," said one official, "has always gone for the drawing-room atmosphere." He said that the new train showed "the modern drawing-room attitude." Perhaps it is because of this emphasis on the drawing-room that the designers are so proud of keeping the passenger's luggage out of sight of anybody looking along the inside of the carriage. There are shelves in the lobby of each carriage for heavy luggage, and the rack above the seats is tilted so that people walking past should not notice the hand luggage. When sitting under the rack the passenger, by looking directly upwards, can see his luggage through slots. The designs on the end walls of the carriages are made of small pieces of wood, metal, marble, and other materials. The artist, Mr George Mitchell, carved each pattern deep in the wood and filled it with these materials. He then ran liquid transparent resin over it, sanded, and polished it. The design sparkles.' (Samples of crockery were sent to the Pullman Car Co. by George Williams the Design Officer in an attempt to get them to agree to 'better table equipment' – *cheapskate Pullman?* The tea set was designed by David Mellor and was initially shown in the Design Centre. Glassware was intended to be dual purpose for both the Blue Pullman trains and on the BTP shipping fleet.)

Next came 'Rail Challenges Air'. 'British Railways today introduce their challenge to competition from air travel between Manchester and London. It is a modern six-coach diesel-electric express train which is to make the journey in three hours thirteen minutes. The train has a top speed of 90mph and will carry 112 first-class passengers. The Midland Region expects it to establish itself quickly as "the business man's special." Originally it was planned to introduce the service early in the New Year but the date was put back for the engineers to make the train run as smoothly as possible.

'Although the train is designed for Pullman service it is a complete break with the heavy Edwardian comfort of the traditional chocolate and cream Pullman coaches. It has a smooth, streamlined, blue and cream exterior and inside in many ways it looks more like the aircraft with which it will be competing than a railway train. The coaches are of open design, with two seats on one side of the gangway and only one on the other. The seats can be moved forward or back, and may be locked in an upright or reclining position. The train is completely air-conditioned and will be heated to a standard 72 degrees. Interior decoration is in shades of pastel blue and grey with red and blue upholstery. Trials were started well before Christmas and the engineers have made full use of the extra time available to deal with teething troubles. Most of these have been slight and easily corrected, but in the middle of January there was still some trouble with the smoothness of the running. In the two centre coaches the ride was exceptionally smooth (it was hard to believe that the train was travelling at 90mph, but there was some sway in the end coaches. The train accelerated rather slowly but once it has reached about 40mph the rate of acceleration increased rapidly. It is limited to its speed of 90mph in many places only by the state of the permanent way.

'The braking system is immensely powerful and hauls the train to a stop in a remarkably short distance. Midland Region will have two of these trains in service initially working on a week-on week-off basis. Three other eight-coach trains are now being built for the Western Region. They will be similar in most respects but they will also carry second class passengers. The cost of the Manchester–London trains is not officially disclosed, but one estimate is that each unit cost about £250,000, and it is believed that they are the most expensive units ever put on the line. A surcharge of £1 in each direction between Manchester and London and also between Leicester and London is added to the normal first-class fare.

'During the working day the train will normally have a maintenance check at Kentish Town depot between 4 and 6pm and it will get another check when it is housed overnight at Reddish, near Manchester. The reserve train will also be held at Reddish. When the trains first come into service fault-finding staff from Reddish will travel on them regularly for a month or two.

'Passenger comfort and punctuality are to be the two main concerns. British Railways' record of punctuality even with expresses on the Manchester–London services is not good, but a tremendous effort will be made to overcome that shortcoming with the new train. The railway people realise that it is vital that they should if they are to win back passengers. The principal attractions are comfortable seats and plenty of room to stretch. Each passenger has a table immediately in front of him, and any meals or drinks will be served without his having to move to a restaurant car. He may press a bell to call the attendant. The bell lights a green indicator above his table and another outside the attendant's pantry, where an arrow shows in which section of the train the passenger is sitting. As the attendant goes to answer the call he turns off the light outside his room and he turns off the light above the passenger's head by pressing a switch under the table. There are many special comforts. All meals from breakfast to dinner will be served, and the bar will be open at all times when the train is running. The windows are double-paned, as part of the air-conditioning system, and as a result will not mist up. Each passenger has an individual venetian blind which rolls down between the two panes.

'The floors are carpeted from wall to wall, and the colours are restful and pleasant. A public address system allows the guard to tell passengers the cause of any delay which may occur and to make any other special announcements, but railway officials insist that it will not be used to bombard passengers with "unwanted chatter." There are door mats to greet passengers as they board the train, and all the doors to the platform open inwards. The dividing doors along the length of the train swing either way and shut automatically when a passenger has passed through, thus eliminating draughts. Perhaps most noticeable of all, the murky concertina-like joins which normally link coaches are dressed up into well-lighted and steady gangways.

'To offset these good points there are only one or two obvious limitations. The more serious of these is the lack of luggage space. Officials counter this objection by saying that since the train will attract principally business men, little luggage will be carried. Some passengers may also object to the lighting. Running down the centre of each coach is a strip of fluorescent light and over each table there is a concentrated iridescent light. On each table is a small single-bulb lamp in a tubular shade. But it might have been a good idea to provide each passenger with a small individual light (again on the aircraft model) behind his head for reading in greater comfort and with less strain. The train is designed in a symmetrical pattern which divides neatly in the middle. The sequence of coaches is; power coach, kitchen car, parlour car, parlour

The Blue Pullman Story

On Friday 1 July 1960, Martin Welch was at St Pancras to record 'Set 2' on its first visit to London. This may even have been the first time a set had ventured this far south although we know 'Set 1' had certainly been on trial for several weeks already. Martin took six views of the train, the three seen here plus three other close-ups of the vehicles. (It was on one of these latter three that we have confirmation of M60093 as the power car at the country end of the station.) The images selected here are those with the most 'public interest' criteria; after all, nothing like that ever been seen before. Both complete LMR sets had been delivered from the builders during November 1959 (See Appendix 11) and consequently we now know that by this time local trials with 'Set 2' had also been completed. The set here appears to be connected to the shore supply – notice the cable on the platform side of the running line. *Martin Welch*

car, kitchen car, and power coach. The power cars seat twelve passengers each, the kitchen cars eighteen, and the parlour cars 36. There is provision for non-smokers. Apart from decoration the two sets of coaches are similar in every way. The total length of the train is 409ft. 1in.

'The kitchen facilities are, for a train of this size, remarkably spacious. Cooking will be by propane or Calor gas as railway kitchen staff apparently dislike cooking with electricity. In each kitchen there is a notice signed by Mr F. D. Harding, Managing Director of the Pullman Car Company, which reads in part, "You know that a smart, clean turnout and unfailing courtesy will rebound to your benefit and satisfaction. Everything possible is done to enable our staff to appear smartly turned out and I count on all of you to maintain this."

'Next to each kitchen is an attendant's pantry and a small room where staff may relax and have a meal. There are also special toilets for the staff. In the toilets for the passengers, plugs are not provided for the wash basins but spray taps are fitted which will run with cold, warm, or hot water according to taste. This is a simple but effective way of removing the possibility of a passenger, towards the end of a journey, finding a basin with a dirty scum mark.

'The most remarkable thing about the driving cabs at each end is the nose. Before the designers finally decided on the present streamlined front they tried and discarded thirteen mock-ups. Inside, the cab is of fairly standard design, although it is more comfortable than most, and has the added attraction of a small stove where the driver and his mate may brew up a cup of tea or grill a piece of bacon. The deadman's control is worked by foot instead of by hand (as in other diesel cars in service) and there is direct spoken contact with the guard through a loud hailer. The cab is also backed with a thick band of acoustic material to deaden the noise from the engines, which are immediately behind the driver's back. It does so very effectively. Each power coach is fitted with a 1,000hp diesel engine built by North British Locomotive under licence from a German MAN design. The alternators are behind the engines and the current generated in them is fed to eight traction motors mounted on the bogies fore and aft. Two auxiliary engines, fitted under the two kitchen cars, provide power for the fluorescent lighting, battery charging, air-conditioning and refrigeration: They are supplied by Rolls-Royce. High speed brakes are supplied by Westinghouse, the electric and control equipment by the General Electric Company of Birmingham, and the air conditioning by J. Stone and Company of Deptford. The main contractors who were responsible for the entire design of the train are Metro-Cammell Carriage and Wagon Birmingham.'

Finally we should mention that in the same newspaper was a piece which concentrated on general carriage design from the earliest days of railways to the (then) present day but without specifics on the new train. Consequently it is of no relevance to the present text and is omitted.

Then on 5 July this from *The Guardian*; 'Pullman shows its paces, a day of early arrivals'. 'From our industrial staff.'

'The train Monday. How did they bring the good news from Manchester Central to London St Pancras?'

'Alderman Arthur Donovan, the Lord Mayor of Manchester, gave half a dozen mighty swipes with a green flag, and the Manchester Pullman (described by a railway official as "showing the flag of railway modernisation", drew out of the station at 8.50am on its first scheduled journey. A rumour had gone round that each of the passengers was to be given an inscribed penknife to celebrate the occasion, but the sight of an inscribed plastic luggage label holder beside each place seemed to indicate that railway modernisation had its limits. The passengers leaned back to the gentle sound of rattling coffee cups. A baby began to cry. But apart from the baby, everybody began the journey in a spirit of loyalty. Soon the reporters were hard at work interviewing each other under the impression that they were all business men. And then over the loudspeaker came the announcement that an attendant would pass down the train distributing, free inscribed penknives, or almost free: to avoid severing a friendship with British Railways, each passenger was invited to follow the ancient superstition by contributing to the railway orphanage. No free food. We now had a plastic luggage label holder and a penknife. But some people are never satisfied. A passenger leaned across the table and asked, "Do we have to pay for the meal?" When told that we did he said that he thought so, but a railway signalman had told him that the £2 extra on a return first-class fare gave the "Midland Pullman" customer the right to claim free food. "I worked it out,' he said. "I didn't see how they could possibly do it."

'We passed through Leicester, the city chosen for the "Midland Pullman's" afternoon run to and from London. There was no sign of excitement being whipped up in preparation for our afternoon visit. It was some consolation when the guard asked for our tickets: his assistant stamped "First run" in red ink on them, and the tickets were returned to us as a memento. In car D, seat 5F, sat Mr J. Royston, Divisional Traffic Manager Industrial Staff for the East Lancashire division of British Railways. He was carrying two letters from the Lord Mayor of Manchester, one for the Lord Mayor of London and the other for the chairman of the London Midland Region area board. There was no letter for the Lord Mayor of Leicester, but then nobody but a souvenir hunter is going to travel from Manchester to Leicester by way of London which is the way the Manchester Pullman does it.

'Alderman Donovan said in both letters that he was writing particularly on behalf of the business community of Manchester in welcoming the new service. He did not mention the alternative air service to which the 'Midland Pullman' is intended to be the railway's chief rival, but the businessmen travelling in the train did. The evidence they gave to the reporters was on the whole favourable to the railways. One man may have expressed the general view of Manchester business men who have been in the habit of flying to London when he said that he would now divide his time between air and rail, travelling by 'Midland Pullman' in the winter and by air in the summer.

Passengers' suggestions. Two suggestions made by people on the train were that the service should include a secretary and a telephone and that the train should leave either two hours earlier or two hours later. The point of this last complaint was that, arriving in London at noon the 'Midland Pullman' prevents a business man from meeting somebody in the morning or from having a convenient lunch on the train before an early afternoon engagement. The official railway reply was that a 7.00am start was too early for most travellers, and unless they could arrive in London at 10.00am or soon after, most business men preferred to give up the idea of working in the morning and to arrange to meet their first client over lunch. As to the suggestion that there should be a secretary and telephone on the train, the reply was that British Railways have learnt by experience on journeys like these. One railway official said: "We are experimenting with telephones, but we do not feel the demand is great. We had a teamed secretary on the 'Comet' (train) between Manchester and London. She never earned her wage. She lasted about a year."

'Proud porters. The train was six minutes early into St Pancras. Proud porters asked us how the journey had gone. A loud-speaker boomed its welcome. Merriment overflowed. But somebody seemed to have overlooked Leicester. At 12.45pm the "Midland Pullman" set off on its first journey from London to Leicester. The stationmaster was there, but nobody waved a large flag. There were no gifts for the passengers. We carried no letter of greeting for the Lord Mayor of Leicester. A man came round stamping "First run" in red ink on our tickets, but not much ink flowed. The train had been nearly full on the run from Manchester to London; now it was nearly empty. Five men, including an opera singer, had arrived with note-books and stop watches in pursuit of their hobby of train-studying. But the only other person who appeared to be there for a practical purpose was a clergyman who was going north on holiday and decided to do part of the journey on the London Pullman to see what it was like. The others were mostly officials. The train was 21 minutes early into Leicester. There we learnt one of the reasons why there was no letter to deliver, apart from railway officials, there was nobody of rank on the platform to deliver it to.

'There was time for a telephone call to the Lord Mayor, Mrs Dorothy Russell, at her home. She said frankly and charmingly that she would love to have taken part in the "Midland Pullman" celebrations but other engagements had prevented her. Every wish fulfilled we were back on the train at 2.33pm, and the man came round again with the red ink stamping "First run" on the tickets and there was a second distribution of inscribed plastic luggage label holders. A woman passenger said she had been travelling on the railways for 70 years and never had she expected to see so perfect a train as the "Midland Pullman". She could think of no improvement necessary.

'We were three minutes early into London, and when the train left for Manchester at 6.10pm, the Lord Mayor of London. Sir Edmund Stockdale, was there to see us off, and to give Mr Royston a letter in reply to Alderman Donovan's. When the train arrived at Manchester six minutes early I had travelled 578 miles in about twelve-and-half hours with three intervals. The net travelling time being about nine hours. I was exasperated to find that the train swayed as much on the Leicester run that I could not write a legible letter. (Returning to Manchester in the same carriage my writing was legible enough over long stretches of the track.) But it is to the train's credit that at the end I felt quite fresh. The quietness, the subdued vibration, the air conditioning, and particularly the well moulded seats, had much to do with this. Another cheering thing was that before the day was over I had collected my third inscribed plastic luggage label holder and a ball-point pen.'

Perhaps it really was a 'slow news week' as the euphoria showed no sign of abating so far as the press were concerned. Witness then the following, again from *The Guardian* on the Friday of the first full week's service (9 July, although clearly penned a few days earlier): 'Manchester to London diesel, 3 hours 13 minutes, by our Industrial Staff.' 'For an extra £1 on a first-class fare, people travelling by train from Manchester to London will be able to do the journey in 3 hours and 13 minutes from July 4. On that day the "Midland Pullman", a diesel-electric express train of six coaches, will start its daily run between the two cities. The reverse journey will take two minutes less than the run from Manchester Central to St Pancras. Bookings are now being accepted for the service, which offers the passenger a comfortable chair, a table, and plenty of room to stretch. The seats can be moved forward or back, and locked in an upright or a reclining position. The passenger can summon an attendant by pressing a button beside his seat. There is a public address system, so that the guard can tell the passengers why (if) they are running late. The train carries 132 passengers. 90mph top speed. It has been estimated that the cost of each unit is £250,000. It was originally planned to have started running last autumn, but Mr J. Royston. divisional traffic manager for the London Midland Region, said he would not accept the train until it was "100 per cent perfect." A member of Mr Royston's staff said in March that all the individual units of the train were perfect, but when running together they were less than perfect. The difficulty was to get the engine and the coaches to work "in cohesion." Mr Royston said at this time that the train would do the journey in three hours five minutes. The train will leave Manchester Central at 8.50am, arriving at St Pancras at 12.03pm, and calling at Cheadle Heath. It will leave St Pancras at 6.10pm, arriving at Manchester at 9.21pm, again calling at Cheadle Heath. During the afternoon, it will run an express service between London and Leicester.'

Not surprisingly, having also 'done it once' so to speak, there appears to have been little real appetite for the press to repeat chapter and verse consequent upon the introduction of the WR sets into service. As a result we are left with recourse to the *Railway Observer* where in their

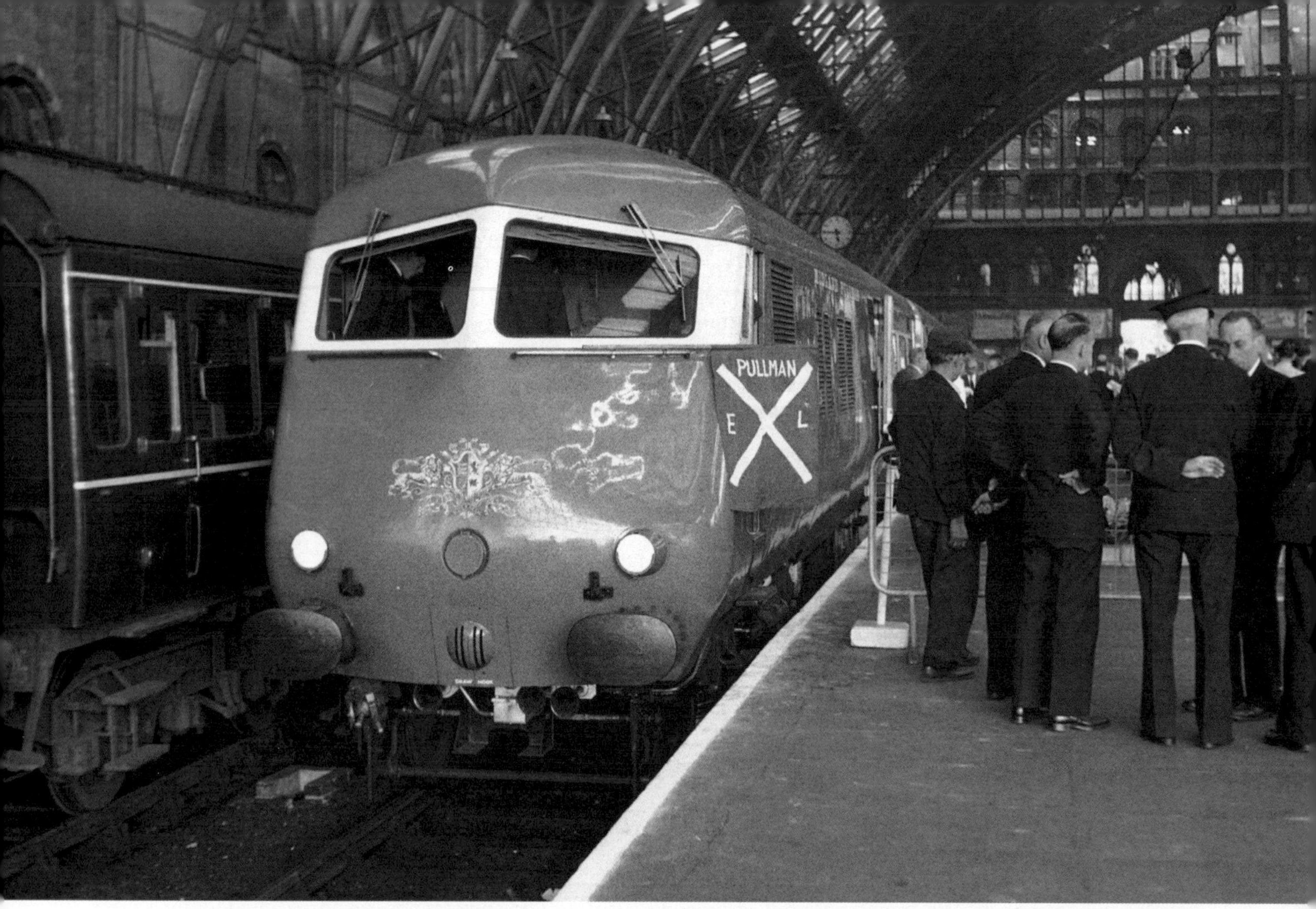
PULLMAN
E
L

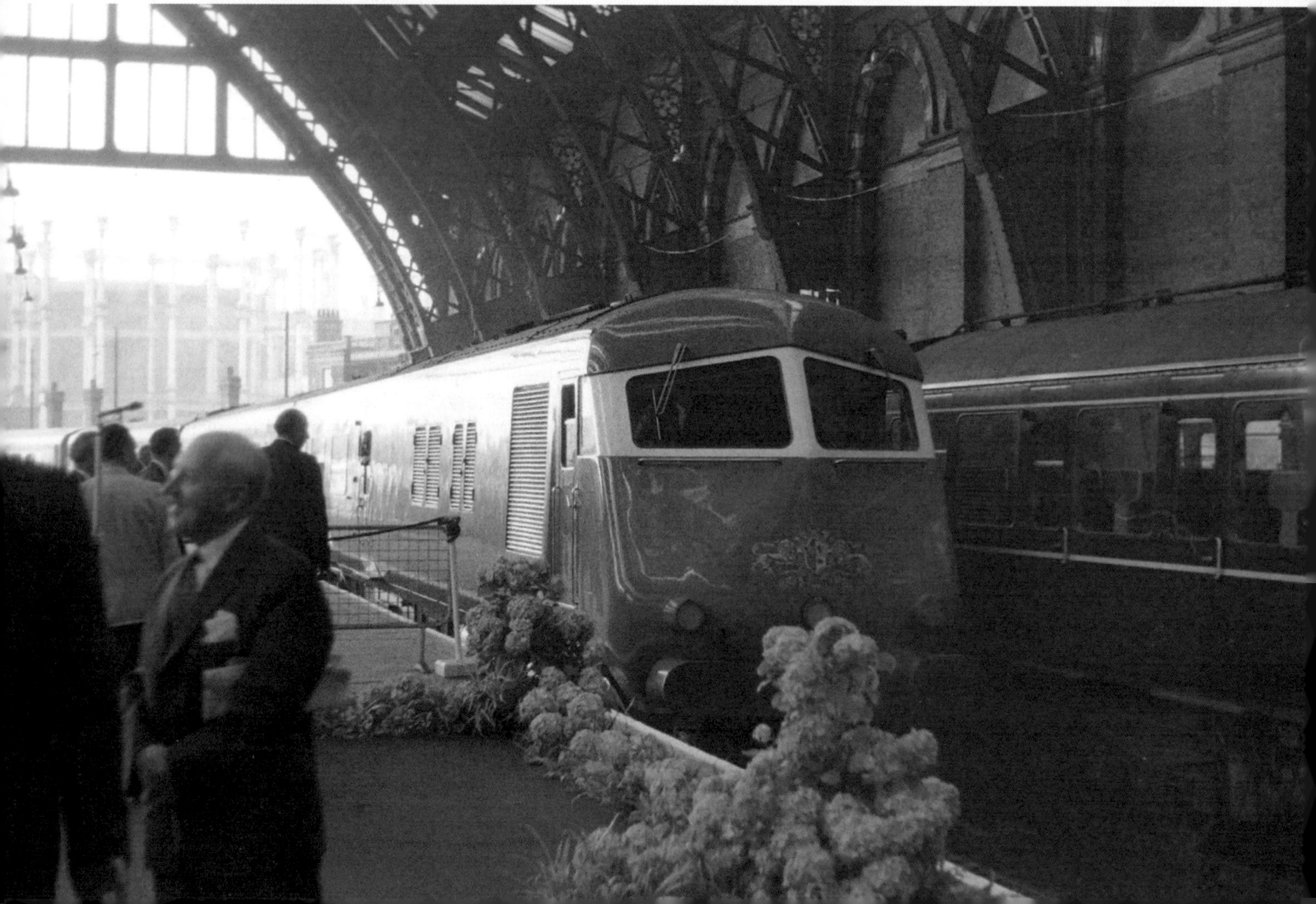

LEFT AND ABOVE St Pancras late afternoon/early evening, Monday 4 July 1960. The stock for the first down evening Manchester Pullman is seen arriving at the station and then seen as the centre of attention prior to departure. Making a speech is the Lord Mayor of London, the Right Honourable Sir Edmund Stockdale, whilst nearby is Mrs Louise Arabin, the Mayor of St. Pancras, and Mr David Blee. Other VIP's include Sir Reginald Wilson, Chairman of the LMR Area Board, Mr R. W. Crawshaw, PR & PO, Mr J. G. Handley, Station Master, Mr R. L. E. Lawrence, District Traffic Manager, and the Deputy Mayoress Mrs R. J. Howell. The clock shows the time as fast approaching 6.00pm with departure scheduled for 6.10pm. Of note is the red-coloured flag attached to the side of the power car – flags were used for this purpose by the LMR whilst under the same circumstances the WR used a metal plate. The driver of this first down service was Mr A. W. Golding of Kentish Town. *The Transport Treasury with caption notes from Terry Bye.*

issue for June 1960 under the heading 'Diesel Multiple Unit Pullman Services' the following was quoted: 'The present intention is for these services *[referring to the WR trains]* to start on 4 July, subject to the staff difficulties being resolved by that date. *[As we of course know, this date was not achievable and the WR trains did not commence until September.]* The set based on Bristol leaves that city at 7.45am and runs non-stop to Paddington, arriving at 9.35am. It leaves again at 10.50am, calls at Bath (11.40/11.43am) and arrives in Bristol at 12.00noon. After another quick turn-round, Bristol is left again at 12.30pm and with a stop at Bath (12.43/12.45pm) Paddington is reached at 2.25pm. The final trip for this set leaves Paddington at 4.55pm. and runs non-stop to Bristol, arriving at 6.45pm. It is greatly to be regretted that the non-stop trips take 110 minutes, i.e., five minutes more than the "Bristolian", on which no supplement is payable. The Pullmans are thought to be capable of covering the run non-stop in 87 minutes, which, with a recovery time of eight minutes, would allow a schedule of 95minutes, ie, five minutes better than last summer's 100 minute "Bristolian". The Wolverhampton set leaves that city at 7am, calls at Birmingham, Solihull and Leamington, and arrives in Paddington at 9.35am, the same time as the Pullman from Bristol is due. It leaves again at 12.10pm, calls at Leamington (1.34/1.37) and arrives in Birmingham at 2.50pm. The 84-minute run from Paddington to Leamington is the fastest ever scheduled between these points. The set leaves Birmingham again at 2.30pm, calls at. Leamington (2.53/2.55pm) and arrives in Paddington at 4.25pm. The final working leaves Paddington at 4.50pm, calls at Leamington, Solihull and Birmingham, and arrives in Wolverhampton at 7.20pm. In view of the fact that it is the Birmingham businessmen who have been demanding a fast morning service to London, it is ludicrous that the up "businessman's" train should take 95 minutes non-stop from Leamington to Paddington (a minute longer than the steam-hauled

Equipment for BRITISH RAILWAYS NEW DIESEL PULLMAN TRAINS

AUXILIARY POWER · AIR-CONDITIONING · HEATING · LIGHTING · ETC.

"Cambrian Coast Express", whereas the 12.10pm. from Paddington performs the journey in 84 minutes. The new services detailed above have, as may be expected, necessitated numerous alterations to other trains, in particular on the Bristol main line.'

We might at this stage comment upon and also respond to some of the points and criticism levied. Firstly if the correspondent to the RO states the sets are able to undertake the run in 87 minutes clearly there must have been trials to prove this point. It is a great pity information on these is not available. A suitably recovery margin though allowing for a 95-minute schedule on the Bristol service does make sense.

So far as the running time of the Birmingham service was concerned, here the slowed scheduling compared to what we are advised had been 'demanded' could simply have been due to available line capacity at that time. Coming to the defence of the WR, they may very well have thought this timing could be improved upon but surely far better to start off 'safe' and improve as experience was gained. Recall too that almost the complete route of both trains was then still operated under mechanical signalling with far less flexibility in train control than is possible in a modern remotely controlled facility. *(Although in the opinion of the present writes – and please forgive the personal input – semaphore signals do look far better!)*

We may conclude this fulsome praise with some words that appeared in an unknown journal albeit penned with a junior in mind. The writer commented, '. . . Railwaymen along its routes call the "Midland Pullman" diesel-electric express the "Blue Streak" … '. A little later the same writer made comparisons with the trains he had witnessed years before on the former Midland Railway main line, a time when 4-4-0, 2-4-0, and 4-2-2 engines were still in use. Surely a definite case of 'Tempus Fugit'. (The equivalent timescale comparisons today would be to compare the modern day electric Manchester service with BP, even if the former now traverses a different route.)

Notes

(1) In the earlier 'Blue Pullman' book it was reported exactly as here, and indeed correctly, that the LMR sets were the first to be completed. But perhaps we should now ask the obvious question, 'why'? And to this there is simply no answer within the files. There is nothing in the paperwork to suggest one region's trains were being given priority over the other, nor that at that time there was anything to suggest an eight-car set was any more complicated to build than a six-car train – excepting of course for the additional two cars required. Possibly the answer is the obvious political one. Had one complete train for each region been built and tested it would have potentially put back the likely introduction into service. The LMR were to operate a single set from the outset, the WR two. Each would require a spare set as well, simpler then to concentrate on the easiest option – the LMR trains and service.

(2) It is not certain if the three WR trains were also sent to Derby or if, following their initial trial running from the builders, they instead went direct to Swindon for 'testing, staff training and familiarisation'.

(3) The test was reported in the *Railway Observer* for November 1959 as follows, 'A special run took place in the early hours of Tuesday 25 August from St Pancras to Manchester and in the reverse direction on Wednesday 26 August. No 45585 *Hyderabad* (14B Kentish Town) on two corridor coaches and the track recording coach *(what the latter vehicle was for the LMR runs is not certain)* put up a remarkable performance on both days. The schedule called for passing times of 60 minutes to Kettering (72 miles) and 84 minutes to Leicester (99.1 miles) but due to pw checks, Derby was passed five minutes late in a shade over two hours. However this loss was made good and arrival in Manchester was on time in a shade over three and a quarter hours. In the up direction the same pw checks were encountered but the loss was more than regained and St Pancras was reached in 3 hours 10 minutes. Presumably the purpose of the runs was to check track reaction preparatory to the high-speed Pullman diesel service over the route. If schedules as this are envisaged some highly interesting running can be expected!'

(4) As this test run does not appear to have been picked up by the enthusiast fraternity and there does not appear to be any reference to it in contemporary journals we are regretfully unable to provide details of the locomotive. 'Timetable running trials' was nothing new but what is perhaps unusual is the limited load provided. The only conclusion reached was that the output of a 'Jubilee' might be said to be in the order of 1,000hp, equivalent then to a Blue Pullman 'half-set'.

(5) Studied in detail, the BTF film shows some interesting aspects of the train. Firstly it was shot on several different dates: this is apparent as in some of the images the Pullman crest has yet to be applied at the front of the power cars. Similarly the kitchen-cars show the partial all-blue livery before this was altered. On-board it will be noted various aspects of technical equipment including a Hallade recorder – the latter located in one of the toilets – may be seen. Some fitting out also appears to be continuing in a kitchen as well (where the ever important kettle is also steaming away!). The interior colour schemes (antimacassars were still be added) are also of note and some seats are vibrating badly. Finally at one point we see one Blue Pullman set passing another. If it is taken that these are both 'Midland' sets, then this would be one of the few occasions when the two sets were in operation simultaneously, albeit on the occasion seen, when both were on test. From the background foliage these latter images were clearly taken in the spring or early summer of 1960 and so confirm filming was on-going over several months. A number of other films available on the same internet channel also show relevant Blue Pullman material.

(6) This statement again raises questions and nothing to do with timescales. The important point must be, 'Where were the WR sets being trialled?' If it was on the WR then we have to state the WR main-line permanent-way was generally reckoned to be the best on British Railways. So if the units were being tested on this modifications of the type suggested may well have had a reasonable amount of success, but it was a thoroughly different matter on the former Midland main-line! Even so as wear developed in service so the situation would simply become worse – everywhere. (But that last statement is to take the story beyond the remit of the present chapter.)

(7) *Design* magazine for August 1960 will come up as being referred to again later.

(8) Shortly after this and in a note from an unknown individual, we learn that at the two meetings Mr Grand attended of the Design Panel, he had also expressed a wish for the WR trains to be in WR/standard Pullman livery. The (unknown) writer commenting, 'It is hardly a matter for surprise that he should still be of that view.' Might this 'writer' have been Howe or potentially even Barman?

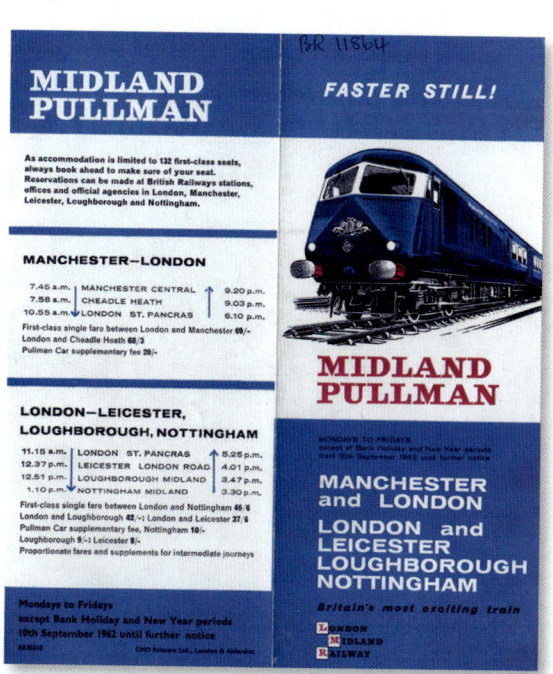

4

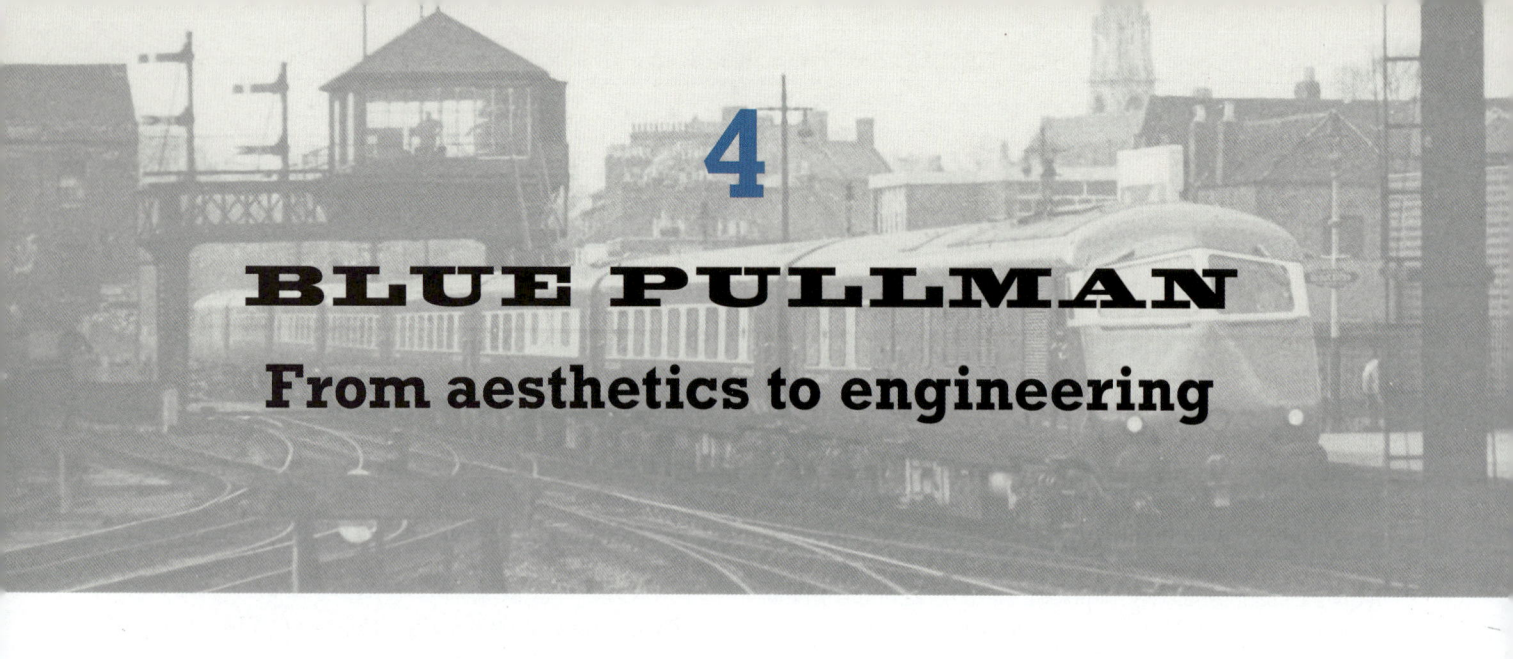

BLUE PULLMAN
From aesthetics to engineering

Before considering the mechanical features of the new trains we need to reconnect with some of the earlier text both from a historic and political perspective and also so far as the actual design was concerned.

The train itself (considering here both the LMR and WR versions) may well have been the mechanical brainchild of Metropolitan-Cammell, but as stated the aesthetics both externally and internally were mainly the responsibility of just one man, Jack Howe.

This influence of Jack Howe was considerable, for example it was he who had especially arranged for the uncluttered appearance of the front end of the trains, including the removal of the four-character head-code panel that had been proposed. Notwithstanding the criticism levied in the *Design* article about the front end appearance, the result was a streamlined train, the like of which had never been seen before in Britain, and which was justifiably presented as the prestige symbol of the Modernisation Plan.

Both externally and internally, the train was packed with innovative ideas and luxury features, and despite the fact that it was Pullman-only, it was genuinely still a considerable advance on anything seen previously. (The counter argument could be that before World War 2, the LMS and the LNER had run, respectively, the 'Coronation Scot' and 'Coronation' services, but while these services easily eclipsed the regular workings of the 1950s, they still did not approach the unashamed luxury that Blue Pullman offered. The only other contender would be the GWR's single train of 'Super Saloons', but these were used either as a complete rake or in restricted numbers solely for very special workings and were not available to the general public. Nor were any of these trains fully air-conditioned, as was the Blue Pullman.) Apart also from where essential components were fitted, the body sides of Blue Pullman were also smooth and clean in detail. Perhaps the least satisfactory features, from a visual perspective, were the gaps between the car and the exposed jumper cables, a particular area where as we know Howe had failed to

Official view of a type 'P2' power car, meaning one for the WR and so having a slightly different side window profile. Under the bodywork and just off-centre to the right may be seen the socket to receive the shore supply. From the refection seen in the gleaming bodywork it is likely this was taken at the MC premises where folklore has it at least one senior member of staff bought a new camera especially to record the trains. We may consider whether the criticism of the front end in *Design* was something Howe had expected. Had he not once proposed something more radical which had been rejected? Tradition also dies hard on the railway (not just Pullman), hence the inclusion of the brackets to take an oil burning tail-lamp.
Richard Moore

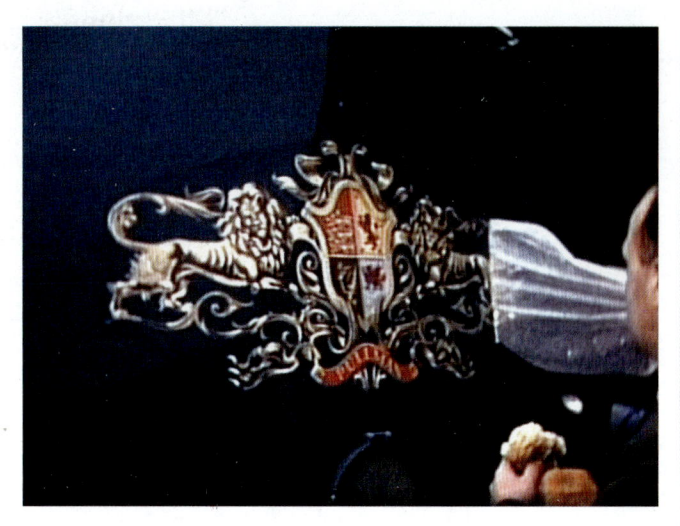

ABOVE Almost the final embellishment to be added were the end crests.

RIGHT The opposite end of the same 'P2' type vehicle – note this and other similar designations seen on what were clearly official MC photographs were copied on and used by BR. It was to hide the 'unsightly' but essential connections between vehicles that Howe had suggested 'bellows' or similar. It would actually take the railways another generation and a bit, before this was achieved and became the norm. Of note also are the buffing plates, physical connection between vehicles – a solid bar requiring bolts – and the pair of builder's plates, one on either side. Few artefacts in the form of hardware survive from the trains: a few seats, and a handful of other items. *Richard Moore*

achieve his aim. Whether his suggestion for rubber type 'bellows' to be fitted would have improved or otherwise the aesthetics between cars will remain a matter for debate.

But even without this external embellishment, at the same point internally there was a vast improvement on the design of the internal gangways. Long regarded as one of the worst features of the traditional railway carriage, invariably dark, draughty and a repository for dirt, instead there was now a clean wide and fluid passageway, mounted on pivots at each carriage end, which formed a semi-floating, rubber-sealed platform, that also prevented any loss of air-conditioning. Indeed if he did find the need to vacate his seat – usually the only time a passenger would do this en-route would be to visit the 'facilities' – then the transition towards the end of or even into the next car was seamless. With booked seats and standing passengers not permitted, gangways were thus free most of the time so allowing for easy access for the stewards. Pullman service meant everything was brought to the passenger. With the exception of the 'half' saloons located within the power cars there was also no end doors of any sort between vehicles. It was another 'first' for carriage design in Britain.

Moving to the interior proper, this was accessed by doors from the outside designed to open inwards in standard Pullman style and provided at the ends only; the early suggestion for centre doors having been abandoned. This change was certainly a good choice, centre doors can lead to large gaps between the train and the platform when stopped against a curved platform. Inside, the traditional Edwardian Pullman, with its timber panelling and marquetry, was (almost) consigned to history. Instead, first class passengers were regaled with grey leather cloth walls, set off by either ebony or polished rosewood partitions, the partitions having inlaid murals by George Mitchell.[1] (The style of panelling was one of the few vestiges of traditional Pullman styling that remained and we may indeed ponder as to how much of this was down to the late involvement of Sir John Elliot. The word 'involvement' is deliberately chosen carefully here, rather than what readers might feel the more appropriate 'interference of'.)

The interior colour schemes varied per half set with first class being either red and black or blue and black. Again this was markedly different to both traditional Pullman and conventional rail vehicles (including the latest build of both locomotive-hauled and DMU/EMU type). Passenger seats were fully adjustable and could be reclined – a deliberate copy of what had come to be expected on a contemporary airliner. (The fact most of the population would not by that time have experienced a modern airliner was a moot point.)

Second class Pullman passengers on the WR sets were not totally forgotten either, although here the seats were fixed, which thus allowed for an increase in seating capacity of 42 compared with 36 in the same area within first class. The use of modern materials was also more prevalent in the second class saloons and avoided the

The Blue Pullman Story

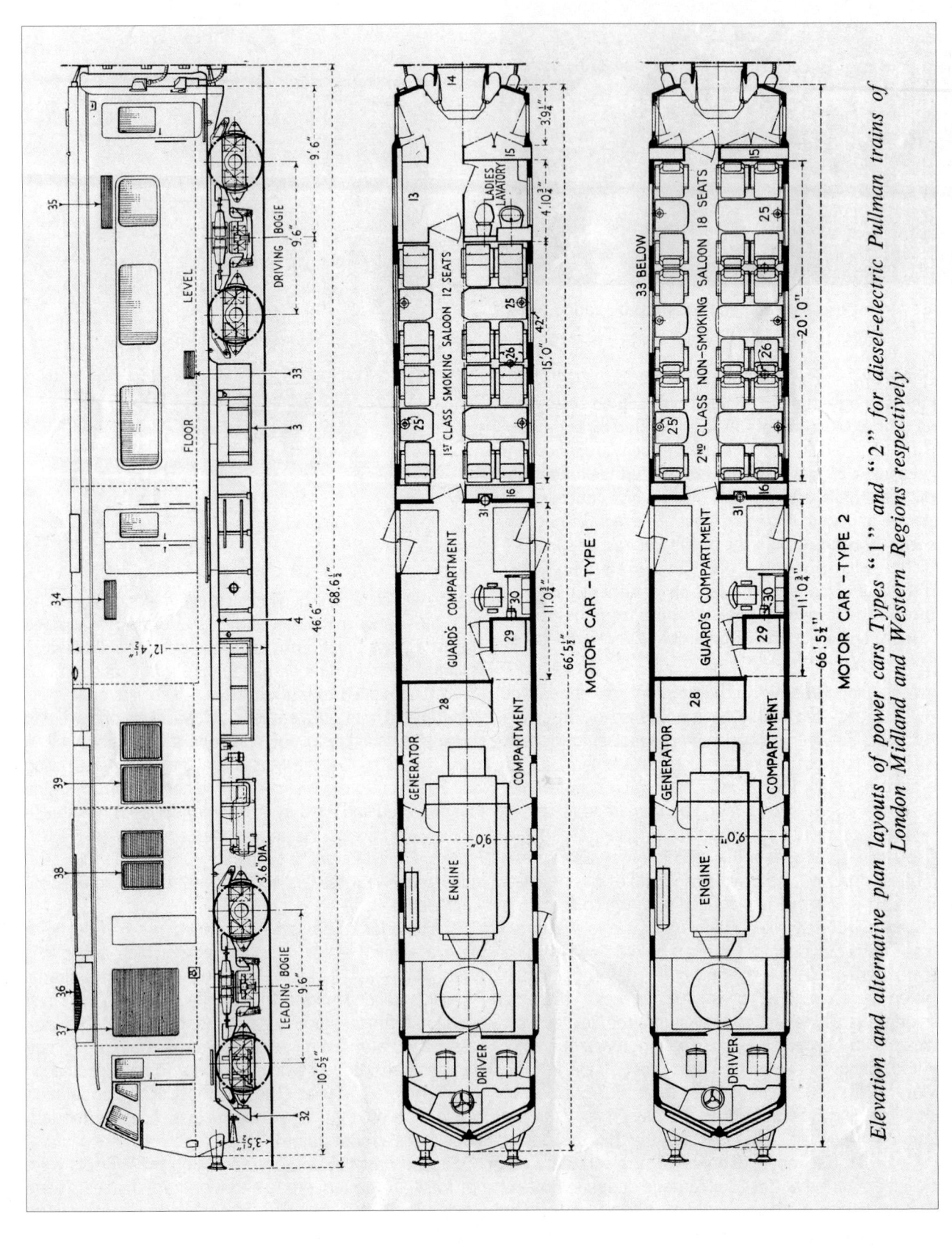

Elevation and alternative plan layouts of power cars Types "1" and "2" for diesel-electric Pullman trains of London Midland and Western Regions respectively

Works drawings for the trains were still being passed from the builders to BR at least as late as September 1963.

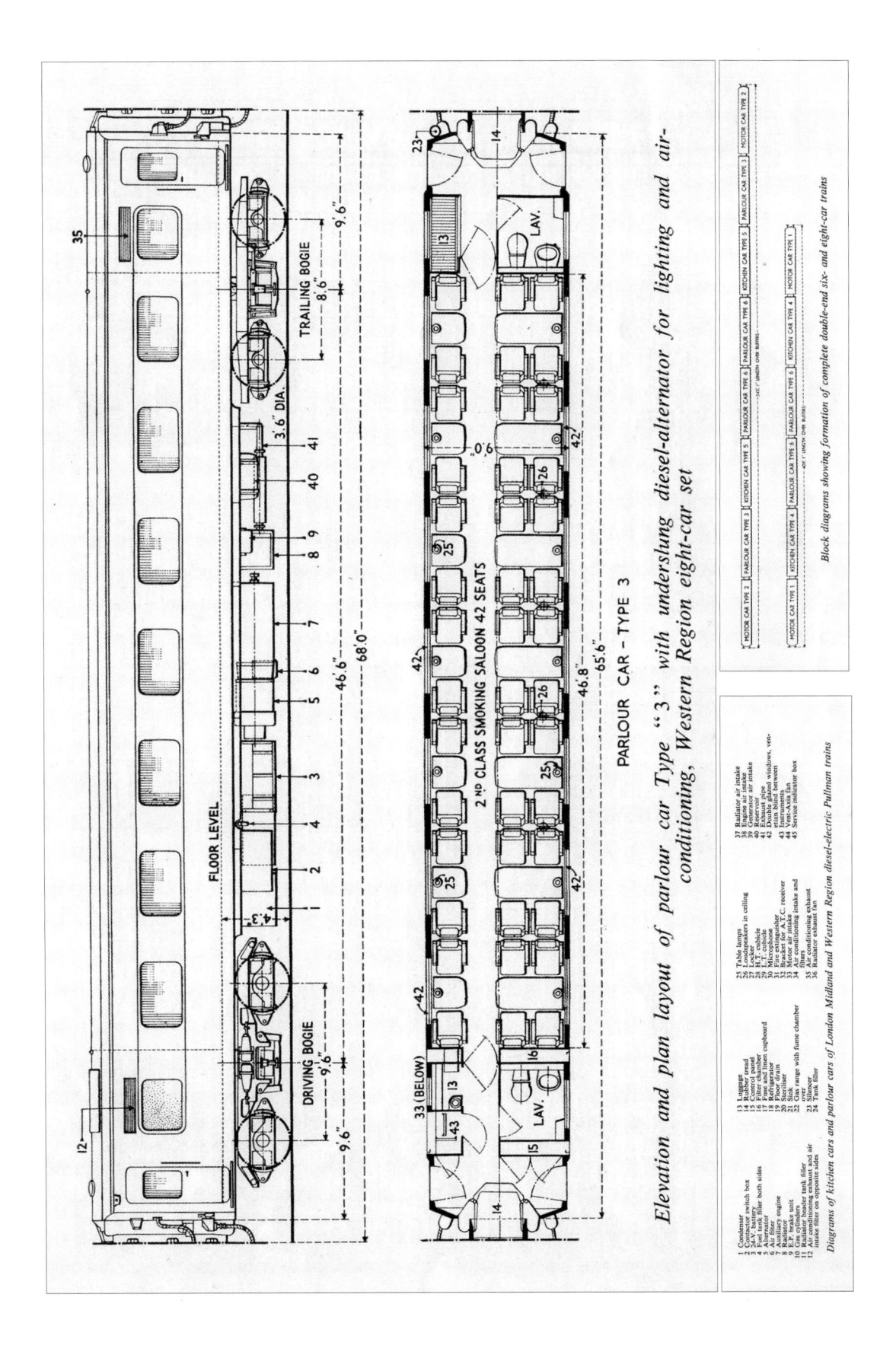

Elevation and plan layout of parlour car Type "3" with underslung diesel-alternator for lighting and air-conditioning, Western Region eight-car set

PARLOUR CAR – TYPE 3

Diagrams of kitchen cars and parlour cars of London Midland and Western Region diesel-electric Pullman trains

1 Condenser
2 Contactor switch box
3 24-V. battery
4 Fuel tank filler both sides
5 Alternator
6 Air filter
7 Auxiliary engine
8 Radiator
9 I.P. brake unit
10 Gas cylinders
11 Radiator header tank filter
12 Air conditioning exhaust and air intake filter on opposite sides

13 Luggage
14 Rubber guard
15 Control panel
16 Filter chamber
17 Fuse and linen cupboard
18 Refrigerator
19 Floor drain
20 Steriliser
21 Sink
22 Gas range with fume chamber over
23 Silencer
24 Tank filler

25 Table lamps
26 Loudspeakers in ceiling
27 Locker
28 H.T. cubicle
29 L.T. cubicle
30 Microphone
31 Fire extinguisher
32 Bracket for A.T.C. receiver
33 Motor air intake
34 Air conditioning intake and filters
35 Air conditioning exhaust
36 Radiator exhaust fan

37 Radiator air intake
38 Engine air intake
39 Generator air intake
40 Reservoir
41 Exhaust pipe
42 Double glazed windows, venetian blind between
43 Instruments
44 Vent-Axia fan
45 Service indicator box

Block diagrams showing formation of complete double-end six-and eight-car trains

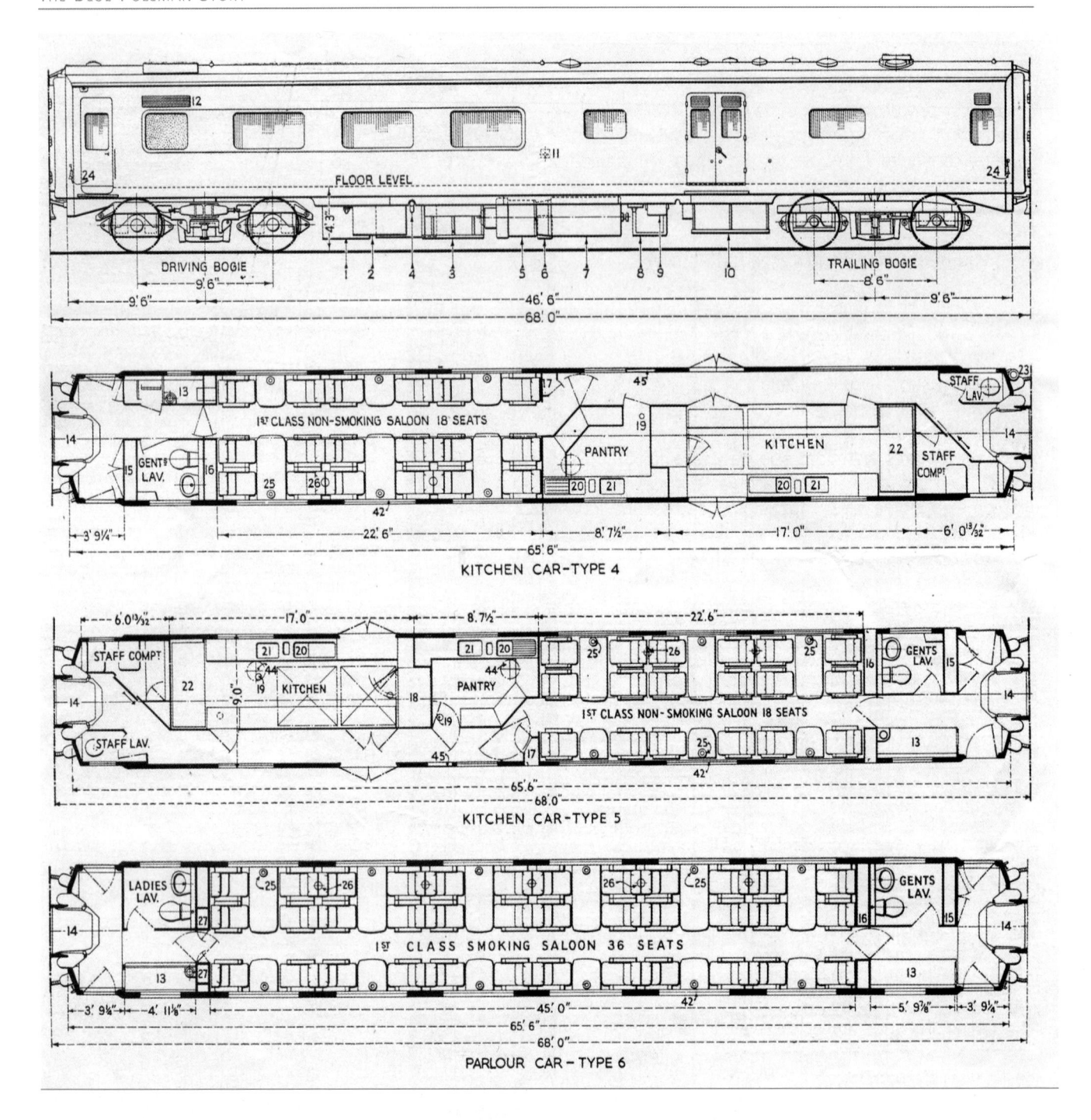

Drawings courtesy Railway Gazette 24 June, 1 July, and 8 July 1960.

more 'traditional' ebony or rosewood for the partition and instead a grey plastic was substituted. It might even be said that the second class was therefore the more modern of the designs although this point is not picked up specifically in contemporary reports.

Wide windows, similar to that on the Cravens prototype coach of 1957[2], were a feature of the design of all the cars – with seats that were in alignment with the position of the windows! The windows were also double-glazed with adjustable passenger-operated Venetian blinds.[3]

Notwithstanding the perceived negative publicity generated from the August 1960 issue of *Design*, others who had been involved in what was seen as 'an icon of the age' (author's words) were keen to capitalise on their involvement. This included Messrs Stones (the sub-contractor responsible for the air-conditioning, as well as some other components) who produced their own booklet featuring the train in order to promote their own involvement. (Subsequently and until the mid 1960s, Stones had a virtual monopoly in the supply of air-conditioning equipment to BR, and according to Michael Harris in his book *British Rail Mark 2 Coaches,* it was a monopoly BR was keen to break.) Perhaps the greatest benefit of the new train, certainly for the benefit of passengers and regardless of their class of travel, was indeed the air conditioning, which was now fitted for the first time to a production train in the UK. In this respect, the new units scored far better than anything that had gone before, but to be strictly accurate, this equipment was what would now be more accurately described as climate-control, rather than air-conditioning. As befitted the prestige train of BR, the attention to detail continued with much of this down to the hand of Jack Howe which including the lighting (excepting the table-lamps of course), carriage litter bins, magazine trays, instruction leaflets for the adjustable seating, antimacassars, the silver plate and glassware with modernized Pullman insignia, plus the signage and notices, all in a modern yet specific Pullman style. In addition there was the actual colour scheme and the use of a mosaic part-tiled wall in the toilet. Howe should therefore be given justifiable credit for the train – in addition to the implied criticism already levelled. Perhaps he just objected to his mosaic idea being included on the toilet floor in addition to the walls!

Some features we might also now take for granted in our 21st century trains similarly showed themselves for the first time: a single spray nozzle in the wash basin and loudspeaker communication throughout the train. For some decades now the generic term used for this type of communication has been a 'public address' system or 'P.A' but at the time the word used was based simply on the manufacturer, namely a 'Loudaphone', the speakers for which were concealed above the luggage racks, and reported as being on one side of each car only.

'Loudaphone' communication was also possible between the guard (and/or Pullman conductor) and the driver on a separate circuit. Even then instructions were given to staff to keep public announcements to a minimum, and if possible, to restrict them to advance advice about arrival points.[4]

Despite the new 'modern' image, traditional Pullman standards of service were maintained, with a push-button to summon an attendant which in turn displayed a green light on the coach side above the relevant two/four seat(s). When the attendant arrived he would extinguish the light by pressing a small button underneath the table on the supporting table leg adjacent to the central gangway.

Later that month, the first of the WR trains was involved in a distance test from the makers in Birmingham working as far as Mangotsfield, several runs being made to this destination via Barnt Green and Gloucester and returning by the same route. The second WR train was delivered, we believe to Swindon, at the end of March, but it was also noted that various modifications were still being carried out. There is even a suggestion that the WR intended to usurp the LMR by being the first region to introduce the new trains into revenue-earning service, although a Paddington memorandum refers to the intended 1hr 50min Paddington to Birmingham timing as having to be postponed indefinitely in April 1960 due to some signalling work not being completed. Exactly what this work was is unfortunately not recorded. In the meantime, the matters of staffing, staff training, infrastructure and maintenance also had to be dealt with, none of which attracted much attention in official documents at the time.

RIGHT Pre-assembled car end for attachment. *Richard Moore*

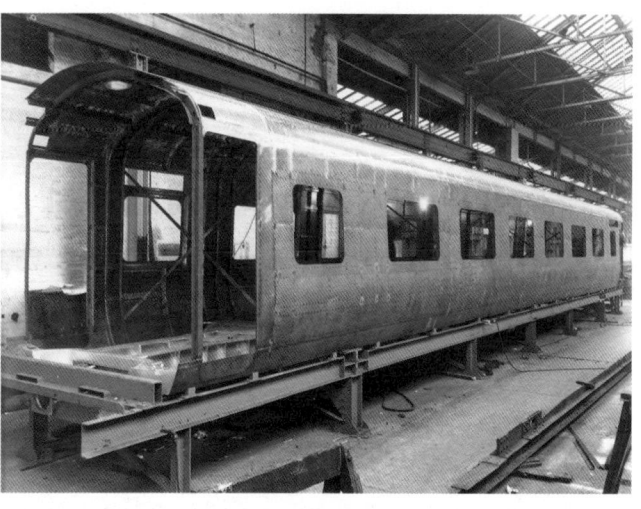

Shell of a first-class parlour car. Under each floor was half-inch limpet asbestos insulation board. *Richard Moore*

Shell of a second-class parlour car. *Richard Moore*

The Blue Pullman Story

Skeletal roof assembly. In a later 1960 newspaper advert there was a feature on steel production which included a mention that the new Blue Pullman trains were made using British steel products. Elsewhere in another publication a correspondent had adversely commented on the use of such heavy grade material whereas lighter metal would have saved weight. There was no accompanying comment about how this would have affected the potential to save fuel as environmental concerns were not the top of the agenda in 1960. *Richard Moore*

Roof panels being fitted. Although we cannot be certain this was likely a parlour car as there are corresponding openings at either end for what may have been toilet water tanks. There was considerable use of welding in the construction. *Richard Moore*

A roof being lowered on to the shell of a Parlour First. *Richard Moore*

'Parlour Car Type 3' under construction for a Western Region train. Six of these were built, the numbers allocated together with their weight and capacity may be seen at the start of this work in the section 'Description of Blue Pullman cars'. *Richard Moore*

Kitchen car bodyshell under construction. Richard Moore

A mechanical description of what was officially referred to as the 'British Railways Diesel-Electric Pullman Trains' rather than the 'Blue Pullman' was given in an extensive article in The Railway Gazette for 24 June 1960. Much of what follows is taken (with due acknowledgement) from that source, and is supplemented by additional items as indicated. Other descriptions, limited in some detail, appeared elsewhere, but the one from The Railway Gazette ranks highly amongst the engineering fraternity and because it is contemporary, was no doubt sourced from the manufacturers themselves. It has been included almost in full (excepting where it duplicates what has already been mentioned in the preceding text) – otherwise comments and deviations from the original text are included in italics within brackets. From the way certain aspects are described, it would also appear to relate more to the LMR sets. There is also a reference to the ladies toilet within the description, as has been mentioned previously.

'Following an extensive period of service trials, British Railways will shortly introduce the first of a batch of de-luxe diesel-electric Pullman trains designed for high-speed travel, with superior standards of comfort and a personal service of meals and refreshments for all travellers. These trains, which have been supplied to British Railways by the Metropolitan-Cammell Carriage & Wagon Co Ltd, are powered by two 1,000bhp NBL/MAN diesel engines, each direct-coupled to a GEC main generator. The complete order is for five trains, two of which are six-car trains for first-class passengers only, and three are of eight cars with first and second class accommodation. The six-car train will run in the London Midland Region, on the main line between Manchester Central, London St Pancras and Leicester, and the eight-car trains in the Western Region between Bristol, London Paddington, and Wolverhampton, Birmingham and Paddington. Passenger accommodation is in enclosed saloons, and all seats on the de-luxe trains are reserved.

'Under-floor-mounted diesel-driven generating sets supply power for lighting and auxiliary services.

'The livery is Nanking Blue *[this was the official name for the colour, although it also had the alternative name, Cambridge Blue,]* relieved by a broad white band extending the length and width of the windowed section along the sides of each car. The rounded nose of each motorcar features the Pullman Car Co Ltd crest, and this is also carried on the white-painted band between the last pair of windows on each vehicle. *[The crest, or more accurately, coat of arms, was applied by transfer. Its presence was suggested by Arthur Wolstenholme and was to a design that was an elongation of the conventional Pullman crest. The revised design was the work of Milner Gray of the independent Design Research Unit – although elsewhere the paperwork refers to Christopher Ironside as being credited! The same modified crest was also used later on the 1960s Pullman vehicles for the Eastern Region.]*

Painting (spray was used) and fitting out of a kitchen car (another BP vehicle is receiving the same treatment in what is clearly a special facility within the Saltley Works). Richard Moore

The Blue Pullman Story

Interior of a first-class parlour car in the process of being fitted out. From the emergence of the wiring it appears the decision has been made over the provision of table lamps at this time. The reader will recall the compliments paid in relation to the quietness of the ride achieved in part by asbestos insulation, a period in history when the perils of this product were not known of. Tragically the dangers would only become apparent years later as per the following journalist's report together with that of a former worker writing in the Birmingham Mail: '… years after its closure, increasing numbers of mesothelioma cases connected to the company have emerged and Birmingham's deputy coroner Christopher Ball last year described Metro-Cammell as one of the city's "asbestos hot spots". The ordinary man didn't know the dangers of asbestos in the 1950s, but solicitors and doctors now claim firms were warned about asbestos before then.' One former worked, identified as 'Barry', adds solemnly. 'We would be eating and breathing in asbestos all day. There were monstrously big sacks of asbestos lying around and it would be shovelled into a machine like a cement mixer before being sprayed on the inside of the carriage like paint. Once it had dried, the apprentices, like me, would chisel bits off to put on the fittings. We even sat on top of sacks of the stuff to have our lunch. We had no face masks; we were only given a white apron and if it wasn't spotless when you turned up in the morning, you were sent home. When my mother was ill, doctors asked me if she'd ever had anything to do with asbestos, which she hadn't, but she would take my filthy apron covered in dust every night and wash it for me. Who knows what harm that caused. It's too late to feel bitter now.' *Richard Moore*

Driver's cab in the course of fitting out. Standing on an adjacent road is another power car – the reason for the apparent 'shuttering' appearing on the cab side door which is in reality the ventilation grills on the side of the adjacent unit. *Richard Moore*

The roofs are painted light grey, the underframes aluminium, and the bogies black.

'Principal dimensions and data are as follows:
    Maximum service speed – 90mph
    Weight of train – six-car 299 tons
    Weight of train – eight-car 364 tons
    Fuel capacity – 1,000 gallons

[Fuel was carried in four tanks of equal capacity, and was considered sufficient for 900 miles in normal service. Interestingly, the LMR quoted that the fuel capacity would be sufficient to cover 1,000 miles, so presumably the difference was due to the variation in weight and consequently range between a 6-car and an 8-car train. The auxiliary engines had their own, separate fuel tanks. Having a 1,000 gallon fuel capacity was the same for the later HST sets as built.]

Length of vehicles over body:
    Motor Car – 66ft 5½in
    Trailer Car – 65ft 6in
    Overall height – 12ft 4½in
    Overall width – 9ft 6in
    Bogie centres – 46ft
    Bogie wheelbase – 9ft 6in

Bogie frame from a trailing bogie seen here turned through 180° for component fitting. The metal here is of 'I' frame type compared with the power bogies and the wheelbase was also shorter at 8 feet 6 inches. As is referred to briefly later in the text of Chapter 6, preliminary riding tests (National Archives AN143/14 and AN 143/23) with a Schlieren bogie were carried out between Derby and Leicester in July 1958. The vehicles used were all of the Mk1 type with comparisons made to several other different types of bogie under different vehicles – but we are not told which. All were Mk1 corridor seconds. Several different types of bogie were then under trial under various coaches at the time, the intention being to find a replacement for the Mk1 which was only subsequently achieved with the Commonwealth type. The Schlieren trials did show that on the same stretch of line in June 1959 on carriages M25281/2, changes were required to the dampers associated with the secondary suspension after some 39,600 miles. Small wonder then that just a few short months later BP riding on the same basic design bogie (accepted to a design modified by MC) with the same type of suspension should suffer similar difficulties. *Richard Moore*

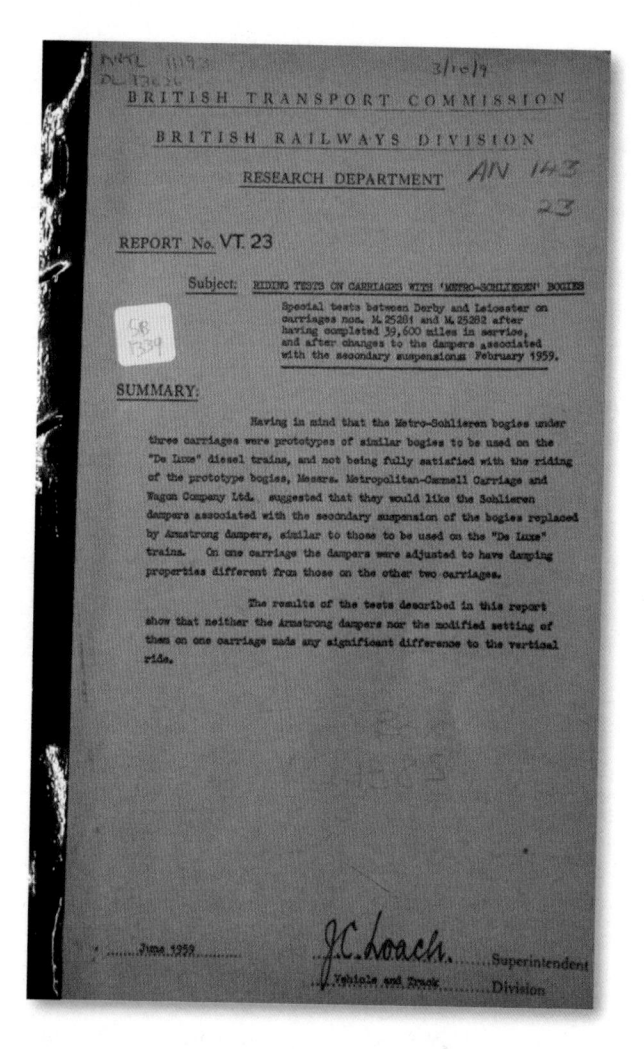

BELOW A completed power bogie with the cables to the traction motor visible. The train could negotiate curves down to a minimum 3.5 chain radius (a quite astonishing 77 yards/231 feet.) The wheel diameter when new was 3 feet 6 inches and with a minimum wear level of 3 feet 3½ inches. As can be seen there were helical springs and hydraulic dampers. *Richard Moore*

'The six-car trains are made up of two power cars, two combined kitchen and passenger cars, and two parlour cars. In the power car, the cooling group, with side radiators and roof-mounted fan, is immediately behind the driving cab bulkhead. A bulkhead across the generator, with doors at each side, divides the engine and generator compartments. Separate cubicles are used for housing the HT and LT equipment. *[Access to the engine for maintenance was by various roller shutters, one larger than the others, on each side of the power car.]* Adjoining the generator compartment is the Guard and luggage compartment, the partitions of which are sound insulated. This compartment has access doors to the passenger saloon and to the power compartment. *[A periscope[6] was provided for the Guard, and double doors of standard BR design gave access to the van and the limited luggage area.]* The saloon accommodates 12 passengers *[18 in the WR power cars, the latter also all second class]*; at the gangway end is a ladies' toilet on one side and a small luggage compartment on the other. *[In the Midland sets, the passenger compartment within the power car was 15ft long. In the WR trains it was 20ft long. The window spacing on the Midland power cars also made them immediately distinguishable from their sister units when later all were operating out of Paddington; the former having two large and one small window on each side. By comparison the WR trains had three windows of equal size and spacing.]*

'The passenger accommodation in the kitchen car is an 18-seat non-smoking saloon. *[Here the reader is referred to the accompanying plans in this chapter.]* At the gangway end is a toilet, and luggage and equipment cupboards. Adjacent to the saloon is the pantry, and at the gangway end of the kitchen is the staff accommodation. In the parlour car, 36 seats are provided, with a toilet and a luggage compartment at each end. In the six-car train, the total seating is 132 first-class. The eight-car train has additional seating in the power cars and two additional parlour cars for second-class passengers. The total seating

ABOVE M.A.N. (originally Maschinenfabrik Augsburg-Nürnberg AG) 1,000hp diesel engine type L12V18/12S working at 1,445rpm. This was a 12-cylinder engine firing in the order: 1, 11, 2, 9, 4, 7, 6, 8, 5, 10, 3, 12. The engines were built in Germany rather than at NBL which appears slightly strange when BR had been loath to import power plants for the WR hydraulic types. To be fair, the MAN engines did give less trouble but then a technician was invariably on hand. Certainly the power units gave less trouble than when identical engines were installed in the WR loco fleet. Possibly this was because they were only pressed to 1,000 and not 1,100hp, hence the peak cylinder pressures and temperatures would be less. A Serck-type radiator was fitted between the free end of the engine and the cab bulkhead. *Richard Moore*

BELOW G.E.C. main generator attached to the end of the main engine output shaft. Note too the bank of resistors in the roof; small wonder the whole of this area was recorded as being so warm. Combined with the traction motors the continuous tractive effort was rated at 12,000lbs. *Richard Moore*

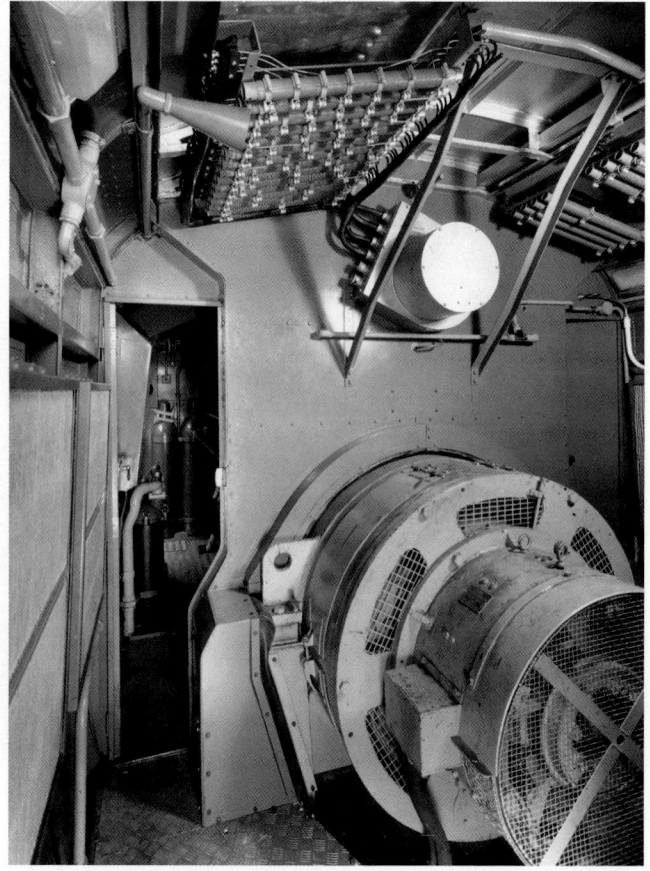

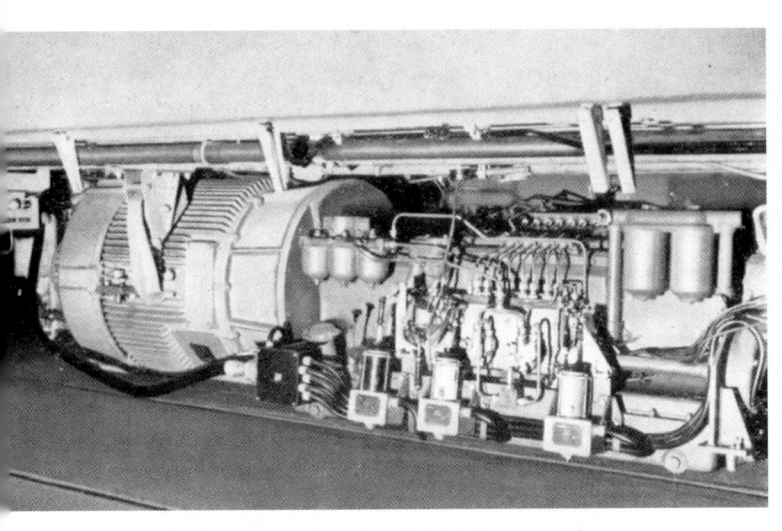

Auxiliary engine fitted under kitchen car. There were, therefore, two per train set although except in extreme cold conditions only one would be used. A separate fuel tank was provided and in this engine the firing order for the eight cylinders was: 1, 6, 2, 5, 8, 3, 6, 4. Each auxiliary engine could generate 190hp and consequently with no demand upon the main engines for auxiliary services a more accurate statement of power output for the train would really be 2,190hp or even 2,380hp. A red light illuminated on the outside solebar if the auxiliary engine overheated the purpose of which was to attract the attention of a signalman who would then send '7-beats' 'Stop and Examine' to the signal box in advance. (See Appendix 3 para 8.). The concept of auxiliary engines, but in this case Deutz 172hp units again for train requirements, was again used between 1971 and 1980 during the time Class 27/2 locos were operating the Edinburgh Waverley–Glasgow Queen Street 'top and tail' workings. *Richard Moore*

Parlour car Type 6 showing the air-conditioning control cabinet. *Richard Moore*

capacity is 228, 108 of which are first class and 120 second class. The entrance vestibules at the ends of the cars are wide and spacious, and the access gangways between the cars are also wider than normal width. The gangways are mounted on pivots at the ends of each vehicle. When joined together, these semi-floating units between pairs of cars form a level platform free from the normal gangway oscillation. Rubber seals cover the outside of the gangways and prevent draughts and loss of air-conditioned air. *[The gangways were of the Swiss-type, 'Metro SIG', and were similar to those on the Swiss Federal Railways light-weight stock. A non-slip rubber floor plate was also provided.]* The complete train is fully air-conditioned with automatic control of air temperature and humidity. The inward flow of air to the saloons from the air-conditioning plant is through outlets in a duct concealed by the central lighting panel. Fully adjustable Venetian blinds are fitted between the glasses of the double-glazed windows. Particular care has been taken to achieve a high standard of sound insulation, and track noise has been reduced to a low level. The insulated floors are fully suspended. *[An explanation of what exactly is meant by the term 'suspended' is not given.]* In each car, the seating is arranged in facing pairs on one side of the passenger gangway, and in facing individual seats on the other, with double or single fixed tables respectively set between them. All seating is of the armchair type, with deep foam-rubber cushions upholstered in red- or blue-striped fabric trimmed with black and grey plastic hide. *[According to George Behrend writing in his book* Pullman in Europe *in 1962, 'The first class saloons are finished off in [one of] two colour schemes. In one, the seats are furnished in red upholstery with navy blue stripes, with a blue and black carpet and rosewood partitions at the ends. In the other, light blue with navy blue stripes is used for the upholstery, and the carpet is red and black, while the partitions are ebony.' Behrend also confirms the colour of the upholstery in the Western Region second class cars as, 'blue with black stripes and the carpet red and black'. A second opinion from Charles Long, confirms that first class on both the LMR and WR sets were either red ribbed or blue ribbed, each half-set being of a different combination; a similar arrangement applied to the LMR power cars. Therefore, depending on whether or not identically upholstered half-sets were connected together, the first-class upholstery could either be half one colour and half the other or identical throughout. On the WR, second class upholstery was always blue, but in a different shade to that used in first class. – refer to Appendix 7.)* The first-class seats can be adjusted from the reclining to the upright position, and are mounted on runners for fore and aft adjustment at the table. In the second class saloon, the seats are of the same armchair type, but are not adjustable.

The Blue Pullman Story

ABOVE 'Interior of second class saloon' (parlour car), identified by the single Venetian blind and fixed – non adjustable – seating. All the cars featured warm white fluorescent lighting concealed by opaque diffusing panels. *Richard Moore*

ABOVE Interior end of a second class parlour car (Western Region). Even when viewed as here in black and white, the appearance is very much in vogue with the styling of the 1960s. Notice the position (top) of the handle for adjusting the blind. *Richard Moore*

ABOVE Interior of first class parlour car: adjustable seats, individual blinds, and wooden end panelling. Because an adjustable seat was something of a novelty, draft instructions were prepared for both passenger and staff use as early as May 1959. 'How to adjust your chair. Your new Pullman chair is adjustable in two ways: Backwards and Forwards to ensure comfortable positions for dining and reclining. This is operated with the lever on the left-hand side of the chair. When it is raised your chair will slide, with slight pressure, forwards or backwards and it is then locked automatically. The angle of the back of your chair is also adjustable in two positions, upright, or reclining. These adjustments are operated simply by lifting the finger grip in the front left-hand armrest. You will find that the best position for dining is with the chair forwards and the back upright.' (Nowadays we might consider such basic instructions facile in view of similar arrangements in the automobile, aviation and rail industries that have been around for decades. But remember, back in 1960 this was likely to have been the first adjustable chair some passengers would have encountered.) *Richard Moore*

ABOVE Looking into a first class parlour car from the gangway between vehicles. Apart from a slight height difference on the actual gangway – with slopes either side – it compares favourably with the more usual moving plates and canvas/rubber bellows on coaching stock up to this time. *Richard Moore*

ABOVE Gangway detail this time seen viewed into a kitchen car with the sliding door leading into the staff compartment. *Richard Moore*

ABOVE End luggage compartment of first class parlour car. Smaller items could of course be accommodated on the racking which ran the length of the passenger accommodation above the seats. *Richard Moore*

ABOVE Vestibule end, probably of the same vehicle seen in the previous view. As per standard Pullman practice, passenger doors open inwards with a 'conventional' door handle. It would usually be the Steward's place to open and close these at stations. (When a palm might also be surreptitiously presented…) Notice too the locking handle on the inside which corresponded with the square key lock on the exterior. It is believed self-adhesive information/instructional notices were added before the trains entered service. *Richard Moore*

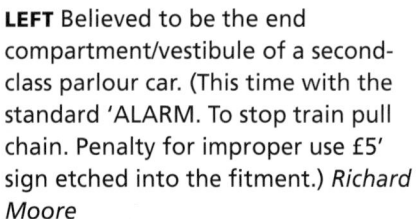

LEFT Believed to be the end compartment/vestibule of a second-class parlour car. (This time with the standard 'ALARM. To stop train pull chain. Penalty for improper use £5' sign etched into the fitment.) *Richard Moore*

BELOW LEFT Passenger toilet. The sign above the rotating knob reads, 'Adjust knob as required. Flow stops after use. Not drinking water'. Four positions are indicated, 'Stop', 'Cold', 'Warm', 'Hot'. The toilets were fed from a 60-gallon water tank, waste discharging on to the track as was then the normal practice. The mosaic tiling curving upwards will be noted. This curvature and continuation of the tiling upwards was another feature objected to by Jack Howe. An electric shaver socket was also fitted. Unrelated to the BP story but worthy of mention is that in October 1962, *Modern Railways* reported one of Mr George Williams team had recently undertook a long journey in a carriage toilet with the sole purpose of observing the behaviour of water in a wash-basin of then new design! *Richard Moore*

ABOVE A staff rest room (previously referred to) and a staff toilet were provided at the end of each kitchen car – its limited size meaning there was perhaps a degree of similarity with the 'heads' on certain naval vessels. In reality, it was simply that space was restricted. *Richard Moore*

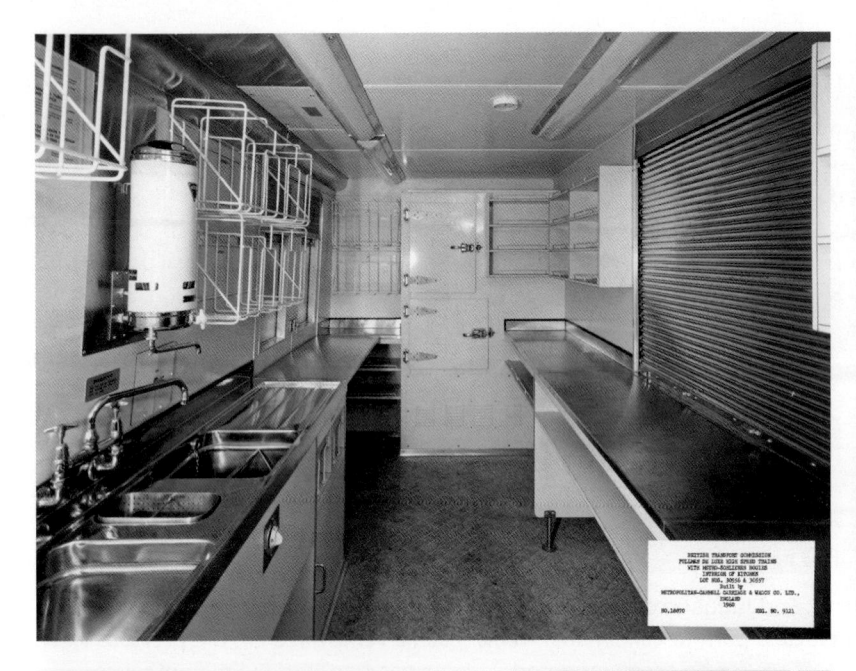

Kitchen area, sink, worktops, range, fridges, and cupboards/racking. The kitchen featured easy to clean plastic surfaces and all utensils and working surfaces were of stainless steel. Other features include a deep freeze plus a constant boiling water supply through the 'Ascot'-type water heater. In each kitchen up to 112 diners' meals might be prepared per trip. The kitchen ranges were propane fired with eight propane cylinders fed from four pairs of twin cylinders located on the underframe. We know gas was easily the most preferred method of cooking by railway staff but it is strange to relate how gas lighting had been considered such a risk in the event of an accident not all that many years before and yet now multiple gas cylinders were again being carried and this time at far faster speeds. There was also a coffee machine in each kitchen as well as a 174-gallon water supply for cooking etc. *Richard Moore*

'The interior decor, which varies from vehicle to vehicle, has been chosen to give pleasing and colourful combinations, mainly of decorative rosewood and ebony veneers, grey plastic hide, plastic seating and contrasting seat upholstery. The partitions forming the ends of each passenger saloon are decorated with wood veneers and abstract plastic inlays. Each partition has glazed panels in the access door, the glass having a vertical striped pattern, ⅜in apart, which acts as a mirror, but allows unimpeded vision at close quarters. *[Later comment by passengers indicated these mirrors were favourably received.]* The bodyside walls are faced with plastic hide from floor level up to the continuous hand-luggage racks running along the length of each passenger saloon. Above the racks, walls and ceiling surfaces are lined with plastic in pearl-grey, with a fine black-line pattern super-imposed, which continues up to the central lighting panel in the ceiling. The exposed parts of the hand-luggage racks, the table edges, and window surrounds are all of anodised aluminium, satin finished in aluminium for the first class, and in pale gold for the second class. The heater grilles, mounted low on the bodyside alongside the seats, are of satin-finished stainless steel. Floor carpets, in Kingfisher blue or Cardinal red, *[again depending upon the corresponding upholstery seat colour]* are fitted on plastic underlay. The walls of the entrance vestibules at the car ends are faced in pearl-grey plastic, with plastic hide trimming around the inter-car gangway entrances. Coir mat floor covering is used in the vestibules. In each saloon, the main lighting is by twin warm-white fluorescent tubes in the centre of the ceiling, supplemented by tungsten lamps fitted in the luggage racks above each table. The fluorescent tubes are placed end-to-end, and covered by flush-jointed diffusion panels. When illuminated, the tubes show as a continuous panel of light running the length of the saloon. Individual table lamps, with glass shades, are mounted on swan-necked pillars fixed to the bodyside just below window level. *[Considerable care had to be given in the placing of these auxiliary lamps, the politics behind which were discussed in a previous chapter. The fact that it would be necessary to change the tablecloths on a regular basis was undoubtedly the reason why the lamps were not stood/ attached directly to the tables. Note the early Tri-ang model of the train had the lamps directly on the tables.]* Battery operated emergency lighting is also installed.

'The kitchen and pantry accommodation is well arranged for ease of working under the most hygienic conditions. The gas cooking range is fitted across one end, and the refrigerator adjacent to the pantry partition. *[In view of the available electric power provided by the auxiliary power supplies it is perhaps a little surprising that electric ovens were not installed although this may well have been a concession to railway chefs who were known to favour gas.]* Two of the four extractor fans are located above the cooker. Worktops are arranged on the corridor side, with the sinks, sterilizing units, and water boilers along the bodyside. All kitchen utensils, sink units, and working tops are in stainless steel. The walls are lined with pearl-grey plastic finish, and the ceilings matt white. The floors are of red composition material set in a two-inch square mesh aluminium grill. A staff compartment and lavatory are provided adjacent to the gangway entrance to the car. *[A single 200-gallon water tank supplied water for each kitchen car, which tank also supplied the staff toilet.]* The equipment of the well-appointed *[passenger]* toilets includes (paper) towel dispensers and hygienic spray washing facilities, which give an automatically timed flow of water. Water temperature of the timed flow can be regulated as required. The walls are plastic faced in flame, clover pink, and grey *[although elsewhere there is mention of mosaic on the walls]*, and the ceilings painted matt white. Coloured mosaic paving is used for the floor. Metal fittings are finished in satin chromium plate, with the exception of the skirting beadings of satin-finished anodised aluminium and the satin-finished stainless steel heater and ventilation grills. Separate toilet accommodation is provided for ladies. *[The water tank capacity for each lavatory was 70 gallons. A minor criticism of the toilet facilities was that the automatic washing facility cut the water off too quickly. However, praise was given for the florescent lighting built into the mirrors.]*

'Power for the main auxiliary generators is supplied by the NBL/MAN, 12-cylinder, supercharged, diesel engine type L12V18/21BS having a 12-hr rating of 1,000bhp at 1,500rpm. Cylinder dimensions are 180mm bore and 210mm stroke. A considerable number of engines of this type are in use for diesel-electric and diesel-hydraulic traction. *[The D8xx, D61xx and D63xx diesel locomotives all used the same type of engine, but at power outputs varying between 1,000 and 1,100bhp. The Pullman engines were built as a V12 design.]* Individual cylinder heads are of the pre-combustion type, provided with two inlet and two exhaust-valves. Supercharging is by a Napier, exhaust-gas, turbo blower mounted above the generator drive. At the free end of the engine is the crankshaft-driven pump for the hydraulic motor fan drive. CAV fuel injection equipment and an Ardleigh governor are fitted. Lubrication priming before starting is by a Mirlees pump driven by a GEC motor. A belt-driven Dowty pump feeds the fuel-service tank. Warning lamps are fitted to indicate low water level, high water temperature, low oil pressure, overload, and earth fault, and the engine idling speed is automatically reduced to idling in the event of high water temperature, overload, or earth fault. In each driving cab is fitted a general warning light and a light to indicate when an engine has stopped. The combined engine/generator unit is mounted on a common fabricated steel bedplate and installed on Metalastik anti-vibration mountings. The use of a quick-running Vee engine results in a good power-weight ratio. The Serck cooling group, comprising vertical radiator panels in the bodyside and roof-mounted extractor fan *[not to be confused with the fan later provided to limit the engine compartment temperature]* is positioned behind the cab bulkhead in the power car. The cooling fan, which is 45in diameter, is driven at the correct speed to suit the cooling required by the Serck-Behr hydrostatic fan drive. The hydraulic fan motor is supplied with oil under pressure by the engine-driven pump and via a thermostatically controlled by-pass valve. Until the engine coolant reaches the minimum operating temperature, the pump delivery is by-passed to the oil tank: during this time the fan remains stationary. At normal operating temperatures the by-pass is closed and the resulting oil pressure rise causes the radiator shutters to open, and the fan to be driven at a speed corresponding to the amount of cooling required. Access from the cab to the power compartment is through the radiator tunnel. The main generator is a self-ventilated, single-bearing machine with windings for separately excited, and self-excited main fields and a series decompounding winding. This also forms part of the series excitation for motorising the generator for engine starting. The continuous ratings at 1,500rpm are 1,700A 383V or 1,250A 523V, 650kW. The armature shaft also carries the armature of the auxiliary generator mounted at the rear end. The ventilating fan at the drive end draws

Top view of body gangway. This was identical between all of the cars and both types of train. *Richard Moore*

cooling air through both machines. The auxiliary generator is rated at 91A 110V, 10kW, the voltage being held within close limits throughout the engine speed range by a Newton automatic voltage regulator. This generator supplies excitation for the main generator and current for starter-battery charging, control circuits, and other auxiliaries. *[See pages 40 and 112 for details of the motors/generators used for on-board auxiliary needs.]*

'The main generator output is controlled by an automatic load regulator, which in turn is controlled by the engine speed governor. This method of control ensures that the full engine output available at each notch setting made by the driver is maintained over a wide range of train speeds. The power output of the generators at each end of the train is accurately synchronized. Protection against wheel-slip is provided by a current limiting relay.[7] The air-conditioning equipment is designed to provide and maintain an automatically controlled clean comfortable atmosphere within established limits of temperature and humidity irrespective of outside ambient conditions. This requires provision for heating, cooling, air filtration, car insulation and a degree of manual temperature selection for service requirements. In addition to the attraction of a high standard of passenger comfort, the air conditioning also keeps clean and fresh the upholstery, fittings, and other equipment. *[There was the belief at the time that fitting air conditioning would eliminate the need to segregate smokers and non-smokers.]* Each car is equipped with a roof-mounted air conditioning unit, floor heaters, automatic control panel, and a refrigeration unit. The conditioning unit filters the air, removes excess moisture, and either cools or heats the air as required. A proportion of the air in the car is extracted by roof ventilators, and this is made up by admitting filtered fresh air into the system. Heating is by electric heaters, and cooling is by flowing the air over the evaporator coils of the refrigerator. Excess moisture is deposited as dew on the cold coils of the evaporator. The motor-driven compressor and condenser are mounted on the underframe, and use Freon 12 or Arcton 12 as a refrigerant. *[Both are CFC (Chlorofluorocarbons) compounds and would not be permitted nowadays. In 1960, the risk such products presented to ozone depletion of the upper atmosphere was not known.]* The condenser is cooled by motor-driven fans. The manual temperature control switch enables the heaters to be switched on at car temperatures of 68°F, 71°F or 74°F, automatic control being by Vapor thermostats.

'To ease the load on the power supply if the air-conditioning compressors throughout the train were switched on simultaneously, a delay switch is fitted to give a sequenced switching throughout the train. Current for lighting, air conditioning, refrigeration, battery charging and auxiliary equipment is supplied by two underfloor generator sets, each set comprising an eight-cylinder, Rolls-Royce, horizontal diesel engine direct-coupled to a Stones Tonum alternator. The output of one set is sufficient for normal summer and winter requirements; the second set is carried for use as a stand-by, and for use under extreme conditions. The engine is rated at 190bhp at 1,500rpm, and the three-phase 50-cycle alternator at 133kVA, 400V. In the six-car train, the generating sets are mounted underneath each of the kitchen cars and in the eight-car trains they are underneath the second class parlour cars. Provision is made for the operation of the lighting, refrigeration, and air-conditioning equipment from an external three-phase AC supply when the train is stationary.

'Static power supply points are being provided at terminal stations on the routes to be served by these trains. *[At first sight, the LMR and WR sets appeared similar externally, other than the fact that the number of cars differed. However, as has been mentioned, there were several differences, such as the window spacing in the power cars, seating, upholstery, and the location of the auxiliary generating equipment. Additionally, due to differences in the formation, the second driving bogie was located under the kitchen first on the LMR trains and under the parlour second on the WR. The requirement to accommodate second class passengers on the WR sets also meant that the space dedicated per passenger was reduced and so the window spacing was altered on the second class parlour cars to seven a side, compared with six for first class. This, at least, afforded each passenger a clear outward view, which was in direct contrast to the standard body-shell used on later BR coaches where some passengers were faced with a blank wall.]* The 400V AC, three-phase, 50-cycle power for lighting and air-conditioning is distributed by two four-wire feeders running the length of the train. Connections between the cars are made through Stone Kleops inter-car couplings, and the circuits so arranged that if a coupling is broken the feeder is immediately disconnected from the power-supply. The bulk of the lighting is supplied at 230V AC by phase-to-neutral connection of the 400V feeders, and the remainder is supplied at 110V AC from a 230/110V lighting transformer. The compressor, condenser-fan motor, and the floor and air heaters are connected to the three-phase, 400V supply. The air-conditioning fan motor and the control circuits are supplied at 24V DC from a three-phase transformer/rectifier unit. This supply is also used to charge a 24V, 216amp-hour battery for auxiliary engine starting and emergency lighting. The bogies are of the Metro-Schlieren type [*this design, with modifications, was used for both the powered and non-powered bogies*], incorporating hydraulically-damped helical springs. At each end of the train formation there are two traction motors in the inner bogie of the power car and two in the adjacent bogie of the vehicle coupled next to it, making eight axles motorised in a train of either six or eight coaches. The unsprung weight on the axle is reduced to a minimum by carrying the motor on a three-point mounting on the bogie frame. To accommodate the relative vertical movement of the axle and motor, the motor drive is taken through a Brown-Boveri spring drive unit. On the motor shaft is mounted a single helical reduction gear, meshing with the axle-drive gear which is mounted on a quill shaft carried on roller bearings. In the face of the gear is a ring of spring-loaded pads which engage with face-dogs integral with a spider pressed on the road wheel hub. Thus the gears are maintained at the correct centres while allowing free vertical movement between axle and motor. The motors are four-pole, self-ventilated machines with a continuous rating of 425A 383V 199hp at 1,360rpm and a gear ratio of 19/67. The two motors in each power bogie are in parallel. Current for the inner-vehicle power-car motors is supplied through cables attached to the adjacent power car. Special features are incorporated in the Westinghouse air-brake equipment to maintain the high efficiency at high speed. Control is by electro-pneumatic valves, and at train speeds at which normal braking is required, the degree of standard brake pressure applied to the cylinders is proportional to the position of the Driver's brake controller. In the high-speed range, the brake pressure is automatically increased to compensate for the lower co-efficient of friction of the cast-iron shoes when operating at high speed. The changeover from high-speed to normal-speed braking, and vice-versa, is entirely automatic, and is controlled by a valve energized by current from the speedometer generator. The de-luxe Pullmans are the first trains to be fitted with two stage EP braking. [*The Electro-Pneumatic brake was universally used by the Southern Region on its multiple unit electric stock and was renowned for its efficiency.*]

'Operating through switch contacts in the controller, the standard brake valve handle is also used to control the automatic brake for emergency use. The brake equipment incorporates the latest type of Westinghouse rubber-seated valves and "O"-ring packings for ease of maintenance. The brake cylinders, fitted with slack adjusters, are externally mounted on the bogie frame, and operation is through compensated clasp brake rigging. [*The leading and powered bogies were fitted with double, clasp type, brake blocks. Single brake blocks were fitted to all other wheels.*] The permanent type of coupling between the coaches, which absorbs both buffing and drawing loads, has been designed to provide a smooth pick-up on starting and stable running at high speed. [*The couplings themselves may be described more simply as being a solid buffing bar stretching the width of the carriage, and fastened to them at the sides by a conventional buffing arrangement. In the centre, the buffing bar was less thick than at the sides. The actual joining of the cars was above the buffing bar where a connection, bolted to the next vehicle, was made. The buffing gear can be seen in detail in the accompanying illustrations of the respective vehicle ends.*] Normal coupling hooks, for emergency use, are in concealed [*folding*] recesses in the nose of each of the leading motor cars of the train only [*not at the passenger end of each motor coach or at either end of the intermediate cars.*] [*As built there was variation in the number of warning horns provided, for example, M60090 had two and M60093 three. The original fitting to the other power cars cannot be confirmed although it appears that as time passed all had a third horn added.*] These de-luxe trains have been built to the requirements of the British Transport Commission under the general direction of Mr J. F. Harrison, Chief Mechanical Engineer, British Railways Central Staff, in collaboration with Messrs S. B. Warder, Chief Electrical Engineer and F. Grundy, Chief Traction Officer, and the Pullman Car Co Ltd. Mr A. E. Robson, Chief Mechanical & Electrical Engineer, London Midland Region, was responsible for inspection and for test running. Mr Jack Howe acted as consultant to the Metropolitan-Cammell Carriage & Wagon Co Ltd on passenger amenities and decor. Sub-contractors included the following:

Traction equipment: General Electric Co Ltd
NBL/MAN engines: North British Locomotive Co Ltd
Air-conditioning and lighting: J. Stone & Co (Deptford) Ltd
Auxiliary engines: Rolls-Royce Ltd
Electro-pneumatic braking: Westinghouse Brake & Signal Co Ltd
Kitchen stoves: Radiation Ltd
Sink Units: James Scott & Co (Engineers) Ltd
Kitchen floor: laid by Durastic Ltd
Toilet commodes and basins: Twyfords Ltd
Bodyside door castings: Deans & Sons (Yorkshire) Ltd
Droplights (kitchen door): Etablissements Georges Klein et Cie
Droplights (Guard's door): Beckett, Laycock & Watkinson Ltd
Carpets (first class): S. & J. Stockwell & Co (Carpets) Ltd
Carpets (second class): Tomlinsons Ltd
Seat castings: G. D. Peters & Co Ltd
Seat cover materials: Edinburgh Weavers Ltd
PVC coverings (first class): Hunt & Winterbotham Ltd
PVC coverings (second class): ICI Ltd
Interior window units: Henry Hope & Sons Ltd
Venetian blinds (Crittal Solomatic type): Crittal Manufacturing Co Ltd
Plastic panels (saloon ceilings): Bakolite Ltd

Plastic panels (toilets): Holoplast Ltd
Interior timber partitions: Edmonton Panel Co Ltd
Body-shell insulation: J. W. Roberts Ltd
Interior insulation: W. Gilmour Smith & Co Ltd
Ascot heaters: Ascot Gas & Water Heaters Ltd
Lavatory mosaic flooring: Carter & Co Ltd
Public address system: Clifford & Snell Ltd
Dunlopillo seat cushions: Dunlop Rubber Co Ltd
Springs: English Steel Springs Corporation Ltd
Axleboxes: Skefco Ball Bearing Co Ltd
Buffer springs: G. Spencer Moulton & Co Ltd
Paint: Docker Bros Ltd
Engine/generator mountings, bogie bushes etc: Metalistik Ltd
Fire protection equipment: Graviner Manufacturing Co Ltd
Heat-demisters, driver's compartment: S. Smith & Sons Ltd
Warning horns: Desilux Electrical Equipment Ltd
Windscreen wipers: Trico-Folberth Ltd

Buffers, hydro-pneumatic: George Turton Platts & Co Ltd
Pipe fittings: British Ermeto Corporation Ltd
Driver's and Guard's seats: A. W. Chapman Ltd
Metallic fittings, locks etc: J. Beresford & Sons Ltd, Jones & Foster Ltd, J. Kaye & Sons Ltd, Taylor & Osbourne Ltd

In addition, there were a number of smaller subcontractors supplying minor items from both the UK and Europe.'

Although the above is not difficult to understand, the technical press was not read by many and in consequence *The Guardian* in its issue of 4 July 1960 published an excellent piece on the 'Mechanics of the Midland Pullman'. Some does repeat the previous and has consequently been omitted, but elsewhere there was useful additional information. 'The use of a German type of diesel engine and a Swiss type of bogie should not be taken as a sign that the Midland Pullman is of a Continental design. At the time the train was being designed there were certain features which were entirely new to British industry, but which Continental firms had worked on. Now, the diesel

ABOVE Type 'P1' Power car (LMR). This is clearly not a pristine train but is dated by MC as being taken in 1960 – possibly returned to the manufacturers for a 'spruce up' following trials and before entering public service. The notice on the Guard's compartment reads 'Load 15cwts distributed,' hence the comment in later years about how the restricted luggage capacity would limit the sets if considered for other routes especially that to the West Country. *Richard Moore*

BELOW Type 6 parlour car (first-class) for the WR. The protrusion from the left-hand bogie on the inside of the vehicle may well be a waste outlet pipe from the toilet. Notice the 'E' plate – indicating the fifth vehicle of the train with the applicable seat numbers shown underneath. *Richard Moore*

ABOVE 'Type 4' kitchen car. Two kitchen cars were provided per train, the Type 4 vehicle being that within the six-car set. For the WR set the kitchen car was designated as Type 5. Internally the passenger accommodation and the actual kitchen were identical and it was on the outside where there were visible as well as mechanical differences. For the LMR trains of six vehicles, one end of the vehicle also had the second driven bogie at one end – seen here to the right. This necessitated the bodywork being cut away to accommodate the heavyweight features required. Again, on the Type 4 the same vehicle housed the auxiliary engine underneath – notice the route of the exhaust finishing vertical at the end of the coach – in similar fashion to conventional DMUs of the period. All this extra equipment added considerably to the weight so making the Type 4 second only to the Power car, weighing in at 49.1 tons. (On the WR trains the Type 5 kitchen had neither the power bogie nor the auxiliary engine.) To maintain symmetry of design, the side bodywork on both the Type 4 and the Type 5 had recessed areas at the kitchen ends although no doors were provided. Within the vehicle, the space immediately where the pseudo door would have opened was instead occupied by the staff toilet on one side and the staff compartment on the other. Finally, on the technical aspects, notice the conventional outward opening doors again at the kitchen end. An identical pair, again outward opening, was provided on the opposite side. Their purpose was for loading stores only, which would have been made more difficult had the doors opened inwards (as per the passenger doors) due to the limited space available both in the corridor and in the kitchen area. (Reference to the plans will explain this point further.) So far as the image is concerned this was reported as taken by MC in 1960. We may also conclude that as with the earlier view of the 'travelled' power-car this was part of a set, having been on trial and returned to MC for 'sprucing up' prior to entering public service. *Richard Moore*

BELOW The 'lightweight' version of the kitchen car, a Type 5 and again for the Western Region. Conveniently the photograph shows the opposite side compared with the Type 4, which also depicts the outlet pipes from the kitchen area. The windows to the kitchen area doors can also be seen to have conventional droplights. *Richard Moore*

ABOVE Type 3 (WR) power car in pristine condition. Whilst the bodywork of the trains could be regularly cleaned in service the underframes were susceptible to the usual brake dust and general grime and consequently the smart black and silver paint would quickly acquire a liberal coating of 'brown dust'. On this vehicle the double doors by the guards/luggage compartment were also inward opening for the Guard and outward opening for luggage. The driver's door was also inward opening whilst the single side door affording direct access to the engine compartment could only be opened from the inside and was used for maintenance purposes only. On this view no 'sideways periscope' is provided for the guard. This fitting, seen on some later images, appears to have been a retrospective addition. *Richard Moore*

BELOW Again for the WR this is a second class parlour car, the righthand end of which had the heavyweight power bogie underneath and also the auxiliary engine attached to the underframe – again note the route and position for the exhaust pipe. A filler cap for (auxiliary) engine coolant is placed slightly off centre on the bodyside. Each eight-car WR set had two such vehicle as Nos 2 and 7 in the formation. Vibration and noise from the underfloor auxiliary engines do not appear to have been a problem, certainly inside the cars. Similarly, whilst BP suffered a poor reputation for passenger ride for anyone sat at the rear of the power car (whilst at the same time the crew would be enjoying a smooth and comfortable journey), this is not mentioned as a particular issue in the SR 'Hastings' units where a similar (power unit at one end) design applied. *Richard Moore*

programme of British Railways has given the incentive to industry in this country to meet the Continental firms on their own ground. It is not at all certain that, if a train like the Midland Pullman were to be designed today, it would need to go abroad for ideas. The development of the diesel engine has had as one of its main objects a reduction in weight while the horse-power is retained or even improved. This is generally obtained by increasing the rotational speed of the engine without increasing the mean effective pressures. The railway modernisation committee decided that the Midland Pullman must be multiple-unit with the power within the set train. To do the journey between Manchester and London in just over three hours the designers had to find a high-speed engine. There were a number of medium-speed diesel engines produced in this country, but these would have been much too heavy for the train. Even on the Continent there were only two suitable high-speed engines available, both from German companies. Maybach and MAN. There was little to choose between them. The MAN model was chosen and North British Locomotive arranged to make it under licence. Since then a similar high-speed engine of greater horse-power than the one in the Midland Pullman has been developed in this country. and prototypes have been ordered by British Railways. *[We are not given further detail.]*

'The Midland Pullman engine, with twelve cylinders of 180mm. bore by 210mm. stroke, is fitted with a Napier exhaust gas turbo-blower giving a boost pressure of 10.4lb. per square inch and has a twelve-hour rating of 1,000hp at 1,500rpm. Each of the two diesel engines, which are 12-cylinder vee-type, is direct-coupled to a GEC composite main and auxiliary generator. The main generator supplies electric power for traction purposes and the auxiliary provides current for exciting the main generator, and for main-engine starter-battery charging, control circuits, air compressors, oil priming pumps and driving cab heaters. When the train is standing in the terminal stations an external electric supply will be connected to it to avoid running the auxiliary engine. This is to prevent the unpleasantness to passengers on the platform of the noise of the auxiliary engine running in a confined space. The supply will lie disconnected and the auxiliary engine started just before the train starts. The auxiliary engines can be started both from the track side and from inside the train. When running they need no attention or control by the driver. An underframe is necessary for the power car to support the main engine and other equipment, but the intermediate cars are of integral construction and built as one structure like a tube. Metro-Cammell's work over many years on this lighter and stronger type of construction has led to the Midland Pullman being of a new type. Much of the body of the intermediate cars is built of low alloy corrosion resisting steel of high strength with extensive spot welding. The structure is heavily insulated in the roof, sides, and floor against heat and sound. In the power car the main engine sits on rubber blocks mounted on the underframe. The electrically driven alternator also has special suspension. The Schlieren type of bogie was taken up by Metro-Cammell and developed for the Pullman diesel expresses. Because it has fewer wearing surfaces than the conventional bogie of the past, it needs little maintenance to keep up a high standard of riding over a large number of miles. It uses helical springs and hydraulic dampers. In each of the four driving bogies the two separate electric traction motors are fully suspended and the transmission from each motor to its respective axle is by a quill-drive. The automatic brake can be applied in an emergency by driver, guard, or passengers, and also works if the train parts. The high-speed brake, which is automatic and superimposed on the other two brakes, is used when the train is slowed to a stop from a high speed. It avoids skidding of the wheels by applying the right amount of pressure for each speed.'

But after all such praise there came a sceptic in the form of the Editorial as appeared in *Modern Railways* for July 1960, 'The British Pullmans. After many vicissitudes, due to staffing, design and construction problems, the well-publicised 2,380bhp diesel-electric Pullman trains of British Railways have been completed and revenue service begun. But there are grounds for believing that the work should never have been allowed to proceed beyond the design stage. For a decade it has been possible to look upon the Pullman Car Co. Ltd. as one of the most efficient and best-run transport organisations in the British Isles. But what economic use can it possibly make of these five enormities of British engineering with which it has now been saddled by its overlord, the BTC? True, its cuisine and personal service are

LEFT End view, Type 5 kitchen car – passenger end. Swing doors protected the toilet and kitchen area corridors at either end and it would in fact be most unusual to see a passenger attempt to walk along this corridor to reach another part of the train. In fact, other than the occasional toilet visit, passengers would hardly move at all and one can probably even imagine the response from a steward, 'Can I help you Sir?' The doors also reduced further the instance of draughts, noise and, so far as the kitchen was concerned, to some extent the aroma of cooking. *Richard Moore*

RIGHT End view, Type 5 kitchen car – kitchen end. The sliding door led to the staff rest room. The maximum height of the train from rail level, both LMR and WR sets, was 12 feet 7 and $^{11}/_{16}$ inches.

Cab layout (LMR) set. The only difference between this and the Western Region trains was the latter had the ATC cancelling button in the place where the circular disc below Nos 13 and 14 is shown.

1 Brake controller, EP/Westinghouse.
2 Window wiper air valve, driver's side.
3 Brake cylinder pressure gauge.
4 Main reservoir/brake pipe pressure gauge.
5 Speedometer.
6 Ampmeter (main generator).
7 Cab heating switch.
8 Engine stopped indicator light.
9 General alarm indicator light.
10 EP brake indicator light.
11 Auxiliary heat switch.
12 Control switch (button).
13 Engine start button.
14 Engine stop button.
15 Overload reset button.
16 Horn valve.
17 Main power controller.
18 Master switch: Forward – Engine only – Off – Reverse.
19 Instrument light switch.
20 Front marker light switch (left).
21 Front marker light switch (middle).
22 Front marker light switch (right).
23 Instrument light dimmer switch.
24 Front marker light repeater (left).
25 Front marker light repeater (middle).
26 Front marker light repeater (right).
27 Loudaphone unit. (Loudaphone communications equipment was also used in some Southern regions EMUs.) *Colin Marsden*

not likely to depart from existing standards, but what administration today can afford 299 tons of service weight to carry 132 first class passengers in six cars, when 200 tons would have been ample? The heaviest of the air-conditioned first-class TEE trains of 1957, on the basis of specific weight, scale 210 tons for 105 passengers, and that surely is enough for the highest standard of luxury. It represents two tons per passenger and 12.7bhp of total installed power per ton of service weight. But now, after three years' grace for progress, we get an increase of 13 per cent in weight per seat to 2.26 tons coupled with a reduction of 37 per cent in bhp per ton to a figure of 8.0, and with fewer design limitations. It is difficult to see how trains of such characteristics can be financially-paying propositions.'

Not surprisingly there was a counter and by no less than D. J. C. Robertson, the Managing Director of Metropolitan-Cammell. Using the same heading and in the following month's issue with a note dated the 8 July 1960 he countered, 'Sir, In your editorial in the July issue, you comment on the weight of the diesel-electric Pullman trains recently

Driver's cab with the door to the engine compartment – heavily insulated for noise of course – also visible. It cannot be denied the space was 'cosy' and whilst access was possible to the compartment from either side by inward opening doors, the seat for the Driver folded forward into the leg/footwell for ease of access whilst the second seat was fixed on a pillar. Out of sight to the extreme right was a small electric cooker and hotplate for crew purposes – but see image on page 133. The large wheel on the desk is the handbrake working solely on one bogie of the power car. *Richard Moore*

brought into service on the London Midland Region. It is important that one compares "like for like". If the comparison was made with the German TEE seven-car train, it is necessary to remember that the Midland Pullman not only has two kitchens but also increased staff and stock accommodation in order to provide full meals at one time for all passengers; whereas the TEE train has only limited dining accommodation served by a single kitchen. In the eight-car diesel Pullman train, which will soon be introduced on the Western Region, there is accommodation for 228 passengers and a working-order weight of 364 tons which represents 1.6 tons per passenger, whilst retaining full meals at one time for all passengers. This represents a reduction of 20 per cent in weight per seat as compared with the figures quoted in your editorial for the TEE train which cannot offer the same catering facilities.'

So to whom do the honours go? For that we leave the reader to decide although not surprisingly the *Modern Railways* Editor managed to have the final word in response to Mr Robertson's letter, 'We fully agree that one should compare only "like with like". That at once eliminates the second paragraph of Mr. Robertson's letter, and was the reason why we did not refer at all to the eight-car Pullmans in our brief weight comparison in July, because first class de luxe should not be compared with first and second class. The question of one or two kitchens is immaterial. The situation is that the British Railways Pullmans need 299 tons weight to carry 132 revenue-earning first class passengers, all of whom can have a meal at their seats; and so the trains weigh 2.26 tons per revenue-earning passenger, yet have no more than 8.0bhp per ton. On the other hand, though built three years earlier, the heaviest TEE train needs 210 tons for 105 revenue-earning passengers, but has an additional 46 seats in the diner and 7 in a buffet, which give a welcome relief on long journeys. Moreover, in the TEE trains certain accommodation had to be set aside for customs officials and train staff. But these trains of 1957 build need no more than 2.0 tons per revenue-earning seat, and have 12.7bhp per ton, values which are respectively 12 and 58 per cent better than those of the British Pullmans.' [8]

If the reader remains undecided – we hope not confused at this juncture – let it be said that BR does not appear to have been concerned over hp per ton or weight per passenger (likely passengers weighed slightly more at the end of a Pullman journey anyway…). What would be the governing aspect in the years to come would not be the passenger to ton weight ratio, nor the catering or even the loadings on the principal routes, that is NOT including the fill in turns, instead it would be the ride comfort, the non-standard equipment, and most of all the fact that as the

From ground level, the jumper and coupling connections between vehicles on an LMR set are shown. Notice that as the complete train was first class only, no designation is shown on the doors. The connected air pipes are the lowest of the pipe connections beneath the gangway. *Sam Lambert*

At the MC works a pair of LMR power cars appear complete and await painting, probably around the summer of 1959. For the record, the first set was reported as 'finished' on 26 October 1959 and according to George Williams, '. . . looks a very fine train.' One of the frustrations associated with the research for this book is that in the National Archives file there an entry similar to that of 27 November 1959 from a Mr Randle which speaks of 'problems' on the trial runs, '. . . as per the attached album of photographs . . .' – but again the latter is missing. *MC/Kidderminster Railway Museum*

A complete WR eight-car set within the works sidings at MC. As noted in earlier views, the condition and presence of the oil tail lamp indicates either the preparation for or the return from a test run with the unit being moved by the on-site works shunter. The purpose of the structure straddling the unit is not known.

A prestige train. At this stage any images taken are without the front crest and also without the final coat of varnish. The Pullman crests were added sometime after 25 February 1960 with mention made at the time that whilst they, '… do not have the effect of a warning to men working on the track … they look very well and enhance the appearance of the car end.' For once also Sir John Elliot appears to have approved. The photographs show an early test run, believed with 'Set 1' at Bedford in January 1960; certainly the condition of the paintwork on the underframe indicates only a limited number of outings had been made. What is also obvious is the final livery of the kitchen car has yet to be applied. One of your authors, in correspondence with former MC Engineer Malcolm Bothan, asked if he was aware of any enquires from other potential buyers? Malcolm replied, 'I do not know of any serious enquiries for further train sets of this design from anywhere. The Blue Pullmans did however leave a legacy in a number of respects. The concept of close-coupled complete train sets was adopted for BR's own high speed train which was developed after the Blue Pullmans, as was double glazing and air conditioning. Some mistakes of the BPs were avoided, eg having a passenger compartment on the power cars. The primary suspension units of the BP Schlieren trailer bogies, which were reasonably successful, was chosen by BR for their B4 bogie for the Mk2 coaches and supplied by MC under licence to Schlieren in large numbers.'

WR set on a longer distance trial between Birmingham and Bristol using the former Midland route, the set being seen at Gloucester on 3 February 1960. As confidence grew in the units so greater distances were covered, allowing familiarity for the manufacturer, operator and of course the staff who would man the train once in service. This was a regular route and test run. Whether LMR sets used the same route and similarly whether WR sets were tested over the same lines as the LMR trains is not known.

years passed so ordinary trains came to equal and even at time surpass the Pullman schedules. Luxury 'at your seat' service was certainly a plus point but it could not compete with the faster trains and services then promised and upon which no Pullman supplement was payable.

The work of George Mitchell could also be seen at the London Barbican Centre and the Co-Operative building in Manchester.

The Cravens coach was one of several built in the 1950s as prototypes for quantity production to follow on from the BR Mark I vehicles and it too featured blinds of the type described. Unfortunately BR considered the vehicle too luxurious, and consequently too expensive, although quantity production would undoubtedly have reduced the cost. In many ways the Cravens vehicle was years ahead of its time, it was also superior in design to what later became the Standard Mark 2 vehicle of the 1960s.

The operation of the window blinds on the vehicles was by hand. A single lever above the window on second class operated a solitary blind whilst on first class handles were provided on either side of the tables. Each is best seen in the accompanying interior illustrations. First class windows are easily identified by the narrow vertical white strip at the window mid-way point. Although more than possible in both first and second class, it is not totally clear how the angle of the blinds within the window was altered.

Staff were issued with suggestions as to the wording they should use when making announcements. One example for the up 'Midland Pullman' was, 'Good morning Ladies and Gentlemen, welcome to the Blue Pullman. In a few minutes we shall stop at Cheadle Heath to take on more passengers, after which breakfast will be served.' Other than a situation arising en-route the second and final announcement was to be, 'In a few minutes we shall be arriving at St Pancras and we hope this has been a pleasant journey.' The evening 'welcome message' for passengers on the down service was, 'Good evening Ladies and Gentlemen – welcome to the "Midland Pullman". Teas and light refreshments are now available and dinner will be served at 7.30 pm.' A final announcement came with the train a few minutes away from Cheadle Heath '… and after that Manchester Central'. For the mid-day fill in turn the announcement was made that '… luncheon will be served immediately if you will please give your order to the attendant.' On the return it was, '… Tea and light refreshments are available throughout your journey…' Indeed even such a small detail as these announcements were necessary to be approved at a senior level and were then agreed by the Pullman company on 16 June 1960. Even so staff were told it was to be considered only as a guide. On the basis of the importance given to such detail it is likely the WR proposed a similar procedure.

This concept meant that the output of the engines need not be sacrificed for auxiliary needs. As a comparison, the later HST sets, albeit with a considerably higher combined power output of circa 4,400bhp, could see a reduction in available power of 10-20%, depending on the demands made according to external climatic conditions. The underfloor engines on Blue Pullman have, in the past, given rise to the incorrect assertion that they constituted an auxiliary 'Power car'. However, as has been seen, this was not the case and they were not in any way wired so as to supplement the output available from the engines mounted in the power cars. This confusion has been heightened as the powered bogies driving the train forward, regardless of six- or eight car type, were always the rear bogie of the power car and the leading bogie of the second vehicle.

The mention of the 'periscope' is interesting. As indicated at the commencement of the technical description, the text for this appears to have been supplied by the builders and it cannot be confirmed this periscope was in fact actually fitted. Careful study of images of the LMR power cars in early days also suggests the small window adjacent to the guards' door/window may not have been an original fitting in all the LMR power cars but could also have been a retrospective addition. Similarly there appears to have been a 'side' periscope fitted to the WR power cars at the same location. A study of photographs is needed to confirm which specific vehicles were so fitted and at what period.

The protection against wheelslip referred to is interesting and may well have been one of the earliest times such facility was provided in lieu of sanding. Whatever, little mention is made of this achievement although it would become a standard fitting on motive power in later years.

The technical magazine *Diesel Railway Traction* in its issue for July 1960 had picked up on the same point. DRT comparing passenger to weight ratio of the 1957 German-built units with BP. Again there followed a swift response from MC in which they cited the meals at seats service on the British trains and served from two kitchens compared with limited catering on the German trains and which were also of seven cars. In the same (July 1960) issue of DRT was reproduced what was probably the most detailed description of the train as appeared anywhere at the time and probably taken from a technical press release issued by the builders. We need not repeat ad-nauseam a further piece similar in many ways to that seen before but it is worth mentioning a few specific points. The first of these being that there was still mention of a separate Ladies lavatory at the passenger end of the power car (LMR only or both six- and eight-car sets?). Also included in the article was a schematic wiring diagram for the train covering both the main and auxiliary circuits and predicted train performance curves.

ns chapter

5

BLUE PULLMAN

Are you being served – or not?
The trials and tribulations of catering on the Blue Pullman

In several areas reference has been made to industrial relations issues affecting the introduction of the new Pullman services.

This (short) chapter does not set out to deliberately repeat all that has gone before, indeed it was necessary in earlier chapters to mention the situation as applied at specific timescales; here though we combine this information using as reference two specific sources. The first consists of extracts with some additions/clarifications from two (of four) articles entitled 'Pullman in Transition' as appeared in the journal of the Pullman Society (Parts 3 and 4) written by the extremely well-informed Charles Long. (We have deliberately included some other items applicable to Pullman but not necessarily directly related to BP purely as Mr Long affords a fascinating insight into the business situation of Pullman during the period.)

The second is sourced from the website of the *Labour Review* for February–March 1960 and is entitled 'Lessons of the Dining Car Strike' by Brian Arundel, see biography for website details.[1]

Starting with Charles Long we learn that on 5 September 1959, Frank Harding the GM of Pullman wrote to David McKenna, then the Assistant General Manager (later the General Manager) of the Southern Region, to express his growing concern about the scale of the losses sustained by Pullman operations on the SR. He said that the need to resolve this problem was becoming all the more urgent because, in connection with the impending introduction elsewhere on BR of new diesel-electric Pullman trains, the NUR was applying increased pressure on the company to bring the generally inferior Pullman conditions of service and rates of pay into line with those of the restaurant car staff employed by the BTHCS.

So far as the SR was concerned the only Pullman services that showed any operating profit were the 'Golden Arrow', 'Bournemouth Belle' and 'Brighton Belle' trains but these profits were being swallowed up *(pardon the pun)* by the heavy losses made by the catering facilities the company provided on other trains on the Region. So far as Pullman as a separate company were concerned, for several years Pullman services on the ER and WR have been subsidising the other SR trains. *(The mention of the WR Pullman service – and there was only the one at the time, the trial 'South Wales Pullman', subsidising the SR services – is most interesting. This tells us straight away the SWP was running at a profit.)*

Even taking into account revenue from supplementary fares, the 23 EMU composite cars on the Central Section of the SR had lost more than £13,000 in the previous year. Mention is then made specifically over BP and it was noted that with some 80% of its restaurant car staff as members of

First class parlour interior, the original probably taken as a publicity view – the flowers on the tables are a nice touch. Even without the table lamps there is a pleasing mix of tradition – the wooden panelling – and the contemporary. Readers will recall there was much discussion about access to the window seats at the four-seat table, the alternative suggested being a 'telescopic' arrangement. This was later discounted for the need to have the tables ready prepared at the start of each journey. Although not specifically mentioned, there was some luggage room available between the backs of the seats.

123

ABOVE Due to difficulties with recruitment, at least four members of staff were seconded from Brighton for the trial, demonstration and inaugural runs of the LMR train in 1960. How long this arrangement continued for is not reported. From a practical perspective lodgings were also no doubt required especially when working to Manchester. Presumably too this would have left the 'Brighton Belle' service short of staff but again this is not mentioned. The names of the individuals were not reported. L to R – Conductor Chris Barnett, Conductor Bert Viney, Conductor Chris Lade, far right unknown. All four were from the 'Brighton Belle' but were loaned to Manchester for training of the new Manchester based crew. 'Brighton Belle' staff were also seen in the official publicity shots and the 'Blue Pullman' film.

BELOW Mr F. D. M. Harding OBE, the Managing Director of the Pullman Car Co., with two of his conductors at St Pancras on 1 July 1960, the first day of services on the LMR. Left is Conductor (designate) Walton in white jacket whilst to the right is Conductor Peate in blue uniform who had been seconded (from the Southern Region?) for instructional duties. *BR/LMR*

the NUR and no agreement on staffing these trains in place, the BTHCS Board plainly sensed there could be trouble ahead. At a meeting on 6 July, it concluded that, '… the implications of this matter were such that there should be the closest integration between the Pullman Car Company's activities and those of the Hotels & Catering Services'.

Indeed, simmering discontent generated by the differing rates of pay and working hours of Pullman and BTHCS staff came to a head at the NUR's Annual General Meeting held at Blackpool later the same month, when the following resolution was passed unanimously: 'The AGM expresses concern at reports that under the Modernisation Plan a number of trains will be replaced by trains with Pullman service and staffed by Pullman Car staff. We demand from the BTC that any new Pullman trains operated on British Railways shall be operated by the BTC and manned by BTC staff, and further we instruct the [union's] Executive Committee to work for the abolition of Pullman Car services operating on British Railways and their assimilation into the Hotels & Catering Services of British Transport.'

Possibly prompted by this development, and avoiding the 'usual channels' (the inverted commas are those of Charles Long and in which is no doubt meant private discussions rather than a more official approach), the BTC Chairman, Sir Brian Robertson, privately asked Sir John Elliot – whom he had recently persuaded to succeed Stanley Adams as Chairman of both the Pullman Car Company and Thomas Cook & Sons Ltd (then still a wholly owned BTC subsidiary) – to prepare a report on how the Pullman Board saw possible future developments. The report, submitted on 1 October, presents an interesting snapshot of the company at a particularly significant moment in its history.

Before it turned to gaze into the crystal ball however, the pages provide for a potted history of Pullman activities in Great Britain and an outline of the company's current operations, accompanied by a note setting out the names of its directors and chief officers, plus a summary of staff numbers and other key information. A statement setting out the financial results for the preceding year (see Table 1) clearly reinforced the concerns that had previously been expressed by Col Harding to SR managers. This gave a far more detailed breakdown than was ever provided in the global figures presented in the company's published annual reports at this time – from which it can be seen that, leaving aside the loss-making services, the 'profit' claimed by Col Harding for the 'Golden Arrow', at only £348, was in truth, wafer thin. It may also come as some surprise to see that the 'Bournemouth Belle' earned more than two-and-a-half times as much (a contradiction from the previous statement) as the 'South Wales Pullman'[(1)], the latter service of course rather more directly related to our story, but setting aside the fact that they were

ABOVE Interior of a second class car. We should take care in suggesting this was exactly as seen for it is more likely to be a pre-service publicity view to illustrate the service available – 'at your seat' – in second-class Pullman as well. Note the passenger sat in the front right-hand seat also has a menu card propped up on the table. Publicity/stills views of this type were commonplace, the individuals depicted usually staff 'borrowed' from the Public Relations Department.

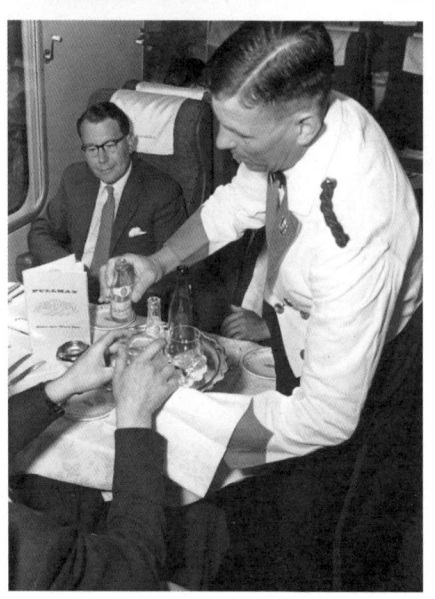

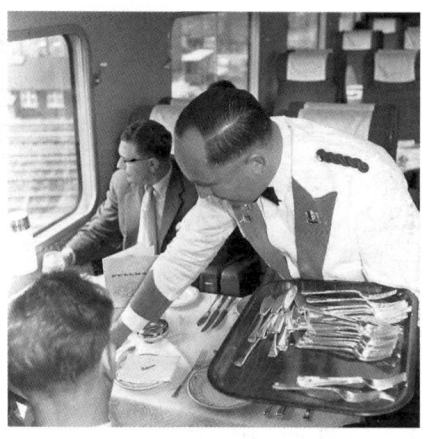

ABOVE LMR Pullman service and again likely to have been a pre-public service. From the discussions that were reported prior to July 1960, reference was made as to the practical need of having the tables laid out and ready before passengers boarded. This view would therefore tend to contradict this requirement but as stated it may well be an exception and was posed purely for the camera.

LEFT A different steward – seen again on page 128 – now pours drinks to perhaps the same 'passengers' seen in the previous view. Images of passengers enjoying the Pullman experience were used extensively in contemporary advertising both in leaflet and newspaper form.

primarily aimed at distinctively different markets, it should be remembered that the former train ran on all seven days of the week compared with only five for the WR service. It might also be noted that, were it not for the company's earnings from supplementary fares, no Pullman services would have shown a profit.

As for the future, the report set out three possible courses of action: 1) continuing to operate current services (plus those already planned) and nothing more; 2) seeking to provide Pullman services on as wide a basis as possible, displacing ordinary restaurant and buffet car services; and 3) examining, with the railway regions, the routes between large industrial and recreational centres that offered the best opportunity for profitable operation by creating and meeting a demand for high-class, high-speed, 'super-comfort' daytime rail services.

With regard to Option 1, the report confirmed that the Pullman Board wanted to be relieved of proven unprofitable operations, such as the restaurant and buffet car services on the Southern Region, while the single-Pullman-car services on the Region's Central Section were not only unprofitable but deemed to be 'out of line with present needs'. These matters were 'in active discussion' with the GM of the SR. Echoing Col Harding (who, newly appointed as Managing Director, was now himself a member of the Pullman Board), the report concluded: 'It is essential that these losses be eliminated at the earliest date possible, otherwise they will cancel out the profitability of the new enterprises such as the Midland and Western diesel trains, and will continue to absorb staff and equipment which could be better employed elsewhere'. In view of the poor margins now exposed it is indeed surprising the new trains were to be designated Pullman at all!

Was Option 2 even put forward seriously? While regular rail travellers might well have had some reservations about BR's publicly extolled 'excellence' of the accommodation provided in contemporary standard BR Mk1 vehicles, could there ever have been any doubt that, in the words of the report, 'such a policy would be unsupported by the large section of the general public which has no desire for greater comfort than that already provided by the excellent modern stock of British Railways, and which, moreover, is unwilling to pay a supplement'?

The route and service which would later turn out to be the catalyst for industrial action. This is the mid-day Leicester 'fill-in' working seen here on the first day of operation, 4 July 1960, with the train in the process of setting back into Platform 3 at Leicester London Road ready to form the 2.33pm departure to St Pancras. An official can be seen riding in the rear cab. It was from this point on when the service was later extended to Nottingham that the chefs and stewards would 'down aprons' and not pick them up until Leicester was reached again on the return journey. *Alec Swain*

As might have been anticipated, the Pullman Board concluded that Option 3 was 'the course which ought to be pursued . . . in line with Commission policy on future passenger services on British Railways'. In addition to the services already planned, it was felt that the following routes were the most worthy for consideration for future Pullman operations: London–Glasgow (via the West Coast route); London–Liverpool; and a Cardiff-based service to complement the London-based 'South Wales Pullman'.

Astonishingly, particularly in view of the plainly growing disquiet among the railway catering grades represented by the NUR, the report made no mention whatever of staffing issues. Only ten days later, on 11 October, there was an unofficial meeting of BTHCS restaurant car workers at Unity House, the NUR's Euston Road headquarters. After a 'long and heated' discussion, it was resolved that, should there be any attempt to introduce any new Pullman services, all Pullman cars would be declared 'black' and they would neither be handled nor serviced. However, behind the scenes, the NUR's negotiating committee had in fact been engaged for some time in talks with Pullman managers (who were themselves doubtless under some pressure from the BTC,

the company's controlling shareholder). As a result of these discussions, the union's sought-after parity for Pullman staff with BR restaurant car staff was conceded and a new agreement was due to be implemented from 1 November. In return, the NUR Executive had indicated that it was now willing to withdraw its opposition to the extension of Pullman operations.

According to a statement published in the *Railway Review*, the NUR newspaper, the BTC had told the union that many businessmen travelled by rail 'only because of the attraction of the Pullman service which was, therefore, a strong selling point and brought additional revenue to the Commission by way of supplementary fares'. Moreover, 'there were no immediate plans for further Pullman services except those scheduled to run between London and Manchester and Bristol and Birmingham. There was also no question whatsoever of doing away with the restaurant car services featured on other trains on these routes and replacing them by Pullman services'.

Notwithstanding these assurances however, restaurant car workers based in Manchester came out on unofficial strike from midnight on 25 October, and over the next few days they were joined by others based at Euston,

Facsimile reproduction of the WR evening menu and wine list from 1960. (Was the same menu used on all the WR evening trains to their respective destinations?) As a comparison the first breakfast menu from the LMR service included 'Scotch Porridge and Cream, – Cornflakes/Puffed Rice/Frosted Flakes – Grapefruit Cocktail – Grapefruit Juice/Tomato Juice/Orange Juice – Poached Haddock Colbert – Grilled Royal Kippers – Omelette to your Choice – Bacon Egg Mushrooms – Oxford Marmalade: Orange or Ginger – Honey – Toast or oven Rolls – Tea Coffee.' The price: 7s 6d. A similar extensive menu was available for afternoon tea and later for dinner which could include such delights as, 'Melon, scampi, cold roast chicken, Yorkshire ham, roast beef, ox tongue, new potatoes, navarin printaniere and kirsch ice cream'. Indeed a 1963 article in Modern Railways referred to the scope for individuality available to the Pullman Chef, '... some items are available direct from Pullman stores but with the Chef also free use discretion as to whether to use the provided supplies or to cook for himself. Each chef on the train, may order independently but they can also draw on the other's supplies if required. Food once cooked was rarely wasted as anything not served was used for staff meals.' The impression then is that the two chefs on each train could in theory be serving different menus but this was not thought to be the case. It is not clear if this autonomy also applied on the WR or how actual Menus might be prepared when individuality prevailed. The Pullman lettering for the new trains was, at Jack Howe's suggestion, originally to have been 'Shaded Extended Egyptian' with the alternative as a modified 'Bodoni', and it is believed that at times these fonts may have been used on both the LMR and WR services.

PULLMAN

Menu and Wine List

Scotch Smoked Salmon with Lemon wedges 7/6
Chilled Fruit Juices: Pineapple 1/6; Tomato 1/6; Orange 1/6
Crème Argenteuil with Golden Croutons 1/6

From the Grill

*English lamb Cutlets 8/6   *Scotch Salmon 8/6
* Fillet Steak 12/6   *Barbecued Chicken à l'Américaine 8/6

* *Price of main dishes includes :*

* Parsley, New and Olivette Potatoes, Sweet Corn, Baby Carrots and Broccoli Mornay

Cold Buffet: Salmon Mayonnaise or
Half a Chicken with dressed Salads 8/6

Fresh Fruit Salad with dairy Cream Ice or
Crème Chantilly 2/-

Continental and English Cheese Tray 2/-

Coffee 8d

Bread Basket of White and Hovis Rolls
Ryvita and Curled Butter 6d

St Pancras, King's Cross, Newcastle and Paddington. From the viewpoint of those taking strike action, the problem of integration still remained. While the new agreement protected them from redundancy, the BTHCS employees feared that, so long as the two catering bodies remained totally separate entities, Pullman staff would be given the better and more lucrative services and that, in consequence, they would be effectively downgraded. At this point, it is perhaps worth reporting the curious fact that the largely non-unionised Pullman on-board staff had been granted a pay rise and reduction in their basic working week from 52 to 44 hours (or, to be pedantic, a basic 88-hour fortnight) and certain other fringe benefits, without having exhibited any industrial muscle, while Pullman services continued to operate normally at a time when there was widespread disruption of BTHCS restaurant car services across the country, triggered by the perceived threat posed by the expansion of Pullman operations. The strike ended on 6 November but only after the President of the NUR had given an assurance that the union would 'insist' that the new Pullman services should be operated by BTHCS staff and would do its utmost to bring about the assimilation of the services operated by Pullman and by BTHCS.

One unlooked-for consequence of the strike was that, because of the sensitivity of the situation, the BTC prevailed upon Metro-Cammell to delay the test-running programme for the first new diesel Pullman units. This is the first time delays to trials are referred to but it shows why, apart from the subsequently found 'technical problems', the planned trip to Marylebone in late November in order to exhibit the trains was postponed. (*Trains Illustrated* for June 1959 had referred to the '...previously forecast introduction of the MP being now in doubt'. The LMR however had advised the Manchester newspapers the delay was due to 'staff training'.)

TABLE 1: 12 MONTHS TO 31 DECEMBER 1958				
	'Golden Arrow'	'Bournemouth Belle'	'Brighton Belle'	'South Wales Pullman'
Commissary Revenue	£12,899	£20,247	£18,670	£20,277
Supplementary Fares	£14,876	£24,851	£33.092	£15,711
Operating profit *(loss)* before taxation	£348	£12,299	£14,362	£4,518

Breakfast – kippers, boiled egg, bread rolls, plus presumably the wine glasses for fruit juice. (Notice too the Players Navy Cut on the table nearest the steward.) Harking back to those lamps again, it could be argued that their position was indeed slightly awkward and in that respect Jack Howe may well have been correct. This is a first class car and presumably the identical breakfast was available in second class (on the WR of course?) It would certainly seem unlikely there was much opportunity for variations on this the first meal of the day.

Beverage time – but this time with an apparent empty first-class seat. The trains clearly made an impact with some of the suppliers of on-board equipment as several asked for facilities to be made available to show potential customers the equipment they could provide in service. This approach appears to have been usually made direct to the Pullman company but who, for whatever reason, were usually cold about providing such assistance. Such requests then appear to have been passed on to the respective region who were somewhat more accommodating.

In passing, it might be noted that it was also considered that it could be advantageous to modify the three 5BEL units so as to have end gangways. There was also a suggestion that, if modified, a number of potentially displaced Pullman vehicles currently operating in 6PUL units might be modified to form an electric 'Golden Arrow'.

The Pullman Car Company and the LMR had originally hoped to inaugurate the 'Midland Pullman' service between Manchester Central and London St Pancras on 11 January 1960. This as we know was delayed due to the various issues discussed elsewhere. In fact, the delay was really something of a blessing in disguise, since it also provided a breathing space in which to try to resolve the still wide-open question of staffing.

The recent round of unofficial strikes by restaurant car staff had done nothing to improve public perceptions of rail travel in Britain and clearly the last thing the BTC would have wanted at this time was for a major falling-out with the same group of disaffected workers and so

First class, this time with coffee being served. The belief that these were publicity type images is exemplified by the interiors always seeming to be fully occupied and with none of the 'passengers' ever appearing to look toward the camera. Would paying passengers have been so keen to have been recorded anyway? Notice too the lights fixed to the underneath of the luggage racks.

LEFT The well known image of the lady adjusting her seat in first-class. This view was reproduced in various brochures advertising the train, sometimes in colour and at other times as seen here. In practice it was necessary to use the feet and knees to propel the seat to the desired position. Notice too the wooden table support.

RIGHT The lady could manage – but the man cannot – and no, it is not a 'tilting' train either. Not sure if this was another 'official' image or one from another source (nothing was recorded on the rear of the original print). It does indeed seem a little strange that the concept of something seemingly so simple as adjusting the seat should have warranted such attention.

scupper the launch of the new Pullmans upon which such high hopes had been placed.

Although the NUR had withdrawn its blanket opposition to the extension of Pullman services on British Railways and the Pullman Company had conceded the union's demands for parity in pay and conditions of service with those of the restaurant car staff employed by the BTHCS, the two catering bodies still remained totally separate entities. Perhaps even more importantly in the present circumstances Pullman had no established presence in Manchester. The union still sought the 'assimilation' of BTHCS and Pullman activities and assurances that there would be no withdrawal of existing restaurant car services as a result of the introduction of the new Pullman train. The fact that a number of BTHCS employees based in Sheffield had been made redundant following the introduction of the 'Master Cutler' in 1958 still rankled with the NUR, which was fearful that something similar might now be in prospect on the other side of the Pennines.

The union's concerns were set out at length at a meeting on 8 January 1960, held at BTC headquarters. This had been convened by the Commission's Manpower Adviser, A. R. Dunbar, in an attempt to cut through the difficulties, and it brought together representatives of all the interested parties – the NUR, Pullman and BTHCS. With Mr Dunbar was C. S. McLeod, the BTC's Chief Industrial Relations Officer. The six-man NUR team was led by the union's pragmatic General Secretary, Sidney Greene, and its Assistant General Secretary, W. Ballantine, whose remit covered the railway catering grades. The Pullman company was represented by its General Manager, Col Frank Harding and its Secretary, E. J. Morris, while the BTHCS was represented by Frank Hole, General Manager, E. K. Portman-Dixon, Chief of Restaurant Cars & Refreshment Rooms, and his deputy, H. G. B. Kelley.

Little positive progress was made at the meeting, although the BTC did put forward a 'suggested provisional arrangement' whereby 'priority in recruitment to staff the new service' would be given to existing restaurant car staff, who would be regarded as being 'on loan' to the Pullman Car Company. This would at least 'enable the train to start running without prejudicing the position in regard to a final settlement'. Further, the BTC representatives said that, together with the union, they would be prepared to consider the practicability of introducing a common promotion and redundancy scheme providing for the transfer of staff between the two organisations. However, discussion of the 'assimilation' of their managements would have to remain firmly off limits while the Pullman contract, which had almost another three years to run, remained in force. Behind the scenes it appears both the Pullman company and BTHCS had tacitly approved the BTC's proposals beforehand, since no comment on them by either party was recorded in the minutes.

A further meeting on 18 February went over much the same ground again. Once more, the NUR team pressed for assurances that existing restaurant car services would not be adversely affected by the introduction of the new Pullman train. They also asked for some indication to be given of the BTC's intentions 'in regard to the assimilation of the two managements, bearing in mind that … the Commission, as successors to the former shareholders of the Pullman Car Company, had the right to acquire the Redeemable Cumulative Preference Shares of that company remaining in private ownership at a fixed price in either June or December of any year after the end of 1958'. In their view, it was essential to resolve both these issues 'before progress could be made towards an understanding as to the manning of the new Pullman services'. The union's negotiators further alleged that the uncertainties surrounding future policy had given rise to feelings of considerable insecurity among BTHCS restaurant car staff.

In response to these concerns, the BTC representatives said that they were now prepared to give an assurance

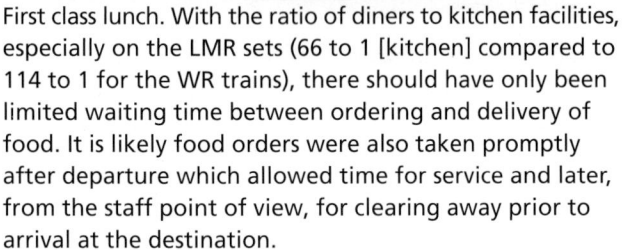

First class lunch. With the ratio of diners to kitchen facilities, especially on the LMR sets (66 to 1 [kitchen] compared to 114 to 1 for the WR trains), there should have only been limited waiting time between ordering and delivery of food. It is likely food orders were also taken promptly after departure which allowed time for service and later, from the staff point of view, for clearing away prior to arrival at the destination.

that, should any employee be made redundant as a direct consequence of the introduction of the Pullman service, every effort would be made to place that individual in a comparable post – either on the Pullman train itself or elsewhere within BTHCS. At the same time they pointed out that the higher staffing levels on Pullman trains should help to cushion the impact of any redundancy – as, it was claimed, had been demonstrated in connection with the introduction of the Sheffield Pullman (?) services. With reference to the union's repeated demand for the assimilation of Pullman and BTHCS operations, on 29 February, Mr Dunbar wrote to Mr Ballantine as follows: 'The Commission regard the standards associated with the Pullman Car Company as having a considerable value in attracting remunerative passenger traffic. It is their policy at present to continue the Pullman Car Company's separate identity'.

At this point, it is perhaps worth reflecting that, had the BTC possessed a crystal ball to foresee the future four years earlier in 1956, when it had received the report of the Diesel Multiple-Unit Main-Line Express Services Committee, it might have spared itself (and the NUR for that matter) its current pains by not focussing on the Pullman brand. After all, that Committee, chaired by Herbert Phillips, had then recommended that the catering facilities on the new trains should be provided by BTHCS, while the Pullman company too had, at that time, appeared somewhat reluctant to become involved in the

Brandy and after dinner coffee perhaps? Few alterations to the interior equipment on the trains appear to have been carried out after they entered service. One change, though, to affect the LMR sets was an improved ash tray fitted with a lid. Exactly when this was carried out cannot be ascertained but it would seem to have been sometime from the summer of 1960 onwards. (An amusing sideline to this was that Jack Howe felt the original ashtrays had been '…designed around Norman Johnson's pipe! Norman Johnson was the Chief Engineer of the Pullman Company. Jack Howe would appear to have been a non-smoker, as in a letter to David Mellor who had been charged with producing a new deeper design of ash tray, Howe comments, 'Also I think it will be necessary to provide a ledge for cigarettes for the benefit of those people who have the disgusting habit of smoking between courses.')

project. We may even wonder, although nothing appears minuted, did BR even ever consider starting their own 'Premium' standard and so by-pass the name Pullman?

For the present, there were a series of further exchanges between the BTC and the union, in which the Pullman Car Company appears to have taken little or no active part. Eventually, on 3 May – almost four months after the launch date originally planned for the new service – Sidney Greene signified the acceptance of the Commission's latest proposals by the NUR's Executive Committee in a letter to A. R. Dunbar. Nevertheless, 'agreement on this matter is on the strict understanding that they will not agree to any further extension of Pullman Car Services (except the two trains contemplated for the Western Region on which separate negotiations are to take place) prior to the complete assimilation of the Pullman Car Company by the British Transport Commission'. The seed for 'downing tools' (or should that be cutlery?) on the later extended Leicester to Nottingham fill-in turn was thus sown.

On 5 May, Col Harding wrote to A. R. Dunbar to thank him for his efforts in getting a resolution to the difficulties that had arisen. 'I am afraid we were unable to do much to help,' he wrote, 'but now I want to say how grateful we all are to you for your patience and skill in sometimes very trying circumstances. We will try to justify this by producing a really first class service – or should I say a really first class Pullman service – and if we succeed I hope you will judge it all to have been worthwhile.'

The selection of suitable BTHCS staff to be 'loaned' to the Pullman Car Company then quickly went ahead and had been completed for the start of the LMR service in July.

As we know the on-board sequences of the supposed 'inaugural journey' shown in the British Transport Films documentary, *Blue Pullman*, were actually filmed prior to the train's entry into service. (How many real Manchester businessmen – or their secretaries – were in the habit of rounding off their breakfasts with a brandy? In one of films it is reported a businessman was also filmed looking at a 'risqué' magazine of the period!) However, most of the individual catering staff featured were, in fact, genuine, long-service Pullman employees who did work alongside the seconded BTHCS staff for a short 'settling-down' period in order to introduce them to the supposed mysteries of the Pullman way of doing things. Apart from Chef Harding, who eventually opted to remain in Manchester, the main players were: Conductor Peart from the 'South Wales Pullman'; and Leading Attendants Chris Lade, Maurice Haffenden, Bert Viney and Vic Barnett, all Brighton men.

After the long-drawn-out stand-off affecting the staffing of the LMR train, the two WR services initially promised to present fewer difficulties. On 2 June, in an internal memorandum to A. R. Dunbar at the BTC, C. S. McLeod wrote, 'The meeting this afternoon went better than I had expected. Ballantine had met representatives of the local restaurant car staff and had apparently obtained their agreement in principle … if all goes well there may still be a chance of introducing the service sometime in July instead of the 8 August as envisaged'.

Unfortunately on 24 June, Roy Hammond, the GM of the WR, wrote to Maj-Gen Llewellyn Wansbrough-Jones, to say that, after all, it would now be impracticable to introduce the Pullman trains before the start of the winter timetable. For its part, the Pullman Car Company, 'despite every effort', was still some way from solving its staffing difficulties, while notwithstanding its earlier verbal assurances, the NUR had not, in fact, yet formally accepted the proposals on the table. In any event, he also felt that the incidence of the Region's heavy peak holiday traffic would make it 'very inadvisable to introduce these important services before the latter part of August. In view of the massive supplementary timetable and special publicity necessary to cover the introduction of the services for the short period of three weeks or so before September 12, it [had been] considered desirable to defer the start to coincide with the Winter timetable…'.

Then there was the issue of a lack of applications to take up posts on the Western Pullmans. This was raised at

Certainly some of the same individuals depicted earlier – we may wonder did they actually get to eat a hot meal? From the background outside it appears this time the train has also moved to different location.

a further meeting between C. S. McLeod and W. Ballantine on 28 June. Evidently, on this occasion, the NUR's Assistant General Secretary had expressed 'his surprise and disappointment that so few names had come forward despite the fact that he had been told by his local people that there would be sufficient applications'.

Neither did matters improve immediately afterwards, as four weeks later, on 20 July, Col Harding wrote to A. R. Dunbar to express his increasing anxiety at the situation that had developed. According to his letter, while eight conductors had applied for two available posts, only six applications had been made for the other 38 vacancies. In addition (so he said), at a meeting at Paddington two days earlier, it had been alleged that the BTHCS was itself so short of staff that it could not afford to release any more men unless its own existing restaurant car services were taken off. 'If these new [Pullman] services are to be staffed in time for 12 September,' he wrote, 'I must now please be set free to recruit in our own way, without being hampered or delayed by further discussions with the NUR or H&C Services'.

Whatever the basis of Col Harding's claims, at a quadripartite meeting hurriedly arranged at the BTC two days later, the NUR yet again insisted that 'the union's policy had not moved from the original principle that the new Pullman services should not be introduced except as additional services'. According to the BTC's representatives however, it had already been explained to the union in early June that certain existing train services on the Western Region's West Midlands main line were uneconomic and their associated restaurant car workings would have had to have been re-examined regardless. The proposed

THE BLUE PULLMAN STORY

More food being served on the move. Stewards became expert at knowing where the less than perfect sections of track were and so would either use their 'sea legs' or avoid dispensing food at those particular locations. Prior to entry into public service, samples of the crockery were sent to the Pullman Car Co. by George Williams, the Design Officer, in an attempt to get them to agree to 'better table equipment' – *cheapskate Pullman?* The tea set was designed by David Mellor and was initially shown in the Design Centre. Glassware was intended to be dual purpose for both the Blue Pullman trains and on the BTP shipping fleet. 'Table furniture' (silver plate cutlery) was intended to be supplied by Messrs Walker and Hall of Sheffield although in the end Julian Morel from Pullman selected what Jack Howe referred to as '… some nondescript Mappin & Webb design'. (This again drew yet another of Howe's abrasive letters aimed at George Williams with a copy to Christian Barman. 'If we are going to make any progress here [referring to the cutlery but no doubt intended also to be a more general comment], it is my opinion that some very high level pressure must be applied by the Design Panel as I am quite convinced that, without it, nothing will be done. Morel has promised to let me have a schedule of quantities required and I, in turn, agreed to try and find the designs which might be acceptable, but I feel that without the support mentioned above, any efforts on my part will be a complete waste of time.')

Genuine Western Region second class interior. Folklore has it that one Pullman steward had perfected the party trick of being able remove the table cloth without disturbing the crockery etc – assisted no doubt by the sheen on the actual linen. Note the antimacassars: these were not always a feature of the early publicity images. We do not know if Pullman staff rotated between the WR and LMR services to cover shortages etc. *Antony Ford collection.*

introduction of the 'Birmingham Pullman' service had simply speeded up this review. They were 'at a loss to understand' the restaurant car staffs' difficulties since a net increase of 24 jobs were on offer; in all, 40 men were required for the two Western Blue Pullman workings which, between them, would represent eight new services daily; against this, it was proposed to withdraw five BTHCS services, displacing 16 men. Draft proposals had already been drawn up to allow for common promotion and redundancy arrangements 'and undoubtedly some provision could also be made for any men who were required to change their home station'. 'After further discussion on the whole of the points raised,' the minutes recorded, 'the NUR representatives finally indicated that they foresaw no difficulty in reaching agreement on the manning of the new trains and indeed the union would co-operate with the management in arriving at satisfactory arrangements.'

And so, indeed, the 'Birmingham Pullman' and the 'Bristol Pullman' services were duly launched on 12 September 1960.

Charles Long adds his own (and very valid) point to the whole affair, 'Even as a junior employee, sharing an office with Frank Chaston, Pullman's Rolling Stock Superintendent (sandwiched between the offices of Col Harding and Maurice Upstone, the company's Staff Superintendent), I could not be other than well aware of the frustrations of this period, if not the detail of what was going on. Revisiting this period through the surviving records in the National Archives, I am struck by how little the company's own managers actually contributed to the negotiations. Was the NUR deliberately aiming to sideline them? Or am I being unduly suspicious?' (Some readers will also already be aware of the subsequent staff issues that affected the extension of the Pullman service from Leicester to Nottingham; this is more appropriately dealt with in the next chapter.)

The website referred to presents a somewhat different perspective in recounting the reasons for the build up to and the consequent actions taken. It is by no means affable to the NUR or the Union Leadership of the time and makes the point that the principle was as much for parity between BR staff and Pullman as it was in opposing the extension of what was seen as a 'private company' operating trains which could therefore risk the employment of union members working on ordinary restaurant car services. The reader is recommended to visit the website in order to gain an appreciation of the opposing argument.

Was there similar disquiet consequent upon the introduction of the original steam-hauled 'South Wales Pullman'? Located files seem not to comment upon this.

Slightly lower down the catering scale, this is the facility available to the loco crews: a small GEC electric oven with hot plate on the top. (Midland power car No 60093.)

6
BLUE PULLMAN
Timeline 1. Pullman on the London Midland Region 1960-1966

The public introduction of the new trains, particularly on the LMR, was carefully stage-managed. Considerable care was taken to ensure that staff were briefed, pantries stocked, and as referred to in the previous chapters advice given as to the suggested wording to be used by staff when making public announcements. (Note the word was 'advice' rather than 'instruction'. Staff could therefore be individuals rather than clones.)

On the LMR, two trains were available, but only one was used, the other being retained as a stand-by. This was a costly exercise, but was no doubt appreciated by the public, whose initial response was almost immediate and universal acclaim.[1] The result was that even with a supplementary fare being charged, business travellers flocked to the service, and loadings were often 100% in this the 'all-first class' train. Ironically, despite the innovation in technology represented by the new units, one throwback to Victorian times still remained, as the London Midland Region (to start with, at least) continued the tradition of using an old-fashioned, oil tail-lamp at the rear. What must Jack Howe have thought of that encumbrance on his aesthetics? (Fortunately the WR however grasped the new technology and used the centre marker light on the trailing power car fitted with a red shade.)

Away from such detail the operation of the service would not have been possible without the agreement mentioned between British Railways and the National Union of Railwaymen (NUR) stating that existing BR restaurant car staff would be seconded to the Pullman Car Co. We should also recall the undertaking given by BR that no further expansion of Pullman services would take place unless until a long-term agreement had been reached over the wider question of rail catering on both conventional and Pullman services. The year 1960 therefore witnessed the introduction of the new trains on both the LMR and WR, and in reality the peak of their success as well, passengers riding (deliberate pun) on a wave of enthusiasm with the trains themselves clearly in what we might now refer to as their honeymoon period.

On the regions the new trains were also referred to by slightly differing names, the 'Midland Pullman' for the service on the LMR, but just 'Pullman' by the WR; these designations were also carried high on the sides of the respective power cars. Unfortunately despite the auspicious start, said honeymoon would not last long as economic pressures came to exert pressure for maximum stock utilization – never to be achieved on the LMR – while as we know the trains were to be plagued by consistent complaints about their rough riding. The peak years were therefore 1960 to about 1965 but at the same time we also know it was not long before public complaints over rough riding came to the surface, hardly surprising when this issue was already known to officialdom. Indeed it could even be argued that it was downhill all the way from 1960 if one was a cynic, although it must also be admitted the re-collections of those who saw or experienced Blue Pullman first hand are very positive. The positive vibes usually emanated from those who travelled once or just on the odd occasion. It was the regular traveller who became the vociferous critic.

But on Monday 4 July 1960 all that was in the future, for this was the start of the public service, commencing from Manchester and utilising what was deemed as 'Set 2' having power car M60092 at the London end of the train.[2]

Manchester's Lord Mayor Arthur Donovan blew the whistle and waved the flag to launch the new service watched by Station Master John Balmer, Mr F. D. M. Harding OBE, Pullman Car Co MD, and other dignitaries. This same set (train) maintained the service for the whole of the first week and, no doubt in a carefully orchestrated plan, arrived seven minutes early at St Pancras after the first up journey – although we can be certain special care was taken to ensure that everything went to plan! (Cynicism is

Public timetable, March 1963.

LEFT The first evening departure – 6.10 pm from St Pancras – to Manchester Central leaves London with an approving and appreciative audience. The LMR would develop this admiration; after all it was also the first regular Pullman service ever to run between the two cities. The journal Diesel Railway Traction for July 1960 carried two articles on the Blue Pullman sets broadly similar to those that appeared in the Railway Gazette around the same time. The first piece was specific to the air-conditioning and auxiliary engines and makes the point, as indeed did others, that the second auxiliary set would normally only be necessary at times of extreme weather but was also '… a standby as necessary'. This also summed up much of the concept of the trains – having a standby 'generator/train available' – almost as if the concept of reliability and availability was still a new idea which the railway had somehow failed to grasp. It must be remember that in 1960 reliability and availability was still rooted in the steam era and it is acknowledged that trying to fit a machine which could operate successfully over a greater number of hours within a 24hr period compared with steam was something the timetable planners were struggling to come to terms with. To be fair of course this was not entirely their fault, attempting to fit diesel traction into existing schedules, the latter dictated by the speed of the lowest common denominator – the steam freight service – was not easy, whilst it must be admitted and was of course later proven, the need for a Pullman luxury trains was restricted very much to daytime/normal working hours. Attempts at running mid-day services were never totally successful either on the LMR or WR whilst no night-time Pullman services are ever believed to have operated. *The Transport Treasury*

135

not intended here; after all why should the LMR not have wanted to put on a good show.)

At St Pancras there was a ceremony to launch the trip back to Manchester with the Lord Mayor of London, the Right Honourable Sir Edmund Stockdale, and Mr J. G. Handley (formerly of Bridlington and Sunderland), the Station Master, leading the event.

The first 'down' run back to Manchester that evening was presumably handled similarly, and it put on a spectacular display, covering the first 40 miles from St Pancras as far as Flitwick in just 32 minutes – a gain of almost six minutes in net running time. Additionally, the speed capability of the new sets, allowed them to breach the summit of the 1 in 119 Sharnbrook bank (between Bedford and Wellingborough) at 70mph – a feat almost unheard of previously.

A young John Huxley witnessed the 'Midland Pullman' in its first week: 'My Dad Richard Huxley worked for an insurance company and travelled by "Midland Pullman" in the first week. My trainspotting pals and I raced to Chorlton cum Hardy to watch this "Blue Streak" race by. My Dad brought back the souvenir brochure. Once the sets didn't have number value for us they sort of became part of the scenery. I did manage to get a pic of an evening run at Chorlton Cum Hardy'.

Derek James was an engineer and travelled throughout Europe on trains. His son Richard recalls 'Dad had travelled on the TEE and thought the "Midland Pullman" compared well inside with the TEE with terrific food served. The downside was the rough ride.'

Nothing quite like the trains had ever been seen in the UK before hence, allied to careful marketing, BR was quick to take advantage of the tremendous publicity they generated. This was in part because of their appearance and vibrant colour, indeed the public could hardly miss the impact both in practical terms as well as in leaflet and newspaper advertising. Posters – those issued by the LMR were of the chrome-litho type printed in nine colours and based on a beautiful design by A. N. Woolstenholme. It depicted a unit at speed passing through the Derbyshire countryside and carried the slogan: *'The New MIDLAND PULLMAN First Class de-luxe travel — Supplementary fares The last word in rail comfort Limited accommodation, book in advance.'*

These appeared at numerous principal stations and were displayed not just at stations on the route of the new trains, but anywhere on the (LMR)[3] system where it was felt there might be the hope of attracting the attention of a wider audience. The posters also appeared on the underground At the time of writing there is a faded and peeling BP poster from 1960 in a disused area of Euston's underground.

Aside from the pictorial grab, the poster showed the original timings of the new service, which was (originally) scheduled to depart from Manchester (Monday to Friday only[4]) at 8.50am, pick up at Cheadle Heath at 9.04am, and arriving at St. Pancras at 12.03pm. The return journey left the capital at 6.10pm, stopping to set down at Cheadle Heath at 9.07pm, arriving at Manchester Central at 9.21pm. Information was also given about the lunchtime 'fill-in' service for the same set: 12.45pm from St Pancras to Leicester (London Road), arriving at 2.10pm. After just a 23-minute turnaround, the train set off on its way back to London, arriving at 4.00pm.

There was even a special archway over the departure platform at St Pancras with the facility to advertise the Manchester and Leicester services.

One set only was required daily, the spare originally kept at Derby (exactly whereabouts is not reported), but readily available should a problem occur with the train currently in use. Derby was just 60 miles from Manchester, but nearly 130 from St Pancras, so it is easy to see why the original decision to base the spare set at Reddish (Manchester) was quickly revised – Leicester would have been more central still and almost equidistant between London and Manchester as well as having the advantage of being the destination for the fill-in turn – whether this was ever considered is not reported. Even so Reddish would remain the 'home depot' for both sets throughout their life on the LMR.

For the first few months of operation, the one set in operation was covering 578 miles daily which included the return Leicester turn. One 'Midland Pullman' driver was Harry Bailey, who at the age of 56 leapt at the chance to re-train at the University of Manchester Institute of Science and Technology (UMIST), this after 40 years on steam at Gorton. Harry's daughter Sandra and nephew David recall Harry was a modest man who was very pleased to embrace the new technology. He went on to become an instructor himself and was always poring over diagrams and pictures of new locomotives.

'He (Harry) found some people's sentimentality for steam unfathomable. They were all anyone knew for a long time and while they were magnificent beasts they were hot and cold at the same time, hard work physically, dirty and he was getting older by this time. By contrast the Blue Pullman was sleek, modern, clean and very comfortable. It was worth the studying for the comfort and my mother appreciated his uniform not being covered in so much grit and grease.'

The drivers peaked caps sported metal 'Midland Pullman' badges although whilst the units were on test and being filmed by the BTF film unit the drivers still had standard 'British Railways' badges.

The 132 first class 'Midland Pullman' passengers were attended to by a staff of 14, excluding the operating staff of four: Driver, Second Driver, Guard and a travelling fitter. The use of the term 'second driver' is interesting, a further reference being made to the same role in 1964, whilst there is reason to believe that this post was common from the outset on both the LMR and WR. It is likely the position was required at the insistence of the unions due to the speed of the trains (unique at the time). A similar arrangement prevailed for some years following the introduction of the later HST sets although then double manning was stipulated when speeds exceeded 110mph. Hence HST schedules at weekends were deliberately slowed to negate the need. Likewise, it is believed (but cannot be

Two days after the start of the public service, the Pullman was still drawing admiring looks from the platform end on 6 July as it departs from St Pancras with the 12.45 Leicester working. These 'official' views taken from the privileged viewpoint of the station signal box show the train leaving the station. Tantalisingly one of the files at the National Archive, 'AN160/70', contains two pages of official photo reference numbers and descriptions, 'DM6839 to DM6849, and DM6852 to DM6857', devoted solely to recording the preparation for arrival and subsequent departure of the first day's service. None of these images appear to have survived. Whilst the majority of the caption information from these missing views refers to the names of those shown and their positions (see Appendix 12), the information for the very first view, DM6839, contains a useful snippet, 'Ticket inspector F. J. Hancock fixes the name board over the specially painted blue cabin at the entrance to No 6 platform watched by Mr J. G. Handley (S.M.)'. We may conclude that Platform 6 was the one regularly used for the trains and that possibly the name board was also a permanent fixture. *LMR PRO* (See Appendix 12).

137

It is indeed a great pity that is has only been possible to access a very few of the LMR (and WR) PRO images for as with the previous views they afford a tempting glimpse of what had once been taken. This pair show the 'Midland Pullman' (the actual service is not reported) in the vicinity of Radlett/Elstree on 26 July 1960. The first image depicts an up – London bound – working, with the second a down train. For the morning up train from Manchester the timings were sharp. There were two reasons for this, firstly the new train had to be shown to its potential customers as having a distinct advantage so far as speed and thus journey time was concerned, but it also had to take opportunities to keep out of the way of other trains. Accordingly the up morning service took just under 3¼ hours and was even quicker heading north in the evening. Passing Bedford, the 49.6 miles up to town were timed for 84mph, which included an uphill section at 1 in 200. *LMR PRO*

On 7 July 1960, the up train is seen passing Silkstream Junction, Hendon and will arrive at St Pancras in just a few minutes. Accompanying the service would be the travelling fitter (this contemporary term is used rather than the modern term 'technician'). Despite the literally hundreds, nay thousands, of papers studied for this work nowhere is there full mention of what his duties might have been on an uneventful trip. We do know that in one of the BP films we see a box of tools being lifted into the engine compartment and it is reasonable to assume there was a similar box located in each power car, otherwise one can almost visualise the scene of a grimy artisan, spanner in hand, purposefully making his way past diners in business suits who are themselves holding glasses of chateau-le-whatever! Hopefully of course there would have been little for the man to attend to but I think we can also assume his duties would not solely be limited to the main engines as he would also have had responsibility for basically everything, mechanical and electrical – possibly even kitchen gas fittings as well. *LMR PRO*

confirmed) that the position of the travelling fitter, a role referred to in more detail when dealing with the WR sets in the next chapter, remained constant throughout the life of the sets, one man being needed per set in service.

Both six-car sets (for car numbers, see 'Description of Blue Pullman cars' at the start of this book) were available for service from the outset but with the one on permanent stand-by, maximum passenger loadings would be required from the outset to achieve any degree of profitability. The trains themselves were rotated weekly and because there was no weekend service, each train was in revenue earning use for just five days out of every fourteen, a usage figure equivalent to 35.7% excluding stand-by time – worst still if the actual journey times were taken into account expressed as a percentage of hours in a fortnight. Here taking 336hrs as the figure representing 100% the usage figure was just 13.75%.

The LMR sets were never intended to work in multiple and consequently no coupling code symbol was given. Technically, no other sets were similarly compatible so as to be able to work with a BP train either. (BR DMU sets were given a coupling code/symbol to indicate which might be coupled together and be mechanically/electrically compatible and so controlled by a single driver, e.g.: blue star; orange star; yellow diamond; red triangle; white circle.) Whenever possible regular maintenance on the BP sets was concentrated on half a train set at a time thus enabling half a train to be still available as a spare if needed – a practice also adopted on some foreign railways at the time. This maintenance work was carried out at Reddish. However if there were faults staff would come over from Derby. Whether the 'mirror' formation of the Blue Pullman trains was intentionally modelled on continental practice is not known, but in any event if a single half-set only were available as a spare there was always the risk it might need to be turned before being available for use.

In order to appeal to the business community, the schedule for the new service had to be fast, and was indeed set at an average of just over 60mph each way (the same figure that had been quoted as desirable back in the planning stage), and this over a distance of just over the 189 miles between Manchester and London. At the time it was claimed to be the train with the fastest average speed operating on BR; in truth, some contemporary Eastern Region and Western Region services might have legitimately disputed this claim, but under the corporate BR banner no-one was going to try to usurp the prestige of the new service.

One of the very few photographs located showing the train at Manchester Central – arriving here as empty stock so we know this was in preparation for the morning departure. This would be train No 3C43, the 6.30am Reddish to Manchester Central, arriving at 07.00. At the end of the day the return ecs working (example given is 11 September 1961 to 12 June 1962) from Manchester Central was 3H81, due to depart at 9.43pm arriving Reddish 10.08pm. Reddish was also the depot for the EM1 and EM2 locomotives working under 1,500V DC overhead electric wires between Manchester and Sheffield hence it is a bit surprising to note that that it was only later that 'electrification warning flashes' were attached to the front of the BP sets. On 16 August 1960 a BP passenger, H. A. Wainwright, wrote to BR complaining about the state of the station at Manchester and also about the track in the area of the Trent valley, which he described as 'rough', although interestingly it was the track and not the train that was being blamed – at this stage. Reminiscences from a railwayman Lawrence Cody about the train also mention the working of the up service: 'I recall a signalman I worked with telling me that as soon as it left Manchester, the Station Master at Cheadle Heath would ring up the boxes all the way to the Peak Forest area, instructing signalman not to do any shunt moves and more importantly "… DO NOT STOP THE PULLMAN". My colleague's comment to me was, "That train was nothing but a nuisance, it stopped the job till it had passed". Mind you, I do not recall him telling me it had a 4-4-6* bell signal but maybe he did. I do know it was my favourite train, but my colleague certainly did not sympathise with me, as far as the job went.' (* was a special LMR bell-code for the Pullman service.) In similar vein, images of the train picking-up/setting down at Cheadle Heath are few although an excellent colour set was taken by the late W. (Bill) Buckley which appears in Backtrack Vol 9 No 2, for February 1995. *Colin Martin*

Example Working Timetable for the evening down departure from St Pancras at 6.10pm. The WTT for 1963 had varied the timing slightly compared with the example given in the caption to the previous view with the complete M-F daily diagram for the set as follows: Reddish Depot dep. 6.55am '3C43', arr. Manchester Central 7.15am. Depart 7.45am as '1C43'. Arr. St Pancras 10.55am, dep. 11.15am as '1D08'. Arr Nottingham Midland 1.10pm. After unloading stable Nottingham Carriage sidings. Dep. Nottingham Midland 3.30pm as '1C71', arr St Pancras 5.26pm. Dep. St Pancras 6.10pm as '1H20' arr. Manchester Central 9.20pm. Depart Manchester Central as '3H81' arr. Reddish Depot 10.08pm.

6 · BLUE PULLMAN – TIMELINE 1. PULLMAN ON THE LONDON MIDLAND REGION 1960-1966

Christopher Lade – PCCo Conductor, *Brighton Belle*
Bert Viney – PCCo Steward, *Brighton Belle*
Julian Morel – PCCo Catering Superintendent
Frank Harding OBE – PCCo General Manager
Pearte – PCCo Conductor

Pullman staff at Manchester Central.

LEFT Reddish depot with one of its more usual residents, 1,500V DC 'EM2' electric No 27006 Pandora.

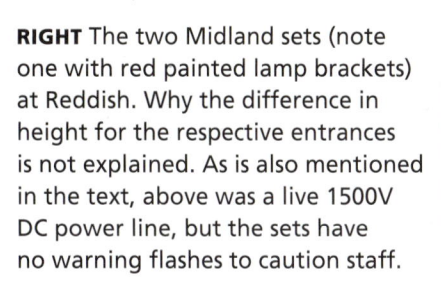

RIGHT The two Midland sets (note one with red painted lamp brackets) at Reddish. Why the difference in height for the respective entrances is not explained. As is also mentioned in the text, above was a live 1500V DC power line, but the sets have no warning flashes to caution staff.

141

ABOVE New (or freshly overhauled) set on one of the outside shed roads at Reddish.

LEFT Shore supply connected at Reddish. This set with red painted horns! A local embellishment perhaps?

Notwithstanding the criticism on the same topic in *Modern Railways*, where the new train did score was in its power-to-weight ratio compared with a conventional locomotive (steam or diesel) and its train. The new 'Midland Pullman' six-car set weighed 292 tons empty, say 310 tons fully laden, a considerable improvement over a steam or diesel locomotive hauling an average 12-coach set, which might turn the scales in excess of 550 tons (albeit with a far greater passenger capacity). Having a fixed formation, maximum loadings were therefore predictable and so with known power outputs from the engines, timetabling was similarly conventional and in consequence schedules easier to maintain.

Of course at that time any comparisons were deliberately made against the relatively pedestrian steam schedules that still existed, the biggest difficulty to the operators not the running of the train itself but attempting to fit a fast diesel service into a timetable where the behaviour especially of steam-hauled freight trains in particular was difficult. This was recognised by David Blee, General Manager of the LMR, in a memorandum dated 12 July 1960 just a week after the train's introduction, and no doubt typical of the frustration that occurred at the time: 'Timekeeping of the "Midland Pullman" MUST be maintained.' Blee's outburst had resulted from a 12-minute delay to the new service caused by a signalman's error on the previous day in accepting the 8.50am Leicester–Wellingborough freight ahead of the up morning Pullman. It wproved the point though; 'one-offs', such as a Press run or the inaugural services were possible even if they required considerable effort on the part of numerous members of staff, a point proved with the deliberately staged early arrivals of both the initial up and down services just eight days earlier. However, a beleaguered man on the ground, under pressure from all sides – Control, the timetable and train crews – could be forgiven for getting it wrong, and the wretched signalman in question was just the unfortunate example. Similar situations no doubt occurred on countless other occasions, but as time passed, perhaps the General Manager was not always informed, or did he become less interested?

But not all difficulties were preventable, such as on 27 July 1960, just over three weeks after the new service had commenced, when a tyre worked loose on the fifth vehicle of the set in passenger use (the exact vehicle and set are not identified). Clearly the situation could have been disastrous, although the report calmly states that, '. . . a fire was caused as a result of the tyre dragging on the adjacent brake block. This was extinguished by the crew, after which the train continued at the reduced speed of 60mph'. *(60mph was a reduced speed . . !)* It might also appear strange in allowing the train to continue but it must be stressed we have no further details of the incident. What is recorded is that the tyres on all the cars were subsequently changed, although from subsequent other (unrelated) reports it would appear the sets were not withdrawn until the work had been carried – again strange without further information. Cross-referencing must also now take place however as we are not told how the WR sets were affected. Presumably they were similarly

Blue Pullman crews probably with a loco inspector; on the extreme left is Driver Edwards. (Edwards had a particular dislike of chewing gum but for a joke the others presented him with a full box of 'Wrigleys'!) The men working the train were from Kentish Town and wore a smart 'battledress' type uniform. They worked 'double home' with an overnight in Manchester. ('Midland Pullman' stewards worked longer hours and basically covered the complete day service.) According to the recollections of Melvin Thorley, on 7 August 1962 the Kentish Town driver was not, for whatever reason, available to take the morning up train. As a result a Gorton man drove to St Pancras conducted by a man from Manchester Trafford Park. (Gorton men were unit familiar as they worked the sets as ecs between Manchester Central and Reddish, although they would not be route familiar through to St Pancras.) Manchester Trafford Park driver Jimmy Gilmour was in charge on another 'awayday' when Preston North End FC hired the set for a special run to Wembley – conductors all the way!

ABOVE Manchester Central. The shabby appearance is hardly in keeping with the prestige train. Seemingly the customer who complained about the station did so with some justification. Just how many times were tickets checked for the service?

ABOVE Individual blind adjustment so clearly first class. Within a year of their introduction a suggestion had been made that the accommodation within the power cars on the LMR be designated 'non-smoking'. This was not acted upon with the chairman of Pullman Frank Harding reporting this was a 'small problem'. Another issue commented upon was the 'rubbery' feel of the table tops; who might have commented upon this is not stated but again no change was made.

modified, or at least checked (if so, this would still have been before they entered public service). The subject of tyres will also come up again later in this chapter.

Despite this incident (which appears not to have attracted any adverse Press reaction), it could be expected that after the first few weeks of operation loadings might reduce. This did not take place, and what occurred instead was a somewhat longer honeymoon for, according to railway figures, loadings were consistently high and amounted to rarely less than 100 passengers per trip. Unfortunately what we do not know for certain is the loading required to achieve break-even in running costs although some clue is possible from the following paragraphs.

Apart from ticket receipts, catering sales were also good and whilst the following was written sometime later in 1963, most of the principles applied from the outset: 'Although not all morning passengers eat breakfast, practically everyone has dinner in the evening … since even the most miserly passenger finds it near-impossible to sit hungry in a coach full of feeders.'

Still (temporarily) forward in 1963 and on the subject of catering, the decision was taken to continue with a full

St Pancras 11.00am and the arrival of the re-timed (earlier) up Pullman once again receiving admiring glances. As mentioned, the LMR continued to capitalise on the look and we must say the popularity of the trains and were similarly determined to keep the service in the public eye. Consequently there was regular press advertising. As examples, *The Times* ran an advert/feature in its 'Reporting Railway Progress' series. BP was No 9 (what were Nos 1-8 and were there others after No 9?). The feature was centred upon the heading, 'Very important Passenger', and described how a business traveller could expect to travel on the new Pullman (both LMR and WR) trains. It was accompanied by a breakdown of the preparation, Pullman service thereon, and departure from the train in the morning with a repeat example on the return run. The whole was illustrated with 11 images of the train and interior. Almost a year after their introduction on the LMR (27 June 1961), there was a three-column advert in the same newspaper. 'Express Success' was once more aimed at the business traveller and ended with the words, 'Midland Pullman – part of the new look of today's London Midland.' There may of course have been other advertising in the interim. Finally we should mention that advertising in the form of eight-inch-depth double-column pieces were placed in the following at different periods, *Evening News/Evening Standard/Star, Guardian, Manchester Evening Chronicle, Manchester Evening News, Leicester Mercury, Leicester Evening, Mail, Times, Telegraph, Financial Times, Observer, Sunday Times, Economist*, (not the *Express, Mail, Mirror* or the *Sketch*) together with various monthly magazines, the titles of the latter were not stated.
Colour Rail DE2998/Trevor Owen.

cooking service on board, rather than the original proposal for pre-packaged food. (Was there a view from 'somebody' that full catering might be dispensed with? If so we know not what, from whom or why.) Indeed readers will recall the discussions prior to the train entering service over the merits, or otherwise, of frozen and micro-waved food versus freshly prepared fare, the decision to retain cooking facilities a factor in favour of the service provided. At the same time there was according to a contemporary (but un-named source), '… much scope for imagination by the chefs themselves', but said without any further elucidation. Indeed it was the evening (return) service that created the greatest demand for catering. Assuming a full load of 132 passengers this would equate to each chef being required to serve up to 66 full dinners. By comparison the London bound service had perhaps an average of only 24 passengers requiring a full breakfast[5], the balance of the catering requirement coming from continental breakfasts and cups of coffee. Later in the day on the 'fill-in' Leicester/Nottingham duty where with an average of perhaps just 30 fare-paying passengers (equivalent to a meagre 22.7% loading), there might be just 12 who would partake of lunch, the reason for this poor take up considered due to several already having pre-arranged (late) lunch appointments at their destinations. The return service from Leicester/Nottingham at 3.30pm would similarly create only a light catering need: 'afternoon tea' or a beverage alone.

Modern Railways in July 1963 reported on the working day for the on-board chefs (and assistants – two kitchens so four men per train) as follows, 'It is a long day for the chefs and their assistants. Departing from Manchester at 7.45am … Arrival in Manchester at 9.20pm ends a 13hr 35min tour of duty. Each crew member has one working day off in five; the relief chef takes over the duties of each of the regular train's crew of four in turn, and thus has one day in five free himself. Whilst the cooking staff appreciate the train's speed and smoothness in acceleration and deceleration; they greatly dislike its occasional exuberance in riding.'[6] This does not take into account preparation and perhaps cleaning time before the start and after the end of service, nor even where the staff might lodge overnight. It could even be said to be an early example of 'flexible rostering', a term which came to cause the railways so many industrial problems involving footplate crews some years later.

For the present and certainly so far as the Manchester service was concerned, it was all good economic news for BR, although it must be cautioned that we do not have access to the loading details at regular intervals. However it was officially reported in November 1960 that the Manchester service would bring in an estimated surplus over expenditure of £46,000 annually, presumably also after depreciation costs were allowed for (although, at this stage, this amount was not stated). Other papers refer to a 16.5% profit on cost for the 'Midland Pullman' between July and November 1960.

This is an interesting statement and it would be even more interesting if it were possible to digest the reported 16.5% profitability – pun definitely intentional this time! Again what we do not know from this 16.5% is if this percentage represented profitability over the two sets or just related to the one train actually being used? If the latter then the spare second set was a depreciating asset potentially achieving zero return for half a year – based on the premise it would only be in use every other week.

Taking into account inflation, it is always risky when quoting actual fares five plus decades later, but as an

ABOVE LEFT Leicester London Road, up working 10 September 1964. *Martin Welch*

ABOVE RIGHT On the same day as Martin Welch took his views of the test working at St Pancras he later took another view of the return working. In his own words, 'I thought I would try and get a shot of it returning through Kentish Town. I hadn't been there before, and so did not realise how grotty [the station] it was. Anyway, here it is for what it is worth. I bet no-one else took a shot here!'

RIGHT A favourite image carried over from the earlier hardback has to be this one of the portable 'contemporary modern office'. The lady, probably a 'top secretary/ p.a.', is dictating from hand-written notes. So far as the trains themselves were concerned, BR were probably very wise to determine how a single, or, in the case of the WR, two out of the available three units, performed in service before going 'all-out' for 100% usage. As we know, this never occurred on the LMR and when it did on the WR there were times when recourse had to be made to the standby trains – see Appendix 8. So a thought – why did BR not consider buying trains that were identical in formation and seating? This in turn might have been easier to justify having a single stand-by set shared between both regions … We also do not know exactly how many times on the LMR (and on the WR up to September 1961), unscheduled recourse had to be made to the spare unit. (On the SR, the three 'Brighton Belle' Pullman sets operated with two in use and one spare for most of their lives. No information is available as to if these services ever had to have loco-hauled substitutions.)

example from the time, the basic first class single fare between Manchester Central and St Pancras by Blue Pullman was then £3 9s (£3.45), added to which was the Pullman supplement of £1, with meals a further optional expense. From Cheadle Heath there was a saving of 9d (4p) on the basic fare only.

Allowing for the Pullman supplement, this was slightly higher than the comparable weekday BEA (British European Airways) ticket for a flight between Manchester and London, which was set at £4 1s (£4.05) single. The air journey also took 30 to 40 minutes less, even allowing for the time it took to get to and from the airports. (Average wages of the period were little more than £13 weekly, so in reality both services were out of the reach of all but the wealthier business class.) Having aimed the new rail service at the business community and charging higher fares as a result, had been a risk, but it was certainly one that appeared to have paid off handsomely. (An even crueller example is when attempting to compare rail with air in late 2019. With discounts and short notice savings possible exact figures cannot be accurately be given but a single first class rail ticket from Manchester around the BP departure time is in the order of £160 if booked on the day and air travel about £180 although for the latter first class is not available.)

'3F' 0-6-0T No 47449 propelling the failed mid-day Pullman service back into Cricklewood Depot on 1 February 1962, following the incident at Haverstock Tunnel. Subsequent examination revealed that only parts of the air-conditioning system were affected. Despite the importance of the various servicing facilities (Cricklewood, Reddish, and, on the WR, Old Oak Common, etc) few photographs have been located of the trains at these establishments. Under normal circumstances, the peak daily mileage for the trains on the LMR, which included the Nottingham fill-in, was 650 miles daily, which was then comparable to a European TEE train. A decade or so later the HST sets in service on BR were achieving 1,000 miles daily. *Alec Swain*

Midland '4F' No 44262 moving what is a half-set and, it appears, a brake van attached to the rear. If so, then this was an unfitted train, which from the headcode is shown as 'unfitted but express working'. It is believed to have been recorded in the Derby area. *J. W. Sutherland*

Economically the gamble appeared to have paid off but on the train itself there were already the first rumblings of discontent and not surprisingly initially over the ride. A reference in the surviving records at the National Archive refers to correspondence on comfort between the manufacturers, the LMR and BRB as early as 5 September 1960, at which time the train had been in service for just nine weeks.

Unfortunately for the present at least further detail is not forthcoming. There may be several reasons for this. Firstly and perhaps the most obvious is that the paperwork simply does not survive and the other is your authors have not been diligent enough to find it! But another option and allied to the first, is that at the time it was simply not considered an important issue, but one likely to go away in time. Possible credence to this theory is that just a couple of years later almost every bump, lurch, tilt, knock, bang, crash, blow, wallop, thump, roll and sway was indeed seemingly recorded. Was it then the case that back in 1960 it was considered either passenger imagination, an inconvenience or more likely down to the track rather than the train? Later on having by then also realised there were indeed serious issues involved it is perhaps understandable that far more notice was taken of vehicle ride allied to passenger comfort than perhaps had been given credence to back in September 1960.

However for the present we return to September 1960 and a complaint not so much about the ride quality as the practicalities of accessing the inside window seat on the train. Surviving files refer to 'comments' and 'letters', both in the plural, over the interiors of the trains, these being sent to either BR or the National Press. (Not necessarily but perhaps sometimes to both.) One example has been located, from a Miss Campbell writing to *The Guardian*, who commented that it was necessary to adopt a 'contorted crab movement' in order to gain access to the inside window seat. The reply from BR was slightly tongue-in-cheek: '. . . seats are moveable so as to ensure that those who have no wish to indulge in the kind of movement Miss Campbell describes, are not constrained to do so' – but from a practical passenger perspective the seats were not that easily moveable unless actually being sat on at the time, so perhaps Miss Campbell did have a point especially if the previous occupant had left the seat in a position close to the table. An easy remedy would have been to ensure staff checked all seats before boarding and to make sure each was set back as far as possible, this seemingly easy remedy was not reported but had it been – and also publicised – then surely useful 'brownie points' might have been achieved. The basic problem was of course the fixed table design, something readers will recall had been considered in the design stage. At that time the argument of having the tables laid ready for meals prior to departure won the day, it would be some decades and a different era before part folding tables – for outside seat passengers – were introduced on some designs to cater for such difficulties. Even so it is interesting to note that the one recorded complaint was from a lady passenger especially at a time when the stated dominance of passengers was definitely from the male gender.

This and the other complaints over the riding also passed across the desk of J. F. Harrison (BR CME). He penned an internal note about the sets, of which unfortunately only the last page survives, but on which this final, somewhat brusque, paragraph is written, 'I am not dealing with the various comments that the public have such a lot of time to write about, such as train seats, etc, because it is all a matter of personal opinion, and anyone who travels by air and does not complain, compared with travelling in the Blue Train, wants their head examined'. Perhaps so, but Harrison missed the point so far as the seating was concerned; BP was a premier service. Airline seats as most will know, are indeed notoriously difficult to access particularly those furthest from the aisle and especially when allocated to an individual of, shall we say, a more corpulent frame. We are not in any way suggesting Miss Campbell might have been of such girth, but instead that she probably did not expect to encounter such a situation on a new luxury train – especially perhaps if she had travelled first class Pullman in the past where the seats were not even sometimes fixed.

From figures quoted in the *Daily Telegraph* during October 1960 (why this newspaper should pick up on this point is not known) it would also seem to appear the full-load honeymoon was now well and truly over. The newspaper instead reporting that passenger loadings were now less than 60%, a figure totally at odds with the 100 passengers per trip figure quoted by BR. (BR's 100 persons figure translates to an average 76% loading, whilst the percentage given in the newspaper represented a passenger loading of just 79 persons. Even so care should still be taken with these numbers as there is no indication as to exactly what the Press were referring to; the 'Midland Pullman' service to and from Manchester only, the addition of loadings on the mid-day 'fill-in' turn, a combination of both, or even taking into account the loadings with the WR trains which by then were also running. It is the opinion of the present author that the numbers quoted by the *Daily Telegraph* are an average of the LMR sets including the fill-in turn. The latter's poor customer patronage from the outset certainly drawing down that 100 average.)

Even so BR (here we refer to both the LMB and BRB) must have been concerned at this leak of what may even have been misinformation. It was out there, in the public domain with the problem now that to issue a strenuous denial could even be taken as reinforcing the poor figures especially at a time when the press were hungry for bad-news stories with which to knock the railway industry generally. 'Twas really ever thus.

LMR half sets, regretfully in both cases at unreported locations. In the facing image power car No 60091 (Set 1) leads, whilst in the colour image, taken in 1963, the part set depicted here appears fresh from overhaul and the corridor blank will also be noted. *Unknown and Colour Rail 284315/Trevor Owen*

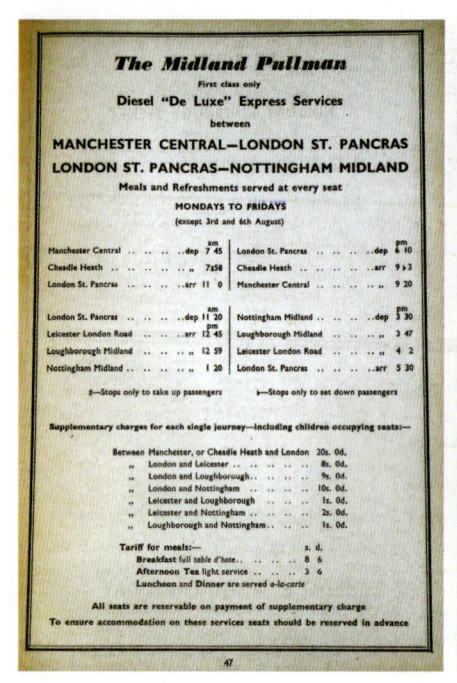

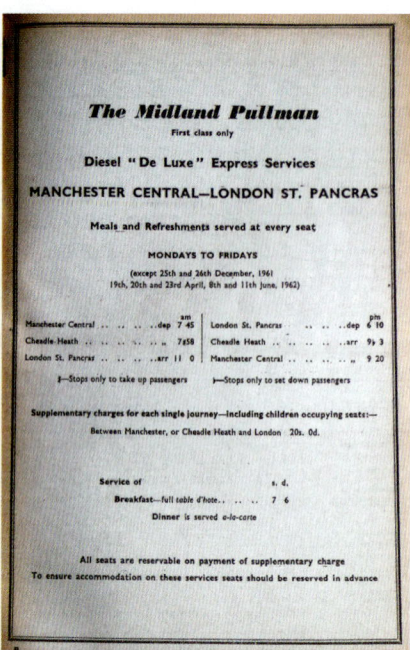

Public timetable/adverts – post 1961.

Perhaps as a semi-public counter the London Midland Staff Magazine for November 1960 carried an article by one Miles Wyvern entitled, 'Quietest, quickest ... that's the "Midland Pullman"'. Much of what followed will not be new to the reader but Mr Wyvern does add a few salient points which are shown in italics although it should be stressed they did not appear in italics in the original piece. Even so we should ask who was this aimed at and what readership might the LMR magazine hope to reach? Certainly not the readers of the *Daily Telegraph*, and we may perhaps instead see it for what it really was, a morale booster for staff, confirmation of the union staffing arrangements, and a reminder of progress in railway modernisation.

'When you board the "Midland Pullman" at Manchester Central, as I did the other day, the first impression you get is one of luxury and soundlessness. Once through the mirror-finished vestibule doors, the familiar station noises are cut off with disconcerting suddenness. You're in a warm air-conditioned world of foot-hugging carpets, clean table-linen and inviting upholstery. Even the conversation of nearby passengers comes through as a mere murmur, so well are the internal acoustics arranged.

'A smart attendant showed me to my seat, seizing my hat and coat and placed them quickly on the rack – presumably lest I should attempt, unpardonably, to do that little chore myself. Since most of my fellow passengers were displaying an air of sang-froid, which apparently bespoke of a life-time of travelling on such a train, I stifled my interest and curiosity with a similar cloak of sophistication. Settling down in the armchair seat and promising myself a session with the two intriguing seat adjustment controls later in the journey, I opened that morning's *Guardian* and attempted to read.

'A smooth start. It says much for that newspaper that, surrounded by so much to distract my interest, I eventually became absorbed. When a few minutes later I looked at my watch it showed 8.51. Good heavens! A minute past departure time and we hadn't moved . . . correction, we hadn't apparently moved. A look through the windows showed the soundless outside world rolling by. We had actually pulled out of the station without the slightest sensation of movement.

'I was able to check the smooth starting of the train after its single intermediate stop at Cheadle Heath, where several more passengers joined the train. The departure was a beauty – and spoke well for the draw and buff gear between the coaches, which was specially designed to assist in the smooth pick-up of speed by the train when starting. Even as we gathered speed there was no increase in noise, no vibration. It was uncanny. Like travelling in a vacuum. Fifty miles an hour felt like five on this train. Trains going the other way glided past the window like ghosts, quickly, silently. The clickety-clack of the rail joints was all but inaudible even in tunnels.

'As we slipped steadily along at 70-80mph leaving Manchester far astern and entering the beautiful mist-shrouded Peak District, it struck me that one of the effects of quietness and comfort inside the train was that passengers tended to take a much greater interest in the passing scenery. They stared with fascination as the views from the windows changed abruptly when the train emerged from cuttings and tunnels. It was all rather like watching a silent film in glorious colour.

'Attracting attention. The windows are double-glazed, so there is no misting, and no penetration by outside noise. In sunny weather Venetian blinds can be lowered and adjusted between the two panes of glass. If you have ever had the luck to travel in a really swish Rolls-Royce you will have an idea of what it is like on the "Midland Pullman" – not only because of the comfort but in the stares you attract from passers-by. For the blue and cream streamliner gets a good looking over from everyone en-route – railwaymen, passengers at stations, farm workers and all manner of trackside rubbernecks. There was even one man, oddly enough in his shirtsleeves despite the chilly morning, who grimly shot us with his cine camera from a perch on the trackside fence near Harpenden. One imagined that he had rushed from his house in mid-shave and then dashed across the damp fields to be in time to record our passing.

'Motorway crawlers. One point in the journey where the sensation of speed intruded for a moment was near Luton where the M1 motorway runs parallel to the line for a mile or so. Cars which must have been travelling in the sixties appeared to be crawling as we swiftly overtook them.

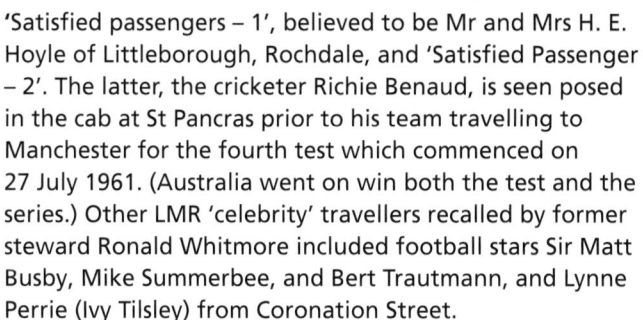

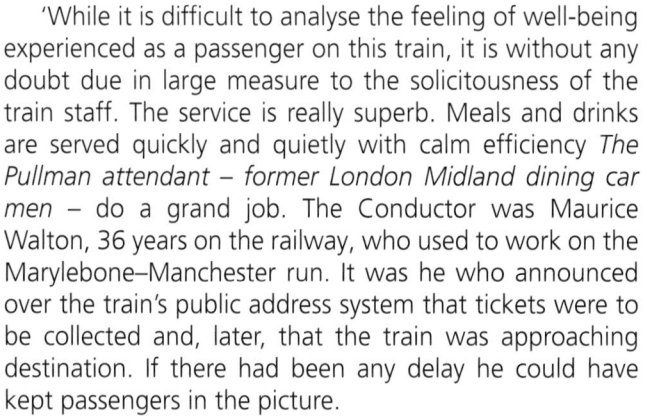

'Satisfied passengers – 1', believed to be Mr and Mrs H. E. Hoyle of Littleborough, Rochdale, and 'Satisfied Passenger – 2'. The latter, the cricketer Richie Benaud, is seen posed in the cab at St Pancras prior to his team travelling to Manchester for the fourth test which commenced on 27 July 1961. (Australia went on win both the test and the series.) Other LMR 'celebrity' travellers recalled by former steward Ronald Whitmore included football stars Sir Matt Busby, Mike Summerbee, and Bert Trautmann, and Lynne Perrie (Ivy Tilsley) from Coronation Street.

'While it is difficult to analyse the feeling of well-being experienced as a passenger on this train, it is without any doubt due in large measure to the solicitousness of the train staff. The service is really superb. Meals and drinks are served quickly and quietly with calm efficiency *The Pullman attendant – former London Midland dining car men* – do a grand job. The Conductor was Maurice Walton, 36 years on the railway, who used to work on the Marylebone–Manchester run. It was he who announced over the train's public address system that tickets were to be collected and, later, that the train was approaching destination. If there had been any delay he could have kept passengers in the picture.

'"But it doesn't do to use the p.a. system too much," he told me. "Our passengers wouldn't appreciate such intrusion. I use it only when I think it will be of help to them."

'The best in Europe. We drew into St Pancras on time feeling like VIPs. For me it was a memorable trip, a glimpse into the future of railway travel. For even though it will be a long time before all main line trains are like the "Midland Pullman", this does represent the ultimate aim.

'The six-coach train conveys 132 first class passengers and loadings on the Manchester–London journeys have been good, and are increasing. It received much favourable Press publicity when it came into service on 4 July last and its reception among businessmen has been outstandingly good. The "Midland Pullman" made a great impression on a team of eight American railway executives who recently visited Britain and six continental countries. They called it: "the best train in Europe"'.

Meanwhile 'on the ground' so to speak, investigation into the considered sub-standard riding was initially centred on the shock absorbers, and understandably so when one was found to have broken as early as August 1960. As a result, all the dampers were replaced on the stand-by six-car train and running trials carried out using this stand-by set. (From this statement alone we may assume the trains were still very much seen as the prestige service and so warranted immediate attention. It is also interesting to note there was sufficient confidence from the operators that a single train was reliable enough to maintain the service whilst the running trials with the stand-by were undertaken.)

The surviving paperwork also contains a note, 'Dampers made by Messrs Armstrong', but it is not clear whether this referred to the new items or those that had been replaced, or possibly even both.[7]

An additional problem was a fractured brake block that was discovered around the same time, although, happily, this was a one-off incident. (This is not thought to be related to the tyre incident mentioned earlier.)

But despite the replacement of the dampers, there was still continuing disquiet from the travelling public. One of the earliest public letters of complaint over the quality of the ride appearing in the *Manchester Evening Chronicle* as early as August 1960, under the heading 'With a Splash', a reference perhaps to soup or beverages. It was signed, 'A disgruntled Manchester Businessman' – a change from the other generic complainer of the time, 'Disgusted of Tunbridge Wells'!

Being serious once more, we may conclude that BR had themselves surmised that replacement of the dampers alone was not the panacea hoped for as further tests were arranged and believed now for the first time to have involved the embryonic BR Research Department at Derby. Accordingly Set 2 (presumably still arranged as M60092, M60732, M60742, M60743, M60733 and M60093) was used for riding trials in both directions between Derby and Leicester. This took place on 2 December 1960 and involved displacement measurement tests of the first six bogies (ie, the first three vehicles), in other words a half set of the complete train.

What was found was that the leading bogie of the power car (M60092) gave a very poor vertical ride, and that the first bogie of the third vehicle (parlour car M60742, over which there appear to have been more complaints generally than any other vehicle) was poor in the lateral

Evening departure time from St Pancras.

direction. However observers on board, who it was noted were also regular travellers on the train, commented on the converse that 'it was better than usual'![8]

At about the same time, additional riding tests were also carried out on what later became the BR test track at Old Dalby. Further tests were made between Derby and Leicester in January 1961, this time involving Set 1 (M60090, M60730, M60740, M60741, M60731 and M60091). Accordingly, the bogies on one set (which one is not known) were modified at Derby Works with long swing links and torsion bars and that at first appeared to offer a vast improvement. Indeed it must be said that notwithstanding the difficulties and failings with Blue Pullman earlier, at this time and also later, BR must be praised for what was a genuine attempt to resolve matters once and for all. The second set was reported as similarly modified in July 1962, after which, on 20 August 1962, further riding assessments were carried out using a 'delegation' of BR staff, again reported as being regular travellers on the service. *(So how many BR staff were regular*

Variations of damper arrangements installed in an attempt to improve the ride quality. In the first view we see Bolster Spring Damper, type AT15 2023, installed on 'B' and 'C' type bogies only. Next is the Bolster Spring Damper fitted on trailer type bogies only. After this is a Lateral Control Damper, type AT15 2027 & 2027/1, installed on all types of bogie, and finally a Primary Suspension Damper, No RW 136 also installed on 'B' and 'C' type bogies only. The actual springs used were colour coded in part to assist identification as visually all were similar. Red and green colouring indicated specific heavy positions, and blue and white for lighter positioning.

passengers – and on 'priv' tickets perhaps? What effect did this also have on the reported loadings?) This time the results were frankly disappointing as it was noted that the initial improvement had not been maintained. We may also question why the long gap between modifying the first train and second. Possibly because the results obtained from the initial modifications were not conclusive but it may also have been that a benchmark had been set against which comparisons might be made.

When published the results of the test runs were probably not unexpected, being heavy on obvious fact but falling short on specific solutions. The main conclusions were that the vertical ride over the leading bogie of the power car was poor. Qualifications then being used stipulated an accepted minimum comfort level of '6' (what this was measured against is not stated); Blue Pullman came nowhere near this, instead affording a figure of between 1.5 and 4.7 at varying speeds between 50 and 90mph. It would also be all too easy to solely concentrate on weaknesses with BP but in its favour it should be pointed out that similar measurements taken at the time on the remaining bogies gave a better vertical ride than the BR standard double-bolster bogie when these latter items were fitted with new tyres, but it was stated that hunting[9] occurred on at least two bogies (which ones were not stipulated but the temptation is to suggest these would be on the driving bogie of the parlour, which vehicle also carried the auxiliary engines) when travelling at 80mph and over, and which led to a riding factor again below '6' at this speed.

Apart from the damper replacement referred to, little else of any substance was done at this stage to improve matters, although it does seems rather pathetic to record that variously-sized pieces of rubber were incorporated in a 'trial and error' attempt to reduce any obvious knocks and banging, hardly a 'high-tech' proposition. These were evidently not considered serious in themselves but it was recognised they were at the very least disconcerting to the passengers.

The vertical movement affecting the leading bogie of the power car was also transmitted to the trailing end of the vehicle resulting in a form of see-saw action. The result was that knowledgeable travellers would deliberately avoid the seating area at the rear of the power car, and instead opted for a place midway along a vehicle. But with a steady stream of complaint letters received from the public, many expressing fears of a derailment, Derby suggested fitting CCTV cameras to the bogies, so that their behaviour could be observed at speed. In itself this would have been a technological innovation for the period but for whatever reason does not appear to have been carried out.

At this stage too we should bring in Malcolm Botham, C.Eng FIMechE, former MC engineer who kindly responded to a number of questions on the trains put to him by the present author.

'The ride problems were wholly with the power bogies. The Schlieren trailers were of good riding although a little short of the ride quality achieved by today's designs. Weight alone was not a fundamental problem, rather more it was weight distribution. But there were some serious design defects:

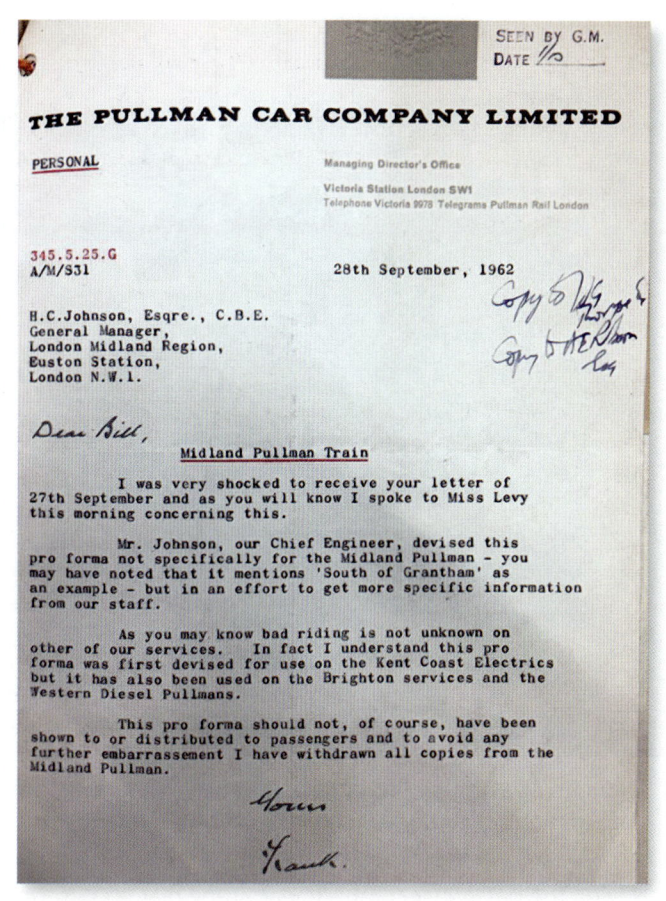

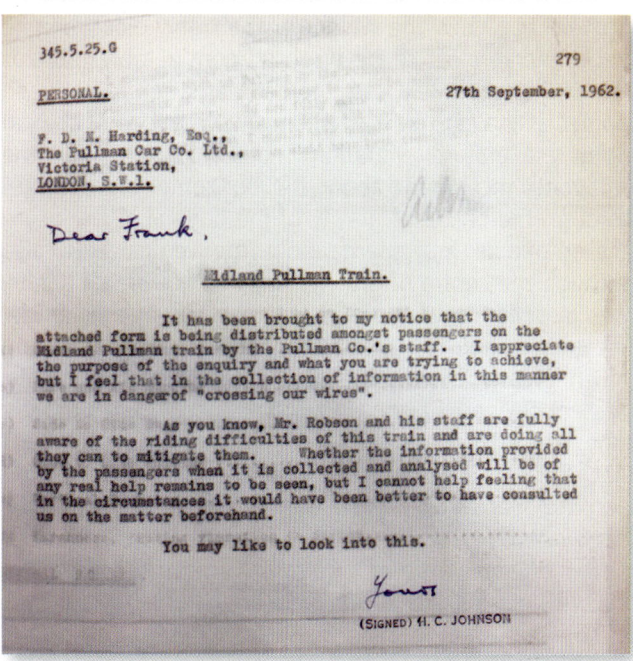

1. Having a passenger compartment at the rear end of the power car.
2. The heavy weight at the leading end of the power car, caused the powered bogies to be located thus, one at the rear end of the power car and the other at the end of the trailer car coupled to the power car.
3. Disposition of the drives between traction motors and axles.

Midland set at Wellingborough – hopefully without too many splashes in the laps of the punters! Notice the red-painted air horns; this was possibly unique to just one set. *Rail On-Line ZF-5438-95371-1-010*

Having the passenger compartment at the rear end of the power car caused the weight of the heavy diesel engine and generator set to be disposed considerably towards the driving cab away from the geometric centre between bogies of the car body. Pitch and yaw motions of the car body are natural vibration modes, pitch being the rotational movement about the horizontal axis laterally through the centre of gravity of the body and yaw being the rotational movement about the vertical axis, also through the centre of gravity. Since this centre of gravity was disposed towards the driving cab end of the vehicle, the movements at the passenger compartment were much greater than those at the cab end. Thus whilst passengers were having their coffee and soup spilt in their laps, the driver was enjoying a comfortable ride. *(PRO AN97/956 of 5 February 1957 comments that the seating accommodation of the LMR power cars could be downrated to second class – was someone aware of potential issues even at that early stage of the design or was this more of marketing issue?)*

The reason for locating the second power bogie on the trailer car was that to put it at the leading end of the power car would have caused the axle load at this end to have exceeded the allowable limit, at this time set at 17.5 tons.

The drives between the traction motors and the axles were of a design by Brown Boveri of Switzerland and as used on Swiss locomotives. The traction motors were attached to the bogie frames and were thus part of the sprung mass via the primary suspension. They drove the axles through quill drives. These were arrangements of coil springs disposed radially around the drives which could thus accommodate the vertical movements between bogie frames and axles. This is believed to have been an innovation to BR where otherwise traction motors were hung partly on the axles and partly on the bogie frames, the new arrangement appealing to the Chief Civil Engineer who was no doubt delighted at the prospect of having less damaging shocks transmitted to his tracks.

It was not the practice in those days to carry out extensive ride tests before vehicles entered passenger service. Indeed, Metro-Cammell had no facilities for such testing and BR had only service tracks on which to do so. The Blue Pullmans thus entered service straight from the drawing board as it were, although there may have been some limited test running, eg between the works and Derby.

Riding tests were carried out on one half of 'Set 2' in December 1960 – although the complete train was still coupled. *(This may even mean some of the undated photographs of the trains supposedly in service on the LMR main line may actually be post service trials. Did they then use the other half set of the formation 'on trial' as a benchmark?)*

Malcolm continues, 'Thus it was, after complaints from irate passengers, that BR decided to run tests between Leicester and Bedford, part of the route operated by the six-car Manchester Pullman. For the purpose, the 'spare' six-car train was stabled at Derby and thus had to run to Leicester for the tests proper to begin. I was deputed always to start with it from Derby.

'I recall the first test run I went on. The senior M-C man present was the Chief Railcar Draughtsman, Charlie Large. The journey from Derby to Leicester was uneventful but shortly after the test proper was started, the ride got rougher and loud staccato banging was heard coming from beneath the floor above the power bogie of the power car. These bangs lasted no more than a few seconds, but recurred a number of times during the run. Charlie and I were at a loss to explain them.

'Also on the test was the representative of Armstrong Dampers, whose firm had supplied the dampers for the primary suspension. He was enormously helpful throughout the tests and I am ashamed to say I cannot remember his name. I will call him Mr A. The Armstrong dampers were arm type, as opposed to telescopic. They were not adjustable without disassembling them and changing the interior valving, but Mr A said he could lay his hands on a set of experimental dampers which were easily adjustable through a knob on the outside of their casings. We eagerly accepted this offer and asked BR to arrange further test runs. This was not an easy and quick thing to do since they had to produce a leaflet giving route and timetable information and circulate it to all operating staff involved, eg signalmen. Thus the tests were carried out over a prolonged period since no-one could predict how many test runs were to be needed. My memory suggests that this was months rather than weeks.

'It should be appreciated that dampers were often misnamed "shock absorbers". They were nothing of the sort, rather were they shock transmitters! Thus the downside to increasing the damping forces was to increase the intensity of shocks coming from transient events in the track, such as rail joints, switches and crossings. Nevertheless such increased damping could reduce the amplitude of vibrations across the springs particularly if a resonant mode was being picked up. Since we are considering the primary suspension, these shocks would be transmitted into the bogie frames, but the car bodies had the added protection of the secondary springs and would not therefore experience so much of these shocks.

'When the next series of tests, with the adjustable dampers began, they were attended by the British Railways Board (BRB) representative, the late, to my mind great, J. L. Koffman. Koffman reported directly to the BRB CM&EE, F. (Freddie) Harrison, and his assistant E. S. Cox. The latter was a prolific writer of articles on railway dynamics published in *Railway Gazette* and other journals, thus I knew him by repute. These articles were usually highly mathematical and were of great assistance and inspiration to me. In those days, railway vehicle design was the preserve of the Chief Engineer, Chief Draughtsman and senior section leaders in the drawing office. Many of them pooh-poohed the Koffman articles since their own designs relied on experience and intuition and anyway, they could neither understand nor apply the mathematical formulae. Lacking their experience, but strong on maths, the Koffman articles were what I needed to be able to make a contribution. When I met Koffman for the first time, it was with feelings of awe and trepidation, but I need not have worried. When I told him I had been trying to apply his formulae to the present problem, he was most supportive and friendly and I was greatly encouraged by this.

'I would always join the train at Derby together with Mr A, who had then fitted the adjustable dampers, and we would then agree the settings for the next test run. We could use one setting for the run from Leicester to Bedford and then change it for the run back to Leicester. To start with all dampers were set to identical strength and these were increased in small steps at a time for subsequent test runs. Koffman would join the train at Leicester, as would my own boss, John Thring.

'The next few runs produced little improvement except that the intensity and frequency of occurrence of the staccato bangings were diminishing with the increasing damping. But there was little improvement in the general ride. Around the same time, I was attempting to do calculations to see if I could determine the source of the problem. I decided it was probably due to excessive bogie frame pitching, but the realisation came that the springs of the Brown-Boveri quill drives were having an influence. Effectively, they were in parallel with the primary suspension springs and because the quill drives were diagonally disposed, they were causing the primary suspension at two diagonal corners of the bogie to be stiffer than those at the other two. The effect of this on bogie frame pitching was to force it to occur on an axis effectively rotated at an angle to the pure lateral axis. The increased pitching motion at two corners was causing these to hit the limiting stops and thus produce the banging. My plan was to increase the damping force at two corners and reduce it at the other two.

'My solution was not a theoretically purist one, which would have required substantial modifications. One cannot alter the stiffness of a spring/mass system by changing the damping force across it. Thus one could not change the frequency of its vibrations, at least not until the damping approached its critical value, which would be quite unacceptable since that would be akin to having no spring at all and the shocks transmitted would be most violent.

'More test runs followed on the basis of trying out this differential damping and, if it proved efficacious in principle, to optimise the damper settings.

'It worked. Koffman agreed to it and perhaps I had acquired some of the experience and intuition previously lacking. Having found the optimum damper settings, the test dampers and all those on the remaining power bogies were replaced by permanently set ones in the differential disposition. Although the ride over the power bogies was never as good as on the trailer bogies, at least the passengers could now drink their coffee and consume their soup without it requiring a massive clean-up operation.

'During the course of the tests, there was one amusing incident. My boss, coming to join the test train at Leicester, had left it a little late to arrive there. When crossing the bridge between platforms, he saw a Blue Pullman at a platform, so without bothering to check the platform number, he dashed down the steps just as the train was starting to pull away. From the window of the test train on the next platform, I saw my boss running along the platform waving his arms and shouting, "Stop, stop.

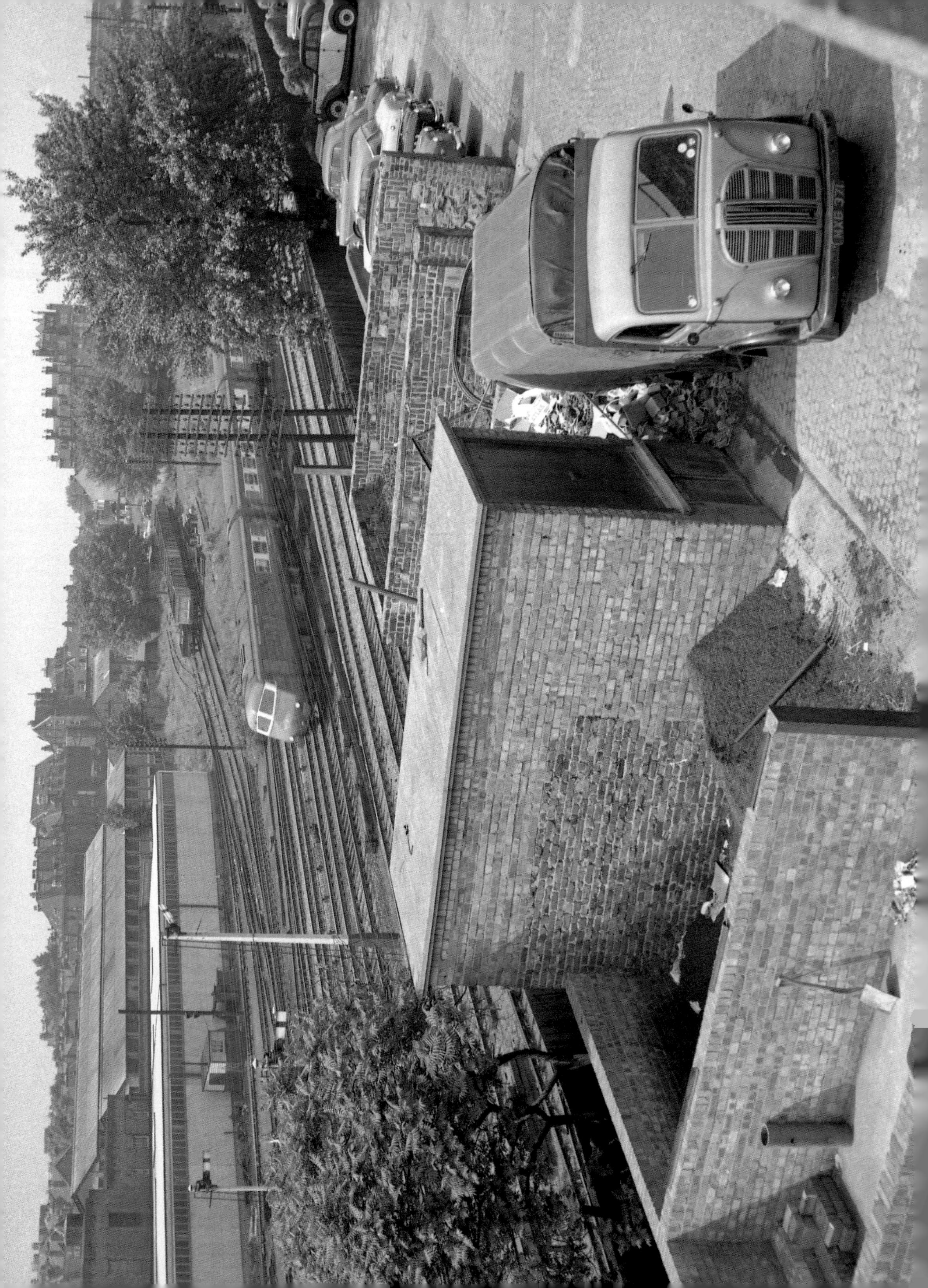

Through the London suburbs at West Hampstead in 1961. Ordinary life goes on whilst a select few are cosseted inside the passing train, shortly to arrive at St Pancras. *Rail On-Line ZF-5438-95371-1-007.*

I want to get on" – as the service train to London pulled away from him!'

Malcolm's final comment is self explanatory, 'I have no personal experience of riding on the eight-car WR sets. I can only speculate that WR tracks were in better condition than those of LMR. Also the eight-cars sets had a higher proportion of good riding trailer cars than did the six-cars. Since BR had one complete six-car unit as a stand-by, the tests were carried out on this, which may have contributed to the impression that their ride was worse. I know of no differences apart from numbers of cars in the consist between the six- and eight-car sets.'

Without access to the correspondence of the period we have to (temporarily) jump ahead to 1963 when O. S. Nock (who together with Cecil J. Allen were the noted writers on train performance of the period), in his regular articles within the *Railway Magazine*, reported on several runs he had made with the sets both on the LMR and WR. At the time of their debut in 1960 he had waxed lyrical about the trains, and when commenting on a cab ride from Manchester at the time, did nothing but sing their praises – but that was in the driver's cab where we know the ride was stated to be excellent. Three years later though he had almost completely changed his tune, likening the ride to 'a peculiar shuddering'. Nevertheless, he made an attempt at a balanced view, and reminded the reader that his preference for loco-hauled Pullmans might have been based on a rosy memory. His final statement, however, was a damming criticism. Having mentioned that his preference for loco-hauled Pullmans had been reinforced while the sets were away for overhaul, he concluded, 'Now, alas, the blue train is back and continuing its purgatorial progress'. To be fair, many contemporary DMUs were equally uncomfortable at speed, but the Pullman, despite its cushioned seats and designed padding for the human anatomy, travelled faster, and this seat cushioning could still not make up for its undoubted pitfalls.

Nock says more in his 1980 book *Two Miles a Minute* when discussing the 125mph potential of the HST's causing him some apprehension before he tried one. This was based on his experience of the 'execrable riding of the Blue Pullmans' although he also slates the frightening ride of the 'Warship' class and refers to a Longsight driver saying 'Ride her Cowboy' in reference to the ride of a Class 86 electric loco. Fortunately he had no problems with the brilliant HST cab ride.

Mike Smith mentioned in the introduction that his father made six trips by 'Midland Pullman' and it is interesting to hear a non expert traveller's experiences. 'My dad Ron Smith (ex RAF Officer) was a Classics teacher at St Bedes College Manchester and was also very active in teaching pupils in out of school activities going on to win competitions in all subjects. He taught high diving, took his F.A. Coaching badges working with Man City, Oldham Athletic and non league teams and importantly for this story he taught Calligraphy and produced beautiful Italic handwriting.

'Thomas Barnard ran the National School's handwriting in conjunction with Mentmore Platignum pens and he judged the competition, along with his fellow judges, the handwriting expert Alfred Fairbank and that great lover of the railways, Sir John Betjeman.

'Dad and his pupils won the competition three years in a row in the early 1960s and in order to get to London for the prize giving it was arranged for them to travel by the "Midland Pullman".

'My Dad was in awe of this stunning looking train and it was a talking point at the school as everyone knew this was a special train. He too didn't realise the train had set off as it silently left Manchester Central.

'Now bear in mind my Dad was someone who had a positive outlook on life and talked of the luxurious Blue Pullman in this way but then added caution over the hazards of train travel at speed almost as if this must be normal on all fast trains. Dad had nothing else to compare it to and his description complete with all the actions of the soup coming out of his bowl and the stewards struggling to keep upright and spilling coffee sadly speaks volume about the poor riding. In reality more Rodeo Ride than Rodeo Drive in reality.

'Even so the experience for him was still a positive one but you can understand why those businessmen and women travelling frequently were irritated by the ride. In 2006 I did take Mum and Dad on the short lived "Blue Pullman" charter train using Class 47s and Mk2 coaches which although it wasn't as handsome as the "Midland Pullman" certainly was a nice experience with comfy seats and great food. It was nice seeing Dad next to the Nanking Blue bodywork with the Pullman logo.'

Contemporary enthusiast Alan Leeke also remembers the trains, his recollection being they looked magnificent at Manchester Central and when he also saw them at Reddish Depot.

Away from comfort (or otherwise) now and back to 1961 and the morning departure from Manchester which was brought forward to 7.45am, both of these taking effect from the first working day of the new year, Monday 2 January. No doubt some shuffling of other services to accommodate the move was also necessary as the overall journey time was maintained and consequently the morning up train arrived at St Pancras 15 minutes earlier than before.

The additional 15 minutes available in London was appreciated by the Manchester business clientele whilst from the railway operator's perspective the bonus was that it also allowed a comfortable schedule for the same set to cover the 100 or so miles on the extended fill-in journey to Nottingham (this compared with slightly under 90 miles from London to Leicester).

Little did the LMR know how they had also pleased one particular schoolboy, Lawrence Cody, as he was able

'Driver and Fireman'; to the left Driver Edwards again. Both would be in the top-link and no doubt also relieved they could go to work and return home clean – although against this was the disadvantage of lodging away from home. The circular badge on the lapel contained the initials 'BR' whilst the metal cap badge proclaimed 'Midland Pullman'. *Harry Edwards*

to watch the 'Midland Pullman' purr into Cheadle Heath each morning before school.

The first time Lawrence saw the set makes for interesting reading and follows a pattern of youngsters being transfixed by the sight of the Blue Pullman: *'My first sighting of one of these sets was at Cheadle Heath heading to Manchester in early 1960. I was near North Box with friends and this "Blue Streak" just appeared from under the bridge, completely taking us all by surprise. It was brand spanking new with orange and white wiring on the frames and white wheel rims. My memory will never fade of that first sighting! It must have been on test and not long afterwards the famous "Midland Pullman" poster appeared at Cheadle Heath. Fifty years on I was in a pub in Birmingham and ended up talking to a railwayman who was on those test runs between Derby and Manchester. Can you imagine my elation at meeting someone involved with the train I have loved since 1960! I would also try and watch the Pullman return in the evening, it looked amazing lit up at night crossing the River Mersey or coming into Cheadle Heath. One evening I was even allowed to look inside it at Cheadle Heath . . .'*

Another from the period who similarly saw the train was John Dickson who would watch the 'Midland Pullman' pass by from a path between the houses off Weston Drive in Adswood, Stockport. Richard Hildebrand of the *Bakewell Yesteryear* page also loved the Blue Pullman and would be there to greet it each morning as it sped through Bakewell Station. Also in Bakewell Vivienne Hawkridge and her friends would wave to the 'Midland Pullman' each morning! Jay Lomas would watch it go around the curve to the three arch bridge in the evenings. Simon Mold could see the blue streak across the valley from his home. Best of all Maureen Weinberg's first date was at Bakewell Station – to watch the 'Midland Pullman' go by!

Alan Davis saw the shortlived fill-in Nottingham run. *'My grandmother lived near Attenborough and she would take me to see the "Midland Pullman" just after lunch time on the Nottingham service. The Blue Pullman seemed so special as it hummed by . . . it was shockingly different to the maroon loco-hauled stock and green multiple units that were the norm. The crest on the nose fascinated me as I didn't know anything about Pullmans then'.*

David Hayes on Flickr recalls, *'I used to watch out for the lunchtime Blue Pullman run to/from Nottingham–St Pancras. The Bobby at Beeston Station would always open the crossing gates well in advance of the train – always a sure sign the 'special' one was on its way, and we kids on the footbridge would be straining to get the first glimpse of the unmistakable blue and white front!'*

Much further south the 'Blue Streak' was having an effect on the youth there too. Steve Povey recalls, *'When I was a kid I had "my bridge" which was Cross Lane Bridge, the first bridge (going under) South of Harpenden. The "Midland Pullman" was stunning to look at with an incredible purr to the engine. There was a speed restriction on approach to Harpenden so to hear it accelerate away on full power away North was awesome. I remember it like yesterday.'*

For his eighth birthday in May 1965 Trevor Jordan was given an interesting present by his Dad, *'I was told I was getting a ride on the "Midland Pullman" from Manchester Central. I pictured sitting there drinking coffee with the waiter serving me . . . but that didn't happen! Having purchased only a platform ticket my Dad made some offer to the guard involving beer and I was popped into the guard compartment of the power car where I had a noisy, bumpy ride to Cheadle Heath!'*

These recollections really do go to show that the vision and image of the Blue Pullman certainly packed a big punch and from this viewpoint was actually a great success in that it did its job of giving the much needed modern image boost to the railway even if only to a youthful general public as opposed to regular travellers on the service.

We return now to the fill-in turn to Leicester. Originally the mid-day turn was just a St Pancras to Leicester service and not surprisingly poorly patronised averaging just 12–15 fare paying 'bums on seats'. In an attempt to increase patronage the decision was made to extend the lunchtime (fill-in) working through to Nottingham which took effect just eight months after launch from January 1961.

Naturally it was hoped this would improve loadings on this fill-in turn, but with a greater distance to cover in the middle of the day, the lunchtime departure from St Pancras was necessarily brought forward to 11.15am, and with the rapid turnaround at the new destination resulted in a 3.30pm departure from Nottingham. Consequently, as with the earlier Leicester only service, the train was unlikely to see the same clientele in both directions on the same day. Unfortunately too the extended lunchtime fill-in turns were now affected by the same previous labour dispute as had existed before, with the Leicester to Nottingham portion of the run taken as an extension of private enterprise. There were threats from the union of further (widespread) industrial action whilst located correspondence appears to refer to the dispute as a 'who cleaned what' rather than a 'who does what'. Indeed there was a genuine fear the BP service as a whole might be 'blacked' by the union – or perhaps that should really have been 'black and blued' . . ?

As we know staffing of the trains was basically a mixture of both BR restaurant car personnel (attired in Pullman uniforms), with five additional Pullman men working on a temporary basis to help to establish the service. The latter were the Train Conductor[10], Senior Chef and three Senior Attendants, who were in charge of stock levels on the train. Meanwhile, the Pullman Car Co was advertising for additional staff from the Manchester area which they were in fact later able to recruit. The threat was that the NUR intended to draw attention to its grievance by the withdrawal of its labour from all BR restaurant cars from 4 January, just two days after the start date of the Nottingham service. BR management had thus to consider their next moves very carefully especially as the travelling public would no doubt have recalled the earlier restaurant staff strike of just 15 or so months earlier in October 1959. In some ways management were between the proverbial rock and hard place: desirous of publicising the new service to attract clientele but by the same token not wishing to antagonise the staff and union.

This staffing difficulty over the proposed extension of Pullman services was just one of the headaches facing BR in the field of labour relations at the time[11] and whilst there is still some confusion from consulted sources, the consensus would appear to be that the Nottingham service did indeed commence (for one day at least) on 2 January but without any form of catering available beyond Leicester to Nottingham and likewise until Leicester was again reached on the return part of the journey. (The service though was quickly curtailed and would only start again in September.)

This led to the somewhat bizarre situation whereby on reaching Leicester, the entire seconded BR catering staff 'downed cutlery' and went on strike – but only temporarily and only as far as Nottingham and then again back to Leicester, during which time they retired en-masse to their kitchens. With such a limited patronage, it is unlikely that very few hungry and thirsty passengers even noticed. More noticeable though was at Nottingham where there was now no one available to facilitate seating in accordance with the seat reservations made for the return journey, hence Pullman clerical staff (who were not in any way party to the dispute) travelled on the train daily to collect the reservations chart at Nottingham and so allocate seats to any late-coming passengers who had arrived without reservations. (We must not forget that in a pre-computer age reservations were made by post or in person. These were then collated and passed to the conductor who would mark allocated seats basically on a chart held on a clipboard. This might sound antiquated now but a similar system worked for all reservations right up to the 1980s. The BR timetables of the period categorically stating that reservations could not be made using the telephone.) At Leicester, the Train Conductor and attendants would reappear as mentioned. None of this would have assisted in endearing the midday train to its potential customers.

Following the general NUR/BR negotiations going on elsewhere, an uneasy truce resulted but the 'on/off' situation so far as the catering was concerned would rumble on, not helped by BR's press announcements over advertising a service which at times was also now having to be curtailed. Clearly management had failed to recall its own words from early 1960 by agreeing not to extend Pullman services, and Leicester to Nottingham was clearly such an extension. In addition to this simmering discontent over perceived private enterprise operation, there were other grumbles, one being that BR staff on loan were required to wear standard Pullman numerical badge identification. Another was over actual duties, the loaned BR restaurant car staff refusing to handle soiled linen on the trains, stating that this was not part of an attendant's task.

Meanwhile *The Guardian* had picked up on the story in its issue of 30 September 1961. 'NUR men decide 'no meals' on Pullman extension.' 'When the British Railways "Midland Pullman" train leaves St Pancras station for Nottingham for the first time *['reintroduced time' would have been more accurate]* on Monday, there will be no restaurant service. The 25 NUR restaurant staff of the train decided yesterday not to work on it because the service – an extension of the Leicester service – was contrary to NUR policy. Mr John Hyland, chairman of the London Midland Regional Council of the union, said that when the new Pullman services were introduced some time ago, it was agreed that there would be no extensions.' 'The position was made clear to the restaurant staff this afternoon and they decided to remain loyal to the NUR decision on this,' he added. 'This decision will affect the services after Monday. Kitchen staff would travel with the train to prepare for the evening run to Manchester to keep existing agreements between the NUR and the British Transport Commission. The main objection of the NUR to extensions of Pullman services was that the Pullman Car Company was a private company within the framework of a nationalised industry.'

A further article in the same newspaper on 9 October confirmed what had taken place although with the slightly incorrect comment that upon arrival at Leicester the catering staff physically left the train, rejoining it on its return. We of course know this to be incorrect and what actually occurred was they simply locked themselves on the train in the kitchen – or elsewhere.

THE BLUE PULLMAN STORY

Two images from the limited selection obtained from the LMR-PRO. Both were recorded on 6 July 1960 and depict the train at 12.03pm close to St Pancras, the reported locations being Dock Junction and Yacht Basin. As we know this was only the third day of public service although earlier in the year the Railway Observer had commented that it was hoped the LMR service would have started on 6 March.

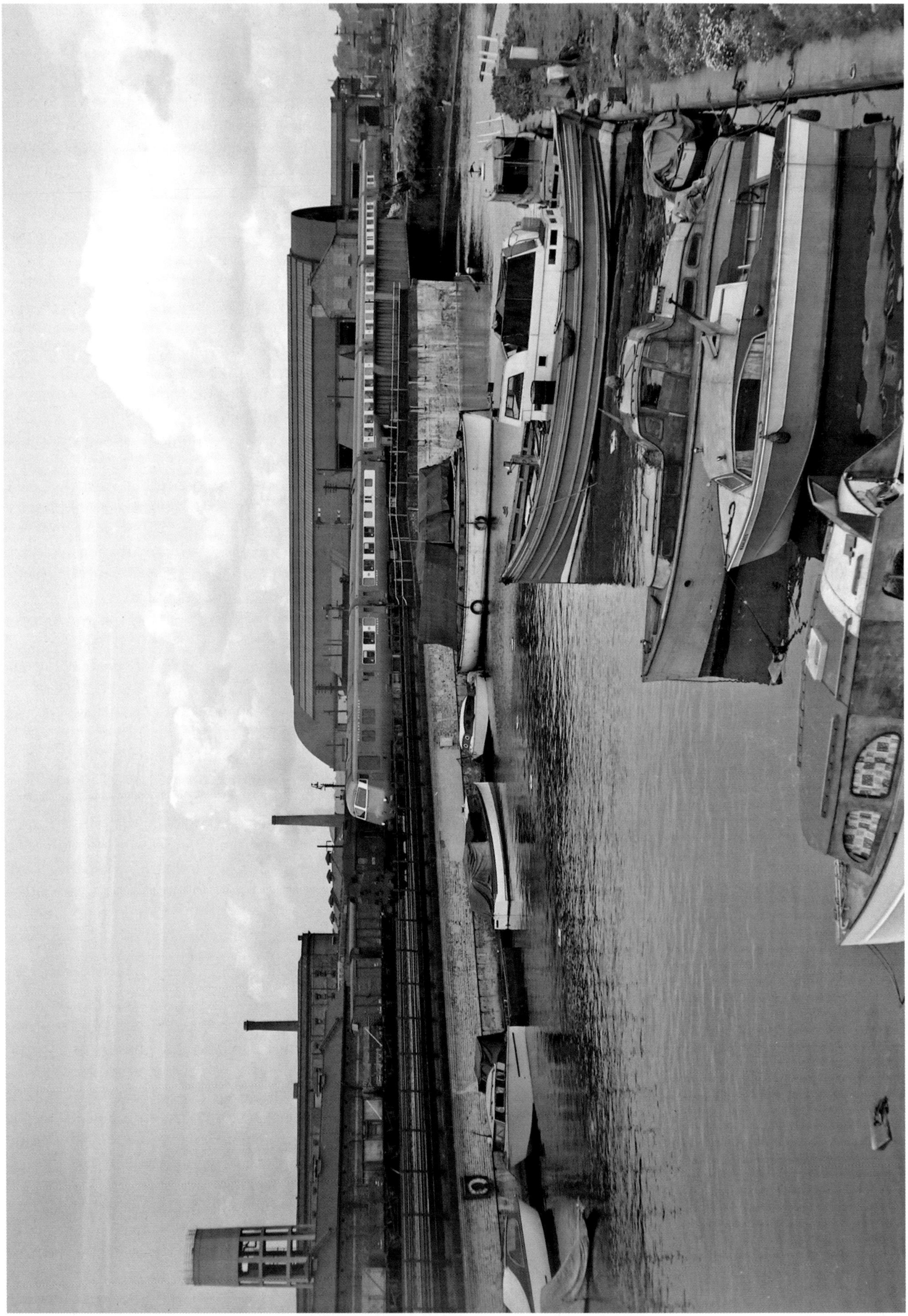

A second image at Silkstream Junction but this time from a different angle. On this occasion the train is running well, but Glynn Waite recalls another day when there was some confusion at Rowsley South Junction due to exactly where the necessary crew change for a down freight was to occur. The result was a 7-8-minute delay to the Pullman service and no doubt a 'please explain' report to both the controller and signalmen. *LMR PRO*

The matter was not easily resolved and as stated the difficult decision was reached to suspend the fill-in turn completely after just the one day of operation – 2 January 1961.

Matters became doubly difficult for the LMR when there was some disquiet amongst the on-board staff that their working day would in future be extended in consequence of the retiming of the train to leave Manchester an hour earlier each day. Whilst this was popular with the clientele some sympathy can also be extended to the staff on this occasion. Fortunately this issue at least was reported as resolved at the end of December 1960 – although we do not know how.

Returning to the mid-day service, the eventual result was that after the short start the Nottingham service was 'temporarily' curtailed and Nottingham did not see a regular weekday Pullman service until 2 October 1961, the service having gone back on/come off in the interim and also subject to periods of temporary withdrawal; curtailment at Leicester; and the lack of a meal service beyond that point. Even so, and so far as Blue Pullman was concerned, there was none of the bad feeling that typified the bitter public disagreements so common on the railways a few years later, the whole situation summed up in a cartoon from the *Daily Mail* (a copy of which was pinned up in at least one of the kitchen cars) in which a railwayman was shown commenting on the dispute: 'Unofficially this is an official dispute. But officially this is an unofficial dispute'. *(Regretfully we have been unable to locate a copy of the newspaper and consequently the cartoon in question.)* When it was finally resolved, it was agreed that the Pullman Car Co, who up to that time had advertised their own vacancies, would first offer them to existing restaurant car staff, and that these men's seniority would be protected if it was later necessary for them to return to their former role. Additionally, it allowed for some BR staff to wear identical Pullman uniforms on non-Pullman services. As an aside we should mention the introduction of the trains on the Western Region had at first involved a similar mixed level of staffing. Such issues though would fall away completely from the end of 1962 with the Pullman Car Co fully vested in BR in that year. Now it was simply a division of BR's Catering and Hotel's business.

1961 also sees the first mention of the use of a 'Midland Pullman' set on charter and excursion work. This appears to have commenced with the idea for a set to provide a luxury service for Leicester City football fans travelling to Wembley for their team's place in the FA cup final against Tottenham Hotspur. Sadly on this occasion it came to nothing due to limited Pullman demand and also because there were already a number of other football special services running that day. (Leicester City were destined to lose 2-0 on that occasion.) Further special workings and charter trains involving the BP LMR set(s) are discussed in subsequent pages. At the same time we should also mention that the Western Region also had some success with charters and specials and which are also in the main discussed later in the text.

Away from services that did or did not run and lunches that might or might not be available, British Railways were extremely conscious that to retain as well as attract patronage to the trains, especially perhaps because of the riding issues, external cleanliness and internal appearance was paramount. In the 21st century it is not uncommon to witness janitorial staff on board certain operator's trains, allied to the short turnarounds of stock now in place. Back in 1960 cleaning was undertaken at St Pancras (as well as presumably at Manchester/Reddish). The limited time available after the morning arrival in London and subsequent departure for Nottingham would not have allowed for much opportunity (although possibly a quick sweep through was undertaken) and instead internal cleaning occupied much of the two hours plus time available after returning from Nottingham and prior to the evening departure to Manchester.

This dealt with the interiors but the exterior was more difficult especially as the manufacturer who had supplied the paint was evidently unaware that the train had been intended to run through a carriage washer. This lack of evident communication between parties might appear difficult to comprehend and on the surface that is certainly the case. In defence of the railway we might also say the whole project involved so many different parties there is perhaps some sympathy to be extended where the individual in charge was simply not aware of what questions might (indeed should) have been asked. The actual automated washing equipment of necessity involved the use of chemicals and this as we know had quickly been found on the Western Region at least to have an adverse

Passing Kettering South signal box in the summer/autumn of 1960. Although tickets were checked at platform entry and departure points they were also, as per tradition, checked en-route. The Pullman company were not happy for attendants to undertake the latter task, feeling it might detract from the efficiency of their service. In response BR suggested the train guard could even collect the Pullman supplement. It appears no decision was reached and this issue remains a grey area when it comes to reporting the actual outcome and 'who did what'. It does not, though, appear to have developed into a 'union' issue. There was also a later staff suggestion which fortunately does throw a little light on the situation when it was reported that at at the time a ticket collector went the length of the train followed by the Pullman man who solely collected the reservation tickets – *does this mean the 'Supplement'?* The suggested example was given that for that time on the ER, on longer non-stop Pullman services, the ticket collector made one pass through the train and was not then utilised for other duties. No reported final decision has been found. *Rail On-Line ZF-5438-95371-1-008*

effect on the external appearance. (See page 83.) Consequently whilst the janitors (or was it Pullman staff?) valeted the inside, the waiting staff prepared the tables for evening dinner, and the chefs, prepared, roasted, carved, boiler, steamed, fried, pureed, stirred, grilled and baked, *(plus whatever else chefs undertake)*, a veritable army of cleaners would be at work on the outside, hand-washing. Indeed this external cleaning could occupy the whole of the lay-over time available. The necessary results whilst perhaps visually satisfactory were obviously both labour-intensive as well as hardly cost effective. (In the original book it was reported that the external cleaning was at first undertaken at St Pancras but subsequently transferred to Nottingham commensurate with the service being extended to that city. With the benefit of hindsight this may not be totally correct for the simply stated fact that with the limited lay-over time at Nottingham there was simply not sufficient time available to undertake the task. Revenue and profit from the actual operation was thus spread ever more thinly.)

How long such a disciplined regime continued is not reported, but it appears from the *Modern Railways* article of July 1963 that it was still being done at least up until that time, an indication perhaps that the Blue Pullmans were still considered to be the jewels in the crown of the LMR a full three years after their introduction and this notwithstanding the riding issues that forever bubbled under the surface (or should that be under the floors?).

Paul Metcalfe, in his excellent article on the trains in *Classic Diesels & Electrics*, refers to the 'Manchester Experiment', where fares were reduced by a third in an attempt to increase passenger numbers. However, this does not agree with the reports of consistent loadings previously mentioned.

Mechanical servicing (and although not mentioned no doubt also included refuelling) was usually carried out at night, and involved two electrical fitters and two mates scheduled as follows: a regular daily check taking 2 to 4 hours, a weekly check taking 5 hours, and every five weeks, a 22-hour check.

The total servicing time each night, involving all staff, which probably included cleaners as well, was seven hours per train-set (the weekly and five-weekly checks usually carried out at weekends). It is not known whether these service intervals were modified later in the life of the trains. An external starter button was fitted to the vehicles carrying the auxiliary Rolls-Royce engines so that that these engines could be checked even if the actual passenger part car was locked. (Was locking commonplace for whatever reason?) Meanwhile, despite pressure from the management of the LMR over timekeeping, schedule reliability rapidly deteriorated as the novelty wore off. This may again have been partly due to the poor riding, and it is interesting to speculate whether the train crew might also have contrived to deliberately slow the service at times – possibly consistent with known bad spots of track, or even when it was known soup was being served – both for their own sake and that of the fare paying passengers, for it cannot even have always been pleasant at speed at the front end (although arguably no worse than on many steam engines). Indeed the LMR reported that by the end of 1960 – and *remember this was just six months after the commencement* – only 65% of Blue Pullman services were running within 5 minutes of 'right-time', compared with 90% when the train had been introduced. (We may take a moment out to analyse that 90% briefly: four trains each day – Manchester/London, London/Leicester, Leicester/London, London/Manchester; consequently 20 trains a week. With 90% running to time this means the equivalent of two services per week were more than 5 minutes late. At 65% that figure is 7 out of the 20 were not running to time.)

However, a year later, the 15 December 1961 issue of *The Railway Gazette* included a brief paragraph under their regular 'Notes and News' feature with the heading: 'Success of Midland Pullman'. It continued, 'The London Midland Region of British Railways has announced that the "Midland Pullman" is attracting an average loading of 95 per cent capacity, and has a record of 95 per cent punctuality'. In reality, the truth was no doubt somewhere between the two extremes, perhaps by simply drawing a line underneath some particularly poor episodes!

What of course is interesting is the reported 95% loadings, although again we may suspect it was convenient just to refer to the Manchester workings. This would appear to be confirmed by the article in *Modern Railways* referred to earlier, in that whilst from the operator's perspective the one train in service needed to be just that, 'in service' for the maximum amount of time possible, the feedback received by the LMR was that passengers were objecting to paying a supplementary fare over the shorter distance when comparing St Pancras to Leicester/Nottingham with St Pancras to Manchester.

This view by a well-respected magazine is in some ways slightly difficult to believe, as the distance between St Pancras to Leicester or Nottingham was comparable with that covered by the 'Bournemouth Belle', and also far greater than that covered by the 'Brighton Belle'. In both the latter cases, there was never any (known) objection to the supplement charge.

Overhaul time at Derby and coinciding with the Works Open-Day – believed to have been in 1964. The public have the opportunity to view the train, entering via the front guard's compartment and exiting from the rear compartment. Further south, the *Railway Gazette* for 9 November 1962 carried an illustration of Sir John Elliot and Mr F. D. M. Harding from Pullman at the opening of the canteen at Pullman's Preston Park (Brighton) Works. Mention was made in the caption that Pullman cars would continue to be overhauled at the works but there was specifically no mention that this would include the BP vehicles. The next year BR announced the Pullman works were to close from 10 July 1963, giving their rationale that there was already a carriage works not far away at Lancing (which was destined to close soon after) whilst other BR works were also well able to take on such work elsewhere. Consequently, no Blue Pullman vehicle or train was ever serviced at Preston Park and, it appears, once in public service no set ever returned to the builder either, instead being maintained and overhauled at either Derby or Swindon. Do note that in the second image both cars bear the same letter designation – 'C' and 'C' – and that electrification warning flashes have also now appeared on the ends of the intermediate vehicles. *RCTS*

Wigstone South Junction, 24 July 1961, near Leicester, the convergence of the Midland main line as well as the Midland line to Market Harborough and the former LNWR line from Nuneaton. Seeing the driver's side droplight partly open we have to say it does not appear the driving cabs had air-conditioning. *The Transport Treasury*

At the time of introduction of the service in 1960, the train had been identified in both the Public and Working timetables as either 'Pullman' or 'Blue Pullman' and was shown a 'Class A' working – meaning an express passenger train identified by two white lights, one above each buffer. With the introduction of four-digit train identification on BR, the morning up departure from Manchester became 1C43 from 12 June 1961, while the 3.30pm up from Nottingham was classified as 1C71. In the down direction, the other designations were, 1D0H (?) for the 11.15am to Nottingham, and 1H20 for the 6.10pm from St. Pancras. We may at this point also pause to ponder one of the original design intentions which had been to incorporate a route indicator panel into the front end of the power cars. Rightly considered aesthetically less than pleasing at the time, just two years after entering service such a fitting would now have been justified although it is hard to imagine how it might have been incorporated without spoiling the visual symmetry of the design. (None of the sets were ever destined to be modified with such a feature but clearly the use of four-digit headcodes was indeed something that was being considered for the future by BR during the latter aspects of the design stage.)

We come now to 1962 and what would be a bad year for the LMR trainsets. It started on 1 February as the down Nottingham-bound service was travelling at speed through the one-mile Haverstock tunnel between Kentish Town and West Hampstead. Driver Edwards was at the controls when they ran over a permanent way jack that had been left by workmen in the 'four-foot' near the south end of the tunnel. The shock to the crew and passengers can only be imagined as they were subjected to banging and crashing coming from beneath them especially as it was initially suspected and reported that there was 'considerable damage to the underneath of the train'. Fortunately no derailment resulted to the credit of the train. Not surprisingly the service was terminated at West Hampstead with the passengers transferred to an ordinary service for the remainder of their journey. LMR 'Jinty' Fowler Class 3F 0-6-0T tank engine No 47449 was used to pull the set to Cricklewood for repairs, where on being examined, the damage was found to be less than first feared and the same set was able to take up its booked working back to Manchester that evening. (Paradoxically the incident was almost an exact repeat of one on the Western Region that had occurred a year or so earlier on 5 December 1960. On this occasion the 'Bristol Pullman' had run over equipment left in 'the four-foot' with consequent damage to the fuel tank. This time the damage was more serious and the train concerned had to be towed to Swindon for repair.)

Just a fortnight later the 'Midland Pullman' was near Sileby in Leicestershire travelling at 70mph when it hit a 4ft log placed on the track by vandals. The train stayed upright but the fuel tank of the lead power car was badly damaged.

Another major concern was the issue of spare parts and the news that some (unspecified) spares were on a delivery schedule 12 months into the future. Contemporary reports cite an example with the Western Region waiting for a spare main engine/auxiliary engine/gearbox and Stones-built equipment. This situation would be worthy of further discussion if other information were available, but without additional records it would be wrong to speculate on cause/blame.

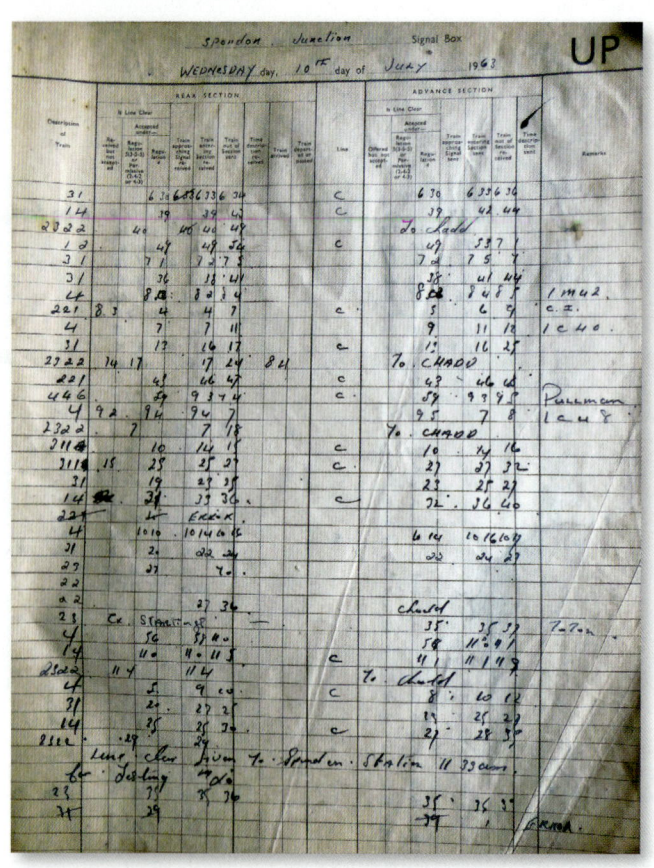

Sample copy of the Train Register from Spondon Junction signal box showing the up (London bound) train 'offered' at 8.59am from the signal box in rear and at which time it was also 'offered on' by the signalman here to the box in advance. Spondon Junction had the train as 'entering section' (from the rear) at 9.03am – again the same time it was sent as 'on line' ahead. 'Out of section' was sent to the rear at 9.04 am and the same code received from the box in advance just one minute later. Clearly some very short block sections! Notice the bell code used '4-4-6' and the duty man has entered the train description '1C48' in the remarks column. *Dr Peter Kazmierczak*

Despite the lack of (some) spares the same year was certainly also the end of the honeymoon period so far as utilisation was concerned. Notwithstanding a realistic marketing campaign intended to attract passengers to the Nottingham service it was still not having the desired results, added to which the viability of having one train on what was effect permanent standby was similarly being brought into question especially as the Western Region were now running all three of their sets on a daily basis.

Consequently the LMR began to cast its eyes elsewhere for places where additional revenue might be gained, with the overwhelming choice for a London to Liverpool service. Neither was this a throw away suggestion, for

St Pancras 1963. A careful look reveals warning flashes have now been added to the white banding around the windows. We might also say the shine was beginning to fade – literally – as witness the grime on the roof above the cab.

The complete formation being prepared for the evening departure. On the platform it appears that the stewards/chefs are in deep discussion – perhaps some of the supplies expected were late. Unseen from here but built into the ceiling kitchen units, were four ventilated fans. For ease of cleaning, the floor of the kitchens was of a red composite material inset within a square mesh aluminium grill. Within the passenger accommodation the lighting has already been mentioned but it should be stated the continuous pattern of light achieved by having a pair of florescent tubes fitted end to end and covered by flush-jointed diffusion panels was possibly the first time lighting in this form had been used in a railway carriage. Emergency lighting operated by battery was also provided. We do not know if this was ever used in practice.

staff working for the Manchester Line Manager were involved in a thorough feasibility study occupying several months, the conclusion reached being that a daily service was very likely to be feasible. A working diagram was thus prepared for the second set which showed a departure from St Pancras at 7.45am; pick up at Luton at 8.12am, running via Manchester (arrive 11.05am) and Warrington (11.23am) to reach Liverpool at 11.45am. This would be followed by a midday fill-in between Liverpool and Manchester. It was later suggested to put the St Pancras departure back to 8.00am, with a corresponding alteration to the other times, intended to give passengers from elsewhere (particularly those off the Southern Region) easier access to the train. The return journey would be from Liverpool at 5.45pm, again with the same stops so as to arrive at St Pancras at 9.40pm. The LMR estimate was for an average 80% loading on the Liverpool service (presumably not taking into account the midday 'Liverpool-Manchester–Liverpool' 'fill-in' which, when viewed nowadays, might seem likely to have suffered a similar difficulty to the Leicester/Nottingham working).

Whilst a Liverpool service was certainly attractive and would get around the rumblings of discontent sporadically emanating from BRB at Marylebone Road concerning under-utilisation, the obvious issue was that with both trains scheduled to operate a daily service there would be no spare available. To counter this, the LMR had been in discussion with the Southern Region about having a spare set of loco-hauled Pullman coaches available if necessary. (These would have come from the pool of Pullman cars formerly part of the 'Golden Arrow' fleet and which by this time, was already no longer restricted to just a rake of Pullman vehicles.) The Blue Pullman set for the Liverpool service would also be dealt with at a new 'intermediate' servicing depot at Allerton, equipped as per Cricklewood. Reddish, however, would remain the home depot for both sets and where more major work would be carried out. Five ex-SR Pullman cars were subsequently sent to Etches Park carriage sidings at Derby; all were first class, the formation being two brake vehicles, *Athene* and *Fortuna*, a parlour car, *Ceteia*, and two kitchen cars, *Thetis*, and *Thalia*.[12]

For the present it is appropriate to mention that the theme of a Liverpool service had been bubbling away under the surface by this time and we will return to this a little later. Suffice to commence by saying it has not been possible to trace a precise timeline as to when Liverpool was first discussed – although we do know it had certainly been mentioned as a potential destination even before the trains had started running. Instead what we can say with some certainty is that in 1962 the feasibility study together with the behind the

165

scenes discussion occupied some months but were brought to a head from August onwards with two internal memorandums. The first was on the technical aspects of the train from an unsigned individual (but clearly with a technical/engineering background) who wrote as follows:

17/8/1962 – 'From the outset the riding of the trains has been highly unsatisfactory and they have been under almost continuous modification since shortly after they were introduced in early 1960.

'The modifications to the power bogies involved the fitting of long swing links and new design dampers to the primary suspension. These alterations have been completed with the exception that the correct setting of the dampers has had to be established by running trials and it now remains for the dampers to be adjusted accordingly. This involves their return to the makers in sequence during the intermediate overhauls now in progress.

'In the case of the trailer bogies these are giving their worst ride at present due to heavy wear in the swing links, trunnions and suspension link pins. During the intermediate overhaul to the trains which are taking place between now and the end of April next, the swing links, trunnions, and suspension link pins will be renewed to a modified design embodying knife edge swing links and trunnions, with the contact surfaces "stellited"[13] to reduce wear. In addition lubrication to the suspension pins will be provided. Here again the correct damper settings to the primary suspension require determining by running trials and returning to the makers for adjustment. All these modifications will be completed during the shopping programme of the two trains over the next five months. The riding will then be very much better but in my opinion will still leave something to be desired, particularly at speeds in excess of 80mph.'

Curiously these subsequent, August 1962, riding assessments were carried out as part of the regular public

Train loadings for the period shown. A slightly earlier record/survey for May 1961 (AN172/294) revealed the 'Midland Pullman' ran on 23 days in the month but did not operate on the Friday before and the Monday of the Bank Holiday, 19 and 22 May. There was of course no service at weekends.

Unknown working. Within the text mention has been made of the spare set being stabled at Derby, certainly for the duration of the trials referred to by Malcolm Botham. Otherwise it is believed the spare train was held at Reddish and, as stated, equal then to just 50% usage of the fleet. Ironically, too, it was either partly or wholly outside as the six-car train would not completely fit inside Reddish depot. BR would also not sanction an extension of the shed for this purpose. No reason for this lack of expenditure is given but a reasonable conclusion would be the LMR did not envisage a long life for the sets with electrification in the offing. Indeed, there appears to be little if any mention of the future of the trains on the LMR once the modernisation of the LNWR main line was complete. As time passed it is believed (but not confirmed) a further spare set of non-Pullman first class loco-hauled stock was also kept in reserve at Manchester, possibly a reaction again to what appears to have been a falling off in the availability of the sets. If this were able to be confirmed it would be a further resource standing idle for much of the time without regular use. We do of course know that at odd times a loco-hauled train had to substituted especially if the failure of the BP set was at the opposite end of the line to Reddish (or wherever). No images have been located to show the substitute LMR train in use, using either Pullman or ordinary vehicles. (Any loco-hauled Pullman service on the Midland main line from 1960 onwards could be reasonably assumed to be a BP substitute as there were no other regular Pullman trains on the route in the period BP was operating.)

service between St Pancras and Leicester, which was also the section over which the 'Midland Pullman' would regularly achieve its fastest average speed. All three types of vehicle forming the six-car sets were assessed, and it was reported that although the motor bogies were reasonable, the trailing bogies appeared to have deteriorated since the report writer's previous trip in May 1962, indeed, they were now prone to giving out the occasional metallic knock. (Now for the first time it was the converse of what had generally occurred in the past – previously it had been the trailers that had ridden better than the motored vehicles.) The engineers charged with the assessments also admitted there was some difficulty in eating and drinking, whilst some passengers were overheard in conversation stating that they would not take lunch, as is was impossible to eat soup or drink coffee at speed – *but not many did, on the Nottingham service anyway!* Even so it was slightly strange to expect unwitting fare-paying passengers to be part of what was admitted to as an 'assessment'. (Again shades of 'Disgruntled Manchester Businessman' from 1960.)

Taken no doubt from personal observation at the time, the writer continued, 'Indeed lunch was quite a hazardous business … almost impossible to write this at speed.' Overall, the report concluded, the ride was generally very jerky, and it was suggested that despite the motor bogies being better than the trailer bogies, it would be worth checking the concentricity of the tyres. It was also suggested (again) that the new medium of CCTV could be used to record bogie movement at speed.

Unfortunately for all concerned such an eminently sensible suggestion was once more ignored. The BR report accompanied by several letters from passengers who appeared genuinely fearful that the vehicles would derail. These daily complaints did not go unnoticed by the train staff either, as at some stage, an internal memorandum (normally reserved for completion by crew members only)

The Blue Pullman Story

Departing St Pancras on an unknown date. One wiper missing from the second-man's side – although the fitting is present, and the important tea can visible! *Lawrence Hassall/KR collection*

168

Despite the wish of the LMR to have the trains available at weekends for hire, special workings do not seem to have been anywhere near as prolific as had been anticipated. The first photographed example found using an LMR set was on 2 May 1964 with a six-car set running from Sheffield Midland to St Pancras – where passengers would de-train for Euston and then Wembley. This ran as '1X34' and was a football special that had originated at Preston – passengers from Preston changing trains at Sheffield. The six-coach BP set is seen passing Rugby Midland on the up journey.
Mike Morant

was distributed to passengers, who were invited to pass comment on the ride. Such action inviting passengers to comment upon the ride did not find much favour with the LMR Board.

So far as the tyre issues were concerned (one failed in the period July–September 1962) there was some suggestion that the general rough riding of the bogies might well have contributed to the failure. Whatever, this appears to be the last mention of tyre problems although without in any way wishing to be cynical perhaps it would be safer to say 'the last time reference has been found'. (Presumably whatever issues/findings had been made with reference to the LMR sets this same information was passed to Swindon but again the WR files are conspicuous in not mentioning similar issues.)

The reader should also not be under the misapprehension that the various repairs at Derby – replacement tyres, modifications to the bogies etc – had in any way cured the riding issues. More likely there appeared now to be a general acceptance that the trains would always behave in this way and the best now had been achieved that was realistically possible. The concluding paragraph of the report into the test runs of 1961 (and which might well have been the conclusion for every test run) was that, '. . . passengers who endured the Pullman were subjected to a "tail-wagging" experience at the end of every coach'.

All this was bad enough and might also have been enough to create sufficient doubt and so preclude the idea of the Liverpool train. Such an assumption is given credence in a memorandum of 19 September 1962 marked: 'Personal – from the Line Manager at Euston to the LMR General Manager'. The memorandum made the suggestion that the region should review the situation very carefully before '…taking the plunge…' and introducing a Liverpool service. 'At the time of writing we are only just able to keep one set in service, and this as you know, is only just on its feet.' (Although tempting, we should again not attempt to elaborate on a statement without further evidence. Consequently it is safest to take it as referring to the general riding issues and having a set under modification/awaiting altered dampers rather than other [unspecified] issues.)

The note continued with the number of days per month since the start of 1962 when no three-car half-set had been available as a standby, notably:

January – 0
February – 11
March – 6
April – 10
May – 8
June – 8
July – 6
August – 3
September (to 18) – 5

Again the above should not in any way be taken to imply that the Manchester service was cancelled on these days, instead it should be read that 'should' a problem have developed on the one set running the public service there was not even a half-set standby available.

As if to back up the warning, attached to the original file are some copies of the riding 'proforma' issued to Pullman Car Staff where they alone could report customer instances and complaints of bad riding. One of these concerned M60742 (Parlour First) on 23 August 1962, as

The mid-day Nottingham fill in turn near Wellingborough in August 1962. (Those former Midland Railway signals are quite superb!) *Martin Welch*

part of the set forming the 3.30pm up from Nottingham to St Pancras. The passenger, D. McConnell, was sat in seat No 5 in what was a first class parlour car and who complained it was impossible to attempt any work at any speed above 50mph. Mr/Ms McConnell had added the staff were: '. . . courteous and helpful – no complaint there at all.' The movement reported included a fore and aft surging motion, side to side sway and side to side rolling, whilst worst of all was a sharp side to side jerking – the same 'hunting' movement described earlier. McConnell concludes, '. . . suspect this is a compromise design to the suspension – the best of everyone's and at the same time the worst of anybody's. As an indication of English railway improvement and the shape of things to come, a sure fire passenger loser even from a hitherto staunch supporter.'

Clearly this was an intuitive statement when it came to identifying the root cause of the poor riding as per his penultimate sentence.

Parlour Car No M60742 appears to have been particularly bad as another complaint was received referring to the same vehicle on the same service on the same day. This time the passenger, A. D. McLean, identified the location of the bad running as south of Leicester and the speed as 70mph. Mr/Ms McLean reported, 'Almost impossible to write this letter.' (Passengers who were given the proforma on the train were informed that to calculate speed: '. . . to count the number of rail joints traversed in 40 seconds'. (*But then any train-spotter could have told them that!*)

None of those who complained had any criticism of the service, décor, or staff, but clearly Pullman (British Railways) were now at risk of losing valuable revenue (and perhaps even more important, 'good-will'), as witness the following un-attributable and undated comment, 'Very jerky at high speed. Some passengers not taking lunch. Overheard the reason for this: almost impossible to take soup or drink coffee at speed. Indeed lunch was quite a hazardous affair.' Exactly the same report from the BR staff reported earlier – perhaps it was even the same people and also repeating the words of Mr Smith snr stated earlier.

We may reasonably assume this last comment was once again directed at the LMR sets. Curiously for this at least, we hear little about similar complaints over the riding of the WR sets although we know they were certainly not perfect and would have suffered similar issues. Why the complaints are centred upon the LMR is for two reasons; firstly and most obviously the referred to National Archives file from which this information is all taken (AN 109/956) relative to the operation of the Blue Pullman sets is predominantly involved with the LMR units. There was also another reason which will not please fans of the LMR, and that was as said before the Western Region permanent way was generally maintained to a higher standard than that of the Midland, and consequently irregularities in riding whilst certainly present would therefore not be deemed so severe.

Complaints from members of the public were bad enough and with seemingly no immediate action

170

BLUE PULLMAN on Tour – 'Liverpool by the sea'

It might not have been the hoped-for regular service but a BP set did reach Liverpool on 5 March 1966. (In the same area a WR train also travelled as a special to Aintree for the Grand National as is described in the next chapter.) In March 1966 the BP set was chartered for a Coventry to Lime Street working and return in connection with the Everton versus Coventry football match. Whether this was for the team, officials and other VIPs or if it ran as an ordinary football charter is not reported. Whatever, no doubt on the way all was euphoria, but as Everton were the victors with a 3-0 scoreline we may have no doubt it was a subdued return. The special is seen arriving at Lime Street with BP man and conductor in the cab, working as train '1Z66'. We then see it carrying the ecs headcode before departing the station. Note in the colour image of this sequence, the connection for the shore-supply is under the left-hand buffer. It was in the same position at each end of the train on both the LMR and WR sets. *All Rail Photoprints*

forthcoming from BR the Managing Director of Pullman wrote to H. C. Johnson General Manager of the LMR on 20 August 1962, thus: 'I am sorry to say we are receiving complaints from passengers because of the rough riding of this train, and our staff confirm this.' 'Sir George Briggs, who has extensive industrial interests, recently complained that the riding had deteriorated very badly and another passenger commented that in various places between London and Manchester the riding was shocking and quite frightening.' '[I am aware that] modifications have been made to the motorised bogies on this train but the bad riding appears now to be equally pronounced in the trailer cars which previously rode much better than the motor bogies. We fear that unless these troubles can be remedied very quickly the loading of this train will be affected.' He continued, 'I enclose a copy of a report made by Mr Johnson [Mr N Johnson – Chief Engineer of the Pullman Co.[14]], following a journey to Leicester and back on 14th August.'

'Report of Riding St Pancras–Leicester 14 August 1962.

Car A 60093 (Unit 3)
Car B 60733 (Unit 3)
Car C 60743 (Unit 3)
Car D 60742 (Unit 2)
Car E 60732 (Unit 2)
Car F 60092 (Unit 2)

171

'On the 14th August in company with Mr W. G. Reynolds, Divisional Traffic Manager, London Midland Region St Pancras, and Mr Alexander of Metropolitan-Cammell, I travelled ex St Pancras 11.20am to Leicester and back.

'On the journey from St Pancras to Leicester we travelled in the end seat of all three types of cars, ie over the motorised bogies in cars "A" and "B", and trailer bogie in car "C" (Parlour Car); in my view and that of Messrs Reynolds and Alexander, the riding over the motorised bogies ("A" and "B") was reasonably good although there were a few occasions on which a metallic knock occurred., but curiously enough, not necessarily when any violent motion was taking place. My own impression was that it was due to some contact being made in the vertical plane.

'The quality of ride in car "C" (Parlour Car) over the trailer bogie seems to have deteriorated since my last journey on 1 June 1962. The car was much too lively both in the vertical and transverse directions; there was also a good deal of sharp rolling and to my mind it was this motion which caused the most difficulty in eating and drinking. On one occasion this was very noticeable when Mr Alexander had a cup of nearly full liquid and was sitting on the gangway seat of a four-seat table (i.e. with his cup more or less on the centre line of the coach); at this time I also had a cup similarly nearly full of liquid but was at a seat near the body side. A sharp rolling motion occurred which slopped the liquid from my cup very violently, whereas that in Mr Alexander's cup was not spilt at all.

'On the return journey from Leicester we were travelling in the vehicles of Unit No 2, again over the motorised bogies and over the trailer bogies in the first class parlour car. During the whole run to St Pancras not a single metallic knock was observed but in general it could be said that the riding over the motorised bogie was at least as good, if not rather better, than over the trailer bogie. I gained the impression that since my last riding in these cars, vertical damping on the trailer cars had been modified or their functioning had deteriorated.

'A check might be made on the concentricity of the tyres, for example on trailer bogies on which the riding has deteriorated. Railway Engineers on the continent experienced with Schlieren bogies stress that this type of bogie is very sensitive to the concentricity of tyres and imbalance of wheels; it is of great importance that the wheels are truly round and correctly balanced if good riding is to be achieved.

'As mentioned above, one got the impression that a sharp rolling motion was the principal cause of spillage of liquids and some of the difficulty in eating and drinking; it might be a good thing if consideration could be given to experimenting with the use of a lateral torsion bar to control the relative deflections of the bolster coil springs – similar to the arrangement which is understood has been tested with good results on the Southern Region Mark IV bogie.'

One thing no one ever seems to have picked-up, or at least mentioned when trial runs were spoken of was that if 'Car No X' was considered to have a poor ride between points 'A and B', and 'Car No Y' sampled when returning back from 'B to A', then recall this would be on a different set of rails albeit running parallel. The point being that the up and down lines could well be different: drainage, cant, etc, could all cause a different set of symptoms dependent upon the actual rails traversed – not just the route. It was never mentioned but was there a difference in ride dependent on whether the bogie was facing the direction of travel or trailing?

Meanwhile away from the difficulties over riding, the publicity machine was still in full swing – privately within BR this was likely considered even more important at this time.[15] Accordingly the LMR issued a Press Release on 28 June 1962 to honour the 100,000th passenger on the 'Midland Pullman' as well as to commemorate the train's second birthday.

'When Mr C. B. Minifie *[there is some doubt as to the spelling, the BR Press Release and internal BR documents showing a variation]* of Cheadle booked his usual Monday morning ticket for the "Midland Pullman" from Manchester to London a few weeks ago, he did not realise that he was in fact the 100,000th passenger to travel between the two cities on this train which entered service on 4 July 1960. (See also page 166 about percentage passenger loadings.)

Luxury travel at half-price? Not quite, as there was no half-price Pullman supplement. Definitely First-class and a good view of the end mural as well, itself a sop to Pullman tradition with its timber and perhaps surprisingly not objected to by Jack Howe, indeed he almost appeared to encourage it. The decorative panels were 'handed' and painted by George Mitchell at his home in Forest Hill, being delivered to him by Metropolitan-Cammell and then returned to the builder for actual fixing. The background wood used was either rosewood or ebony. Another point of note not mentioned previously is the tip-up armrest nearest the gangway. Definitely an 'action' shot as notice the trees flashing past. We have to admit we have no idea if this is Midland First-class, or Western first-class – it matters not. Note the table is also not laid, so perhaps not the evening Manchester service. No name either but from the pen and notebook possibly a spotter. *Rail On-line ZF-5438-95371-1-011*

TOP RIGHT Incognito power car at Derby on 28 February 1965. Possibly after overhaul/repaint with the running number – usually sited immediately below the grill behind the cab door – yet to be added. Electrification warning flashes are added and note the red 'Not to be Moved' flag on the front bogie. The LMR retained one 'A' type bogie as a spare whilst reconditioning of the bogies took place every nine months and wheel turning, if the latter were considered necessary, at 12monthly intervals. 'General Repairs' as they were then known were scheduled for every 36-48 months. The point about wheel turning is interesting, as more than once LMR engineers suggested checking the wheels for concentricity in an attempt to resolve the riding issues. This in itself raises questions that cannot be answered, namely did small flats occur due to uneven braking and consequent wear? Tantalisingly, whilst questioning the wheels, no answers are given. *The Transport Treasury*

RIGHT Excluding those shown earlier, images of the trains at Reddish depot are few – but do also see p43 of Blue Pullman Pictorial. Instead we have this view of a *very* junior driver supposedly taken whilst the train was at the depot, possibly during its weekend stopover. Reddish had opened in 1954 on what was the Fallowfield Loop. At the time its main function was as a maintenance and servicing facility for the EM1 and EM2 1,500V DC electric locomotives working between Manchester and Sheffield via Woodhead. It also dealt with EMU sets operating on the same voltage and later the Blue Pullman and conventional DMU sets. As also mentioned, normally the spare set would be held at Reddish and this was highlighted in Modern Railways in July 1962 referring to an incident that had occurred on 28 May the same year when the up morning service had burned out one of its main GEC generators. As a consequence the mid-day Nottingham trip was cancelled and the train turned on the Cricklewood triangle ready to return to Manchester on one engine. We are not informed if it did indeed return north in its booked evening slot in this fashion or if the spare set (assuming this was available) was hurriedly made ready and sent south as an ecs working.

'To mark the occasion and to celebrate the train's second birthday, the London Midland Region, British Railways and the Pullman Car Co. decided to make Mr Minifie their "guest for the day" and to present him with a small memento of the occasion the next time he travelled.

'On Monday next, 2 July therefore, Mr Minifie will be greeted at Manchester Central by a deputation of Railway and Pullman Car Officers and escorted to his seat. He will travel to London as their guest, and be met at St Pancras by another party of Officers including the Divisional Manager, Mr W. O. Reynolds MBE, who will present him with a suitably engraved ashtray. *[The ashtray was engraved with the words 'Midland Pullman'. Some reports say he was also presented with a cake – or was it just a slice (!) – see next paragraph.]*

'To round off the occasion a birthday cake *[which we learn was baked on the train]* has been prepared suitably decorated and this will be presented to the driver, fireman and guard and the technicians[16] who work the train.'

The figures by the Press Department unwittingly give us some information from which to gain perhaps the most accurate analysis of loadings to date. The figure of 100,000 passengers in two years was just referring to the Manchester–London service (and return of course). Allowing for the service operating five days a week and also removing the eight public holidays as applied each year in 1960-2, we are left with an approximate 590 days actual service. Divide the passenger (100,000) number by this figure and we get an average daily loading of 169.49, or basically 85 passengers each way, a daily equivalent loading of 64.39% on a train capable of carrying 132 passengers.

Having 'dealt' with Mr Minifie and – perhaps unwittingly so far as said gentlemen was concerned 'used him as the catalyst' – the main theme of the publicity in the form of an advert followed: 'After two years the popularity of Britain's luxurious super train the "Midland Pullman" shows no sign of abating and it is evident that the service from Manchester (Central) at 7.45am and return from St Pancras at 6.10pm, with nearly seven hours in London for business or pleasure in between, has provided a much welcome link between the two great cities. Facilities will be available at both Manchester

For his birthday young Ted Buckley was taken by his father Bill to see the exciting new Midland Pullman at Cheadle Heath on 29th September 1960. A present many of us can only dream of today! *Ted Buckley*

The Manchester suburbs: Cheadle Heath. *G. A. Worth and Andrew Lance*

Central (before departure) and St Pancras (after arrival for interviews and photographs.' (Regretfully it has not been possible to locate any photograph of the occasion on the day.) We may also ponder whether Mr Minifie had ever or was asked to comment on the ride – assuming he was a regular passenger of course.

It is interesting to note that included in the press release some old habits had been resurrected: notably the reference to a 'fireman' instead of the earlier 'second driver' term, whereas more correctly he was of course a 'second man' or 'driver's assistant'. We learn also that a travelling technician was also still being carried. We speak more on this role in the Western Region chapter.

But whatever may have been the public persona it continued to be very different behind the scenes, as witness a series of correspondence which continued on from a note

Watched by an admiring group of 1960s spotters – with pencil, notebooks, duffle bags, satchels, sandwiches etc., and perhaps one or two with the obligatory Ian Allan spotters book – a Blue Pullman trails through Derby station. This was not the normal route for the service trains, so may have been a diversion, special working, test or works visit.

of six days earlier '25-9-62, from Line Manager LMR, "With the present condition of the BP stock there is a real risk of the breakdown of the existing service … ought we not to assemble a spare train?"'

This was followed a day later with a note from H. C. Johnson at Euston to John Ratter at the BTC expressing concern at the condition of the BP trains. Johnson starts by stating the LM are developing a proposal to run a Liverpool service using the second set with a loco-hauled train available as a stand-by. He adds that the LMR CME reports the present mechanical and electrical condition of the trains in the following terms:

'During the past two months two major troubles have arisen, firstly a fractured leading bogie tyre, followed by another similar incident, has revealed that all the tyres on both the trains will require to be changed immediately, and secondly the main generators have been giving progressively poor performance in recent months and it now seems that there is progressive internal breakdown of insulation which means that all the generator armatures must be rewound by the manufacturers as a matter of urgency.'

From this we can see that the proposed Liverpool service had not been forgotten although it would seem as if Johnson was disinclined to proceed and was almost looking for an ally at BRB whom he might use in the future should further pressure be exerted over usage/capacity.

What follows is an understandable postponement of the Liverpool working confirmed by a response from Ratter at BRB to Johnson at Euston as set out in a letter from the former of 4 October 1962. Commenting on the present mechanical condition of the units and the units generally he states, 'There is no option but to "shop" the trains for maintenance and modifications. They were originally conceived as an experiment with the thought that further sets would be ordered, if successful, and proper spares built up. Another ten trains, even if working in two or three regions, would change the whole problem. We made the job more difficult by having different trains on the Western Region.'

Was this an admission of failure on the part of BR and the start of the higher echelons looking to distance themselves from the sets? Possibly yes, but for the present Euston were still keen to promote their positive points especially as the LMR was then under regular criticism for poor service on the LNWR main line at the time being rebuilt for electrification. The LMR had attempted to counter these complaints with regular positive updates but it was an uphill battle not least as on their prestige express services Stanier's 'Duchess' class had been largely superseded by more modern yet distinctly less powerful Class 40 diesel locomotives which with slower schedules did little to promote the 'modern' railway.

Rutter continued, 'I think you would probably agree that there is no case to build more [meaning Blue Pullman] of them. If we wanted more de-luxe trains, a conventional locomotive-hauled Pullman would be a more flexible and economic solution. The cars could be modelled on the "Blue" train pattern and amenity.' The note further continues: 'I think the answer is:

1) To face up to the fact that the Liverpool service can be put back until the major overhauls of the "Blue" train are complete. It should then run for two years without major overhaul.

2) To examine the case for an extension of "Blue" train type service, in conjunction with the Western Region and possibly Eastern Region, so providing a capacity margin for maintenance. These could be built fairly quickly if a case was proved.

3) As an alternative to "2", we will have to face up to periodic withdrawal for maintenance, running old-type Pullman cars in their place, which will not please the customers, although we may be able to give the old cars a "face lift". I shall be grateful for your views and will start talks going here on the lines above if you think the same.'

It would seem as if Ratter did indeed consult amongst his colleagues at the Board for shortly after his own note something appears from a very perceptive Gerry Fiennes at the time in his role of Chief Operating Officer at BR Headquarters. Fiennes sent his own memorandum to Euston in which he suggests running a 2,500hp loco-hauled 'Liverpool Pullman' to gauge demand. He also suggests a costing exercise, and continued with these prophetic words:

'… whether in fact it would not be better to replace both Blue Pullmans by locomotive hauled stock, so that in 1966 you do not have them around your neck.'

Fiennes also makes the hint that if not wanted for the East Coast – presumably he meant post 1966 – they would be sold to Peru.

This was also the very first time any reference is made to the post-1966 situation and indicates that the Blue Pullman trains would in fact be redundant after that (post electrification) date. From this we may take it that a decision had already been made to replace the current diesel Pullman with an electric version operating on the newly upgraded LNWR route. But where does Peru fit in? Likewise the East Coast (although more on the latter later)? One thing is certain, the connection with Peru is not clear. Had Fiennes or someone else already made or even received an approach? We are unlikely to find further on this topic although it shows that even at this early stage – *just two years after entering service* – clouds were already gathering over the future of the sets themselves and perhaps serious consideration was being given to ridding BR of what was becoming an ever more problematical train. (Whether BR might have wished to dispose of the WR sets as well we can only imagine.)

For now we must come back to fact instead of conjecture and report that the repairs envisaged for both LMR sets were based on an intermediate overhaul and would involve:

'1 – Wash down, touch up and varnish paintwork. Refurbishing of interior bodywork etc. Testing refrigeration, air-conditioning and lighting equipment. Lifting for examination of suspension and dismantling and examination of brakework. Check roller bearing axleboxes. General inspection of the electric traction equipment, turbo-chargers to be removed and bearings renewed. M.A.N. engine to be tested for rated output. Rolls-Royce auxiliary engine and alternators to be re-conditioned.

2 – The eleven defective Brown-Boveri gear wheels [this defect is not mentioned earlier] have not yet been replaced The replacement wheels are available and will require to be changed during the intermediate repair. The risk of scrapping an axle during this operation cannot be entirely ruled out.

3 – Modifications: Fitting of AWS equipment [at last, but which still meant these, the latest, trains had been operating on the LMR for two years in all weathers without this vital safeguard and at average speeds greater than before]. Modifications to trailer bogie, swing links, i.e. fitting of means of lubrication to swing links and trunnions. Modifications to Stones/Rolls alternator suspension bracket. Riding trials are required as soon as possible to determine the optimum settings of the various dampers, after this all dampers will require to go to the manufacturer's for setting and then re-fitted to the cars.'

Desborough 1964. LMR set passing Desborough south of Leicester in July taken on the not ideal colour film of the period. The point of the image – again apart from the lovely MR signals – is to show that some unofficial individuality still survived as per the red-painted lamp brackets. Regretfully, we have no indication as to the actual vehicle(s) involved. *Colour Rail 211807*

LMR at Derby North Junction in 1960 – sparkling train in every way. At the time the through service was the only regular passenger working over the Chaddesden loop – normally just used for goods services avoiding Derby station. *Colour Rail 211815*

It was noted that on 2 November 1962 a main generator had failed whilst the other set was in Derby for heavy maintenance and modifications.

Johnson at Euston also points out to BRB (presumably Ratter) that during this work not even a half-set will be available as a spare, particularly a problem with the main generators, as '. . . only two are serviceable and one of these is doubtful.' He continues with what is almost a desperate plea: 'The reported condition of the existing sets, however, caused serious concern, not only as regards the Liverpool venture, but as regards the continuance of the existing service. I have asked the Pullman car people to let me have the spare loco hauled set as quickly as possible to stand by. Anything you can do to help will be appreciated.' At a meeting on 6 November it was promised at least a half set would be available and which so appears to confirm that Midland sets did indeed swap half sets.

The timescale for the maintenance work was likely to take three months per complete train and which it was naturally hoped would then lead to improved riding. But it is interesting that nowhere in located papers is the single word 'cure' used when it came to addressing the riding issues which leads to the conclusion that Euston were aware the best that might be achieved was instead 'some improvement'. Consequently the scratch set of locomotive-hauled Pullmans was now prepared and held (presumably as originally discussed at Derby) as a reserve set. What we are not informed of with any certainty, although again this is spoken of later, is how often it was actually required in the six-month time span it took for both sets to have their respective works visits.

With one set now out of use and undergoing repair at Derby, Euston received a report on 7 January 1963 that a collapsed bearing had been found on motor coach No M60730. We are not told which type of bearing was involved: wheel/motor/generator etc. Presumably this was actually on the set then undergoing repairs as there does not appear to be any mention of a service failure or necessary use of the stand-by set as a result. The report added the actual bearing would be examined at Derby; no doubt it was but again a gap in the paperwork does not provide a result.

What we do learn later in the same month (28 January 1963) is the spares situation as applicable to major components. An internal BR report states there was just a single '1,100hp' (1,100?) MAN diesel and generator to cover all five train sets operating on the LMR and WR – equal to the provision of a 1 in 10 back up. The report added that two more had been ordered. The position so far as the auxiliary generators was the same, with just one available and so again two further sets had been ordered. Finally on the topic of spares there was a '...similar situation with bogies.' It was noted that the delivery of these spares was taking longer to arrive than anticipated.

But these statements need both clarification and explanation. Was this limited number of components the norm or had it been allowed to reach such a low figure either deliberately or by choice – necessary economy/actual usage etc? Why the mention of '1,100hp' MAN engines; surely those specified, and genuinely believed fitted to the trains were at the lower rating of 1,000hp? And finally the bogies: what was the actual spare situation so far as bogies were concerned as of course each train had of necessity several different types? Regretfully this remains another topic on which we are now never likely to achieve full amplification.

Meanwhile the LMR had still not totally given up on the idea of Liverpool as a destination. It is slightly unusual to report then that Gerry Fiennes' idea of assessing demand with a loco-hauled set was not proceeded with, especially as the WR had successfully used this same concept to prove viability for a 'South Wales Pullman'. Fiennes it will be recalled had used the words 'diesel hauled' and '2,500hp'. No doubt his phrasing was carefully chosen to ensure that an 'old-fashioned' steam engine was not used (unlike on the WR), One of the issues may have been the LMR simply did not have a spare 2,500hp diesel at their disposal or for that matter access to any further loco-hauled Pullman cars, what spares there were now being held at Derby in reserve as the spare set for the existing service. (It is slightly strange that spare loco-hauled Pullman vehicles could be held at Derby but the spare BP was by now being stabled at Reddish.)

Whatever, it was around this time, late 1962/early 1963, that the LMR Board, we may also say probably reluctantly, came to the decision not to proceed with Liverpool as a destination for Pullman, either with a loco-hauled or Blue Pullman set. Having known that some rumour as to a Liverpool Pullman set would likely have already leaked to the media and the public, the excuse was used that this was due to potential disruption with the ongoing electrification works. Privately though the reason was likely just as much due to the ongoing complaints of poor riding which had not diminished; after all, why leave themselves open to another train full of potential whingers?

But this decision was certainly not welcomed by all sides, especially it seems by the Manchester Line Manager. Considering that the Manchester–St Pancras service was still operating successfully, the decision not to go ahead with the Liverpool service can be considered slightly surprising in view of the good business case that had been prepared for the utilisation of an expensive and depreciating asset that was otherwise earning nothing. It will come as no surprise to report that on 13 March 1963 Dr Beeching as Chairman of British Railways had himself questioned the limited use of '. . . this expensive asset'.

Unaware no doubt of how the wind was blowing in London and in the genuine belief that the service was about to be approved, or was it to spur the LMR Board into action, the Manchester Line Manager had a few months earlier and it seems off his own back begun publicising the new Liverpool service with a proposed start date from the autumn 1963 timetable. (The long lead-time was considered necessary in order to have, amongst other things, the necessary servicing infrastructure in place.)

In the heart of the Peak District, the morning service passed New Mills South Junction. As is known the sets contained two auxiliary engines for on-board train requirements. The actual engine was basically similar to that used as a traction unit for diesel railcars and included many interchangeable components with other RR fitted equipment – one of the few features where interchange did exist. For ease of servicing and likely equipment needing attention, this auxiliary engine was so arranged as to be accessible from either side and all scheduled maintenance could be carried out without the need to gain access through the floor or by removal of the engine unit. The unit had cast iron cylinder heads formed in two four-cylinder units attached to a hardened steel crankshaft running in nine bearings.
The Transport Treasury

Down Manchester service in full flight at near Kibworth North, 16 May 1961. As mentioned, advertising for the trains continued for some time. One feature from 3 October 1960 was an advert/report on British Steel and how their products were used in the train. It also quotes from two members of railway staff under the heading, 'First of Britain's new crack expresses'. Rolling stock Inspector Barker was quoted as stating the train had more than lived up to expectations, and that, 'Everybody is highly delighted with its performance. It has kept its times and mostly even been ahead of them'. There was also a quote from Driver Bone, who said, '[he] Wished he had trains to drive like this when he became a driver 26 years ago…'. There was a similar positive quote from an un-named Chef. *Stephen Summerson/The Transport Treasury*

Not surprisingly the announcement was picked up and reported on in a number of newspapers, as well as contemporary railway magazines. However rather than confirmation or even a change of heart by Euston, said Manager was instead rebuked with specific instructions that he was to advise all concerned that the Liverpool service would not now commence. No doubt he did – and of course it never did. (Pullman services did eventually reach Liverpool but not with a BP set. Instead from around the summer of 1965 four Pullman cars were added to a morning and evening Liverpool train – an almost exact repeat of one of the proposals from years before!)

Unfortunately, while the LMR Board might have viewed a Liverpool service as having been merely an idea or proposal, there were those on Merseyside who were certainly less than satisfied with the decision, especially in view of the publicity already given. An article in the *Liverpool Daily Post* for 23 August 1962 had the headline: 'Progress marches backwards on Liverpool–London line'. It was accompanied by a publicity photograph of a six-car Blue Pullman set together with the caption, 'The train that could provide additional passenger accommodation over the main line through Matlock'. It took a private meeting between BR and (it was stated) 'journalists from Liverpool' to resolve the situation, after which nothing else appears to have been mentioned. To be fair, the Liverpool press did have a point; in 1962 their best service to London now took 4hr 5min, slower than compared to 3hr 20min as had existed in 1939. The proposed Pullman service would have been 3hr 55min down, and four hours in the up direction, only a slight improvement so far as 1962 was concerned but on the plus side at least it would have been in luxury. Somehow the local press had not picked up the fact that timings would hardly have been improved; the existing schedule appeared to be their main gripe. It would have to wait for electrification a few years later for honour to be satisfied, the whole probably not helped with the occasional visit to the Liverpool area and indeed at least once to Lime Street station of a BP set on a charter working.

In reality the start of 1963 saw the situation on the LMR and their two six-car Blue Pullman little different than the start of the service in July 1960. Still only one set was in regular use, added to which there was also now a spare set of five loco-hauled Pullman cars on stand-by at Derby. The maintenance of the sets also had to be done by April 1963 and consequently the ride was definitely starting to get rough and in more ways than one.

But we are left to ponder as to whether Liverpool as a destination really was dead, for in March 1963 an unaccredited note appears on the file stating that a decision as to the new service was (still) urgently needed in preparation for the printing of the timetable, the service being planned to start in September 1963. For the first time we are also informed as to some details as to the proposed actual working which in the down direction at least would have had intermediate stops at Luton, Manchester Central and Warrington Central. Servicing would have been at Allerton at a cost of £32,000 for

179

equipment plus the cost of training staff and additional staff required – the latter implied as one fitter and one artisan. So was this a last ditch attempt by Manchester, the Line Manager, or even Euston to resurrect a new working? Commendable perhaps in some ways but whoever or whatever was behind this late attempt was still seemingly ignoring the mechanical and reported reliability issues. In the event it took another four months before the definite decision was made, as on 12 July 1963 in an internal note signed by A. J. Johnson, the LMR Commercial Manager, came what was the final statement: the Liverpool option would NOT go ahead – the recipients of Mr Johnson's note were not stated.

So, whilst Liverpool as a destination from London may have been ruled out this was certainly not the last idea as to extending the sphere of operation for the trains and with it an attempt at full utilisation. Indeed we know that at the same time, early 1963, closed discussions within BR had come up with the idea of a luxury service between either Manchester or Liverpool and Glasgow although subsequent discussion would rule this out due to line capacity and the very practical view that over this distance air-travel would have a distinct advantage. (Had either of these gone ahead we might wonder about the reaction of Liverpool at seeing their own luxury London service usurped. Recall too the previous comments by Charles Long over victualling Pullman services away from the Capital.)

A somewhat more feasible alternative was put forward by an unnamed member of staff in a note dated 13 February 1963. This person suggests the second set work an 'up morning Derby to St Pancras train' – it will be recalled the Manchester service whilst by-passing Derby did not call there either in the morning or in the evening. A return St Pancras–Derby working would be scheduled for the evening. It does not appear much, if any, discussion took place over likely patronage and instead it almost appears as if the hierarchy now looked for reasons not to proceed, with excuses along the lines of, '… suggested pathway may conflict with flagship "Condor" freight service. One existing DMU service would also have to retimed to run five minutes later. Other services would have to be altered or retimed unless … (whichever) … could reach … (wherever) … by this time … etc'.

Towards the end of the same year, 1963, there was even mention of a Birmingham–Glasgow or even a slightly fanciful Newcastle–Bristol working but again air-competition would appear to have been one of the factors against such a service together with the likelihood that there would be insufficient passengers and fewer still being prepared to pay the necessary Pullman supplement. What is not totally clear is if these ideas were perceived for the present time or post 1966 train-set use. All of these suggestions seemingly glossed over the reliability and ride issues that still prevailed.

So once again we come back to resigned acceptance amongst the hierarchy that the riding issues would indeed never be satisfactorily resolved and the idea of expansion on the LMR was thus (permanently as it turned out) shelved. It might seem as if the Fiennes prophecy was also coming to the fore as comments were also made that the life of the sets was limited following electrification.

Before leaving the topic of projected services, we should mention that Charles Long, in his later May 1973 article in *Railway World*, commenting on the proposed Liverpool service, stated, '… basically, it was lack of agreement with the unions on staffing that prevented the introduction of a London-based "Midland Pullman" using the stand-by six-car diesel unit'.

Charles Long continues, 'The union dispute over the Nottingham extension was still going on, and with the new Liverpool train having to run beyond Manchester, this could have been seen as displaying a "red" flag to a bull.' (Should that perhaps have been a 'blue' flag?)

At this stage the reader could be forgiven for believing the operation of the 'Midland Pullman' has been little short of problematical from the outset and more of a millstone to the LMR than an object of pride. But this would not be strictly correct for as we have seen whenever the opportunity arose every effort was made to not only promote the trains but also to enhance their prestige. Witness then the early summer of 1961 when the LMR entered into an agreement with the Messrs Victor Britain Ltd. to provide a chauffeur service for passengers to meet passengers arriving off the up Manchester service, and take them in luxury on the final leg of their journey to their London destinations. It was hoped by all concerned

Speeding through Market Harborough on 25 March 1963, another power car seemingly without identification number. Personal needs were not forgotten for the guard either as his compartment in the power cars contained a food warmer.

Getting ready for the evening departure from St Pancras; and two views earlier in the day preparatory to the Leicester/Nottingham working. Seen from this angle the 'standard' type opening doors leading to the kitchen area somehow look decidedly out of place. Again, it is surprising there was no comment from Jack Howe on their design. With the droplights down we might only begin to imagine the cooking aroma emanating. *Antony Ford collection.*

(although certainly not drivers of the famed London black cabs) that the clientele from the Pullman would favour such a service, and discussions took place from 18 May 1961. Evidently, they were quickly concluded, for the new arrangement commenced as early as 5 June 1961. Publicity was provided by advertising cards that were handed to each passenger on board the train. Unfortunately the take up was nowhere near as good as had been expected, and with an average patronage of just one person a week, it was inevitable that the service would be withdrawn. No actual date is given for this, but it was unlikely to have been protracted. Interestingly, the same car firm had successfully operated a similar service some years earlier, it is believed from Paddington, but it eventually suffered a similar fate. It is believed the charge was around 25s per hour's travel with a subsequent comment in *Motor Sport* for July 1962 that Victor Britain's '. . . new V8 Daimlers are said to be so quiet that tape-recorders can be used therein without picking up road noises.' *Modern Railways* in their July 1963 issue illustrate a Victor Britain Jaguar MkX 3.8 with a customer in the driving seat and the door held by a uniformed driver with a self-drive Morris 1100 behind them.

Taking a break now from specifics and instead returning to general and particularly loading issues, we know that loadings on the Leicester/Nottingham service

181

were of course poor and as if to prove the point BR announced that for a trial period in the autumn of 1963, a special first class single fare would be available on the Nottingham train which was reduced by the equivalent of the usual Pullman supplement. This would apply from 7 October, Mondays to Fridays on journeys by the 11.15am 'Midland Pullman' from St Pancras to Leicester, Loughborough and Nottingham.

The normal fare to Nottingham of 46s 6d (£2.32½) was therefore reduced to 36s 6d (£1.82½) but still plus the 10s (50p) Pullman supplement. (This was half the original £1 supplement originally applied on this route. When the reduction was made is not reported.) It was also the second attempt to boost custom, as from 10 September 1962 the Nottingham service had been accelerated to 115 minutes from St Pancras, and in consequence had become one of the fastest schedules on BR at that time. This acceleration was in many ways an unfortunate and perhaps not particularly well thought out piece of marketing – attempting to attract extra passengers particularly considering the ride characteristics which we know became worse as speed increased.

What we do not hear anywhere with complete accuracy are tales of passengers being unable to obtain a seat on the Manchester workings (recall standing passengers were not permitted) whilst in similar fashion there is no general information as to how loadings might have varied on differing days of the week. Was it possible to book a Pullman 'season ticket' for the Manchester working if desired?

The fact the trains were still in operation and similarly being publicised would have appeared to the public at least as showing the trains were a business and financial success, but behind the scenes their long-term future on the LMR was already being considered. A memorandum from an un-named source at the BTC (Ratter perhaps as the use of the word 'experiment' is repeated again) dated 4 October 1962 sounded a note of warning: 'The trains were originally conceived as an experiment, and present difficulties exist over withdrawing them for periodic maintenance, as there are only a very few units and consequently this cannot be overcome. Possibly the sets could provide information on new fittings for other vehicles in future, and also lead to other stock being upgraded to a similar standard.'

We may read this in two ways: another attempt by BR to distance themselves from an issue which for too long had rested in the 'too difficult' tray but also a hint as to what could well follow in the future and here we cannot ignore 'HST' – we will return to that particular theme in the final chapter. No doubt had the spate of problems which had plagued Blue Pullman not been as widespread and long lasting then the word 'experiment' would likely not have been used.

On this issue, it is also difficult to separate the LMR operation from that of the WR – which will be discussed in the next chapter. Perhaps even the BTC were preparing the ground for a feared outcome even if, at that time, it was still a few years into the future. Further discussion on the train's future, on the LMR at least, would subsequently occur at intervals right up to 1966 – and beyond. More immediately, the subject of what do with the sets over the 1962 Christmas Holiday was under discussion, BR deciding as early as June 1962 that it intended to cancel the service between 20 December 1962 through to 2 January 1963, and likewise on, and surrounding, the other Bank Holidays in 1963. Not surprisingly The Pullman Car Co objected to this, and cited its objections as based on a serious loss of revenue. However BR's justification for its intended action was supported by revenue and passenger figures from the equivalent period from the previous year. Accordingly it is now that we obtain one of the very few details of actual passenger numbers covering the period Monday 4 December 1961 to Friday 26 January 1962. In summary it shows that on the down Manchester journey from St Pancras for December 1961/January 1962 numbers dropped from a peak of 125 to just 40 paying passengers. The up train, though carried its maximum complement of 132 passengers on one occasion and over 120 on several other days. Indeed, over the 37 days surveyed, the loading was only below 100 persons on seven occasions, but also with a minimum of 31. The Nottingham service was (usually) very poor by comparison, with a maximum of 112 leaving St Pancras (certainly higher than we might have been expected to believe on any occasion) but also down to a minimum of just six. The return journeys back to St Pancras were also poor: a maximum of 53 and a minimum of eight. While these figures must be read as representing just a sample and covering just one period, they do support the later decision to curtail the Nottingham working. Unfortunately, from the limited data provided it is also impossible to draw valid conclusions on which days it was reasonable to expect profitability and on which it was not. What was stated and is interesting to note, is that a number of passengers only ever booked single tickets on the 'Midland Pullman'. Hence it would appear the train was not just being used as a *luxury commuter* service but instead perhaps as a *luxury connecting* service; or might the well-informed have found their dry-cleaning bills a little on the excessive side due to slopping soups and beverages!

Pullman's own concern about 'loss of revenue' applicable to curtailing the service on certain days around bank holiday time must also now be considered. For as mentioned previously, most passengers consumed food in the evenings whilst during the morning a full breakfast was served to the minority – not the majority – and yet it was the morning 'up' train which had the greatest patronage. Small wonder Pullman was unwilling to give up any chance of securing a few more 'crumbs'. We may even wonder about the amount of food that was wasted in consequence – purchased by Pullman in case of need, stored, prepared, but then not served and eaten. Then there was the issue of the number of staff to be paid but with a patronage as low as just six on one occasion what did they do? We know BR were adept at 'creative accounting' in other areas of their operation far removed

Almost everywhere it ventured it seemed BP received admiring glances; spotters would eagerly try and record vehicle numbers; cameras would be pointed at the train both stationary and in motion; whilst even more would simply stand and watch – as indeed here at Dock Junction not far out from St Pancras on 24 September 1960. *Rail On-Line ZF-5438-95371-1-003*

from Pullman, so we might equally wonder how Pullman was justified to continue in its present form.

In the opinion of the present writers perhaps there was indeed consideration given to curtailing the Pullman aspect of the train but would this have really saved much? By stopping the 'meals at seat' service, provision would have to have been made for a separate dining car with consequent loss of general seating. Then there was the issue of the two kitchens already in place: keep both, close one, or replace/rebuild with seating? Finally, the image perspective: if the train were downgraded to ordinary first class would this have a knock-on negative effect on Pullman services concurrently operating elsewhere?

Away from conjecture and supposition, we again now have to refer back (text-wise if not in strict date order) to July 1963 when A. J. Johnson had formally curtailed the Liverpool idea. From a note just 11 days later, on 23 July 1963 we learn that the LMR are now admitting BP was 'not thoroughly reliable' and there had been the need to run the stand by set, itself 'not a very good one' far too often[18]. It added that any rather hazardous attempt to run extra services using the sets 'would involve a lot of expense for a comparatively limited period . . . on balance we should be well out of pocket.' The intended recipient is not clear. The same note made what were now becoming common references to what will happen after electrification of the 'LNWR' route and in consequence the potential remaining limited life and operation of the trains. Perhaps it was the same un-named (senior?) LMR person who had penned an earlier note on 13 June 1963 and who appeared to ask why with two train sets available just one was making a single return trip daily? Clearly at a certain level (or in a certain position) a lack of knowledge of what actually went on – referring to the mid-day fill in service – had not been a barrier to promotion.

With what follows we can almost come to the conclusion that there existed on the LMR (and likely to have involved BR Headquarters as well) two distinct camps so far as the Blue Pullman trains were concerned. On the one side we have Mr Johnson (it is not certain if this is the LMR or Pullman 'Johnson' but probably the LMR man) admitting on 23 November 1963 that even after modifications made to the bogies the ride at 80mph plus was likely to be inferior to an ordinary coach running on BR 'Commonwealth' or 'B4' bogies. But then on 12

Reported as at Roman Road on 15 June 1962. *M. Mitchell/The Transport Treasury*

Leaning to the curve at Bedford in 1965; probably the up morning service from Manchester. *Rail On-Line ZF-5438-95371-1-005*

December 1963 an unsigned note refers to a proposal for the second LMR set to run a reverse St Pancras to Manchester service leaving St Pancras in the morning! (There would have been a corresponding Manchester to St Pancras train in the evening.) Clearly the train still had its advocates.

We may suspect the earlier words of Dr Beeching were also still resonating so far as maximising usage were concerned, perhaps confirmed by another (frustratingly) undated note from the BR Chairman at Marylebone Road to the respective General Managers expressing disappointment at not making full use of the BP sets. 'It was appreciated that there were certain commercial objections to putting them into general service, but embarrassing political and public criticism could be made if the extent of their non-utilisation were known. The Board wishes the General Managers to take immediate action to secure sensible use of these train in service…'[19]. This was a bit unfair on Paddington as from September 1961 all three of their trains were in daily use; perhaps this undated note preceded that of September 1961 or was it another case of lack of information at the top?

Indeed the public through the media had (fortunately) remained totally ignorant that 50% of an expensive asset (on the LMR) remained unused all of the time: a somewhat unusual situation when they would certainly have been party to the same information back in July 1960.

Had the reverse St Pancras to Manchester morning working proceeded we are again given detail as to costs of additional fixed assets. These were additional shore facilities at Cricklewood and now Reddish plus some new facilities at Derby. The estimated cost being £20,000. There was mention of an anticipated 50% loading but how this figure had been arrived at is not explained, even so there was some doubt as to whether it would have been sufficient to cover costs. No mention is made of pathways. One ticketing initiative for the proposed new working was a suggested 'out by Pullman return by ordinary train' – something, presumably not offered on the original Manchester/Leicester–Nottingham workings – but only stated as such because it has not been found to have been mentioned. (Perhaps this initiative was as a result of learning not all journeys booked for the existing train were returns and because of the poor take-up of the return Manchester train.) As with the exiting Manchester working, the proposed 'reverse' working was not suggested to run at weekends, with this stated as due to the potential for unreliability caused by likely weekend engineering works.

As can probably be guessed, once more nothing came of the idea and which we can also state with conviction as being the final recorded attempt at intensifying the Blue Pullman service on the LMR.

Post 1964 until the end of operation on the LMR, there was little further of note to report. From the public's viewpoint the trains continued to operate to the usual pattern[20], patronage, perhaps remarkably (but this not in any way intended as a sarcastic comment), was as before and the only continuing difficulty was presumably the ride issue (although there is no located correspondence on this subject after this date). Instead, activity was concentrated behind the scenes, the LMR working flat out towards the electrification of the former LNWR line out of Euston, leading to the electric service being seen as the preferred option to serve Manchester instead of running locomotive-hauled trains (or a Pullman DMU) over the former Midland Railway route. How and when this preference developed is not reported but from the available evidence it appears rooted in electric over diesel and was certainly policy prior to 1960 – possibly even going back to 1955.

Even so the continued level of patronage was at least equal to the type of figures quoted previously and which in itself did pose the LMR a dilemma. Were they simply to abandon the service in favour of electrification or continue to earn revenue from what was still a premium working, even if it was slowly becoming dated by comparison? Was there even the opportunity to run both, perhaps for a time at least?

But in 1964 at least, the choice was for everything to be concentrated on the electrified railway, and this is confirmed in papers lodged at Kew which state that BR, by implication the LMR but that is not 100% certain, would use the Pullmans even when the ex-LNWR line was electrified. (We cannot be certain if this meant just a locomotive hauled electric Pullman service or even a transfer of the diesel Pullmans to the LNWR line. The file is completely ambiguous on this important but salient point.) In the event it was academic, for by the following year a decision had been confirmed and it was stated categorically that there was, 'no question of using the diesel Pullman on the electrified line'. However, Pullman would perhaps have the last laugh, as (possibly as a direct result of the general success of the diesel Pullman service) a batch of new locomotive-hauled Pullman vehicles had been built from 1962 onwards.

Even at this late stage we have once again to revert back to 1960 and the situation as regards the location of the spare set, for should a failure occur then it was simple pot luck as to geographically where the failure occurred and consequently whether the spare BP set was in a position to take over the working – or whether recourse had to be made to the 'scratch set' of Pullman cars. There is some suggestion that where use of the spare Blue Pullman was not feasible (or perhaps even possible), passengers were simply shepherded on to an ordinary working, no doubt to rumblings of discontent. With a refund perhaps . . ?

We do know of one spectacular but fortunately safe outcome to a failure that occurred on 27 February 1966. On this occasion, the rear power car of the down 6.10pm from St Pancras suffered a seized traction motor bearing which resulted in the associated wheelset locking solid (the running number of the power car involved is not known). The precise location where this occurred is also not recorded, but a clue can be gleaned from the subsequent report which states that the damaged power car was later observed at Bedford depot. This time the spare Pullman set was not available (we are not told why) and a replacement service consisting just ordinary Mark 1 coaches hauled by a 'Peak' class diesel was used for the next two days.

Meanwhile both LMR sets had been overhauled in 1964, at which time they were also due to repainted. This time George Williams was quick to point out to Derby that care should be taken to use a clear varnish so as not to unduly discolour the white paint underneath. We may safely say that after 1964 the LMR Blue Pullmans appeared post-overhaul in a slightly different colour to when they had first entered service. We might also raise a wry smile as following the repaint it was discovered that no one on BR had kept a record of where the front-end transfers had been obtained from – although there must have been some frantic and eventual successful searching as this omission was subsequently rectified.

Withdrawal was now only a matter of time, but there was also a possibility that the Eastern Region had considered taking the two LMR sets to use as a separate portion of their own 'Yorkshire Pullman' train, intended to run from King's Cross a few minutes behind the main service, but instead destined for Hull. In the event it is hardly surprising to report the ER was not satisfied with the riding qualities, and the proposal was abandoned; the involvement of the ER in the trains is also discussed further later on.

The only other change came in March 1966, when BRB decreed that the Pullman crest be abolished, in line with the intended new corporate image. It is thought this decree was never followed through with the LMR sets which ended their operational days on the region still in basically the same external livery as they started. Finally on Friday 15 April 1966, the last departures took place from Manchester and St. Pancras, and compared with less than six years earlier, seemingly without celebration of any sort. The new electric locomotive-hauled Pullman service began

In the final months of BP operation on the Midland, a set passes Beeston (Nottinghamshire) and even after several years was still being watched – perhaps this was in the final days of working on the LMR. Alongside, the siding into Shipstones Maltings has clearly not been used for some time, its rails rusting, as indeed would be the fate of the BP trains in a few short years. As is mentioned in the next (final view) for this chapter, the last BP services on the LMR operated on 15 April 1966; ironically too at the same time the trains were also almost half way through their operational lives. *Rail On-Line ROS-CB013*

This time to what is an empty auditorium, the very last London-bound BP service passes the closed station at Heaton Mersey, running on time just before 8.00am en-route to St Pancras. The station here had closed to passengers in 1961 and would close to all traffic two years later. The route too would later be closed and like the train all would consigned to history. Heaton Mersey station is now an industrial estate. *John R. Hillier*

from Euston the following Monday, 18 April.

After this and until June 1966 at least the two sets were held in store (where is not reported but most likely to have been Reddish where they also would hopefully have been under partial cover) pending a decision as to their future – the phrase now is to be held in 'warm-store'. We can be certain that considerable discussion took place behind the scenes about a suitable future use, and this is referred to in the subsequent chapters. What is not believed is that for the moment at least there was any further move to sell them to Peru or indeed any foreign railway, the sister units to the two 'Midland Pullman' sets still operating favourably on the WR at this time.

With the eventual decision to transfer both six-car sets to the WR, they were officially withdrawn from LMR stock, and moved sometime in the late summer or autumn of 1966, it is believed initially to Old Oak Common, although formal transfer to WR stock would not take place until March 1967. Somewhat prophetically the former route taken by the BP sets on the LMR between Derby and Manchester via what we now term the 'Midland line', was closed in June 1968. Manchester Central, the northernmost destination of the Blue Pullman service, also closed from 5 May 1969, the site subsequently becoming a scruffy car park until 1978. Work then started in 1982 to transform it into the Greater Manchester Exhibition Centre (G-Mex) which Queen Elizabeth II opened in 1986. Since extended, this iconic building was renamed in 2007 as Manchester Central.

St Pancras remained a railway station and has prospered. Whilst no longer the London home of the 'Midland Pullman' it has been totally revamped, with the buildings now housing a 5-star hotel, a champagne bar on the concourse and more importantly now, as St. Pancras International has a dual role serving not only trains to Nottingham and Derby but also as the UK terminus for the Eurostar operation via HS1.

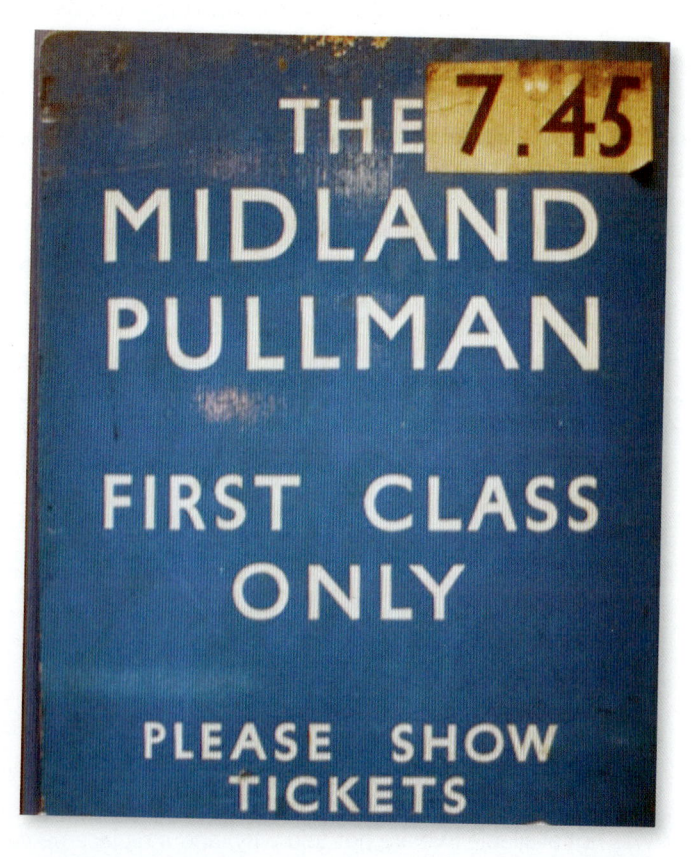

Notes

(1) The word 'appreciated' here is used with caution. First thoughts might well be the same as rail passengers would have today if a new train service and new stock were brought into use – we would naturally assume there was sufficient of this stock to maintain the service with little thought given as to necessary 'down-time' for servicing etc. So did the LMR promote the fact that there was a spare, 'standby' set available? If so it was certainly not done openly in the various items of publicity for the period, neither was it noted in contemporary media reporting. Possibly to do so would have been a risky strategy, on the one hand such information might well be best intended as a reassurance to the business user that the railway was ensuring the new (and for its time radical) train service could be maintained at all times, but against this was the risk that such information might, especially to the uninformed, imply there was almost an expectation failure was expected. It could also lead to speculation that half the investment was being underused.

(2) 'Set 2' appears to have been used as a temporary official designation. Set numbers were certainly never displayed on the trains (either LMR or WR units) and instead identification was by vehicle (car) numbers. Another reason set numbers were not given was so as to facilitate the swapping of half-sets. We do at times have reference to 'Train 1' or 'Train 2' but the make-up of these could of course have varied at times although always of six cars and comprising two 'mirror' half sets.

(3) There was little point in displaying the 'Midland Pullman' poster in areas where potential traffic was unlikely to be generated and in consequence they were mainly seen at or near to both the stopping points of the morning, lunch-time, and evening service. Some may also have appeared at principal stations on other regions no doubt in the hope of enticing potential customers needing to make a trip to one of the train's destinations.

(4) The service was only ever operated on weekdays with weekends given over to the maintenance.

(5) Mention is made in the text that, '… the most miserly passenger finds it near-impossible to sit hungry in a coach full of feeders.' No doubt this was true and in consequence to the benefit of the profitability of the service, but it is then perhaps surprising that there was not a similar response to the allure of cooked bacon on the morning train!

(6) We are not informed what duties were worked by the driver and second man (second driver), likewise the guard. Whilst the turn may well have been one where mileage/overtime was regularly achieved could it have been that the crews only worked one way and returned on another duty? Without access to crew rosters there is a case for both scenarios. Bear in mind that with no mid-point stop either from or to Manchester the Manchester/London crew would have to work straight through and sometimes stayed over. So far as the catering staff were concerned, the four continuous days referred to meant they worked 54hrs 20 minutes over that period, some of which was undoubtedly overtime. (The years in question are long before the period of modern day 'flexible rostering.') Assuming there was little or no preparation time in advance of the morning departure, the breakfast and subsequent luncheon/tea requirements were relatively straightforward although preparation would have been required in anticipation of the evening return. We are not told but it would also appear likely there would have been some mutual assistance provided between catering cars should this have been necessary. Presumably also each chef served what was an identical meal on the evening service? Finally consider the cost of the waiting staff, chefs and of course the food – 18 staff and one conductor – viz: 9 staff including the chef and his assistant per 'half-set'; small wonder on board catering prices were high.

(7) There is no reference as to whom the original dampers for the trains were supplied by.

(8) This is a curious comment and in some respects slightly worrying. Who were these regular travellers: public who had been coerced into taking part or more likely railway staff? If the latter, and probably the more likely, then they may have become 'numbed' into the train's behaviour, compared with the irregular passenger, or maybe more tolerant of any shortcomings. Might it even have been test staff whose previous assignment could have involved something far worse and in consequence anything, including Blue Pullman, was infinitely better!

(9) 'Hunting' is a swaying action whereby the set of wheels and/or the bogie moves left and right to the limit of its permitted movement. Quoting from Wikipedia, 'A classical hunting oscillation is a swaying motion of a railway vehicle (often called truck hunting) caused by the coning action on which the directional stability of an adhesion railway depends. It arises from the interaction of adhesion forces and inertial forces. At low speed, adhesion dominates but, as the speed increases, the adhesion forces and inertial forces become comparable in magnitude and the oscillation begins at a critical speed. Above this speed, the motion can be violent, damaging track and wheels and potentially causing derailment. The problem does not occur on systems with a differential because the action depends on both wheels of a wheelset rotating at the same angular rate, although differentials tend to be rare, and conventional trains have their wheels fixed to the axles in pairs instead.'

(10) The term 'Train Conductor' should not be confused with the role of the Train Guard, each being totally separate. The 'Train Conductor' was the equivalent of the 'Maître D' and whose role was as the person in charge of the catering and service on the train. The equivalent on a conventional train where meals were served would be the Head Waiter. On Pullman the difference was also that whilst a Head Waiter might well occupy himself with waiting at tables, on Pullman the Maître D was more of an overseer.

(11) The railway unions were at the time threatening various strikes both regional and national. BR for its part made offers with the intention of either resolving or at least postponing such action. The situation was not assisted by ongoing inter-union rivalry. Three parties were eventually involved in resolving the issues, the TUC, Sir Brian Robertson, and for the Government, the man who would later become Prime Minster, Edward Heath. In general it was not a happy period so far as industrial relations were concerned, BR's own attitude at times doing little to cool an already simmering situation. The matter was not helped when an unnamed BR official when referring to the staffing issues on the Blue Pullman was quoted as saying, '… there is some substance to their claim'. (For more on the subject of BR industrial relations during the period, the reader is referred to p238 et-sec of British Railways 1948-73, A Business History by T. R. Gourish.)

(12) With the exception of the first two named, they would subsequently find their way into the WR 'Wells Fargo' spare set. According to Chares Long, '. . . originally eight pre-war cars were transferred from the Southern to the London Midland in anticipation of both the potential Liverpool service and to cover maintenance periods. Because of weight restrictions laid down by operating authorities, the proposed traffic formation was, in fact, no more than five cars, and in order to provide a seating capacity equivalent to the diesel units, the vehicles selected (although all nominally first class) were a mixed bag of traditional-style firsts, with massive armchairs 1+1 each side of the central gangway, and former seconds which, while being refurbished internally, retained a 2+1 fixed-seating layout. In keeping with former Pullman practice, the ex-seconds were all named when 'up-classed'. The names chosen had a strong classical flavour and were drawn from a list suggested by the London Midland. I cannot recall all the rejected names, but one does stick in the memory – 'Terpsichore'. Not surprisingly, the Pullman management felt it would not be appropriate for a railway vehicle to commemorate the Greek Muse of dancing!'

(13) 'Stellite' is a range of cobalt-chromium alloys designed for wear resistance. It may also contain tungsten or molybdenum and a small but important amount of carbon. It is a trademarked name of the Kennametal Stellite Company and was invented by Elwood Haynes in the early 1900s as a substitute for cutlery that stained (or that had to be constantly cleaned). (Wikipedia).

(14) No connection believed with Mr H. C. Johnson of the LMR.

(15) Whilst the railways had at the time what were then termed 'Public Relations Departments', with the benefit of hindsight the more modern terms of (departments for) 'spin' and 'hype' would certainly seem more appropriate here. It easy to see how the LMR were perhaps desperate (or is that perhaps too strong a term?), for positive media coverage for the trains to counter the type of negative feedback that could appear in the press at any time. Very surprisingly no record of such negative news over the riding appears to have reached the broadsheets, although again we must be honest and simply say perhaps it did and has simply not be found.

(16) The use of the word 'technicians' in the plural is interesting in that there were two but one was Electrical and one Mechanical. Although they worked on a rota basis one often became experienced in his colleague's area of expertise.

(17) We may reasonably assume the overhaul/repairs of the sets commenced around November 1962 for on 16 January 1963 there is a note that the 'major programme of overhauls and modifications was scheduled to be completed by the end of April 1963 and until then only one half-set was available as a spare'. This would tend to imply that despite the earlier comments not even a half-set would be available perhaps there had been a change of heart and one was.

(18) This is almost the only reference made to the use of the stand-by loco-hauled Pullmans having been used and unfortunately without being detailed further. We are left to ponder on the response of the travelling public, whether schedules were kept, what locomotive type might have been used and also whether there were any comparisons made as to the ride. This statement also counters a comment made in the original work and repeated here where it was stated there were likely only three weekdays between July 1960 and the cessation of the service when the stand-by train had been required. Assuming this to be the case then it is a credible record especially when taking into account the various difficulties referred to and occasions when a complete train was out of service for repair, modification or overhaul. Perhaps a particular individual (unfortunately unnamed) was trying to make a point. By January 1964 it is believed a second stand-by set, this time consisting five first class vehicles (catering facilities are not mentioned) was also being held in reserve at Manchester.

(19) With the note undated we cannot be certain if this originated from Dr Beeching or his successor Sir Stanley Raymond. It would seem slightly strange that whoever it originated from would sent it to the 'General Managers' in the plural, especially as by this time the WR were already using their three sets in daily service, albeit with layovers during the day.

(20) It is believed the Leicester/Nottingham service may not have continued until the end of 1966 so leaving both sets available to cover the single weekday Manchester–St Pancras working.

District Motive Power Superintendent
J. A. KNAPMAN

Telephone
EAST 1811
Ext. 73

Our Reference
Your Reference G/33

BRITISH TRANSPORT COMMISSION

B.R. 32600/19

District Motive Power Supt.
London Midland Region
British Railways
Manchester South
(Gorton)

8th August, 1962.

Passed Fireman B. Nuttall,
TRAFFORD PARK.

MIDLAND PULLMAN, 7.8.62.

My attention has been called to the ready manner you took over the duty of pilotman for the above train, when, owing to a breakdown in the diagram working, the train had to be worked to London by a driver unfamiliar with the road.

I want you to know how much I appreciate your efforts which were in the best tradition of the service.

Your action avoided a heavy delay to this important train and I would like to take this opportunity of expressing my sincere thanks to you for a job well done.

J A Knapman

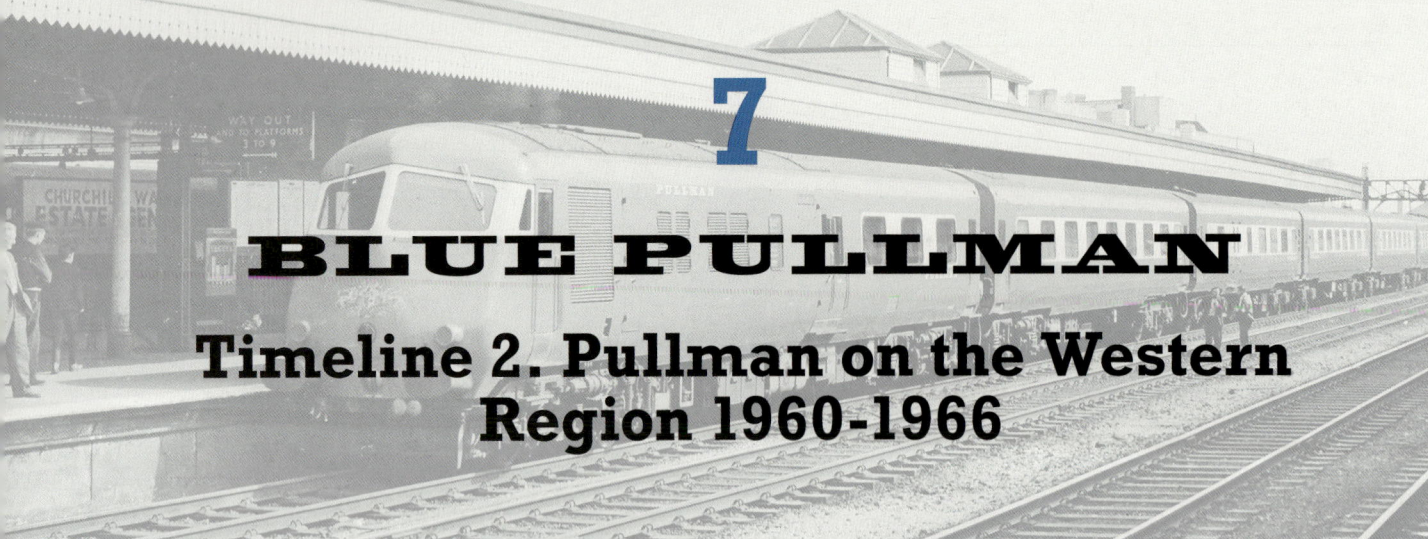

7
BLUE PULLMAN
Timeline 2. Pullman on the Western Region 1960-1966

The reader could be forgiven for expecting the chapter on Blue Pullman running on the Western Region to start on 12 September 1960, the very day public service of the Bristol and Birmingham services commenced. But instead we need to step back slightly for whilst it is indeed reasonable to assume that basic inter-regional rivalry would suggest the WR would at the very least be desirous of starting on the same day as the LMR, events would conspire to prevent this happening.[1]

Rather than speculate on this page on what might and might not have been, let us deal in fact instead. The new Blue Pullman trains were the first 'high-speed' air-braked sets designed to operate on the WR which were also fitted with the (G)WR type of Automatic Train Control (ATC).

Previously on the (G)WR, ATC had been successfully used on all main line routes with the proven ability to stop a train without intervention from the driver should he fail to respond to a 'caution' aspect given by a distant signal. This was achieved by a shoe under the locomotive coming into physical contact with a ramp laid between the train prior to or at the distant signal (the ramp was placed at the distant signal if both a stop and distant signal were mounted on the same post) and which, if the distant signal was 'clear', was energised and caused an 'all clear' bell sound in the cab. If however the signal was 'on' or if a failure occurred then no electric contact was received, the action then of raising the contact show under the locomotive (unit) as it passed over the ramp instead sounded a siren and if not acknowledged by the driver the brakes were automatically applied.

The system had worked well for over half a century and had often been held up as the 'gold-standard' by Board of Trade (later Ministry of Transport) inspecting officers when investigating accidents caused by signals being over-run. Despite having been introduced in the early part of the 20th century the principals of ATC still held good; indeed a high speed test run had been carried

LEFT 'From the front'. Western Region cab with the controller fully open and speed up at 90mph – the speedometer was numerically graduated at 0-20-40-60-80-100. The driver has his right hand on the main power controller and his left hand on the horn valve. In the centre between the two is the ATC cancelling button. ATC was fitted to all three WR trains in both cabs from the outset. *Ivo Peters*

RIGHT Not quite pristine but still an icon of the period. A 1965 view of one of the sets – Bristol, Birmingham, or South Wales departing from Paddington. *Paul Cooper collection*

out in late 1947 as one of the last acts of the old Great Western Railway, proving that the system worked perfectly satisfactorily with speed in the high 90s.

So why the concern now? Well simply that the Blue Pullman train was fitted with air-brakes whereas up to now all fast passenger trains operating on the WR had been equipped with vacuum brakes.[2]

Accordingly, with regular 90mph running planned, the Ministry of Transport wished to ensure the ATC system would work satisfactorily with air-braked stock. Why this should have been the case is not certain but Brigadier Charles Langley of the MofT stipulate that these tests were required before he would grant approval of the trains for use.[3]

Thus on Thursday 16 June 1960 a demonstration was run. We know the power cars involved were Nos 60098/99 (no doubt at the front and rear of the standard eight-car formation) and that the actual testing was to take place on the Badminton line between Swindon (Wootton Bassett) and Stoke Gifford.

At the time the brake pressure being used was 50psi on all bogies up to 30mph but this automatically increased to 70psi above that speed throughout the train except on the power cars and the driven bogie of the auxiliary power car.

We are not informed as to the prevailing weather conditions but the test results were evidently satisfactory: at 59.8mph on the down line at Badminton the train stopped in 665 yards whilst on a 1 in 300 falling gradient. In the same direction other tests were carried out at varying speeds at Coalpit Heath, Winterbourne, and Stoke Gifford. In the up direction similar braking tests were carried out at Winterbourne and Chipping Sodbury culminating in a test from 89.8mph at Badminton. This time the train was on varying gradients but came to rest in 1,525 yards.

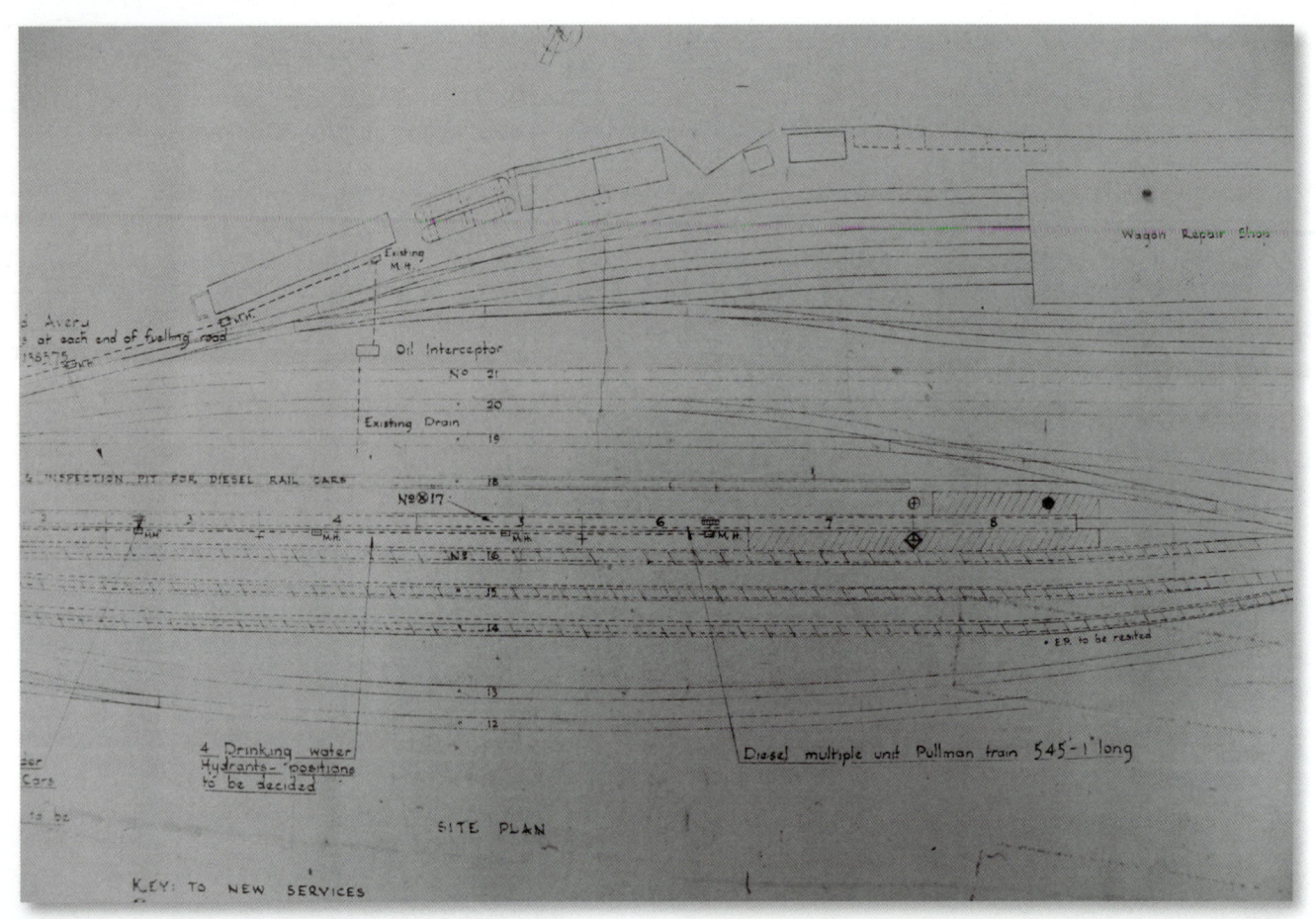

Facilities for the new trains included a new three-road shed at Old Oak Common – ironically it was still being referred to as the 'Pullman' shed decades later – as well as at Dr Day's, Bristol. At the latter location a small canopy was provided at what was a new fueling point. Similar work may also have been carried out at Tyseley (Birmingham), Wolverhampton and later at Swansea. In addition 400V shore supplies were provided at Paddington, Bristol Temple Meads, and likely Birmingham Snow Hill, Wolverhampton Low Level, and again later at Swansea.

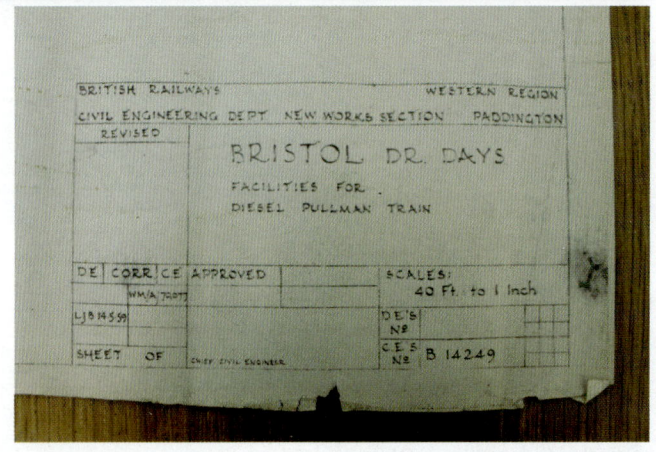

If there were any problems that were specific to the Western Region these are not mentioned and we may reasonably assume that with one complete train-set being delivered in consecutive months from December 1959 onwards, the Western Region were now both familiarising themselves as well as 'playing' with their new toy. Such a statement might appear to both patronise and belittle the trains (can an inanimate object be patronised?) but it is still said with some foundation, especially quoting from earlier, the October 1959 inspection, 'The General Managers were like kids with a new toy …'. After all why should they not be? Blue Pullman was probably seen as much as a morale booster on the WR as it was on the LMR, these positive vibes filtering down from the very top. Possibly the only time it took a dent was prior to the June 1960 Marylebone press inspection concerning the issue of cleanliness – again referred to previously. Whatever the problem was over cleanliness, again it was resolved as the sets positively gleamed when the Western Region service commenced three months later.

Moving away from the trains themselves for a moment, we need to discuss the matter of servicing and maintenance. On the WR major maintenance work was scheduled to be undertaken at Swindon whilst Old Oak Common would be the home base for the three sets.

In this area we fortunately now turn to Brian Wharton, who on the 'Blue Pullman' Facebook group comments: 'My connection with the Blue Pullman goes back to 1959/60 when I was a young man training to be a civil engineer with BR (WR) at Paddington. I was the Junior Assistant Engineer on site at Old Oak Common where one of the existing carriage sheds was converted to provide maintenance and servicing facilities for the Pullman units. From memory I think the shed was previously a carriage paint shop which had a timber floor (presumably to reduce dust). We had to strip that out and lay concrete floors. There were three roads in the shed, one of them now provided with a full-length concrete inspection pit. At the same time we provided a fuelling station for main diesel locos in front of the old loco erecting shop. Another part of our contract was refurbishment and repair of the rooflights and glazing plus repair of the access walkways.'

This special carriage shed at Old Oak Common that was converted into a purpose- built shed was to the north of and fairly close to the main running line. The shed, only accessed by rail from the London end, was of light and airy construction and afforded similar facilities to other contemporary diesel depots built on the WR: Laira, Bristol Bath Road etc. As well as the pits and walkways referred to there was an office, stores, messing and general maintenance facilities. In design it was more conventional than the new build diesel depots having a hipped roof compared with the concrete being used elsewhere at this time. Unfortunately despite being contemporary with the trains, no images of the construction and opening of the shed have been located. Instead the website http://www.derelictplaces.co.uk/main/misc-sites/9855-oak-common-loco-depot-nigh.html is useful where several views of the shed, extant and still in railway use, may be found. Fuelling facilities for the diesels were available at Old Oak as well as Bath Road, (later at Dr Day's sidings Bristol), and for Birmingham services at Tyseley. Indeed the spread of diesel traction generally across the Western (and other) regions had meant that fuel bunkering was not a problem, so allowing the units scope to roam considerably on special workings over the years.

Further memories come from Mike Woodhouse who started work as an apprentice engineer at Old Oak Common in January 1960 aged 15 years. He recalls the stunning sight of the first Blue Pullman arriving just a month later in February 1960. 'She was parked up in the newly converted long carriage shed, from now on to be known as the Pullman shed. When the Pullman first arrived the shed was locked up and none of us were allowed to go in. My tutor was one of the top men of the new diesel era and had just returned from a stint at Swindon. In less than two years I was made part of the team that looked after the Blue Pullman! This train was so ahead of its time and was beautiful inside. It smelt new and we had to wear rubber booties over our workboots before entering the Pullman. A light brown/beige carpet protector called a Drugget had to be put down first as well. It was noticeable that the Pullmans were usually cleaner around the engine bay and the quality of the German M.A.N. engine, built in the famous Augsburg factory, was far superior to the ones built under licence by N.B.L in Scotland. The difference was noticeable in the Class 22s and the first "Warships" (as D600 and D601) had the German engines whereas the rest were NBLs. The

Reported as a set inside the Pullman shed at Old Oak Common on 18 September 1960 although this must be perhaps slightly open to question. What is certain is the train fits inside neatly but if we believe the date this was just six days after the commencement of services, and already the train looks decidedly grubby. After the demise of the Pullmans, the building was used to keep both prototype HST and APT units out of sight whilst undergoing trials. Later still and following the closure of Swindon Works, some staff were transferred to OOC, undertaking repainting work which took place in the short road of the Pullman Shed. The 75-ton breakdown crane was also kept in this building between call-outs. The structure was eventually demolished in late March 2009. *J. Archer/ARPT*

NBLs suffered a lot of seizures and the machining, casting and drilling were very rough by comparison with the MANs. The N.B.L. iron crankcases were too thin and later on Swindon had to make improvements to quality. [Author's note - this reminds one of the difference in quality between the UK built and Romanian built Class 56s]. The diesel fitters were told there were to wear white overalls but it never happened for us and we stayed in blue overalls until the safety conscious orange came in by which time I was at Laira with the beloved HSTs . . . The drivers of the Pullmans were proud of their smart new white uniforms but of course they were nicknamed ice cream sellers and milkmen. The biggest problem with the Pullmans in service was the rough riding. From a repair and servicing point of view there was no doubt whatsoever that these trains were special and huge pressure was placed on us by management to give the Pullman units priority hence we would be taken off other work on "Westerns" and the like to get a Pullman back in service. For us the biggest problem with the Pullmans was getting the spare parts. The majority of parts were held at Swindon and Derby. If a part wasn't available the phone would be red hot and the Chief Engineers for BRB Marylebone, the Western Region and at Old Oak 81A would want to know why a Pullman was being delayed. Sometimes parts would come from Metro-Cammell or

This one we know is most definitely within the new shed although undated. Ordinarily only the spare set – until the South Wales service went over to BP operating in late 1961 – would be stabled here, as later all three trains would overnight at their respective destinations ready for the morning up runs. In consequence it was not unusual to find WR diesel locomotives and DMUs being serviced within, one road almost semi-permanently given over to diesel-shunter maintenance. In its final years and following the demise of the BP trains, special coaching stock and various engineering operator's equipment was housed within.

Derby. We had to keep a spare set of older Pullman coaches called the "Wells Fargo" set usually with a "Western" loco in reserve just in case the Blue Pullmans couldn't run. This steam-heated stock was fully prepared, serviced, gassed up and ready to go! In 1966 I moved to Laira and worked on the Diesel Hydraulics, Diesel Electrics and ultimately the HSTs until I retired in 2001. At first all three Pullmans were kept at Old Oak Common travelling ecs in the mornings and evenings but as confidence in them grew they were stabled overnight at their starting points. For Birmingham this could be at Tyseley or the Wolverhampton sidings and for Bristol usually Bath Road but later at Dr Days. There was talk of swapping the three sets around to balance out the mileage but this never happened. Strangely the 'South Wales Pullman' was usually the set that got into trouble on my watch and it consisted of W60094, W60644, W60734, W60744, W60645, W60735, W60745 and W60095.'

Colin Finch also remembers his colleague Gwynne South was the Travelling Fitter on the South Wales route.

Going back to 1960 the Western Region units, were as with the Midland sets, originally trialled around Birmingham although as confidence grew so they were to be seen on secondary main line and lightly used routes. We know this involved the Bristol–Birmingham via Barnt Green and Evesham section and also the North Warwickshire line to Henley in Arden. Possibly the Cheltenham–Honeybourne–Stratford–Tyseley routes were used too. Initially these trips would have been out and back from Metropolitan-Cammell but following formal handover of each train from manufacturer to British Railways (it is regretted that no date for this has been established other the arrival of the first Western set at OOC in Feb 1960) it is likely the tests and familiarity/training trips originated from WR locations. Other than initial trials around the 'Birmingham circuit' there is no evidence that the LMR sets were ever trialled on WR metals and vice versa.

What we do know is that during this 'working-up' period, visits to Swindon – and presumably also Metropolitan-Cammell – were made on occasions, presumably for modifications and adjustments, which would have applied to all three WR trains. The earlier report by A. E. Robson on the LMR sets may have meant that a number of the points raised were already remedied before the trains reached WR metals whilst we can be sure than there was a steady flow of information between Metropolitan-Cammell, British Railways generally and the regions. We might also surmise that planned trips were also cancelled or curtailed at short notice when an urgent modification was required although it should be stressed no records have been found of breakdowns or resultant delays caused by one of the new trains during this trial period.

Apart from the bedding in of the mechanical aspects so as to provide for a hoped-for reliable service, there was also the issue of crew familiarisation and training. This requirement occupied the spring and early summer of 1960, that is until Paddington announced themselves also ready to begin public operation in July 1960. Probably they had in mind a joint launch with the LMR?

Assuming this announcement was made following the Marylebone press launch of June 1960 it will now come as some surprise to report that a delay then occurred. This cannot have done the PR image of the Western Region much good at all with Kenneth Grand also believed to have received a strong rebuke from 'The Kremlin'. In reply, Paddington cited in their defence the considerable difficulty they had so far experienced in finding men both willing to transfer to the new trains, as well as new catering staff to recruit.[5]

From what followed it appears as if at the time there was an embargo on outside recruitment although quoting now partly from the earlier *Blue Pullman* book, 'There appears to have been far less union resistance over the manning of the WR sets, although one suggestion is that potential staff were not prepared to transfer to the new roles for fear of becoming embroiled in an ongoing labour dispute. It was relatively easy for Headquarters at Marylebone

Publicity for the new trains consisted of posters, leaflets, newspaper adverts and even cardboard representations of the train such as the type seen here – this was with a travel agent. Many of these views were based on photographs taken in Sonning Cutting east of Reading. Press advertising also continued beyond launch day, as an example *The Times* for 26 October 1960 carried a two-column advert for both the services then operating – Bristol and Birmingham – complete with the respective timetables. *John Metters*

Road Headquarters to pontificate at a distance away from day to day practicalities at the same time exerting pressure to find staff as quickly as possible.' We may take it that footplate (should that not really be 'cab' staff by now?) and guards were not a problem. We quote again now a brief extract from *The Times*, Friday 24 June 1960: '… 18 staff and one conductor will provide for 228 passengers on an eight-car train', so meaning the staffing levels for the WR units had been set as the same as for the LMR units, although remember of course the latter had less seats. Remember too that the WR trains were both first and second class – clearly second class passengers were not to be given the same personal attention![6]

Recruiting (or transferring staff) was eventually successful and the Western Region service was finally (re)advertised in August 1960 to commence in the following month. Whilst in appearance the pre-launch paperwork followed similar themes as per the LMR trains it must be said to appear to have been slightly lower-key. Whether this was by accident or design is not certain but even so the results were certainly not derogatory and the new workings (excluding for the present a diesel 'South Wales Pullman') finally commenced as planned on Monday 12 September 1960.

An advance boost to the new service was provided in a brief report in *The Times* for Friday 9 September under the heading, 'New Diesel Pullman Service: London to Bristol and Birmingham'. It was accompanied by a view of the train passing through Twyford station. 'New diesel Pullman services from Paddington to Bristol and Birmingham in under two hours at speeds up to 90mph are to begin next Monday. Yesterday, on a demonstration run to Swindon, the 77-mile journey was completed at just over a mile a minute, in spite

Sonning Cutting with a down BP set running on the fast line – the WR kept its fast and slow lines separated with the down fast and up fast both on the left of the picture. This particular image was taken on 11 June 1963. Whilst it must be said the riding on the sets on the WR was perhaps never quite as bad on that region compared with the LMR – even so it was far from perfect, and time and time again engineers called into question the concentricity of the wheels. We are never told the answers although we may note that whilst one vehicle, W60732 was later the first to be taken out of service due to 'flats' (see page 294), this should not be taken to confirm the suggestion. 'Flats' can be caused for a number of reasons although the most common is when the wheel locks up under braking. *M. Morant collection*

of the train having to slow down at Twyford and Reading stations and between Pangbourne and Goring and Streatley. On these new trains venetian blinds, double-glazed windows, air conditioning, and fitted carpets are of the most modern designs. The seats are adjustable, lights on the tables are controlled by passengers, and even at the highest speeds it is still possible to eat and drink in comfort without ending up with most of the meal on the floor or in your lap. *[We may say this is a slightly strange comment to make. Almost as if it implies spilt food was an otherwise common occurrence and yet the WR – and of course the other regions – had been*

195

The 'Lawn' at Paddington, albeit on 2 March 1964, nearly three years after WR services commenced, but depicting the illuminated signs for the trains. The Pullman services would usually be seen on Platforms 4 and 5 at the station. *John M. Boyes/ARPT*

running dining cars on trains at speed for numerous previous decades.] British Railways say that so far as is practicable their schedules have been designed to meet the requirements of the business executive. The trains will run twice daily in each direction from Monday to Friday.' Altogether a useful note from which we learn about this specific demonstration run and one not previously reported – it also of course begs the question, how many other similar runs might there have been as well?

As with the LMR at St Pancras and Manchester Central – perhaps also at Leicester/Nottingham – (or perhaps not at the latter as the timetable was such that the waiting time at Nottingham was severely limited), an external 120Kw shore supply was available at Paddington to provide power for auxiliaries. Similar equipment was also installed at the new depot at Old Oak Common, at Bristol Temple Meads, Dr Day's Sidings (Bristol) and Cannock Road Sidings Wolverhampton. Unusually perhaps Birmingham Snow Hill was not mentioned. Gerald Williams recalls similar provision was made at Swansea in the Maliphant sidings at the top end of '5' road London end when the Blue Pullman service was extended there in 1961.

The initial Western Region programme involved the operation of two out of their three Blue Pullman sets each weekday. As with the Midland both were 'up' workings (meaning towards London), the first train commencing from Wolverhampton Low Level at 7.00am calling at Birmingham Snow Hill, Solihull and Leamington Spa before continuing non-stop to Paddington via the Bicester route. The second service was non-stop from Bristol Temple Meads at 7.45am running via the Badminton line. Both trains were scheduled to arrive at Paddington at 9.35am. Fill in turns were provided for both units as will be described shortly.

Aware of how good publicity can be turned to maximum advantage (and following the same theme for publicity adopted by the old GWR) the operators planned a simultaneous arrival at Paddington, and for the first day at least this was a literal simultaneous arrival with the two sets deliberately converging at Old Oak Common – *on parallel lines of course!* Old Oak Common was the convergence of the Bristol and Birmingham (via Bicester) routes, after which both trains would run side by side for the final leg into Paddington, arriving also on adjacent platforms. Contemporary records refer to a signalling inspector being present in OOC for the first morning at least although to ensure a concurrent arrival there would undoubtedly have been much influencing of other trains well before Old Oak Common was reached. Whatever, the end result was achieved and as intended the Wolverhampton and Bristol trains ran together for the final three miles to destination. (But also see the accompanying illustration, as evidently the hierarchy were not all privy to the arrangement!)

Former Western Region employee Michael Farr then working at Paddington was a regular traveller on the morning up service from Bristol, and recounts that for the first day, and indeed for several days subsequently, there was a general euphoria amongst the passengers over what they all perceived to be something rather special. On the first day (or days) the passenger complement was also often supplemented by reporters and photographers,

> Outwardly, these new Western Region Pullmans will be readily recognised, in their livery of Nanking blue, relieved by a broad white band along the side of each car and with the Pullman Car Company's colourful crest emblazoned on the front of each driving unit.
>
> The services, commencing on September 12th, Monday to Fridays only, will be :-
>
> **"THE BIRMINGHAM PULLMAN"**
>
> WOLVERHAMPTON & BIRMINGHAM TO LONDON
>
> | | | | | |
> |---|---|---|---|---|
> | Wolverhampton | (Low Level) | Dep | 7.00 a.m. | |
> | Birmingham | (Snow Hill) | Dep | 7.30 a.m. | 2.30 p.m. |
> | Solihull | | Dep | 7.40 a.m. | |
> | Leamington Spa | (General) | Dep | 8.00 a.m. | 2.55 p.m. |
> | London | (Paddington) | Arr | 9.35 a.m. | 4.25 p.m. |
>
> LONDON TO BIRMINGHAM & WOLVERHAMPTON
>
> | | | | | |
> |---|---|---|---|---|
> | London | (Paddington) | Dep | 12.10 p.m. | 4.50 p.m. |
> | Leamington Spa | (General) | Arr | 1.34 p.m. | 6.19 p.m. |
> | Solihull | | Arr | | 6.44 p.m. |
> | Birmingham | (Snow Hill) | Arr | 2. 5 p.m. | 6.55 p.m. |
> | Wolverhampton | (Low Level) | Arr | | 7.20 p.m. |
>
> **"THE BRISTOL PULLMAN"**
>
> BRISTOL TO LONDON
>
> | | | | | |
> |---|---|---|---|---|
> | Bristol | (Temple Meads) | Dep | 7.45 a.m. | 12.30 p.m. |
> | Bath Spa | | Dep | * | 12.45 p.m. |
> | London | (Paddington) | Arr | 9.35 a.m. | 2.25 p.m. |
>
> LONDON TO BRISTOL
>
> | | | | | |
> |---|---|---|---|---|
> | London | (Paddington) | Dep | 10. 5 a.m. | 4.55 p.m. |
> | Bath Spa | | Arr | 11.40 a.m. | * |
> | Bristol | (Temple Meads) | Arr | 12.0 noon. | 6.45 p.m. |
>
> * Via Badminton
>
> (It should be noted that the above times are experimental and are subject to review).
>
> Cont'd.......

> 3.
>
> In addition to the ordinary fares, a supplement is payable by each passenger, the maximum being 10/- First Class and 5/- Second Class between London and Bristol, and between London and Birmingham or Wolverhampton.
>
> These new Western Region trains have been built at the Birmingham Works of the Metropolitan-Cammell Carriage & Wagon Company, Ltd., under the direction of, and in collaboration with, the British Transport Commission and the Pullman Car Company, Ltd.

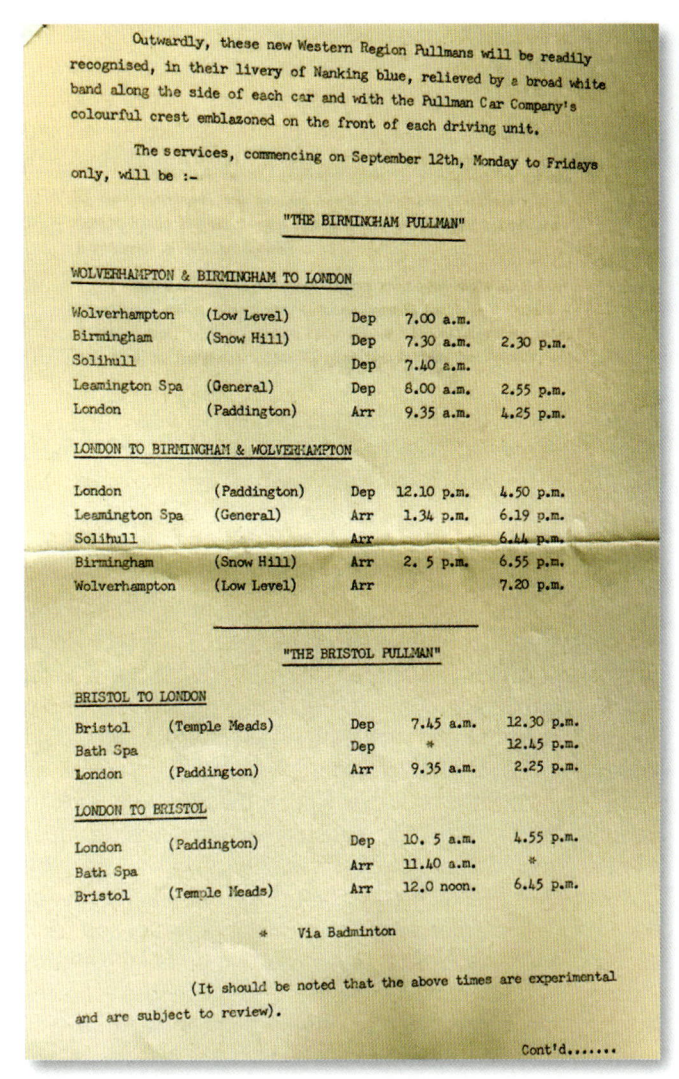

although Michael recalls that the ride was not particularly smooth even when the sets were brand new, as indeed was reported in the previous chapter. (In all probability a similar mix of public/press had occurred on the Wolverhampton working and likely at the time of the introduction of the Midland sets into service.)

An ominous portent for the future came within a very few days when Michael noticed an absorbent paper doily had now appeared between the cup and the saucer. The stewards too seemed to be adopting a policy of not filling cups to the same level as before. There were two obvious and to be fair beneficial results, the first being the earlier incessant rattle of crockery was reduced, and secondly, slops of liquid from the cup were less noticeable. (See also "With a Splash" on page 150).

Regardless of the goings on within, the new trains scored with the traveller in exactly the same way as had the Midland sets. This is from Brian Wharton: 'I experienced several trips to Bristol on the Pullmans and I remember one particular return from Bristol. I had been surveying with a senior colleague at Severn Tunnel Junction all week and we planned our return to Paddington via Bristol. We were travelling 1st class and we took lunch on the train – very civilised, happy days!'

BELOW The deliberately contrived arrival on the first day, with both trains seen here running parallel over the final few yards into Paddington. According to a letter in the National Archives dated 4 October 1960 from the WR Chairman, who signs himself 'Reggie' Hanks, addressed to Sir James Dunnett at the Ministry of Transport, Mr Hanks quotes, 'This was not organised, but the drivers spotted one another at Old Oak Junction and showed commendable enterprise by continuing the journey to Paddington together.' We may say with certainty Mr Hanks was perhaps not completely informed as to what was a careful planned operation. In the photograph, the ex-Bristol service is on the left and that from Wolverhampton on the right. (The latter was also always known as the 'Birmingham Pullman' despite its place of departure.) We have no details as to what vehicles were used on that first day. Presumably also the WR referred to the trains by 'Set' numbers but again this is not confirmed and certainly no other identification other than vehicle/car numbers was ever shown on the actual trains on either region.

At rest at Paddington; note too that Platforms 5 and 6 have been used. Taken on the first day of service, and from a glimpse of the throng alongside the Wolverhampton arrival, we may assume some form of celebration/discussion is going on alongside the power car at least. Again note that the underframes of both trains are nowhere near as clean as were displayed on the first day of LMR service. Finally look at the buffers of the Bristol arrival. These have clearly been rubbed against another vehicle – or a set of buffer stops. *Colour Rail 215031*

Philip Littler went several times from Bristol to London and back with his father and remembers the excellent service as does Peter De Lacey on the later (Paddington) Reading to Cardiff run. Stuart Williams watched them coming into Bristol Temple Meads and eventually managed a ride on one. Stuart thought of them as D.M.U.s albeit 'fancy' but preferred locos such as the 'Westerns'/'Warships' and 'Hymeks'.

Jerry Howlett, later to work for BR at Swindon, was mad on trains as a boy and recalls witnessing the Pullman stopping at Chippenham. 'It was the first time we spotters heard an engine roar then the coaches followed by another roar. When leaving the station it really had a smooth sound . . . I remember an attendant once threw Pullman sugar lumps at us with the Pullman wrapping on. One of those sugar cubes lasted for ages at my parents' but I guess one day it finally went into a cup of tea!'

Paul Sheppard was eight in 1961 and first saw the 'Bristol Pullman' from the footbridge at Corsham Station in Wiltshire. 'This was my favourite train and I was thrilled when one appeared on a card I collected from "Rice Krispies". I would see the Blue Pullman on its way to Bristol and would run from one side of the bridge to the other . . . the memory of it growling away towards Box Tunnel is a sight and sound embedded in my memory.'

John Ford was a travelling fitter working on the 'Bristol Pullman' between 1960 and 1967. He was interviewed some years later at the age of 86. John was initially trained on the electrical aspects of the train, his opposite number an expert on the mechanics, although as time passed each would also learn from the other. 'My fellow technician, Ivor, was a shift supervisor at the Swindon Running shed. We would do two and a half runs on a shift then would change over at Bath. For a while there was also a longer run to Weston Super Mare.' [This was an extension of the mid-day fill-in working.] 'The make up of our train was 60099 at the London end and 60098 at the Bristol end. The staff were two stewards in second class, a Chef and Sous Chef in the kitchen and two stewards for first class plus a leading steward. This was repeated at the opposite end plus one conductor (usually George Johnson), a guard and two drivers plus the one technician. The conductor George was the chief as he was a BR man and the technicians were treated as a member of the team which Ivor and I appreciated. We both lived in Swindon so on a Sunday night I caught the 21.00 from Swindon to Bristol so as to be ready for the first Up train on the Monday morning. We were both graded WS2 and consequently had a first-class all stations pass.

'Upon arrival at Bristol we walked the lines from Temple Meads to Dr Day's sidings and inspected the train; we checked maintenance was done then went for a kip! We were back on duty at 06.30, met the drivers and then helped the Pullman staff to prepare the train (my job was polishing glasses) and eventually ended up in 60098, the kitchen car for hot buttered toast and tea. It was then up to Bristol and off to Paddington sat mostly with the drivers. After arrival in London, we firstly connected the shore supply. Then after disconnecting we went ecs down to Old Oak for a full English breakfast with the lads. This was followed by another train inspection before going back to Paddington for the 12.15 to Bristol (and later Weston Super Mare). I would then enjoy silver service lunch with the passengers in the kitchen car first class until changeover at Bath with my partner tec. Then he went to Bristol and back to Paddington with a silver service dinner on the return journey. [The schedule for the sets varied over the years for at one time it was the Up Wolverhampton set that was used on the mid-day Bristol turn.)

'On a normal week on the way from Paddington, Ivor would get on at Chippenham and I would leave the train at Bath to go home until the next day at Chippenham when I took over again. For holidays and sickness we used to cover each other … we only bothered Paddington bosses in an emergency.

'This meant we could be on the train continuously for weeks at a time. Sometimes I also covered on the Wolverhampton set – Paddington to Birmingham Snow Hill – which was stabled at Wolverhampton Ford Houses at night. I was not so familiar with these Pullman staff as my mates were really at Bristol and with conductor George Johnson. I would go the pub with the Bath Road guys. How the Pullman staff covered holidays and sickness I never thought about but to me they always seemed to be on duty all of the time!

'Despite maintenance being carried out by Bath Road depot we came under Paddington management where we had two direct bosses. We were BR employees and had no training from Rolls-Royce or NBL on the engines on the train. I started in AE shop at Swindon and had worked on the electrics of all the NBL-engined machines; both types of 'Warship' Class 41 and the old Class 43 plus the Class 22s. As far as the ride was concerned it was a bit rocky but remember this was a luxury train at 90mph running on short section rails. It was much improved with continuous (welded) rail and staff still managed to pour the coffee ok! I would say the ride was about six out of ten compared to the best stock we had at the time being eight out of ten. Maybe I had got used to it over time. Regarding the maintenance, the train wasn't always the easiest to work on sometimes. As an example, on the underside there were some double brake-block hangers which were very difficult to remove when it was necessary to fit new blocks.'

Over on the 'Birmingham Pullman' a young Cadbury's manager, Paul Hotchkiss, was required to travel from Birmingham to London for meetings with various advertising agencies. He recalls his many trips: 'I was just 20 years old and had been a trainspotter as a boy, helped by the fact my Dad was a railwayman. I now worked as an Assistant Product Manager for Cadbury's so all my travel was arranged for me and paid for by the office. To put the London trip into perspective I had no car and I walked into work each day. I did have a Lambretta for local trips but the train made much more sense for me to get into London.

'I picked up the "Birmingham Pullman" at Snow Hill and looked forward to the excellent breakfast, the service really was fantastic from the uniformed stewards. There was certainly a posh ambience of smart business travellers and if passengers weren't tucking into the tasty breakfast their heads were buried in newspapers. The power cars emitted a sort of mid frequency "thrum" and were well insulated.'

When asked about the ride he replied: 'Well yes it was noticeable and at lower speeds the carriage was affected by a fore and aft sensation. This made the serving of breakfast . . well shall we say "exciting"! The poor stewards had to adopt a wide legged diagonal stance in order to balance themselves against the movement. What went on your plate and on to your lap varied! As the speed rose the train would start to sway side to side. You might think all the passengers would be talking about the bad ride but that didn't happen and I think the most important aspect is that there wasn't much alternative. A loco-hauled Mk1 coach wasn't that comfortable either so at the time the fastest and nicest way for me to get to London and back was by using the Blue Pullman.'

The Queen Mother travelled from Paddington by 'Birmingham Pullman' on 1 November 1960 on the 10.10am run. *(HRH was not asked for her comments!)*

Further reminiscences came from David Direktor who remembers seeing a set at Snow Hill on display. He was then aged 10 and was able to travel on the Pullman in second class with his mother and grandmother. He recalls having to gulp his drink down at the Leamington stop as it was quite difficult to do so beforehand due to the rocking side to side of the coach as it gathered speed. The return trip was by a conventional locomotive-hauled train.

Iain Fanthom and his mother Val would travel from Stourbridge by DMU to Snow Hill where Iain would be excited to meet his Dad Ron returning from London on the 'Birmingham Pullman': 'The lighting effect at Snow Hill showed the Nanking Blue paintwork off a treat and they looked really special, I fell in love both with them and with Snow Hill. They had their own unique sound, a powerful smooth thrum when departing and conversely otherwise silent – bar the final brake screech when coming to rest. My Dad loved travelling on the Pullmans and found the blinds useful whilst working. He would bring home the biscuits served with the coffee and I recall seeing some menus. He did say there were some rough lengths of track on the journey and the ride was rough at times but he thought the supplement for Pullman travel was worth it for the excellent service.'

As referred to earlier, the Bristol and Birmingham sets had a midday 'fill-in' turn, the third retained, for the present, as a spare in the new shed just down the line at Old Oak Common. So far as the set morning up train from Wolverhampton was concerned, this was quickly restocked (and presumably cleaned) whilst in its earlier arrival platform at Paddington and after just 30 minutes later departed again, now as the 10.05am to Bristol – exactly the type of turnaround as had been envisaged for this type of working a few short years earlier.

Power car destination blind. Blinds were provided on both sides of each power car and were (presumably) the responsibility of the guard – who was a BR and not a Pullman employee. The wording to be used in the destination panels had been set by the WR in December 1958 whilst even something seemingly as basic as this came in for criticism by Jack Howe. It seems likely he had at some stage attempted to create his own version, as the records show a letter to the Design Panel from E. S. Cox at the BTC: 'These instructions are to be followed in every respect and no variation is permitted'. Howe had wanted the destination station to read from top to bottom with the word 'Pullman' at the bottom. He could also not resist a touch of sarcasm when writing to George Williams over the wording on the blinds and states, 'Since I have produced this exactly as required I am assuming it will not be necessary to submit them again to Mr Harrison or the Western Region. I feel that this would only be inviting them to change their mind again'. As on the LMR, neither the power cars or individual vehicles carried names, a complete break with tradition for Pullman as in the past all First-Class cars had been named.

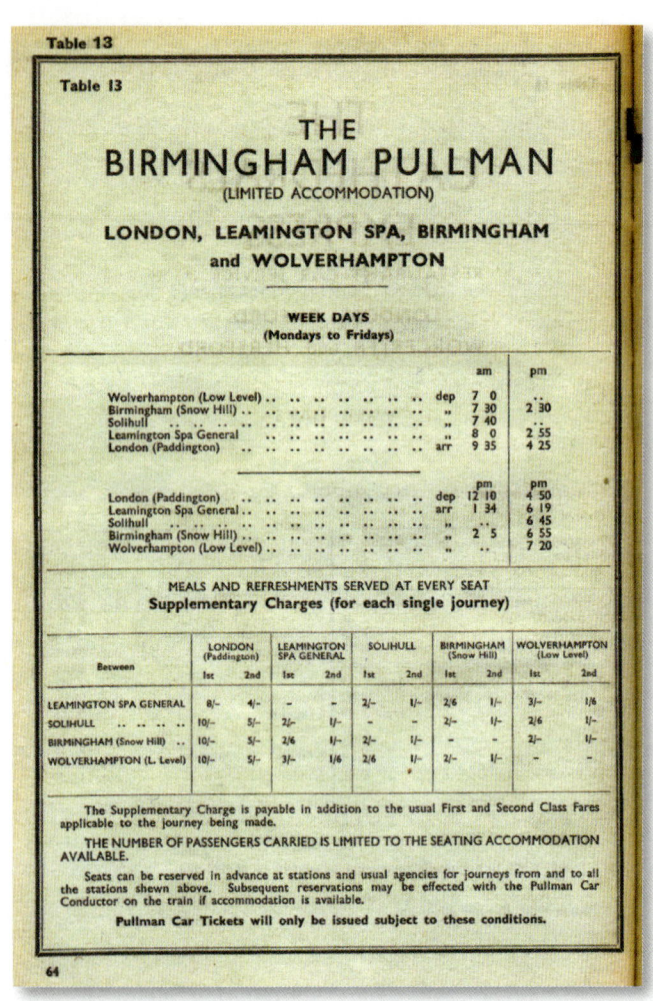

Sample pages from the public timetables, both circa 1962, by which time the Bristol service had also been re-routed away from the Badminton line and was instead running via Bath.

At Bristol there was another short turnaround with a scheduled departure at 12.30pm but now re-routed so as to call at Bath. This also added five minutes to the journey time with the result that the set arrived back at Paddington at 2.35pm. Back in London, probably this time now at OOC, the set was serviced, cleaned and restocked ready for its final departure at 4.55pm, again for Bristol and once more running non-stop via Badminton.

The fill-in for the Bristol arrival was conversely working north-westwards, forming the 12.10pm Paddington to Birmingham Snow Hill and return calling at Leamington Spa only in both directions. After this the train formed the early evening departure for Wolverhampton Low Level. Each train set in use was therefore covering a similar distance of around 480 miles daily. We are not told as to whether similar special arrangements to ensure timekeeping as had applied in the morning were similarly in force for the first day's return journey. We are also not informed which two of the WR three sets were used on that first day.

Interestingly the mid-day 84-minute allowance between Leamington and Paddington was commented upon most favourably and was also the fastest schedule ever between these two points. Less positive comment came over the Bristol service where the non-stop working was still five minutes slower than the contemporary diesel-hauled 'Bristolian' working which critics were also quick to point did not necessitate a supplementary change. To counter this it could be said Pullman offered a far higher standard of service, meals and other refreshments being brought direct to individual seats, but even so it was an argument that would never really go away and was also destined to return with greater weight later.

Of course as we have seen, before any new service was instigated careful research was carried out to confirm a likely need. In that respect the respective regions mostly got it right. Commenting on this particular period we could say that all three of the main starting point/destinations for the trains, viz Manchester, Wolverhampton and Bristol, were correctly chosen, but the Western Region had made one error and that was to omit Bath from the schedule so far as the peak hour Bristol services were concerned. The burghers of Bath were similarly quick to become vociferous when learning their own previously existing fast morning service to Paddington had been necessarily retimed to accommodate the new working. 'Thou shalt not upset Bathonians' might well have been the phrase rapidly echoing around the corridors at Paddington with the result that the morning and evening trains were both re-routed and retimed so as to incorporate a Bath stop even if this did add yet another five minutes to the schedule. It was also clearly viewed as a serious situation at Paddington for with the new Winter timetable only five weeks old the position and routing had been altered, to take effect from Monday 17 October 1960. We might add that the renowned railway correspondent of the period O. S. Nock lived at Bath and worked at Chippenham and was a regular traveller on the Pullman. Might we wonder if he was one of the complainers, or did he instead just sit back and observe? Certainly he was not backwards in coming forwards with his views generally.

Unfortunately what is missing from the records of the first season of operating are details of timetable alterations covering the Christmas period and it would certainly not be totally safe to assume that the WR and LMR followed suit with each other so far as the suspension of services around the holiday period. We also lack one major piece of information and that is the loadings on the WR trains. It is easy to surmise that these were reasonable, based on the continuation of the workings both at peak times and as the mid-day fill-ins, however it should also be stated that there was every likelihood the mid-day turns would have suffered the same restricted take up of food and for exactly the same reasons as on the LMR Leicester/Nottingham service.

The reader will of course be aware that the principal differences between the LMR and WR trains was the mixed accommodation and provision of two extra cars in the WR formation, so making an eight-car set. Again this consisted of two mirror halves, each half comprising: power car with seating for 18 second class passengers, parlour car with seating for 42 second class passengers, kitchen car with seating for 18 first class passengers, and a parlour car with seating for 36 first class passengers. As befitted the social fashion of the time, the two smaller saloons within the power cars seating 18 passengers each were the only ones designated as non-smoking.

Below the underframe the equipment carried was again basically identical on both the region's train's although visually there were subtle differences in the bodysides to the power cars and parlour cars on the respective regions. Viewed sideways on, the respective power cars had, on the LMR two and a half windows for the passenger compartment, whereas on the WR there were three windows. The difference was explained by the substitution of the lavatory on the LMR trains for an additional bay of seating on the WR. Similarly the first class parlour cars on both the six- and eight-car sets had seven full windows per side, whilst the WR second class parlour cars had eight windows – equivalent to 'more bums on seats' and slightly less legroom. To be really clever when identifying individual types, look for the vertical line that existed down the centre of the first class windows. This was the demarcation between having an individual Venetian blind in first class whereas there was only a single blind per window in second class.

Comparisons of the available lavatory accommodation may also be made. So far as the LMR was concerned the

Western Region Blue Pullman drivers in their distinctive white coats at Paddington on 17 May 1961 with Locomotive Inspector Whitley behind. The three men had been in the cab with Ivo Peters when the latter travelled from Bristol. The white coats issue quickly gave rise to the men being referred to as either 'milkmen' or 'ice-cream sellers', the latter a connection to then popular brand of 'Druid's' iced confectionary. Not surprisingly this gave rise to some ribald comments between crews working the Pullmans and others and may well have contributed to a reversion to a more conventional driver's attire from around the mid 1960s onwards. It is believed the driver on the left may be Ernie Morris, who as one of the first WR men to be trained (passed) on the Blue Pullman sets also featured in the 1962 BTF Let's Go to Birmingham film. Sadly Ernie together with two others were killed in the Knowle and Dorridge crash on 15 August 1963, when an up 'Wells Fargo' Pullman deputising for the normal BP set was in collision with a freight train. *Ivo Peters*

original intention had been to have eight lavatories for each six-car train, designated each for male and female. This was until it was realised that female travellers would likely be outnumbered somewhat so none were in the end gender specific. Eight toilets per trains was an equivalent average of one per 16.5 passengers, the staff having their private facilities.

On the WR with its higher potential loading, 228 passengers, the ratio was also higher at one per 22.8

NOTE:—

This booklet is intended as a guide to Railway staff and those of the Pullman Car Company who may be concerned with the working of Multiple-Unit Diesel Pullman trains and it must be clearly understood that it does not replace or supersede the instructions relating to the observance of the rules and regulations applicable to the working of Diesel Multiple Unit Pullman Trains as contained in Circular No. 544, "Working of Diesel Pullman Trains".

C. W. POWELL,
OPERATING OFFICER,
PADDINGTON.
September, 1960.

CONTENTS

	Page
Description of Trains	5
Train Name and Destination Indicators	7
Half Set Identification Arrangements	7
Driving Cab Layout	8
Access to Cars	10
Seating Arrangements	10
Seat Reservation	11
Blinds at Passenger Windows	13
Attendant Call System	13
Parcel and Luggage Racks	14
Guard's Compartment	14
Travelling Technicians	17
Westinghouse Electro Pneumatic Brake with High Speed Control	17
Automatic Warning System	22
Auxiliary Diesel Engine Generator Sets and 120KW Shore Supply	25
Lighting	32
Air Conditioning Equipment	33
Coupling and Uncoupling	36
Reversing and Propelling	37

On the Western Region at least staff were issued with a small 'A5'-size booklet intended to bring together every aspect of the operation of the trains and every (anticipated) potential issue. Some instructions were also repeated from other instructional paperwork. As an example, this referred to the 'Loudaphone communication': 'The loudaphone apparatus is a means by which the Driver and Guard may speak to each other, or exchange bell signals, but it does not relieve staff from their obligation to carry out the relevant Rules and Regulations. A bell, which is actuated by the depression of the "call" button on the loudaphone, is provided in both the Guard's and Driver's compartments and the bell communication must always be used for the exchange of signals in accordance with the standard code shown in the Instructions for Working Multiple-Unit Mechanical Diesel Trains. An additional bell push which will ring the bell in the Driver's cab is provided over the door of each Guard's compartment. Standard bell codes will be used for all normal movements but the Driver, if requiring to speak to the Guard, or the Guard, requiring to speak to the Driver, must send on the call button the code 3 pause 3 "Guard required to speak to driver", or "Driver required to speak to Guard", and the man at the other end must acknowledge by repetition as detailed in the Instructions referred to above. Conversation may then proceed provided both men keep the "Speak" button depressed. The apparatus must only be used for essential conversations on matters affecting the working of the train and, except in the case of emergency, should not be used when the train is in motion. The apparatus may also be used by shunters, in the absence of Guards, in order to communicate with drivers in connection with shunting operations. In order to avoid any possibility of unauthorised use of the apparatus in Driver's cabs, the door leading to the Driver's compartment must be kept locked when the Driver's cab is not in use.' (Circular No 544 referred to was a set of stapled instructions, dated 12 September 1960 and marked with the usual 'For the use of Employees only' dissemination across the top. It included instructions as to the stopping points at the various calling points – including Bath Spa even though that was not on the original schedule.) *See also Appendices 3 and 4.* (The use of a BP set as an eye-catching image was repeated by BR/WR in 1966 on the cover of the booklet 'Craft Apprenticeships – British Railways Workshops'. *Evidently they considered the train was modern and inspiring enough to gain the attention of spotty adolescents!*)

passengers. As originally planned these were again to have been gender specified, four for gentlemen, one for ladies, plus two in the second class parlour car (one at each end) 'non gender specific' – perhaps the term 'unisex' would be a better description. Before entering service it is believed all were relabelled simply as 'Toilet'; again staff had their facilities.

Unfortunately just five months on from the June 1960 ATC tests which it will be recalled tested the braking (as much as the ATC response) there is mention of brake troubles – the details of which are not fully clear – with the paperwork almost implying these troubles had been present from very early on. So does this mean from the start of the running trials in early 1960, from the start of the public service, or is it more simply a cross-reference to the brake issues previously found by the LMR? Surviving paperwork is not clear on this point but we may realistically assume had it been the first then something would most likely have been mentioned at the time of the ATC tests. Thus it may be reasonable to assume it had probably come about in the light of service conditions. Accordingly on Tuesday 22 November 1960 a series of brake tests were conducted using the spare set between Old Oak Common and Swindon at speeds from 70mph upwards with incremental increases in 5mph stages up to 90mph. Power cars 60098 and 60099 were again used on a standard eight-car train – the same pairing as had been

	Page
Kitchen Cars	37
Maintenance and Daily Servicing	38
Battery Charging	39
Fuelling	39
Water Supply	39
Carriage Cleaning	40
Route Restrictions	41
Station Stops	41
Loudaphone Equipment	42
Public Address System	44
Train Identification Indicators	44
Reporting of Defects	45
Access Routes at Depots for Pullman Car Company Staff	46
Regional Appendix Instructions Relating to the Working of Diesel Pullman Trains	46

NOTE: A diagram of the Pullman Train Set and a more detailed index of the items included in this booklet will be found at the end.

4

INTRODUCTION

The Multiple Unit Diesel Pullman trains have been introduced by British Railways (Western Region) as part of the "Plan for the Modernisation and Re-equipment of British Railways." They provide services to the highest standards of speed and passenger comfort, and incorporate many new features in design and equipment.

DESCRIPTION OF TRAINS

The trains consist of eight-car sets and have been built to entirely new standards of Pullman comfort with specially designed decor. All the vehicles are painted blue externally with white edging to the windows. Diesel-electric is the method of traction employed.

See diagram at back of booklet.

Each set will be a self-contained train and will consist of the following formation:—

Motor Car (Second Class) with main engine and generator, above floor; also Guard's accommodation.
Parlour Car (Second Class) with auxiliary engine generator set, below floor.
Kitchen Car (Kitchen and First Class seating).
Parlour Car (First Class).
Parlour Car (First Class).
Kitchen Car (Kitchen and First Class seating).
Parlour Car (Second Class) with auxiliary engine generator set, below floor.
Motor Car (Second Class) with engine and generator, above floor; also Guard's accommodation.

5

utilised for the earlier ATC tests. No 60098 being at the Swindon – the country end – of the train.

From information available it appears the trouble was heat distortion as the words 'thermal troubles' are mentioned – once more a similar replication of that experienced on the LMR. Also, either before or perhaps in consequence of this, the maximum brake force permitted was/had been reduced to 2.5T per brake block – somewhat frustratingly an equivalent psi pressure is not given so we unable to make the direct comparison with the LMR experiences of a year before. Again an example of lack of consistency in reporting issues between the regions or simply lack of communication?

Whilst this may have resolved the issue so far as BP was concerned there was in consequence a penalty to pay and that was the results now achieved at this reduced pressure setting were such that the stopping distances being obtained were not as good as per a locomotive hauled train – stated as diesel hydraulic hauling BR standard rolling stock operating with 25in of vacuum – but they were still within signal stopping distances and similarly stated to be within the BR 'S'(?) curve. All braking was carried out on level track with BP coming to rest from 80mph in 1,093 yards whilst from the same speed the locomotive-hauled train stopped in 835 yards. (We are not told if the results from the locomotive-hauled train were recorded at the same time or if these were figures previously available, nor for that matter and in the case of the former, what locomotive type/number was used.)

Apart from the obvious differences in formation between the trains running on the WR and the LMR, a further external detail difference was the provision of a mechanical route indicator roller-blind located in the guard's compartment of the power cars. Originally this could be set to read either 'Bristol Pullman' or 'Birmingham Pullman', for as we know the rostering of the sets meant they could be used on either of the two routes. Similarly, the carriage sides were simply lettered 'Pullman', without specifying Bristol, Birmingham or Wolverhampton. Pullman staff uniforms were identical for the catering staff on both the LMR and WR, but instead of 'battledress' for the loco crews on the LMR, the WR drivers were issued with white knee-length work coats and matching white hats that quickly led to them being given nicknames of 'ice-cream sellers' or 'milkmen', together with associated ribald comments, although we should note that both John Ford and Mike Woodhouse say the drivers were proud of their uniforms. To some, such clothing was considered as trivialising the impact of the new trains. Despite these comments, some WR crews were still wearing the white uniform as late as 1966 and perhaps even beyond that date. Notwithstanding the earlier comments officially the travelling fitter was supposed to be based in the unoccupied guard's compartment of the train. (The train guard being at the other end. 'Loudaphone' communication was, though, available to him should he be required.)

The year 1960 concluded with the incident of 5 December, referred to briefly in the previous chapter. The train affected was the 10.05am 'Bristol Pullman' from Paddington, which was immediately taken out of service at Swindon with the passengers continuing their journeys on the steam-hauled 'Merchant Venturer'. The afternoon return from Bristol was covered by 'Castle' class 5056 *Earl of Powis* and a 10-coach set, although further details of the vehicles used are not known. (The spare Pullman being miles away at OOC.) For the evening working, the spare Pullman set from OOC was used, and remained in use for several days. The derailment of an unrelated train near Swindon on 10 February 1961 saw the up service from Bristol diverted via Devizes – believed to have been the first time one of the sets worked over this route although it was a recognised diversion (via Bath, Bradford-upon-Avon, Bradford Junction, Holt Junction, and Devizes to join the up Berks & Hants line at Patney & Chirton and thence via Newbury and Southcote Junction to Reading West and so rejoin the main line again at Reading [General]).

BLUE PULLMAN

Bristol service passing Christian Malford Halt between Chippenham and Dauntsey in 1961. Aside from modernisation in the form of the train, the trackwork has been partly upgraded as well with flat-bottom rail on one side only, but even so it was still jointed track. It was suggested later that running on jointed track rather than continuously welded rail was one of the causes of the sub-standard ride. *Paul Strong*

In Colour on the Western

Up Bristol service paused at Bath Spa – contemporary 'modern' BR platform lighting on the concrete pillar behind. Track rationalisation is taking place in the centre although mechanical signalling remains complete with the station's lofty signal box just visible on the left. *Tony Woodforth collection*

BLUE PULLMAN

On the up platform line at Reading General – at the time numbered Platform 5 – in August 1964. Initially the trains did not stop at Reading but from the number of destinations shown on the (unfortunately unreadable) destination blind on the side of the power car, this was later altered with the mid-day fill-in turns. Do also notice the position of the Pullman crest on the front of this particular vehicle which appears placed distinctly higher than on other power cars. Notice the damage to the covers of the air horns. *Rail Photoprints*

In Colour on the Western

Down Birmingham service passing through High Wycombe on 30 August 1962 – compare the position of the front crest with that of the previous view. Note also the 'weathered' livery on the vehicle sides with brake dust adhering. It must be said that in general terms the WR sets were not externally always as pristine as those operating on the LMR. *Colour Rail DE521*

BLUE PULLMAN

A slightly puzzling view at Leamington Spa with the simplest explanation being that the steam train has been cautioned into the already occupied down platform. The date is 1963 but other details are not known. *Kidderminster Railway Museum*

In Colour on the Western

Against a decidedly smoke-grimed station backdrop, the well-filled morning up Pullman awaits departure from Bristol Temple Meads sometime in August 1963. As we know, and as per the LMR, the WR attempted to maximise revenue from its trains by operating mid-day 'fill-in' turns. Clearly these were not as popular as had been hoped for as far back as May 1961 (considering the sets had only been in operation since September 1960) Trains Illustrated was reporting that in April 1961 the WR had offered reduced price travel to school parties on the midday Bristol and 'Birmingham Pullman' services. ('TI' did not elaborate but finished their report with a simple series of full stops: no doubt thinking then exactly as we do now, that something was wrong when there was a need to attempt to attract custom – *almost any custom* – to the 'fill-in' workings.) If they had but known, it did not bode well for what would happen just a few years later with five Pullman sets concentrated in an even more restricted operational area. *Colin Maggs/Colour Rail DE1169*

BLUE PULLMAN

ABOVE Empty stock or poorly patronised 'Bristol Pullman'? Passing through Platform 4 at Reading in March 1965 shortly before Multiple Aspect Signalling (MAS) was introduced in the Reading area. *Mike Upton*

RIGHT Up 'Bristol Pullman' passing Swindon on a dull 31 March 1964. Within, all would no doubt be suitably snug, with silver service available to those who desired such attention. Just a few days later on 2 April 1963 during a routine examination at Tyseley, cracks were discovered by a fitter (name not known) in a bogie bolster. The information was immediately passed to the LMR whilst at Swindon the problem was confirmed. (It is not clear if the Swindon confirmation concerned the aforementioned set from Tyseley or others from the fleet as well.) Similar cracks, again with further elaboration, were also found on the LMR trains. For whatever reason no further mention is made of this situation although the fitter concerned was commended for his action. We know that all the WR units were out of action on 11 April so it is likely this was the day full checks were being made. Without further reference being found, we may assume necessary remedial action was quickly undertaken. (A similar bogie issue had occurred not long after the WR Gas Turbine 18100 entered service with bogie cracks being found.) *Paul Cooper*

7 BLUE PULLMAN – TIMELINE 2. PULLMAN ON THE WESTERN REGION 1960-1966

In Colour on the Western

The Blue Pullman Story

BLUE PULLMAN

In Colour on the Western

ABOVE The Paddington of the early 1960s – 30 July 1964 to be precise. Steam was giving way to diesel on the principal services, as witness the Blue Pullman set which has recently arrived, whilst almost hidden from view is a maroon 'Western' on what could well be '1A86' working. The Pannier Tank is on OOC (Old Oak Common) shunt duty No 4. On the WR at least the BP sets were also used on at least one occasion in connection with commercial – unconnected with the railway – advertising. This one occasion known of was on 30 July 1963 involving Messrs Fry's Chocolate. This company had rail access via a private siding at Keynsham near Bristol. Whether filming was undertaken there or elsewhere is not reported, but the Paddington 'C' list of images records that images No 42023-5 were taken by BR to record the occasion. (Does anyone also remember the long running advert for Horace Bachelor from Keynsham on Radio Luxemburg with his 'infra-draw' method of winning the pools?) Whether an advert or not, there is also a supposed scene in one of the films of the train showing a businessman openly reading a copy of a contemporary risqué magazine. *Rail Photoprints*

BELOW Paddington arrival. There were three principal external differences between the LMR and WR power cars; on the latter the cantrail designation was simply 'Pullman', there was a destination blind on the side, and finally the passenger compartment had three windows of equal size. Regardless of the Pullman service, upon arrival at the terminus an office junior would be present to meet the train and obtain details of the loadings. Presumably a similar task would be undertaken for trains working in the reverse direction – or did the Pullman Conductor simply retain this information for when he arrived back at Paddington next time? *The Transport Treasury*

The Blue Pullman Story

BLUE PULLMAN

Blue Pullman service reported as near to Claverham, south of Bristol, on 25 September 1964. Reports indicate that at varying periods post June 1963 the mid-day Bristol service was extended to Weston-Super-Mare without, it seems, appearing to attract dissent from the unions. *Mark Warburton courtesy Mrs M. Warburton*

A down Pullman approaches Reading facing into the glare of the evening sun. Visibility was difficult at such times; equally in the morning on the up runs, the GW main line ran almost directly east-west. The train has not run through signals at 'Stop', for look carefully and the distant signal for the down main is just returning to danger in consequence of the train hitting the track-circuit ahead of the signal. *Bob Treacher*

In Colour on the Western

Paddington on 30 July 1964. A most interesting view as on Platform 6 we have a Blue Pullman set recently arrived as well – identified as an arrival due to the red light on the rear (the WR being satisfied it was able to use an electric tail light instead of the earlier oil lamp). From the clock partly visible on Platform 1, this would appear to be mid-afternoon and so the return of the mid-day fill-in turns, possibly those from Birmingham (left) and Bristol (right). In the centre is 'Castle' No 5076 Gladiator in well-travelled condition. At the time allocated to Southall, it had but six weeks to work before withdrawn on 14 September. *Rail Photoprints*

BLUE PULLMAN

In Colour on the Western

LEFT Paddington arrival. Without (control/motive power) records from every day the diesel Pullmans trains were due to operate, it is impossible to say exactly how many times a loco-hauled replacement was utilised but in general terms between September 1961 and the start of 1967 it appears to have been an average of a couple of occasions per month – excluding scheduled 'time-outs'. One such occasion was on 26 August 1964 when 'Brush Type 4' (Class 47) No D1690 was used to head a locomotive-hauled substitute 'Birmingham Pullman', the formation of which included three modern East Coast Main Line Pullman vehicles. Because of the make up, this was possibly a pre-supposed stand-by although that was certainly not the case on 3 October 1966 when the up morning BP set failed at Banbury. As a result of this the 10.10am departure from Paddington was hastily formed of rather grubby standard stock without even refreshment facilities. An eleven-minute late departure was announced as '. . . due to lack of crew to work the diesel locomotive.' According to an (obvious) quote from a correspondent in Railway Observer who reported the incident: 'Not a brilliant performance for one of BR's prestige trains.' *Amyas Crump*

ABOVE Paddington departure – the direction of travel for the second set on the right would appear to be similar. Careful study of various images reveals one early modification was the fitting of covers to the air horns; these also appear to have been susceptible to damage – notice the image of the train at Platform 5 at Reading seen earlier, and also here where just two covers are in place and the third missing. Again BP is in typical external WR condition and notwithstanding this is from a slide taken 50-plus years ago the Nanking Blue livery also appears to have faded in service.

BLUE PULLMAN

ABOVE Passing Southall on a down service. Vehicle numbers were shown on the outside of each car and also within, the latter on an engraved aluminium plate having black lettering placed above the corridor entrance to each passenger saloon. The sets had not been in service for many weeks on the WR when even on the generally excellent permanent way of the 'Western' comments began to filter through about ride quality. These same rumblings likely reached the ears of several senior officials as, perhaps almost in an attempt to counter these, a note was sent from T. H. Summerson to R. F. Hanks on 19 October 1960. It read, 'I travelled on the Blue Pullman from Paddington to Birmingham on Thursday night last week. I was in a trailer car in the middle of the train and had an altogether admirable ride. It could hardly have been better, both for smoothness and silence. When I checked the speed at one point I found it difficult to believe that we were travelling at nearly 90 miles per hour. Why cannot this quality of riding and service be made universal in all our express passenger stock?' *Colour Rail DE20*

BELOW Less than six months after entering public service another grimy WR set is seen, this time passing St Anne's Park, east of Bristol, on 1 February 1961. The Bristol set would overnight at Dr Day's sidings where, as stated in the text, new fuelling services were provided in connection with the trains. Folklore has it that in extreme winter conditions the set so stabled would on occasions freeze and be unable to be used in the morning. A signalman who worked the signalbox at Dr Day's also recalls coming to work at 6.00am to see the Pullman derailed on the catch points protecting the relief road. Apparently the set had developed a fault in one of its cabs and the decision was made to turn the train around so the good cab would face the London direction ready for the up service. What should have happened was the Pullman was to reverse out of the sidings on to the down main towards Lawrence Hill. Then using the good cab, drive around the loop on to the London line and reverse into Temple Meads. In theory this was perfectly easy and straightforward; in practice it was not. In the sidings the driver was at the far end and so reliant upon the shunter to give him a hand signal as to when to set back. The shunter always said he received a hand signal from the signalman. The signalman denied it, saying why should he give a hand signal, when there is a dummy signal on the ground to tell the shunter when the road was set? The long and short of it was the catch points worked just as they were intended to – admirably! By 9.00am the box was 'full of suits', much to the annoyance of the signalmen who had to still do their own work – 2.00pm and the end of their shift could not come around quick enough! *Mark B Warburton courtesy Mrs M Warburton*

In Colour on the Western

Lawrence Hassall's classic image of the train entering Leamington Spa on a down Birmingham service. No covers on any of the air horns this time! Modern Railways in its issue for April 1962 included a letter from T. E. Velvick from Eastbourne who stated that with the exception of one Chef, all staff on the WR BP sets come from BR restaurant cars, they wear Pullman uniform but are paid BR rates and that they are all specially trained for the job, the cost of which was met by the Pullman Car Co. (Who was Mr Velvick?)

The Blue Pullman Story

BLUE PULLMAN

Birmingham Snow Hill in March 1961. In true Pullman style a steward waits by the door of the second class parlour car. Turnaround for the trains at both Paddington in the morning and later in the day at Birmingham Snow Hill was fast for the period. The initial up service from Wolverhampton arrived at Paddington at 9.30am and departed again north at 10.10am. Arrival at Birmingham was at 12.05pm where it would remain for 55 minutes before departing again at 1.00pm. Necessary preparation by the on-board crew were probably undertaken in the platform although passengers would not be permitted to board until nearer the departure time. On Platform 5 at least standard enamel signs with the words 'Pullman A' etc were hung indicating where passengers would need to stand when waiting for a specific Pullman car. *Colour Rail*

In Colour on the Western

The lunchtime up service from Birmingham service heads south through the Birmingham suburbs: a modern train passing signals on old wooden posts. Three men, all in 'ice-cream' coats, are in the cab, likely undergoing route-learning/set familiarity. Natural staff turnover and link movement meant this was not an uncommon occurrence. *Colour Rail*

The Blue Pullman Story

BLUE PULLMAN In Colour on the Western

RIGHT Pullman set leaving Bristol at the start of its 1 hour 55 minute/2 hour, journey to London. With the exception of the first two weeks, all the Bristol services ran via Bath but in exceptional conditions could also operate from Bath via Westbury and the Berks & Hants line should operational conditions dictate this need. *Amyas Crump*

222

ABOVE The diesel 'South Wales Pullman' was introduced from 11 September 1961 exactly a year (less one day) from the start of the Bristol and Birmingham services. A London bound service is seen here passing the conglomeration of sidings that once existed at Severn Tunnel Junction. As an aside there was for many years at Neath a café on the station appropriately named the 'Blue Pullman Café', the name presumably dating from 1961 but which continued with the same identification for more than 40 years after the trains ceased to operate. *Maurie Graves*

LEFT AND RIGHT Seen here on Platform 3 at Bristol Temple Meads is Syd Synnuck a former Top Link driver from Bristol Bath Road depot and amongst the first on the Western Region passed to drive the Blue Pullman. Syd retired in September 1962 just two years after the start of the service. *Andrew Synnuck*

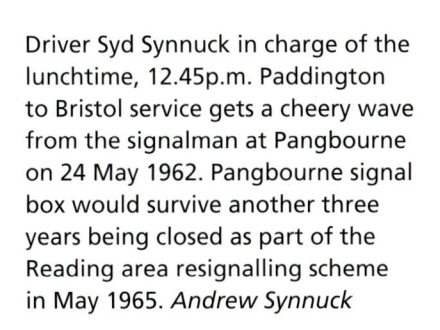

Driver Syd Synnuck in charge of the lunchtime, 12.45p.m. Paddington to Bristol service gets a cheery wave from the signalman at Pangbourne on 24 May 1962. Pangbourne signal box would survive another three years being closed as part of the Reading area resignalling scheme in May 1965. *Andrew Synnuck*

223

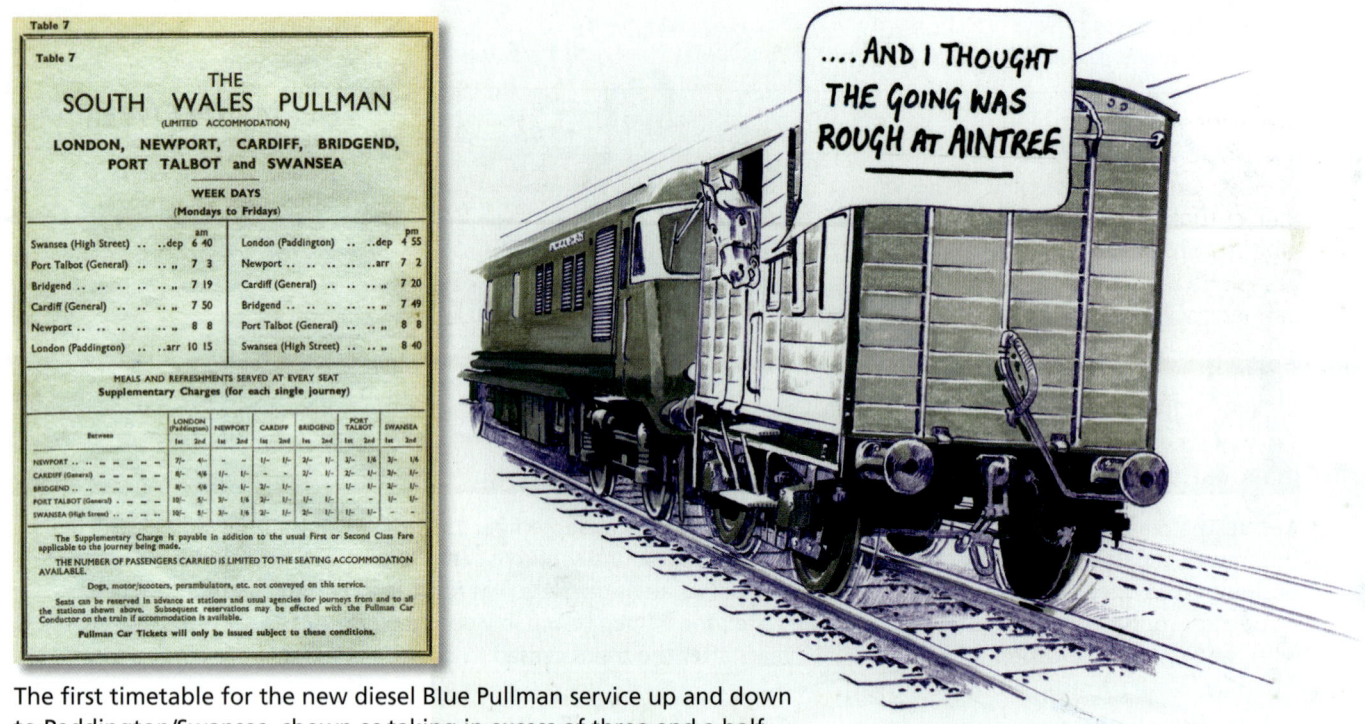

THE BLUE PULLMAN STORY

The first timetable for the new diesel Blue Pullman service up and down to Paddington/Swansea, shown as taking in excess of three and a half hours. As a comparison the steam-hauled 'South Wales Pullman' took around four and quarter hours whilst today's service is under three hours.

We may also look back nearly half a century at two other points of note. The first is that in the public timetable, great prominence was given to the trains, a single coloured page at the start of each issue devoted to each Pullman working. It is also important to remember that in the working timetable the concept of a fixed-formation express service was to a great extent unique and in consequence it was necessary for the operating rules to be succinctly explained (or reminders given) to staff so there might be no ambiguity. Before detailing further, remember that nearly all services were then made up of individual vehicles formed into rakes which could, and often did, vary, the only fixed rake trains then in use being the diesel multiple units operating the various suburban services. Ordinarily then should a party or group booking be advised it might, dependent upon the train and existing loading, result in an extra coach or more being added to the train – subject to stock availability and the maximum weight for the train/engine and route to be taken.

Even a DMU might be strengthened at times – with another single or twin diesel of compatible type but more specifically 'tail traffic' could be added – for example a fitted parcels van – again up to a stipulated maximum load. ('Tail traffic' meant another vehicle[s] added on the rear and certainly not something 'with a tail' – BUT see next paragraph!)

The Blue Pullman sets were of course different. Not only could they not (at that time) work in multiple but more specifically they could not have additional vehicles added either within the fixed formation or as tail traffic. Hence to ensure this was confirmed to all staff, the symbols ♠♠ appeared in the working book with the meaning, 'Four wheeled vehicles must NOT be conveyed on this train'. (It might equally have been said ANY additional vehicle may not be conveyed by this train. The thought of a shunter attaching a horse box or cattle truck to the rear of a Pullman set, let alone said vehicle bouncing along at 90mph, is perhaps best left to the imagination!)

The same public timetable also included a note that 'Dogs, motors/scooters, perambulators, etc are not conveyed on this service'. Again some of these may seem obvious, not least due to space constraints, but in the first days of operation it was quite acceptable to arrive at Paddington, Bristol or Birmingham with 'Pongo' (or updated for this revised edition to 'Shelby Cooper' in honour of Mike's Cockapoo), and he would be carried accordingly – *was there a similar 'Pullman Supplement' applicable to the dog ticket but who might then be provided with an 'at dog bowl' meals of Bonio or the like?*

To begin with, 'poochipoo' was probably carried within the passenger vehicle, but it was soon changed to dogs being required to travel in the front guard's compartment. This change possibly came in consequence of a complaint or perhaps an unpleasant event/occurrence. Being totally serious now, this latter method of travel was certainly the case one day, when two German Shepherd dogs belonging to one of the passengers were secured in the front guard's compartment, itself a somewhat noisy area. Unfortunately on that occasion the travelling fitter needed to gain access to the front engine compartment but was prevented from doing so by the two dogs driven to panic from the roar of the 1,000hp MAN engine just a few feet away. We may have sympathy with all three. The incident informs us of two points as well, firstly the guards' compartments were not fully insulated against sound, and secondly there was indeed access from this compartment into the engine room. Dogs were barred in-toto shortly afterwards; however this later changed to dogs being allowed in the passenger areas at the Conductor's discretion and presumably dependent upon the size of the tip!

On another occasion, a Bristol-bound set suffered a defect (unknown) but so serious that the crew was wary about stopping the set to gain assistance for fear of being unable to start moving again so they keep moving. Somehow this was communicated to the operating staff along the route (the traditional method of a note on a piece of paper attached to a lump of coal, and lobbed out near a signal-box, was clearly inappropriate – perhaps they used a sandwich?) with the positive result that the train was diverted through the platform lines at Swindon at slow speed and a door held open for a fitter to join the rear of the unit without it stopping. Whatever, having successfully gained access to the train, the next stage was for the man to make his way through the passenger accommodation to the front power car and hopefully remedy the defect; but he was then prevented from doing so by the Pullman Conductor, unless and until he covered the top of his overalls with a jacket. (It is not known why the travelling fitter could not fix the problem, assuming of course there was one on that service, or it may have been that the man picked up at Swindon was carrying a necessary spare part.)

There was a final amusing sequel to the incident of the dogs which occurred in the bad winter of 1962/3. It appears that HRH Princess Margaret, together with Lord Snowdon and their entourage (which included two Sealyham dogs), were stranded at Birmingham, unable to return to London by their planned aircraft due to the prevailing weather. Accordingly, a rapid change of plan resulted in the party finding their way to Snow Hill where space was to be found for them on the Pullman service. This change had been notified to Paddington, but there was still a genuine fear that the particular conductor on the service (known to be something of a martinet) would very likely refuse the Royal party access purely due to the presence of the dogs. Paddington therefore spent some considerable effort attempting to raise Snow Hill, and in particular the Station Master or a Senior Inspector, to advise them of the situation. Of course Paddington were already extremely busy due to the numerous delays resulting from the weather and it all resulted in further

Like on the LMR, the Western Region would no doubt have been glad to have their Blue Pullman sets occupied with special workings at weekends, as up to September 1961 all three would otherwise stand idle from Friday evening until Monday morning. One early exception is illustrated here, a WR set at Coventry on Sunday 5 March 1961 with the headcode '1Z66'; unfortunately no other detail is given as with others described in Appendix 10. Whilst in regular service the trains never carried a formal headboard in everyday service – perhaps such an idea was seen as 'outdated' by 'Jack Howe & Co'.; one was certainly pictured at Bristol with a small embellishment prior to working a Bristol to Leeds football special. (Some of the football specials are known to have had a special menu printed with the word 'Pullman' included.) Additionally the 'Educational Special of April 1970' (depicted later) also carried a small rectangular board. *RCTS*

As well as that mentioned earlier came an outing in connection with a Rugby Union County Championship match, Durham County versus Warwickshire, being played at Hartlepool on 13 March 1965. Two trains were operated, the first a WR BP set commencing at Coventry and thence via Birmingham new Street–Aston–Lichfield–Burton-on-Trent–Sheffield–York–West Hartlepool. The return journey was a reversal of the outward run. The second special departed a few minutes after the Pullman and was steam hauled by 'Britannia' No 70020 Mercury from Coventry via Nuneaton to Burton-on-Trent and then on to the same route. (Warwickshire were the victors with 15 points to 9.) Especially unusual was the use of the Western Pullman set for the train in particular as Coventry was 100% LMR territory. Might it have simply been because of the required number of seats? Whatever, the train is seen at its northern destination, the external condition of the unit again doing little to showcase WR cleaning standards. This does though also raise the question of were there other occasions when sets were borrowed between regions? The answer is probably no, although we must of course discount the post 1967 period when the sets were to be seen over a far greater operating area. It almost appears as if the two regions kept their trains very much under their own control whilst correspondence also suggests even the perhaps obvious suggestion of pooling spares was considered impractical although this may have been as much to do with where such items were stored. In which case why not concentrate all overhauls for all the trains at the one specific location, Derby or Swindon being the obvious choices? *R. F. Payne/ARPT*

delays to several other services simply because of the time spent ensuring all would go smoothly with the Royals. The final twist is that, regardless of their best intentions, the control office staff were later criticised over the time spent and the additional delays that occurred elsewhere.

There is no record as to where the dogs did eventually travel on that particular day; perhaps 'in comfort' would be a fitting tailpiece to this particular occurrence.

It has been suggested that at least one other individual was afforded a similar VIP service, this time on a London-bound Pullman service from Cardiff, the person being the Welsh singer Shirley Bassey. On this occasion all 18 second class seats in one power car were set aside for the sole use of Welsh singer, together with her own travelling canine companions.

Whilst on the subject of VIPs or well known passengers travelling, this also led to some pleasant experiences for John Ford on the 'Bristol Pullman'. 'We had the freedom of the train and on the afternoon shift we were served silver service dinner with the passengers and that was when we met most of our important people and friends, 99% of them were really nice and interesting. We did not forget that we represented BR and Pullman. The staff and customers really got on well to mutual benefit. I had afternoon tea with the singer Alma Cogan, sat with Tony Hancock the comedian and chatted with Charles Hawtrey of "Carry On" fame.

'The evening departures had quite a few MPs and Ministers, such as Lord George Brown returning to the West Country. I have to say Lord Montagu of Beaulieu was very keen on transport and invited the wife and I to

Beaulieu. Was he ever allowed in the cab? I couldn't possibly say!

'I had a good job before working on the Pullman repairing locos and running trials but being on the Blue Pullmans really was a wonderful experience for me and I was very lucky to work with such a good bunch.

'We got a good wage too but I left the trains upon taking a promotion in 1965 to become Electrical shift supervisor at the diesel test house in Swindon. I think someone replaced me from Bath Road Depot as the travelling fitter. To be honest I really preferred the Blue Pullman fitter's job.'

With three sets initially available on the WR, one was kept as a spare, normally in the new purpose-built three-road Pullman shed erected at Old Oak Common located between the former steam shed and the carriage sidings. (Incidentally, decades later the structure was being used by one of the privatised rail infra-structure maintenance companies, but was still being referred to as 'The Pullman Shed'.) Utilisation up to the summer of 1961 meant that two of the three eight-car sets were in use, and allowing for the spare set, this meant that each train was in service for ten days out of 21. As stated, loading figures from BR sources for the WR trains in the early days are not known, so instead we have to quote from a *Daily Telegraph* article of October 1960 which stated the 'Midland Pullman' as running at less than 60% capacity, 70% for the Bristol service but as high as 90% for the Birmingham service. (Doubtless, the traffic originating at, or continuing on to, Wolverhampton was considerably less.) Without in any way wishing to be sceptical we should remember that this was just one month after the commencement and as such these numbers were still very much in the WR's own 'honeymoon' period.

What was not good was that despite having a 33.3% spare capacity, it appears that on the WR, at least, there were times when both the two booked sets and the stand-by train were unavailable, possibly due even to the spare set being inconveniently placed to cover a breakdown – as indeed we saw at Bristol earlier. Despite this and regardless of the reliability or otherwise of the trains, Paddington still apparently had far more confidence in the sets with the result that an expansion of the diesel Pullman operation was scheduled for the start of the autumn timetable in 1961. This was in the form of a modern diesel replacement for the steam-hauled 'South Wales Pullman' commencing on 11 September 1961 (although another report refers to the Swansea service beginning from 31 August). In reality the WR really had little choice but to change the service to diesel, a steam-hauled Pullman service and its traditional-style stock was definitely seen as 'old-fashioned' when compared with the swish services operating to Birmingham and Bristol.

The diesel 'South Wales Pullman' service operated on weekdays between Swansea and Paddington and called at major stations each way between Swansea and Cardiff, before running non-stop from Cardiff via Badminton to Paddington. As with its steam predecessor it was a commercial success from the outset although it did now mean there was no longer a spare diesel set if it were needed.

The popularity of the trains amongst the enthusiast fraternity was confirmed when Messrs Ian Allan chose a Mike Mensing image of a WR set for the cover of the Summer 1962 'abc Combined Volume'. A BP set also featured on the cover of the August 1960 issue of *Railway Magazine*. (The actual image used was probably taken at Solihull.)

It was a similar case with the WR Staff Magazine, the region still seeing the Blue Pullman sets as being at the top of their prestige services. Sonning Cutting is again being used.

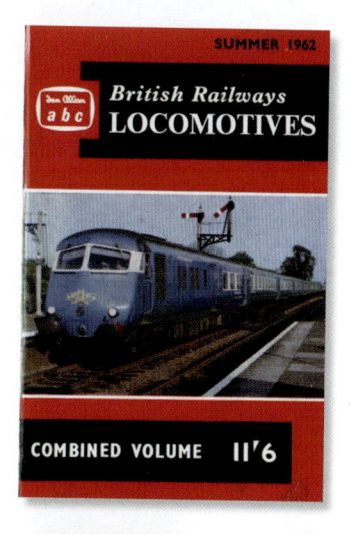

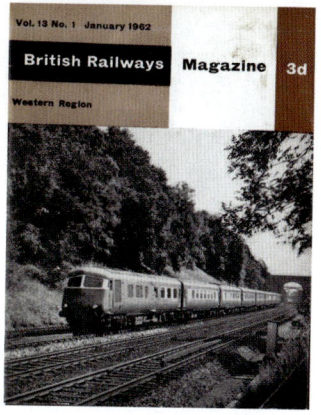

Paddington was clearly alert to this possibility for although the regular loco-hauled Pullmans were now withdrawn from daily service, most were retained as a standby train set. Although not stated this was likely to have been based at Old Oak Common, and in its earliest stand-by form now included two BR standard Mark 1 open firsts. The fact that the WR was still forming its other named trains in traditional chocolate and cream livery also meant the authorities were very anxious that the two Mk1s should exactly match the rest of the train. Accordingly, a supply of authentic Pullman umber and cream paint was despatched to Swindon to apply to the Mk1s, but the result was anything but satisfactory with no attempt made to apply any type of lining whatsoever, nor even to emulate that on a conventional BR vehicle, let alone the more elaborate Pullman style. At a later stage, the spare train set was re-formed with traditional Pullman vehicles only and with the suggestion that they should be named after rivers. Among the names selected were 'Wye', 'Severn', 'Thames' and 'Avon'. According to R. W. Kidner in *Pullman Trains in Britain*, the formation of the spare set was originally vehicle numbers: 27, 249, 169 and 54 plus *Cecelia*, together with Mk1 first opens: W3093 and W3094. Unlike the diesel trains, the formation was not 'fixed' and is known to have altered at various times, such as on 26 August 1964, when three second class Eastern Region cars (Nos 340, 352 and 344) were used as stand-in first class accommodation on the 1.00pm

'The Western will ... *be in the black this year.*' So stated the then WR General Manager, Gerry Fiennes when interviewed by G. Freeman Allen for *Modern Railways* in January 1965. Fiennes was what one might nowadays call a 'progressive' manager and whose name has of course already cropped up in this text previously. His views were at times radical and he was certainly not always popular with passengers or staff but it could not be said he did not speak his mind. In three pages of question and answer almost the whole topic of traffic on the WR was discussed with this short section on the Pullmans. Allen asks, '. . . is there a good market for Pullmans?' Fiennes: 'It seems so. In the principal business paths of the day we run most successful Pullmans between South Wales and London, and between Birmingham and London, and a not-quite-so-successful but still very rewarding Pullman between Bristol and London. Indeed, the mid-day 'South Wales Pullman' working as far as Cardiff, which we have only introduced this winter, is loading to over 60 per cent of capacity in one direction and to over 50 per cent in the other.' The lead image to the article was one by George Heiron and showed the down Bristol Blue Pullman set at St Anne's Park. *(So had things changed that much between the time of Gerry Fiennes and when John Palette was interviewed a few years later? And of course, there is the obvious question: if Bristol is the weakest how could that service then subsequently justify a 12-car train?)*

service from Birmingham. The reason for this was officially stated to be that the available seating more closely matched that of the eight-car WR Pullman sets.

Whenever a spare set was in use, the catering staff nicknamed it the 'Wells-Fargo' set, a somewhat unkind reference to the contemporary 'Western' television series then popular which featured a locomotive and rake of elderly Pullman cars and to which the spare set was perceived to bear a striking resemblance(?). If one of the stand-by sets was in use it was also not unusual for some passengers to object to paying the Pullman supplement due to old fashioned stock being used, official policy in such cases being that they would be refunded without question. One specific passenger complaint from the time came from a man who when seeing his mother off at Paddington on a stand-by set stated, 'I am paying extra for her to travel, just to watch a man walk up and down the coach in a white suit.' As mentioned in the previous chapter, by 1962, the LMR also had a spare set of locomotive-hauled Pullman vehicles at its disposal, courtesy of the Southern Region.

Backtracking slightly, the first use of these vehicles was both unforeseen and, to say the least, difficult. Charles Long recounted a story in relation to the 'Birmingham Pullman' shortly after the WR West Midland lines were transferred to the LMR: 'Some fault had been discovered during the routine weekend examination of the rostered diesel unit. Bear in mind also that the seating layouts and numbering in the older style loco-hauled Pullmans was also totally different compared with the diesel cars. Consequently the previous carefully prepared equivalent seating diagrams to match a five-car loco-hauled rake to the six-car, first class "Midland Pullman" were useless when it came to substituting for the eight-car first and second class Birmingham train. Having also likely seen the stand-by set for the first time only a short while beforehand, the Conductor had quite a job sorting out his customers (interesting that Mr Long uses the modern day term 'customers') on the well-filled Monday morning journey to Paddington. Confusion was confounded en-route, as regular passengers, expecting their normal diesel unit, waited in their usual places at intermediate calling points, first-class towards the centre, second class at each end. Since the 'genuine' first-class locomotive-hauled cars included both brake-ends, many second class ticket-holders found themselves enjoying unexpected armchair luxury, while certain first-class passengers were somewhat less-lavishly accommodated in the sometime seconds.'

The increase from 66.6% to 100% utilisation achieved by the WR from the autumn of 1961 was in stark contrast to the continuing 50% utilisation on the LMR, raising a number of questions, the first and most obvious being why if the WR could have all its sets ready for use, did the LMR still feel unable to do so? Did the idea of a Liverpool service on the LMR stem from the observation of the 100% utilisation being achieved by its neighbour? Likewise, was maintenance on the ground an issue, and was it this that prevented the LMR from operating at full capacity?

We do know some servicing difficulties were reported as early on as 20 September 1962 but these again mainly concerned the availability of spare parts. Mike Woodhouse confirmed the LMR and WR did indeed assist each other with spares when necessary, and the manufacturer helped too although official information about the number of spares held, as well as difficulties obtaining specific items, is contradictory in the surviving paperwork. As both types of unit were similar, the WR worked to similar maintenance and inspection schedules as their colleagues on the LMR and again as per manufacturer guidelines, although regular checks and maintenance was likely to have taken slightly longer on the WR for the simple reason of the additional two cars; again this work was scheduled for weekends.

On the WR we are lucky in that some examples of failures are recorded. As mentioned before a P-way jack was run over on 5 Dec 1960 on the LMR. In September 1962, 'Hymek' D7023 was observed with a locomotive-hauled Pullman set deputising for the up South Wales set – the reason for the non-availability of the diesel set is not given. Another example was when D1006 *Western Stalwart* was in charge of locomotive-hauled stock on the Birmingham service (whether morning or midday is not reported).

In contrast to modern-day behaviour, an incident for which the railway was clearly not responsible warranted a rapid response by the operators and minimal disruption to traffic. An example of this was when an unfortunate individual jumped in front of the up 'Birmingham Pullman' at Seer Green. Notwithstanding any shock sustained by the crew, the train continued to Old Oak Common where it was paused briefly for the front to be quickly washed down, so allowing it to continue to Paddington with minimal delay. (An accident also took place on an unreported date, resulting in the death of a platelayer at Uffington who was mown down by one of the Pullman sets.)

In the same year, 1962, but on an unreported date, a brake block became detached from one of the bogies on the power car when working a down service and ruptured the fuel tanks. The fitter evolved a very makeshift repair by stuffing handkerchiefs into the holes and the train made its way, cautiously, to Swindon – having apparently turned down the offer of a 'shove' from *City of Truro* then stabled at Didcot!

Mike Woodhouse recorded his jobs on the Blue Pullmans at Old Oak Common: 'On 14 November 1962 I was on the early shift (7am to 3pm which later [became] 6am to 2pm) which was also my first day on the Blue Pullmans. In those days communication was by a message was sent to Control at Paddington by a signalman or a station master. We heard that the 6.40am from Swansea High Street was down to one power car after 60094 shut down. The travelling fitter suspected low lube oil pressure. The failed set limped into the Pullman shed and was plugged into the shore supply. I tested the fuel and diagnosed poor fuel dilution to the fuel injectors plus an oil and oil filter change were required. Twenty-four hours later I was back starting up the power car and checking all the new injectors for leaks before refitting the rocker covers and joints and joyously recording 60lbs of oil pressure. The "Wells Fargo" set had stood in for the set on the 14th and 15th November.

'I also heard that on 8 January the "South Wales Pullman" had left mechanical pieces all over the track but we didn't get the repair job so no further details.

'On 2 April 1963 a message came through for the same power car, 60094, to come in for a fuel injector change after running on the down "South Wales Pullman" service. 60094 was actually due be changed anyway according to its maintenance schedule. (MAN injectors were changed at intervals of 1,500hrs operation). We were told to finish up on a diesel hydraulic to avoid delay to the Pullman service. The parts were in stock and we booked out 12 fuel injectors, seals and joints along with the special MAN tool for extracting fuel injectors. It was a hard job for four of us, two either side, to extract the injectors from an extremely hot engine but we got all 12 out before signing off!

'The demolition of the steam shed was just starting as we left, knowing the next two shifts would carry on with 60094 to ensure there was minimal delay before the power car could return to service.'

The worst known day for BP availability on the WR was 11 April 1963, when all three sets were out of action because of the bogie bolster cracks found earlier by John Ford on a particularly freezing day.

'In the 1963 deep freeze I failed the set on inspection at OOC because of a small crack in the bogie where the brake rod passed through on 60099. I remember the panic having reported it about 11am and having to get the "Wells Fargo" set ready for the 12.15 run.'

On this particular occasion, the Birmingham service was in the charge of D1006 *Western Stalwart*, the Bristol service had D834 *Pathfinder*, and the South Wales train had 'Hymek' No D7066. Rolling stock details were not recorded, but presumably use was made of both the WR and LMR loco-hauled rakes as there is certainly no evidence that a BP Pullman set was ever the subject of an inter-regional loan. *(How did they get the spare LMR set across in time?)*

An unusual means of publicising the sets also took place in 1963, when public announcements were made referring to the impending withdrawal for overhaul of some of the sets. The cleverly worded announcements ensured that the trains still remained in the forefront of the minds of the clientele with the wording: 'After intensive service since their introduction in September 1960, the WR Blue Pullman diesel expresses are undergoing their first complete overhauls. The 'Bristol Pullman' which was withdrawn on May 8, is the first of the three luxury trains to be treated. This express, which runs twice daily on Mondays to Fridays between Bristol and Paddington, has now run over 370,000 miles. (The intermediate service will be extended to Weston-super-Mare from June 15.) Overhaul of each train will take about six weeks, and will be carried out in the Swindon workshops. During this period, a substitute train, consisting of traditional Pullman coaches hauled by a diesel locomotive, will maintain the schedules. On the return to service of the Bristol set, the 'Birmingham Pullman' will be withdrawn, but the "South Wales Pullman" will not be withdrawn until next year.'

The truth though was not exactly as stated as the 'Bristol Pullman' had already been out of service between 26 February and 12 March 1962 for heavy maintenance. With little or no notice given to passengers there was much chagrin from regular travellers. The new 'negative' publicity was therefore a bold and we may say proactive approach turning a disadvantage into an advantage; and what is more it worked as well. On the subject of repairs (spares), in 1963 the WR was reported as having no spare bogies for their train sets, although these were on order at the time. We know there had been spares available in 1960 so the only conclusion has to be they had been used in the interim (by the WR or LMR?), possibly in an attempt to over-come riding difficulties. It does though seem strange that a 'bogie' needed to be ordered; more likely surely were spare bushes, bearings and other parts, but again why was a supply of these major components not kept in stock?

It was also in 1962 that probably the most remarkable 'might have been' involved the train. This was on 29 August 1962 when a regular 'Bristol Pullman' passenger, Mr John E. Collins of the Bristol Building Centre, asked Frank Harding, the Pullman Car Company MD at Victoria, if a Blue Pullman set could be hired for a Study Tour to Paris and back. As all three Western sets were now in use Harding enquired if the LMR would be up for loaning a six-car set for the tour.

Neither was this a 'pie in the sky' idea (do pardon the pun for what follows), for Collins had previously paid £9,00 to hire a plane to take 137 people on a study tour to New York. Apparently the Southern Region had already paved the way for the Pullman to travel and planned to split the six car set into its two half sets and park them

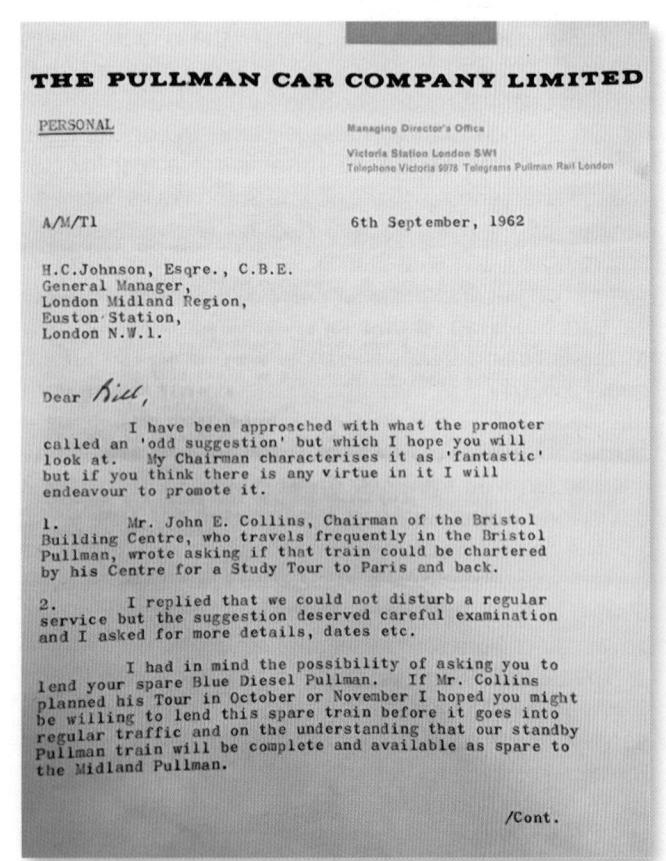

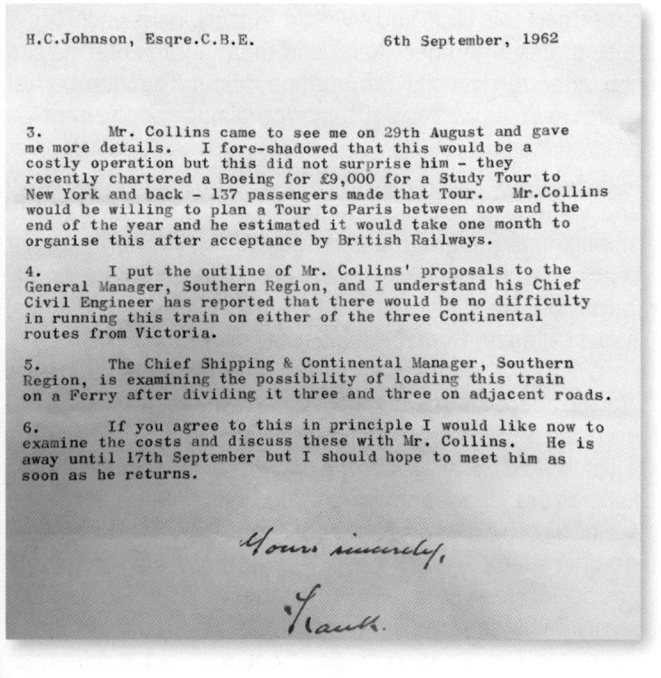

Truth is indeed stranger than fiction.

side by side on the train ferry. Unlike Mr Collins' New York trip, as can be imagined the idea sadly never did get off the ground, and we are left to wonder quite how 'Le Pullman Bleu' would have fared on French rails.

In one respect we might say the actual trains led a charmed life although not the service. To explain this we must report on the tragic accident as occurred to the up mid-day turn of Thursday 15 August 1963 formed of the Wells Fargo set.

Mike Woodhouse recalls: 'The Blue Pullman was stuck at TY [Tyseley] due to a running repair and we received a request at Old Oak Common to send the "Wells Fargo" set ecs to Birmingham. Upon arrival the train became the 1.0pm Birmingham Snow Hill to Paddington service. The umber and cream steam-heated stock was pulled by our own 81A allocated Class 52 "Western" loco *Western Queen* D1040 finished in Maroon BR livery.'

As No D1040 powered towards Knowle and Dorridge at 80mph the crew sighted the distant signal at 'on'. A full brake application was made but despite this the locomotive collided with a goods train carrying brand new Land Rovers which had shunted 'wrong road' on to the main line. Special instructions existed at the location when dealing with fast trains and this the signalman at Knowle & Dorridge had failed to comply with.

Several witnesses, including school children estimated the Pullman was still travelling at about 20mph at the point of impact. Luckily all four crew on the freight train (hauled by a pannier tank) jumped clear but sadly the three Wolverhampton men in the cab of *Western Queen* were not so lucky and all perished. In addition chef Peter Harrold was badly scalded in the kitchen car. Ironically, the co-driver of the diesel was Ernie Morris who was one of the first drivers trained on the Blue Pullman and had been the star of the speeded up *Let's Go to Birmingham* film. The driver was Sid Bench and, covering for a sick colleague, was secondman David Corkery. The strongly built rolling stock from 1923 stood up well with the train remaining upright and intact. The subsequent enquiry absolved the train crews of all blame, and instead focussed blame on the signalman in the Knowle & Dorridge box, Evan Jones. There were some later comments made about the braking characteristics of the train, which despite the age of the rolling stock, implied that it was still better than on the diesel Pullman.

Mike Woodhouse recalls again: 'On the 15 May 1963 I was actually in the OOC "factory" working on *Western Pathfinder* D1001 [allocated to] 84A changing a turbocharger and its 375 exam when my supervisor said the "South Wales Pullman" was in trouble. This time kitchen car 60745 was emitting a noise from the frame. We rushed to get the line drawings as most of us only knew the power cars in detail. On arrival we saw the exhaust joint had blown off and the manifold was loose on the auxiliary Rolls-Royce engine. There were no spare joints in stock so we made our own from gasket jointing using scissors and hole punches.

'We were offered overtime to carry on and finish the repair so the "South Wales Pullman" could do the evening run and the "Wells Fargo" would not be needed. Shortly afterwards on 25 June 1963 it was the turn of the trailing power car 60095 to misbehave on the "South Wales Pullman" due to total loss of coolant. Once in the Pullman shed I poured raw water into the engine and we quickly saw the coolant pipe had split between the engine and cooler group. We drained the coolant and cut off the offending hose. We had the parts in stock and again we were offered overtime to ensure the "South Wales Pullman" could be back in service for the evening 4.55pm departure.

'On another occasion, 1 July 1964 and just after breakfast, we heard that 60095 was giving a rough ride in the cab as the non powered bogie was oscillating at high speed. My workmate and I were in the Pullman shed and had just finished replacing the final drive torque arm rubbers on 'Western' D1047(allocated to Canton 88A) so looked over the line drawings of the non powered bogie. The Pullman had by now been berthed in the long shed so we had to get all our tools, hand lights etc from the Pullman shed. We checked the treads for flats and damage and went into the inspection pit to examine flange wear but there was nothing apparent wrong. After that we examined the main bogie which was all the springs, dampers, riding heights and the underframe. We found the left-hand vertical damper between the leading trailing wheel had damage and the rubber doughnut was missing. The vertical damper was also leaking so we needed to replace all the affected components. The parts were out of stock so our supervisor had to inform Paddington the Pullman couldn't run that evening. On the Western Region we operated a scheme called U.V.S. (Urgent Vehicle Standing) which gave priority to obtaining parts. The Chief storeman would then ring Swindon followed by all the main Western Blue Pullman depots. Questions were being asked as to how could the Western Region not have a vertical damper between them and after we left we were told the phones were red hot. Metro-Cammell sent the part by overnight courier and the next day we found out our supervisor had promised the part would be fitted within an hour of arrival! The next morning the Pullman was still berthed but the night shift had fitted the vertical damper and she was back in service that morning. It was then back to routine work and we then serviced and carried out a brake adjust on *Western Warrior* D1017 (allocated to 88A Cardiff Canton) ...'

John Ford also recalls a few more incidents. "Although I was the electrical fitter after a time you got to know if the engine sounded right. One day I called down my two bosses at Paddington to come and listen to the engine but they reckoned nothing was wrong. Within the next couple of runs the engine failed at Swindon ... A con rod had gone straight through. Next we had a problem with the engine governor. As it moved up to increase revs, an external lever on the governor moved with it. For a time the governor would increase but not the associated spring return; so we helped it out with an elastic band ... in fact we actually ran like that for a while, no big deal! We had more elastic bands for safety and yes, there were other breakdowns, like a sparking generator commutator, failed traction motors which had to be uncoupled by us so we could keep running until Swindon's was ready to take the job. We had plenty of pheasants hitting the windscreen on the

THE BLUE PULLMAN STORY

INFORMING YOU . . .
this Pullman diesel electric train will be taken out of service for a period of approximately six weeks as from May 7 for mechanical overhaul. It has run a total of 478,000 miles.

During this period a standby train giving you Pullman standard of comfort will be running in its place.

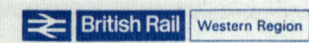

British Rail | Western Region

ABOVE See also Appendix 8.

ABOVE Blue Pullman set at Tyseley with a contemporary 'Cross Country' DMU alongside, 18 February 1962. Tyseley was the WR Midlands area depot for servicing the sets although when this was not required overnight berthing was at Cannock Road sidings, Wolverhampton. With two and later three trains stabled away from London overnight we might even question what was the point of the new shed at OOC in the first place. Note also the two views were NOT taken on the same day and do not show the same set, he first image being particularly interesting as the position of all three air horns has been modified and point lower to the ground. *Rail Online ZF-5438-95371-1-014, and unknown*

"Bristol Pullman". Sadly the South Wales technician and two other drivers I know also had to deal with suicides whilst on the Blue Pullmans.'

Interestingly, *Modern Railways* recorded that when recourse had to be made to the loco-hauled stand-by Pullman set, loadings were not adversely affected. Pre-booked passengers of course would be unlikely to be aware that the usual diesel set was unavailable, so continuous use of the standby set over a protracted period might well have had a different effect on the loadings. It was stated in the same magazine that up to late 1964 the three diesel sets operating on the WR had failed in service (does this mean failed 'en-route' or were not available?) on a total of 19 occasions since 1960.

The renowned writer Adrian Vaughan in his various pronouncements also refers to his knowledge of the working of the train during his time he was a signalman at Challow. According to Adrian, the point to point timings for the Pullman between Badminton and Wootton Bassett were often credited with periods of 100mph running – notwithstanding the official 90mph limit that applied. It was also not unknown for the occasional part to detach itself (as indeed occurred regularly from the transmission of the early GWR diesel railcars). So far as BP was concerned such an incident took place at Hullavington on the down 'South Wales Pullman' but without further detail being given. Further west the 'South Wales Pullman' was diverted around the Vale of Glamorgan line on occasions as a young Chris Ware found out in 1965: 'We were so excited to hear the Pullman was going to pass near my house and had to wait ages at Porthkerry Tunnel but it was well worth it …'. The train also ran over the former Taff Vale mainline through the Taff and Rhondda valleys and on to Swansea via the Rhondda and Swansea Bay route. Still with the same train but moving ahead to 1964, there was an occasion on 14 January when a power car on the 06.50 ex Swansea burst into flames just as the train was leaving its starting point. The passengers were detrained and transferred to the 07.20 up London service. Meanwhile with the fire extinguished the set left light for Paddington with the intention that it would take up its booked return journey. Unfortunately the fire erupted again at Bridgend and consequently this time the train was understandably taken out of service. Adrian Vaughan comments that the stand-by set of coaches had to make a quick dash to Paddington which both John Ford and Mike Woodhouse say were mostly kept at Old Oak Common. (Where else might they have been stabled?)

A few other incidents may also be reported. The first of these was on 25 July 1963 when the 17.45 down 'Bristol Pullman' from Paddington hit some hounds from a fox hunt near Maidenhead. John Ford was on the Travelling Fitter on the train. 'We were travelling at speed when the drivers were confronted by a pack of hunt dogs crossing the line. The drivers told me they hit quite a few dogs and there was a huge gory mess. The force of the impact also opened an air cock and snapped the handle. The air was blowing all over the ballast and mess with lots of passengers

232

Caption (left photo): Corridor blank in place for use whenever less than a set with power cars either end was being moved. The observation window – for shunt purposes – will be noted whilst there is also provision for the regulatory tail-lamp. *Derek Everson*

Caption (right photo): Half-set passing Didcot in December 1964, the destination almost certainly Old Oak Common. Various combinations of trains – full, half, two power cars and two trailers, two powers alone, and even a single power car – are known to have operated between OOC and Swindon or Swindon and elsewhere. In the case of a single power car travelling alone, power would have been extremely restricted as just one power bogie and consequently two traction motors were all that would have been available. Former OOC fitter Derek Everson recounts that if an engine failure were discovered on one of the BP power cars which was not possible to fix at the depot, the defective vehicle would be towed to Swindon and invariably returned ready for its next day's duty. 'Swindon must have had an ace gang of fitters who worked through the night. At OOC we did engine changes on "Warships" but not on BP.' Just visible on the sides are car identification plates which read A/H–B/G–C/F–D/E. 'A' and 'H' were the power cars with 'H' always at the London end of the train. This half set conforms exactly with E-F-G-H visible. No public service ever operated using just a half set. *Rail Photoprints*

staring out of the window at the carnage! I isolated the front power car then put one driver in the back cab for power and put the second man in the damaged front cab to act as watchman. We needed to clear the line ASAP and 'bogged' it to Reading. I got a right rollicking for splitting the drivers which annoyed me. As for hunt party it soon disappeared as he obviously should have had more control. The power car ended up at Swindon for repair.'

An unrelated source continues with the rest of the episode. At Reading those on the train who were partaking of dinner were unceremoniously turfed out on to the platform with the intention that they would continue their journey west on a following Bristol service being stopped especially to pick them up. The damaged BP set in the meanwhile was taken into the Reading carriage sidings. Unfortunately the train intended to take on the Pullman passengers, the 18.45 departure, was already full to capacity and there was simply no room for up to 224 additional passengers. With no spare vehicles available at Reading, the Control Office had no choice but to call back the damaged BP train from the sidings and after its passengers had been reseated (and as Adrian Vaughan puts it '… reunited with their by now cold dinners') proceeded to Bristol where they arrived a mere three hours late.

As has been reported should the 'Wells Fargo' set be required then invariably, but not exclusively, this was diesel hauled. Examples of the train with 'King' and 'Castle' haulage are also shown in the accompanying illustrations. It should also be recalled that the Western Region were very keen to throw off their steam heritage and it therefore must have caused not a little embarrassment when steam had to come to the rescue – in fact as late as 15 May 1964. On that occasion the standby coaches were in use for the 08.15 ex Bristol hauled by a 'Western' diesel. This was declared a failure at Didcot and the only available substitute motive power was a decidedly grubby member of the 'Hall' class, No 6937 *Conyngham Hall* which it transpired was also just seven months away from being withdrawn and condemned. Despite hardly being prepared for its task, No 6937 and especially its crew set about the task in hand, so much so that they even beat the scheduled Reading to Paddington timing set for the BP set by two minutes.

A final tale from Adrian Vaughan concerns the Pullman trains at Challow. The train itself was always signalled using the old GWR code for an express diesel, '4-1-13', rather than what might have been thought the ordinary '4 bells' for an express passenger train. As on the LMR, 'double-block' working was also in force for down Pullman trains meaning the block had to be clear for two sections ahead of the train. Whether this just applied at Challow or at other locations on the WR is not certain. (Might this also not just have been due to signal spacing and speed but also due to the proven inferior braking characteristics as compared with a locomotive-hauled train?)

In Adrian's own words, 'It was an ambition of the signalman at Wantage Road and Challow to contrive to route the Pullman on to the relief lines. One day the opportunity occurred when the down Pullman [*whether a Bristol or South Wales service is not stated*] arrived at Challow with both engines failed. Already waiting at

The Blue Pullman Story

Power cars receiving attention in Swindon Works. General wear and tear could cause considerable minor body damage as witness (what we think) is W60094 in the works on 23 May 1965. Of necessity, with all three trains scheduled for weekday working, a 'Wells Fargo' set would concurrently have been in operation. The second image is taken slightly earlier in August 1964 and is receiving what appears to be light repairs. As time passed so it was admitted that obtaining paint colours identical with the originals was not possible. Jack Howe also commented on the inside colours (during we think c1962) that, '… replacing three patterns used on the original trains supplied by Holoplast is impossible as they are now obsolete, namely: pale Pink Filigree 111.C matt, Paynes Grey Filigree 113.C matt, and Flame Carousel 502.B matt. Replacements advised as Warerite: Tessata Coral Pink matt, Moresco Silver Grey matt, and Morasco Scarlett.' Mechanically, a top engine overhaul was specified to take place every 9-12 months. *Brian Dale and Colour Rail 211840*

Challow ready to follow the Pullman was the scheduled 18.01 Didcot to Swindon passenger stopping train with '61xx' 2-6-2T No 6136 at the head of two coaches. A bit of 'discussion' took place and it was agreed that the 61xx and its two coaches would attach to the front of the Pullman and tow it to Swindon – which they did.' As Adrian pointed out, 'It was probably totally against all the rules not least because the steam train was vacuum braked and the Pullman air-braked, likely meaning there was no braking available on the eight-car Pullman train.] Adrian concludes by asking, '… I wonder what the Pullman passengers must have thought as their train made various chuffing and whistling sounds as well as stopping at all the intermediate stations between Challow and Swindon!'

Ralph Cousins worked in the GEC Traction Machines Department and oversaw the repair of failed main generators. 'I'd been to see the Blue Pullmans being built using our equipment. I looked after the repairs of failed main generators which usually meant on the NBL Type 2s. However, once we went to Wolverhampton to carry out a temporary repair on the "Birmingham Pullman". Exhaust bends used to fail and blow the exhaust back into the back ends. I did have a nice cab ride in a diesel Pullman and I'm sad they didn't preserve a set.'

A few other incidents, some of a serious nature, occurred and this ex BR employee who worked on the Blue Pullmans was prepared to talk to us but even after more than 50 years asked for his identity to be withheld. 'On one Up Pullman journey between Slough and Paddington there was a long relief loop that we didn't normally use. One day we were put into this loop via a gantry signal and after some miles released by a ground signal. This different type signal could and did disorientate a driver on one of my trips and we were lucky to have it pulled off just in time.'

He continues: 'Ordinarily the "South Wales Pullman" was due to leave Paddington before the Bristol service but there was an occasion when the SWP was delayed and instead they released the Bristol train first. All went well until Wootton Bassett where the South Wales line diverges to the right and in mechanical signalling days the signal for the junction was somewhat obscured by the platform and footbridge. There was also a speed restriction of 60mph across the junction on to the Badminton line to Wales. I was told by my colleague that the signalman had assumed the trains were still running in the right order and that the approaching Blue Pullman was for South Wales not Bristol. Instead the "Bristol Pullman" whipped around that bend at 90mph – fortunately remaining upright. They had to get a wrong line order and reverse to regain their normal route! What I do know is that the drivers always treated this signal with great care afterwards!

'A Blue Pullman also hit the buffers at Paddington one day. The Pullman had two types of brake, an engine-only air brake that you could apply in snatches like on/off then on/off whilst if this brake failed there was still the normal train brake. The technique with the train brake was totally different and you had to apply it first then release for the air pressure to build up again, hence no rapid on/off then on/off or you would simply lose your brake! So on this particular day the Pullman lost its brakes and kissed the buffers.

'The engines were 1,000hp MAN engine driving a GEC generator which supplied power to four traction motors. When they failed on a journey we crossed our fingers they would not seize and we could carry on for the rest of the day – then unpin them overnight which of course meant with one disconnected less power was available. If I remember rightly the maximum pull away current was 2,400 amps at each end! There was also an acceptance that the MAN engines blew out plenty of oil into the engine room and sometimes there was a little fire although you didn't to have to schedule an oil change as often as you did on those Maybach engines.

'Another thing I do remember is bringing the train back to Swindon empty from Wolverhampton at midnight with a new driver who did not want to drive even though he knew the road. I'm not going to admit to driving that night but we did get to Swindon in one piece . . .'

Perhaps we should now look at the early years of the Western Pullmans from an observer and passenger's point of view. John Wilson was one of the lucky few: 'The Blue Pullman was totally different to anything I'd ever seen. I used to see it pass the Eagle recreation ground four times a day! It really did look amazing in that beautiful blue. It was 1961 when I caught the "Birmingham Pullman" as my firm paid for me to travel to Paddington quickly so I could meet a coach on its way back from Holland. The seats were extremely comfortable, the train was quieter and faster than the steamers. For me it had a smooth ride despite reports to the contrary and I remember the luxurious interior was so clean.'

Watching with his school pals was Graham Anderson: 'My school, Islip Manor First in Northolt, was very close to the old "Birmingham Pullman" Route and between 1961 and 1965 my school pals and I would race down there to watch the trains go by. Next to the 'Kings' and 'Castles' the new Blue Pullmans really stood out with that vibrant colour and regal crest on the front. We used to place pennies on the track and wait for the Pullman to thunder by completely flattening them . . .'.

1962 view of John Ford, Travelling Technician (in the suit). The tall attendant is Ron Spring or Springer. John thinks the older guy with the pants up over his waist is a driver (but no ice cream outfit!).

Memories ... Nicky and Buster (right) at Leamington in late 1963.

Tony Llewellyn often saw the 'Birmingham Pullman' at Wolverhampton Low Level as well as the sets travelling ecs to Cannock Road Sidings.

More personal memories follow, this time first from Buster Hewitt: 'In late 1963 my Dad Peter Hewitt took my big brother and I to Leamington Spa Station. My Dad and the two of us were mad on trains. We lived in Seascale, Cumbria and were visiting grandparents in Leamington Spa. My Dad built up the trip to the station up by telling us we were going to see a VERY special train which of course was the Blue Pullman and it did absolutely blow us away. It is one of the most treasured memories I have of Dad and childhood.'

Greg Maxwell Collett says: 'Although my Dad Howard worked at Metro-Cammell I don't think he ever got to travel on the Pullmans. However, he took me along to stations to note the numbers. I know he was very proud of the product and when we were on holiday in 1964 at Weston-Super-Mare I saw the Blue Pullmans head off towards Bristol. My notes from the time show I had seen the following vehicles in Nanking Blue: W60094, W60095, W60096, W60097, W60098 and W60099 plus W60644-9 and W60734-9. They had a unique sort of hum to them as they pulled away'.

From the summer timetable of 1964 the 'Bristol Pullman' started to make intermediate stops at Reading and Swindon on the off peak runs. In June 1965 Chippenham was also dropped from the timetable.

Neath GWR Retired Staff Club member David L. Phillips was a guard on standby duty on 16 December 1965 when for the only time in his career he was told to jump on the 'South Wales Pullman'. 'I knew something important must have happened for them to use the Blue Pullman as emergency transport. It turned out I was in fact on my way to relieve the guard of the breakdown train that was attending the tragic accident that had occurred at 2.30am that morning when a landslip on the up side of Bridgend

The Blue Pullman Story

BLUE PULLMAN

ABOVE Another dingy station view, this time with power car W60096 leading the line-up at Snow Hill in 1962. Notice the cover over the coupling has been removed and the group of keen young spotters on the platform. The train is being made ready for a return to Paddington. *Rail Online ZF-5438-95371-1-013*

LEFT 'South Wales Pullman' or a very early Bristol working? The former is more likely. The service is on the Badminton line near Westerleigh. Notice the differing uniforms for the crew and just two covers to the air horns. *Lewis Coles*

In Black and White on the Western

Grand National day, 27 March 1965. The service was a special working from South Wales to Aintree. The views show the train entering Shrewsbury; stationary, either waiting the road or perhaps for a crew change; and finally the return working across the Cheshire plain just before passing Crewe.
Martin Welch

BLUE PULLMAN

LEFT Again on the Badminton line, this time near to Chipping Sodbury. Did the WR staff on board the trains act in similar fashion to their LMR counterparts with regards to the air-conditioning when it came to meeting a steam train travelling in the opposite direction in the tunnels at Alderton, Chipping Sodbury, under the River Severn and at Box? *George Heiron*

BELOW The 4.50pm 'Birmingham Pullman' (actually the Paddington to Wolverhampton Low Level working) leaving Solihull station on 6 July 1961. Mention has already been made in the early chapters of this book of how the railways needed to adapt to both retain traffic and find new markets. The diesel Pullmans were obviously one plus point but compare that with the goods yard in the background – weed strewn track and little real traffic apart from coal, and that would of course reduce as the number of houses with open fires started to diminish. Partly related to the BP sets and partly to the change then taking place with reference to corporate livery and symbolism, came this letter from (Mr?) G. Rheam of Leamington Spa who wrote to BR in January 1965, 'The Blue Pullmans are first rate for short journeys, but the seats are too narrow for long ones.' The said passenger adds a few (not Pullman specific) comments which are relevant to the period, 'I had an opportunity of making a quick visit to the Design Centre … Haven't you got your priorities wrong? Who cares about your symbol! At least the old one incorporated the British Lion – this new one is meaningless … You could do a lot I believe in restoring good service to the public if you could improve the morale of the staff by de-centralising responsibility. In the old days everyone was proud of their railway, now the old timers have lost all their one-time pride and just wait for retirement – who cares?' *Michael Mensing*

In Black and White on the Western

Another image with plenty of detail from the photographer. This is the 3.15pm 'Bristol Pullman' to Paddington, seen here passing Moreton Cutting east of Didcot on 22 September 1961. Just visible by the Guard's window is the small mirror requested to be fitted to the WR sets so the Guard might be able to observe signals as necessary. In the background 0-6-0PT No 8430 waits to leave the yard with an up freight. *Michael Mensing*

Through Swindon with clear signals – the clock on the exterior of the signal box was possibly unique and it appears no one was ever able to truly identify the reason for its presence. *The Transport Treasury*

BLUE PULLMAN

Getting into its stride westbound at Subway Junction just outside Paddington.

Awaiting departure from Swansea, is the passenger enquiring as to the train or commenting upon the uniform coat? As mentioned in the text, on 6 December 1968 there was some discussion over reducing the South Wales service to seven vehicles; however this was vetoed on the basis of a potential loss of revenue estimated to be some £20,000pa and resulting from having less second-class accommodation available. For interest sake and still on the topic of catering, around the time the 'Birmingham Pullman' ceased operation, a survey was also undertaken relating to the average food/drink profit generated per passenger/class on the Pullman services. This came out as 'Bristol Pullman' 7s 4d and 1s 11d, 'Birmingham Pullman' 7s 4d and 2s 8d, and on the 'South Wales Pullman' 7s 4d and 3s 9d. The higher figures for the South Wales service are explained by the greater distance and time travelled, with passengers also needing 'top-ups' en-route!

In Black and White on the Western

Bristol bound at Wootton Bassett. This was the convergence/divergence of the Badminton line through to Patchway and eventually South Wales – seen in the tracks passing behind the signal box. Nowadays the station, signal box, signals, and of course the train, are long gone but the junction still survives remotely controlled from the Thames Valley Signalling Centre.

Blue Pullman set at Banbury. The point of note here has to be the white painted buffers, something seen as well on one LMR set at one stage. Clearly done for a special working, in the opinion of your authors they enhance the appearance. We may wonder if Jack Howe ever felt the same?

BLUE PULLMAN

Paddington arrival, once more past a group of spotters. Possibly this is a train from Birmingham.

7 — BLUE PULLMAN – TIMELINE 2. PULLMAN ON THE WESTERN REGION 1960-1966

In Black and White on the Western

Perhaps a final test run – or perhaps a Press trip – seen at Cardiff on 8 September 1961 just three days before the diesel South Wales service was inaugurated.

243

BLUE PULLMAN

A neat platform with no apparent passengers. The date is May 1961 and if the single lamp above the left-hand buffer is to be believed, then the code is 'Light Engine'. Possibly this is then an empty stock arrival. *The Transport Treasury*

In Black and White on the Western

Another special working 1Z65 on 28 January 1967. The view was taken near Chelford north of Crewe with a WR set used to bring Walsall fans to their teams FA cup match against Bury. (Bury won 2-0.) As also seen in the image on P241, this was the set with the embellished buffer heads. *Martin Welch*

We conclude this chapter with the repeat of an image seen before but from feedback received also a definite favourite with many. The occasion was a 1967 publicity photo shoot with 'Miss France 1966' Monique Boucher, and the presentation of a certain brand of brandy. The expression on the face of the driver in particular is priceless. As a comparison in expressions, the Pullman conductor on the left is in the new Pullman uniform recently introduced consisting a navy blue suit with new style cap having gold braid and piping. *Antony Ford collection*

station forced a Class 47 (D1671) on ecs duty from Swansea to Cardiff into the path of the Cardiff to Margam coal train hauled by a Class 37 (D6983).' The Class 47 hit the other train head on and rose over the top killing the Landore-based crew of the 47, Donald Brock and his co-driver. Neath member Ron James was in the cab of the 37 and feels the built-up longer front saved him and his colleague.

When the Blue Pullman arrived at the location near Bridgend, David was met by a member of the fire brigade who suggested he went straight to the guard's van of the breakdown train and didn't look at the scene. In the middle of the night brave volunteers to help clear the debris included Neath member Gerald Williams who has been so helpful with 'South Wales Pullman' information.

Notes

(1) Possibly the word 'conspire' is slightly strong to use here, but it does raise several questions, none of which are answered by located surviving paperwork. We know the actual Western Region sets were delivered later than those destined for the LMR. In addition we also know there were staffing issues relative to the catering. This time it was probably not just industrial relations problems – as it would certainly appear strange if these had been confined solely to the LMR – but on the Western Region at least the problem was as much towards actual recruiting. Was this staggered introduction then a deliberate ploy by British Railways hierarchy to 'drip feed' the trains into service and so maintain public interest? Could it also have been that (more) lessons (and necessary modifications) now being learnt from the LMR trials were having to be incorporated into the WR sets? Or was it simply the question of waiting until the winter timetable?

(2) Air brakes had first been introduced to the WR with the advent of the D600 'Warship' class. The design, however, allowed for air brakes to apply on the locomotive alone, with a following train still using vacuum brakes.

(3) This requirement by Brig Langley indicates the power the Ministry of Transport had over the operation of a British railway as well as its stock. In very basic terms, this was one government department overseeing another. The point that might be made though is slightly different. Satisfying the requirements of the Inspecting Officer for the WR sets we might well say was indeed a good idea – but the LMR trains were running at the same speed and they did not have any form of ATC/AWS at all! (At least not for some years.)

(4) Testing, running-in, driver/crew familiarisation trips over lightly used routes was nothing new; an example a few years earlier was when Swindon had used sections of the former Midland & South Western Junction Railway line to test DMU units built at the Wiltshire works.

(5) According to official government statistics available at www.ons.gov.uk/ons/rel/lms/labour-market.../unemployment-since-1881.pdf etc., the percentage of the workforce unemployed for the period January to September 1960 was between 1.4 and 2.2%, the higher figure applicable during the winter months was no doubt due to seasonable considerations. This must be read as an average national figure and there would of course be areas where a greater or lesser percentage applied. The late Harold Gasson in his reminiscences book Signalling Days (OPC 1989) recounts how in the late 1950s and 1960s signalmen (and others) were leaving the railway to find or take up more lucrative employment in factories, British Railways being unable to match pay rates available in outside industry.

(6) It would be interesting, although also perhaps a little pointless, to undertake statistical analysis of 'attendants per customer' on the LMR compared with the WR trains and even first class versus Second class. Suffice to say the parameters that might be considered are almost infinite as this would also depend on the number of travelling passengers as well as those actually taking refreshments or requiring service of whatever type on board. On a very crude basis the average number of passengers per member of staff, excluding the conductor but including chefs, was 7.33 on the six-car, and 12.44 on the eight-car units. We also have no information as to relief crews to cover absentees etc.

(7) Despite the considerable publicity surrounding the day, we cannot be 100% certain which train actually arrived 'on the block' at OOC first. The consensus appears to indicate it was the Wolverhampton working but only by a few seconds – although might it even have been that from Bristol? Whatever, their respective drivers, probably each accompanied by a traction inspector for the day, had been instructed to slow or accelerate as necessary so as to achieve the desired parallel working, signal indications permitting of course!

PULLMAN DIESEL TRAINS

THE SOUTH WALES PULLMAN
THE BRISTOL PULLMAN
THE BIRMINGHAM PULLMAN

8
BLUE PULLMAN
Timeline 3. The years 1966-1973: 'Just *too many* trains'

Any positive gain from attracting the occasional charter work was of course a bonus but whilst the accountants may have been rubbing their hands at this additional revenue, elsewhere dark clouds were gathering and these foretold of the dilemma that British Railways would shortly be facing – simply what to do with the whole Blue Pullman fleet on completion of the electrification of the LMR route from Euston?

The reader might be forgiven for thinking this was something just affecting the two LMR sets but in reality it was far more widespread, for in addition the WR would be losing their Paddington to Birmingham train, regional boundary changes meaning Birmingham was now firmly under the charge of the LMR and in consequence Wolverhampton and Birmingham services to London would in future be catered for by electric traction operating between Euston and New Street.

As far as the WR was concerned it would also mean Paddington potentially being in a similar situation to the one they had been in 1960 with just two sets in daily use, although now serving Bristol and Swansea. As to the question of the future of the two six-car LMR units, while with hindsight the concentration of all five sets on the WR might seem both simple and obvious, there were definite reasons why such a decision was not immediately taken, the most important being that to do so could 'over-Pullman' a restricted area. (The term 'over Pullman' might not easily roll of the tongue but it was the very phrase used by the higher echelons of BR.)

Much work had taken place behind the scenes in 1965 and 1966 by BR as to the best way to ensure best utilisation of the Blue Pullman fleet, the most obvious problem being what to do with the LMR pair once services started on the West Coast electrification routes. In reality there was concern about the whole fleet.

In 1966, BR had conducted a survey into the character of Pullman travel[1]. This was conducted across the network with no noted breakdown as to region or service. As such whilst proving a useful snapshot of society at the time, it was perhaps (understandably) loaded more towards the results BR wished to hear rather than as a truly objective summary. Even so some of the conclusions reached were as follows:

First class business – between and third and half of those who travel Pullman do so when someone else is paying.

Most have made the same journey by road/air.

Gender breakdown was mostly male: 92% male passengers in first class, 76% male passengers in second class. (Probably only marginally improved – if at all – from the percentage of travellers in 1960 and so confirming the justification for not segregating the sexes when it came to toilet accommodation.)

The name 'Pullman' implies fast comfortable travel, and implied prestige compared to other passengers (the report in its conclusions added the words 'snob factor' at this stage).

A reminder of times past – exiting Reading General (as it was before successive rebuildings). For the trains, from 1966 it was downhill all the way. John Ashman/Paul Cooper

Second class Pullman passengers were an 'unstable audience'. (And we do not mean because of the ride!)

The speed of travel was important, but so were actual start and end times.

A total of 1,469 questionnaires were given out, surprisingly perhaps not just to Pullman passengers alone although we conclude the majority were. Just 11% of these who travelled Pullman said they did so for social and not business travel. (Might this then be a clue as to why the 'Devon Belle' had failed to attract sufficient clientele – it was simply not a 'business' service with little in the way of 'business' in the west of the country.) Forty-eight per cent of first class Pullman passengers were regular travellers who regularly travelled first class Pullman (despite the ride!) A general comment was, 'One feels expected to eat on a Pullman'.

With no breakdown by actual train services surveyed was it even really a fair representation? We do not even know what day of the week or month of the year was used.

A far more accurate result would have been to repeat the questions more than once. No doubt to encourage completion of the survey, all of the 51 questions asked were of the then modern multiple choice (objective) type whilst certainly not all would have applied to all groups. One perhaps obvious question was also missing – probably because BR would not have liked the answer – what would be the reaction of the passenger if a substitute non-Pullman train were provided? (Or to BP passengers alone if the 'Wells Fargo' stock were used, although we probably know the answer so far as BP was concerned judging from the reaction of the Bristol passengers when they had lost their train for maintenance years earlier.)

The whole might have been a useful PR exercise but with hindsight it was little more than a smokescreen which did little to assist the dilemma British Railways would shortly be facing –- simply what to do with the whole Blue Pullman fleet on completion of the electrification of the LMR route from Euston?

As mentioned before one might be forgiven for thinking this was something just affecting the two LMR sets but in reality it was far more widespread, for in addition the WR would be losing their Paddington to Birmingham train, regional boundary changes meaning Birmingham was now firmly under the charge of the LMR and in consequence Wolverhampton and Birmingham services to London would in future be catered for by electric traction operating between Euston and New Street.

The other regions were therefore asked to consider a Pullman service on whatever route might be considered viable (in itself almost seen as a desperate plea), whilst it was only the Eastern Region that appears to have seriously considered the option. It was for a Leeds to King's Cross working using the LMR sets and to test the practicalities that a running trial was arranged for Saturday 16 October 1965.

A formal plan for a test working was thus issued which involved a former LMR six-car set consisting M60090, M60730, M60740, M60741, M60731 and M60091 running

Following the end of services between St Pancras and Manchester, the two LMR sets were sent to store at Reddish pending a decision as to their fate. Nothing has been located to suggest withdrawal and/or scrapping was being considered at this time and similarly no evidence has been found to suggest a potential sale to a third party either although that is not to say any of these options were not being considered – just that no evidence has been found. Consequently both sets were placed into what we might nowadays refer to as 'warm store' (the term used at the time was they were 'mothballed'), not necessarily literally in a warm building as it may have been outside storage but they were still maintained and available to use at short notice. This probably meant running the engines and auxiliary equipment at regular intervals and possibly even short trips within the depot confines. An interesting 'paper' transfer had actually occurred back on 1 January 1963 in consequence of a change to regional boundaries in the Birmingham area. This had seen power cars W60096/7 moved to the LMR simply because they were based at Tyseley for maintenance purposes and that depot was now under the control of the LMR. No physical renumbering of the vehicles took place. This also does not mean that these two power cars were the only ones ever seen on the Birmingham runs for, as before, operating diagrams saw all the WR sets working on all three routes in rotation. (W60097 is reported to have had its last major overhaul between July and September 1967.) Physical movement of the former LMR sets to the WR from Reddish took place on an unreported date but by November 1966 the second ex LMR set had arrived at Old Oak Common via Swindon where it had also acquired experimental yellow ends. No M60093 is seen here with the doors and cab roof painted whereas M60092 at the opposite end had a smaller area painted as can be seen on page 262. *Derek Everson*

ecs from Reddish to Leeds via Huddersfield, Mirfield, Low Moor and Laisterdyke. The schedule and (précised) other details were stated as under:

Leeds, Platform 5: dep 11.22
Doncaster: arr 11.56 dep 11.57 – Eastern Region Officers to join
King's Cross, Platform 7 arr 14.08
King's Cross, Platform 10: dep 16.05
Doncaster: arr 18.14.5 dep 18.17.5 Eastern Region staff depart
Leeds Central Platform 5: arr 18.54

'Senior officers to join the third vehicle from the front as from London. Other staff will be accommodated in the second vehicle from the front from London. Technical staff with their apparatus in the trailing vehicle in the direction of travel. Luncheon will be served at 1230. Tea will be served on the return journey.' The timings of connecting services were also given.

The Leeds – Kings Cross trial seen passing Knebworth, 16 October 1965. *Michael Downes*

The test train at Dryclough Junction near Halifax, 16 October 1965. *A. R. Wilson*

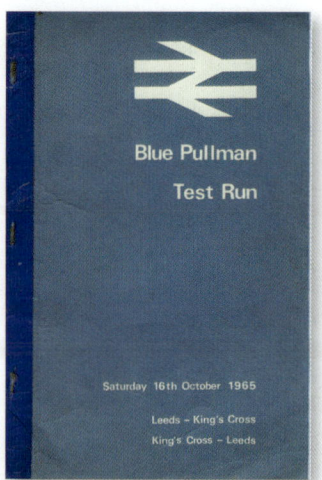

The passenger list includes two from the BRB (names not given), 12 from the North Eastern Region including the General Manager Mr A. Dean, and seven from the Eastern Region, including the General Manager of that region, Mr J. R. Hammond. Also travelling was Mr E. J. Morris from the Pullman Car Division.

The train left Doncaster on time but was reported as 1½ minutes late arriving at King's Cross. On the return journey again the special left King's Cross on time but was one minute late arriving at Doncaster, at which point the individual who was keeping time also left the train. Whether these delays were the fault of the train or conflicting outside factors is not reported.

Crucially, what we do not know is how the timings were set. Was it even based on 'Deltic' timings? If so BP would be disadvantaged from the start. (The 'Deltics' with a top speed of 105mph were then the fastest diesels operating on the ER, indeed BR as a whole.) Surely it was unlikely the minute or so delay on schedule would have made up the minds of the regions not to take the sets and so there remain too many unanswered questions to draw specific conclusions.

In reality it would appear as if the ER were to some extent pressurised into agreeing to the trial but which also had the potential promise of providing a modern fast Pullman service which could well have attracted additional revenue. Commercially this would surely not have been refused but the same issues as plagued the LMR in the past would have applied; namely either run one set and so have only 50% utilisation, or risk two and the need for a permanent stand-by set of loco-hauled vehicles. Why also the presence of representatives from the NER? Was there even consideration for a Pullman service north of York? (The Eastern and North Eastern regions already operated loco-hauled Pullman trains so may well have had spare stock available; in any event the spare set formerly on the LMR would of course now be available as well.)

The eventual conclusion, although we have no detail as to when this was made (or by whom), from the ER – and presumably the NER – was that they would not take the train based on their riding qualities. For the ER to say this on what was an extremely well maintained main line south of Doncaster really does say something about the BP sets. Remember too it was the LNER main line where years earlier the SR 'River' class tank engines were tested following the disastrous Sevenoaks derailment of 1927 and with history due to repeat itself just two years later from the BP test run when an SR 'Hastings' unit was run at speed on the ER following the 1967 accident at Hither Green. In both cases the former LNER route was found to be faultless. On board BP in October 1965 comparisons were no doubt being made against the 'Deltics' as well as the behaviour of existing loco-hauled vehicles. It did not bode well for the future. Indeed with the passing of years since 1965 it might even be tempting to say this was the ER being forced into trying out

From *Modern Railways* of December 1965 came this image by D. L. Percival showing the trial run crossing Welwyn viaduct. 'MR's comment at the time was that we may see such workings in the Spring, although as is known nothing would come of the idea. (Another view of the same special was published elsewhere showing the train at Little Bytham and credited to P. H. Wells.)

the train when they had already made their decision anyway. A case of simply 'going through the motions' – but having a good day out in the process! According to Simon Lee, the other former LMR set also ventured away from Reddish on the possibility of providing a service between Hull and King's Cross. Simon writes, '. . . my brother and I went on a day trip to Bridlington. Imagine our surprise as we passed (Hull) Botanic to see a Blue Pullman set stabled on the depot. When we returned that evening, the set was still there. When we arrived home my brother hot footed round to his friends and came home triumphant with the set numbers M60092 + M60093 + M60732 + M60733 + M60742 + M60743. Years later we found out that the reason for the visit was the threat of a new business air service from the Hull area to London and the NER had found a spare set off the LM and brought it to Hull. Unfortunately there was no one local who knew the unit, so it stayed a week and returned from whence it came around the 30 April. I would dearly love to find a photo of the set in Hull but I guess it is in the same league as rocking horse manure.'

Whilst this might appear to be reminiscences of a youthful spotter, there is certainly credence in Simon's story and we take it seriously for the simple reason BR went so far as to install a shore supply to '3' road in the shed. Clearly then there was far more going on than it has been possible to unearth. We even know that a BR man from Hull, Lawrie Scrivener, had been selected as the Technical Inspector and technical manuals supplied. It has been suggested by Pullman historian Antony Ford that two further trials involving (it is believed) a six-car set also took place around this time, one on the North Eastern Region – possibly that mentioned above – and the other to Harwich. Regrettably,

The special working seen at King's Cross ready for the return working on 16 October 1965. We may never know but perhaps a 'no' decision had been reached even before the day was over. As far as is known this was also the only time a BP set was seen at King's Cross and possibly also the only time one ran on any part of the former Great Northern main line.

no further information on these runs, if indeed they actually took place, has been located. However further credence to the thought of BP running at least on the NER is given in an exert from the NER Sectional Appendix – see Appendix 5. Clearly the text is standard wording probably copied from a similar set of rules applicable to the LMR, but why go to the trouble of even preparing this unless there was a serious intention of taking the trains on the NER? It might also explain the presence of the 12 representatives from that region on the October demonstration run.

'Oxford Pullman'. With five trains available one of the attempts at utilisation was a mid-day Oxford service, seen here being ceremoniously flagged away from Paddington on its first day of operation on 5 March 1967. In theory at least there was every wish tourism would be the main money spinner for this service; accordingly, it was targeted at visitors from North America. Air Vice Marshall William Foster MacNeece Foster, the Lord Mayor of Oxford, is seen in charge of proceedings, accompanied by Mr Jack Herfurt, Consul General at the United States Embassy, and Mr David Pattison, BR(WR) London Division Manager. Other guests on the first run included the London Manager of the American Express organisation and representatives of nine travel agencies. On arrival at Oxford, the party toured several of the university colleges followed by a civic reception at the Town Hall.

The concern over ride quality was still an important issue at this time, for as mentioned previously various modifications had been made to the bogies, and after 1962 there are fewer complaints reported on ride quality. We must also be fair and say that certainly some improvement had been achieved, whether by design, modification, 'bedding in', luck or even an acceptance that the trains were riding 'as well as can be expected', although as we know it was seemingly still not good enough for the ER. In fairness we will hear later that in April 1967 it was an ex LMR set that the 14-year-old Chris Head rode on as a treat from Reading to Bristol and he was shocked to find it had a 'rocking and rolling' ride even on the 'GWR billiard table' which is how WR permanent way was often referred to.

So with potential additional Pullman services on the Eastern and North Eastern Regions ruled out, the alternatives that remained were the Scottish Region, Southern Region and of the course to concentrate all the trains on the WR. Perhaps slightly surprising is that there does not appear to have been any reference to an overseas sale at this time. Possibly 1962 had been forgotten and to be fair BR had not been exactly pro-active in attempting sale of much, if any, surplus equipment overseas for some time. (What sales that were made around this period were either of redundant assets to scrap merchants, locomotives to industrial concerns and intended for further use, and of course to the preservation movement.)

Even so BR did recognise that to have any potential chance of success in operating the LMR trains as the premier brand 'Pullman', let alone a restricted all first-class train, it would need to find an area with a potential large traffic flow, which obviously meant between large conurbations. Consequently this tended to rule out most of the Scottish Region and the London Midland did not seem willing to consider the trains running on any other service on their region. Truth be told they may even have been glad to rid themselves of the units, although this last statement must be stated to be conjecture on the part of the present writers and is certainly not born out by fact or any located documentation. Consequently almost as a last resort all eyes turned towards

Pullman at speed: the Oxford service accelerating hard away from the station on the journey back to Paddington in March 1968. As far as is known this working was always given to one of the former LMR sets. One passenger noted, 'I made several journeys on the up 'Oxford Pullman'. The supplement was fairly cheap, and for that you got a seat in what had been Pullman First when the unit ran the Manchester Pullman. Afternoon tea, complete with toasted teacakes, was an affordable luxury, but it was necessary to make sure that you didn't have a full cup of tea over the pointwork at Didcot East Junction, Reading, or Slough.' Harking back we may recall Keith Farr's own comment on the first few days on the 'Bristol Pullman' with instructions evidently given to the stewards on board not to fill cups more than about half full whilst a paper doily was also placed between the cup and the saucer.

Readers will recall from the caption in the previous chapter how Gerald Fiennes commented upon the profitability of the Birmingham and South Wales services being the greatest, with Bristol being in last place. Strange to relate then how WR management felt confident enough to increase the formation to 12 cars on the Bristol working (the two six-car former LMR cars coupled together) for the morning and evening peak workings, which would have also necessitated almost a doubling of the crew numbers as well. To achieve this working multiple unit jumpers were fitted at either end which it must be said did nothing to enhance the sets' previous smart appearance. The down Bristol service formed as described is seen here passing Thingley Junction signal box. Both sets are also still in original colours excepting the provision of yellow ends.

the Southern Region and a modern replacement for the existing locomotive-hauled 'Bournemouth Belle'.[2]

Again it was as if the wheel had turned full circle, as it was of course similar to the suggestion made by Hugh Barker back in 1954 (see page 17). However, the Southern Region itself was at this time in some turmoil as work accelerated towards the completion of the Bournemouth electrification scheme which would result in the abolition of steam from the area, and the ending of the locomotive-hauled 'Bournemouth Belle' service. (Electrification to Bournemouth was originally scheduled to be completed for 1 January 1967, but was subsequently put back to June and finally July 1967.) Again it was a suggestion destined to come to nothing, with the otherwise mild-mannered David McKenna, General Manager at Waterloo, determined to have nothing to do with a second-hand replacement Pullman. On the Southern at least it could not be argued that Blue Pullman would be slower than the new 4REP sets due to introduced even though both trains had a rated maximum of 90mph. As the Bournemouth suggestion was not even a paper exercise there is no evidence that any trials took place on the SR. One set did work from Paddington to Brockenhurst for Lord Montagu on 25 March 1971, but this was as a special. On at least one other occasion a BP set was seen at Southampton and a third occasion saw a set visiting Surbiton, Woking and Guildford on an educational tour (see Appendix 10 for details of charters). Waterloo or Paddington to Exeter were other options which might have been worth considering in the area, with the latter being perhaps the more likely, but surprisingly there does not appear to be any reference to these being mentioned. Instead and certainly as far as the SR was concerned, memories of the failure of the 'Devon Belle' to attract sufficient passengers all the year round were no doubt recalled.

It might be worth considering for a moment a Blue Pullman running on a similar schedule as existed on the Bournemouth line after July 1967 (Waterloo to Southampton in 70 minutes, and Waterloo to Bournemouth in 100 minutes). So might it have worked? The answer could well have been yes provided the public were not already falling out of love with Pullman generally – and that is one of the questions which we discuss in the final chapter. We also do not have loadings details for the 'Bournemouth Belle' in the period 1966/67. Then we have to consider the obvious 'lively' ride on BP. Here it would be useful to have first-hand experience of BP (which neither writers have) and be able to compare with a REP/TC. But what Kevin does have is years of having to endure REP and TC sets out of Waterloo. These too could certainly be said to be 'entertaining' especially at places like Worthing Junction, Farnborough and Hampton Court Junction, hence the thought of a 90mph Pullman on the same line brings positive shudders to mind. Indeed the phrase 'With a Splash' (see page 150) might even have to be replaced by 'With a Deluge'. BR was therefore left with little option: the WR it had to be, the only other alternatives being sale or scrap. (It is for similar reasons there is no located correspondence for use on the Central or Eastern sections of the SR. A modern day replacement for the 'Brighton Belle' is a thought that appears not to have been discussed.)

Paddington was thus the best of a poor set of options and to some extent this did make sense. Certainly the sets were non-standard so far as all other trains and units operating on BR were concerned, but if all were to be concentrated on the one area (region) then the issue of spares, servicing and above all familiarity was improved. Mechanically as well as operationally it made perfect sense but the problem still remained of what to do with them – three spare train sets (two LMR and one WR, the latter previously on the Birmingham route) each capable of a prestige service but other than the occasional special working was there really the potential for regular traffic on the WR, either as they presently existed or perhaps even in a reformed fashion?

Enter then the Western Region Movements Department whose records of discussions are accessible at the National

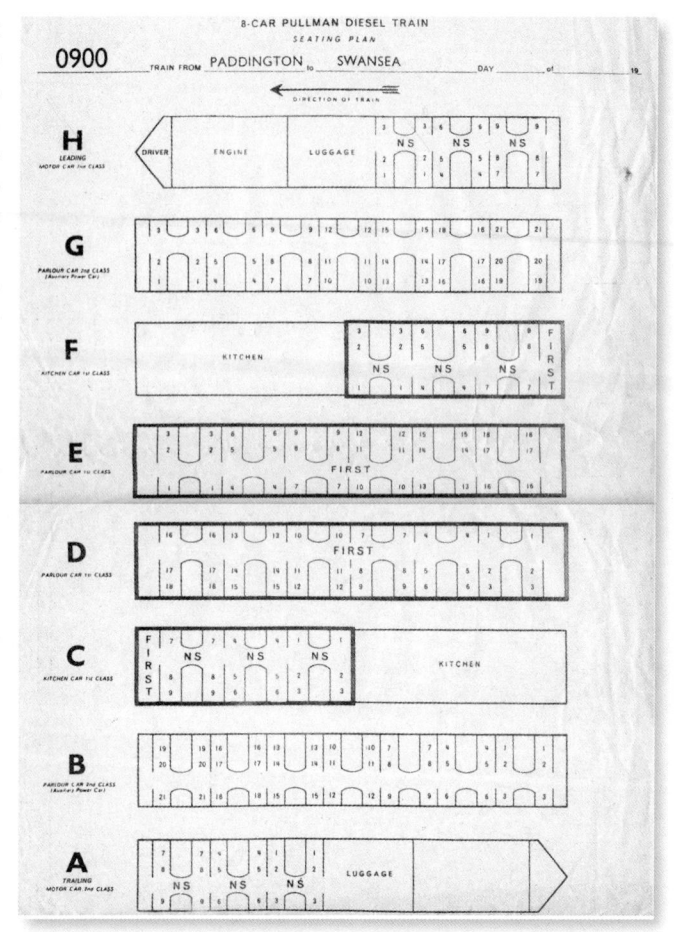

An unused copy of the train seating plan; this one is for the 'South Wales Pullman'. This item was first reproduced on p116 of the original hardback with the comment that with likely in excess of 16,000 were issued over the life of the trains, with this the only one so far located. The same statement remains true today. A seating/usage plan was also provided on the occasions a scratch set was in use.
Ian Shawyer collection

TABLE 1					
Type	Seats	Bogie Type	WR	LMR	Running Numbers
1 – Motor 2nd	18	A-B	6		60094-60099
2 – Parlour 2nd	42	C-D	6		60644-60649
3 – Kitchen 1st	18	Trailer – Trailer	6		60734-60739
4 – Parlour 1st	36	Trailer – Trailer	6	4	60740-60749
5 – Kitchen 1st	18	C-Trailer		4	60730-60733
6 – Motor 1st	12	A-B		4	60090-60093

TABLE 2					
Train	Car Types	Seating 1st	Seating 2nd	Total	Original Allocation
A	1-2-3-4-4-3-2-1	108	120	228	WR
B	1-2-3-4-4-3-2-1	108	120	228	WR
C	1-2-3-4-4-3-2-1	108	120	228	WR
D	6-5-4-4-5-6	132	-	132	LMR
E	6-5-4-4-5-6	132	-	132	LMR

TABLE 3

OPTION ONE

Train	Car Types	First Class	Class Seating	Total
A	1-2-3-4-4-5-6*	108	72	180
B	1-2-3-4-4-5-6*	108	72	180
C	1-2-3-4-4-5-6*	108	72	180
D	1-2-3-4-4-5-6*	108	72	180
E	1-2-3-4-4-3-2-1	108	120	228

OPTION TWO

Train	Car Types	First Class	Class Seating	Total
A	1-2-3-4-4-3-2-6*	108	114	222
B	1-2-3-4-4-5-2-6*	108	114	222
C	1-2-3-4-4-5-1	108	78	186
D	1-2-3-4-4-5-1	108	78	186
E	6-5-4-4-5-6	132	-	132

OPTION THREE

Train	Car Types	First Class	Class Seating	Total
A	1-2-3-4-4-3-2-6*	108	114	222
B	1-2-3-4-4-3-2-6*	108	114	222
C	1-2-3-4-4-4-5-1	144	78	222
D	1-2-3-4-4-4-5-1	144	78	222

OPTION FOUR

Train	Car Types	First Class	Class Seating	Total
A	1-2-3-4-4-3-2-6*	108	114	222
B	1-2-3-4-4-3-2-6*	108	114	222
C	1-2-3-4-4-5-4*-1	108	114	222
D	1-2-3-4-4-5-4*-1	108	114	222

OPTION FIVE

Train	Car Types	First Class	Class Seating	Total
A	1-2-3-4-4-3-2-1	108	120	228
B	1-2-3-4-4-3-2-1	108	120	228
C	1-2-3-4-4-3-2-1	108	120	228
D	6*4*5*-4-4-5*-4*-6*	72	132	204

Archive as well as having been expertly assimilated into the following tables by Paul Metcalfe. Tables 1 and 2 describe the original makeup of the sets. Note that in Table 2 the reference to 'Train A' etc is included purely for ease of reference.

Table 3 gives the alternatives that were considered by BR, including it will be noted in 'Options 1 and 2' rakes of seven-car trains. In all cases both first and second class seating would have been provided. The * symbol refers to a first class vehicles that would be downgraded to second class – but presumably without any attempt made to reduce legroom and incorporate extra seats? Options 3, 4 and 5 also indicate one pair of power cars would not be used, and which in many ways was a sensible precaution. In addition with the same consideration two kitchen cars would be surplus and stand idle.

In the choice available it was recognised that whilst the region could run all five trains it was not felt all five would be economic if operated in this way – a lesson that was clearly soon forgotten. The best arrangement was felt to produce four trains (options 3, 4 and 5), even though this left two motor and two kitchen cars '. . . with only limited value as spares.' Here there seems to be a wish, nay perhaps an obsession, to achieve maximum utilisation although again with the benefit of hindsight would it not have made sense to have done this, thereby reducing the potential for uneconomic operation, but perhaps reducing to nil the need to keep a 'Wells Fargo' set on standby?

Option 4 was indeed the best that could be considered; each train was identical so far as passenger capacity was concerned and could be achieved at the limited cost of £2,000 in converting certain first class to second class

Pullmans on the Berks & Hants line. In the first view we see a former LMR six-car set with M60093 leading, still for the present with the designation 'Midland Pullman' on the side of the power car (the word 'Midland' was later removed from all four similar LMR vehicles) on a crew training run in November 1966. We do not know for certain when the actual paper transfers and movement of the sets occurred from the LMR to the WR but it was certainly quick as they ran last on the LMR in April 1966 and the first sight of the trains at Swindon was just three months later. Even so it appears likely the WR were reluctant to formerly accept the trains at first in the vain hope an alternative home might be found for them. Whatever, with all five sets now on the WR crew training was essential as more sets would be working, the B&H line being a favourite for this practice, often operating a circuit from OOC through Reading to Heywood Road (Westbury) and then either via Bradford Junction and Thingley Junction back to Old Oak, or via Bradford-on-Avon and thence to Bristol. In the second view we see another service passing Newbury, this time an WR eight-car train on what may well be a scheduled Bristol working but diverted via Reading West and the B&H and which will rejoin its normal route at Bathampton. The B&H was then a recognised diversion route for Bristol trains – indeed it remains so today. *E. C. Paine Ltd and David Canning*

although a visual gap would exist between the 2+2 seating of second class Pullman and the 2+1 seating of first class by having a kitchen car in-between. (No doubt the canny passenger would soon have worked out where it was best to travel anyway!)

Otherwise the report repeated much of what had been concluded back in the 1950s concerning the three main uses for a Pullman train, the first as an additional service using a completely new path, the second as a replacement for an ordinary train or an existing service, and finally as a stand-by for those Pullmans already in operation.

The stand-by option was quickly discounted whilst the obvious statement was that any additional service would have to cover its own costs. These costs were quoted as a defined £95,000 a year although this is perhaps a slightly strange comment as surely there were variables with costs proportionate to the miles run. Whatever, the WR worked out that if the Pullmans drew traffic from existing services, they would have to carry 190,000 passengers per annum to obtain sufficient in supplements, and food and drink profit, to cover costs. But if 10% of its passengers were new business to rail, then only 150,000 persons would be needed yearly. The routes with the highest Pullman potential had been identified as those to South Wales and Bristol, but the same report, and it should be noted carried out *before* the transfer of the two LMR sets had been undertaken, also made it clear that the only hope of employing further Blue Pullmans profitably was to use them to replace existing services rather than attempting to create new ones. As such there would be a need to encourage existing passengers to the service. Even then, replacing a loco-hauled service would mean the Pullman having to cover an additional cost of between £33,000 and £38,000 a year, depending on whether the existing service had a restaurant car. To make a profit of £10,000 a year, the Blue Pullman would have to carry some 90,000 passengers from existing services. If 10% of its passengers were new to rail, the figure was reduced to 70,000 a year, but if substituting an existing service for a Pullman made passengers look for other modes of transport, then 110,000 passengers would be needed to make the same profit. It was a big ask and an equally big gamble.

The consideration of routes also turned out to be a major headache. The report having come out in favour of Option 4 decided that the existing services on the Paddington-Bristol/South Wales routes were already making sufficient money for the region to justify continuing them. South Wales might also be served by a 'reverse' Pullman running out from London in the morning and returning later in the day.

Assuming there were to be just four trains in service, only three possibilities were really acceptable. Out of these options, the one with the greatest potential for profit was to run a reverse service on the Paddington–Bristol route starting from London in the morning. However it also warned there could be serious problems associated with having such a high proportion of Pullmans on that route. The same applied with the reverse Paddington–South Wales service already mentioned.

The third case was a new service on the WR's other principal route, that to the West Country, with the suggestion that a Pullman might take over the existing 'Golden Hind'[2a] service. It was, though, quickly pointed out that the majority of passengers on this service, notwithstanding the prestige brought about by the name, travelled second class. Limited luggage accommodation on the Pullman might also be an issue. Both factors could also have a knock on effect by creating capacity problems on the 'Mayflower'[2b] operating on the same route.

Enter then 'Motive Power' who added that the electric transmission of the Pullman sets was not considered acceptable for regular use over the South Devon banks although naturally a six-car set would be more reliable than one of eight vehicles.[3]

The obvious and existing point was also made that if a BP set were able to be used on a profitable morning and evening return (wherever on the WR) it would thus be available for a 'marginal cost' mid-day fill-in turn and to this end Paddington to Oxford was suggested.

The case for the 'Golden Hind' was further hindered when it was stated an eight-car set did not have sufficient power to maintain the timings of the existing train and re-diagramming was out of the question, not least as it would have caused major knock-on problems west of Plymouth. Traffic on the 'Golden Hind' was also averaging under 300 passengers a day during the period and that was considered insufficient for a profitable Pullman operation; indeed the limited patronage of first class passengers on the route meant it was very unlikely many would be prepared to pay an additional supplement anyway. Once arrived at Plymouth there would have been little potential either time-wise or service-wise for any fill-in duty in the area. Consequently, surprisingly a Liskeard to Looe mid-day shuttle was never likely to have been considered! (The last statement is definitely tongue in cheek!)

The report thus concluded that the only two feasible uses for the two LMR Pullmans were to provide reciprocal services on the existing BP Western Region routes or to replace the 'Golden Hind' but the latter was at considerable risk. The authors (un-named) covered themselves by stating, 'Each of these possibilities require further consideration, however, as at this stage there was not a clear-cut case for any of them.'

The matter was formally discussed in BR Headquarters Report Number 077 of May 1965 (see Appendix 9), which undertook, 'To examine the problem of determining the best use for the 36 Blue Pullman cars'. Like the Paddington options, the BR report was again full on facts and short on solutions, the impression being given that the WR had made a success of its previous Pullman operations and were therefore best placed to succeed again. It was a definite case of 'Pass the buck', which may perhaps appear to be a little unfair, but by also failing to mention it, the various contributors seem to have ignored the fact that the success of Pullman on the WR was in no small part due to the revenue accrued from the Birmingham service, which as we know was due to be withdrawn.

The Awarding of New Colours

ABOVE In accordance with BR policy on visibility, yellow ends started to appear on the Pullman sets from late 1966. No definitive record has been found as to which power cars were dealt with first but it is possible the new paint coincided, on the LMR sets at least, with the fitting of jumper cables as seen here. From various images, there were also variations to the amount of yellow applied: here the paint only reached as far as the cab windows, and yet on M60093 the yellow extended over the top of the roof as well. Perhaps the latter additional paint was simply added to that seen here. Notice too the word 'Midland' has been hastily painted over whilst a metal destination plate is attached to the bodyside by the Guard's door. Other points of note are the repositioned horns – necessary for regular access to the couplings – and the cut away panel to reveal the actual coupling hook. Missing are the Pullman crest – this was never reinstated when the ends were repainted yellow – and also the electrification warning flashes. The set is depicted at Bristol Bath Road depot on 6 April 1968. All five trains were eventually repainted in the revised Pullman (reverse) livery. To some this revised front end colour scheme gave rise to the sets being referred to as having, '… a custard dipped front end'. *Colour Rail DE328*

ABOVE Another 'custard dipped' set (with tears and 'Bet Lynch' earings), possibly an Oxford working, seen in Sonning Cutting. Aside from the centre red light not being covered – the blanking plates were kept in the cab/Guard's compartment – note too the word 'Pullman' on the bodyside has been repositioned compared with the previous view.

RIGHT No longer the esteemed train of just a few years past. Three covers on the air horns, but none on the lights. No electrification warning sign either. Swansea 1967.

LEFT Former 'Midland Pullman' six-car set at Bristol probably on the mid-day fill-in turn, 24 November 1968. As a prestige brand the set was badly in need of a repaint – at least. Hardly the prestige image it was desirable to portray. In general terms, and referring to the early years of the trains, we know that on the LMR, at least to start with, the exterior of trains was hand washed, whereas on the WR they went through a standard carriage washing plant. It was this procedure that affected the paintwork as much as the elements, blue being a less than ideal colour under the circumstances. *Mark Warburton courtesy Mrs M. Warburton*

The Awarding of New Colours

A slightly cleaner WR set seen at Old Oak Common but with the cover hiding the coupling missing. (Some fitters reminiscences mainly concerning the Class 22 diesel type but with reference also to BP may be found at http://project22society.co.uk/wp-content/uploads/2018/10/Lister-D6303-Autunm-2018-.pdf)

WR set inside the Pullman shed at OOC alongside a diesel Inter-City unit. In this view we might mention the massive buck-eye coupling hanging down from the DMU compared with the standard three-link retained when the LMR sets were converted to multiple unit working. The BP sets were not connectively similar to any other units and consequently would never have needed to work coupled to another diesel unit. Although not dated this is likely to have been taken c1967. Early in the same year, on 10 January it was reported the original three WR sets were due for shopping which included renewal of the upholstery. A check at Swindon also revealed there was no stock remaining of the original carpet in the stores with six rolls having disappeared. (Police later raided a property in Wootton Basset but nothing was found.) Consequently the decision was made for the interior of the trains to be brought into line with the new Pullman vehicles then running on the LMR having orange/black carpets in first class and seats in Peacock Blue. For second class the existing colours should be used but as the original wool/Worsted mix was also no longer available this would now be in a wool/nylon mix. *Amyas Crump*

ABOVE Six-car ex LMR set passing Reading on the down Oxford service, 29 April 1969, the last week of operation for this mid-day turn. It has not been possible to ascertain what market research might have been carried out to suggest, for example, Oxford as a potential Pullman destination or is it again being cruel to suggest with so many trains and so little potential almost any idea was grasped upon? What might not have helped the cause was that the Pullman was scheduled to return from Oxford at a time during the afternoon when there were no other trains to London – and accordingly it was not specifically advertised as a Pullman service. Hence when a passenger for London arrived at Oxford he was stung with the supplementary fare – or the choice of waiting 45 minutes for the next ordinary service. Those were the days when there was just one fast and one slow train between Oxford and Paddington per hour. This particular set at least appears reasonably clean externally but the comparison with the set seen at Bristol (four or so images back) means that at the same time the 12-car Bristol service would have had one externally reasonable and one poor set conjoined. On the right is the then single bay platform for electric services diverted from the closed Reading (Southern) station. (Nowadays there are three bay platforms at the east end of Reading devoted solely to services to the former Southern Region.) The dent in the front end remained for the life of the power car. *Colour Rail 211861*

RIGHT Motive power of the Western Region in June 1967: Bath station with the Pullman departing west and a 'Western' arriving with a Paddington service. Again the external condition of the recently transferred and modified LMR set may be noted. Also, just visible to the right of the Guard's compartment door is the metal destination plate. *Colour Rail 215029*

So now the question might be asked, *why* was the Birmingham service to be withdrawn? The answer is that BRB Marylebone and the LMR at Euston had made what was perhaps the questionable decision to concentrate all London to Birmingham traffic on the newly-electrified former LNWR route from Euston whilst at the same time the former GWR route via High Wycombe was to be reduced to secondary status – leading in Birmingham of course to the subsequent closure of Snow Hill.

Whilst the likes of Sir Felix Pole might have been justifiably turning in his grave at the very thought of such action it should be recalled this was at a time when alternative or duplicate routes were simply not considered necessary and to attract investment money from government it was necessary to prove savings in other areas. Hence the widespread cuts of the period were the price to pay.

With hindsight, it would have made sense to retain the Pullman service, and operate it between Birmingham New Street, Coventry, Leamington and Paddington. Line capacity in the Birmingham area, however was a problem in addition to the same situation that had occurred when the new trains had been introduced to Bristol in 1960 – a faster service would be available (in this case via the electrified route) with no surcharge to be paid. In the event, the Paddington to Birmingham service subsequently ended on 3 March 1967.

In reaching its 'non-conclusions', BR Report 077 also provides some interesting details relating to expenses at the time. Figures for 1964, the last complete year for which they were available, give receipts for the trains operating on the WR as £104,000 (South Wales), £134,000 (Bristol) and £157,000 (Birmingham) – the latter clearly the most profitable. This was against a total operating cost for all three trains of £95,000, a third of which was maintenance. The result was a gross operating profit of £300,000 – in the order of 76% and an admirable figure, although it does not appear that depreciation had been factored in at this stage. Report 077, however, only afforded options – not decisions – and the final problem of what to do with the trains was *still* to be resolved.

The wheel of decision had turned full-circle and as Birmingham ended so the two LMR sets were similarly sent to store, and, apart from their limited outings to Hull and Leeds/King's Cross, mothballed until the time came for their despatch to the WR.

Another variation of yellow end and which this time we can definitely identify as belonging to unit M60092, recorded at Old Oak Common in November 1966; M60093 was at the other end. Yet to be removed is the word 'Midland' whilst jumpers and clips for the side destination board have still to be added. A personal memory from Pete Nichols of OOC is that there were three turns, 06.00 14.00 and at 22.00, known as the 'Pullman shunts'. 'After about a week at the depot I looked at the roster and saw I was down for the 06.00 Pullman. Oh wow, I thought only been here a week and I'm on the Pullman. The lads in the Hostel said yes cracking job that – so best pale blue overalls, shiny boots, shiny hat and down the bank I went probably half hour early to meet up with my mate. Unfortunately the trains were not quite as I had expected and the required checking was dirty to say the least. By 06.30 I was covered in oil grease and general filth.' *Derek Everson*

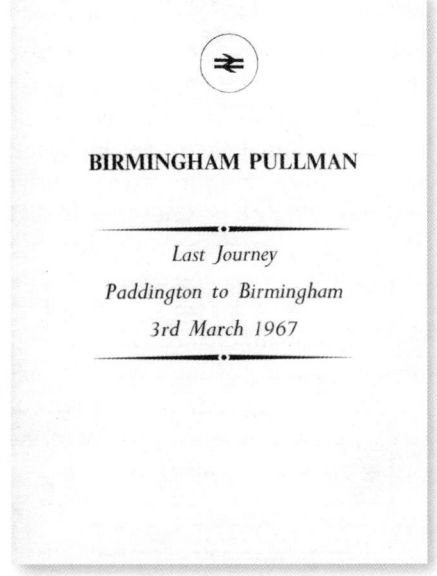

The 'Birmingham Pullman' ended on 3 March 1967 and to commemorate the occasion the WR had a special menu printed. Gone, though, was the Pullman coat of arms and in its place was the standard corporate logo. It is almost tempting to suggest Paddington were a little reluctant to see the end of the service as they sent out the official photographer to record the occasion. Files at the NRM record that in the 'Paddington C' photographic register, negatives 49886 Nos 1-4 recorded the last run but without further elaboration as to detail.

An almost direct 'before and after' comparison with the same power car: M60092 in a similar position at OOC, this time with a date of 9 May 1969. The changes mentioned have been made, plus, now m/u connections and associated cut-away coupling access, resited (and re-covered) air horns, the word 'Midland' removed, and the yellow colour scheme continued around to the cab doors in what became the standard design. In the background within the Pullman shed lurks the second former LMR set. *Alec Swain*

We should mention that both Paddington and we may suspect BRB at Marylebone were indeed still trying to come up with practical suggestions for usage. Dependant now upon the perception of the reader what now follows will either be seen as exploring every possible avenue or at the opposite end of the spectrum – sheer desperation! (The authors will not give their own opinions as to which stand-point they ascribe to!)

In 1966 the dilemma of what to do with the train might have been slightly eased had a proposal to use one LMR set (or part set) as a test bed for gas-turbine operation come to fruition. Clearly BR had not been put off by the trials and tribulations of the WR gas turbine engines, 18000 and 18001. The discussion commenced in public with an article by the railway journalist Brian Haresnape and referred to the proposed installation of Rolls-Royce 'Dart' turbines as well as new lightweight Budd-type bogies and mechanical drive. The new power plant would have provided for 1,500bhp per powered bogie. The same idea was mentioned in *Modern Railways* in 1968 in an article by E. L. Cornwell under the title, 'New BR scope for Gas Turbines'. In his article Mr Cornwell first discusses the merits of the gas turbine engine and compares this with electric and diesel traction. He then continues, 'Blue Pullmans are the ideal guinea-pigs: of existing BR stock one of the five Blue Pullman trains would make an interesting first subject, particularly one of the eight-car formations, which have a working weight of 364 tons and are harder pressed to maintain their schedules than the 299-ton six-car trains. With 1,500hp two-shaft Darts and direct mechanical transmission to new bogies, in place of the original … it would be possible to make a systematic examination of the overall economics of providing similar prestige inter-city stock capable of substantially higher sustained performance than that of any current non-electric stock'. The article was accompanied by an illustration of a six car Blue Pullman set at St Pancras with the following caption, '… Before the concentration of all these sets on the Western Region, it has been suggested that one of these units should be experimentally converted to gas turbine mechanical traction, but this now seems impossible because of WR commercial requirements'. Remember the article was seen in print in 1968, at which time all five sets were on the WR but could well have been written anytime between 1966 and this time.

David Clough in his book *APT – The Untold Story* also states that sometime later, on 18 March 1969, H. O. Houchen wrote to the CM&EE (BR or WR, it really matters not) to say that one of the Blue Pullmans could be taken out of service and used as a developmental train. Houchen judged that a decision could be made in 1970 whether to convert all of the five Blue Pullmans or build more orthodox trains. A week later he sent a memo to the BR Deputy Chairman to give his views on future high-speed traction policy.

Mixed livery set departing Paddington, May 1969. *George Woods*

Nothing, though, came of the idea at this time, nor a similar suggestion later that instead of using a BP the idea was now to use an existing four-car Swindon built DMU for trials. According to Colin Marsden the reason for not using the Swindon-built set was due to structural integrity and the strain the anticipated power would place on the underframes. The idea for further gas-turbine propulsion would have to wait until 1972 and APT-E which was fitted with four individual Leyland truck gas-turbine power units. As to what might have been with Blue Pullman, three years later on 10 August 1975 the gas-turbine APT-E would achieve a then record for speed on the BR of 152.3mph on the GWR main line.

We now have to deal with the 'politics' concerning the demise of the BP sets and which involves pulling together all the discussions that had been going on behind the scenes in the years leading up to withdrawal. Without in any way also seeming to make this an apology – which it is not – we have of necessity to also repeat part of what was presented in the previous chapter.

The thoughts (and conclusions) were that there was also no potential for a cross-country service such as Birmingham to South Wales via Gloucester whilst again the problem of limited luggage space was raised. (This could have been overcome by extending the guard's space or converting one or both of the passenger compartments in the power cars to luggage but with a consequent loss of seating in return.) A modern-day 'Cheltenham Spa Express' and even a premier service to Worcester and Hereford might have been considered but the located paperwork does not appear to record such thoughts. (Decades later, luggage space seems to have been conveniently ignored by twenty-first century train operators especially on inter-regional [cross-country] services and we regularly have to put up with attempting to step over bags left in gangways and so be denied the delights of the refreshment trolley.)

Whilst Headquarters might have been pushing for 100% daily usage what does appear to have been overlooked was the necessary regular down time required for servicing. Weekday and weekend maintenance would of course continue but a complete train would also need to be taken out of service for seven weeks every time a general overhaul was necessary – the timescale for this was stated as every 36–48 months. The same report also spoke of a main engine overhaul taking place every 9 to 12 months, which in itself would have seemed to have made the case for having spare power car(s) available. Repairs to the auxiliary diesel engine were scheduled for every 18 months. The advantage of running just four sets was that with two spare motor coaches (albeit first class) a train could be released from repair earlier, while if only three sets were in regular operation, the stand-by train could possibly be used at weekends, although the traffic potential was small. Whatever variation on a theme was chosen, it would still mean that part of the overall asset would be under-utilised, echoing the position of the LMR in trying to find regular additional/special traffic for the second 'Midland Pullman' train. For the first time the report also dealt with depreciation and so gives some idea about the initial capital cost involved. The cost of the units in 1960 was put at £1,662,000, and spares at £336,092 (not corrected for inflation to 1965. After all the furore over non-availability of spare bogies etc a short time before, we may also ask what were these spares back in 1960?) This £1.6 million figure related to just the 36 vehicles and presumably with workshop facilities, shore supplies, and so on an addition. Depreciation was quoted as £31,000 per annum. (In 1960 it was said to be £11,250, the larger figure taken from the WR report on 1964 train receipts, so it is not clear whether the figure for the increased depreciation figure was simply an adjustment for inflation, or a means of deliberately reducing the time taken to write off their capital cost.) Assuming each set to be roughly the same value (and so conveniently not taking into account the variations in depreciation of a six- or eight-car train), it can be said that

Charging away out of Paddington c1970. The crew too are now in a different uniform, the days of the white coats consigned to the past. *J. H. Ashman*

the expected minimum 'book' life of the trains was just under 13 years, this being the time needed to write off their original cost excusing maintenance. This timescale should not be regarded as the length of their useful lives, although ironically, they would almost achieve this 13-year lifespan. BR also identified that the sets had a relatively small scrap value, and again being non-standard only a few minor components were capable of being re-used in other trains. The Western Region had been backed into a corner, forced to take the additional two sets and financially with no option but to retain the trains in some form or another for the foreseeable future.

A financial comparison with BP reported at the same time showed that ordinary 'train stock' (presumably Mk1 vehicles?) in a pool of similar vehicles depreciated at £20,000 annually. The operating cost of a Blue Pullman was understandably higher, as this included the cost of travelling technicians, so a suggestion was made that these men be replaced by 'Platform Inspectors' although it is not confirmed whether this actually took place. Something in favour of the Blue Pullmans was that their fuel and lubricant costs were lower than a comparative train, although this might have been because the cost comparisons were based on 255 days use per year for the Pullman, compared with 307 for an ordinary train.

Having little option, the WR came up with an innovative decision which was to modify the two LMR sets for multiple unit operation by the necessary addition of jumper connections at each end and the fitting of a permanent screw coupling. Minor work was also necessary to relocate the air horns. It is believed this work was carried out at Swindon and which would then see a 12-car formation operating from Bristol to Paddington in the morning with a similar return service in the evening. We do not know loadings for the morning Bristol service but clearly Paddington felt more might be encouraged to travel if more seats were available. But at what costs with the additional staff presumably carried?

Aesthetically these front-end alterations did nothing to enhance the appearance of the trains whilst it is almost certain Jack Howe was not consulted. What his feelings may have been can only be imagined.

Physically in August and then November 1966, respectively, the two sets were transferred from Swindon, where they had been in store since their arrival from the LMR around June, to Old Oak Common for crew-training purposes. Clearly, the WR appeared to be in no great hurry to effect the transfer, perhaps even holding on to the vain hope that some other use elsewhere might be found; indeed they remained on the books of the LMR until March 1967. As converted and upon arrival at Paddington from Bristol in the morning, the now 12-car train from Bristol (the two six-car sets) would divide with one making a mid-day return run to Oxford (on the day of the launch the rear six-car set was used as Coach 'K' [11th vehicle of the morning 12-car set] can be seen in a photo of the train being flagged away), covering the 63.5 miles non stop via Didcot in one hour, start to stop. The other six-car set would operate a mid-day turn to Bristol, and on the 1.15pm return journey would call at the railway town of Swindon as well as Reading, so giving the Wiltshire town its first ever regular Pullman service. (Shades of the pre-war Cheltenham Spa working perhaps, and in this respect is almost the only suggestion from the 1965 report that was actually converted into practice.) This still left the original three WR eight-car sets. It was decided to use one as a reverse working on the South Wales service, meaning there would be morning and evening trains each way on the route. The third eight-car set would be held in strategic reserve, not mothballed but as a stand by, sometimes at Maliphant and sometimes at Old Oak Common. Later still, a mid-day Paddington to Cardiff and return working was introduced using an eight-car formation, but it is not clear whether this used the spare set, or the one that had worked up from Swansea in the morning. Shortly afterwards, a reverse direction working was introduced to Bristol using an eight-car set down in the morning and up in the evening. This meant that all five sets could be in use daily, but with no spare capacity as by the same time the WR had finally rid itself of the loco-hauled 'Wells Fargo' sets, most of which vehicles were then scrapped. Subsequent details of any substitutions are not known, but they were obviously covered by standard loco-hauled stock. One interesting thought for which no answer has

Eight-car Western Region set in revised livery working the 13.15 up 'Bristol Pullman', 19 July 1968. As is commented elsewhere, the light colouring did look smart when new but in practice wore rapidly. On a clean train however and with the sun shining off the side they were now sometimes referred to by a new name, the 'Silver Pullmans'. Just discernable underneath the four engine compartment ventilator slats of the power car is the BR 'double-arrow' symbol and the word 'Pullman'. Apart from the reversed livery (reversed compared with the blue and grey which was then being applied as the standard colour scheme for ordinary coaching stock), this single word was the only means of identifying the standard of service as something different, all other crests that had previously adorned the vehicles were no longer applied. Alongside is another icon of the WR, a member of the 'Hymek' diesel class, No (D)7040. *G R Hounsell*

Platform 1 at Paddington with three distinct styles of passenger stock on view. Right to left we first have the Pullman, next on Platform 3 a 'First Generation' DMU, and finally just visible on the extreme left, probably on Platform 6, a locomotive-hauled train of Mk2 coaches. Vehicles of this type were delivered with air-conditioning from 1971 onwards, were smoother riding than BP and often operated on schedules that were as fast if not faster. Consequently, the principal advantage of the BP sets – air conditioning – was being usurped by the proletariat, at a cheaper cost but of course without the advantage of a full meal-at seat-service. Times do indeed change – somehow I cannot quite see a trolley service of 'drinks and light refreshments' working on a Pullman! This was a South Wales working recorded on 11 March 1973 with just eight weeks of operation left. *David Canning*

The photographer Paul Cooper was a Management Trainee with the Western Region for a time during the last years of the Pullmans (we cannot really call them the 'Blue Pullmans' any more) and admits at times he would make his way to the platforms to record the trains. Here an empty but still impressive looking set awaits its next move from an otherwise deserted platform – with every one of the 'table lamps' visible switched off.

Journeys' end at the curved platforms of Bristol Temple Meads with the roof of the original straight train shed behind; faded livery in every sense and again, as seen, standard BR Driver's attire. The position of the multiple unit piping either side of the indicator lights together with the sloping top to the windscreen was said to resemble a sad appearance. This LMR set at least retains a cover for one of the indicator lights.

Freshly painted inside the Pullman shed at OOC. What we do not know is if the repaints – full repaints were undertaken at Swindon – also included a mechanical overhaul as well. This particular unit appears clean on the underframe and consequently may have had a full service.

been found relates to the 12-car Bristol service. Should one of these six-car sets fail, was an eight-car unit the only substitute or might the patronage have warranted two separate trains, one of six and the other of eight cars? (We can say for certain that a 14-vehicle formation was not possible as the eight-car sets were not of course equipped for multiple working.)

But before any of these changes could take place there was a need for additional trained crews, hence crew training on the former six-car 'Midland Pullmans' began between Paddington and Westbury mainly using the Berks & Hants line in late 1966. Three of the trainers were George Watts, Jack Nurse and Noel Butcher and at this time were based at Newburn Sidings, Swindon.

Lester Watts, George's son, was a lucky boy and had an extremely memorable, possibly scary, fast ride in the cab from between Bristol and Swindon aged 13. This was in an eight-car Nanking Blue WR set and later Lester and his mother were treated to Pullman service whilst Dad was teaching a driver up front.

It was generally felt that the cab was small. Lester recalls the drivers saying they disliked the earlier ice cream man white uniform and also says there had been talk of installing a crew toilet under the driver's seat but ASLEF objected. Lester must have enjoyed these early experiences as for 47 years he's been a train driver and George lived on until 2016 and the grand old age of 95.

It has been suggested that around this time, a trial took place between Bristol and Plymouth, possibly as a prelude to a regular Plymouth working discussed in the earlier proposals, and no doubt also intended to assess (or confirm the unsuitable) performance of the sets on the steep South Devon banks. However, this trial cannot be confirmed unless information was gleaned at the time of the Plymouth runs described next.

The suitability of the units to maintain schedules on the Plymouth services might excuse a slight digression at this stage. On the WR the weight of a full eight-car diesel Pullman set, with a power output of 2,000hp, was in the order of 358 tons, which was also the maximum trailing weight allowed for the WR 2,000hp diesel-hydraulic locomotives of the 'D6xx' and 'D8xx' classes over the steepest part of the banks (although here, the weight of the locomotive was not included). The same limit applied to the 'King' class steam engines over the same stretch – a 'Castle' could take less at 315 tons. The weight quoted for the Pullman was empty, but even if a complement of passengers was added, the weight would only come up to perhaps 380 tons – still less than a locomotive plus its rake of coaches. A six-car diesel Pullman set would have had an even better power to weight ratio.[3] A six-car set did later work to Plymouth on 24 December 1970, but as a special in connection with the opening of a new Holiday Inn hotel in the City (see Appendix 10). It returned empty to Bristol. Whilst it arrived at Plymouth seemingly without assistance the operators were taking no chances on the return as a pilot was provided for the return run over the South Devon banks in the form of a 'Western' class diesel-hydraulic.

ABOVE Eight-car set leaving the access/egress from Old Oak ready to work ecs to Paddington and its passenger duty.

BELOW The six-car down mid-morning Bristol service still in blue livery emerging from St Anne's Park tunnel, 26 September 1967. From this angle we can see this particular set has lost all three air horn covers. From the number of views of the trains minus this fitting it is clear such an omission was common. *P. J. Fowler*

A few days later on 28 December the return special ran; Bristol to Plymouth empty – Plymouth to Kensington Olympia loaded for the return. It was also formed of a six-car set, and was piloted – we may assume this time in both directions. (The weather may also have played its part in 1970 with, according to historic Met Office records, cold and snow showers on both of the days referred to.) What is even more surprising was that at the same time the following year, 1971, an eight-car set repeated the journey ... see the accompanying photo section.

Plymouth Photo Special

We are fortunate that railwayman Bernard Mills was on hand to record the arrival of the first Pullman set to arrive at Plymouth (North Road) at 14.20 on Christmas Eve 1970. Bernard was on late-turn that day and took his photograph from the fourth floor of the adjacent tower block. He recorded the vehicles as being an ex LMR set, Nos 60091, 60731, 60741, 60740, 60730, and 60090, forming the 1Z03 11.55 from Kensington Olympia. The return 5Z03 ecs working to Dr Days sidings at Bristol departing at 15.50 had D1054 attached at the front – thank goodness for that front coupling and air pipes!

We next see the return (loaded) working formed as 1Z03 to Kensington Olympia – what route was used in 1970/71 for the loaded runs via Bristol or via the Berks & Hants is not reported. This was on 28 December with D1032 assisting. The 'Western' came off the front at Exeter. On the down (ecs) run the set was noted as having left Bristol and travelled via Weston-Super-Mare where observer Ian Chancellor noted it pause at the station for two minutes. Why the WSM route was taken is unknown.

The following year on 24 December 1971 another special from Kensington Olympia to Plymouth was operated. No views of the down loaded run have emerged after which the set returned ecs again to Bristol for stabling, but we do have these two images of what is clearly an eight-car train with an LMR power car at either end – W60092, W60732, W60742, W60743, W60740, W60741, W60733, W60091 – on the return (28 December loaded) run and being piloted. (A 12-car set had originally been proposed but insufficient tickets were sold.) We see it first passing Laira and then to quote Bernard, 'I ran across the road to get the going away shot, something impossible now due to the dual carriageway and sheer volume of traffic. The works to the left are the road works for the construction of the dual carriageway from the Marsh Mills Roundabout to Laira, these on the site of the recently filled in tidal inlet and Blagdon's Boat Yard. In the distance are the twin viaducts of the Plympton bypass opened 18 months earlier, to the right the estuary of the River Plym with the wreck of the *Antelope*.' The down, loaded run operated as 1Z08 leaving Olympia at 11.30 with D1010 assisting presumably west of Exeter – or might it even have been from Newton Abbot? The WR deliberately swapped the usual power cars for LMR types to facilitate piloting. One minor detail was that the destination blind on at least one power car read 'Bristol Pullman'. Despite these new and unique images some questions still remain. Clearly the fact ticket sales are mentioned reveals this to have been a commercial exercise by the hotel company, and buoyed by their success in 1970 they hoped to at least equal and perhaps even better the 1970 venture. Unfortunately, there was no repeat (using BP at least) in 1972. More pertinent is why had there been no assistance for the set on the down run? Perhaps the answer was that it was not considered necessary – or might it have been an unofficial test? Could it even have been it was the driver who reported it as having been 'uncomfortable' over the grades in the down direction? Finally, why did the unit have to travel ecs back to Bristol instead of being stabled at Plymouth? About the only possible reason has to be restocking the train for the return run, but then surely supplies could have been brought down early on departure day so saving the cost of all that ecs working? *Colour images courtesy Bernard Mills*

Apart from the mechanical modifications to the ends of the former LMR trains, aesthetically too the units generally were changing. The Pullman logo was now considered outmoded and the decision was taken to radically alter the external paintwork, basically to the reverse of what it had been previously. We know Jack Howe was not in favour of this revised colour scheme, indeed he had tried to have the same Nanking Blue livery applied to the Mark 2 Pullman stock, unsuccessfully as it turned out. Additionally, yellow ends were provided; some of these changes are easily identified in the accompanying illustrations. At first, there were also considerable variations in the way the yellow was applied to the ends of the power cars, not all details of which are known. For example one of the former LMR power cars, 60093, is known to have had the driver's doors painted yellow (as per one of the Bachmann sets), with the colour extending to the bottom of the cab. Nos 60090 and 60092 certainly had an apron style of yellow nose. It has been suggested that the painting of the LMR sets could have been carried out while the set was in store on the LMR so consequently there may well have either been a lack of understanding of the livery to be applied on the WR or it could be that the LMR and WR had their own interpretations. At the point of these experimental yellow noses the 'Midland Pullman' lettering remained. Operationally though, when in service on the LMR both six-car trains ended their days externally in exactly the same livery as at the commencement in 1960.

After the training runs and as befitted their new role, the former LMR sets had the word 'Midland' obliterated from their sides, although for the present they still retained their coach numbers prefixed by the letter 'M'. Interestingly, it was suggested that MKFL (Motor Kitchen First with Lavatory) 60730 from the original 'Midland Pullman' Set 1 had at one point temporarily acquired the prefix 'NE', but this has not been confirmed.

An article by Adrian Curtis in the July 2002 issue of *Traction* magazine, confirms details of the formal allocations in January 1967, with both former LMR six-car sets being based at Bristol Bath Road.

It states W60094, W60095, W60644, W60645, W60734, W60735, W60745 and W60746 were at Newport (Ebbw Junction), although the Newport allocation is somewhat strange, and might have been on paper only, as the Welsh set was still actually stabled at Maliphant sidings, Swansea, where Gerald Williams worked.

The remaining two WR sets were at Old Oak Common. It was in this form that the five sets entered the final period of their working lives.

The year 1967 was destined to be one of mixed fortunes. To start with the January 1967 issue of *Modern Railways* speaks of a 'National Traction Plan' which looks forward to the future but succinctly makes no mention of the Pullman sets. It does, though, hint towards the demise of the hydraulics. This was justified by a reliability figure down to just 20% at times when referring to the original North British A1A + A1A type but adds that overall the figure for locomotives with hydraulic transmission was never likely to exceed 70%. On the face of it then BP should have been more secure, save that is for its lack of mention and the additional note that BR considered it presently had 910 DMU units that were surplus. Really? Did BR even have 910 DMUs in total anyway? But that was the figure, that was the quote and perhaps somewhere in those figures the BP sets (or was it even an individual vehicle count) were part of that number.

March saw some accelerations in the timetable but a deceleration of the Pullman between Paddington and Bristol. There were also some changes made to the stopping points on the mid-day Bristol service.

Also in March the 'PR' department at Paddington was busy with images of 'top people's secretaries' being taken for a day out by Pullman, Mr Lance Ibbotson, then the General Manager of the WR, being photographed with Miss Doris Proctor next to the BP train. Miss Proctor was employed as private secretary to Lord Robens, Chairman of the National Coal Board, so it was certainly not all railway secretaries who were involved.

Shortly after this on 13 April 1967 Christopher Head recalls his first trip on a Blue Pullman: 'My school friend and I were both railway enthusiasts. We didn't go trainspotting, but we did like to travel on different routes and trains. Most of this was local to me around the Woking and Guildford areas, going on the Reading to Tonbridge line, or the maze of tracks around Frimley and Farnborough, and down the Christ's Hospital line as far as Cranleigh (before Dr Beeching closed it! We thought the Pullmans must be very glamorous indeed and it would be really great to ride the Blue Pullman, so we saved up for a trip.

'On Thursday, 13 April 1967 we had our 28 shilling "Special Day Excursion" tickets from Reading to Bristol and back, plus an extra nine shilling Pullman car supplement and seat reservation. I remember standing on what was Platform 4 at Reading, gazing down the line towards Sonning Cutting waiting for a first glimpse of the Pullman's arrival. When it pulled into the station the attendant for each car stood by the door to check passenger's tickets and reservations.

'Stepping inside was a big change from the BR Mk1 coaches and remaining pre-nationalisation stock that we were used too. We were seated in a kitchen car and had bought second-class tickets so at the time I thought that first class must be even more luxurious. (It is only recently via Mike's "The Blue Pullman" group on Facebook that he found out that these six-car sets were actually the former LMR stock.) The set was still Nanking Blue, the nose was painted yellow and it had been fitted with the ugly jumper cables. This set of course had formerly been all first class. The Western Region had nominally downgraded some areas by removing the number '1' although the seats and wood panelling remained the same! I remember the venetian blinds between the panes of double-glazing, and a funny handle to wind it up and down. The table was laid out with a self-patterned cloth. I don't recall us running to lunch on our budget, but a photo that my friend took of me shows the Ridgway Lucerne patterned coffee cup which was a change from the standard pale green Bakelite stuff we were used to from afternoon teas in the Mark 1 restaurant cars.

'Unfortunately perhaps my over-arching memory of the trip was the awful ride quality of the carriage. It rocked and rolled, and was certainly out of keeping with the 1960s style chic of the car's interior. It was certainly worse than the D.M.U.s and only half as good as the Class 47 loco-hauled stock we rode back.'

On 16 May 1967 a major failure was reported as having occurred to the up 'South Wales Pullman' at Cardiff when it was taken out of service with a fractured frame. This information comes from the *Railway Observer* of July the same year but tantalisingly does not give details of the failure nor the vehicle involved. (As no withdrawals took place it was obviously subsequently repaired.) Whatever, a substitute train consisting of seven coaches of 238 tons tare behind D6881 (Class 37) had to be provided. Leaving Newport at 15.01 there was a severe check on the ascent out of the Severn Tunnel but thereafter a clear road permitted the 113 and a quarter miles from Patchway to Paddington to be covered in 86 minutes at an average of 79mph. The Badminton–Didcot section in particular was covered at an average of 90mph *(which allowing for the necessary Wootton Bassett junction slowing would have meant the speed would have needed to be well in excess of 90 in places.)*

The final major overhauls and full repainting into the new reverse livery started at Swindon in July 1967 and involved half set W60096/W60646/W60736/W60744. This newly repainted part train appeared at the Old Oak Common Open Day on 15 July along with the still Nanking Blue W60097/W60647/W60737/W60747 other half. Combined half sets in Nanking Blue and reverse grey/blue livery were seen in service over the next three years until the last set was finally repainted in the new livery. Unfortunately but hardly surprising, the new 'reversed' livery weathered very quickly and below the window line the grey quickly looked grubby. Whoever had thought a pale grey was a suitable colour was clearly not practically involved in railway operation but then this same colour scheme also now applied to loco-hauled Pullman cars on the LMR and ER as well. (On the Southern the 'Bournemouth Belle' retained its umber and cream Pullmans until it ceased operation on 9 July 1967. The 'Brighton Belle' would similarly end its days in a modern Pullman livery.)

One benefit of seeing a car in the new livery was not outside but within, as at the same time the cars had received a face-lift with seat covers and carpets renewed and the interior decor of the first class accommodation coming into line with the contemporary Mark 2 Pullman fleet. All the other sets were similarly dealt with when they were next at Swindon for overhaul. Whilst in work the power cars, with the exception of W60095 and W60099, were fitted with dual WR and BR AWS, the exceptions having the original WR contact system only.

On 1 September the next half set, W60097/W60047/W60737/W60747, was being overhauled and repainted soon after as witnessed again by Christopher Head: 'I was lucky enough to have a school trip to Swindon works on 30 September 1967 and saw the brand new reverse livery paintwork freshly applied to Western power car W60097'.

Later the same year *Modern Railways* for November 1967 carried a piece by John Palette who was then in the role of Passenger Manager of the WR.[5] In an article entitled 'The Evolution of an Inter-City service London to Bristol and South Wales' and a subsequent sub-heading 'The role of the Pullmans', Mr Palette stated, 'In June, 1955, the "South Wales Pullman" was introduced between Paddington and Swansea. From then on the Pullman type of service has gradually won increased favour. This had its biggest impetus in September 1960, and September 1961, when the diesel Pullman m.u.s were introduced on the Bristol and South Wales services respectively and attracted an immediate response from the travelling public for this type of luxury travel, particularly to London in the morning. It is not possible to make strict comparison of the amount of Pullman travel year by year, owing to the variation of and additions to schedules since the Pullmans' introduction. For example, the 1967 figures will have to recognise the major revision of schedules which took place in March, when the complete BR fleet of diesel Pullman m.u.s was transferred to the WR. But comparing 1966 with 1964 there has been an increase in value of supplementary fares collected of 99 per cent on the Bristol route, and 137 per cent from the South Wales services. The Pullman service now offered on both routes can be regarded as a permanent de-luxe feature of the WR timetable between major centres of population, and at the same time utilising this very expensive equipment in a sensible and extremely productive manner. As the units are of fairly recent construction, they are expected to continue in service until the late 1970s. It is recognised in BR passenger policy that there will be a durable demand for high-class luxury travel, but the future design of equipment to replace such trains as the diesel Pullmans is as yet not definite.'

John Palette had commenced his article by commenting that up to recent years both Bristol and Swansea had only ever been served by trains en-route to elsewhere and it is only since a rescheduling of services to give priority to destinations such as Bristol and Swansea and by making them the final destination rather than an en-route stopping place, that increases in traffic have been achieved.

Back in South Wales Gerald William's colleague Val Berni was a Maliphant-based Service Driver: 'I was sent on a three-day Blue Pullman course in 1968 with Driver-Inspector Alun Vickers. From this I was added to the Blue Pullman ferrying link roster which allowed me to drive the Blue Pullman from the Maliphant sidings to Swansea High Street station, a distance of about three-quarters of a mile. This was without a second man and I never exceeded a speed of about 10mph. What I remember is there was no real difference at that speed to other diesel locomotives that I had driven and the vision from the cab was very good.

'Only the Pullman link driver wore a white overall and a special cap and the same applied to the second man. I never took the Pullmans on a long run but I know the link drivers would face a number of speed restrictions starting at Landore viaduct with a 20mph slowing and each station approach would be down to 40mph. After this the driver could open

Railway enthusiasts Keith and Sue Long chose to travel by the 14.20 South Wales Pullman from Cardiff on 20 November 1968 after a trip to the scrapyard at Barry. They travelled in second class parlour car W60648 on Keith's free pass and display a look which is the epitome of 1960s' style. *Keith and Sue Long*

up the Pullman at Raglan Moors right up to 90mph. The Severn Tunnel however was restricted to 65-70mph.'

On 1 July 1968 half set W60099/W60649/W60739/W60749 went in for heavy overhaul/repainting followed in October by W60098/W60648/W60738/W60748 and then in December it was the turn of W60095/W60645/W60735/W60745.

On 20 November 1968 a recently married young couple, Keith and Sue Long caught the 14.20 Cardiff to Paddington 'South Wales Pullman' service: 'My wife Sue and I were on a day out from Leeds to Barry Island to view the famous scrapyard. It had started at York the previous evening with an overnight ride on the Sleeper to Bristol then across to Cardiff and Barry Island using my free pass. As I was a railwayman (subsequently a signalman for 45 years) travelling on a free pass we were in second class but the interior was really modern and far superior to anything else I'd seen on British Railways at that time, even better than the Met-Camm Mk1 Pullmans which were built in the early 60s and used between Yorkshire and King's Cross.

On decent modern welded track the ride was very good, but in 1968 it wasn't as it is today and there were a lot more points, crossings and jointed track and on this there was a vibration which made the salt and pepper pot slowly walk across the table. This was first noticed when running through the Severn Tunnel which was noted for its poor track. There were very few passengers on our run and as far as I can remember we were the only ones in our coach; probably if the train had been full the vibration wouldn't have been as bad although it didn't spoil the journey. It was great to have had the chance to have a ride on one and we wouldn't have missed it for anything.'

Sue is just as keen as Keith on trains and she too is an experienced traveller: 'I remember dressing up seeing as it was the "South Wales Pullman", you did in those days! I must say it was impressive but a bit bouncy at times.

I preferred the proper loco-hauled Pullmans like "The Master Cutler". We never did manage to do the "Midland Pullman" despite Keith being a Midland man.'

Around this time an 18-year-old BR catering worker Chris Price leapt at the chance to be a last-minute stand in for the Pantry Boy on the 'Bristol Pullman'. 'I was sat spare in the office at Bristol Temple Meads when Mr Stan Klift, who was the Chief Steward for the London end of the "Bristol Pullman", asked my manager if I could cover for the pantry boy. It was still Nanking Blue at this point. We left at 8.15am and although the ride was rough I loved it. There were two ladies from Weston-Super-Mare working as stewardesses along with stewards Billy Williams and Ron Springer.

'At the other end the Chief Steward was a Hungarian chap called Steve Cziener. We went to depot 81A and after a nice breakfast I had a really good look around Old Oak Common. As a BR employee and not Pullman staff I couldn't believe I was working on the Pullman. Having loaded up from the underground stores at Paddington we left at 5.45pm back for Bristol.'

Chris's story confirms that the previously 'males only' world of the Pullman train staff now had women working on the trains. (Clearly the bastion had been broken and female staff were now regularly seen on the train as witness an entry on page 134 of the original hardbook where there is a chit from the fault book for W600736 dated 26 November 1971 that refers to a missing food drain cap in the pantry that may be dangerous for female staff wearing high heels.)

WR half-set in revised livery running through the closed station at Horfield (closed 23 November 1964) between Ashley Hill and Filton Junction. Clearly a stock movement, this may well have been one of the regular transfers of half sets then taking place between Old Oak Common, Swindon and Bristol Bath Road, recorded on Sunday 18 May 1969. *P. J. Fowler*

An even shorter stock working of just two vehicles from a former WR set led by W60096. Specific instructions running to six typed pages were issued to both the LMR and WR relative to the uncoupling and coupling of vehicles within the sets. Paramount was the need to ensure the handbrake was set on the portion to remain stationary, an obvious point perhaps but the railways were always, and indeed still are, specific in their working instructions so as to ensure a 'clear understanding' is achieved by all concerned. Another equally important point was to shut down the main and auxiliary engines and, if appropriate, ensure no shore supply was connected. Handbrakes were only fitted to the respective power cars, any intermediate car(s) left standing on its or their own for any reason would need to be chocked. *David Birt*

On a day steeped in railway history, 7 October 1971, a half-set returns towards Old Oak Common past the bulk of the former Reading West Main signal box. The gathering of photographers is there for a specific reason, and from the glum look on several faces, *not* to photograph the Pullman! The group were actually waiting for the appearance of No 6000 King George V on a trial run to test if BR would allow the return of steam for special workings on the main line. *Martin Welch*

275

The Glory Fades

ABOVE With no destination blinds fitted to the LMR cars (or retro-fitted upon their transfer to the WR), it was necessary to provide brackets and fit the then standard metal plates affording destination details. (Evidently the LMR did not consider there would be confusion between departures from St Pancras for Manchester or Leicester/Nottingham.)

ABOVE RIGHT Bristol Temple Meads and a fully booked service. The photographer has the date down as 6 October 1966 but this must be open to question. In the background an original Western Region set is departing. *D. L. Percival*

TOP LEFT 'Top Secretaries sample "Top" Trains', so stated the caption to this view from the Paddington PRO of March 1967. 'Some of the 20 London "top" secretaries who travelled from London to Cardiff and back on Thursday (March 9) as guests of British Rail. They were sampling the new London to South Wales Blue Pullman morning service which was introduced last Monday (6 March). Miss Elizabeth Barling (second from left), secretary to the Western Region's General Manager, acted as hostess to the party at Paddington before joining the train.' (I think we can count 18 pairs of shoes.) But there was a serious side to the day as well, as it was no doubt hoped the luxury service now available would be advised to their respective bosses. Pro-active marketing or almost a sign of desperation?

BOTTOM LEFT The morning up 'Bristol Pullman' awaiting departure from Bristol Temple Meads, 5 June 1968. With the service made up of the two former LMR units, all of which were originally classified as First-Class, those 'in the know' would deliberately choose a former first class seat now downgraded to second, the actual seating configurations or number of seats never being altered. On the basis of economics, the two conjoined sets now also contained four kitchen/parlour-cars. Were these all staffed and indeed now many train crew were on board? *Colin Maggs*

ABOVE August 1968 and a special working in connection with the opening of the Gulf Oil Refinery at Pembroke Dock by HM Queen Elizabeth II. It is not known if the unit, a clean set in original livery, was used by the Royal party – or *lesser* VIPS. This is almost certainly the furthest west into Wales a set ever ventured. *Antony Ford collection*

The Glory Fades

Another 'westward' trip was that to Plymouth (twice) in December 1970. A six-car set with power cars W60092/3 running as '1Z08' is seen here alongside the sea wall at Dawlish – the return working (5Z03) of 28 December from Plymouth to Bristol. It might seem strange that the WR went to the bother of ecs mileage when the Pullman was hardly likely to have been required for any other use on 25-27 December. As we know it was also 'piloted' over the South Devon banks as far as Newton Abbot for the return but as can be seen here is running alongside the Dawlish Sea Wall without assistance. This and the similar working the following year were the only occasions a 'Blue Pullman' would venture into Devon. *David Canning*

This time on Southern metals: the 26 April 1970 run of a WR set from Surbiton to Carmarthen seen here on the outward leg having just left Woking for Guildford. The headboard which was carried throughout read, 'Gilks-Grenside Educational Special No 8'. *RCTS*

TOP RIGHT News of the strangers' appearance at Guildford had been passed along the 'bush telegraph' and as can be seen cameras were at the ready! After picking-up, the service would reverse to make the journey to Reading and towards its westwards destination. *Trevor Owen/Colour Rail*

CENTRE RIGHT Journey's end – for the Pullman at least – at Carmarthen. Conductors (Pilotmen) would have been required for several parts of the route, notably to/from and whilst on Southern Region lines and possibly west beyond Cardiff. *Trevor Owen/Colour Rail*

BOTTOM RIGHT Visit of a WR power car and train to Newbury Racecourse on 31 July 1972 (certainly not 1974 as was stated in the original hardback). At this late stage it is best to exercise caution when attempting to describe the train for whilst it is certainly a WR power car, exchanges were the norm at the time so this might even be at the head of a former LMR six-car set. There is certainly no confirmed information that other than six- or eight-car trains were operating at this time. The Newbury race specials had once been the province of the former GWR Super Saloons heading the 'Members' train from Paddington – lesser special workings were also provided! Whether the Pullman sets were seen annually on this prestige working is not certain, it may simply have been that this was a one-off with BR glad to take the revenue. Andrew Snowdon on 'Blue Pullman facebook' recounts, 'I started at 81A (OOC) in 1971. I did a few turns on the Pullman as secondman. These were specials as normally two drivers were involved if I recall. Our shed shunting turns were always known as the Pullman shunts. We actually did shunt the sets which had their own shed, known of course as the Pullman sheds! Sadly, never took a camera to work; very few of us did. At Old Oak the Pullman jobs were top link. They did not work nights, so if a power car needed to be put in the factory for repair we had to use a loco to shunt it. The cab was a bit cramped. I think a Rolls-Royce technician accompanied the train? One of my jobs was a Newbury race special. After arrival we stayed until the return. Admission tickets were given to the traincrew.' *David Canning*

The Glory Fades

Possibly the last time a Blue Pullman set traversed the Berks & Hants line seen here heading east and approaching Thatcham. This is reported to have been a charter working on 24 March 1973 but further details are not known. *David Canning*

Another mystery trip and reported visit, an eight-car set supposedly recorded at Bromley South on 15 July 1972. Nothing appears on the 'SixBells' site and so far it has not been possible to ascertain further information. *Foxley Slides/Southern Electric Group*

The Glory Fades

An unusual trip from 1971 was on 25 March, believed to have been the only time Messrs Ian Allan sponsored a tour using one of the trains. Marketed as 'Dinner with a Difference' the journey was from Paddington (depart 18.45) calling at Reading and then via Reading West and Southcote Junction on to the Southern Region through Eastleigh and Southampton Central to Brockenhurst, where buses were laid on for dinner in the form of a medieval banquet at Beaulieu Abbey. Seen here the set used (no details unfortunately) is passing Eastleigh on the outward run. The service was worked by an OOC Driver and Paddington guard, piloted south of Reading by an SR crew. The return followed the same route with a photograph of the train at Basingstoke on the return run depicted on p132 of the original hardback. This may have been the only time a BP set operated south of Basingstoke and it would be interesting to know what the passengers thought of the ride. Of course it might not have been the only time had the suggestion for BP as a modern day 'Bournemouth Belle' replacement been taken up a few years earlier. *Ian Shawyer collection*

On 25 January 1969 a football special was run for the fourth-round FA Cup tie between Aston Villa and Southampton. The away fans are seen arriving at Southampton in a WR set led by W60096.

Details of the ordinary service workings over the final years have been more difficult to locate, possibly for the simple reason the sets were no longer in the news. In addition the WR reverted to an interchange of certain vehicles between the former LMR and WR sets to make up the eight-car operations. In a memo of 6 December 1968 the Paddington General Manager, J. Bonham-Carter, suggested the formation of a seven-car set that would have been achieved by inserting an additional Parlour First into each of the existing six-car trains which sets would then take turns to have heavy repairs at six-monthly intervals from May 1969 onwards. The suggestion of a seven-car train was circulated to the Catering Department who, while recognising the difficulties, were far from convinced that this was the best option. Instead, they suggested adjusting the workings so that an eight-car train was used. An interesting fact to come from British Transport Hotels Ltd within the same correspondence concerns the profit made from catering on the diesel Pullmans. This had clearly dropped, compared with previous years, with the words, '. . . from a pure catering viewpoint they [the trains] lose money, and it is only the addition of 50% of the supplementary fare that makes them viable'. From the same report, it appears that industrial unrest was still a consideration: 'We do have trouble working the Western Region Pullmans; staff are not keen to accept positions on them and consequently, they are run with men below the standard we would choose to employ on what should be our best services. A total of 68 staff are required to work the South Wales runs and 28* for the Bristol workings, and there would be some redundancy in the event of the withdrawal of the Pullmans."' (*Is this figure of 28 the total number of staff required per day for Bristol or the actual number of staff required on the conjoined two six-car sets?)

As late as 1971 the Western Region issued a (revised?) route availability sheet for the Pullman sets which included the WR main line as far as St Austell as well as access on to other regions. Should a set be required to work 'off-piste' then special dispensation and if necessary tests/calculations were carried out. Whilst the sets did indeed traverse some of the routes referred to, the paperwork should not be taken to read a Pullman set did work over them all.

Should one or both of the two former Midland sets not have been available then recourse had to be made to an eight-car set (with resulting loss of accommodation). How this affected intended patronage (and similarly, how the running of the 12-car formation had affected patronage, if at all) is not reported. No doubt some Bristol punters appreciated being able to pay second-class Pullman prices, yet travel in what had been first class accommodation.

On 24 February 1969, the first step in the eventual withdrawal of the units took place in the form of a memorandum, again from the WR General Manager, J. Bonham-Carter, at Paddington to the BRB. It was specifically addressed to the Chief Operating Manager, Chief Passenger Manager, Chief Engineer and Rolling Stock Manager, with copies circulated to other senior interested parties including the General Manager of British Transport Hotels.

The memorandum ('report' would perhaps be a better word as it ran to four closely-typed sides) first described the history of the sets, and then set the scene for what was to come: 'To assess the value of the Pullman in relation to ordinary services, market research has been carried out. This has shown, clearly, that the Pullman service has no special influence on the majority of our customers' mode of travel; they would travel by train in any event. In fact, there is evidence to suggest that some, who had travelled second class Pullman, would have travelled first class in a traditional service running at Pullman time.' (The report added that, 'Copies of the Market Survey are available at BRB Headquarters' – *so was this the same survey referred to earlier from 1966? If so Mr Bonham-Carter has interpreted its findings in a very different form.*)

He continued, 'It is also particularly relevant that there is now little difference in the general standard of comfort between Pullman and the latest type of conventional coaching stock, apart from the facility of meals being served at all seats and air-conditioning being provided in the Pullman.' (*Given that the ride of the Blue Pullmans remained the same, this must refer to the fact that the ride of Mark 2 stock of the period was actually more comfortable than the Pullmans!*) 'If the Pullman services were withdrawn, catering arrangements on the replacement services would require examination to ensure adequate facilities were available, depending upon the time of day. In other words, it might be sensible to have a 'reserved seat in the restaurant car' situation on particular trains, and a 'fluid service' on others. Equivalent schedules on the same timings as those for the present Pullman services could be covered by the rearrangement of engine and coach workings with the addition of one Type 4 locomotive and nine Mark 2 coaches. In view of all the foregoing considerations, the financial case for withdrawing the Pullman units and replacing them by conventional stock of the newest type has been examined … the most advantageous course financially to be the complete withdrawal of the Pullmans in May 1970.' The report continued with an assessment of the likely financial impact on revenue, and concluded that the overall loss in revenue annually was likely to be in the order of only £3,190. There was no mention, at this time, of savings on maintenance having been considered. But even if the financial case was strong, Paddington did display an amount of regret over their conclusions: 'The (WR) Board have reached this conclusion with considerable regret because of the "modern image" of the units and the fact that they have been in service for only nine years. The Board also appreciate that, if the proposal to withdraw is adopted, there will be a great deal of criticism of one sort and another, and the matter would, therefore, have to be handled very specially, with extreme care from a Public Relations point of view. Criticism will undoubtedly come from regular passengers who like the Pullman, although they would continue to travel by rail if the units were withdrawn, and no doubt there would be some criticism of the Board for scrapping relatively new equipment.' The report concluded with the view that it was unlikely that another region would be prepared to take over the trains, and in this Paddington were correct – but we do not know for certain if even at this late stage they were actually asked? As mentioned before, this had been found to be impractical in 1966, and consequently it would surely have been next to impossible in 1969. It was now up to the British Railways Board to have the final say, their decision having some degree of urgency, due to the necessary forward planning for the 1970/1 timetable.

Less than two weeks later, on 7 March 1969, the BRB met to consider the WR's request. Six members of the hierarchy were present chaired by Mr W. O. Reynolds. The other attendees Messrs D. M. Howes, G. Crabtree, T. C. B. Miller, G. T. Smithyman and P. B. Johnson. Also present and representing the WR, were Messrs T. R. Barron, S. Ridgway, and John Palette.

The case for withdrawal was first outlined by Mr Barron, who also outlined the capital cost of the trains, presumably including their associated spares and shore/servicing facilities which was put at £2.6 million. Allowing for depreciation to date, it was estimated that the amount to be written off was in the order of the familiar £1 million figure. No decision was made at this time, the only comment being that the Chairman would discuss the matter with other BRB officers, while recognising the need for an early decision.

At this stage matters again become somewhat convoluted, and it is interesting to try and unravel what might have been going on behind the scenes. Indeed other than that mentioned before, there is no other located correspondence from the WR or BRB over the planned withdrawal at this time, one possibility being that a decision was delayed pending full delivery of Mark 2 stock to the WR.

As a compromise the WR were recommended to reduce fleet maintenance, despite the ongoing major overhauls which had the knock-on effect of seeing the curtailment of the fill-in turns with effect from the May 1969 timetable. Gone then were the mid-day Oxford service, as well as the other midday fill-in workings to Bristol (and Reading/Swindon), Cardiff (and Newport), the morning Paddington to Bristol and evening Bristol to Paddington workings.

Interestingly there was also a much longer gap before the next half sets went in for painting and overhaul, not totally surprising perhaps seeing many were now standing idle for much of the day. Consequently, there must have been a conscious decision to get the most out of the stock before the inevitable withdrawal.

It was November 1969 then before W60094/W60644/W60734/W60746 entered the workshop and were swiftly followed by the two ex LMR trains. December saw W60092/W60732/W60733/W60743/W60742/W60093 and then nearly three years after the first repaint the final Nanking Blue vehicles were, in March 1970, sent into the workshop to be transformed into reverse blue/grey Pullman livery. These were W60090/W60730/W60740/W60731/W60741/W60091.

Away from the norm though the sets were still sought after for some interesting tours over routes that would never normally see a Blue Pullman (should that really now be a 'grey' Pullman?) Hence on 25 April 1970 an educational 'Gilks-Grenside' Educational Tour to West Wales was run reaching Carmarthen.[4]

Back though at Paddington and Marylebone it had been confirmed there was still nowhere else on the British Railways network considered suitable for the trains and even if there had been, the potential risk of labour relations was still bubbling under the surface.

However, looking further afield was worth investigating, perhaps with a chance of recouping some of the Blue Pullman's costs to help with future developments such as the HSDT.

The files report on 30 July 1970 a reply to earlier correspondence from Mr R. Long, then the Executive Director for BR Passenger services, in the form of a memo to Mr I. D. Gardiner, the BR Commercial Director, with regard to selling all 36 Blue Pullman vehicles to the former Yugoslavia.

Gardiner answers on 18 August 1970 with a couple of suggested approaches that might be made, both quite different in nature.

The first one almost seems ridiculous in that the sale price should be based on the cost of the new HSDT prototype, plus a profit, plus modifications to the 36 cars for use in Yugoslavia and in addition a 7.5% inflation figure to cover any increase in costs in wages, materials etc for building the HSDT. The amount quoted is an unrealistic £2.3 million.

The second more realistic figure was based on the new price of the 36 vehicles back in 1960 and which including spares had been £2,066,000. Allowing for both inflation and depreciation to date the end of 1970 value for the five trains was £1,033,000 to which Gardiner adds £200,000 (approx £5,555 per vehicle) necessary for preparing them for Yugoslavia and then a final 25% profit margin.

This gave a total price of £1.5 million but even so Gardiner points out to Long that the BR Board are keen to sell and more importantly this price may still seem too high for 10-year-equipment. A price of '£1 million or even less' is therefore suggested. BR almost appeared desperate.

But in hindsight even £1 million was a good price. With the benefit of hindsight if BR had received an offer of half of that they should have grabbed it with open arms for the eventual sale for scrap (and it is appreciated we are moving ahead somewhat) secured a paltry £48,000 and this was after the MAN engines had been removed.

How and why Yugoslavia should have been mentioned at all is not answered. Who had made the approach; had representatives from that country been to the UK and inspected/travelled on the trains; how serious was the approach? All of these are questions we simply do not have answers to.

What is reported is a note from Gardiner in which it is stated that by giving a good price now to the Yugoslavs may open the door to sales of the new production HST trains in the future.

ABOVE W60092 (presumably with the rest of the set attached) stored at Cardiff Canton, 24 June 1973. Assuming the dates to be correct the fact this set is in the location given is contrary to information given previously (p142 of the original hardback) that at the end of services in May it had been stored at Bristol Bath Road. Seen here is clearly a former LMR power car; we may note that the original numerical digits have been retained although the prefix has been changed from an 'M' to a 'W'. Discussion on the internet in February 2019 has come up with a comment that a six-car set was used on a Wales to Paddington service in April 1974. The contributor is adamant it was a six-car set being operated as an ordinary train but with no table lamps. The same information was for a time repeated on Wikipedia. There is though no firm evidence that other than stock movements to Swindon and later power cars into Bristol Temple Meads etc (as discussed later), any former BP set operated a passenger service post May 1973. Stock movements could equally have been as loco-hauled ecs. *Rail Online ZF-5438-95371-1-012*

RIGHT Final days: an eight-car set just west of Subway Junction on an unknown working. It must be said that even allowing for restricted maintenance in the final years the riding of the sets was far better after 1962 than it had been for the first couple of years. The real problem was the fitment of heavy motor bogies under the power cars and also at the outer end of the auxiliary power car, both of which rode so badly that consumption of drinks on the train became hazardous. These motor bogies also carried the body weight on a centre pivot instead of on two outside bearers working in an oil bath after the usual Schlieren pattern, and were thus affected by the unequal weight distribution of the coach body and the rigid couplings and enclosed gangways. Preliminary investigation had also shown only limited improvement by the fitting of telescopic hydraulic dampers across the primary springs. More intensive study carried out by the Western Region (the full report for which has not been located) produced answers which substantially bettered the riding of the power cars on the WR sets and the same modifications were then applied to the Midland sets. Wearing plates between the bolsters and frames were removed and to restore the free lateral movement the latter were located around rubber-mounted torsion bars. The bolster suspension system was also redesigned with much longer swing links of 24 inches mounted on rocking washers and fitted with transverse hydraulic dampers to reduce the period of lateral movement. The disparity in weight between the two ends of each power car was of course a design issue that remained, whilst it was discovered that the brand of flexible traction motor drive on the Pullman units also tended to stiffen the primary suspension. (Source – Modern Railways Editorial January 1962.) *John Morgan*

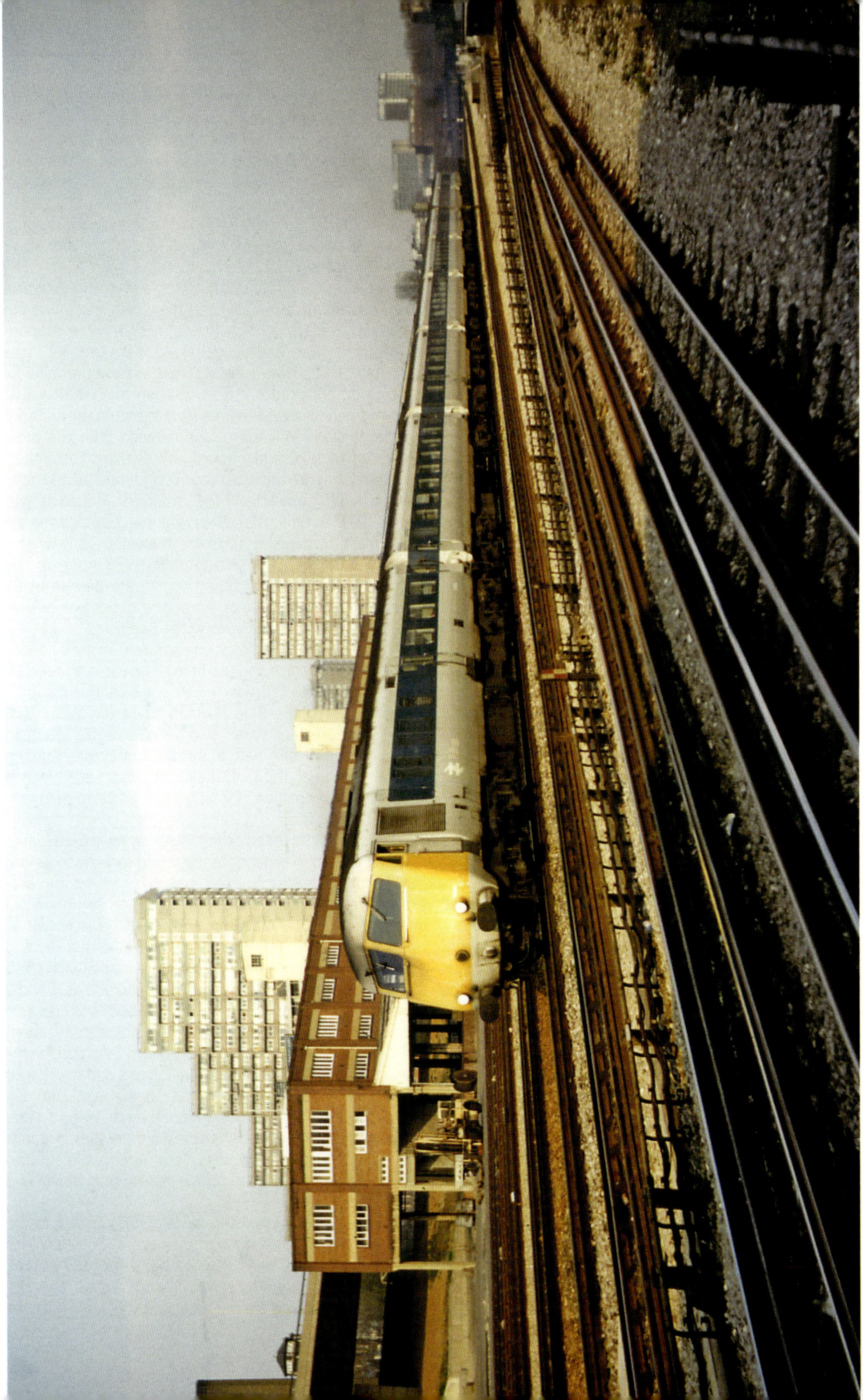

It is surprising to relate Paddington now raised an objection to the potential sale on the basis they had nothing to replace the Pullmans with. This was communicated to the BRB and board member Mr J. M. W. Bosworth in correspondence dated 26 August and whilst he sympathises with the problem of replacement stock he reminds Paddington that not so long ago (1969) the Western Region had presented the case to the board for withdrawing all the Pullmans! Bosworth also backs up Gardiner's view that a sale could lead to further sales to Yugoslavia in the future.

Long's response on 28 September is that £1 million is the lowest that Gardiner can sell the trains for and on 6 October Gardiner responds by saying he takes their confirmation of £1 million as being the acceptable figure as the go ahead to commence negotiations with Yugoslavia. Gardiner also asks that the vehicles be released from traffic in Spring 1971 for the refurbishments to start.

Yugoslavia was at the time part of the communist bloc within Europe so might it even have been a further case of 'reverse engineering' as indeed was to be the case with the 4,000hp *Kestrel* diesel in 1971? *(More on this engine in the final caption of this chapter . . .)*

In concluding this aspect of history it appears the Yugoslavs were not happy with the price and consequently no deal was done leaving the Western Region to continue operating a diminishing fleet for a further three years.

The potential for a sale though appears to still have been running below the surface for there is an oblique reference to the Greek railways but without elaboration. The fact that two countries are mentioned does tend to suggest it was BR who was making a trawl around potential customers rather than an approach having being made to the UK. Might even the railways of these two countries have been the ones to have shown the most interest in the trains when new? It was not mentioned who might have been 'tempted' back in 1960 but it must be considered as a possibility?

Internal discussions within BR appear to have dragged on, but it was noted that in October 1970 negotiations were taking place with another purchaser (who, it is not stated – so might this even have been Greece?), and it was hoped that these would again lead to the WR releasing the stock for the necessary 'overhaul and modification' in the spring of 1971. Again the correspondence also noted that a total figure as low as £1 million might be accepted, but this was said to be the absolute minimum.

Despite the optimism raised, this is also the end of the paper trail and, we assume, also the discussion. For whatever reason, no deal was ever struck. However, it could be that the very fact that there was a sale in the offing actually resulted in the trains remaining in service longer than had been intended. Vandalism and decline were far more likely to take place had they been stored in some out of the way location awaiting a decision.

Considering briefly, if we recall the projected 1970 scrap value of all the trains was put at just £48,000 we will probably never know why the sale abroad failed. BR would obviously have been aware of the likely scrap value compared with the sale value and so the question might well be asked, why did they not consider a far lower asking price, such as £500,000, still around ten times that of scrap value. It may well have been to simply save face. Having likely communicated the £1 million price tag to the customer, should the asking price then suddenly drop by half it is understandable the potential customer will ask a very big 'why'?

Devolving itself of an asset having a seven-figure write-down value and especially one for which there was no immediate replacement in the form of a more modern replacement was always going to risk bad P.R., the proverbial 'hot potato', to BR. Then as now the railways were being criticised – it really matters not what was in the news headlines at the time for if there was any chance to portray bad news about the railways then the press were sure to take that opportunity. Perhaps fortunately for the railway all this was kept confidential at the time and no leaks appear to have occurred. Indeed it was stated at the time that a permanent withdrawal/sale would have to be carefully 'stage managed', but what is interesting to report is that later in 1973 none of the major dailies appear to picked up on the demise of BP after such a short life. For once it was positive railway news, the HST, that was making the headlines.

Before then drawing conclusions solely on the evidence presented in the preceding text (and chapters), it is necessary to return briefly to February 1969, at which time it should be remembered the Blue Pullman trains (or as we said earlier, the 'Grey Pullmans') had been in service less than nine years, and still had a further four years running ahead. This final third of their lives was very much a shadow of the prestige in which they had been held only a short time before.

Having also moved to South Wales by now Christopher Head continued to experience the sets in service soon after: 'My Reading to Bristol return in 1967 was not my only experience of riding the Blue Pullman. Later at university I was sent to South Wales for an industrial placement at Llandarcy refinery between Neath and Swansea. By this time (1971) the train's livery had been swapped around so it was mainly grey with blue around the windows. I had a bedsit flat in Neath with a view of the railway and was able to photograph the "Grey Pullman" passing opposite. I used to go to Swansea by train to stock up on food, and I thought that it was fun to use the Pullman and in order to do so I paid the small supplement (I think it was 25p). On the relatively short trips I don't recall the ride being so bad on these short trips although these were the Western units as opposed to the ex-LMR units. I still have fond memories of this glamorous train, and for me at least it spiritually lives on in the HST sets.'

Schoolboy Brian Rolley also made a note of some of the formations and unusual movements in South Wales occurring in the final years: 'On Monday 3 May 1971 at the former Ely Mainline station (West Cardiff), I saw "Hymek" number D7083 slowly towing an eight-car Blue Pullman set made up of W60094/W60644/W60734/W60746/W60749/W60739/W60649/W60099. Five days later on 8 May 1971 a half set of W60096/W60646/W60736 and W60744 was at Cardiff Central. The Swansea set would sometimes travel ecs to Canton at 22.50 FO. Half sets would run between Canton and Maliphant/Landore quite often.'

Brian lived in Cardiff and he got an idea of the working hours of a Pullman Steward from his neighbour: 'One of our neighbours would catch the bus just after 6am from Pentrebane Road and then get to Swansea "on the cushions". Then he would work from Swansea to Paddington and back before going back to Cardiff and catching the bus home about 8pm.'

The paired 12-car Bristol train continued until 4 October 1971, after which time it reverted to the original status-quo of an eight-car set for the remainder of the life of the service.

From the introduction if the Winter 1971 timetable there were also now only three Pullman services: up from Bristol in the morning and returning in the evening, but a down as well as an up on the South Wales line in the morning with the reverse in the evening. The name 'Swansea Pullman' as well as 'South Wales Pullman' appears to have been used around the time. Each of these consisted the former WR eight-car sets leaving the two former LMR trains as spare and likely concentrated at OOC. Consequently, swapping of stock became an ever increasing feature as time passed and with it maintenance declined.

Western Region driver Andrew Snowdon joined OOC 81A in November 1971 and as a secondman travelled on the now Grey Pullmans a few times. 'The diesel Pullman was still a very futuristic looking design when I started in November 1971. By contrast the cab was more old fashioned with solid power controller etc. I found it cramped, quite noisy and the ride was not great. To work the Pullman was still seen as a prestige job for top link drivers. My involvement was usually shunting them or on charters and the performance was not "electric". [Brian now is comparing this with his many subsequent years on the HST sets.] I worked on the HST Prototype and of course the production HST which was much roomier and much better to drive.'

This swapping around of cars can be confirmed by Brian Rolley who noted the following different sets at a cold Cardiff leading up to Christmas 1971: '15 Dec, W60097/W60647/W60737/W60747/W60746/W60736/W60646/W60096. 23 and 24 Dec, W60094/W60644/W60734/W60744/W60745/W60735/W60645/W60095.'

Then following year on 10 May 1972 from the same observer it was: W60096/W60646/W60736/W60746/W60743/W60742/W60732 and ex LMR W60090.

Further proof of the integration of ex LMR vehicles comes from Keith Riley at Bristol Temple Meads in June 1972: LMR W60093/W60648/W60738/W60748/W60749/W60739/W60649/W60099 which by the last day of operation still had those trailers on the Cardiff-based stock. Meanwhile No W60093 stayed on the Bristol stock and W60099 was sadly the first power car to die of natural causes on 1 October 1972.

Next in the reminiscences dealing with stock movements Brian Rolley observed this interesting move: 'The smallest Pullman train I saw was in the Canton sidings when carriage shed pilot D3421was used to turn W60093 on the Penarth Curve's triangle on 8 July 1972.'

With discussion going on behind the scenes as to their future, the diesel Pullman sets were now unquestionably living on borrowed time. Technological progress and engineering development meant that a number of their previously innovative features were already somewhat dated, while in addition, the cost of maintaining a fleet of just five (or should that really be three?) individual train-sets was, doubtless, a major consideration, even if no figures have been located.

Reports of defects as a snapshot of some of the issues that occurred in June and again in August 1972 are recorded below. It is emphasized this should be seen as only a sample and would appear to relate solely to one set, possibly that employed on the South Wales service, but this is not confirmed. What is interesting is the number and variety of defects. One reference may be highlighted for special mention, that of 18 August relating to the checking of the dampers, indicative yet again of poor riding being experienced. (All were reported as 'repaired'/'no fault found'/or to be 'kept under observation'. Might some of these even indicate the run down of maintenance that had being going on beforehand?)

One of the principal difficulties was the promise of air-conditioned Mark 2 locomotive-hauled coaching stock just around the corner (the Mark 2E and Mark 2F vehicles), while slightly further ahead, the APT project and what would morph into HST trains were in the offing. All these were intended to afford far faster and more comfortable travel to the masses and it was unlikely that a business clientele (which was the main market for the Pullman) would continue to support a service that was both more expensive and also potentially slower – and one with a ride that remained poor by comparison. In that respect alone little had changed from 1960, recalling that even then the 'Bristolian' was a faster service to and from Paddington.

The reader will recall that withdrawal had first been suggested by the WR back in 1969 but at which time there was nothing available to replace them other than standard stock: 'from silver service to ordinary service' might even be the appropriate maxim.

Regardless of what was going on behind the scenes at the time, the Pullman branding still represented something special in the eyes of the travelling public. Witness this tale from railway author Colin Scott-Morton, 'In the early 1970s, I was sitting on a DMU at Paddington awaiting departure for Slough. A reverse livery Blue Pullman set was awaiting departure from the adjacent platform. In the next seating bay of my train, a pair of American ladies were admiring the Pullman through the window, and commenting on the luxurious interior. "Gee", said one, "that's a real smart train. Where do you think that's going?". Her friend thought for a moment, and then replied, "Scotland" . . !'

Before the end there had been yet another attempt to redeem the trains albeit perhaps not for Western Region clientele; clearly BR continued to search around attempting to find alternative or additional uses for the sets. It was almost as if certain individuals and departments accepted the inevitability of eventual withdrawal unless, and it was a big ask, some other use could be found for what was still regarded as, internally and by at least one (American) passenger at least, a prestige brand and prestige train.

But the fate of the trains was effectively sealed on 17 August 1972 with a damning note from the Chief Executive (Railways) to the Chairman of the British Railways Board. In it, the inevitable comment was made that the trains had now reached the stage where an estimated £300,000 was needed to be spent on the sets (the three in regular use or does this mean all five trains?) in order to fully overhaul them to an acceptable standard, the formal wording being, 'substantial expenditure for overhaul and renovation is required', and that this would be needed in 1973. No elaboration is given to explain or justify this statement except to say that the last major overhauls were reported as having been started, as we know, back in 1967.

The second paragraph of the note contained the fatal words, 'I have, therefore, agreed that the Pullman trains should be withdrawn from the timetable of 1973, and be replaced by locomotive-hauled, air-conditioned stock', and as if to further justify the decision, the report continued. 'Even allowing for some loss of revenue because of the service revisions, which will involve a small reduction in the number of trains, there should be a net benefit over the years 1973 and 1974 of over £350,000'.

This in itself is interesting when mentioning such a saving as it appears the BP sets had thus gone from operating profit to operating loss in a very short period. We are almost tempted to say this was figures being manipulated to justify a decision – no proof but it did (and still does) happen.

Publicly we know no formal announcement was made until the winter of 1972 but the *Railway Observer* in its edition of December 1972 reported a rumour that the 'Bristol Pullman' would be withdrawn in May 1973. It continued, 'Traffic on this train has sadly declined recently to an extent that now on average only 26 people use the service from Bristol daily. Some traffic may have been lost to the M4 but principally it is believed that passengers are using the 07.40 from Temple Meads which after picking up at Parkway runs non-stop to Paddington.' In that last sentence the failure of the train had in effect been summarised: it was a slower service, and although not mentioned, one on which you paid a supplement to travel as well. The original attraction of the meal at your seat service had literally gone stale.

Around the same time as the 'RO' appeared, a formal announcement of the cessation of services pending withdrawal was made on 20 November 1972. Co-terminus instructions were issued to reduce maintenance still further (which we know had been going on for some time anyway) so that when the final date eventually came certainly not all the sets were still serviceable. The earlier run down and instruction to limit maintenance on the trains, although issued around 1969, had not really had much of a marked effect for some time. Indeed up until June 1972 all five trains were still available (just) although as we know only three were required for the remaining service extant at the time. We have also seen some swapping of serviceable vehicles and cannibalisation took place, by which means the WR were able to maintain a fleet of three eight-car sets until the end although certainly not formed of all original WR allocated cars. In fact one of these trains was comprised of a WR half set and an assortment of other vehicles including a former LMR power car to make up the other half. Whether this combination affected the seating capacity is not reported.

Ex LMR kitchen firsts W60732 and W60730 were the very first vehicles to be officially taken out of service on 1 June 1972, this following complaints over rough riding and associated flats on the wheels. (We may joke slightly that it must have been truly bad for each to achieve this melancholy distinction.) Wheel-turning, though, did take place as late as 25 February 1973 (the last dealt with being kitchen first W60734 at Cardiff) which would almost indicate a desperate need to 'maintain the best of a bad lot', perhaps with no other alternative vehicle available. With four parlour-first cars now not in regular use and formed in what had been the LMR trains it was no major issue to simply effect a substitution.

Four months later, on 1 October 1972, Old Oak Common placed former WR power car W60099 in store with a thrown con-rod along with W60095, which was due its E service. W60091 was stored a little later with backlash in the valve timing gears; none of the three would run again. Cannibalisation was being resorted to for all sorts of components, proof yet again if it were needed that maintaining a serviceable level of spares for a non-standard product was both costly and time-consuming. Similarly three complete spare engines had been removed from depots to Swindon, all needing work, and they too were destined never to be used again.

In addition to the original ten power cars there had originally been a single spare engine from new but over time two more had been obtained giving a total of 13 engines used in the Blue Pullman fleet. Now, though, there was little point in going to the expense of repairing a power car for it to potentially continue to stand idle.[1][2]

Mentioning of how eight-car sets were now sometimes appearing as per their original formations recalls a time some years back, circa 1961, when a 'modified' type of Pullman unit had been considered. Again this was at the instigation of Gerry Fiennes, this time in his role as General Manager of the Eastern Region, who asked Metropolitan-Cammell to prepare a scheme for a very high speed six- and eight-car DMU service. The results are held at York and reveal plans for trains of this type with the following details: six-car : 84 first class and 172 second class passengers, plus 33 seats in a single dining car. All were also to be 'open' type coaches. The eight-car unit had the same dining and first class facilities but this time with 256 second class seats, both classes in a mix of both open and compartment facilities. No specified power unit details were given but it was fitted with an underfloor engine

Date	Veh No.	Veh type.	Detail
19/6/72	60090/1	Motor brake first	Both engines stopped at Swansea. No fault light in cab of 60091 . . . (remainder illegible).
18-8-72	60737	Kitchen first	Kitchen corridor double platform door – double slam lock defective and left-hand door twisted.
18-8-72	60090/1	Motor brake first	Both power cars main primary damper oil levels to be checked also transverse dampers removed and tested.
18-8-72	60090	Motor brake first	PA equipment rectifier vale defective.
18-8-72	60737	Kitchen first	Kitchen domestic fridge compressor head joint blowing.
18-8-72	60747	Parlour first	Rolls engine lub. oil leak on bearing housing; drive engine end of fuel injector pump.
18-8-72	60646	Parlour first	Rolls engine Serck oil leak on delivery flange. Securing threads stripped in pump body.
18-8-72	60090	Motor brake first	Air conditioning system through control contactor sticking.
18-8-72	60090	Motor brake first	'A' bogie brakes to be adjusted; arms touching top of wheel flanges.
20-8-72	60090	Motor brake first	AWS conduit going into shoe switch adrift.
21-8-72	60091	Motor brake first	'A' bogie r/h side trailing wheel coil spring; nuts are missing.
21-8-72	60090	Motor brake first	MAN engine 7-12 manifold gaskets and/or 'plugs to be checked for exhaust leaks.
21-8-72	60646	Parlour first	Rolls engine stopped with low water level. System filled at Paddington but engine stopped again at Slough.
21-8-72	60646	Parlour first	Brake linkage arms hitting stops (trailing bogie).
22-8-72	60747	Parlour first	Water leak at hot water tank behind mirror in London end toilet.
22-8-72	60090	Motor brake first	MAN engine coolant glass to be removed/cleaned.
22-8-72	60091	Motor brake first	Driver reported unable to cancel AWS whilst train is in motion; no fault when stationary.
22-8-72	60091	Motor brake first	'A' bogie l/h side coil spring safety bracket securing nuts are missing.
22-8-72	60090	Motor brake first	'B' bogie r/leading brake is cracked. Please fit worn block of a suitable size!
22-8-72	60090	Motor brake first	PA system, please refit cable to plug for hand microphone.
23-8-72	60091	Motor brake first	Cab door lock defective, right-hand side.
23-8-72	60091	Motor brake first	Please check AWS slipper height and rectify if necessary.
23-8-72	60091	Motor brake first	'A' bogie r/h side coil spring safety bracket is fractured.
24-8-72	60737	Kitchen first	Please supply one h/p (1kw) element as per pattern.
24-8-72	60090	Motor brake first	Driver's cab brake controller isolation valve defective, not isolating air supply.
25-8-72	60090	Motor brake first	Exhaust blow No 12 cylinder.
25-8-72	60090/1	Motor brake first	60090: 'A' and 'B' bogies both r/t brake block equalisers to be refitted. 60091: 'B' bogie, r/t pedestal safety bracket bolts to refit.
25-8-72	60737	Kitchen first	Kitchen electric hot cupboard element to be changed (larger wattage element to be fitted). Supplied by Landore.
25-8-72	60090	Motor brake first	Air compressor noisy when under load. (Same defect reported twice.)

with seating in both power cars. An outline drawing of the specification was provided but without much details – and a front end design that definitely needed the attention of the Design panel! No details were given as to whether this might have been a Pullman type train but on the basis of the available information it appears unlikely.

The impression given from Mr Fiennes enquiry was that it should at least equal and hopefully surpass 'Deltic' performance. Each intermediate car would have its own underfloor engine and transmission – of a type not specified but believed to have been diesel-electric. What we do know is that Rolls-Royce engines were envisaged. As will be gathered the idea was not, for whatever reason, progressed. It would be another generation and more before the modern day equivalent of this 1961 idea materialised in the form of the Class 180 sets (named 'Zephyr'/'Adelante' sets by GWR) built in 2000/01 by Alstom, the successor to Metro-Cammell at Washwood Heath. These Class 180 vehicles were to be plagued with many technical problems and GWR eventually managed rid themselves of all 14 units to other operators.

In the final months of operation we once more turn to Brian Rolley who on 16 April 1973 observed the following combination at Cardiff: Ex LMR W60090/W60645/W60735/W60745/W60744/W60734/W60644/W60094. This was an OOC based set which was destined to remain

The Blue Pullman Story

Final Days, courtesy of Bernard Mills

FACING PAGE Following the arrival of the 16.45 ex Paddington service at Bristol, on 11 January 1973, the set was worked as ecs to Dr Days Sidings (or was it by now Bath Road?) for servicing and made ready for the following morning's up working. Here we see the ecs set at the platform, certainly with ex LMR power cars and possibly a 4+3 combination. In the rear view, note too the travelling safe on the opposite platform. *Bernard Mills*

RIGHT AND BELOW The very last public departure of a Blue Pullman set from Paddington was the 16.45 Bristol service from Platform 6 on Friday 4 May 1973. Here the stock is arriving at the terminus consisting W60098, W60648, W60738, W60748, W60749, W60739, W60649 and W60092. Fortunately Bernard Mills had realised the significance of the occasion and was on hand to record the event. It appears he was either the only one or certainly one of only a very few who witnessed the event. He also noted there was no form of official commemoration or announcement by the Western Region. *Bernard Mills*

ABOVE A definite BP 'scratch' set seemingly in public service but with a mixture of former WR and LM vehicles – the most obvious being the position of the two kitchen cars. We would appear to have (left to right): WR Power car/Parlour second/Kitchen car/Parlour first/Parlour first/Parlour first/Kitchen car/LM Power car. Presumably some downgrading of accommodation took place otherwise the seating total would have been 126 first and just 90 second. The location is not given but the Bristol area comes to mind. The external condition speaks for itself. As an aside, the end of the Blue Pullman's sets also marked the end of second-class Pullman travel on BR. *David Allen/Booklaw Publishing*

ABOVE Blue Pullman failure/rescue? An apparent 'South Wales Pullman' service at Paddington attached to an unidentified Class 47. Unfortunately no date or details are given. From the position of the loco at the head of the train nearest the buffers, the conclusion would appear to be a failure somewhere en-route with the Class 47 then attached to complete the journey. BUT, was this a former WR power car (without jumpers) so was it thus possible to attach the air supply and so work the train? With a BP set having two power cars this would also tend to imply a failure of both, as a single car would normally be able to work the train albeit at reduced speed. Generally, though, and according to an individual from the Divisional Control Office at Paddington (before this was moved to Reading), the BP sets were considered to at least be operationally reliable. (One of your authors was on a legitimate trip 'up front' on an HST some years ago from Swansea to Paddington when the front power car failed upon leaving Swansea. We continued but were naturally unable to maintain the schedule with consequent loss of time and speed accumulating especially on the gradients after the Severn Tunnel and then between Bristol Parkway and Wootton Bassett. Arriving late at Swindon a clearly disgruntled passenger expressed his disgust at the crew in pseudo Churchillian manner).

in the same form through to the last day including use on the farewell tour.

Throughout these later years the 'South Wales Pullman'/'Swansea Pullman' carried on but of course with maintenance having being reduced there was a noticeable effect on the stock if not the efforts of the staff who still maintained a pride in what they at least regarded as the premier service.

Stewart Alison Reilly has worked on the HSTs since the 1980s between Swansea and Paddington, a family tradition as several of Alison's family worked on the trains including the Pullmans and she was well aware, even as a little girl, that the Pullmans were very special trains with the most important aspect always being the service given to the customer.

From a customer perspective, Robert Thomas used the 'South Wales Pullman' many times from the late sixties through to the end. 'These Pullmans were still pretty smart inside but once the train was at speed the ride was the worst I've encountered on British Railways – with the exception of the Pacers. It was jagged, sometimes bumpy and was definitely inferior to a Mk1 or Mk2 coach.'

Robert also saw the OOC based South Wales stock at Neath on 2 May 1973 led by W60094. 'The Pullmans were sometimes chosen by parents to send children away who were travelling alone – all due to the excellent service and care given by the Pullman staff.'

Two eight-year-olds, Peter De Lacey and David Lewis, both experienced the 'South Wales Pullman' at Cardiff and David also the 'Bristol Pullman'. David says 'I recall it was very plush and the Pullman brand seemed iconic but the ride was so rough'.

Peter was quite amused at his experiences: 'We went from Reading to Cardiff return in first class more than once. I remember the joy of pressing the button to call the waiter to order a drink. I couldn't help but giggle at the poor waiters trying to serve food as the carriage bounced about and my orange juice spilling as it was put down on the table much to the annoyance of the steward'.

Cliff Blackwell, a railwayman himself at Stratford, took the opportunity to travel from Paddington to Swansea on the ageing units. 'I travelled first class in the luxury interior which was pleasant with the reclining seats and we had a lovely breakfast. However the venetian blinds wouldn't wind and the set was groaning and creaking as we rode along. I'm very sad that one wasn't preserved though, a real luxury train of its time.'

Regular timetabled services were due to end to coincide with the introduction of the summer timetable on Friday 4 May 1973. Paul Strathdee wanted to have a ride on the last Blue Pullmans: 'I managed to ride both the "Bristol Pullman" and the very last Up "South Wales" Pullman on 4 May 1973. Yes, the ride was a bit rough over the bogies but inside they were a lovely place to sit and the staff, despite their services ending, were absolutely great.'

Clearly too some at Paddington still had the spirit of publicity in mind as following the end of public working a remarkable special and, as it turned out, final working was arranged for the next day. This was indeed to be *the* final run and marketed as an 'Enthusiasts' Safari'. Paddington were clearly aware of the potential for revenue from the enthusiast at this time, this Blue Pullman special just one of a number of officially organised enthusiast specials although the only one related to BP. (Coincidentally another official special at around the same time had constituted the last trains on the Lambourn branch, which were also hugely successful.) The Pullman 'Safari' was advertised for a price of £10 to include all meals and was apparently well-filled. As mentioned, the set used was the London-based 'South Wales Pullman' stock from Old Oak Common: W60094/W60644/W60734/W60744/W60745/W60735/W60645 and finally W60090 at the country end.

Departure from Paddington Platform 1 was at 8.53am, the train running via High Wycombe to Banbury and Leamington Spa, so far replicating the route of the former 'Birmingham Pullman', before taking the LNWR line to Kenilworth, Coventry and on to Birmingham New Street. Reversal followed and it now went via Cheltenham Spa, Bristol Temple Meads (reverse) and Severn Tunnel Junction to its destination at Swansea (2.19pm arrival, 5.10pm departure). The return was via Cardiff (3-minute stop for a crew change), Newport, Bristol Parkway, Didcot and on to Paddington. Such an itinerary encompassed elements of all the original WR Blue Pullman routes previously operated by the trains when in general service. The final leg from Swansea saw the train arrive six minutes late at Newport, but some fast running resulted in an arrival at Paddington at 8.02pm, 18 minutes earlier than the scheduled 8.20pm, an astonishing average speed of 81mph from Newport, and no less than an 88mph average between Swindon and Reading! 90mph maximum? – we may doubt it! Whether or not such a performance had been intended by BR was a moot point; hopefully it was just the crew 'having a final fling', but, whatever, it was still an excellent bit of income producing marketing for the period. After arrival at Paddington, the passengers de-trained and the set left for the sidings at Old Oak Common where the engines were shut down; the last time a diesel 'Blue' Pullman would ever be seen at Paddington.

The Blue Pullman Story

Two Pullmans at Paddington, Platform 5 and Platform 1 being occupied. Definitely the blue/grey period, Mk1 stock abounds and notice the men trackside on Platform 6 – not a high-visibility jacket to be seen. A note from S. Gaskell on the 'Railcar.co.uk' website mentions that in July 1968 (either) power car 60091 cr 60093, was found to have been throwing oil from the exhaust and with metal debris found in the sump. *Paul Cooper*

The 'toy train set' – as it was sometimes called when looking down on the railway at Reading in 1972 from the then London Division Headquarters at Western Tower – demolished in 2017/8. The Pullman set is arriving from Paddington and seen passing Platform 4A for Southern services. To the right the cars are parked on what had formerly been the area occupied by Reading Southern whilst on the opposite side of the line the former Reading Goods Shed is now the province of National Carriers. *Paul Cooper*

The Blue Pullman Story

British Railways

to: R.G. Hole Esq., General Manager, B.R. Catering, St. Pancras Chambers, London S.W.1.

Copy to: Movements Manager.

o/t 108/KU/GX70
date 6.12.68
from General Manager, Paddington
ext 27104

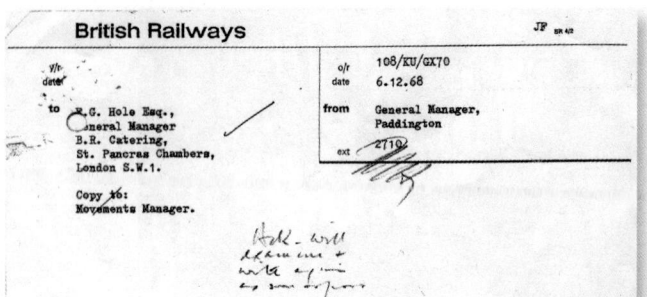

Blue Pullmans.

From May 1969 for approximately a year heavy repairs will be undertaken to the two six-car pullman sets which work the 08.20 Bristol and 17.40 Paddington daily trains.

Three cars at a time will be under repair and arrangements will be made for the three eight-car sets to work the regular service.

This will mean that there will not be a pullman train of sufficient seating capacity to act as a standby for use on occasions when one of the regular sets is out of use.

I therefore have it in mind to use one of the six-car sets as a standby with an additional parlour first inserted from the remaining set making a total of seven vehicles.

I appreciate this is not an ideal arrangement for you but I would much prefer a pullman set as standby to a set of traditional stock and I would hope that it would not have to be brought into service very often; even when it had to be used it would, of course, not necessarily be for the heaviest loading trains.

Perhaps you will be good enough to examine the proposal and let me know that you will be able to make the necessary arrangements.

For your information the seven-car formation would provide 108 first class and 60 second class seats.

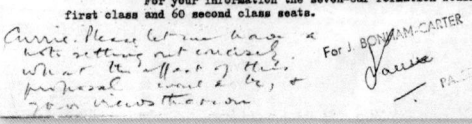

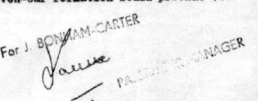

For J. BONHAM-CARTER
PASSENGER MANAGER

British Transport Hotels Limited

To: F.G. Hole Esq.
c.c. Mr. Shaw, Mr. Simpson
From: W.J. Currie
20th February, 1969
Ref RC/28   Ext. 125

SUBJECT: PULLMAN DIESEL UNITS : WESTERN REGION

With reference to the letter from Mr. Bonham-Carter and its enclosures, returned herewith, the case from the railway viewpoint would seem to be a valid one and must rest on this. The Field Manager himself would have fewer troubles if these trains were not Pullmans. I agree, however, that customer-reaction would be considerable; an example is the Master Cutler situation.

On these circuits, from a pure catering viewpoint they lose money and only the addition of 50% of the supplementary fare makes them viable. Of course, the loss of receipts with the May 1969 timetable will worsen the position.

We do have trouble in working the Western Region Pullmans; staff are not keen to accept positions on them and consequently, they are run with men below the standard we would choose to employ on what should be our best services.

68 staff are required to work the South Wales runs and 28 for the Bristol workings and there would be some redundancy in the event of the withdrawal of the Pullmans.

The introduction of non-fluid seating would, of course, be expensive to us as a Department - this would naturally be a subject for detail examination. A further point to be settled would be the quality of the catering vehicles which would be available on the Western Region in 1970; we might have to think in terms of some improvements if only in the way of 'face-lifting.'

Under the Pay and Efficiency agreement, Pullman Saloon Stewards would be upgraded to Chief Stewards I and the point arises whether we should do this now and then have, perhaps, a number of redundant men in that grade. Maybe we could upgrade on a temporary basis to start with in the knowledge of these possible withdrawals.

I am passing a copy of this letter to Mr. Shaw so he may be aware of the position.

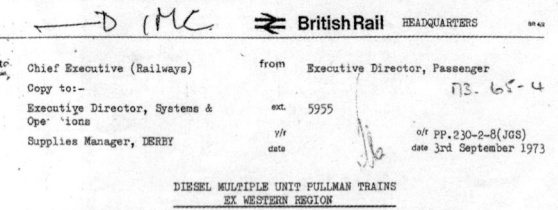

British Rail HEADQUARTERS

to: Chief Executive (Railways)
Copy to: Executive Director, Systems & Operations; Supplies Manager, DERBY
from: Executive Director, Passenger
ext. 5955
o/t PP.230-2-8(JGS)
date 3rd September 1973

DIESEL MULTIPLE UNIT PULLMAN TRAINS EX WESTERN REGION

Bearing in mind the difficult situation for Type 4 locomotives likely to arise this winter, I have been considering further the possibility of making use of the Pullman trains now awaiting disposal after displacement from W.R. services.

I am told it would be possible to make up sets with the following formations:-

		SEATS	
		1st Class	2nd Class
1.	Motor	2	18
2.	Parlour	1	36
3.	"	1	36
4.	Kitchen	2	18
5.	Parlour	2	42
6.	"	2	42
7.	"	2	42
8.	"	2	42
9.	Motor	2	18
		90	204

Such formations would be suitable for two workings now in use between London (Paddington) and Birmingham, provided that the power units could manage the extra trailing car. It is suggested that it would take a minimum of three months to bring the sets to a suitable state for use, and that heavy expenditure would be required. However, Executive Director, Systems & Operations may consider that for the limited period of regular use envisaged a smaller amount of work would suffice. Renovation of the sets might then open the way for their use for high quality excursion work, again involving relatively low annual mileage - scenic tours in Scotland for example - rather than that they should be sold for £48,000 as scrap.

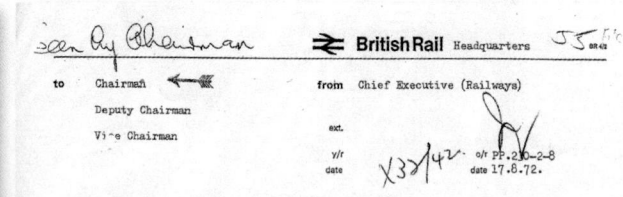

British Rail HEADQUARTERS

to: Chairman, Deputy Chairman, Vice Chairman
from: Chief Executive (Railways)
o/t PP.20-2-8
date 17.8.72.

BRISTOL AND SOUTH WALES PULLMAN

The diesel Pullman trains working between London and Bristol/South Wales have now reached the stage where substantial expenditure for overhaul and renovation is required. About £300,000 would be needed in 1973 for this purpose. Before this time a number of new air-conditioned coaches will have been introduced into the Bristol and South Wales services. These vehicles offer a standard of service in many ways superior to that afforded by the Pullman trains and their use at peak time will certainly improve the seating capacity which on the Pullman trains is restricted.

I have, therefore, agreed that the Pullman trains shall be withdrawn from the timetable of 1973 and be replaced by locomotive-hauled air-conditioned stock. Even allowing for some loss of revenue because of the service revisions which will involve a small reduction in the number of trains, there should be a net benefit over the years 1973 and 1974 of over £350,000.

CHIEF EXECUTIVE (RAILWAYS).

RECEIVED 18 AUG 1972 CHAIRMAN'S OFFICE

[Memo reproduced:]

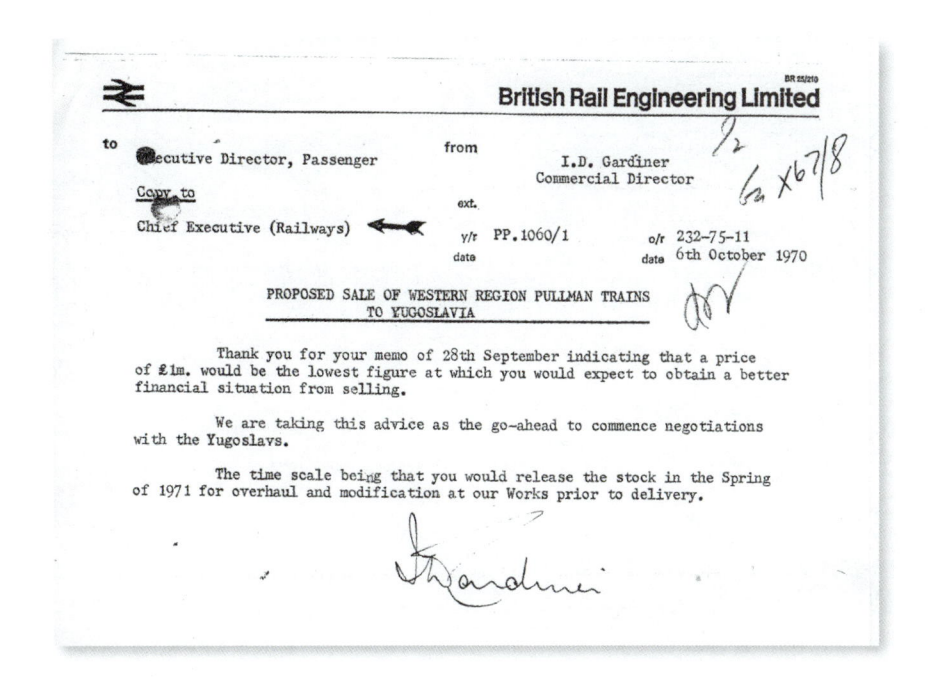

British Rail Engineering Limited

to: Executive Director, Passenger
Copy to: Chief Executive (Railways)

from: I.D. Gardiner, Commercial Director
y/r: PP.1060/1
o/r: 232-75-11
date: 6th October 1970

PROPOSED SALE OF WESTERN REGION PULLMAN TRAINS TO YUGOSLAVIA

Thank you for your memo of 28th September indicating that a price of £1m. would be the lowest figure at which you would expect to obtain a better financial situation from selling.

We are taking this advice as the go-ahead to commence negotiations with the Yugoslavs.

The time scale being that you would release the stock in the Spring of 1971 for overhaul and modification at our Works prior to delivery.

Notes

(1) AN173/19 at the National Archives.

(2) The same suggestion for a diesel-hauled 'Bournemouth Belle' service but running from Paddington to Bournemouth via Reading and Basingstoke was made by (Mr) M. Newman in a letter to Modern Railways that appeared in the April 1967 issue.

(2a) and (2b) – Both these named trains operated from Paddington to the West Country. The 'Golden Hind' ran all the way to Penzance, and the 'Mayflower' to and from Paddington Kingswear/Plymouth. Whether the former would have been curtailed at Plymouth is not stated as there is no mention of the Pullman ever operating all the way to Penzance – none ever did.

(3) The issue of traction power on the steep gradients of the South Devon banks is not one just related to engine output or simple engine horse power. Much is also dependent upon gearing and the torque available, which is why the diesel-hydraulics performed better than their later replacements with electric transmission. Consequently restrictions on loads applied to loco-hauled services hauled by the Class 47 and Class 50 types which were inferior to those of a 'Western'. Limiting trailing loads is not possible with a fixed formation train and it has been known for a 20th century HST set even with 4,400hp at the controller to become stuck on these same South Devon banks under certain conditions. Hence even in 2019 the Bi-mode 'IET' stock designed for the West of England are specifically designed to cope with this natural obstacle.

Ecs to Paddington passing Royal Oak on 29 August 1972. WR power car W60099 is at the rear.

(4) Details in Appendix 10 and The 'Six Bells Junction' rail tour site here: https://www.sixbellsjunction.co.uk/70s/700425gg.html

(5) The author had the pleasure of meeting John Palette many years ago, long before he had any idea of recording the history of BP. John Palette was the son in law of Tom Palmer, former signalman at Welford Park and later Cholsey & Moulsford at a time when Kevin was researching the Lambourn line. (Welford Park is on the Lambourn branch.) John left an indelible impression on the author as a man of integrity and honour and one who would be severely taxed in later years when elevated to the BR Board and placed in charge of personnel and negotiation.

(6) AN173/19 at the National Archives.

ABOVE RIGHT Friday 4 May 1973 and the final down South Wales service departs from Platform 1 at Paddington. At this late stage all we can really confirm is the presence of a WR power car at the London end. Obviously by this time all that was left were the Bristol and South Wales services, Birmingham having ceased to be a Pullman destination from Paddington some years before. Even so it is interesting to note that in Terry Bye's regular 'Pullman Car Services' newsletter, a contributor, D. Lindsay, reported on a visit to Banbury on 8 September 2016 there was found a sign attached to a door marked 'Birmingham Pullman, Driver's Lounge' coloured in blue with white lettering and incorporating the BP crest.

BELOW RIGHT Former LMR set at Bristol Bath Road – undated. Converted from a former steam shed, the depot here in turn became life expired with the demise of locomotive-hauled trains. For a time in the 1960s and beyond, regular open days were held by the WR (and other regions) at their various depots. So far as the WR was concerned the presence of a Blue Pullman set was often seen as the star exhibit, such events known to have taken place at Old Oak Common, Tyseley, Bath Road and Worcester as well perhaps elsewhere.

ABOVE An extremely rare shot by Western Region driver Chris Guntripp of a single power car running 'light engine' in this case W60096 passing through Reading on 27 September 1972. Speed was reduced when running in this way due to lower braking force being available. *Chris Guntripp*

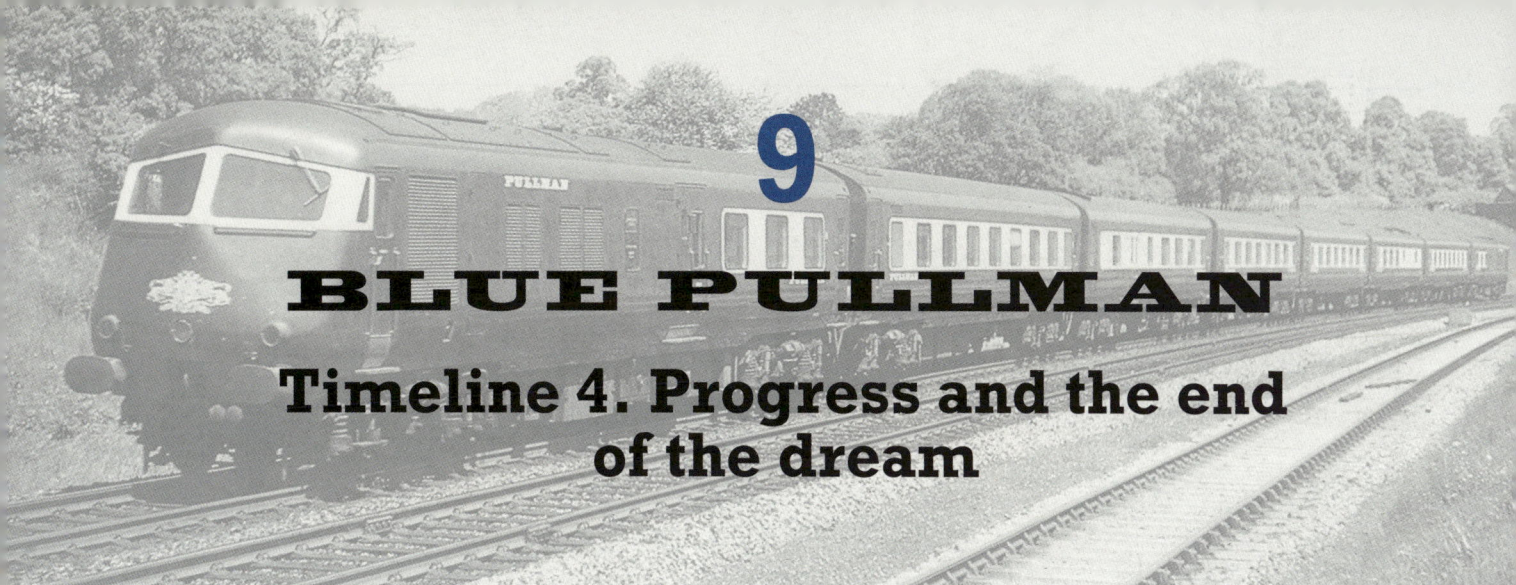

9
BLUE PULLMAN
Timeline 4. Progress and the end of the dream

Following the end of public service the vehicles were at Old Oak Common, Cardiff and Bristol although the Bristol set later moved to Swindon alongside the works and was visible from the main line.

Sadly, though, for the Blue Pullmans, life as living, working machines was over and here we try to follow their progress from the end of service to final scrapping/burial.

We commence with the status of the three available sets at the very end of service which were as follows:

Old Oak Common: W60094/W60644/W60734/W60744/ W60745/W60735/W60645/W60090. This was the South Wales set that had regularly worked the reverse train (Paddington–Swansea) each weekday morning and was also the one that was used for the Enthusiasts Safari last run detailed in the preceding chapter.

Meanwhile, at Bristol Bath Road was: W60096/W60647/ W60737/W60747/W60743/W60742/W60731/W60093.

The third eight-car train was at Cardiff Canton consisting: W60098/W60648/W60738/W60748/W60749/W60739/ W60649/W60092. This had been the 'South Wales Pullman' that left Wales in the morning and after withdrawal also later moved store at Swindon for a time.

On the final day, Saturday 5 May 1973, Old Oak Common actually played host to 20 BP vehicles, of which 12 vehicles, including four power cars, had not been in use for some time, plus then of course the eight-car set mentioned above from the last run. Thus we should list the OOC figure as including: W60094/W60644/W60734/ W60744/W60745/W60735/W60645/W60090 plus power cars W60091/W60095/W60097 and W60099.

Former LMR and later WR Bristol/Oxford power car W60091 and set at Old Oak Common. Whilst we know in the very last months an LMR power car could run attached to a WR eight-car set, there is no evidence that the former LMR sets ever worked on the 'South Wales Pullman' duty although three of the former LMR powers certainly did, attached to the ends of former WR 8-car sets. *Neil Ruffles*

It is interesting to note that at the end, power cars W60096 and W60097 had run some 450,000 and 445,000 miles respectively since their last heavy overhauls six years earlier, an average of around 74,500 miles per annum (likely to have been more, dependent upon when they last worked).

The last power cars to have heavy overhauls in March 1970 were also the oldest vehicles in the fleet, the ex LMR Nos W60090 and W60091 which had each run 180,000 miles in just over two years.

Rather than despatch the vehicles for scrap immediately, with no potential interested buyer found it appears they were 'withdrawn – but stored' at this stage.

In *Traction* magazine (July 2002 edition) Adrian Curtis interviewed Mike Stephens, head of the WR's Shopping Control Office at the time, who recalled that a complete

The Blue Pullman Story

ABOVE Former LMR power car W60091 stored at Old Oak. The vertical streaks down the side of the power car may well be oil stains blown from the exhaust. *Derek Everson*

RIGHT From the rust on the rail surface it appears to be some time since this particular vehicle, W60090, moved. Is that a cover on the left-hand light? A replacement cover for the middle air horn has been fitted, clearly these were being 'lost' on a regular basis.

breakdown of the condition of all the sets was required very quickly as again there was a potential buyer from abroad (no details given) but this came to nothing.

W60092 also was seen 'poking its nose out' at Cardiff Canton a few weeks later on 24 June 1973 presumably with the rest of the set still behind it. A couple of weeks later on 10 July 1973, eight-car set W60096/W60647/W60737/W60747/W60743/W60742/W60731 and W60093 was photographed at Marsh Junction by David Gilbert.

The first power cars to be officially withdrawn were Nos W60095 and W60099, both former original WR stock, seen parked nose to nose at Old Oak Common on 11 August 1973. It also appears that for several months afterwards a potential resurrection for use was a considered possibility. Perhaps this was also the reason the Bristol set were moved to open store at Swindon where there was less likelihood of damage. Most surprisingly, this was being considered by BR itself – even if this contradicted their own recent conclusions that there was no place for the Pullman to run parallel with trains made up of new Mark 2 coaching stock.

How this twist came about is referred to in a memorandum from the Executive Director (Passenger) to the Chief Executive (Railways), at BR Headquarters dated 3 September 1973 – four months after the last service. The first sentence reveals everything: 'Bearing in mind the difficult situation for Type 4 locomotives likely to arise this winter, I have been considering further the possibility of making use of the Pullman trains now awaiting disposal after displacement from WR services.' The '… difficult situation …' referred to was of the railway's own doing and had been created by the wholesale withdrawal of various former WR diesel-hydraulic classes. The 'Warship' classes had gone by the end of 1972, with considerable inroads having been made into the 'Hymek' class and the first 'Westerns' were already laid aside.

The note continued with a proposal to reconstitute two Pullman sets, augmented to nine cars each in the following formation: Motor-Parlour-Parlour-Kitchen-Parlour-Parlour-Parlour-Parlour-Motor. (Just the one kitchen car is mentioned so it was likely to be run as an ordinary train and certainly not with Pullman type catering.) A projected seating capacity of 294 was given, 204 of which would have been second-class. As this was only a proposal no specific vehicle numbers were given but we obviously conclude they would be chosen 'from the best of a bad lot'. We might also say there is an interesting parallel to the similar ideas of varying rake suggestions made back in 1966.

The report included an assessment that it would take three months to prepare the trains for their new use, and although no costs were mentioned, it was admitted that necessary 'heavy expenditure], would be required. Their intended use was also given, ironically between Paddington and Birmingham, but with no further elaboration. Two other comments from the note are also interesting; the first was that if the trains were required for only a limited period of regular use, a smaller amount of work on them might suffice. It was also stated that, 'Renovating the sets might then open the way for their use for high quality excursion work, again involving relatively low annual mileage – Scotland for example'. All these comments are worthy of further discussion, the three-month timescale in particular. The report as we know was dated September 1973, hence if the anticipated motive power situation was due to occur in the coming winter, the three-month timescale necessary to get the sets ready for use would mean they would not have been available until half way through the winter timetable anyway. The mention of Scotland and tourist work is a pleasing and perhaps underestimated idea; we will never know just how popular this type of Pullman tour might have been – *again apart from with two American ladies at least!* (But consider again for a moment how the trains might have fared on some of the Scottish gradients.)

Further correspondence on the topic does exist. This is dated a fraction more than two weeks later on 20 September, and expands slightly on the earlier note, referring this time to the creation of four sets, each of nine vehicles, two to be ready in January/February 1974 and the remaining two in March. This time a cost of £200,000 is quoted (basically similar to the renovation costs quoted at the time of Yugoslav/Greek discussion and obtained, it was stated, verbally, from BREL). It was also acknowledged that costs would rise due to, 'vandalism and ageing of equipment' while in storage. It was also suggested that one of the four should be kept as a spare.

This was confidential at the time but it did eventually leak out some time later in June 1974 when the *Railway Observer* reported that Nos W60644/W60645/W60646/W60647/W60648/W60649 and W60731 were 'to be retained for development purposes', although as we know that did not occur.

Clearly, there was other paperwork (not located) as there is mention of the preparation of timings over the proposed Birmingham route. There is also an acknowledgement that the sets in a 2+7 formation would be likely to be poor timekeepers. Elsewhere, there is mention of further difficulties with the sets not being cleared to run into Birmingham New Street – *but we know one had on the last day Safari!* It was as though some factions were already against a resurrection (perhaps hardly surprising), as the difficulties it seems were being accentuated rather than there being a will to succeed.

This scepticism is borne out in a reference to the renovation of the sets and where it should take place. 'Presumably BREL would carry out the work at Swindon, which has traditionally dealt with them, although I must point out that this will certainly pose industrial relations problems due to the agreed run-down of facilities at that works'.

Swindon did not finally close in 1986 but it becomes clear that the decision to do so had been taken at least twelve years prior to this. It was also noted that while servicing could be carried out at the Pullman shed at Old Oak Common, this very facility was shortly to be used for maintaining the prototype (diesel) HSDT and the gas turbine APT-E set and it was considered that, '. . . there would certainly be a risk to running both forms of traction which I would not be prepared to take'. This last comment is difficult to comprehend, and can only be seen as another obstruction to the re-introduction of the trains.

First class saloon on the final day 5 May 1973. Maybe not a professional image but useful for showing the condition within after almost 13 years of service. *John Morgan*

One thought is that the reverse livery was now carried by the HSDT prototype and silver/blue on the APT-E so having the aged Blue Pullman sets in the same livery may have detracted from the image of the new technology. Colour schemes should have had no bearing on whether to renovate the train but who knows what was going on in the minds of some at the time.

Finally, what of the comment about running the sets between Paddington and Birmingham? Were the principal services on this route not concentrated on Euston, the former WR line via High Wycombe having been reduced to a secondary service? What also of the possible involvement of and views of the LMR? None of these issues was addressed in any of the papers.

In the event it was all irrelevant and for whatever reason (although it appears from later notes that industrial relations were again the main sticking point) the trains were not reintroduced. Instead they remained in store, suffering from the ageing and vandalism that had been referred to, until, eventually, scrapping was the only option.

There were, though, two straws still in the wind. The first was a chance they might have been saved for overseas service nearer to the UK for, according to the *Irish Railfans News* Vol 19 No 4, for November 1973. 'The Irish national rail and bus operator Córas Iompair Éireann gave "serious consideration" to acquiring (and so, by implication, regauging) the Blue Pullman sets but ultimately decided against it.' https://en.wikipedia.org/wiki/British_Rail_Classes_251_and_261 - cite_note-7

Meanwhile the vandalism and indeed deterioration referred to by the BR hierarchy had indeed occurred as witnessed in contemporary reports, this from 'Sir Bob' on the Wigan World forum: 'In about 1973-74 in my train spotting days I was having a jaunt in London, going to the Old Oak Common Rail Depot in West London, which covered the Western Region of the then British Rail. There I was expecting to find a horde of diesel-hydraulic locos,

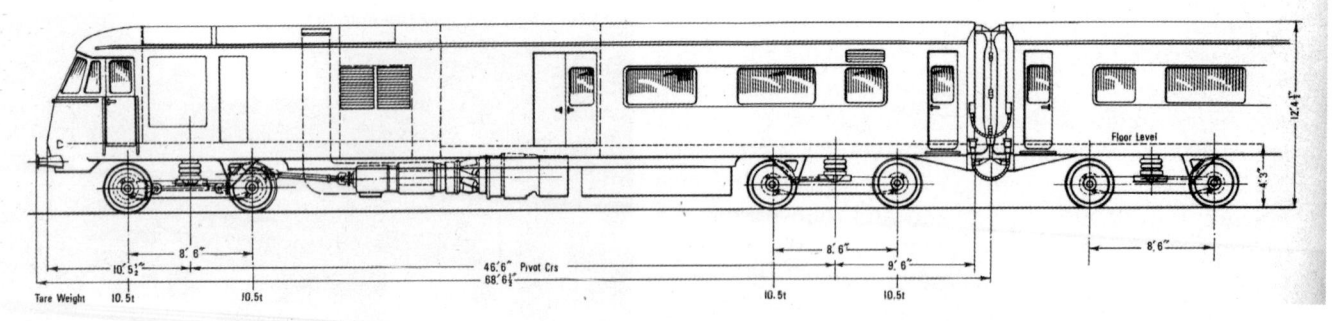

The 1968 proposal for conversion of a BP set to gas-turbine propulsion with mechanical transmission running on lightweight Budd bogies. BP would have been an ideal candidate although the choice of mechanical transmission was probably for cheapness rather than long term practicality. (The later BR Gas Turbine prototype APT which used gas turbines delivered their power via traction motors.) Mention is made of the use of a Rolls-Royce Dart turbine producing 1,500 hp – presumably one in each power car – which then also obviated the need for an auxiliary engine. With an improved power to weight ratio, just 42 tons now for the power car compared with the existing 67.5 tons, and each intermediate vehicle running on lighter bogies and without the weight of the auxiliary engine, an eight-car set would produce 3,000hp for a tare weight of around 260 tons. The potential then for speed and probably an improved ride was considerable. Little other than what has already been published has been discovered on this idea although we know Rolls-Royce were keen on sponsorship, that is until rising fuel costs vetoed the proposal. In developing its own gas turbine APT only a few years later, BR probably felt it was easier to start with a clean sheet rather than attempt to effect the modification of an existing unit.

which would have included "Western" and "Warship" classes of locos. I also found the recently withdrawn Class 251 and 261 Pullman units which were on a siding in the depot. Myself and the friend I was with boarded one of these trains and there we found the luxury Pullman interiors. We walked along the train and came to the Restaurant Car and entered the kitchen part of the car. The way it had been left made it obvious that the train had done its last journey, as the kitchen contained rotting food and dirty crockery and cutlery. From what we saw it was plain that after the last meals were served on the train the staff had not even bothered to wash up or throw away any unwanted food items. It was disgusting and obvious that these trains were going to be scrapped, but at the time this was not reported in contemporary railway magazines. The kitchen did look filthy with ingrained grease and grime over everything and I suppose people who leave food to rot like that, will not have been much cleaner in their everyday work practice. And this was a "Pullman" train, supposedly a high quality, high class service.'

Joseph Pestell on RM Web had a similar experience: 'I was never much of a shed basher but I did tag along on our school rail club's (916 club) outings. We did OOC while the Blue Pullmans were there in 1974 and were allowed to have our lunch sitting in them. We had to remove broken glass from the seats! Would never happen these days!'

Nick Tozer was able to get some photos of the stock and even cabbed a power car, noting the smashed and vandalised driver's desk. Nigel Ratledge also got in the cab and recalls the smell being akin to musty old books left in the damp.

This was also around the period of the infamous power-cuts associated with industrial disputes and the 'three-day week' from 31 December 1973 to March 1974. Accordingly certain redundant power and auxiliary power cars were stationed at Bristol Bath Road, Bristol Temple Meads and Cardiff to act as emergency generators. Cardiff had trailers W60648 and W60649 whilst Bristol Bath Road had power car W60093 and trailer W60731.

Jon Porter saw W60096 run under its own power at Bristol Bath Road on 13 January 1974 (was this the last time a power car ran?) before being shunted into the fish dock by a Class 03.

Stabled at Platform 4 of the neighbouring Bristol Temple Meads station were W60096 and W60647, where Michael Pember recalls: 'I was 12 and had started train spotting in 1973. My gramp brought me the *Railway Magazine*. That had regional reports in the rear of the magazine with readers' info so I was aware the Pullmans were finished. I knew Tri-ang Hornby did a model of them in the last livery. Then during the miners' strike in Feb 1974 a power car, W60096, and another car, W60647, were used at Bristol Temple Meads. They were parked in the fish dock in the station (where the 'King' No 6023 sat for a year or two). I was surprised to see them there and thought it unusual that a trailer was kept with a power car. I was with a group of local lads and we were amazed the trailer was unlocked when we went to look. It was a horrible cold day and we thought we would sit inside as we had a view of coming and goings . . . but it had a rancid stink. The smell was the damp smell similar to the one in your car when the air con is broken. We walked through to the power car and then got out.'

Dave Redfern travelled from the opposite platforms and also noted the Pullmans in Platform 4. From Cattle Market Road looking up at the part of the platform that sits on a bridge over the road the front half of a dirty W60096 was visible.

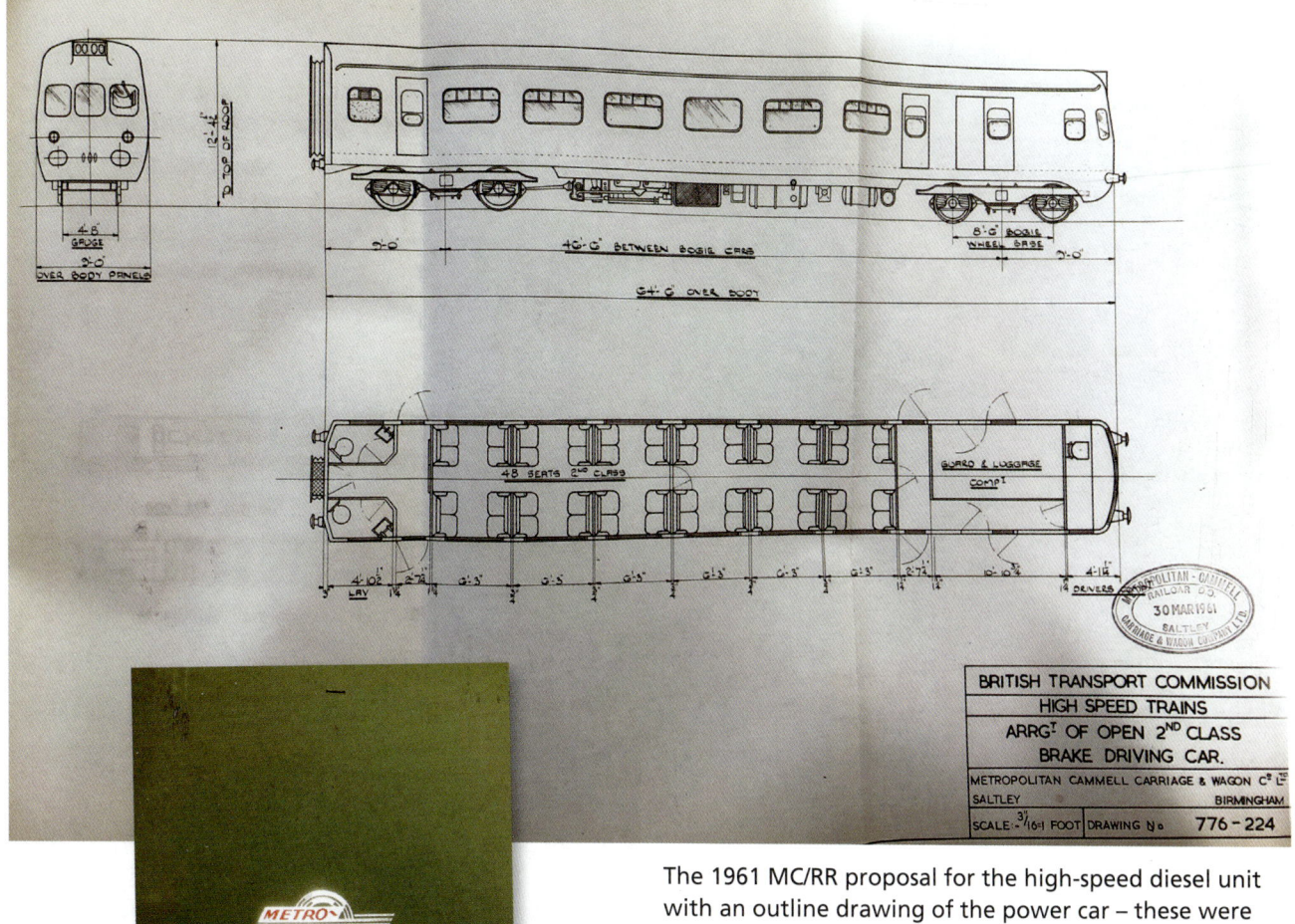

The 1961 MC/RR proposal for the high-speed diesel unit with an outline drawing of the power car – these were common in design to both the six- and eight-car units. But it is definitely in need of some attention in the front-end design!

Dave Harris spotted W60647/W60731 and W60091, although we think the latter was a mistaken identity and was actually W60093, at Bristol Marsh Junction. He took a silver menu folder as a souvenir from the kitchen car and remembers seeing the Bristolians had kedgeree on offer for the last day!

Still, though, there was one very last ray of hope and the subject of a widely reported preservation attempt on another of the sets. This was reported upon in the *Railway Magazine* for July 1975: 'Ten Blue Pullman carriages, withdrawn from service by the Western Region in May 1973, have been saved from scrap by a private group with the principal intention of making a train of six or more of them available for charter over British Railways. They comprise the first two (and the last surviving) of the diesel-electric motor brake firsts Nos W60090/1, two kitchen firsts M60731/3, and six parlour seconds W60644-9. All are to be towed to BRE Glasgow workshops for complete renovation and repainting in the "Nanking Blue" livery carried when they were supplied by Metropolitan-Cammell in 1960. Because the number of drivers experienced in their operation is limited, initially operations will be limited to the WR, probably from sidings rented from BR, but they could eventually be accommodated at a preservation centre when not on main line charter work. To assist in

On 24 March 1974 W60096 was seen with the trailer on the other side of the station. When in use as standby power generators at Bristol etc., the reason for having two cars at each location was that the power cars were the only ones with normal couplings but it was the second vehicle at each end of the set that contained the three-phase alternator, powered by the 180bhp Rolls-Royce engine. This tends to imply that they were shunted into position rather than by being moved using the actual power cars. Whether any, or all, were used for their intended power-generation purpose during the dispute is not certain.

Shortly afterwards Keith Riley spotted W60096/W60742/W60743/W60747/60737 and W60093 (so missing the two generator standbys) a few lines away from the platforms at the station. Later, on 16 April 1974

305

The dream that literally faded: a WR eight-car train in very close to as-new condition but with the typical windscreen wiper trait visible of 'flying off at an angle' Part of the appeal of the new trains was, undoubtedly, the striking colour scheme of Nanking Blue body-work with white window surrounds. This was surmounted by a specially redesigned Pullman coat of arms, and shaded, Egyptian slab-serif lettering, the whole very different from the traditional umber associated with Pullman vehicles up until that time. By comparison, the remains of this 'Midland Pullman' poster were discovered in a disused underground tube tunnel at Euston half a century after the service had ceased to operate on the LMR.

maintenance, the Blue Pullman Group is seeking official drawings, circuit diagrams, running manuals and so forth, which might now be in the hands of collectors.'

It should be remembered that this was a period when the private use of steam locomotives on BR was banned and it would also be many years before a privately owned diesel would be permitted.

At such a recent point in the Blue Pullman story, it might be expected that information on the preservation attempt would be easy to locate, but again the reverse is the case. No details have come to light about the preservationists referred to in the *Railway Magazine*, nor how close they might have come to achieving their aim. Some years later Doug Parfitt wrote to the contact address given in the RM but to no avail.

Another suggestion from the same period was that power car W60091 alone would be saved by an organisation called the 'Blue Pullman Group' (the same name as the group in the *Railway Magazine* article so perhaps the original ambitious aims had of necessity been reduced from a train to single car?). It seems quite strange that W60091 was considered given it was stored early with backlash in the valve timing gears.

By the end of May 1974, though, the vehicles were truly entering their last chapter, some literally ending their short life at this time. The trains were now sold off as scrap to Birds of Morriston (near Swansea) and Cardiff. Investigation had shown the cars all contained a large quantity of blue and white asbestos, which back in the 1950s was still the preferred material used for insulation, hence this had delayed the sale. Due to their condition some were impounded at Cardiff Ninian Park Sidings after which it appears they were sold on to two local yards, George Cohen's (600 Group) of Morriston and Thomas W. Ward's in Briton Ferry. Moving forward, the activities of the scrappers over the years led to curious repercussions later as land that had been used was found to have been contaminated at both sites.

Whether Messrs Birds initially took the vehicles and then deliberately sold some on in the course of business

It was surely not beyond the wit of man to find a viable use for the trains post 1973. Preservation was a hoped for but perhaps not really practical solution but as a cross-country service, demoted from Pullman, refurbished perhaps to give a greater emphasis to second class and with just a single restaurant/kitchen car and enhanced luggage accommodation, the opportunity for a longer life must have been available. If it were possible to challenge the then management of BR (not just the Western Region), no doubt the response would have been that the trains needed considerable maintenance/overhaul. But who was to blame for this? Surely BR themselves for running down that very same maintenance over several years. Concentrating all five sets – four perhaps if one was even to be cannibalised for spares – and maybe even making four six-coach trains, it was to many an opportunity lost. Neither is this just a rose-tinted view of what might have been, for at least one unfortunately un-named official was heard to comment along the lines of, 'We got it wrong somewhere, there must surely have been an alternative to withdrawal and scrap.' This is Paddington and the arrival of a set in what has to be the better of the two liveries carried. *The Transport Treasury*

Jack Hancock's view of a WR set at Ryecroft shed in Walsall. This was the occasion of a visit on 14 March 1964 on a football special. Even a decidedly wet day cannot diminish the impact of the train.

or whether it was for work load or asbestos reasons they were moved around is not known. What we do know is the scrap value in 1970 was just £48,000 for all 36 vehicles. Maybe in 1970 it would have been better to have reduced the price to Yugoslavia (or anybody!) by a substantial sum after all and retained a few hundred thousand pounds.

Inflation in the early 1970s was such that by 1973 £48,000 would equate to over £63,000 but there is no record of the actual amount paid by Birds nor the sell-on prices to Cohens or Wards. In 2019 this would represent about £20,000 per vehicle. However BR paperwork from 1973 still refers to the scrap value as having been the original £48,000.

In the event, 14 were sold to George Cohens (600 Group). With W60648 and W60649 at Cardiff as generators the remaining vehicles at Swindon – W60098/W60738/W60748/W60749/W60739/W60092 – were hauled away on 22 May 1974 to the scrapyard at Morriston.

Amusingly Jerry Howlett recalls: 'The Swindon Shed foreman rushed out with the Blue Pullman's brass EP starter keys that had been hanging on an anglepoise desk light for a months as he thought "They might need them" – this as the lifeless and now dirty grey Pullman set was dragged off to the scrapyard by a Class 37'.

On 13 July 1974 the power cars used as generators also left for Morriston along with some trailers. This time the formation was W60093/W60742/W60743/W60737/W60747/W60096 and W60093, which could later just be seen from the outside from passing trains under the bridge leading into Cohens. Pictures of the scrap vehicles in this position taken on 3 January 1975 by Rev. M. R Connop-Price later appeared on page 185 of the April edition of *Railway Magazine*.

Graham Court was 16 at the time and had seen the article. He deliberately travelled to Swansea then walked back to find the scrapyard which was located on the defunct branch line that ran from the docks to Morriston East. Beaufort Road ran next to the River Tawe and there was a small bridge over the river that led to the scrapyard where Graham was welcomed by the staff and recorded his visit by taking photos.

Mike Floate and his pal Peter Moore also purchased seats from Cohens Scrapyard: 'We bought first class seats from a massive pile for £5 each which we loaded into Pete's old van. The ex LMR power car was up against the fence. I did all my degree work sat in mine and now have it in my summerhouse where I enjoy my retirement. It is also the single most comfortable seat I ever sat in.'

Jeremy Turner remembers travelling in and out of Swansea on the train and says, 'Not far away on the train out of Swansea just after the metal bridge you could see more Pullman vehicles in Cohen's yard at Morriston with a jumper-cabled power car near the entrance'. (This was W60093.)

307

ABOVE Llanharen bank west of Cardiff with the westbound Pullman on the final leg of its journey to Neath and Swansea. In the immediately foreground is an occupation crossing where, according to the photographer, a farmer had just shepherded a flock of sheep across the line without seemingly taking the trouble to advise the signalman! In general terms the reported behaviour of some of the most senior members of staff on British Railways must also be called into question at times; likewise Sir John Elliot – in the case of the latter might it simply have been almost a last chance at wielding power and influence? *Alan Jarvis/ Stephenson Locomotive Society*

LEFT Again the final day enthusiast special: LMR power car heading up the eight-car set. Appropriately as well, it is at Platform 1 at Paddington. *John Morgan*

RIGHT May 1963, apart from the air horn covers – again – an otherwise pristine set runs through Twyford westbound. Just a decade later the trains would be no more. Students of contemporary WR diesel history will be aware that certain other WR diesel classes had similar engines to BP – but not believed to have been interchangeable. The engines on BP were basically reliable, far more so than the MAN engines built in the UK. BPs engines had a builder's plate attached with the simple initials 'M.A.N.' The engines built at NBL had the initials 'N.B.L.-M.A.N.' *Mike Morant collection*

Old Oak Common, old (right) and new liveries on display in the depot. Unfortunately we are still no closer to knowing what the notice on the buffet stop set reads!

Mike Smith also has a fully working first class seat with antimacassar, a venetian blind winder, kitchen car build plate and ashtray which came from long term Bluebell Railway alumni Tony Harris who recalls his own trip to the scrapyard at Morriston. 'It was after a day that had been spent recovering spares for Maunsell coaches in the scrapyard in the winter's cold and gloom and I was knackered. Two Pullman units were standing at the far side of the yard and had been mostly stripped internally by this time. The manager of the scrapyard said that some of the hardwood panelling, tables and fittings had been recovered and sold to luxury yacht builders. A lot of the seats were in store and he was seeking buyers such as cinemas or theatres. Perhaps there are some around in a cinema somewhere? The bodies were still intact awaiting cutting up, but I think valuable/saleable parts like the engines, control gear and electric motors had been stripped out. We (about six members of the raiding party) asked the manager if it was possible to buy a seat? He said £10 each, choose from the seats still in the units. I have this lasting memory of individuals staggering about 300 yards across heaps of scrap metal each carrying a Pullman seat in the gloom of a winter's evening, encouraged by the shouts of the other members of the party (what on earth are you doing?!?) and the scrap yard people who just wanted to lock up and go home for the night. We could only just lift these seats – Blue Pullman seats are incredibly heavy – we joked afterwards that only BR could make cast aluminium that was heavy! The next challenge was to find space and weight distribution in already overloaded transport. Six made it back to the Bluebell Railway to be utilised as mess room seating but I know some were thrown out after a while. I also saved an ashtray and blind winder from the floor and a couple of antimacassars plus a Met-Camm build plate from a kitchen car. I am told I must have saved more parts from a Blue Pullman than anybody else in the world. That's a nice thought 45 years on!'

Tantalisingly ex emergency generators W60731 and W60647 were moved to Cohens of Morriston where they were buried on their sides around July 1975.

Mike Smith obtained his own second class seat, removed from power car W60096, directly from Lee Hanford who worked for George Cohen's and Lee also took him to the site where the last two coaches were buried.

Lee comments: 'Some of these Pullman sets were scrapped at George Cohen's at Morriston. I worked there as a moulder in the iron foundry. The Managing Director was Colin Maliphant (sadly no longer with us). I used to socialise with him quite often at the original Woodfield club in Morriston where he was chairman for many years. He had two of the seats removed from the Pullman cars and used them in his office, one being trimmed in black leather and the other left as original. He knew I had an interest in the Pullman cars so he offered one to me. I clearly remember that two coaches were left in the yard for a very long period due to problems with the removal of the blue asbestos cladding present. One of the foremen in the yard, a Mr Gordon Bennett (yes really), who I knew very well, informed me that two large holes were excavated and they were simply buried on their sides at the back end of the yard.'

Going back in time to Old Oak Common the *Railway Observer* reported in the September 1974 edition that the following vehicles went extant to OOC in July 1974:

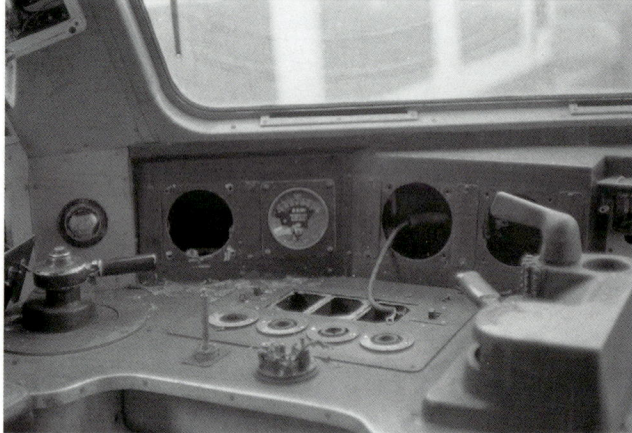

ABOVE RIGHT A final visit to the Pullman shed on 26 July 1974. Power cars Nos 60091 and 60099 have had their engines removed prior to scrap.

ABOVE LEFT Old Oak Common, W60091. *Nick Tozer*

LEFT Vandalised instrument panel of W60091. Official or otherwise? *Nick Tozer*

BELOW Eight-car set outside Swindon works alongside the main running lines, 11 May 1974, more than a year since the final public runs. Was it here for evaluation, pending sale to somebody, or simply stored? *John Tolson/The Transport Treasury*

Old Oak Common in May 1973 with two sets visible; unfortunately details of either are not given. The railway press seems to have almost completely ignored the demise of the trains. Little if any mention appears in Railway Magazine and instead in the July 1973 issue the only reference appears to be the car numbers being shown as 'Withdrawn'. Modern Railways was the same, but then contrary to the name of the magazine, Pullman was yesterday's train and all talk was now towards HST/APT and air-conditioned services. The set nearest the camera had been used on the final special run.

Power cars W60090/W60091/W60094/W60095/W60097/W60099;
Trailers W60730/W60732/W60734/W60735/W60736/W60740/W60741/W60744/W60745/W60746.

Of these Nos W60099 and W60091 were in the Pullman Shed on 26 July 1974 and the other vehicles were stored outside on 31 July 1974.

With the exception of W60090 and W60091 all these vehicles went straight to Briton Ferry via Gloucester and Mark Alden witnessed the long train pass close to Tuffey Junction in Gloucester. 'The formation saw a Class 47 pulling the vehicles with a power car either end and two in the middle nose to nose. There was a brake van at the rear and these scrap runs were classed as 9X. Consequently they were not allowed to run through the Severn Tunnel and had to go the long way via Gloucester.'

The units were seen first at Briton Ferry in the sidings near the station partly covered by a tarpaulin. There are three reliable sightings of Blue Pullman vehicles partly covered by tarpaulins being moved through the night.

So why the covers? Were BR so embarrassed at their early scrapping that they wanted to keep it as quiet as possible? Unlikely, for they were happy to leave disgustingly unclean Pullman vehicles visible in Bristol Temple Meads and in sidings. The scrapyard workers spoken to certainly do not recall any arriving with tarpaulins.

Upon arrival the two 'sets' were certainly separated as the first was then shunted out of the sidings at Briton Ferry towards the scrapyard across the Port Wallaroo crossing at Church Street and under the A40 road bridge before coming to a halt by a grassy hill called the Warren.

Robert Thomas came across this set with W60094 at the back (the very power car Robert saw in service on 2 May 1973 and one that was part of the last day Safari set). By now of course the windows were smashed and the damaged venetian blinds were sitting at various angles. The access line to Wards then had a horseshoe shape around the base of the hill and once around the bend would run back towards Neath along the riverside past the alloys works and into the breakers yard. Here there was an extremely sharp horseshoe bend as the land jutted inwards and large ships were often docked in the opening and cut up there. Schoolboy Andrew Lane and his Dad saw the set parked up by the River Neath. Andrew says, 'The set was partially under the A48 bridge but stopped before the entrance of the alloy works. We walked through the set from power car to power car and were surprised at these

311

modern luxury units being trashed and seeing the luxury fittings covered in litter and broken glass.'

Robert Thomas says 'I went back and saw a pile of seats and asked if they could cut a deal for use at the Rugby Club but the asking price of £10 per seat (around £95 today) was way too much for our purposes.'

Alan Williams was in his 20s and worked for T. W. Ward for 13 years until the yard closed. He worked on the scrapping of many ships and railway vehicles. Alan recalls: 'The first of the Blue Pullman vehicles arrived from British Rail and then they were moved into the scrapyard by Ward's own shunter. They were lifted off the tracks by crane and put in a corner of the yard.' Alan's last job of the day was to set the vehicles alight and leave them to burn themselves out. The power cars had arrived engineless but still there was a lot of wood to burn out of the coaches. As the yard was quite full 14 vehicles minus bogies were then taken by crane out of the yard to waste ground near to where the access line curved around, doubling back on itself. The bend of the horseshoe is next to the old Tinworks engine house on the bank of the River Neath and the second set joined them making a total of four ex-Western power cars and 10 coaches.

These scrap Blue Pullmans were observed, explored and filmed by the then 11-year-old schoolboy Jeremy Turner and his younger brother Dominic who were regularly taken by their parents and Grandad to see the ships and railway vehicles being scrapped. Jeremy says: 'I had seen these "long" DMUs with rounded ends before running past my Grandparent's house in Briton Ferry and I had no idea they were near the end of life being so modern looking. I also didn't know the Pullmans were once Nanking Blue and two sets had been on the Midland route. During our summer holiday in 1974 we could see some Pullman cars amongst the goods vehicles in Briton Ferry Sidings but the next day they were gone so we followed the access line across Church Street to see where they had ended up. The access line went under the A48 road bridge and turned diagonally right heading towards the tinworks and the River Neath. Just about where the M4 support pillars are now it would bend back round to head along the riverside. We were very surprised to see all 14 Pullman vehicles (five first class parlour cars, five first class kitchen cars and four power cars) part way round the bend where the substation is now. On further inspection you could see some had been de-railed on the way round but still had their bogies. We went back over the next couple of days and the Pullmans had been removed from the rails and lifted on to the waste ground but without their bogies. This waste land was fully accessible to the public with none of today's Health and Safety precautions whereas Ward's yard was pretty hard to access with huge ships and railway wagons being scrapped riverside. Back on the grassy wasteland the stranded Pullmans were a truly amazing sight. The condition of the units varied and some had been damaged by the crane lifting them on to the ground. They still looked modern to me and it was incredible to walk all the way through them. They still had most of their seats and fittings in but they had vandal damage such as broken windows with some smelling musty and smoky but a couple seemed ok. The kitchen cars were a complete mess with pots, pans, utensils, cutlery and broken crockery everywhere. There was lots of stuff we could have taken but we didn't have permission so we left everything as it was. The four power cars had no engines in; there were lots of wires and electrical equipment. I clearly recall going into one cab and it all appeared to be in good condition with its windows intact. I really wanted to press the starter button to see what happened! The two power cars on the left were facing us, then the coaches lined up and then another two power cars facing away. The line-up was at 90 degrees to the track. On the next school holidays they were still there complete but burnt out and getting rusty. The next trip saw the power cars cut down to their frames and some coaches were burnt but were not cut yet. I, like the units, was completely gutted. There was one cab cut in half on its side and a windscreen in perfect order lay there unsmashed. I wanted to take it home but it was too big. There were also strands of blue asbestos everywhere, on the floor and on the bushes'.

The *Railway Observer* for December 1974 reported a further sighting of some withdrawn vehicles from 29 September: power cars W60090/W60091 now at Birds Cardiff together with W60644/W60645/W60646/W60733/W60648/W60649/W60731.

Nos W60090 and W60091 were taken to Briton Ferry sidings around December 1974 where they stayed until eventually they were moved into T. W. Ward's riverside site for cutting in May 1976 (as mentioned earlier these were the two power cars earmarked for saving by the Blue Pullman Group). Jeremy Turner recalls: 'In the Christmas holidays of 1974 we saw two power cars in the sidings adjacent to the main line in Briton Ferry and filmed them from the road as we passed them. The two power cars had jumper cables and were in the sidings for a long time after. By now the sidings were much less busy and the power cars could be seen clearly with broken windows. 'They were there for months and months but eventually disappeared so we took a walk down the canal path and could see them inside T. W. Ward's riverside site. Eventually they seemed to be amongst other scrap piled around them and they were certainly still there in Easter 1976.'

Alan Williams remembers these last two power cars stayed basically intact for quite a while as fresh scrap came in and was dumped on top of and around the two vehicles. Once the units were ready for cutting, the Ward cutters would reduce them to 5ft by 2ft sections as this was the ideal size for the furnace.

Neath railway man Mike Buton recalls being transferred to Swansea Street in 1975 during the re-organisation of railway signalling. He recalls that whilst working at Swansea Dock and Burrows signal box he used the Dan-Y-Graig depot's shunters mess room in which there were two Blue Pullman chairs. From the mess hut it was possible to see a few reverse livery Blue Pullman coaches stabled in

Scrap Yard Pictorial

THIS PAGE AND OVERLEAF It still seems hard to comprehend that the journey from luxury train to hunks of scrap was less than half the lifespan originally intended. Had one of the sets managed to linger on towards its more anticipated life it is very likely one at least would have been saved. We can only imagine the feelings of those whose work had contributed to such a luxury product if they viewed it again in a sea of scrap. *Graham Court*

The Blue Pullman Story

Scrap Yard Pictorial

314

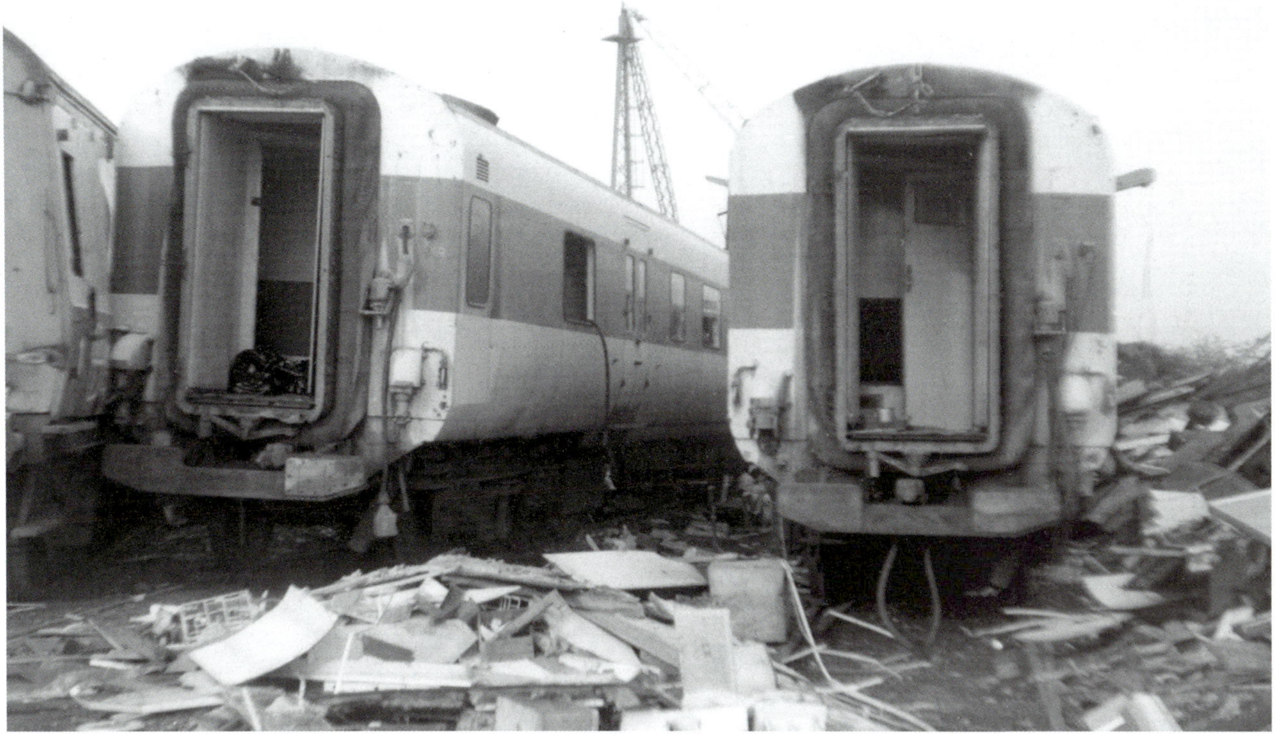

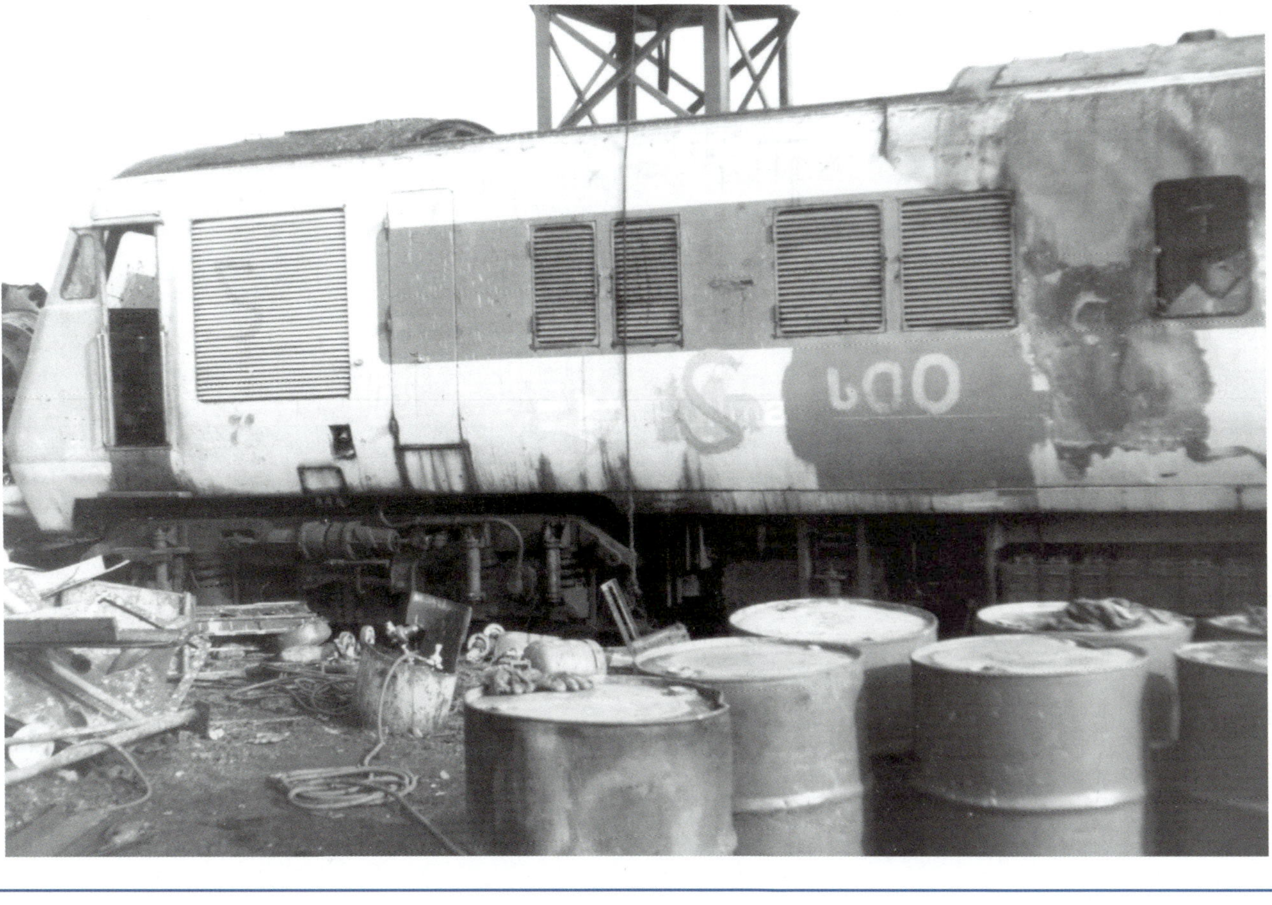

	Metropolitan-Cammell	Pullman	DMBSL
60090	11.59	5.73	T. W. Ward, Briton Ferry 5.76
60091	11.59	5.73	T. W. Ward, Briton Ferry 5.76
60092	11.59	5.73	G. Cohen, Morriston 5.74
60093	11.59	5.73	G. Cohen, Morriston 5.74

	Metropolitan-Cammell	Pullman	DMBS
60094	2.60	5.73	T. W. Ward, Briton Ferry 7.74
60095	2.60	5.73	T. W. Ward, Briton Ferry 7.74
60096	4.60	5.73	G. Cohen, Morriston 5.74
60097	4.60	5.73	T. W. Ward, Briton Ferry 7.74
60098	5.60	5.73	G. Cohen, Morriston 5.74
60099	5.60	5.73	T. W. Ward, Briton Ferry 7.74

	Metropolitan-Cammell	Pullman	MPSL
60644	2.60	5.73	G. Cohen, Morriston 5.75 OR Bird Group, Cardiff 5.76
60645	2.60	5.73	G. Cohen, Morriston 5.75 OR Bird Group, Cardiff 5.76
60646	4.60	5.73	G. Cohen, Morriston 5.75 OR Bird Group, Cardiff 5.76
60647	4.60	5.73	G. Cohen, Morriston 7.75
60648	5.60	5.73	G. Cohen, Morriston 5.75 OR Bird Group, Cardiff 5.76
60649	5.60	5.73	G. Cohen, Morriston 5.75 OR Bird Group, Cardiff 5.76

	Metropolitan-Cammell	Pullman	MSLRK
60730	11.59	5.73	T. W. Ward, Briton Ferry 7.74
60731	11.59	5.73	G. Cohen, Morriston 7.75
60732	11.59	5.73	T. W. Ward, Briton Ferry 7.74
60733	11.59	5.73	G. Cohen, Morriston 5.75 OR Bird Group, Cardiff 5.76

	Metropolitan-Cammell	Pullman	TFLK
60734	2.60	5.73	T. W. Ward, Briton Ferry 7.74
60735	2.60	5.73	T. W. Ward, Briton Ferry 7.74
60736	4.60	5.73	T. W. Ward, Briton Ferry 7.74
60737	4.60	5.73	G. Cohen, Morriston 7.74
60738	5.60	5.73	G. Cohen, Morriston 5.74
60739	5.60	5.73	G. Cohen, Morriston 5.74

	Metropolitan-Cammell	Pullman	TPFL
60740	11.59	5.73	T. W. Ward, Briton Ferry 7.74
60741	11.59	5.73	T. W. Ward, Briton Ferry 7.74
60742	11.59	5.73	G. Cohen, Morriston 7.74
60743	11.59	5.73	G. Cohen, Morriston 7.74
60744	2.60	5.73	T. W. Ward, Briton Ferry 7.74
60745	2.60	5.73	T. W. Ward, Briton Ferry 7.74
60746	4.60	5.73	T. W. Ward, Briton Ferry 7.74
60747	4.60	5.73	G. Cohen, Morriston 5.74
60748	5.60	5.73	G. Cohen, Morriston 5.74
60749	5.60	5.73	G. Cohen, Morriston 5.74

the Burrow sidings waiting to be scrapped. The remaining BP vehicles appear to have been 'ringfenced' both here and at Cardiff (reportedly for asbestos reasons) whilst records show they were finally scrapped by either Cohen's at Morriston in July 1975 or Bird's at Cardiff in May 1976.

So was the Blue Pullman story one that ended with the premature withdrawal of the trains? Were they really life-expired, given that when first introduced it was predicted that they have a standard 30-year life span and so still be active in 1990? Were there simply too many innovations in the one design? Indeed, was the whole Blue Pullman story actually just a poor business decision?

An independent assessment is really not possible, unless it were to be based purely on subjective opinion. There are several issues to consider; hence it is necessary to refer back briefly to some of the topics discussed previously.

Firstly, there was Pullman itself. Originally an independent company, this autonomy slowly changed with the absorption of Pullman into BR so that by the 1960s the remaining hierarchy at Pullman were almost fighting a rearguard action to both justify their continuation as a separate concern and at the same time promote the Pullman ideal. It may be summed up in an article that appeared in the *Railway Gazette* of 14 June 1963 by E. J. Morris. 'The close liaison which has for years existed between those who cater for Britain's railway travellers has become even more effective since the integration in January of the Pullman Car Company's activities with those of the British Transport Hotels Co. Ltd. Changes on this scale cannot be accomplished overnight, and the full benefits they will bring to day-to-day Pullman operation, in terms of greater efficiency and economy, have yet to be fully realised. Nevertheless, many of the broad advantages of the merger are already apparent – notably the streamlining of management. The process began with the retirement of the board existing in 1962 and the formation, of a smaller board, under Mr. F. G. Hole, who is also the General Manager of the Hotels Company. The re-organisation is cutting out duplication of some behind-the-scenes activities on which the quality of service so largely depends. Pullman laundering, for example, previously carried out in the company's own plant at Battersea, is now done by one of the Hotel Company's main laundries at Willesden. Simplification of victualling arrangements are in hand; the stores depot activities are integrated with the larger unit in the Catering Services organisation. These are some of the initial results of the merger, but the long-term objective is to expand Pullman operations where a demand exists or can be established. The Pullman type of individual seat service will always find favour, especially on the middle- and long-distance trains between London and the provincial centres. It is particularly attractive to the businessman, whose custom the railways are now so vigorously seeking in their drive for viability.

'The hallmark of Pullman service is constant service, provided by a highly trained crew whose object is to ensure the comfort of passengers from the time they reach the train to when they reach their destination. The attendant helping a departing passenger with his coat makes a doubly favourable impression if he follows up with a helping hand at the coach door. It is important that this tradition of personal service, built up over the company's 89 years in Britain, is continued and this will be done by ensuring that every attention, is given to the passenger in a Pullman car.

'The regular Pullman traveller appreciates such attention all the more because it comes from someone he knows, and so far as possible the trains keep the same crews. This results in the atmosphere in many Pullman trains resembling that of a good-class club.

'Attractive features. Although the basic appeal of Pullman travel lies in personal service, speed, reliability, convenient departure times, and that rail termini – unlike most airports – are situated in or near city centres, are equally telling characteristics. The prestige which traditionally attaches to Pullman travel is equally important. Keeping up these high standards, and where possible their improvement, will undoubtedly be a factor in the competitive years ahead of British Railways. The "pulling power" of de-luxe services has been well illustrated by the Blue Pullman diesel units. From the inception of these roughly two years ago *[we may assume Mr Morris really meant three years]*, the streamline blue-and-white liveried trains caught the public's imagination as an example of modern design and good taste in future railway operation. These luxury unit trains were produced in the early phase of railway modernisation and had many new features such as air conditioning, sound insulation, tip-up adjustable seats and double-glazed windows with venetian blinds between the panes. The trains are well suited to regular inter-city 'prestige' travel. Motive power at each end permits a quick turn-round, and a reserve of power enables them to make up time; an exemplary punctuality record has been built up. The two six-car trains are doing brisk business on the London Midland Region's Manchester-St. Pancras route, also fitting in a mid-day run to Nottingham. Three eight-car sets are at present used on the Western Region linking Paddington with Birmingham, Bristol, and South Wales. This enterprise has been worthwhile.

'Future trains are to be locomotive hauled. Lessons learned from operating the Blue Pullman trains indicate that to permit of greater flexibility in train formation, future Pullman trains will be locomotive hauled to meet changes in traffic density. The 44 cars of the more traditional types built by the company since the war have been well received on practical and aesthetic grounds, for excellent riding, and for a combination of the best of the customary Pullman features with modern design and materials. Experience has shown that Pullman cars are most suited to complete train operation, as this enables the conductor to patrol the complete train to ensure that every passenger is receiving individual attention. Fourteen all-Pullman trains are in service; these include the 'Queen of Scots', between King's Cross, Edinburgh, and Glasgow;

the 'Master Cutler' linking Sheffield with London; and a formation which enjoys an international reputation, the 'Golden Arrow', which carries passengers to Dover en route to Paris.'

Regrettably, Mr Morris, though whilst accurate for the time, could not foresee the social changes on the horizon. At a time when utilitarian travel was becoming the norm, the days of Sir John Elliot's 'Gentleman's Club' type vehicle were rapidly fading into history.

On balance, BR was undoubtedly right to attempt to capture the luxury market, but whether using luxury trains with very limited use was the right approach is not so clear-cut. The difficulty in drawing conclusions decades after the demise of the sets, and more than half a century since they were conceived, is that opinions are based on the standards of today.

With hindsight perhaps a better solution would have been to improve a number of front-line services on all lines but in reality this was just not possible. Hampered, as they were, by years of under-investment (a familiar cry today), the luxury train concept would inevitably be restricted, simply because it was required to operate amongst other services on existing tracks, competing with them for space, and taking their share of delays. In the skies perhaps 'Concorde' was another example: a stunning flagship but enjoyed only by the privileged few and which, since its demise, has not resulted in a clamour for equally fast travel but instead for the movement of more of the masses in the same 'cattle-class' discomfort.

However, without realising it at the time and notwithstanding the comments of Mr Morris, BR with its ever increasing fleet of EMU and DMU sets and of course the Blue Pullman trains had shown that the concept of a fixed-formation train was a well-balanced approach, especially at a time when costs were rising and all means had to be found to reduce them. The ability to dispense with shunting movements, so saving on locomotives, staff and turnouts and resulting in quicker turnaround times (exemplified when a spare or replacement set was needed in a hurry) was a factor that was very much in the BP trains' favour.

It is appropriate therefore to now explore the fixed-formation idea further. As far as the LMR is concerned, we should look at something that happened on 13 January 1961. On that day it was reported that the up 'Midland Pullman' had rapidly lost power near Bedford (the actual reason is not known and is irrelevant in the present context, safe to say one of the power cars failed) it resulted in an arrival nine minutes late at St Pancras. It was now after midday, and the return service was due to leave St Pancras for Manchester just six hours later. Meanwhile, the spare set was at Reddish near Manchester, over 180 miles distant, and yet it was immediately sent for. It worked south, and arrived in London in time to be restocked ready to take up the booked return working.

The Western Region too could also rise to the occasion when required, this time at Paddington on 9 February 1962, when the 10.10am 'Bristol Pullman' departure failed after travelling no more than a few yards along the platform. Within just 25 minutes, passengers had been transferred to the diesel Pullman set that had arrived from Swansea, which then managed to regain a further five minutes (net) to Birmingham; this was despite suffering some severe signalling checks due to its path now conflicting with other trains – the BP set now running well out-of-course – as well as coping with a number of temporary speed restrictions.

The other advantage in favour of the fixed formation was its predictable performance. The percentage increase in weight between a part load and a full load was negligible when plotting timetable paths, and compared favourably with the loading variations that applied to the locomotive-hauled services of the period.

Having described best practice, it is only fair to refer to the opposite as well. We know from earlier in this book that 11 April 1963 was a bad day for the WR, as all three of its diesel Pullman sets were out of action for various reasons, resulting in loco haulage of various 'scratch' standby sets. But arguably even worse was the situation that beset Paddington on 1 December 1960, just three months after the publicity surrounding the introduction of the WR service.

On this occasion, the 10.10am 'Bristol Pullman' service consisted of nothing better than ordinary coaching stock that had previously arrived as the 9.38am from Henley-in-Arden. 'Castle' class 4-6-0 5043 *Earl of Mount Edgcumbe* was put in charge, but for unknown reasons managed to lose a further 20 minutes westwards on top of its 10-minute late departure. It was also hauling ordinary – not Pullman – coaching stock.

Finally, it should be said that the Midland lines were not devoid of difficulties either, as on 21 December 1960 the down service from St Pancras was formed of six ordinary coaches and a 'Peak' class diesel! Post September 1961 the WR was perhaps more likely to suffer failures as from that time their three sets were being used far more intensely. The temptation is to look back at the Pullman sets with revered admiration, but we should recall they were certainly not perfect.

Without doubt, the jewel in the crown as far as the WR was concerned was the service to Birmingham and Paddington seemed oblivious to any sensible planning when it came to introducing the new trains to and from Bristol in 1960. The new 110-minute Pullman service to Bristol, on which the supplementary fare was charged, was a whole ten minutes slower than the erstwhile 'Bristolian'. It is true that fears over the behaviour of the 'Warship' class diesels heading the 'Bristolian' later led to the service being slowed to 105 minutes, but pre-service trials had shown that the Pullman sets were easily capable of an 87-minute schedule. Add, say, eight minutes recovery time into the timetable, and the result could have been a very attractive 95 minutes timing – bettering the 'Bristolian' by five minutes.

Both these fast services were routed via Badminton rather than Bath, but the WR scored another own goal by setting the evening Pullman departure time for the Bristol service from Paddington in a path previously used by a fast service that a number of influential Bath commuters patronised. These travellers were vociferous in their complaints that their return from London now involved a journey time extended by no less than 40 minutes, in addition to having to endure a change of trains. The result was that, just over six weeks after the Pullman service began (from 17 October to be precise), it was rerouted via Bath, and a stop at that location was added. The fact that the printed public timetable had to be heavily revised mid-way through its currency was not helped by at least three other unconnected services also having to be retimed for varying reasons. But perhaps Paddington did have the last laugh, as they could now charge those same Bath commuters a supplement to travel home!

The Bath route was now the preferred choice for the diesel Pullman services, and moving ahead in time, it should be mentioned that the 'Bristol Pullman' service was accelerated in 1968 to 100 minutes inclusive of the stop at Bath. The train was slowed slightly to 105 minutes for its last months of operation from 1972, but this was due to an additional stop at Chippenham. (Similar rumbles from 'disgruntled of Tunbridge Wells' would echo through the offices at Paddington/Waterloo/Euston/King's Cross should the regular traveller feel he was ever being 'short changed'. Indeed for many years there was a tacit acknowledgment by the various regions' timetable planners that, '… thou shalt not upset the commuters of Bath, Newbury, Winchester – wherever'. [Or do so at one's peril.]).

Clearly, Paddington had learnt a harsh lesson, and they were determined that these same mistakes would not to be repeated with the introduction of the diesel 'South Wales Pullman'. Trials had shown that it was possible to shave no less than 35 minutes from the schedule of the steam-hauled 'South Wales Pullman', which dated from 27 June 1955. (The steam service had commenced two weeks later than intended, due to an ASLEF strike at the time.) The new diesel Pullman meant that Swansea was now a minimum of 3hr 35min from Paddington. (Unfortunately we have no details of these diesel trials.)

Having dealt with the services, what about the trains themselves, and in particular the ride quality and were they really as bad as has been made out? Recall the same type of bogie had been used extensively on the continent including under vehicles operating the prestige SNCF 'Mistral' express in France. It has been suggested that even before the Pullmans ran, trials of the new bogies under Mark 1 stock did reveal some deficiencies, but this was possibly accentuated by the generally shorter length of British coaches compared with their European counterparts, together with the weight of extra equipment required to be carried by the home-grown product. Some of the Pullman vehicles were certainly in this category, while others appeared to ride better than their neighbours. Generally speaking the trailers were the most acceptable of all.

This situation with the bogies is really quite surprising for it would appear to indicate that this totally new bogie was tested, found not to be completely suitable, and yet was still used under the new trains. Without implying blame or criticism of either BR or the manufacturer, the later riding problems must surely have been foreseen. No doubt the trials, and the subsequent decision to use an unsuitable product, generated an inordinate amount of correspondence, but none has been located. Was the design of the new trains simply too advanced technically? (Remember, the order was placed with Metropolitan-Cammell in December 1956.) We should of course recall that it was not just the BP sets that suffered from, shall we say, a less than ideal ride and the Swindon built Inter-City DMU sets necessitated subsequent modifications to the single bolster bogie originally fitted. So far as BP was concerned once the trains were in service BR and the manufacturers probably did as much as was realistically feasible with the original Metro-Schlieren main suspension supplemented with hydraulic or friction types of damper.

If so, and without any evidence to support or refute these beliefs, what follows is a painful but true comparison. Less than a decade earlier than BP took to the rails, the Southern Railway, and its successor the Southern Region under Mr Bulleid, had persisted in the use of sleeve valves in the design of the 'Leader' locomotive, even when experiments with this equipment on a 'Brighton Atlantic' had proved them to be less than ideal. The situations appear identical; in both cases tests were carried out which showed up the deficiencies, and yet even while the tests were being undertaken, the intended design on which the item was to be used was still being proceeded with without any major modification. In both cases too it appears the respective designs were simply too far advanced to effect change. This is little different then to locomotive examples from the 1955 Modernisation Plan with new locos ordered in quantity straight off the drawing board without having the opportunity to test a prototype – although one might argue that the five BP sets were in fact all prototypes in their own right.

In reality, the Swiss bogie just did not suit British trackwork. The WR sets, while poor at times, did not attract as much criticism and for two reasons. First, there were more lightweight trailer vehicles per train, and second (although this will not necessarily be appreciated by devotees of the LMR), the standard of track maintenance on the WR was far better than that out of St. Pancras. (It was not much better out of Euston either in later years, but this was as a result of the punishing behaviour of some of the AC electric locomotives with their nose-suspended traction motors.) It is not for nothing that the main line out of Paddington is still known as 'Brunel's billiard table' even today. At the risk of upsetting the Western diehard, however, it should also be noted that the East Coast main line out of King's Cross was even better, and to complete the picture, the least said about certain examples of Southern trackwork of the period, the better.

As a partial defence, the tests with the Metro-Schlieren bogie might not just have been intended to verify their suitability for the Pullman sets. At the time, BR was seeking a new bogie design for its main-line corridor stock. The final result was the B4 type, but an interim solution was the heavy 'Commonwealth' bogie, which, because of its weight, was also expensive. Had the Swiss bogie come up to expectations, it might have been adopted as standard. Latterly, the BR double-bolster bogie gave a better ride at 90mph than did the Pullman bogie at a lower speeds, while by the end of the 1960s, the BR Mark 2D coaches, with the B4 bogie, were giving passengers a far better ride, to faster schedules and without the necessity to pay the supplement. It would not, though, be the end of Schlieren on BR for the bogie of the Class 56 type locomotives was based on the Schlieren design but this time with modified coil springing and flexicoil secondary suspension. We should probably leave the final word on the ride quality of BP to BR's John Ratter who on 11 November 1960, just a few months after the trains entered service, wrote a personal letter to Sir John Elliot stating: '(there is . . .) no hope of a rapid solution to riding problems'. Sadly it was to turn out to be an all too true statement as well.

The Pullman sets also lost out due to their limited utilisation when first built. This could easily have been overcome if more had been built, but it must have been obvious that, in the cost-conscious 1960s, there was no way the railway could sanction a spare train set almost permanently held in reserve.

Accordingly, full utilisation was required, but the question remains how was this to be achieved? Had the two sets remained on the Midland, perhaps Liverpool was indeed the logical choice but electrification still meant that on the LMR the trains would be redundant so in some ways it did make sense to concentrate all the units in one place, where staff were familiar with them.

The Blue Pullman services might perhaps be remembered as a useful 'stop-gap', and one that saved a (very) limited amount of business for the railway in the interim between the steam age and the age of electrification and the future HSTs. On balance, BR was probably correct in believing (for a while, at least) that the appearance of the diesel Pullmans alone was enough to justify a slower schedule.

One aspect of Blue Pullman that came late in the research was some sound recordings where the sets sounded amazingly like the early HSTs fitted with Paxman Valenta engines.

When posted on the HST enthusiast groups on Facebook most members thoughts they were listening to an HST but then two ex BR drivers identified the sound as Blue Pullman. You can understand why those who witnessed and heard the Blue Pullmans in action would think of the Blue Pullman as HST forerunners.

But by the late 1960s, it was only a matter of time before someone decided, 'enough was enough'. A warning of this had come in 1969 when all the mid-day fill-in turns disappeared whilst the sets were nowhere near as smart and neat as they had once been. This was partly a change of fashion, but in the opinion of many, the corporate livery did nothing to help. Blue and white was far more preferable to white and blue, and perhaps the biggest error BR made was this livery change. White and blue changed the appearance of the sets overnight from something previously special to something dowdy and aged. It was the same when the traditional Pullman livery disappeared from the 'Brighton Belle'. One day these electric trains – the only other multiple unit Pullman service ever built – were still smart in their individual livery which so suited their external styling, the next day in blue/grey-white, it was a case of 'mutton definitely dressed up as lamb'.

In their book *Disconnected – Broken links in Britain's Rail Policy* by Chris Austin and Richard Faulkner (Ian Allan 2015), the two authors describe Blue Pullman as '… providing the inspiration for the Inter City diesel train of the future – the HST …', but, as we have said, inspiration, yes for the fixed formation unit, but it should not be seen as the prototype. Indeed fixed formation trains had been around for decades before in the form of the various (mainly Southern) emus. The change with Blue Pullman was that for the first time it was a fixed formation *express* diesel (electric) service although we might well say there were comparisons with the SR 5BEL, 6PAN, 6CIT and 4COR/4RES units – and the last named rode none too well either!

Ironically the very first phase of the LMR overhead electrification scheme around Manchester Piccadilly, which would eventually oust Blue Pullman from its role as the premier train between the two cities, came into use when BP had only been in operation for three months! This is proof of the earlier statement that Blue Pullman could be regarded as the stop-gap intended to retain and hopefully attract clientele.

With hindsight would it even have been better to develop a single prototype to iron out any faults first? The trouble was that something akin to Blue Pullman was really needed fast. BR were haemorrhaging passenger traffic at an alarming rate, hence the closure of branch lines and the oft stated validation that if the various regions wanted to modernise (and therefore invest) in new trains and equipment on their principal services, there would have to be equivalent savings elsewhere, so rationalisation and closures it had to be.

We may also ask was Jack Howe, although an undoubted gifted and considerate designer, the right man for the job, and was it that he simply became more frustrated as time passed? Or was his behaviour at times bordering on the obsessive, little more than that of a petulant child? It can safely be said that the incident concerning the wording of the blinds to be shown on the side of the WR sets sums up much of what would affect the design of the Blue Pullman trains throughout their gestation – obsessive attention to detail rather than ensuring they were right from an engineering perspective.

Maybe, though, Jack Howe was indeed responsible for all the best bits of the Blue Pullman whereas the design engineers were responsible for the troublesome items such as the bad ride.

Subjectively it is all too easy to place the blame for this (and countless other tantrums) with the builder/manufacturer(s), design panel, consultant, the Pullman

George Cohen's (600 Group) scrapyard in Morriston with W60093/ W60742/ W60743/ W60737/ W60747/ W60096 and W60096 nearest the camera. Phil Trotter

W60093 almost appears as if she is crying tears near the entrance of Cohen's scrapyard. Phil Trotter

Car Co., British Railways, suppliers – the list is almost endless. But away from the facile, might this almost be taken to be the start of the troubles the train would experience in service, whereby an inherently suitable design was in the end 'tinkered' with by so many the final result pleased no one?

Reading copies of the various items of correspondence in the research period for this work (2016 to 2019), a question also comes to mind in so far as to what exactly was Jack Howe's role in the whole story. Yes, he was the capable design consultant, but how far did his remit go, and was he even attempting to stretch his involvement beyond what he had originally been commissioned for? The fact is, of course, that we do not know what that remit originally was. Was it to advise the Design Panel; advise on Design etc.? It could be extremely cruel to suggest that he was attempting to secure additional work (and with it fees) by appearing to make himself indispensable.

The problem also is the particular file at the National Archives (AN160/70) that deals with all these concepts is literally a 'copy of correspondence file'. We sometimes see both the original letter and its reply, whilst at other times only the one side of the correspondence. Equally frustrating are the numerous occasions when mention is made along the lines of, '… I enclose the photographs you requested …', or '… please return the colour slides when you have finished with them …'. These illustrations are just not present! (An example occurs on 18 November 1959, a time when we know that at least one of the LMR sets was running trials, which involved a letter heavily marked 'Private & Confidential' sent from the builders Metropolitan-Cammell' to George Williams, Chairman of the Design panel at the BTC Headquarters in Marylebone Road. 'Regarding your request to borrow slides for a talk you are giving to the Commission on 7 December on the work of the Design Panel, as you probably know, all publicity in connection with this train has been frozen until a new date has been determined for the handing-over ceremony at Marylebone. Whilst Mr. Large is quite willing to lend the slides, I can only agree to their being released if you can obtain permission from the Chief Publicity Officer of the BTC, to your showing the films and to you giving a personal undertaking: that in no circumstances will they be shown or given to any member of the Press.' The mind boggles, as this meant the Chairman of the Design Panel of the BTC was not permitted to borrow illustrative material on the new trains to show to the BTC! (Clearly this was 'security too far' and Williams was able to borrow the necessary material subject to the necessary undertaking that it would not be shown except as indicated and would be returned not later than 10 December. Unless this might also refer to parts of the BTF film 'Blue Pullman', it would also appear that what was shown on 7 December has not survived.)

Indeed, the number of files available in the public domain specific to the Blue Pullman trains is surprisingly few, and that takes account of records from the builder and British Railways. As mentioned in the introduction, whilst the new papers now available do reveal much new information, there remain gaps which if ever answered will be left to another to describe in the future.

The Blue Pullman concept showed the way and was probably never intended to be more than an experiment, a stop gap and a prototype for the future. The sets were not alone at having an early demise either, as proved by some of the contemporary Inter-City diesel sets although as BP was more obvious it is the one that has attracted the most interest, and I hope still does! The HST from the mid-1970s would be the next big step forward and remains the most successful move away from the conventional

The classic HST, March 1982. Successor to Blue Pullman? Well, this depends entirely on one's viewpoint. Successor, yes, in the form of a fixed-formation diesel passenger unit intended for Inter-City use; the difference was it was not a restricted service limited to Pullman passengers only. BR had also learnt from the positioning of the power unit, consequently the power cars contained no passenger accommodation. Of course, with the successor to the HST in the form of the IEP (InterCity Express Programme), the reverse is the case and the power cars do now contain passenger accommodation. *Alan Edwards*

locomotive and coaches. In the opinion of many the HST was also the saviour of the railway system, for without it Serpell and his contemporaries might have had their way. (The Serpell Report proposed the wholesale closure of almost the whole railway network, save for a section of the East Coast main line.) It is a matter of regret that, as the 21st century continues, the same timetabling difficulties that beset the operation of the diesel Pullman services still affect services today. This is despite cutbacks to local services over the years and the closure of wayside stations and uneconomic branch lines, all of which (allied to modern signalling) should have reduced line congestion. It is surely ironic that, despite all this, the railways generally seem ever more incapable of delivering the service wanted by their customers.

The final words really belong to General Sir Brian Robertson and Dr Richard Beeching, both of whom were in favour of luxury train sets for business travel. The Blue Pullman style of train (not necessarily exactly as the original design) was intended to woo the business traveller, with the intention of similar trains being introduced on other routes to create a pool of similar vehicles. This did happen later – but not for the business traveller, instead for the masses in the form of the HST. (The approval of the luxury train concept by Dr Beeching is perhaps the most difficult to reconcile, as he is on record as disapproving of anything different from the regular service, as shown by his well-documented attempts to dampen peaks in holiday and seasonal traffic. However, in

Precursor to the next generation, APT-E and HSTD inside the Pullman shed at OOC. What a great pity a Pullman was not available to complete the image.

The HS 4,000hp Kestrel. Was this even more of a direct successor to BP? According to David Lawrence the design certainly was! See page 329.

1963 he spoke on behalf of the BRB to the effect that future plans for an extension of the Pullman network had been predicted, although no plans for the actual construction of the trains had yet been prepared.)

The relentless march of technology and innovation throughout the 1960s meant that finding suitable work for the Blue Pullman sets was becoming more difficult every day. It cannot be said either that BR did not make all reasonable efforts to find gainful employment for the sets. The story that at some time in the middle of the night one or more sets were spirited away to a secret store in rural England under Box Hill Tunnel (although there are military stores in such places of course) or Wales is nothing but a myth. In fact in writing this book we have discovered rare photos of the scrapping to dispel the myths. Physically then the demise of the trains might have taken place from late 1974 through to 1976, but it had really begun at least five years earlier. The trains with their unique Nanking Blue livery have now been consigned to history for far longer than they actually existed. Their lifetime was short, their peak years even shorter, and their true usefulness is likely to be debated for years to come. What is certain though is that the unashamed beauty of the units in their original Nanking Blue, and for that we must acknowledge Jack Howe, has left indelible images and memories in the minds and hearts of so many who saw them.

Notes

(1) What follows now must not be taken to appear to criticise British Railways for the sake of it, but most students of railways will be aware of examples, both mechanical and structural, where repairs/maintenance/overhauls have taken place, only for the item never to be used or used for just a very short time. Infrastructure wise we may cite the station at Highclere south of Newbury which was repainted just a few months before being closed to passengers – justification being given on the basis that on a rotational basis repainting was due, but with no communication from one department to another railway office, with the latter considering closure. Locomotive wise SR 4-4-2 'Atlantic' No 32039, previously used by Mr Bulleid for his sleeve valve experiments, was also given a full overhaul and new boiler, plus repainted in black and renumbered, only to be never used and scrapped. No doubt there are other examples.

(2) According to Adrian Curtis, an audit of spares and equipment for the trains in May 1973 revealed that there were three complete spare power units at Swindon, although not ready for use. It is not stated exactly when this audit was carried out, one possibility being when the possible sale to Europe was under discussion. The fact that three spare engines are referred to, together with two (there had originally been three) spare auxiliary power units, is the very first time that concrete figures are given for major spares held for the sets.

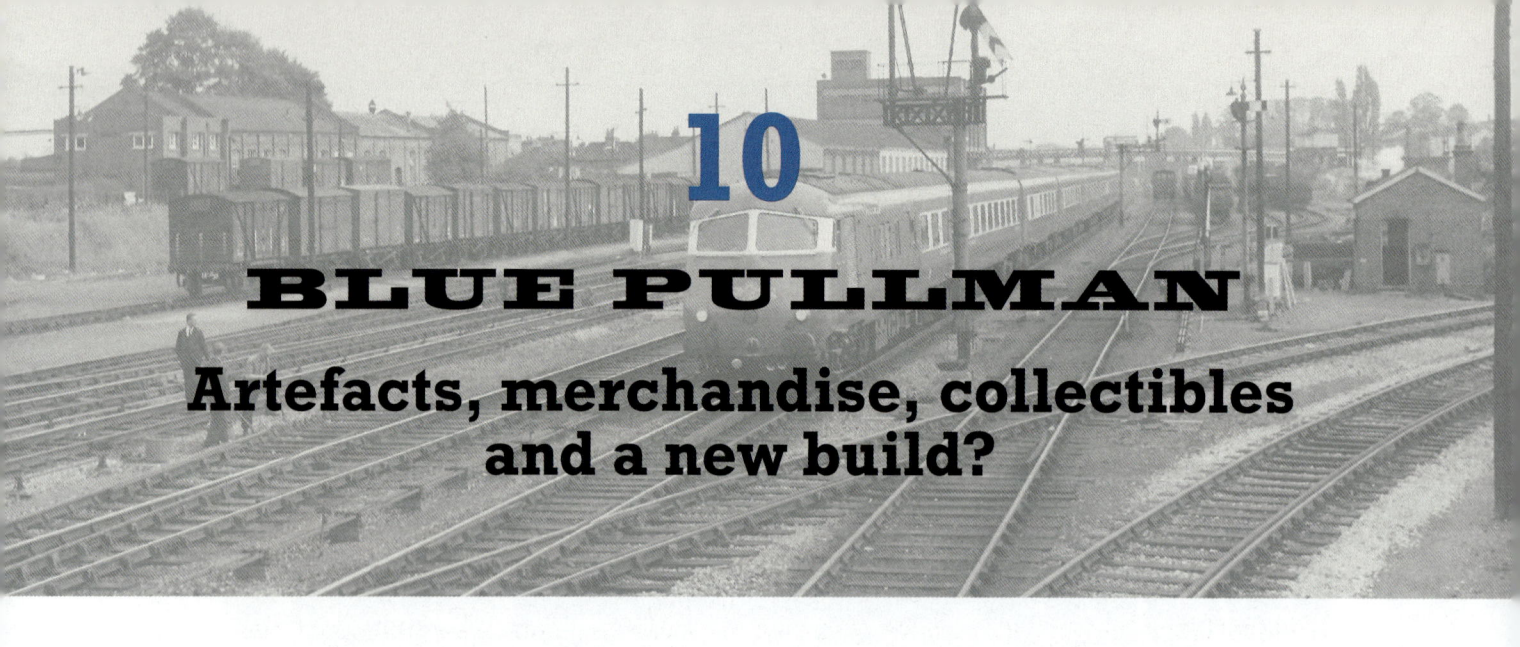

10
BLUE PULLMAN
Artefacts, merchandise, collectibles and a new build?

So whilst we have may have concluded the present story of the actual trains, it may be appropriate to take time to look at what still exists from the sets that we can enjoy.

We hope that in what has gone previously we have already added some nuggets to the little that had previously been known to survive, and not, as has been the norm for many years, to end an article (or book) on the topic with the tag line 'all that is known to remain of the Blue Pullmans is a seat unit at the Bluebell Railway'.

We start then with seats. When researching *Blue Pullman Pictorial* a Rowan Millard photograph revealed the existence of three first class seats on the Bluebell railway, albeit in poor order. Further questioning has discover that at one point there were actually six seats, all located in the carriage works mess room at Horsted Keynes and which had been obtained from Ward's in Briton Ferry. Two of the seats were later repatriated (in 2012) to more of an appropriate location in the south Midlands and currently reside with Messrs Bachmann. They remain there today.

Co-author Mike Smith has also saved the only known surviving second class seat, this from WR power car W60096. Using social media Mike then made contact with fellow enthusiasts Mike Floate and Tony Harris, each of whom also had first class seats from M/W60742. Hence we are back up to a total of six whilst it is suspected a couple more are out there. Can anyone confirm this?

Simeon Gaskell got lucky when bidding on some metal engine plates at auction and ended up buying the only known builder's plate from a Blue Pullman engine. The plate shows 'MAN NBL' on it and indeed the parts were machined by MAN but were then sent to NBL in Scotland for assembly under licence, hence both names on the plate.

The actual engine number was 307072, identified as the original spare engine for the whole fleet but subsequently fitted to W60094 on 17 October 72 and remaining in the same power car until withdrawal. Simon takes up the story, 'In the early days of internet auction sites someone was selling his late father's collection of items obtained during a career on the railways. I thought they were all from the Class 22s and in fact I bought D6354's plate from him. After seeing the 1,500rpm rating I investigated and was delighted to have a Blue Pullman plate. You can still see traces of Nanking Blue paint on it.'

Lyn Jones, who volunteers at the Severn Valley Railway obtained a number plate from the vestibule end of LMR and Western power car 60092 on a visit to the famous 'Collectors Corner' at Euston.

Howard Fisher made the nice discovery of one of the circular ashtrays made for the Blue Pullman and interestingly it has 'PULLMAN' engraved on the bottom, suggesting it was given as a gift by the Pullman company to a customer.

Mike Smith also has an ashtray but this time from the actual unit, along with a builder's plate for a Western kitchen car (Lot 30557) and a winder for the venetian blind that Tony Harris picked up from Ward's in Briton Ferry. Another builder's plate from a Midland kitchen car (Lot 30556) is pictured in Issue 24 of Terry Bye's *Pullman Car Services* news. Richard Matthews also has a window blind winder that he purchased at the Swindon open day in 1976.

There are few actual relics surviving from the BP sets: a builder's plate or two, paperwork of course, some individual vehicle numbers, crockery ('Lucerne pattern')/silverware and a few seats. A suggestion has also been made that a number of the wooden panels from first class were sold to a luxury yacht maker. *Mike Floate*

Simeon Gaskell's engine plate came from 307072 which was the fleet's spare engine. It ended up fitted installed in W60094 on 17 Oct 1972 remaining as such until withdrawal. Simeon obtained the plate at auction as part of a job-lot.

One of the 'Bristol Pullman' destination roller blinds is known to have survived and can be seen here: https://www.flickr.com/photos/63616124@N06/27705457596/in/photostream/ Railway silverware is another popular collectable, the David Mellor Sheffield designed items made by Walker and Hall are particular sought after, especially those with the Pullman crest, but it should be noted that this was not the only silverware used on the Blue Pullman trains as the same items seen in BR Hotels appeared.

Chinaware for Pullman was often made by the Staffordshire Company Ridgway as part of their 'Lucerne' range and it is this that is frequently seen in contemporary photographs of passengers eating and drinking on the Pullman sets. The price per items varies but individual items as well as complete sets have ranged in recent years between £40 and £100.

General Pullman memorabilia is also sought after, anything from complete uniforms to individual badges. The National Railway Museum are now the custodians of the Chris Lade Archive including his Pullman badges and epaulettes. Chris of course features in this book serving passengers as well as being one of the stars in the BTF Blue Pullman film (who can forget his demonstration of the first class seat adjustments.)

We see Chris and his team serving the tempting breakfasts on the film and menus from the trains are popular, with several surviving from the earliest days through to the Enthusiasts Safari on the last day. Early examples portray the Pullman Crest and Egyptian Pullman slab serif lettering whilst it should be noted there were differences for the Midland and the Western region sets. By the late sixties the British Rail double arrow logo appears with the later PULLMAN branding.

First class seat from M60742 saved by Bluebell Railway Stalwart Tony Harris and now belonging to co-author Mike Smith complete with genuine antimacassar. *Tony Harris*

Individual menus were also provided for (some) charters. Stephen Field treasures his menu from 18 September 1967 when as an Aston Villa supporter he travelled from Birmingham Snow Hill to Liverpool Lime Street. Andrew also kept his tickets – as did Chris Head and others who travelled on the various trains. We continue to hear what a special feeling it was to travel by Pullman, which almost seems to counteract the bad ride experience.

Publicity (the term used in the 1960s – nowadays 'marketing' would be the phrase) was achieved though the many brochures, timetables and special signs produced for Blue Pullman by BR and also Metro-Cammell and its suppliers.

Some were almost works of art in themselves with excellent use of colour as well as drawings or photographs. The National Railway Museum has one of the wooden sign boards from Manchester Central showing the 7.45am departure time whilst a beautiful sign survived at Leicester for many years showing a 4.02pm departure – in its latter days it was simply turned around and used as an ordinary notice board.

Brochures regularly appear in internet auction sites and in Railwayana auctions. Postcards and even postal first-day covers were produced. Mike Smith has one that was carried on the 'Bristol Pullman' between Swindon and Paddington on 1 March 1968. Illustrations of Blue Pullman trains have also featured on other first day covers even when the Pullman service was not an original Blue Pullman set but the later loco-hauled pseudo Mk2 and 3b stock.

Terry Bye's excellent Pullman Car Society newsheets contain lots of information on Pullman and readers have often sent in illustrations of Blue Pullman (and other) items located sometimes from the most unlikely of sources and previously unknown of or long forgotten. See also http://www.semgonline.com/coach/coupe/

One of the most well known of the marketing items has to be the stunning 'Midland Pullman' poster

Speedometer from co-author Mike Smith's favourite power car M/W60090, the first vehicle built. This treasure was removed at Old Oak Common in 1974. Mike's collection also includes two of the exceptionally rare Triang Minic model M521 Birmingham Pullman 'Push and Go' Power Cars, a pair of Walker and Hall silver jugs, a builder's plate from a Western Restaurant car, a window blind winder and an ashtray. *Left: Mike Smith Right: Howard Fisher*

by Arthur Woolstenholme, of course seen in the BTF Blue Pullman film. The NRM sells a reproduction of this artwork although the original will be considerably more. There were also a number of other promotional posters for the various services although it should be noted that some do not even feature an illustration of the actual train.

The train also lends itself to the skills of the modern-day painter, one such example by artist Carl Henderson GRA depicting a Midland set passing Chee Dale changed hands at the GW Railwayana auctions event in November 2017. Other earlier paintings adorned the cover of some railway books and annuals from the 1960s including *Trains* published by Nelson in 1961, the *Deans Gold Medal Book of World Travel* from 1962 and the *Eagle new book of trains* 1963, with the latter authored by Cecil J. Allen. The cover of *Locospotters Annual 1965* also shows a Midland Pullman passing a Class 45 diesel; this is from a work by Victor Welch.

One of finest artworks ever done of the 'Midland Pullman' features in this book and is available as a print at the time of writing. Stephen Millership's artwork adorns the back cover of this book and is available in many sizes and can be ordered as a print or on a canvas. This artwork can also be put on T-shirts or mugs when ordering from Redbubble or the famous poster shop Athena. His paintings of *Mallard* and the 'Coronation Scot' make a nice blue trio. See https://athenaart.com/art-prints/the-blue-pullman-by-stephen-millership/ and https://www.redbubble.com/people/smillership/works/27563089-the-blue-pullman?p=poster

Nick Harling was commissioned by Simon Altham of the BRCW group to do a fantastic painting of the 'Midland Pullman' in the snow also at Chee Tor and prints of these can be bought through The Blue Pullman group on Facebook for a good cause (more of which later) and from BRCW at www.bluepullman.brcw.co.

Other works are Mike Turner's painting 'The New Image Takes Over at Bristol Temple Meads' which shows a 'Warship', a 'Western' and a 'Bristol Pullman' in the train shed. There is also Alan Ward's work of a Western unit at Chipping Sodbury.

Malcolm Root FGRA did a painting the 'Bristol Pullman' and this image often appears on cards and posters with a similar image used for jigsaws produced by the firms Good Companion and Champion jigsaws whilst Victory jigsaws offer both artwork showing a Pullman on a bridge above road traffic and a photograph of a unit at speed.

The Blue Pullman also appears as a little metal pin badge; both new and vintage are available in blue and reverse livery.

Some beautiful Blue Pullman teddy bears, made to honour Attendant Chris Lade and the 60th anniversary of the trains were dreamt up by Mike Smith. These have hand-made uniforms that take one craftsman 15 hours to make and each has its own number. Join the Blue Pullman group on Facebook or email mikeastons@hotmail.com for details but 'bear' in mind they are very limited so be quick!

Some readers also love model trains and as both a child's toy and an adult's hobby the various Blue Pullman models have been quite significant to many, some even citing the models as the start of their interest in the full-size trains.

One of the earliest mass-produced models was from Rosebud Kitmaster, a short lived brand that started in May 1959 and was sold to Airfix models in 1962. Post 1960 they produced three Blue Pullman vehicles.

No 31 (in their range): 'Midland Pullman' Power Car Type 1 First Class No 32: 'Midland Pullman' Kitchen Car Type 4 First ClassNo 33: 'Midland Pullman' Parlour Car Type 6 First Class

Each were self-assembly plastic kits and from a collector's perspective are very sought after rare products today. An illustration of the packaging together with an expertly built model may be viewed at: http://www.kitmaster.org.uk/Pullman.htm

Lines Brothers, based at the Tri-ang works in Merton, had their own model railway system called Rovex and sold model railways under the Tri-ang Railways brand. The Tri-ang brand later moved to a factory in Margate and in 1963 launched a generic three-car Blue Pullman set aimed at the mass market.

Tri-ang catalogue numbers were R555 representing power car W60097 (non motorised), model No R556, representing W60095 (powered) model, and R426 representing parlour car W60745. The three were available as a set whilst individual cars might also be sold separately.

For 1964 the Tri-ang Minic (Minic was the electric model car section of the company) catalogue featured on the cover a Blue Pullman train together with a model of a Jaguar MkII, the Blue Pullman now available in a train-set model, No RS52. 1965 and 1966 saw no change other than in 1966 the branding of the company was changed to Triang-Hornby (Tri-ang had by now acquired the Meccano business and with it the Hornby brand name) whilst in 1967 it appears the parlour car was dropped as a stand alone item. For 1968 both the train set and the individual power cars were now produced with yellow ends.

For 1969 there were big changes, reverse livery for the first, and although the model number stayed the same it was now sold as the Diesel Pullman set. The power cars were now only sold in pairs (one having a motor and one not) with the model number R555-C. The parlour car also returned with the same R426 model number although again in revised livery. For 1970 the set changed to RS652 and was then dropped from the 1971 catalogue although stocks of the two-pack and parlour car were still for sale.

Loughborough Departure board. *Phil Lindsey*

ABOVE Lyn Jones snapped up a bargain at Euston's Collector's Corner years ago when she spied the vestibule number plate from this ex LMR power car.

As with the real thing the glory had faded from the model by 1972 and 1973 and all the models were dropped but bizarrely they reappeared in 1974 with the new style Hornby branding for the Pullman, this time in blue with yellow ends and a bizarre strip of white paint along the power car together with an extra Pullman crest in white that never appeared on the real train! The individual power cars were also back again in blue using their old numbers of R555 and R556 whilst the parlour was again back but still in the newer reverse livery – we may rightly wonder what was going in the minds of those at Margate! With the subsequent sale of the business (although it rose again later), the tooling for the models was subsequently destroyed/lost.

Moving forward, the modern day Hornby company, in an effort to keep up with the times, produced in 2007 and 2008 models of the short-lived pretend FM Rail/HRT Blue Pullman train. This was available as a set, R1093, and featured a Class 47, *Dionysos*, two Mk2 coaches and a Mk2 brake coach. An enlarged four-coach pack model No R4310 was also available in 2007. In 2008 Hornby Collectors Club members could also buy a limited edition model R2783, a Class 06 shunter loco No 06008 painted up in blue and white Pullman colours. These had the stock code M521.

Reverting to the 1960s there existed what is now an incredibly rare O gauge Minic (Tri-ang) Push and Go set of two Blue Pullman power cars.

Between 1974 and 2010 there was no ready-to-run OO gauge Blue Pullman available until in May of the latter year Olivia's Trains of Sheffield announced that they were to team up with Heljan to create a Blue Pullman model. Shortly after in July 2010 Bachmann announced they too had been working on a model of the 'Midland Pullman' (great minds think alike?), intending to produce a six-car Midland set in two versions, one with the original Pullman crests (item 31-255DC) and unusually one with full yellow ends (item 31-256DC) as per the experimental design that only ran during driver training on the Western Region in late 1966.

By November 2012 both the Bachmann models had appeared, the quality of which was superb as indeed we had come to expect from this manufacturer. The model came as a full train set with track and controller. (At this stage the reader is referred to *Blue Pullman Pictorial* where ten pages are dedicated to the model including information on the design and development.) *Model Rail* magazine for November 2012 gave the product a huge 98% rating (it lost 2% for not having sound as standard)

Ridgway Pottery in Staffordshire sold the Pullman Car Company it's Lucerne range and some still survives.

and added *'For many modellers this is the most exciting new "OO" gauge release in recent years'*. An N gauge set to the same standard was also available.

The sets were re-launched in June 2016 as special collector's edition (item No 30-425) with extras such as new box artwork, a separate print of the box artwork, a reproduction menu, a specially produced booklet detailing the history of the trains plus a pack of Stewards and Train Crew. The Bachmann 'Midland Pullman' Stewards and Train Crew were also available separately as item No 36-420.

In 2018 Bachmann announced that it was modifying the tooling of both the OO and N gauge models to incorporate the jumper cables and other front end modifications that were added subsequent to the Midland Region sets being transferred to the Western Region. 2019 saw the release of the N scale model No 371-742 in reverse BR grey and blue livery as a six-car multiple unit and a similar release of the OO equivalent in a prestige train set. In OO scale the model is an impressive 1.5 metres in length; item No 30-420 now features independently configured sound-fitted power cars, separately controllable head, tail, cab interior and saloon table lighting functions and a Dynamis Ultima operated circuit of track.

For followers of the larger scales, Messrs Westdale produced a very good set of body parts for many years; a train made from these kits features on the cover of John Emerson's 2016 book *Modelling Railways in O Gauge*. The kits were built by Richard Dockerill. The firm L. H. Loveless has also advertised future ready-to-run six- and eight-car diesel Pullmans but at the time of writing nothing had yet appeared.

Other models, perhaps not quite to scale, include a set constructed from Lego: https://www.eurobricks.com/forum/index.php?/forums/topic/80775-moc-blue-pullman/

Messrs Mardyke created a ride on Blue Pullman petrol Hydrostatic in 2006 made up of the main locomotive, parlour car, kitchen car and dummy power car. It seated twelve passengers and ran for a while but has since disappeared from public view. http://www.mardyke.co.uk/latest1.htm and http://www.mardyke.co.uk/fabricat.htm

YouTube has several films of various Blue Pullman type models in operation.

Computer technology has also allowed train simulators to appear on the market, some details are again available on YouTube.

There are also those who have sought out travel over the routes formerly taken by the Blue Pullman sets. All three Western Regions routes are accessible in 2020 although more than one operator is involved between Paddington and Birmingham whilst the original Snow Hill is no more and likewise Wolverhampton low Level, although part of the trackbed is used by the West Midlands Metro.

At the former Wolverhampton Low Level station the old buildings have been restored as a beautiful banqueting hall. Some of the platform and the old metal bridge survive; an ideal place to imagine the ghost of the 'Birmingham Pullman' arriving or departing.

But to imagine the ghostly passing of a Blue Pullman the best place has to be the old 'Midland Pullman' route. Manchester Central station is now a large exhibition centre but it is still possible to see where in the BTF film the Nanking Blue beauty leaves the station, albeit without rails or platforms.

One side of the former station is now used by the Manchester Metrolink and it is possible to hop on to a tram right there at Deansgate-Castlefield and follow the 'Midland Pullman' route through Chorlton Cum Hardy as far as East Didsbury near the Manchester-Stockport border.

Amazingly when the route was closed in the late 1960s Manchester City Council through it prudent to not build on the trackbed – just in case it was needed again in the future, and 40 years on it was.

However, Stockport Council did not have the same vision and they did replace the track with construction; hence an old A to Z is required to continue past the likes of Cheadle Heath. After this the route heads out towards the Peak District and it is possible to follow the route after Buxton and enjoy the magnificent Monsal Trail either on foot or by bicycle.

This section is replete with several of the former station buildings still standing whilst the tunnels have been re-opened and are illuminated. Highlights include Millers Dale station (which has a picture of the Blue Pullman) with the two iron railway bridges, Monsal Head, Great Longstone, Bakewell station and thence on to Rowsley and the start of the Peak Rail Heritage Railway where a heritage steam or diesel train takes the route of the 'Midland Pullman' with lots of interest for railway enthusiasts. Darley Dale is a lovely station with a level crossing and a museum and the line goes through to Matlock.

This is also an interchange to the national rail network which continues the route of the Pullman through to Derby. Highlights include Ambergate, once one of the three triangular stations in the UK and which featured prominently in the BTF Blue Pullman film. From Derby the Midland main line continues to the beautifully restored St Pancras (International).

For some the fact there is no longer a Blue Pullman to be seen 'in the metal' on these routes may appear to be off putting, but those who have visited and have an interest in the train visit often comment on the atmospheric feel of the route especially between Buxton and Belper with thoughts of the Blue Streak speeding by quite easy to imagine.

With the success of 'new build' loco projects in the 21st century the thought of resurrecting a Blue Pullman train has been discussed several times with thoughts given to using one of the two surviving NBL engines.

One of these is earmarked for a Class 22 new build and Doug Parfitt and Mike Woodhouse are very involved with that project.

So would a 'new' Blue Pullman succeed? The 2006 attempt with a Class 47 and blue/white painted coaches was reasonable but hardly the real thing. Perhaps an HST set repainted in full Nanking Blue would in the opinion of many be a better option; it would certainly make for a popular charter train for both HST and Blue Pullman fans. However, maybe what is really needed, and also an idea that is practical, is a cosmetic Blue Pullman set, one that to the eye is a 1960 Blue Pullman set but underneath is a modern eco-friendly machine with excellent riding capabilities.

Such an idea is not a pipe dream either, see www.bluepullman.brcw.co .We wish them the best of luck . In the meanwhile a campaign has now been launched to raise funds for a wooden mock up power car cab, again similar to those seen in the original BTF film.

APPENDIX 1
Biographies of the principal players

Christian Barman *1898-1980*
Educated at the University of Liverpool School of Architecture. Editor, the *Architect's Journal* and the *Architectural Review*; Publicity Officer, London Passenger Transport Board, 1935–41. Public Relations Adviser, GWR, 1945–47; Chief Publicity Officer, British Transport Commission, 1947–62; Executive Member, BTC Design Panel, 1956–62. Author of several other transport and architectural related books.

Sir John Elliot *1898-1988*
Educated at Marlborough. War service in France, 1914, 3rd The King's Own Hussars. Assistant Editor of the *Evening Standard*, 1922-25. Public Relations Assistant to Sir Herbert Walker (GM) on the Southern Railway. Assistant Traffic Manager Southern Railway 1930-38. Assistant General Manager SR from 1938 and then Acting General Manager c1946-48. Chief Regional Officer British Railways Southern Region 1948 and later in the same role with the LMR. Chairman of the Railway Executive 1951. Chairman London Transport 1953-59. Chairman of the Pullman Car Co. from 1959. Sir John wrote his own biography *On and Off the Rails* (George Allen & Unwin 1982) but there is only a very brief mention of Pullman and nothing whatsoever on the BP trains.

Kenneth Walter Chamberlain Grand *1900-1983*
Joined the GWR in 1919, was the GWR representative in the United States and Canada from 1926-29. Rose to become Assistant General Manager to Sir James Milne at the time of Nationalisation. Chief Regional Officer BR(W) 1948 then General Manager British Railways Western Region until 1963. Grand was a vocal opponent of the BTC and took every opportunity to follow an independent approach on the WR. He is quoted as commenting that, '…standardisation stifles innovation'.

(Sir) Henry Cecil Johnson *1906-1988*
General Manager British Railways London Midland Region. Commenced his railway career as a Traffic Apprentice on the LNER in 1923. Assistant Superintendent Southern Area LNER in 1942. 1955 appointed Chief Operating Superintendent BR Eastern Region and then in 1958 GM of the Eastern Region. 1962 GM of the LMR and Chairman LMR 1963-67. Vice–Chairman BRB 1967, then Chairman 1968-1971.

E. J. (Ted) Morris *1904-1994*
Messenger Pullman Car Co 1921. Appointed Accountant for the Pullman Car Co. 1927/28. Chief Accountant and Company Secretary 1940. Appointed General Manager 1962.

George Williams *?– 1965*
Joined the Design Panel in 1957 working for Christian Barman with two design officers for industrial/graphic design and research, tasked to prepare briefs for external consultants who would then do the bulk of the actual designing. Williams had begun his career designing passenger and racing cars and also commercial vehicles and led the team organising the road, rail, sea and air display for the Transport Pavilion at the 1951 Festival of Britain. It was Williams who would later commission Wilkes & Ashmore as consultants for the design of locomotive superstructures. (From *British Rail Designed 1948-1997* by David Lawrence, published Ian Allan Ltd.)

And of course, **Jack Howe** *1911-2003*
(See: https://en.wikipedia.org/wiki/Jack_Howe_(architect)) Howe was consulted/commissioned by Metropolitan-Cammell over the external design of the train together with many of the internal fittings from a very early stage. Although he is not believed to have been a member of the BR Design Panel, from the outset he maintained close relations with several members as well as liaising directly with other senior railway staff. As such he may be said to have had a unique and privileged position when it came to the finished trains. What we do not know is exactly what his formal remit was so far as Blue Pullman and if, as is discussed in this book, he achieved or was even over-zealous in his brief. (He was invited to join the Panel in June 1960 in connection with what later became the BR Mk2 coach design. It would appear Howe may also have had a hand, certainly in the initial stages of planning replacement [electric] stock for the Western Section of the Southern Region.) Although not a household name outside of his speciality, he was nevertheless a gifted and capable individual and was responsible for several iconic designs including the first ATM cash dispensers. So far as British railway design was concerned, Howe was responsible for relieving the bland front-ends of the 'Metro-Vick 'Co-Bo' diesels by introducing curved front windows – similar to the 'Clacton' electrics. Unfortunately this curved glass did not stand up well in traffic and a flat and tasteless alternative was later substituted. He also made changes to the position and style of the side grills on the same machines together with the styling of the grills and nameplates on the 'Peak' Type 4 diesel locomotives. Interestingly Jack Howe had no involvement in the external styling of the 'InterCity 125' trainsets a decade or so later, this instead being in the hands of Sir Kenneth Grange although it is interesting to report that Grange had worked in the offices of Jack Howe at the time the latter had been engaged in the design of Blue Pullman. The profile of the HST prototype certainly had a look of reverse livery Blue Pullman from the rear three quarter view but it was the unions that led to Grange rethinking his cab design to the recognisable HST cab we see today.

Comment by railway author David Lawrence – see credit above – adds, 'The original artworks for BP were undertaken by Peter Ashmore of Wilkes & Ashmore, to aid Jack Howe's design work. Howe was an architect, and therefore not best placed to design a train, whereas W&A were vehicle designers. I suspect there were several pub conversations between the men as BP progressed, co-ordinated perhaps by George Williams at the BTC Design Panel. What is not widely known is that the design of *Kestrel* began as a single-fronted tractor unit for a DMU, and is therefore the direct successor to BP. *Kestrel* came from W&A!'

In attempting to analyse the work of Jack Howe, undoubtedly gifted that he was, it is invariable that we come to attempt to analyse the man as well. What comes through is that he simply did not like having his designs being changed by engineers and others who he felt just did not understand design. Likely it was Christian Barman who introduced him to the Design Panel but could anyone ever really control him? An example was BR's attitude that they could not produce the rounded ends for the trains he had originally wanted. Might we say the final result was like a camel – the proverbial horse designed by a committee – or should that even be a 'Metropolitan-Camel'?

APPENDIX 2
Sample logs of runs and comments thereon

From *British Railways in Transition* by O. S. Nock.

'Last of all, in this necessary wbrief survey of multiple-unit expresses I come to the Pullman trains. Despite the operating convenience of the multiple-unit type of train for short distance, for cross-country and for long-distance residential and seaside traffic, as exemplified by the Brighton, Hastings, Portsmouth and Kentish services of the Southern Region, it does seem a very different matter when it comes to apply the principal to long-distance luxury services, for which supplementary fares have to be paid, and which entail continuous running for long periods at speeds of 80mph and more. Taken-all-in-all, the multiple-unit trains of this country are not famed for their smooth riding, whereas the principal business expresses have an excellent reputation to keep up. While the business man is prepared to pay for increased speed he would be less inclined to do so if speed is obtained at the expense of comfort, and by comfort I do not necessarily mean the luxury of the appointments. There is a great deal in the "atmosphere" of a train-de-luxe, and in this respect I feel that the diesel-electric Pullmans, for all the lavish attention that has been poured upon them, fall considerably short of the ideal.

'For one thing, the open saloon is not everyone's choice. One is constrained to sit at a table, and any occasion to reach dispatch cases or other light luggage from the racks entails an upheaval. A table for four may be admirable for a party, but on a long run of two hours or more three total strangers may be irksome, without the occasional relief of a leg-stretcher in the corridor. Again, nothing can be more nauseating than having to sit through a meal in which one is not participating, particularly the atmosphere and aroma of breakfast, at which time one's sense of peace with the world is not at its greatest! All this is to suggest that the luxury Pullmans would have been more likeable on the trains if at least some compartment-type stock, without tables, had been included, like the admirable formation of the inter-city expresses working between Edinburgh and Glasgow, and like that most cherished of pre-war train memories, the "Silver Jubilee".

'Those of us who have had occasion to use the new Pullman trains at all regularly have been aware of their initial shortcomings in the way of riding qualities. Their action can best be described as a "shuddering" effect. The novelty of much of the equipment amply explains such teething troubles, and a great amount of research and attention has been given to bogies and running gear subsequently with the result that opinions of the travelling public today are much more favourable. As to speed, there has never been any question. By the invitation of the Western Region authorities I was a passenger on a demonstration run staged for the civic authorities of Bath and Bristol, and for the local press, before the "Bristol Pullman" went into service. On the return trip from Reading, as shown in the accompanying log, we ran the 70.9 miles to Bath in 53 min. 59 sec. start to stop; indeed, after an easy start over a section subjected to a temporary restriction of speed, we ran the 49.8 miles from Cholsey to Corsham at an average speed of 89.3mph. This was remarkable, seeing that the maximum imposed upon these trains – 90mph was strictly enforced, save for a fractional excess to a top speed of 91mph down Dauntsey bank. The up morning "Bristol Pullman" has had two changes in its working since its introduction in the winter service of 1960. At first it ran non-stop from Temple Meads to Paddington via Badminton, on an easy schedule of 110min. for the 117.6 miles. Next it was diverted via Bath; leaving my home station at 7.57am it became a very convenient business train, with its arrival in London at 9.35am. I travelled by it on many occasions, and the journey, though nearly always punctual, was often rather rough. The actual booked time of 98min. for the 106.9 miles from Bath to Paddington was fractionally slower than the best scheduled between the two cities with steam, from 1954 onwards, and consequently was not difficult to maintain with the ample power built into the diesel-Pullmans.'

'The most impressive piece of running I have experienced with these trains was on the up Manchester service when I was privileged to travel in the driver's cab throughout from Manchester to St Pancras. The engine power is the same on both the six-car Midland trains and on the eight-car Westerns, and as the tare weights of the respective sets are 299 and 364 tons one would naturally expect faster acceleration and comparatively higher uphill speed on the Midland. Both train sets are powered by two 1,000hp NBL/MAN engines each directly coupled to a GEC main generator. The log of my run, as far as Leicester, is tabulated herewith. Figures apart, it is really difficult to convey one's impressions of travel at the head-end of this remarkable train – at any rate in the terms usually associated with the running of high-speed express passenger trains. For the most part we were travelling so smoothly and placidly that from time to time I had to make some quick mental calculations to make sure we were running to schedule. It is certainly true we had a trip singularly free from incidental delays. Not once in the run was an adverse signal sighted, and in difficult and congested areas like the environs of Derby and Leicester, and inwards from Hendon, the road was kept absolutely clear. The one out-of-course check, for relaying at Bakewell, had an almost negligible effect, so that this run shows the minimum in the way of speed that is needed to keep the schedule. With no permanent-way restriction to come the driver chose to even out his running, to lose a little on the most sharply timed sections, and regain it over the stretches where there is a recovery margin. In this way,

Down 'Bristol Pullman' passing Slough West, 10 October 1963. *R. C. Riley/The Transport Treasury*

WESTERN REGION – THE 'BRISTOL PULLMAN'			
Demonstration run on 6 September 1960			
Eight-car Multiple-Unit train			
Miles		Min. sec.	Mph
0.0	Reading	0 00	
5.5	Pangbourne	7 20	Easy
12.5	Cholsey	13 15	83
17.1	Didcot	16 24	90
24.4	Wantage Road	21 17	89
30.5	Uffington	25 22	90
35.5	Shrivenham	28 46	88
41.3	Swindon	32 39	90
46.9	Wootton Bassett	36 24	90
51.7	Dauntsey	39 35	91
58	Chippenham	43 46	90
62.3	Corsham	46 41	89
65.9	Box	49 07	Eased
70.9	Bath	53 59	

of course, the passengers are given a much more 'even' ride. There is ample power for time recovery if necessary, but it was not needed on my trip. My friends in the cab, Driver A. Bailey, of Kentish Town, and Inspector Barber, told me that in the earlier weeks of the schedule two very heavy slacks were in force on the up road – one at Great Glen and the other at Radlett. Day after day they were going all-out up the long bank from Bedford to Leagrave, sustaining 90mph for most of the way. The schedule time over the 19.6 miles from Bedford to Luton requires an average speed of 84mph, and on a run timed by Mr F. G. Cockman the speed gradually rose from 84mph passing Bedford to 89 at Ampthill Tunnel. The controller was then eased back to avoid exceeding 90mph on the short level past Flitwick, but speed was thereafter held at 89mph up the 1 in 202 towards Leagrave summit. The initial booking of 10 minutes for the 9¼ miles to New Mills South Junction appears about a minute on the tight side. The speed limit of 60mph through Disley Tunnel does not concern XL Limit and Special Limit trains, which are rarely doing

O. S. Nock in second class on the occasion of the WR press run referred to in the text. *W. J. Mayo collection*

LM REGION – THE 'MIDLAND PULLMAN'
Cheadle Heath–Leicester
Six-car Diesel Pullman set
Load 298 tons tare
Driver A. Bailey (Kentish Town)

Miles		Schedule	Min. sec.	Mph
0.0	Cheadle Heath	0		
4.0	Hazel Grove		6 30	61
7.0	Disley		9 38	58½*
9.1	New Mills South Junction	10	11 17	70
10.8	Buxworth		13 08	45*
11.8	Chinley	12½	14 20	
13.8	Chapel-en-le-Frith		16 33	55
15.0	Dove Holes Tunnel Box			58/50*
17.4	Peak Forest	18½	20 50	50
22.0	Millers Dale	25	20 57 pws	15
31.8	Rowsley	35½	37 30	
43.1	Ambergate	50½	50 27	25*
45.6	Belper		53 41	80/72
50.2	Little Eaton Junction		57 18	78
52.8	Derby North Junction	60	60 05	20*
54.8	Spondon Junction	68	65 20	20*
58.8	Draycott		69 57	72½
61.5	Sheet Stores Junction	74	72 18	40*
69.7	Loughborough	81	79 55	82
77.5	Syston		85 51	78
82.2	Leicester	93 pass	90 55	10*
* speed restriction				

Appendices

ORIGINAL 'MIDLAND PULLMAN' SCHEDULE					
Miles		Up	Down	Up	Down
0.00	Manchester Central	8.50			9.21
1.5	Throstle Nest E. Junc.	8.55			9.17
3.55	Chorlton Junc.	8.58			9.14
7.9	Cheadle Heath	9.02*/9.04			9.07+/9.08
17	New Mills South Junc.	9.14			8.58
19.7	Chinley	9.16½			8.55 (3#)
25.4	Peak Forest	9.22½ (3½#)			8.46
29.95	Millers Dale	9.29			8.40½
39.75	Rowsley	9.39½			8.28½
44.2	Matlock	9.43½			8.24½
51	Ambergate	9.54½			8.16½
60.8	Derby North Junction	10.04			8.06½
62.85	Spondon Junction	10.12			7.58 (4#)
68.85	Sawley Junction	10.17½			7.49½
69.45	Sheet Stores Junction	10.18			7.49
77.55	Loughborough	10.25 (2#)			7.43
90.1	Leicester	10.37	2.10	2.33	7.32
106.25	Market Harborough	10.52½	1.53½	2.49½	7.18½
111.1	Desborough	10.57½	1.5	2.54½	7.15
117.2	Kettering	11.02	1.45	2.59	7.10
114.15	Wellingborough	11.07	1.39½ (4#)	3.04	7.04½ (4#)
119.45	Sharnbrook Summitt	11.12 (2#)	1.31½	3.09 (2#)	6.56½
139.45	Bedford	11.21	1.24½	3.18	6.49½
158.95	Luton	11.35	1.11	3.32	6.36
169.35	St Albans	11.42½ (4#)	1.03	3.39½ (4#)	6.28
182.25	Hendon	11.55½	12.53½	3.52½	6.18½
187.65	Kentish Town	12.00	12.48½	3.57	6.13½
189.2	St Pancras	12.03	12.45	4.00	6.10
* Calls to take up only					
+ Calls to set down only					
# Recovery time (min)					

as much as 50mph on this severe incline. With the Pullman, however, it is another matter. We had accelerated to 61mph at Hazel Grove, and the controller had to be eased back considerably to avoid exceeding 60mph through the tunnel. Once through, speed was quickly worked up to the 70 limit permitted past New Mills South Junction, but, even so running at the maximum speeds permitted by the road we were 1½ minutes down at this point. Next came the 55mph restriction round the Buxworth curve. Here, it is true, the slack was over-emphasised, but after a further splendid acceleration on the 1 in 90 above Chinley, to all but 60mph at the LNWR bridge, the motors had to be eased down again so as not to exceed the statutory 50mph through Dove Holes Tunnel. Driving up this toilsome grind of an incline, with memories of Class 3 Belpaire 4-4-0s, of compounds, and even the quite recent memory of a 'Britannia' badly up against it on the 'Palatine', this quite effortless ascent was something quite new in railroading. It was the same sort of feeling that one gets taking a powerful motor car up some hill that is hallowed with memories of youthful struggles on a push-bike! Rain was driving across the high moors of Kinder Scout, but with the screen-wipers in action we had a perfectly clear vision of the line ahead, and the gloomy aspect of the hills, the low cloud and the dive into the very mountainside at Dove Holes Tunnel, all seemed to emphasise the complete mastery of the railway over wild nature – at any rate so far as this train is concerned. We were 2½ minutes late past Peak Forest, but with the subsequent recovery allowance we were less than a minute late through Millers Dale. The effect of the Bakewell check was easily recovered, and Derby North Junction was passed exactly on time; but although not classed as recovery time the schedule over the avoiding line presumably anticipates something in the way of checks. Here the two miles between Derby North Junction and Spondon Junction are allowed eight minutes, and even though we were crawling at mostly below 20mph we only took 5½ minutes. Thus we passed Sheet Stores Junction nearly two minutes early, and this was the prelude to the first piece of appreciably fast running.

Entering Red Hill Tunnel the controller was put into the eighth notch, out of a maximum of ten, and this gave us an average speed of 79mph over the 7.8 miles from Loughborough to Syston. As we swept along, riding with smoothness and a very slight but pleasant buoyancy, there was really no sensation of speed. It not only seemed easy; it was easy.'

PADDINGTON–BIRMINGHAM. DIESEL PULLMAN – 8 CARS

Actual timed runs but no dates other than sometime between September 1960 and December 1960

Miles		Sch. Min.	Actual	Speed (mph)	Actual	Speed (mph)
0.00	Paddington	0	0.00 Sigs		0.00 pws	*15
3.25	Old Oak Common W. Junc	6½	12.11		8.13	*35
7.8	Greenford	11	16.55	68	13.27	70½
10.05	Northolt Junc E.	13	18.59	78	15.33 pws	71½/75 *33
14.8	Denham		22.46		20.53	
17.45	Gerrards Cross		25.04	72	23.27	65
21.7	Beaconsfield		28.33	73	27.06	75/83½
26.55	High Wycombe	28	33.15	*32	32.00	*30
28.8	West Wycombe		36.47	47	35.40	44
31.55	Saunderton		39.39	60/69	38.43	60/69
34.7	Princess Risborough	37½	42.36 pws	*61 *16	41.40	*60
41.1	Haddenham		49.08	87	46.04	88
44.05	Ashendon Junc.	44½	52.02	*60	48.59	*60
47.45	Brill		55.12	90/91½	52.13	88
53.4	Bicester		59.12	85	56.42 pws	76½ *32
57.2	Ardley	55	61.58	76	59.48	
62.4	Aynho Junc.	59½	66.13	*59	65.24	*60
67.5	Banbury	65	70.23	72	69.55	77½
71.1	Cropredy		73.21	77	72.50	75
76.25	Fenny Compton		76.58	77½	76.48	83½
81.2	Southam Road		Pass 80.22	85	80.37 sigs 83.18 pws	Sigs *20
83.55	Fosse Road		81.59	88	87.59 pws	
87.35	Leamington Spa	84	85.26		93.43	
1.95	Warwick		3.26	61	3.22	60/65
6.1	Hatton	9	7.27	61	7.28	*50
10.3	Lapworth		10.56	81½	11.29	
12.85	Knowle	15	12.52	82	14.03	82
16.25	Solihull		15.16 sigs.	87 37*	16.10	79
20.0	Tyseley	21½	19.08		19.07	*69
22.0	Bordesley		21.33	64	20.54	
23.3	Birmingham SH	28	23.05		22.50	

* Speed restriction

Chris Head logged his first trip on the 'Bristol Pullman'.

BLUE PULLMAN READING TO BRISTOL TEMPLE MEADS, THURSDAY 18 APRIL 1967				
Fare: 28s + 9s Pullman supplement				
Train: six cars (former 'Midland Pullman' stock), 2000hp				
Distance: 82.35 miles				
Time: 75 minutes overall, 73 minutes 45 seconds net				
Place	Miles	Schedule	Actual	Approx. MPH
Reading	36	11:18	11:18:00	
Tilehurst	38.63			60
Pangbourne	41.5		11:22:30	80
Goring & Streatley	44.75			
Cholsey & Moulsford	48.38		11:27:30	84
Didcot	53.18		11:30:45	80
Steventon	56.38			
Challow	63.83			
Uffington	66.53		11:49:45	
Shrivenham	71.55			65
Swindon	77.25		11:58:00	70
Wootton Bassett	82.95		12:02:30	60
Chippenham	93.88			
Corsham	98.34			65
Box	101.95		12:14:15	40
Bath a	106.88		12:19:00	
Bath d			12:32:00	
Saltford			12:26:15	
Keynsham	113.75		12:28:15	72
Bristol Temple Meads	118.38	12:40	12:34:00	

APPENDIX 3
Operating instructions WR: 'Working of Diesel Pullman Trains'

British Railways (Western Region) Circular No 544
Working of Diesel Pullman trains
To come into operation 12 September 1960

The following instructions will apply in connection with the working of Diesel Pullman Trains on the Western Region:-

These trains are fitted with three-tone warning horns at each end. The three tones must always be sounded when it is necessary to give a warning. For standard or local whistle code purposes the lower note only must be used.

All concerned must warn men employed under their supervision who may be required to work on the permanent way or to walk upon or cross running lines, of the importance of observing the warning and that they must be prepared for the trains to approach quietly and at high speed. Upon hearing the warning, the Driver should be given an acknowledgment whenever possible. It is important that men engaged on permanent way work etc., shall move promptly to a point of safety upon sighting or receiving audible warning of the approach of a train. If it is necessary for Diesel Pullman trains to work over a section of line where they are not normally scheduled to run, Drivers of such trains must sound the three-tone warning horn in accordance with Rule 127 and when approaching curves, level crossings, barrow crossings, overbridges, Ganger's huts and other buildings adjacent to the line upon which the trains are running. In such cases prior advice must, where possible, be issued to all concerned, particularly permanent way staff, by means of printed or other notice. In emergency, when it is not possible to issue prior notice, the Drivers of such diesel trains must be advised.

The speed of trains must not exceed 10mph when proceeding along carriage or repair sidings, or sidings in Motive Power Depots. Before entering sheds, Drivers must bring their trains to a stand and give a warning signal on the horn to staff who may be at work inside. The speed of trains inside a shed must not exceed 5mph.

STATION STOPS
In all cases, owing to the use of a standard formation, the trains should come to rest at the same position every day and this will enable the station staff to assist passengers in taking up a position as near as possible to the entrance of the coach in which their seats have been reserved. Station stops and turn-round times have been kept to a minimum consistent with the duties to be carried out and it is essential, therefore, that station staff and train crews should do all they can to avoid delays.

The following stopping points have been laid down:
BATH SPA At the 9-car station stop signs on both Up and Down platforms.
BRISTOL (TM.) Platform 9, at the point opposite the white ring indicated on platform support pillar opposite the Chief Inspector's Office. Other platforms at the normal stopping point for main line trains.
LEAMINGTON SPA At the 8-car station stop signs or both Up and Down platforms.
SOLIHULL At the 8-carstation stop signs on both Up and Down platforms.
BIRMINGHAM (S.H.) At the 8-car station stop signs on both Up and Down platforms.
WOLVERHAMPTON (L.L.) At the 8-car station stop signs on both Up and Down platforms.

1. WORKING INSTRUCTIONS
1. The Rules and Regulations are applicable to Diesel Pullman trains except as modified below:–

(i) Rules:–
127. Each driving compartment is equipped with a sealed detonator case with a red flag. The Driver, when taking over, must ensure the seal is intact. The Driver must have with him in the driving compartment a handlamp with red shade.
141. The Guard's signal to start the train will be given in accordance with the bell code shown in Instruction No. 6.

(ii) Brake Regulations.
Diesel Pullman Trains operate on the Westinghouse Electro-Pneumatic compressed air brake.
The following Regulations will apply: – Reg. 1 – Description – The normal brake pressure is 70lbs. per square inch and is indicated in the Guard's Brake Vans and Driving Cabs.
Reg. 297 Before starting from Depot etc. – The Driver must advise the Guard when he is ready to make the brake test with him from the rear Guard's compartment; the Guard must check that: –

(a) The brake pipe is charged to 70lbs. per square inch.
(b) On opening the Guard's valve and reducing the brake pipe pressure to zero, check with the Driver that the brake cylinder pressure rises to at least 45lbs. per square inch.
(c) Must return the Guard's valve handle to the closed position and see that the brake pipe pressure is restored to 70lbs. per square inch.

The arrangements for conducting the test will be carried out on the Loudaphone equipment.

This test must be made daily before the train is taken into service.

The Guard will be held responsible for satisfying himself the brake has been tested in accordance with these instructions and is continuous throughout the train.

2. HEAD CODES

Electric head lamps exhibiting the standard Class 'A' or 'C' head code will be carried.

3. AUTOMATIC WARNING SYSTEM ON DIESEL PULLMAN TRAINS.

The Apparatus in the Train, which is air braked, varies from that for vacuum braked trains as previously described, although the audible signals are again produced by a bell for the 'all clear' aspect and a siren for the 'caution' aspect. The operation of the contact shoe is also similar on air and vacuum braked vehicles.

The cab apparatus is placed behind the driver on the bulkhead with the handle of a Sealed Isolating Cock projecting slightly from the face of the enclosing cabinet. The associated Timing Reservoir and Application Valve are situated in close proximity below the cab floor. The A.W.S. Power Governor is fixed beside the A.W.S. Battery Box on the other side of the bulkhead. A Reset button is situated on the Driver's desk and above it is an A.W.S. IN/OUT of USE Switch and an A.W.S. IN/OUT of USE indicator.

The shoe switch is connected with an electrically controlled valve in such a way that whenever this valve is opened, air will be released through the siren from the brake pipe thus sounding the siren.

This occurs when a train passes over a 'dead' ramp, associated with a Distant signal showing a 'caution' aspect resulting in the brakes being fully applied together with a cutting off of the power to the traction motors and the diesel engines reverting to idling, and this will happen within three seconds of the siren first sounding if suitable action is not taken in the manner described hereafter.

The Driver, by depressing and releasing the Reset button within the 3 second warning period, can acknowledge the warning given by the siren, stopping the siren sounding and avoiding the brake application and cutting off of traction power.

If the caution signal is not acknowledged as described above within the 3 seconds warning period, the ensuing brake application can only be cancelled by first returning the power control handle to the Notch 0 position and then depressing and releasing the Reset button. The traction power, which was cut simultaneously with the brake application, can only be reapplied when the brakes have become fully released.

When the train passes over an electrified ramp, which is associated with a signal displaying the 'all clear' aspect, the bell will ring.

The Reset button cannot be used to forestall the sounding of the siren. If the Reset button is depressed at any other time than after receiving the caution warning from a 'dead' ramp the siren will sound and, if held depressed for more than 3 seconds, the effect will be the same as for an uncancelled warning.

If the train is proceeding very slowly over an unelectrified ramp, or is standing on an unelectrified ramp, the siren will sound, but the full brake application and cutting off of the traction power can be avoided by the Driver holding down the Reset button, which will stop the siren sounding. When the shoe clears the ramp the siren will sound again and the Reset button must then be quickly released if the Driver wishes to regain full control of the train.

When the Driver takes charge of a train, before moving the train he must observe the following rules:—

Non-driving Cab.
(a) The Main battery isolating switch must be 'IN'.
(b) Check that the A.W.S. isolating cock is sealed.
(c) The A.W S. IN/OUT of USE switch must be in the OUT of USE position, and the Indicator must read A.W.S. OUT of USE.

Driving Cab.
(a) The main locomotive battery switch must be 'IN'.
(b) Check that the A.W.S. isolating cock is sealed.
(c) The A.W.S. IN/OUT of USE switch must be in the IN USE position and the Indicator must read A.W.S. IN USE.
(d) The A.W.S. apparatus must be reset by depressing and releasing the Reset Button.

If the A.W.S. is not switched into use the siren will sound after the Forward/Reverse handle is moved from the 'OFF' position, until the A.W.S. is engaged as above.

After resetting the A.W.S. or when recharging the brake pipe from a low brake pipe pressure, with the A.W.S. reset, the Application Valve will vent to atmosphere for a short period of time until its reservoir is charged sufficiently to reseat it.

The working of the A.W.S. equipment on the train must be tested before the train is moved from its stabling point and at any other time as may be deemed necessary.

The following procedure must be carried out in each driving cab: – Depress Deadman's Pedal and select direction (Forward or Reverse).

Allow A.W.S. siren to sound and after 3 seconds delay note that the Brake Pipe Pressure falls at least 30lbs. p.s.i. and the Brake Cylinder Pressure rises to at least 45lbs. p.s.i.

Place A.W.S. IN/OUT of USE switch to the A.W.S. IN USE position when A.W.S. Indicator must show IN USE and reset by depressing and releasing Reset Button. After a short delay the Brake Cylinder Pressure will fall to zero and the Brake Pipe pressure will rise to 70lbs. p.s.i.

When the Driver leaves the Driving Cab, the following procedure must be observed: – The A.W.S. IN/OUT of USE switch must be placed in the OUT of USE position when the IN/OUT of USE Indicator must read A.W.S. OUT of USE.

If the A.W.S. IN/OUT of USE switch is moved to the OUT of USE position before the Forward/Reverse handle is moved to the 'OFF' position the siren will sound between the two movements.

Any irregularities must be dealt with as described under Section IV (a) Clause 7 of the Regional Appendix.

If it is not possible to reset the A.W.S. due to a failure of any part of the A.W.S. equipment on the train, the A.W.S. must be isolated by breaking the seal and turning the handle of the Isolating Cock. Movement of this cock to the Isolated position causes the IN/OUT of USE Indicator to read A.W.S. OUT of USE irrespective of the position of the IN/OUT of USE switch. Breaking of the seal and use of the Isolating Cock must be reported.

4. LOUDAPHONE COMMUNICATION

The Loudaphone apparatus is a means by which the Driver and Guard may speak to each other, or exchange bell signals, but it does not in any way relieve staff from their obligation to carry out the relevant Rules and Regulations.

A buzzer, which is actuated by the depression of the call button on the Loudaphone, or the signal push above Van doors, is provided in both the Guard's and Driver's compartments and this communication must always be used for the exchange of signals in accordance with the standard code shown in the Instructions for Working Multiple-Unit Mechanical Diesel Trains. An additional signal push which will operate the buzzer in the Driver's cab is provided over the door of each Guard's compartment.

Standard bell codes will be used for all normal movements but the Driver, if requiring to speak to the Guard, or the Guard, if requiring to speak to the Driver, must send on the call button the code 3 pause 3 'Guard required to speak to Driver', or 'Driver required to speak to Guard', and the man at the other end must acknowledge by repetition as detailed in the Instructions referred to above. Conversation may then proceed provided both men keep the 'Speak' button depressed.

The apparatus must only be used for essential conversations on matters affecting the working of the train and, except in the case of emergency, should not be used when the train is in motion. The apparatus may also be used by Shunters, in the absence of Guards, in order to communicate with Drivers in connection with shunting operations.

In order to avoid any possibility of unauthorised use of the apparatus in Driver's cabs the door between the generator compartments and the Guard's compartment and the exterior door of the Driver's compartment must be kept locked when the Driver's cab is not in use.

5. DIESEL PULLMAN TRAINS MUST NOT CONVEY TAIL TRAFFIC

6. COMMUNICATION BETWEEN GUARD AND DRIVER

The following code of bell signals between Guard and Driver must always be used by means of the bell communication provided: –

1. Stop
2. Start
3. Set-back
3-3. Guard required by Driver
   Guard or Driver attend telephone (where provided)
4. Slow down when propelling
5. Driver or Guard leaving train in accordance with rules
6. Draw up

These bell codes must be acknowledged by repetition.

In cases of failure of the bell communication, hand signals must be used except as indicated in the second paragraph of Instruction No. 10.

7. PROPELLING

Except during shunting operations, propelling must only be resorted to where specially authorised.

When propelling, a speed of 5mph must not be exceeded and the Guard or Shunter must ride in the leading driving cab, keep a good look-out, operate the warning horn when necessary, and be prepared to stop the train as required by application of the emergency brake. The Guard or Shunter must carefully observe all signals and signal to the Driver as may be necessary in accordance with the bell codes shown in Instruction No. 6. In the event of failure of the bell communication the train must be driven from the leading end.

Trains must be driven from the leading end when proceeding on to another train or entering Carriage or Repair Sheds.

8. FIRE PRECAUTIONS

In the event of an engine becoming overheated, a small red light will be exhibited on the solebar on the side of the vehicle concerned. Should this red light be observed by a Signalman, he must endeavour to bring the train to a stand but if the train enters the section ahead the provisions of Block Regulation 17 – 'Stop and Examine Train' must be carried out.

Each driving cab is equipped with two hand operated fire extinguishers of the CO_2 gas type; each Guard's compartment and each trailer is provided with one two-gallon CO_2 water type hand operated extinguisher. In addition, automatic fire extinguishing apparatus is fitted on the underframe of motor vehicles. In the event of a fire developing in one of the engines, the extinguishing equipment will come into operation and at the same time ring a bell in the Driver's compartment. After the train has been stopped in accordance with Rule 188, the Driver must proceed to the affected engine and take with him a fire extinguisher and, in the case of trains conveying passengers, must carry out the duties allocated to the Fireman under Rule 188 after satisfying himself that the fire is being dealt with.

When there is a fire, Drivers and Guards must act according to the best of their judgment and ability in the circumstances. After ensuring that the fire has been extinguished, the small metal tab on the front of the fire alarm control box should be pulled off. This will uncover a

(Private and not for publication)

BR 31451/5

BRITISH RAILWAYS
WESTERN REGION

ROUTE AVAILABILITY — DIESEL LOCOMOTIVES

Paddington
February, 1971.

G. GRAHAM,
Movements Manager.

F.4

DIESEL MULTIPLE-UNIT PULLMAN TRAINS

6, 8 or 12 Car Diesel Multiple-Unit Pullman Trains are authorised to work over the undermentioned sections of line. When they are required to work over a route not shown the authority of the Movements Manager is to be obtained.

8 Car sets cannot work over rising gradients steeper than 1 in 68, and 6 and 12 Car sets must not work over rising gradients steeper than 1 in 50.

Unless otherwise shown the Western Region Automatic Warning System apparatus is to be maintained in the operative (Down) position.

Routes Authorised	Sets Authorised
WESTERN REGION ROUTES	
Paddington to Cogload via Bristol or Berks & Hants Line	
Bristol—Westbury	
Didcot—Oxford.	} 6, 8 and 12 cars.
Wootton Bassett—Swansea.	
Swansea—Milford Haven (via Cockett).	6, 12 cars.
Swansea—Milford Haven (via crossover at the East End of Port Talbot, and District Line).	8 cars.
Cogload to St. Austell*	} 6, 12 cars.
Aller Jcn. to Paignton.	
INTER-REGIONAL AND OTHER REGIONS ROUTES	
Oxford—Banbury	
Old Oak Common—Birmingham New Street.	
Bristol—Barnt Green—Birmingham New Street—Dudley Port—Wolverhampton—Stafford—Crewe.	} 6, 8 and 12 cars.
Newport—Craven Arms—Crewe.	

* Subject to clear run guaranteed over Hemerdon, Rattery and Dainton inclines.

F.5

Routes Authorised	Sets Authorised
Crewe—Liverpool Lime Street.	6, 12 cars.
Crewe—Warrington—Preston—Carnforth—Milnthorpe—Oxenholme—Windermere.	
Barnt Green—Camp Hill Line—Saltney—Water Orton—Whitacre or Kingsland Loop—Wichnor Loop—Derby—Ambergate—Clay Cross—Hasland—Rotherham—Doncaster.	6, 8, 12 cars.
Doncaster—Hull.	
Doncaster—York—Middlesborough.	6, 12 cars.
Wath Road Junction—Darfield—Normanton—Leeds.	
Acton—Acton Wells—Neasden Junction—Dudding Hill Junction—Cricklewood—Carlton Road Junction—Upper Holloway—South Tottenham Junction—Temple Mills—Channelsea Junction—Northumberland Park.	
Acton Wells—Watford.	
Westbury—Salisbury—Portsmouth.	
Reading—Basingstoke—Eastleigh—Southampton.	
Salisbury—Woking.	6, 8, 12 cars.
Reading—Guildford.	
Old Oak Common—Latchmere Junction.	
Latchmere Junction—Clapham Junction—Point Pleasant Junction—Putney.	
Latchmere Junction—Norwood Junction—Selhurst.	
Latchmere Junction—Charlton.	
Reading—Ascot—Feltham—Putney.	
Clapham Junction—Byfleet Junction—Guildford.	
East Putney—Wimbledon. (**)	(**) A.W.S. shoe removed.

Richard Matthews

switch which should be operated to stop the alarm bell and extinguish the warning light. It will also render it impossible to re-start the affected engine and after this has been done the train can proceed.

The alarm isolating switch referred to does not cut out the re-setting thermostat and should this operate through a recurrence of fire on the engine or fluid flywheel, the alarm bells will ring and the warning light will be lit. In this event the fire will not be extinguished automatically as the extinguishing agent will have been previously discharged. It is essential, therefore, for the remaining hand operated fire fighting equipment to be used as a matter of the utmost urgency after the train has been stopped.

The fire extinguishing agent used in the auxiliary power cars is Chlorobromomethane. The vapour given off from the liquid is heavier than air and will therefore tend to settle at ground level but will be dispersed rapidly if there is a free current of air. Therefore an extinguisher going off normally in service is unlikely to constitute a hazard. Chlorobromomethane is not highly toxic and no dangers are likely to arise. Should an extinguisher be discharged accidentally and persons sprayed with the liquid in an enclosed space, the following simple precautions should be taken: –

1). Remove patient from the discharge area into the fresh air. Apply artificial respiration if necessary.
2). All clothing soaked by the liquid should be removed and where the liquid has splashed on the skin it should be washed off with water or, if available and the skin is not broken, by a saturated solution of bicarbonate of soda.
3). If the liquid enters the eyes wash freely with water.
4). Summon medical aid as soon as possible, notifying the doctor that the patient has been in contact with Chlorobromomethane and that oxygen therapy may be required.
5). If the liquid enters the mouth give the patient an emetic, such as one pint of saturated solution of bicarbonate of soda.
6). All clothing contaminated with the liquid should be laundered before being used again.

9. DEADMAN'S PEDAL
A Deadman's pedal is provided in all driving compartments and should the Driver release the pressure, the power will be cut off and the brakes applied.

10. DRIVING APPARATUS DISABLED
In the event of the driving apparatus in the leading compartment becoming disabled, and the Driver being able to regain control of the train from the other driving compartment the train must be driven at a reduced speed of not more than 15m.p.h. from the most convenient driving compartment and proceed with caution to the nearest point where the train can be taken out of service. In such cases the Guard must ride in the leading driving compartment, keep a good look-out, operate the warning horns when necessary and practicable, and be in a position to stop the train as required by application of the hand brake. The Guard must carefully observe all signals and signal to the Driver as may be necessary in accordance with the bell codes shewn in Instruction No. 6.

11. ASSISTING DISABLED TRAIN
In an emergency, disabled Diesel Pullman trains can be assisted by any type of train or engine, but in such circumstances the trains must be worked cautiously and at reduced speed.

When a Diesel Pullman train is being assisted, the working must be in accordance with the special instructions included in the Driver's handbook and according to the type of train or engine which is providing the assistance.

In the event of an air brake defect the Guard must be prepared to ride in the rear driving compartment and operate the hand brake under the direction of the Driver as may be necessary.

Each Diesel Pullman train is provided with a draw hook at each end.

12. DERAILMENTS
In all cases where Diesel Pullman cars are derailed they must be rerailed only under the supervision of and by Running and Maintenance Department staff.

13. FLOODING OF THE LINE
The movement of Diesel Pullman trains is restricted during flooding of the line as Indicated in the Weekly Permanent Way Notice (K2/530) and the Regional Appendix, dated 1 October, 1960, page 89, as for Diesel Electric Multiple Units.

C. W. POWELL,
Operating Officer.
August 1960

APPENDIX 4
Extracts from BR (WR): 'Multiple Unit Diesel Pullman Trains'

For the information of Railway and Pullman Car Company Staff

TRAVELLING TECHNICIANS

A Travelling Technician from the Chief Mechanical & Electrical Engineer's Department will form part of the train crew of each train. He will travel in the leading Guard's compartment, in which a small cupboard for his tools and equipment has been provided. He will be responsible for:–

(i) Deciding which of the auxiliary engines should be used.
(ii) Changing over auxiliary engines en route.
(iii) Switching on the second auxiliary engine when requested by the Pullman Car Conductor during excessively cold weather.
(iv) Taking action when 'fault' lights appear.
(v) Dealing with technical faults in traction equipment upon request from the driver.
(vi) Supervision of connection and disconnection of 'shore' electrical supplies. Where provided at terminal points.

CARRIAGE CLEANING

The following carriage cleaning arrangements are applicable to the Diesel Multiple Unit Pullman trains:

EXTERIOR
Standard arrangements for British Railways Stock.

INTERIOR
Daily:
Vestibule, lavatory and corridor floors, using diluted suitable disinfectant. Chrome fittings wipe with damp rag. Empty Ash Trays at end of each day, and at the end of each individual journey during the day.

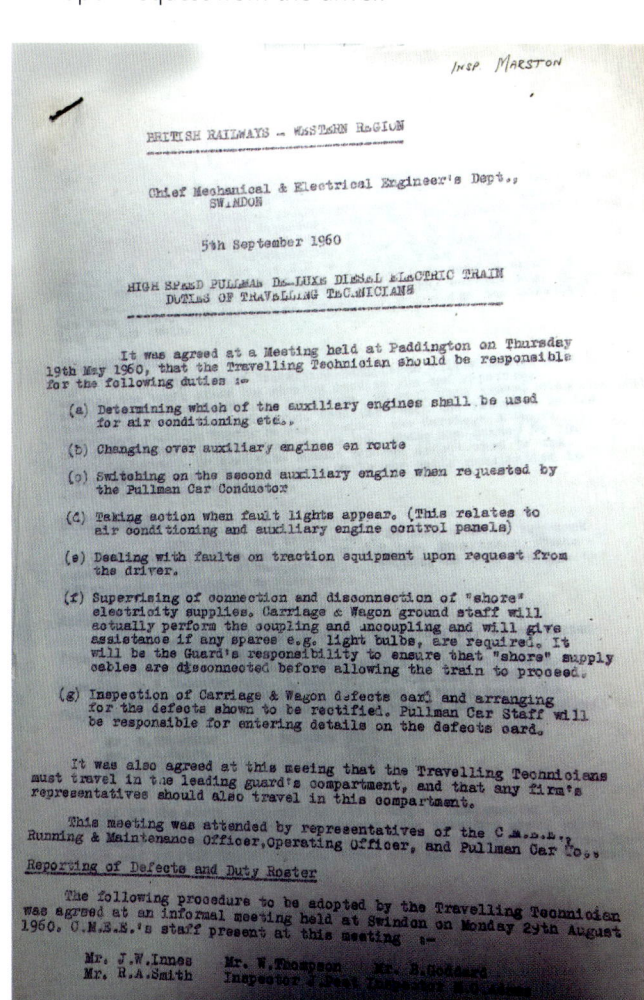

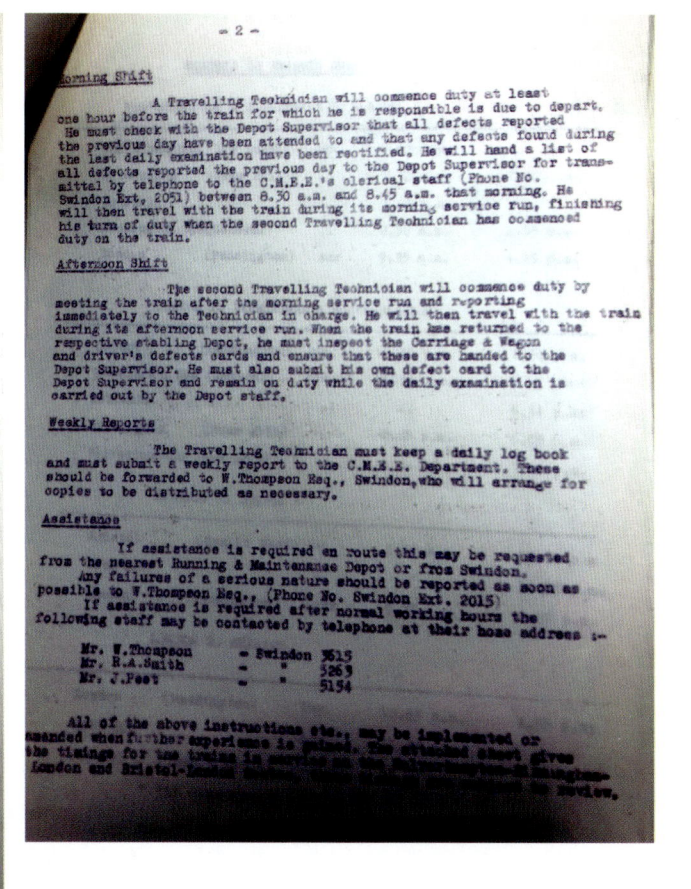

Weekly:
Carpets and upholstery, vacuum clean and remove stains as necessary.
Toilet walls (plastic), sponge down and dry off.
Aluminium fittings, dust off and clean with lanoline.

Fortnightly:
Plastic panels, i.e., saloon ceilings, second class partitions, sponge down lightly with clean water and dry off.
First class partitions (wood veneer), clean and polish with a good furniture polish.
Lanide panels (body sides and table tops), sponge down using a diluted solution of soap flakes or similar detergent, dry off with clean cloth.

Note: Acids must not be used for the cleaning of Pullman Cars.

The Pullman Car staff is responsible for equipping the lavatories with toilet rolls, soap, hand towels and the provision and changing of antimacassars in the Cars.

ROUTE RESTRICTIONS

These trains are built to the C1 loading gauge with the exception of the traction motor gear cases which are to the Ll gauge, and may work over running lines and sidings normally used for coaching stock, subject to the restrictions shown in the appropriate instructions.

STATION STOPS

In all cases, owing to the use of a standard formation, the trains should come to rest at the same position every day and this will enable the station staff to assist passengers in taking up a position as near as possible to the entrance of the coach in which their seats have been reserved. Station stops and turn-round times have been kept to a minimum consistent with the duties to be carried out and it is essential, therefore, that station staff and train crews should do all they can to avoid delays.

APPENDIX 5
Excerpt from BR North Eastern Region Sectional Appendix, 9–22 April 1966

GENERAL INSTRUCTIONS AND NOTICES
MISCELLANEOUS NOTICES
DIESEL-ELECTRIC PULLMAN TRAINS – WORKING INSTRUCTIONS

The following instructions will apply in connection with the working of Diesel-electric Pullman trains running on the North Eastern Region. These trains are fitted with three-tone warning horns at each end. The three tones must always be sounded when it is necessary to give warning. For standard or local whistle code purposes the lower note only must be used. All concerned must warn men employed under their supervision who may be required to work on the permanent way or to walk upon or cross running lines, of the importance of observing the warning and that they must be prepared for the trains to approach quietly and at high speed. Upon hearing the warning, the Driver should be given an acknowledgment in accordance with Rule I l(b). It is important that men engaged on permanent way works, etc., shall move promptly to a point of safety upon sighting or receiving audible warning of the approach of the train. If it is necessary for these trains to work over a section of line where they are not normally scheduled to run, Drivers of such trains must sound the three-tone warning horn in accordance with Rule 127 and when approaching curves, level crossings, barrow crossings, overbridges, Ganger's huts and other buildings adjacent to the line upon which the trains are running. In such cases prior advice must, where possible, be issued to all concerned, particularly permanent way staff, by means of a printed or other notice. In emergency when it is not possible to issue prior notice, the Driver must be advised. The speed of trains must not exceed 10mph when proceeding along carriage or repair sidings, or sidings in Motive Power Depots. Before entering sheds. Drivers must bring their trains to a stand and give a warning signal on the horn to staff who may be at work inside. The speed of trains inside a shed must not exceed 5mph.

1. RULES AND REGULATIONS
The Rules and Regulations are applicable to Diesel-electric Pullman trains except as modified below.

(i) Rules 120
Diesel-electric Pullman trains must display one electric tail lamp at all times whilst on running lines and. For this purpose, the centre lamp position must be used. 126. A Driver is forbidden to leave charge of his train without: – (a) stopping the main engines, (b) removing the controller key (c) putting the hand brake on hard. 127 Each driving compartment must be equipped with not less than 12 detonators and 2 red flags. The Driver must have with him in the driving compartment a hand lamp with a red shade. 129(iv) (c) It will be the duty of the Driver to ensure that the handbrakes have been dealt with in accordance with the Driving Instructions. (BR 33003/81.) 141 The Guard's signal to start the train will be given in accordance with the buzzer code shown in instruction No 5.

(ii) Brake Regulation
Diesel-electric Pullman trains are equipped with, and operate only on the Westinghouse Electric-Pneumatic brake. The following Regulations will apply: – Reg 1 – Description. The normal brake pipe pressure is 70lbs per square inch and indicated in the Guard's brake vans and driving cabs. Reg 2 – Before starting from Depot and/or Carriage Sidings – The Driver must advise the Guard when he is ready to make the brake test with him from the rear Guard's compartment: the Guard must: – (a) Check that the brake pipe is charged to 70lbs per square inch, (b) On opening the Guard's valve and reducing the brake pipe pressure by at least 25lbs per square inch, check with the Driver that the brake cylinder pressure rises to at least 45lbs per square inch. (c) Must return the Guard's valve handle to the closed position, advise the Driver when this has been done and see that the brake pipe pressure is restored to 70lbs per square inch advising the driver when this is accomplished. The arrangements for conducting the test will be carried out on the Loudaphone equipment. This test must be made daily before the train is taken into service. The Guard will be held responsible. For satisfying himself the brake has been tested in accordance with these instructions and is continuous throughout the train, by observation of brake pressure gauges fixed externally on intermediate vehicles, must ensure that the pressure of 50lbs per square inch is available on those vehicles.

2. HEAD AND TAIL LIGHTS
Coloured discs are provided at each end of the train for use as shown below: – Three blue-for blanking out any lamp position. Two white-for headlights. One red-for tail light or for working in wrong direction in emergency. (a) The standard Class '1' or '3' headcode must be displayed at the front of the train by means of white discs inserted into the appropriate lamp positions. After sunset or during fog or falling snow, the appropriate lamps must be illuminated. The Driver must see that the proper headcode is displayed and illuminated as necessary, and also that the electric tail light is illuminated. (b) The Guard will be responsible for the insertion and removal of the red disc

forming the tail lamp indication. (c) An oil tail lamp, cleaned and trimmed ready for use must be carried in each Guard's compartment and the Guard will be responsible for the fixing of a lighted oil lamp when the train is stabled, also in emergency on any miming line in the event of failure of the electric tail light. (d) When the train is stabled on a line which has access from either end, a lighted oil lamp must be fixed at both ends of the train.

3. LOUDAPHONE COMMUNICATION

The loudaphone apparatus is a means by which the Driver and Guard may speak to each other, or exchange buzzer signals, but it does not in any way relieve staff from their obligation to carry out the relevant Rules and Regulations. A buzzer, which is actuated by the depression of the 'call' button on the loudaphone, is provided in both the Guard's and Driver's compartments and this communication must always be used for the exchange of signals in accordance with the standard code shown in Instruction No 5. An additional signal push which will operate the buzzer in the Driver's cab is provided over the door of each Guard's compartment. Standard codes will be used for all normal movements but the Driver, if required to speak to the Guard, or the Guard, if requiring to speak to the Driver, must send on the call button the code 3 pause 3 'Guard required to speak to Driver' or 'Driver required to speak to Guard' and the man at the other end must acknowledge by repetition as detailed in the Instructions referred to above. Conversation may then proceed provided both men keep the 'Speak' button depressed. The apparatus must only be used for essential conversations on matters affecting the working of the train and, except in the case of emergency, should not be used when the train is in motion. The apparatus may also be used by Shunters in the absence of Guards, in order to communicate with Drivers in connection with shunting operations. In order to avoid any possibility of unauthorised use of the apparatus in Driver's cabs the door between the generator compartments and the Guard's, compartment and the exterior door of the Drivers compartment must be kept locked when the Driver's cab is not in use.

4. TAIL TRAFFIC

Diesel-electric Pullman trains must not convey tail traffic.

5. BUZZER COMMUNICATION

The following code of signals between Guard and Driver must always be used by means of the buzzer communication provided:–
 1. Stop. 2. Start. 3. Set-back. 3-3. Guard or Driver attend telephone. 4. Slow down when propelling. 5. Driver or Guard leaving train in accordance with Rules. 6. Draw up. These codes must be acknowledged by repetition. In cases of failure of the buzzer communication, hand signals most be used.

6 PROPELLING

Except during shunting operations, propelling must only be resorted to where specially authorized for the Diesel-electric Pullman train.

When propelling, a speed of 5mph must not be exceeded and the Guard or Shunter must ride in the leading driving cab, keep a good look-out, operate the warning horn when necessary, and be prepared to stop the train as required by application of the emergency brake, i.e. move the air control handle from the SHUT DOWN to the EMERGENCY position and leave it in that position until the train has come to a stand, returning it to the SHUT DOWN position when again ready to move. The Guard or Shunter must carefully observe all signals and signal to the Driver as may be necessary in accordance with the code shown in Instruction No 5. In the event of a failure of the buzzer communication the train must be driven from the leading end. Trains must be driven from the leading end when proceeding on to another train or entering carriage or repair sheds.

7. FIRE PRECAUTIONS

In the event of fire occurring at an auxiliary engine, a small red light will be exhibited on the solebar on the side of the vehicle concerned. Should this red light be observed by a Signalman, he must endeavour to bring the train to a stand, but if the train enters the section ahead, the provisions of Block Regulation 17 – Stop and Examine Train – must be carried out. In the event of the fire warning bell sounding, the train must be stopped in accordance with the provisions of Rule 188, and the Driver must proceed to the affected engine taking with him a fire extinguisher. In the case of a train conveying passengers, when the train is single-manned, the Driver must carry out the duties allocated to the Fireman under Rule 188, after satisfying himself that the fire is being dealt with. Drivers and Guards must, however, act according to the best of their judgment and ability in the circumstances attending the fire. When a fire extinguisher has been used, this must be reported on the Driver's defect sheet. (a) Main and Auxiliary Engines. Automatic fire extinguishing apparatus is fitted, and in the event of a fire developing at one of the main auxiliary engines, the extinguisher equipment will come into operation and at the same time ring an alarm bell and brightly illuminate a red warning light in the Driver's compartment, giving an indication which engine is affected. After ensuring that the fire has been extinguished, the Driver must pull off the small metal tab in front of the fire alarm control box which will uncover a switch which must be operated to silence the alarm bell and extinguish the warning light. (b) Auxiliary Engines. The fire extinguishing medium used in the automatic apparatus is chlorobromomethane, a toxic gas which dissipates very rapidly when exposed to the open air. Care should be taken, therefore, to avoid contact with or inhaling of the vapour. If, however, contact is made the following precautions must be taken:–

(1) Remove the person concerned from the discharge area. (2) Summon medical aid as soon as possible, notifying the doctor that the person has been in contact with chlorobromomethane and that oxygen therapy may be required. (3) If contaminated with liquid, ALL clothing, wrist watches, rings, etc., must be removed and the patient washed freely. (4) Arrangements should be made for contaminated clothing to be thoroughly cleaned. (5) Fresh

air is essential and artificial respiration may be necessary. (6) If a quantity of chlorobromomethane enters the eyes or nose, wash affected parts very freely with plain water. (7) If a quantity of chlorobromomethane enters the mouth give an emetic. (8) There may be certain delayed effects of chlorobromomethane poisoning and every case of contamination therefore must be referred to the Regional Medical department for observation. (c) Main Engines. The fire extinguisher used in the automatic apparatus on the main engines is CO2 gas. If a fire is detected in the engine of the generator room, care must be exercised before deciding to enter, as when the temperature rises above normal the automatic extinguisher equipment will come into operation. Similar conditions will exist if a false alarm is given and the same discretion should be exercised. (d) General. Each driving cab is equipped with two hand operated fire extinguishers of the CO2 gas type and one hand operated C.T.C. type; each Guard's compartment and each trailer is provided with one two-gallon CO2 water type hand operated fire extinguisher. In the event of a small outbreak of fire being detected by sight, sound or smell, the hand operated extinguishers should be used. The CO2 extinguishers should only be used against internal fires, and the C.T.C. extinguishers against external fires.

On no account must C.T.C. or CO2 water type extinguishers be used on electrical equipment which is still alive.

8. DRIVER'S SAFETY DEVICE

A Driver's safely device is provided in both driving compartments and should the Driver release the pressure, the power will be cut off and the brakes applied unless the holdover button is depressed. When the train is single-manned, should any defect arise to make the Driver's safety device inoperative, the Guard must ride with the Driver until another competent man can be provided or the defect remedied.

9. DRIVING APPARATUS DISABLED

In the event of the driving apparatus in the leading compartment becoming defective, the Driver can regain control of the train from the other driving compartment. The train must be driven at reduced speed from the rear driving compartment and proceed with caution to the nearest point where the train can be taken out of service or reversed. In such cases the Guard must ride in the leading driving compartment, keep a good look-out, operate the warning horns when necessary and practicable, and be in a position to stop the train as required, by application of the emergency brake as indicated in Instruction No 6 or by the hand brake. The Guard must carefully observe all signals and signal to the Driver as may be necessary in accordance with the codes shown in Instruction No.5.

10. ASSISTING DISABLED-DIESEL ELECTRIC PULLMAN TRAIN

In an emergency a disabled Diesel-electric Pullman train can be assisted by any type of fitted train or locomotives, but in such circumstances the train must be worked cautiously and at a reduced speed. When a Diesel-electric Pullman train is being assisted, the working must be in accordance with the special instructions included in the Driving Instructions (BR33003/B1) and according to the type of Train or locomotive which is providing the assistance. The Guard must ride in the rear driving compartment and operate the hand brake under the direction of the Driver as may be necessary. Each Diesel-electric Pullman train is provided at each end with a draw hook without shackle. No connections for heating or automatic brake are provided on the outer headstocks. The Diesel-electric Pullman trains must be coupled to the assisting train or locomotive by means of a screw shackle.

11. DIESEL-ELECTRIC PULLMAN TRAIN ASSISTING DISABLED TRAIN

The Diesel-electric Pullman train may be used to assist (either by drawing or propelling) any other type of fitted train within the following limits.

Gradient	Total weight of train being assisted must not exceed
Rising 1 in 90	160 tons
1 in 200	500 tons
1 in 500	800 tons
Level	1,000 tons

The Diesel-electric Pullman train and the train being assisted must be coupled by means of a screw shackle.

12. DERAILMENTS

In all cases where Diesel-electric Pullman cars are derailed they must be rerailed only under the supervision of and by Motive Power Department staff.

13. SIGNALLING

Diesel-electric Pullman trains must be signalled by the special 'Is line clear' signal, 4-4-6.

APPENDIX 6
WR train reporting numbers 1960 to 1967

UP TRAINS				
Service	Dates	Departure Time	Reporting Number	Notes
ex-Bristol	12-9-1960 to 10-9-1961	7.45am	1A00	
ex-Bristol	12-9-1960 to 10-9-1961	12.30pm	1A50	
ex-Wolverhampton Low Level	12-9-1960 to 10-9-1961	7.00am	1A01	
ex-Birmingham Snow Hill	12-9-1960 to 10-9-1961	2.30pm	1A78	
ex-South Wales	11-9-1961 to 8-9-1963	6.40am	1A06	
ex-Bristol	9-9-1963 to 14-6-1964	8.15am	1A14	
ex-Bristol	9-9-1963 to 14-6-1964	3.15pm	1A83	
ex-South Wales	9-9-1963 to 14-6-1964	6.50am	1A11	
ex-Wolverhampton Low Level	9-9-1963 to 14-6-1964	1.00pm	1A55	
ex-Weston-super-Mare	15-6-1964 to 13-6-1965	2.50pm	1A66	
ex-Wolverhampton Low Level	15-6-1964 to 5-3-1967	7.00am	1V02	Ceased to run after this date
ex-Wolverhampton Low Level	15-6-1964 to 5-3-1967	1.00pm	1V16	Ceased to run after this date
ex-Bristol	14-6-1965 to 5-3-1967	8.15am	1A10	
ex-Bristol	14-6-1965 to 5-3-1967	1.15pm	1A50	
ex-South Wales	14-6-1965 to 5-3-1967	6.55am	1A11	
ex-South Wales	14-6-1965 to 5-3-1967	2.30pm	1A64	

DOWN TRAINS				
Service	Dates	Departure Time	Reporting Number	Notes
to Bristol	12-9-1960 to 10-9-1961	10.05am	1B07	
to Bristol	12-9-1960 to 10-9-1961	4.55pm	1B17	
to Birmingham Snow Hill	12-9-1960 to 10-9-1961	12.10pm	1H13	
to Wolverhampton Low Level	12-9-1960 to 10-9-1961	4.50pm	1H30	
to Bristol	11-6-1961(?) to 14-6-1964	12.45pm	1B13	1B15 from 18-6-1962
to Bristol	11-6-1961(?) to 5-3-1967	5.45pm	1B25	
to South Wales	11-9-1961 to 8-9-1963	4.45pm	1F60	
to South Wales	9-9-1963 to 14-6-1964	4.40pm	1F60	
to Birmingham Snow Hill	9-9-1963 to 14-6-1964	10.10am	1H09	
to Wolverhampton Low Level	9-9-1963 to 14-6-1964	4.50pm	1H30	
to Weston-super-Mare	15-6-1964 to 13-6-1965	11.45am	1B13	
to South Wales	15-6-1964 to 5-3-1967	11.00am	1T32	
to South Wales	15-6-1964 to 13-6-1965	5.40pm	1F60	
to Birmingham Snow Hill	15-6-1964 to 5-3-1967	10.10am	1M11	Ceased to run after this date
to Wolverhampton Low Level	15-6-1964 to 5-3-1967	4.50pm	1M21	Ceased to run after this date
to Bristol	14-6-1965 to 5-3-1967	10.45am	1B10	
to Cardiff General	14-6-1965 to 5-3-1967	11.00am	1F60	

APPENDIX 7
Interior finish and paint schemes

Scheme 1. First Class

Ceiling	Plain colour Polar White matt
1 Lavatory wall including door	Flame Carousel, 502B Matt Decorplast
3 Lavatory walls	Paynes Grey Filigree 113C Matt Decorplast
Floors	Tenazzo

First Class saloon:

Saloon Ceiling	Warerite Plastic A79/9. Grey with Black stripes
Saloon Walls	Lanide French Grey 41 on 3/16th thick Polyurethene plastic free backing
Partitions, including doors and reveals	Rio Rosewood veneer. Stock No 10812/12
Seat Back etc.	Hide to match Lanide Grey 42
Seat Arm Sides	Lanide Black 43
Seat Pedestal	Lanide Black 43
Seat Upholstery Fabric	Trial No W73/2. Red stripe vertical
Saloon Carpet	Cortina as 1/2953. Kingfisher width 24in
Table Tops	Lanide French Grey 41
Lighting Fittings	Satin Chrome plate
General metal work	Anodised aluminium,. Silver bronze
Heater grills	Stainless steel with satin finish
Window blinds	Venetian blinds between double glazed windows.

Scheme 2

Ceiling	Plain colour Polar White matt
1 Lavatory wall including door	Clover Pink Hopscotch, 303C Matt Decorplast
3 Lavatory walls	Pale Pink Filigree, 111C Matt Decorplast
Floors	Tenazzo covering

First Class saloon:

Saloon Ceiling	Warerite Plastic A79/9. Grey with Black stripes
Saloon Walls	Lanide French Grey 41 on 3/16th thick Polyurethene plastic free backing.
Partitions, including doors and reveals	Macasser Ebony Veneer. Stock No 6507/24
Seat Back etc.	Hide to match Lanide Grey 42
Seat Arm Sides	Lanide Black 43
Seat Pedestal	Lanide Black 43
Seat Upholstery Fabric	Trial No W73/3. Blue stripe vertical
Saloon Carpet	Cortina as 1/2953. Cardinal width 24in
Table Tops	Lanide French Grey 41
Lighting Fittings	Satin Chrome plate
General metal work	Anodised aluminium, Silver bronze
Heater grills	Stainless steel with satin finish
Window blinds	Venetian blinds between double glazed windows

Schemes 1 and 2. First Class Vestibules

Vestibule Ceiling	Plain colour polar white matt
Vestibule Walls	Warerite 'Tessuto' pearl grey
1 Lavatory partition, door in vestibule	Formica Tapestry Design. Exc 252 (Special) matt finish Pompadour blue 60767
1 Lavatory partition, door in vestibule	Formica Tapestry Design. Exc 252 (Special) matt finish Pompadour red 60156
Vestibule carpet	
Scheme 1	Cortina as 1/2853. Kingfisher width 24in
Scheme 2	Cardinal as 1/2953. Cardinal width 24in
Gangway connections	Lanide French Grey 41

Lavatories. First Class

Scheme 1
Ceiling	Plain colour polar white matt
1 Lavatory Wall including door	Flame Carousel, 502B. Matt Decorplast
3 Lavatory Walls	Paynes Grey Filigree, 1130 Matt Decorplast
Floors	Tenazzo

Scheme 2
Ceiling	Plain colour polar white matt
1 Lavatory Wall including door	Clover Pink Hopscotch. 3030 Matt Decorplast
3 Lavatory Walls	Pale Pink Filigree. 111C Matt Decorplast
Floors	Tenazzo covering

Icons of different eras. Inside the Pullman shed at old Oak Common a WR set rests whilst alongside former GWR 4-6-0 No 4073 'Caerphilly Castle' awaits its road journey to the Science Museum. *R C Riley/Transport Treasury*

Scheme 3. Second Class Saloon

Ceiling	Warerite Plastic A79/9, Grey with black stripes
Walls	'Vynide' Quality V31, Colour GY 70, Design 409, Finish 1022 on 3/16th thick Polyurethene plastic from backing.
Partitions	Plastic Jester Pattern, Exc/245 (Special) Matt
Doors and Reveals	Warenite Green No 537
Seat Back	'Vaumol' Crushed Grain Grey VM 3393
Seat Arm Sides	Lanide French Grey 41
Seat Pedestal	Lanide Black 43
Seat Upholstery Fabric	Trial No W37, Colour 1. Stripe vertical
Table Tops	Lanide French Grey 41, as for seat arm slides
Lighting fittings	Satin Chrome Plate
General Metal Work	Natural Satin Silver
Heater Grill	Stainless Steel with Satin finish
Window Blinds	Venetian

Scheme 3. Second Class Vestibules

Ceilings	Plain colour Polar White matt
Vestibule Walls	Warerite 'Tessuto' pearl grey
Lavatory partition and door in vestibule	Warerite 'Tessuto' pearl grey
Vestibule Carpet	Design & Colour 38/9600. Worstead Persian Yarn in Devon Weave. Width 24 inches
Gangway connections	'Lanide' French Grey 41

Scheme3. Second Class Lavatories

Ceiling	Plain colour Polar White matt
1 Lavatory wall including door	Chinese Blue Hopscotch 318B. Matt Decorplast
3 Lavatory walls	Paynes Grey filigree. 113C Matt Decorplast
Floors	Tenazzo finish

Venetian blind handle. *Richard Matthews*

APPENDIX 8
The 'Wells Fargo' workings. Extracts from Pullman Car Services Archive 'The Blue Pullman Standby Pullman Sets' by Terry Bye

(See also additional notes within the various chapters.)

1. Diesel Multiple Unit – Blue Pullman Operations.

The Blue Pullman operations were as follows:
The 'Midland Pullman' 4 July 1960 to 15 April 1966.
'Birmingham Pullman' 12 September 1960 to 3 March 1967.
'Bristol Pullman' 12 September 1960 to 4 May 1973.
'South Wales Pullman' 11 September 1961 to 4 May 1973. (Steam service ceased on 8 September 1961.)
'Oxford Pullman' 6 March 1967 to 2 May 1969.

It was identified that in the event of a unit failure or works visit, covering arrangements would be required to be supplied by the Pullman Car Company, and in response the Company put together two locomotive-hauled sets, one to cover the 'Midland Pullman' and the other the Western Region.

2. The Blue Pullman Standby Pullman Sets Stabling Point.
The Midland Region standby set was allocated and stabled at Etches Park Carriage Sidings, Derby.
　The Western Region standby was allocated to and mostly stabled at Old Oak Common London although it was sometimes kept at Swindon.

3. Western Region Locomotive Hauled Set – September 1961.
　Vehicles allocated:
　188. AVON. 66. Parlour. K. (Plated by 1960).
　226*. CETEIA. 73. Parlour. K. (1928 Steel car).
　210. HEBE. 105. Kitchen. K.
　227*. MELANDRA. 74. Parlour. K. (1928 Steel car).
　215. SEVERN. 60. Kitchen. K. (Plated by 1960).
　211. THALIA. 106 Kitchen. K.
　216. THAMES. 61. Kitchen. K. (Plated by 1960).
　212. THETIS. 107. Kitchen. K.
　193. WYE. 35. Parlour. K.

The plan was for the cars to be interchangeable between both the Midland and Western Regions. No Pullman parlour brake cars were allocated to these formations – although at least one photograph would tend to contradict the parlour brake comment.
　Information Source: *Pullman* by Julian Morel. We know they were used on the WR through the images we have obtained.

Additional Notes:
Cars 105, 106 and 107 were originally MARCELLE, SYBIL and KATHLEEN, but had been converted in 1946 from 1st to 3rd class (all originally built 1927).
*CETEIA and MELANDRA were both 1928 built all steel cars.
Information Source: 'PCS-Archive'.

1961:
Western Region – 25 September 1961
WR standby train first recorded use, with No 6020 *King Henry IV* noted hauling the morning up 'Birmingham Pullman'. Only one Pullman car identified in the formation – CAR No. 27.

26 September 1961
WR standby train consisting of five Pullman cars and two BR Mk1 FO coaches painted in umber and cream noted passing Acocks Green.
Information Source: *Trains Illustrated* November 1961.

1962:
26 February to and including 12 March 1962
The 'Bristol Pullman' multiple unit is withdrawn for overhaul. It is replaced by a locomotive-hauled seven-coach set. This includes four second class Pullman cars, one First Class car 'CECILIA' and two ordinary second opens.
Information Source: *Railway Magazine* May 1962.

28 April 1962
Noted at Old Oak Common, Pullman cars 54, 169, CECILIA, 249, 27 and two BR Mk1 coaches W3093 and 3094 in chocolate and cream.
Information Source: K. Gunner, 11 January 2010.

12 July 1962
The 'Birmingham Pullman' multiple unit is withdrawn for overhaul, the standby set hauled by a six-day-old D1006 *Western Stalwart* included Pullman cars 27/249/169/54 in the formation plus First Opens W3093 and W3094.
Information Source: *Railway World* May 1973 and Philippa Dudek-Mason.

16 July 1962
D1001 *Western Pathfinder* spotted at Snow Hill
Information Source: *The Railway Magazine* February 2017.

7 January 1963, the standby Pullman working the Birmingham Pullman service at Acocks Green behind D1046 Western Marquis. *Warwickshire Railways.com*

10-14 September 1962
The 'South Wales Pullman' service is covered by the locomotive-hauled set.
Information Source: *Modern Railways* November 1962'.

14/15 November 1962
The 'South Wales Pullman' service is covered by the locomotive-hauled set.
Information Source: Mike Woodhouse OOC 81A

Winter Timetable 1962
The locomotive-hauled set. The two BR Mk1 FO have been removed from the set.
Pullman Kitchen First cars AURELIA, CECILIA, CHLORIA, MEDUSA and ROSAMUND are returned to the Southern Region.
Four second class Pullman cars are converted to first class and allocated names.
Parlour WYE Ex CAR No. 35.
Parlour AVON Ex CAR No. 66.
Kitchen THAMES Ex CAR No. 61.
Kitchen SEVERN Ex CAR No. 60.
The train formation will consist Brake 2nd, Kitchen 2nd, Kitchen 1st, Parlour 1st, Kitchen 1st, Kitchen 2nd, Brake 2nd.
Information Source: PCS-Archive.

1963
Loco-hauled 'South Wales Pullman' with 'Western' diesel at its head failed four miles east of Swindon. No 7906 *Fron Hall* was in the goods loop with a freight. The engine was not prepared but took over the working making 45-50 past Challow whilst the fireman 'got the fire right'. 'They let rip from Didcot and made a fast run to Paddington'. Information source: Adrian Vaughan.

7 January 1963
The 'Birmingham Pullman' hauled by D1046 *Western Marquis* with eight Pullman cars noted at Acocks Green.
Information Source: Warwickshire Railways.com.

2 April 1963
Two Western Region multiple units out of service; two locomotive-hauled sets standing in.
Information Source: *Modern Railways* June 1963.
One was the 'South Wales Pullman' and the other was the 'Birmingham Pullman'
Information Source: Mike Woodhouse OOC 81A

11 April 1963
The up 'Birmingham Pullman' locomotive hauled by D1006 *Western Stalwart*.
Information Source: *Railway Magazine* August 1963.

16 April 1963
D834 *Pathfinder* noted with locomotive hauled down 'Bristol Pullman'.
Information Source: *Railway Magazine* June 1963.

17 April 1963
D7066 noted at Paddington with the 'South Wales Pullman'.
Information Source: *Railway Magazine* July 1963.

3 June 1963
'Birmingham Pullman' noted on Hatton Bank hauled by D1002 *Western Explorer*.
Information Source: *Heyday of the Westerns* by Derek Huntriss

6 June 1963
'Birmingham Pullman' noted passing Bentley Heath hauled by D1002 *Western Explorer* with CAR No. 27.
Information Source: M. Mensing.

15 August 1963
D1040 *Western Queen* hauling the 'Birmingham Pullman' collides with a goods train at Knowle & Dorridge station. The three-footplate crew were fatally injured.
Information Source: *Railway Magazine* October 1963.

8 May 1964
'Bristol Pullman' set withdrawn for approximately six weeks, to undergo a complete overhaul at Swindon works. This was followed by the 'Birmingham Pullman' and lastly by the 'South Wales Pullman' set which was due in 1965. The locomotive-hauled set covered for the withdrawal period. Information Source: *Railway Magazine* June 1964.

2 June 1964
The up 'Bristol Pullman' arrives at Paddington behind 'Hall' class No. 7916 *Mobberley Hall*. Information Source: *Railway Magazine* September 1964.

1 July 1964
'South Wales Pullman' service is covered by the locomotive-hauled set.
Information Source: Mike Woodhouse OOC 81A

30 July 1964
'South Wales Pullman' service is covered by the locomotive-hauled set.
Noted at Paddington

25 August 1964
The 'Birmingham Pullman' standby set was noted at Snow Hill. Pullman cars within the formation were CAR No. 54, CAR No. 106, CAR No. 340*, CAR No. 352*, CAR No. 344*, CAR No. 105 and CAR No. 55.
*These three cars are BR Mk1 1960/1 Metro-Cammell Pullman cars acting as first class with 2x1 seating. Two cars from the 'Midland Pullman' standby set CAR No. 105 and 106 were included in the formation. None of the pre-1960 cars carried the allocated names as detailed in 1962.
Information Source: Ian Breeden, 8 February 2010.

26 August 1964
The 13.00 'Birmingham Pullman' consisting of the standby set was noted at High Wycombe hauled by D1690 with

A 1962 view of the stand-by set at the same location, Acocks Green: seven vehicles made up of five Pullman cars and two BR Mk1 carriages. The first of the 'Western' class, D1000 Western Enterprise, is at the head. *Michael Mensing*

The Blue Pullman Story

Bath on 29 May 1964, D1005 Western Venturer has nine cars on the down 'Bristol Pullman' service. This was during the six-week period the Bristol set had been withdrawn for overhaul. *M. B. Warburton courtesy Mrs Margaret Warburton*

Solihull 1964, this time eight vehicles, comprising from the front, Cars: 27, 105, 340, 352, 344 and the last three BR-built Pullman vehicles from the Eastern Region, Nos 107, 106 and a BR Mk1 brake. At the head is an unidentified 'Brush Type 4' (later Class 47). *Michael Mensing*

Pullman cars CAR No. 54, CAR No. 106, CAR No. 340*, CAR No. 352*, CAR No. 344*, CAR No. 105 and CAR No. 55. Information Source: *Pullman Travelling in Style* by Brian Haresnape.

31 August 1964
Noted passing Solihull, D1683 with the standby set on the 16.50 Paddington to Wolverhampton service. Information Source: *Trains Illustrated – Express Train* 1977.

7 May 1965
The 'South Wales Pullman Set' is withdrawn for approximately six weeks, to undergo a complete overhaul at Swindon works. The standby set covered for the withdrawal period.
Information Source: PCS-Archive.

4 July 1966
Both ex-'Midland Pullman' six- cars sets noted at Swindon. This allows the withdrawal of the standby train formations.
Information Source: PCS-Archive.

3 October 1966
The up morning 'Birmingham Pullman' set failed at Banbury. The 10.10am departure from Paddington was hastily formed of rather grubby standard stock without even refreshment facilities. An eleven-minute late departure was announced as '… due to lack of crew to work the diesel locomotive.' According to an (obvious) quote from a correspondent in *Railway Observer* who reported the incident, 'Not a brilliant performance for one of BR's prestige trains.'

3 March 1967
The 'Birmingham Pullman' service using a 'Blue Pullman' set is withdrawn.
Information Source: PCS-Archive.

6 March 1967
The 'Oxford Pullman' service using a 'Blue Pullman' set commences.
Information Source: PCS-Archive.

6 March 1967
The 'South Wales Pullman' service now all 'Blue Pullman' operated (only one set allocated since 11 September 1961 working with a loco-hauled set).
Information Source: PCS-Archive.

March 1967
Locomotive-hauled replaced by the two surplus 'Midland Pullman' sets which transferred to Western Region following the withdrawal of the 'Midland Pullman' service in 1966.
Information Source: 'PCS-Archive.

Midland Region Locomotive-hauled set – September 1962.

The second stand-by train is formed for the Midland Region operations of the 'Midland Pullman' set.

248 ATHENE Ex CAR No. 248 Brake Parlour
212 THETIS Ex CAR No. 107 Kitchen
226* CETEIA Ex CAR No. 73 Parlour
211 THALIA Ex CAR No. 106 Kitchen
161 FORTUNA Brake Parlour
253* JUANA Parlour
227* MELANDRA Ex CAR No. 74 Parlour
HEBE Ex CAR No. 105 Kitchen
*1928 All-steel car.

The set was never used, and in January 1963 was being used on the 'Birmingham Pullman'. Information Source: *Traction Magazine* November 1997. *(The holding of a complete spare train on the LMR, plus a rake of five*

Steam to the rescue! 'Birmingham Pullman' substitute – note the words 'Birmingham Pullman' on the cantrail of the first coach and the missing table lamps in this vehicle – running behind a 'King' near Acocks Green. This would appear to be a different member of the class to that referred to of 25 September 1961, when No 6020 King Henry IV worked the service. Apart from the other mentioned incident involving No 7916, 'Castle'-type steam engines are also known to have hauled the spare set when required, including an updated view of No 5036 on the down Birmingham service. (The reader is also referenced to Pullman Profile No 2 – *The Standard 'K' Type Cars* for further information on the vehicles used in the stand-by sets.

Pullmans and a set of first spare first class coaches at Manchester, can only be described as a shocking waste of a resource – KJR)
1962, five BR Mk1 Pullman Cars allocated to the Western Region from the Eastern Region as direct substitutes to cover failures and works visits of the 'Blue Pullman' services out of Paddington.
Second Class Kitchen CAR No. 340, 341, 342, 343 and 344.
Second Class Parlour CAR No. 348, 349, 350, 351 and 352.
The Western Region 'Birmingham Pullman' locomotive-hauled set formed of:
Parlour Brake Second CAR No. 65. Built 1920.
Pullman Kitchen Second CAR No. 106. Built 1927.
Mk1 Pullman Kitchen Second CAR No. 340. Built 1960.
Mk1 Pullman Parlour Second CAR No. 352. Built 1960.
Mk1 Pullman Kitchen Second CAR No. 344. Built 1960.
Pullman Kitchen Second CAR No. 105. Built 1927.
Parlour Brake Second CAR No. 55. Built 1923.
Spare locomotive hauled cars:
Parlour Brake Second CAR No. 27. Built 1923.
Kitchen Second CAR No. 249. Built 1925.
Kitchen Second CAR No. 169. Built 1924.
Parlour Brake Second CAR No. 54. Built 1923.
Kitchen First CECELIA Built 1927.
In addition two BR Mk1 First Opens Nos. W3093 and W3094, in Western Region chocolate and cream livery.
Information Source: 'PCS-Archive'.

APPENDIX 9
British Railways Board, Operational Research Department. Blue Pullmans (Western Region) May 1965, Report No O.77. Blue Pullmans Western Region.

(Note, this official BR[WR] report includes separate appendices. To avoid confusion with appendices contained in this book, those within this report and the references thereto have been changed to Roman numerals.)

The project was undertaken at the request of the Assistant General Manager (Movements), Western Region, with the following terms of reference:

Operational Research are to examine the problem of determining the best use, from 1967 onwards, for the 36 Blue Pullman Cars then available to the Western Region. In making recommendations they will consider the overall profitability of the Pullmans (i.e. for the Western Region and the Pullman Division combined); they will also take account of possible new routes, the appropriate standby arrangements and the possible conversion of cars to make suitable formations.

The problem will arise after the completion of the L.M.R. electrification, when the Paddington–Birmingham route will no longer be available to the Western Region for Pullman services, and when it is proposed that the Western Region should take over from the London Midland Region its two diesel-electric multiple-unit Pullmans. This will leave the Western Region with two of its existing Blue Pullman routes (Paddington–Bristol and Paddington–South Wales) and 36 Blue Pullman cars, at present arranged in three eight-car trains and two six-car trains.

The basic approach has been economic. The cost and revenue data used are discussed in Appendix I. They are rough averages designed to assist in making broad policy decisions on the use of the Pullmans. Further costing will be necessary following regional decisions on the details of operation of any specific services selected for closer examination.

This report first considers appropriate train formations for operation in the Region, then the general uses to which these formations can be put and finally discusses potential routes for Blue Pullmans.

TRAIN FORMATIONS

Appendix II lists possible arrangements of the 36 cars to give train formations and considers their suitability for use on the Western Region. The detailed examination in this appendix shows that, although there are sufficient motive power and kitchen cars for five trains, the possible formations are such that not all of the five could be run economically on the Region. The best arrangements therefore produce four trains, even though this leaves two motor and two kitchen cars with only a very limited value as spares.

Of possible four-train arrangements, some are rejected because of unsuitable class composition or unsuitable seating layout. The best seems to be an arrangement with four eight-car trains with identical capacities of 108 First Class and 114 Second Class seats (six less Second Class than the present W.R. trains). An alternative leaves the three WR trains as they are and gives a fourth train with 72 First and 132 Second Class seats, Both these alternatives (arrangements 5[ii] and 6 [ii] in Appendix II) involve a conversion cost of £2,000, and both involve the use of First Class cars as Second Class although they are separated by the kitchen from the cars used as First Class.

GENERAL USES

There are in principle three uses for a Pullman train:
- as an additional service using a completely new path
- as a replacement of an 'ordinary' train on an existing service
- as a standby for the Pullman trains in operation

a) Standby

Standby requirements are discussed in appendix III and an attempt is made to assess the economic value of using a Blue Pullman as a standby instead of the present old hauled Pullman stock. The value is small on the assumption that old stock will be available for a standby in future [reasonable in view of the modernisation of the Pullman Division's fleet]. A Blue Pullman standby would retain the traffic lost by using inferior stock, mainly during the seven-week overhaul for each Pullman in service which takes place every three years. Experience in 1964 shows this to be small, with an estimated maximum loss of revenue of about £2,500 p.a., in economic terms therefore a Blue Pullman would be better employed in service, if a profitable route could be found. The seven-week overhaul plus breakdowns are together expected to keep each Blue Pullman out of service in future for an average of 18 days per year (routine maintenance is all planned for 'out of service' times, mainly at weekends). If all four trains were in service, the old standby would be in use, somewhere in the Region, for over a quarter of the year. Consideration of the 'railway image' might be held to outweigh these economic considerations.

b) Additional Service

When operated as an additional service, a Blue Pullman would have to cover its full costs, which are shown in Appendix I to be around £95,000 p.a. Using the broad average receipts in the same Appendix, we can make the following very rough calculations. If the Pullman drew all its traffic from existing services it would have to carry 190,000 passengers p.a. to obtain sufficient in supplements, and food and drink profit, to cover its costs. If say 10 per cent of its passengers were new to rail, (producing additional fares) it would have to carry about 150,000 passengers p.a. This compares with 1964 carryings on the present W.R. Pullmans of:

South Wales	£104,000
Bristol	£134,000
Birmingham	£157,000

These are the routes with the highest Pullman potential in the Region, so that the only hope of employing any further Blue Pullmans profitably is to use them to replace existing services rather than as additional services.

c) Replacement Service

Appendix I shows that a Blue Pullman would have to cover an additional cost, compared with the ordinary service which it replaces, of roughly £33,000–£38,000 p.a. (depending on whether the existing service has a restaurant car). Average receipts are again used to make crude estimates of the traffic required. In this context the profitability of the Blue Pullman is assessed by the addition to the net revenue resulting from its substitution for an ordinary service.

To make a profit of say £10,000 p.a,, a Blue Pullman must carry some 90,000 passengers p.a. if they all come from existing services. If 10 per cent of its passengers are new to rail its carryings need to be 70,000 p.a. If on the other hand its substitution for the ordinary service deters say 5 per cent of existing passengers so that they leave rail for other transport, it would need almost 110,000 passengers per year to make the same profit.

POTENTIAL ROUTES

Appendix IV discusses, in the light of the above conclusions, routes within the Western Region on which the four Blue Pullmans might be used.

On the basis of the crude costing used here, the existing services on the Paddington–Bristol and Paddington–South Wales routes are making sufficient money for the Region and the Pullman Division combined to justify continuing them.

For the remaining two trains only three possibilities emerge for further consideration. The one with the greatest potential for profit is to run reciprocal services on the; Paddington–Bristol route, starting from Paddington in the morning. There may, however, be serious problems associated with having such a high proportion of Pullmans on this route.

A reciprocal service is also possible for the Paddington–South Wales route, although a somewhat more variable traffic might create greater difficulties than on the Paddington–Bristol route. The risk of going beyond the 'saturation point' for Pullmans is present on this route too.

Thirdly there is a marginal case for considering the replacement of the 'Golden Hind' with a Blue Pullman on the South West route. The existing traffic is not ideally suitable for Pullmans and probably would need a train with a high proportion of Second Class accommodation. Replacement of the 'Golden Hind' is likely to produce capacity problems on the 'Mayflower on the same route. If a Blue Pullman ran profitably on one return trip a day on this route it would be available at marginal cost for a shorter return trip from Paddington the middle of the day. Paddington–Oxford might be considered for this.

If, in the light of the comments in Appendix IV and of general policy considerations, it is decided to examine further any of these potential additional services, it will be necessary to formulate specific operating proposals and submit them to a detailed costing of train operation including the conversion and terminal costs involved. If, on closer examination, not more than one proposed operation can be shown to be practicable and profitable, then the best use within the Region for the fourth Blue Pullman would be as a standby.

GENERAL COMMENTS

The economic examination in this report assumes Pullman supplement charges to be similar to those on the present Pullman services. Any change in the future is not likely to effect the general arguments used here unless it produces a large increase in receipts. If, for example, Second Class supplements were raised to the level of First Class, a Blue Pullman run as a replacement for an existing service would make £10,000 p.a. profit with 70,000 passengers p.a. instead of the 90,000 passengers p.a. shown previously.

Maintenance costs constitute about a third of total Blue Pullman operating costs and there is a strong incentive for pursuing any proposal to reduce them. For instance, the value of the travelling technicians has been questioned. With a full complement on four trains they would cost some £15,000 p.a. and their replacement by platform inspectors might reduce this to a third. This would not affect the general arguments in this report but would be a welcome contribution to the profitability of Blue Pullmans.

If four Blue Pullmans are put into service, it would be worth investigating the possibility of reducing the time taken for the three-yearly overhaul, so that the use of a standby of inferior stock can be minimised. Closer study perhaps using Network Planning techniques might show that the overhaul could be planned so that it is only the engines that need to be in the workshops for the whole of the seven weeks and, by use of the spare Motor Firsts, a train could be released for service earlier. If only three Blue Pullmans can be put into profitable service and one is used permanently as a standby, a train could be made available for week-end working despite the maintenance requirements. The potential traffic is likely to be small compared with the weekday services discussed in this report but it could make the use of one set as a standby more profitable.

CONCLUSIONS

From this general survey of the problem it is not obvious that the Western Region can make profitable use of all the 36 existing Blue Pullman cars.

With the technical limitations on possible formations and with the present Pullman charges, it appears that the Region could operate economically only four trains made up from the existing five trains.

This leaves two motor and two kitchen cars as spares with a value that is limited, even if further examination shows that they can be used to give somewhat higher utilisation of the four train formations.

Two trains can be used profitably for the existing services on the Paddington–Bristol and Paddington–South Wales routes.

For profitable use of the other two trains, the crude costing used in this report has excluded all but three possibilities (reciprocal services on the Bristol and South Wales routes and replacing the 'Golden Hind'), and each of these is doubtful as a practical proposal.

If more detailed examination shows the doubts to be well-founded for more than one of these possibilities, then the best use for one of the four Blue Pullman trains would be as a standby, even though the economic case for this is slight.

APPENDIX I

BROAD COMPARISON OF COSTS AND REVENUE FOR 'NOTIONAL' BLUE PULLMAN AND ORDINARY TRAINS

The presentation of costs and revenue here is intended to enable crude estimates to be made of the profitability of Blue Pullman operation in varying circumstances. Any specific proposal for a particular service will obviously require more refined costing before implementation.

The cost estimates are based on information obtained from the Regional Traffic Costing Department. The revenue estimates are based on an analysis of Pullman receipts from existing W.R. services in the last seven periods of 1964.

COSTS

For the Blue Pullman, these relate to an eight-car train which, with the present formation, gives 108 First Class seats and 120 Second Class seats. The 'notional' ordinary train has a Type 4 locomotive, hauling 10 coaches in a formation with 178 First Class seats and 256 Second Class seats.

Costs are considered to be of three types: those related to time (annual costs not greatly affected by the way in which the train is operated); those related to train mileage (fuel, lubricants and some of the maintenance), and those related to the number of passengers (Pullman costs for food and drink). It is more convenient to consider passenger costs together with receipts so as to give an average gross profit per passenger. This is done in the discussion of revenue at the end of this Appendix. Time costs and mileage costs for a Blue Pullman and an ordinary train are compared below with an explanation of how they were built up.

	Blue Pullman	Ordinary Train
Time Costs Train	£50,000 p.a.	£42,000
Pullman	£25,000	
	£75,000 p.a.	£42,000 p.a.
Mileage Costs	£0.207/train mile	£0.208/train mile

Time costs for the train are stock provision, stabling and servicing, certain of the maintenance costs and crew costs.

Stock provision costs are derived from the original capital cost and cover depreciation and interest on the original investment. They are relevant to the consideration of whether to replace existing stock because in the long run the capital used must be replaced and must earn a return. In the present situation, however, where we are considering how best to use existing stock, the capital expenditure which these costs represent has already been made and cannot be 'unmade'. In these circumstances the cost of providing stock for a particular service is the 'opportunity cost' of the value of the stock in alternative uses. Blue Pullmans, by their nature, are specific to the very restricted type of service considered in this report. They have virtually no scrap value within the Region since they have only minor components in common with other stock. Therefore the 'opportunity cost' of using the 36 existing cars can be regarded as nil. On the other hand, both locomotive and coaching stock for the ordinary train can, in effect, come from a common pool which serves many uses (i.e. train services). The addition or deletion of any one of the services supplied with stock from this pool can be reflected fairly quickly in renewal costs. Therefore the 'opportunity cost' of using an ordinary train is the depreciation and interest for new stock. In line with this reasoning the conventionally calculated stock provision cost is not included above for the Blue Pullman (£31,000 p.a.) but is included for the ordinary train (£20,000 p.a.).

Time-based maintenance costs and stabling and servicing add up to some £35,000 p.a. for the Blue Pullman and £15,000 p.a. for the ordinary train. For the Blue Pullman they include the costs of the travelling technicians and the standby train. Train crew costs are not completely related to time and are more dependent on the manner of operation. On any route, however, they will be higher for the Blue Pullman than for the ordinary train because the former has another driver instead of a second man and because Blue Pullman drivers form a separate link. The cost of around £15,000 p.a. per train for present Pullman operation is therefore reduced to £12,000 p.a. for the ordinary train.

The costing from which the time costs for each train were derived had been built up on a different basis. The Blue Pullman costs are for one set operated 255 days a year, as at present, with normal planned maintenance taking place at weekends. The time costs for the ordinary train represent the cost of having locomotive and coaching stock available for 307 days a year (i.e. the normal basis of costing exercises). Some adjustment is obviously necessary to make the costs for the two trains comparable, but the exact amount by which the ordinary train's time costs should be reduced depends upon the detailed diagramming for any service examined. This Appendix, however, aims to build up rough estimates which can be used in a preliminary costing of several routes. For this purpose the ordinary train's total of £35,000 p.a. for stock provision, time-based maintenance, stabling and servicing has been reduced to £30,000 p.a., which with the addition of train crew costs, gives £42,000 p.a. With the exclusion of stock provision explained above, the equivalent costs for the Blue Pullman total £50,000 p.a.

The Pullman time costs of £25,000 p.a. cover the Pullman crew and establishment costs (fuel, water, linen services and overheads). The 'notional' ordinary train includes a restaurant car so that it has costs of the same type. These are not shown above, however, because in any comparison with the Blue Pullman, restaurant car receipts would have to be offset against these costs. The extra amount that a Blue Pullman would have to earn to compensate for the loss of restaurant car profit on the service which it replaced would differ on different routes, but it seems unlikely to exceed £5,000 p.a.

Mileage costs for the Blue Pullman (£0.207 per train mile) are virtually the same as for the ordinary train (£0.208 per train mile) since, although the Blue Pullman mileage maintenance cost is higher, its fuel and lubricants cost is lower.

For passengers transferred from an existing service to a Blue Pullman. the extra revenue is in the supplement and in the profit made on food and drink. Receipts under these headings have been calculated per passenger for each of the present three W.R. trains in the last seven periods of 1964 (i.e, after the latest increases in supplement charges).

Supplement Receipts per passenger obviously depend on

	Supplement Receipts per Passenger	Food & drink Profit per Passenger	Total extra Receipts per Passenger
'Bristol Pullman'	7s 4d	1s 11d	9s 3d
'Birmingham Pullman'	7s 4d	2s 8d	10s 0d
'South Wales Pullman'	7s 9d	3s 9d*	11s 6d
Average	7s 6d	2s 9d	10s 3d.

*Average of last four periods in 1964, after the introduction of the mid-day service

the class composition of the traffic but this is much the same for the three existing routes. The average is understandably higher for the South Wales route since the maximum supplement charged is 12s 6d compared with 11s 0d on the other two routes and the length of the journey seems to induce a higher consumption of food and drink. Any class difference in food and drink profit per passenger appears from the analyses to be outweighed by other factors (distance travelled, time of day, etc.).

The average supplement receipts shown above are based on the present level of charges. If the charge for Second Class passengers were raised to the level of the present First Class supplements, it is estimated that supplement receipts per passenger would rise to 10s 3d and the total extra receipts per passenger would therefore be 13s 0d.

If the introduction of a Blue Pullman leads to a change in the rail traffic (i.e. either attracts new passengers who previously did not travel by rail or loses existing passengers who will not pay the supplement and cannot travel on another service), then we must consider the effect on fares receipts as well as the additional Pullman revenue. Allowing for the recent increase in fares, the average fares receipts per passenger on the present blue Pullman services are estimated to be 35s.

CONCLUSIONS

Talking in very rough terms, the above figures indicate how much additional revenue a Blue Pullman service needs to bring in (to the Region and Pullman Division combined) if it is to pay for itself. If it is a completely new service, it breaks even when it brings in £75,000 p.a. plus £0.207 per train mile. With four trips a day over a 100-mile route this means a total of over £95,000 p.a.

If it replaces an existing ordinary train service the mileage costs virtually cancel out. To break even it must result in earnings £75, 000 — £42,000 = £33, 000 p.a, more than the existing service and up to £5,000 more if the existing service has a restaurant car.

For the same purposes of rough calculation we can reckon the effects on receipts of introducing a Blue Pullman service to be as follows:

For every existing passenger who transfers to the Pullman we gain 10s 0d

For every new passenger attracted to the Pullman we gain £2 5s 0d

For every existing passenger lost to the railway we lose £1 15s 0d

For every existing passenger who transfers to another service there is no change.

APPENDIX II

The table below analyses by type the 36 cars available to the Western Region from 1967 onwards|:

Thus, the present W.R. and L.M.R. trains have only one of

Type	Seats	Bogies	No. of Cars		
			W.R.	L.M.R	Total
1 Motor Second	18	A B (power)	6	-	6
2 Parlour Second	42	C (power) D	6	-	6
3 Kitchen First	18	Trailer Trailer	6	-	6
4 Parlour First	36	Trailer Trailer	6	4	10
5 Kitchen First	18	C (power) Trailer	-	4	4
6 Motor First	12	A B (power)	-	4	4
			24	12	36

the six types of car in common (Type 4, Parlour First), and none of the other cars in the L.M.R. formation is completely interchangeable with any car in the W.R. formation. The W.R. Motor car has Second Class seats while the L.M.R. equivalent has First. Although Kitchen cars in both formations are First Class, the L.M.R. type has a powered bogie and the W.R. type does not. The W.R. train has its power bogie on the Parlour Second which has no equivalent in the L.M.R. train. The Motor cars are designed to be placed at the ends of a train and two of these provide sufficient motive power for a train with a maximum of eight cars. Feasible formations within these restrictions are considered below.

The 36 cars include sufficient motive power and kitchen cars for five trains. (Arrangements 1, 2 and 3).

ARRANGEMENT 1

Type	Car Types	Seats		
		First	Second	Total
A	1 – 2 – 3 – 4 – 4 – 3 – 2 – 1	108	120	228
B	1 – 2 – 3 – 4 – 4 – 3 – 2 – 1	108	120	228
C	1 – 2 – 3 – 4 – 4 – 3 – 2 – 1	108	120	228
D	1 – 2 – 3 – 4 – 4 – 3 – 2 – 1	108	120	228
E	6 – 5 – 4 – 4 – 5 – 6	132		132
F	6 – 5 – 4 – 4 – 5 – 6	132		132

These are the formations of the present eight-car W.R. trains and six-car L.M.R. trains

This arrangement gives three trains of eight cars and two of six cars. It is feasible only if the six-car trains can be operated profitably in the Region. The profitability is assessed by a rough calculation similar to that used later in the main body of the report.

The six-car train has a seating capacity of 132 seats, all of which are First Class. Any route which could provide a sufficient amount of First Class traffic would have considerable Second Class traffic as well. The six-car Pullman would therefore have to be operated as an extra service, not as a substitute for an existing service.

It is estimated that the cost of a six-car train would be some £15,000 p. a. less than for the eight-car train costed in Appendix I. To justify its introduction on a route the Pullman would therefore have to earn extra revenue in the region of £80,000 p.a. Its additional revenue per passenger would be higher than the average shown in Appendix I but not much higher than 15s -d. Therefore, if the six-car Pullman's load was composed of traffic attracted from existing services it would have to carry 107,000 passengers a year. This would mean two trips a day with a completely full load every day and a further two trips with an average of nearly two-thirds load. This is a far better performance in relation to First Class capacity than the existing Western Region Pullmans achieve, and these have only 108 First Class seats and are operated on the most favourable routes. Fewer passengers would be required to break even if some were newly attracted to the railway by the Pullman service, but as will be seen later there are no routes in the Region where existing First Class traffic seems a large enough base on which to build up this traffic.

ARRANGEMENT 2

Type	Car Types	Seats		
		First	Second	Total
A	1 – 2 – 3 – 4 – 4 – 5 – 6*	108	72	180
B	1 – 2 – 3 – 4 – 4 – 5 – 6*	108	72	180
C	1 – 2 – 3 – 4 – 4 – 5 – 6*	108	72	180
D	1 – 2 – 3 – 4 – 4 – 5 – 6*	108	72	180
E	1 – 2 – 3 – 4 – 4 – 3 – 2 – 1	108	120	228

No conversion is necessary, but four First Class Type 6 cars marked (*) are used as Second Class

This arrangement gives four trains with seven cars and 180 seats and one with eight cars and 228 seats. Its adoption would mean at least one of the two existing Pullman services (Bristol and South Wales) would have a reduction of 48 seats in its Second Class seating capacity from 120 to 72. The effect of this reduction has been estimated from an analysis of carryings during 1964 on the Bristol and South Wales routes. This is confined to the morning and evening trains since the midday trains are not heavily loaded.

A capacity of 72 would be inadequate for Second Class passengers on 230–240 days a year on each of the morning trains and 130 days on each of the evening trains. In total some 12,000 passengers per annum would be unaccommodated in Second Class seats on either of the two routes and only about half of them could have First Class seats, even if they were willing to pay the extra supplement and fare. If all of them were completely lost to rail travel it is estimated that this would represent a loss of revenue of approximately £20,000 p.a. on each route. If all travelled on alternative rail services the loss would be about £5,000 p.a. Some might travel First Class on the Pullman; on the other hand others might be deterred from using the Pullman even when accommodation was available.

The risk of losing possibly £20,000 p.a. on one of these two existing routes would have to be justified by finding

363

three profitable new routes for the remaining trains in this arrangement. As will be seen later this is unlikely.

ARRANGEMENT 3			Seats		
Type	Car Types	First	Second	Total
A	1 – 2 – 3 – 4 – 4 – 3 – 2 – 6*	108	114	222
B	1 – 2 – 3 – 4 – 4 – 3 – 2 – 6*	108	114	222
C	1 – 2 – 3 – 4 – 4 – 5 – 1	108	78	186
D	1 – 2 – 3 – 4 – 4 – 5 – 1	108	78	186
E	6 – 5 – 4 – 4 – 5 – 6	132	-	132
No conversion is necessary, but two First Class Type 6 cars marked (*) are used as Second Class				

This arrangement includes one six-car train of 132 First Class seats and so is subject to the same argument as Arrangement 1.

We are then left to consider arrangements giving four trains. All of these leave two spare Motor Firsts and two spare Kitchen Firsts. As will be seen from Appendix III they have limited value as spares since the longest time when trains have to be taken out of service is for the three yearly seven-week overhaul when all cars are worked on together.

ARRANGEMENT 4			Seats		
Type	Car Types	First	Second	Total
A	1 – 2 – 3 – 4 – 4 – 3 – 2 – 6*	108	114	222
B	1 – 2 – 3 – 4 – 4 – 3 – 2 – 6*	108	114	222
C	1 – 2 – 3 – 4 – 4 – 4 – 5 – 1	144	78	222
D	1 – 2 – 3 – 4 – 4 – 4 – 5 – 1	144	78	222
Spare	6 6 5 5			
No conversion is necessary, but two First Class Type 6 cars marked (*) are used as Second Class				

This arrangement gives four trains of 222 seats but two of them have 144 First Class and 78 Second Class. This is the wrong balance for the two existing services, where the 120 Second Class seats are more often full than the 108 First Class seats. Other potential routes for Blue Pullmans are likely to have an even lower ratio of First to Second Class.

ARRANGEMENT 5			Seats		
Type	Car Types	First	Second	Total
A	1 – 2 – 3 – 4 – 4 – 3 – 2 – 6*	108	114	222
B	1 – 2 – 3 – 4 – 4 – 3 – 2 – 6*	108	114	222
C	1 – 2 – 3 – 4 – 4 – 5 – 4 – 1	144	114	222
D	1 – 2 – 3 – 4 – 4 – 5 – 4 – 1	144	114	222
Spare	6 6 5 5			

This is the same as Arrangement 4 except that two Type 4 cars are reclassified as well as two Type 6 cars. The Kitchen cars are also repositioned to make formations C and D similar to A and B. This can be achieved either (i) by running power cables through the Type 4 cars to feed the traction motors on the Type 5 cars; or (ii) by fitting the Type 4 cars with power bogies from the two spare Type 5 cars (and making the necessary alterations to their underframes) and by removing the traction motors from the two Type 5 cars in use and re springing their motor bogies. The two spare Type 5 Kitchen cars would be unusable without expenditure on bogie changing.

The cost of either (i) or (ii) would be £2,000, but (ii) is preferable because the Type 5 car can be placed so that the kitchen divides the reclassified Type 4 car from the First Class accommodation.

This arrangement gives four trains, all with 108 First Class seats and 114 Second. This is six fewer Second Class seats than on the existing W.R. formations. The effect of this reduction in capacity on the Bristol and South Wales routes has been estimated from an analysis similar to that mentioned in the discussion of Arrangement 2 above.

With a capacity of 114, the Blue Pullman services on each route would fail to accommodate about 700 Second Class passengers per annum. At the worst, if all of these passengers were completely lost to rail, revenue on the two routes combined would be reduced by £2,500 p.a.

ARRANGEMENT 6			Seats		
Type	Car Types	First	Second	Total
A	1 – 2 – 3 – 4 – 4 – 3 – 2 – 1	108	120	228
B	1 – 2 – 3 – 4 – 4 – 3 – 2 – 1	108	120	228
C	1 – 2 – 3 – 4 – 4 – 3 – 2 – 1	108	120	228
D	6* – 4* – 5* – 4 – 4 – 5* – 4* – 6*	72	132	204
Spare	6 6 5 5			

Trains A, B and C are the present W.R. trains, Train D is made up from L.M.R. First Class cars but the three cars at each end marked (*) are reclassified Second Class. The Type and five cars at each end are treated in the same ways as in trains C and D of Arrangements 5(i) and 5(ii) to produce Arrangements 6(i) and 6(ii). The necessary conversions could be made at the same cost of £2,000.

This arrangement leaves the three Western Region trains, each with 108 First Class seats and 120 Second, and provides an extra train with 72 First Class seats and 132 Second Class seats, which might be useful on routes where the preponderance of Second Class traffic is greater than on the present routes. It would need more passengers per year to break even, however, to compensate for lower average supplement receipts than those on the existing W.R. Pullmans.

ARRANGEMENTS 7 and **8** *(no accompanying table was provided.)*

These are the same as Arrangements 5 and 6 except that the two Type 4 cars reclassified as Second Class would be properly converted to have 42 seats instead of 36. For Arrangement 5 this gives trains C and D the same capacity as the present W.R. trains. For Arrangement 6 it raises train D's capacity to 144 Second and 72 First Class seats. The total cost in either case would be £10,000 – an additional £8,000 to the £2,000 referred to above.

To make these converted Type 4 cars and the Type 5 Kitchen cars completely interchangeable with the W.R. Types 2 and 3 cars, the auxiliary engines and fuel tanks would have to be transferred from the Kitchen cars to the Parlour cars at a cost of about £11,000. Even this would not make the converted Type 2 cars identical with W.R. Type 2 cars; although seating would be the same, their windows would still be as for a First Class layout. In fact many of the seats would not be next to a window.

The two spare Type 5 L.M.R. Kitchen Firsts could be made inter-changeable with Type 3 W.R. Kitchen Firsts at an extra cost of about £1,000.

Thus these arrangements give a total of 12 extra Second Class seats more than Arrangement 5 or 6, at a minimum cost of £8,000, but they both seem to be ruled out because they give supplement paying passengers sub-standard accommodation in respect of window layout.

CONCLUSIONS
From the broad approach here the best formations seem to be those in Arrangement 5(ii). Existing services are not affected greatly and there is the additional advantage that all the four trains are inter-changeable.

If it is difficult to find enough First Class traffic for four trains, Arrangement 6(ii) is an alternative. This would save a small potential loss of revenue on the two existing services and would give one train with a 2:1 ratio of Second to First Class seats.

Both these arrangements involve a relatively small capital cost and both involve using First Class seating as Second Class although the Kitchen separates the reclassified from the true First Class.

For the purposes of this report the operating costs of these formations can be taken as the same as those in Appendix I.

APPENDIX III

STANDBY REQUIREMENTS
Normal planned maintenance on Blue Pullmans is all scheduled for non-operating time at weekends. In addition there is a three-yearly major overhaul lasting seven weeks. Last year two trains were overhauled within a period of 4½ four and a half months but in future it is intended to spread these overhauls more evenly over time.

In some periods in the past breakdowns have been frequent, but this has been largely due to faults which it is hoped are now rectified. The pattern in 1964 can be taken as representative of the future. Then the days or part days when trains were out of service due to break-downs totalled 19 for three trains.

With 35 working days lost for overhauls every three years, average standby requirements per train per year are 19/3 + 3 5/3 =18 days.

Allowing for the fact that overhauls can be planned not to coincide, the statistical probability is that four operating trains will require one standby train on 63 day a year and two standby trains on four days a year.

On purely economic grounds the quality of train required as a standby depends upon the effect on receipts of using inferior stock. Up till now the Western Region has been using 35-year-old hauled Pullman cars as a standby. Traffic in 1964 has been analysed in an attempt to determine the effect of using this stock. There was no discernable effect on the odd days when breakdowns occurred – these, are in any case relatively infrequent. During the major overhauls of the 'Birmingham' and 'Bristol Pullmans' in the summer of 1964 any effect is obscured by a seasonal downward trend in passenger carryings. The slight falling off in these periods is matched by a similar pattern in 1963, when the Blue Pullmans were in operation. Any additional loss of traffic due to the use of the standby would seem to be at the most 150 passengers a week. If all these are completely lost to rail the revenue loss is about £2,500 for the seven weeks. If there was any effect it was not permanent, since on both services passenger carryings reached their highest levels in the autumn.

The time taken for the overhaul of a Blue Pullman might be reduced by the application of Network Analysis to the problem. This technique has already been applied successfully to the overhaul of locomotives in workshops. The incentive, for attempting a reduction in overhaul time on the Western Region depends upon whether a Blue Pullman standby train is available.

CONCLUSIONS
The use of a Blue Pullman train as a spare might save at the most £2,500 for each train in service every three years. In purely economic terms this is not justified unless there is no service on which the Pullman could be operated at a profit. Other factors may be considered to outweigh the economics in the final decision, however, particularly when having all four trains in service means that, for over a quarter of the year, at least one will be out of action.

POTENTIAL ROUTES FOR BLUE PULLMANS
It has already been shown that, ideally, routes need to be found for four Blue Pullman trains, and that to operate profitably each of them must carry something of the order of 90,000 passengers a year. With five-day operation this is roughly 350 passengers a day. They need a route with a high proportion of business traffic, indicated by a high proportion of First Class passenger.

Their potential use is thus confined to routes in the Region between principal centres. On the widest definition these could be defined as London, Birmingham, Bristol, South Wales, the South West and just possibly, Cheltenham/Gloucester and Oxford.

Of the cross-country routes, not even Birmingham–Bristol and Birmingham–South Wales have nearly enough traffic on existing services to justify replacement by a Blue

Pullman. Attention must therefore be concentrated on routes radiating from Paddington. The three of these most likely to have Pullman potential – Birmingham, Bristol and South Wales – each already have two Blue Pullman services a day in each direction. Paddington–Birmingham, however, will not be a Pullman route for the Western Region after the completion of the L.M.R. electrification. On the other two routes the profitability criterion described above is satisfied, with carryings of 134,000 passengers p.a. on the Paddington–Bristol route and 104,000 p.a. on the Paddington–South Wales route. If, on this basis, these services arc continued, new Pullman services will have to be introduced to employ two trains.

In principle a reciprocal Pullman service could be added to either of the two existing routes, starting from Paddington in the morning. An indication of the traffic which might be available for each service can be obtained from looking at the 'Bristolian' and 'Capitals United Express', although the present timings of these trains would not fit a working of four trips a day and the 'Capitals United Express' in particular, returns to Paddington too early in the afternoon. It seems possible that there might be as much potential traffic for reciprocal services as there is for the existing Blue Pullman services. Both these trains have average carryings in both directions of around 400 a day but the 'Bristolian' has a somewhat higher proportion of First Class passengers (over 40 per cent). Carryings on the 'Capitals United Express' are more variable and there is a high proportion of days when a Blue Pullman's Second Class capacity would be inadequate. On either route adding a reciprocal Blue Pullman service of four trips a day would mean that in the daytime period, 40 per cent of the trains in each direction were Pullmans. It must therefore be considered whether this is beyond the saturation point for Pullmans – whether, in fact, sufficient existing traffic could be attracted to the additional services, whether the travelling public might not feel that the change represented a concealed increase in fares, and whether the reduction in total carrying capacity resulting from Pullman operation can be afforded. There may also be a problem with parcels traffic which cannot be carried on Blue Pullmans.

On the South West route it has been suggested that the 'Golden Hind' might be replaced by a Blue Pullman. The eight-car train discussed earlier, however, has not sufficient motive power to maintain the present timings of the 'Golden Hind'. Even with present timings four trips a day could not be worked on the route and any attempt to do so would involve considerable rediagramming as other present services work through beyond Plymouth. Traffic on the 'Golden Hind' itself (averaging under 300 passengers per day) is insufficient for profitable Pullman operation, but there is a larger volume of traffic on the 'Mayflower' (timed 1hr 25mins later on the up service and 1hr later on the down service). In considering whether sufficient traffic is likely to be attracted from both services combined to form a reasonable basis for Pullman operation, it is significant that total First Class passengers on the two services average less than 100 in each direction and on some days are less than 50. There are also occasions, particularly Mondays in the up direction and Fridays in the down direction, when the 'Mayflower' is more than fully loaded in the Second Class and the 'Golden Hind' is carrying 40–60 more Second Class passengers than the capacity of W.R. Blue Pullmans. If a Pullman service were introduced, it might be better to use the formation (described as train D of Arrangement 6(ii) in Appendix II) which gives 72 First Class seats and 132 Second Class seats. Average revenue per passenger would be lower with more Second Class and would tend to cancel the effect on revenue of the route being longer than is assumed in the average shown in Appendix I.

On the Paddington–Cheltenham/Gloucester route the only likely existing service for replacement by a Blue Pullman is the 'Cheltenham Spa Express'. On average this carries a total in both directions of over 450 passengers a day, of whom only about a third travel First Class. The Pullman with the 132 Second Class seats would therefore seem more appropriate for the route, but, even with this, Second Class accommodation would be inadequate nearly every day. As the time gaps between the 'Cheltenham Spa Express' and other trains are large, particularly on the return trip, there is a serious risk of losing a significant number of passengers on the route, even if a high proportion of them could be persuaded to use the Pullman.

The Paddington–Oxford route cannot justify a Pullman service of its own but it might be used for a return trip in the middle of the day in conjunction with a Pullman replacing the 'Golden Hind'. If enough extra revenue to cover the time costs had been earned on the Plymouth route, the Oxford route would have to bring in extra revenue to cover only the mileage costs (about £7,000 p.a.), unless it replaced an existing service in which case all extra revenue would be profit.

CONCLUSIONS

Two of the four available Blue Pullman trains could be used profitably for existing services on the Paddington–Bristol and Paddington–South Wales routes.

The only feasible uses for the other two trains appear to be in providing reciprocal services on these same routes or to replace the 'Golden Hind'. Each of these possibilities, however, require further consideration as there is not a clear-cut case for any of them.

APPENDIX 10
Charters, special runs and BR open days

As we know there were several pre-launch runs involving the train for press and VIPs from this country and overseas as detailed earlier. Perhaps with confidence in running achieved regardless of the ride, other uses were sought for the units which quickly led to travel on to the BR other regions. Here we focus on the use of the Blue Pullmans for charter work, bringing in welcome extra income instead of otherwise lying dormant at the weekends and the occasional appearances at BR Open Days.

It appears the Western Region managed to hire their trains out far more than the Midland Region (unless someone has a secret list of Midland charters we don't know about!)

The first known use of a Pullman unit for such work was quite also a spectacular occasion. On the morning of Saturday 4 March 1961 there was much excitement on Platform 3 at Paddington as 120 specially invited guests for *The Music Man* were welcomed by a brass band and four 'Show Biz' girls dressed in drum majorette costumes from the show. The girls were holding up special directional signs and a large display board was erected to advertise the event. *The Music Man* was a successful American musical brought to the UK by the impresario Harold Fielding and the celebrity guests were to be whisked to Bristol at 11.50am for a matinee performance of the show.

Once on board it was entertainment all the way and the Pullman's public address system was used to play a welcome message from Van Johnson, the star of the show, followed by the music from the show. Fifty disc-jockeys and journalists were on board to hold interviews with the guests and the event had been publicised so on arrival in Bristol many fans turned out to see who was on board. The Fishponds British Legion Band struck up as soon as the Pullman arrived and played 'Seventy-six Trombones', a hit from the show. The cast included 13-year-old Dennis Waterman, later of The Sweeney and Minder fame.

Mr Fielding, the Western Region and Pullman Car Company all rose to the occasion and so impressed was one of the members of the Beverley Sisters singing trio that upon the subsequent return to Paddington she said she now wanted all their future contracts to have a clause inserted that all necessary rail journeys must now be made by Pullman Diesel Express!

Van Johnson later sliced off the top of his finger in a railway carriage scene on stage. Despite this the show moved to London and enjoyed a long run.

It has been suggested that, on 14 April 1963, a charter was arranged on behalf of the Bristol and District Railway Society running between Bristol and Plymouth (out via Okehampton, and return via Newton Abbot) but this has not been confirmed. As this was also only three days after the date when it is reported that none of the sets was available, its operation should be questioned.

The following year on 14 March 1964 the regular eight-car 'Bristol Pullman' set using: W60097/W60647/W60737/W60747/W60746/W60736/W60646 and W60096 ran from Swansea to Witton near Walsall for the FA Cup Semi Final at Villa Park between Swansea Town (later City) and Preston North End, a match that Preston won 2-1. The journey necessitated traversing the Lickey incline near Bromsgrove with the Pullman set banked by 0-6-0PT No 8415. According to Mike Woodhouse the Pannier tank engine only buffered up to the Pullman whose driver would sound the horn when he was ready. The Pannier tank then give an answering whistle and all moved together to the top at Blackwell where the Pannier tank would stop. The stock ran ecs to Ryecroft shed for cleaning before the return journey.

The following Saturday, 21 March 1964, Mirabel Topham, the owner of Aintree, ran a Grand National special using a different set comprising W60094/5, W60644/5, W60734/5 and W60744/5. The make up of the cars in each mirrored half is not confirmed. By this time one of the power cars was showing a large dent on the corner of the cab.

The special ran from Swansea to Aintree Sefton Arms station and was stabled at Kirkdale carriage sidings during the day. On the return journey from Aintree to Swansea there were quite a few celebrating, for the winner 'Team Spirit' ridden by G. W. Robinson had the attractive odds of 18-1.

Football involved the next outing on 2 May 1964. Having beaten Swansea to get to Wembley, Preston now chartered 'Midland set 1' to take the team, officials and VIPs to London. Jimmy Gilmour was the driver. Preston lost 2-3 to West Ham Utd.

Banking on the Lickey 14 March 1964. Alan Spence was the fireman on No. 8415 that banked this Swansea to Witton Charter for the Swansea v Preston FA Cup Match 14 March 1964 using the Bristol Pullman stock, Nos W60097, W60647, W60737, W60747, W60746, W60736, W60646 and W60096. (The result was Swansea 1 – Preston 2.) *Alan Spencer*

Hereford 21 March 1964: the Grand National special using W60094/5.
Kidderminster Railway Museum

The date 15 August 1964 was the Derby Works Open Day and the 'Midland Pullman' 'set 2' (with power cars M60092 and M60093) was fresh from overhaul and opened up to the public. Steps were erected at either end to allow a walk through the train.

Then on 13 March 1965 a WR set went from Coventry to West Hartlepool for the Rugby Union Final where Warwickshire beat Durham 15-9. From Coventry the route was via Birmingham New Street, Aston, Lichfield, Burton on Trent, Chesterfield, Sheffield, York, and on to the destination at West Hartlepool. On this occasion cars W60097/W60647/W60737/W60747/W60744/W60736/W60646/W60096 were used.

Two weeks later on 27 March 1965 Mirabel Topham again hired a WR set charter to run from Swansea to Aintree, presumably once more with banking assistance on the Lickey.

The final known event for 1965 was on 23 October 1965 when a set was displayed at the Bristol Bath Road Open Day.

The next year specials started early, and on 15 January 1966 Robert Thomas believes a set ran from Swansea to Hanwell (buses to Twickenham) for a Wales versus England Rugby Special.

More definite was the run of 12 February when a Western Region set took the unusual step of being used from Walsall to Norwich for an FA Cup Fourth Round match. Walsall were the losers, being beaten 3-2. The route was reported as Walsall, Ryecroft Junction, Sutton Park, Water Orton and Norwich.

The following month, 5 March saw the football pundit and then Chairman of Coventry City FC Jimmy Hill hire a WR eight-car train running as 1Z66 from Coventry to Liverpool Lime Street. The purpose was a match against Everton which the home side won 3-0. The vehicles used were W60097/W60647/W60737/W60747/W60744/W60736/W60646/W60096. It should be noted that the route taken very likely involved LMR metals throughout, so we may ask why the WR stock? The likely answer was that it was simply down to seating capacity.

The end of the year saw another WR set on display at the Bath Road open day.

Next was 28 January 1967 when Walsall FC were off to Bury. It is thought the train let its passengers off at Bury Knowsley Street station before being seen later at Bury Bolton Street station. The 'Six Bells Junction' website includes a comment by a passenger John Stanley who writes: 'The route was a complete mystery, but I do recall an incident on the return journey when we went round a sharp curve too fast in the Stoke-on-Trent area and all the crockery in the galley crashed to the floor.' The train ran as 1Z65 and again the home side were the victors 2-0. Trips such as this taking a train (WR or LMR) off its home territory would have involved a BP familiar driver with a pilotman in the cab on unfamiliar lines whose role was to advise the set driver of speed restrictions, signal placings etc. Clearly here the latter was perhaps not quite keeping an eye on proceedings.

The following month, on 18 February, Aston Villa fans including Stephen Field travelled from Birmingham Snow Hill to Liverpool Lime Street only to see their team lose 1-0 to Liverpool. Stephen kept his ticket and menu showing he was in second class coach 'G'. The menu also now used the BR double arrow sign instead of the traditional Pullman crest.

Later in the summer of that year, on 15 July 1967 the Oak Old Common Open Day had different liveried half sets on display. Cars W60097, W60647, W60737, W60747 were in Nanking Blue whilst W60744, W60736, W60646, W60096 were in new reverse grey/blue livery. We are not told if the two halves were in fact coupled into a complete train.

Robert Thomas thinks a set ran from Swansea to Hanwell again (buses to Twickenham) on 20 January 1968 for another Wales versus England Rugby Special. The belief being, as in the previous case, that his father had travelled by the special working.

One of the few occasions when a headboard was carried on one of the trains was on 9 March 1968 when an ex LMR unit was chartered by Bristol City for their FA Cup tie at Leeds United. The (wooden) headboard carried the words 'The Chairman's Special HD11'. The 'HD11' referring to chairman Harry Dolman's 11 players who went on to lose the match 2-0. The set then was still in Nanking Blue but with yellow ends.

Royalty was involved on 11 August 1968 when on the occasion of Her Majesty Queen Elizabeth II opening the Gulf oil refinery at Milford Haven two sets were chartered. Both a Nanking Blue set and a reverse livery set were involved and each carried large 'Gulf' stickers on their cabs. The trains were hired to bring in VIP guests to the event although it is not clear if HRH also travelled by one of the services.

In the summer of 1968 a Mr Peter Hughes of Buntingford hired an eight-car WR Pullman set to convey guests from Paddington to Weston-super-Mare for his son's wedding, his intention being to avoid the guests being penalised by the recently introduced breathalyser test for motorists. The WR also entered into the spirit of the occasion with the entrance to Platform 6 at Paddington especially decorated, and a red carpet unrolled beside the train; four cooks and 14 stewards attended to the 200 guests. (Presumably there was a later return journey although this is not mentioned.)

On 25 January 1969 Aston Villa chartered an FA Cup Special for their Fourth round game against Southampton which they drew 2-2 but subsequently went on the win the reply 2-1 four days later. This was a reverse livery set led by W60096.

One set was also photographed at Newbury racecourse around this time, presumably on a special working and most likely the 'Members' train, in which case it would have started from Paddington and would return at the end of the meeting.

We know for certain that on 22 March 1969 West Bromwich Albion chartered both ex LMR sets for their FA Cup Semi Final against Leicester City which they lost 1-0.

The following month a LMR Nanking Blue set including power car W60091 (complete with its dented custard-dipped nose and jumper cables) together with W60731/W60741/W60740/W60730/W60090 was on display at the Worcester 85A open day of 12 April. This was a rare if not unique occasion so far as a BP set was involved; photographs of the occasion can be seen on page 68 of *Blue Pullman Supplement* plus online (the 12th photo down) at: https://www.freewebs.com/brdiesels/thejdscollection1.htm and https://www.flickr.com/photos/glevumblues/5556233791

Another set was seen at Bristol Bath Road open day held on 18 October.

Moving now to the final years and we first report the tour of 25 April 1970. This was a 'Talking of Trains Surbiton Educational Special No 8' sponsored by John Gilks and Harry Grenside. (Was this in fact the railway enthusiast and photographer J. Spencer Gilks?) The tour was from Surbiton to Carmarthen. 'Talking of Trains' is the Surbiton, Kingston & Malden branch of the Workers Education association who

Bristol Temple Meads 9 March 1968 complete with headboard. *David Wharton*

still meet today. The route was necessarily convoluted from Surbiton, Woking. Guildford, Wokingham, Earley, Reading General, Didcot, Swindon, Wootton Bassett Jn, Westerleigh Jn, Patchway, Severn Tunnel Junction, Newport, Cardiff General, Bridgend, Port Talbot, Court Sart Jn, Felin Fran, Morlais Jn, Llandilo Jn, Llanelli and Carmarthen, involving several reversals en route. Full details of the formation are not given although we know No W60096 was one of the power cars involved. A DMU set took the group from Carmarthen to their final destination Newcastle Emlyn.

The BP set was again used for the return from Carmarthen to Surbiton. A square headboard was carried with the words 'Gilks-Grenside'.

Another Paddington to Newbury Racecourse Members Only special operated on 15 August 1970.

The operation of a six-car and then an eight-car set to Plymouth on 24 and then again 28 December 1970, and again on the same dates in 1971, has already been referred to in the text. Full details for the 1970 run at least are that it was referred to as the 'Holiday Inn Express' and worked (loaded) between Kensington Olympia and Plymouth even at this late stage breaking new ground for a Pullman diesel. (The hotel had only just opened on 15 December 1970 and survives today as the Crown Plaza.) Four diesel locomotives are referred to as having assisted the sets; we know three of them as 'Western' class Nos D1010, D1032, and D1054. A class 47 was involved also on one occasion, No D1655, this assisted the down working on 24 December.

January 1971 witnessed another charter to Liverpool This was a football special on the 23rd of the month when Swansea City were playing Liverpool in the Fourth round of the FA Cup; Liverpool won 3-0. It is believed three BP sets were involved, the two LMR sets operating in multiple and an unreported WR train. The trains were observed at Shrewsbury by Wilbur Bruck and by Robert Thomas near Margram.

Then in March, the 13th of the month saw a Rugby Union Special, Wales versus Ireland at Cardiff Arms Park. What working – from and to – is not referred to although we learn from Brian Rolley an eight-car set was involved: W60094/W60644/W60734/W60746/W60745/W60735/W60645 and ex LMR W60091.

We now move away from the WR to the Southern Region when 'Dinners With A Difference' was organised by Messrs Ian Allan. This operated from Paddington via Reading to Basingstoke and thence on to Brockenhurst where guests where loaded on to coaches for a feast at Beaulieu. This was an evening tour (and return).

Two tours only are referred to in 1972, the first on 15 January 1972 when Bristol Rovers chartered a train for their FA Cup match against Leeds Utd. They lost 4-1. Interestingly at this stage the set used a mixture of WR and LMR vehicles: W60093/W60738/W60748/W60749/W60739/W60648/W60649 and W60099. Taking their history into account, using a diesel Pullman set for a football charter almost seemed to guarantee the team would lose.

Next on 15 July 1972 a reverse livery set was pictured at Bromley South, this time the route, purpose etc are not reported but it is included here as there would appear to be little other reason for it to be seen other than on a charter working. (Unless by chance the SR were finally considering a diesel replacement for the 'Golden Arrow' – unlikely at this late stage.)

Another and, as it turned out, the penultimate London Paddington to Newbury Racecourse Members Only Race Special was operated on 31 July 1972. (The last was on 24 March 1973 using an ex LMR set although it is not known if this was a Members' or other charter to the same race event.)

The final open day appearance was on 2 September 1972 for the Old Oak Common Open Day and involved a WR unit.

Then on 20 January 1973 an eight-car set was observed near Reading. As this was a Saturday it is possible this too was a charter but of unknown origin. (We are not informed whether passengers were seen on board.) The vehicles were W60098/W60648/W60738/W60744/W60734/W60644/W60094.

The very last special was of course the 5 May 1973 BR 'Enthusiasts Safari' which was also destined to be the final run of a Blue Pullman in revenue-earning service. The cost was £10 to include afternoon tea. The set used was the Cardiff-based 'South Wales Pullman' W60090/W60645/W60735/W60745/W60744/W60734/W60644/W60094.

Although covered earlier full details of the route were not given but this was from Paddington to High Wycombe and thence via Banbury, Leamington Spa, Kenilworth, Coventry, Marston Green, Birmingham New Street, Selly Oak, Kings Norton, Bromsgrove, Stoke Works Junction, Abbotswood Junction, Cheltenham Spa, Standish Junction, Yate, Westerleigh Junction, Bristol Parkway, Stapleton Road, Bristol Temple Meads, Filton Junction, Patchway, Severn Tunnel Junction, Newport, Cardiff, Bridgend, Port Talbot, Neath and Swansea. The reverse direction was from Swansea to Neath, Port Talbot, Cardiff, Newport, Patchway, Bristol Parkway, Swindon, Didcot, Slough and London Paddington. Famously an elderly gentleman was ejected at Neath who didn't have a ticket for the special whilst some very fast running occurred thought to be exceeding 100mph.

The engines are still growling away on the rare clips of the day.

Also in 1964, the Western Region celebrated 400 years since the birth of William Shakespeare with some special fares for the 'Birmingham Pullman' from Paddington that included onwards travel from Leamington Spa to Stratford-upon-Avon.

Memories

Amazing shots showing 14 year old Chris Head having been served with tea in a Ridgway Lucerne cup sat in an ex Midland first class coach but downgraded to second class on the Western Region. (see also pages 272/3.) The power car seen at Bristol has just been fitted with jumper cables and 'custard dipped'. *Christopher H. Head/Head Forward Consulting Ltd.*

LEFT A visit to Swindon on 30 August 1967 reveals a WR power car receiving attention and its first repaint into the new livery. *Christopher H. Head/Head Forward Consulting Ltd.*

THE BLUE PULLMAN STORY

Memories

'Grey Pullman viewed from my bedroom window at Neath, 7 September 1971; London-bound crossing the road bridge at Neath, Autumn 1971'. At this time the South Wales set was serviced at Maliphant sidings, Swansea. In the background is the former Hafod Copper Works. *Christopher H. Head/Head Forward Consulting Ltd.*

RIGHT AND BELOW The short lived Blue Pullman tribute charter train operated by FM Rail/Hertfordshire Rail Tours using Mk2 coaches and top 'n' tail Class 47's. It was on this this train that co-author Mike Smith treated his parents Ron and Sheila to a day out from Kings Cross to York and back on 4 March 2006. Memories flooded back for Ron of his trips on the Midland Pullman. Ron sadly passed away on 10 January 2020 but he did see a sneak preview of the book cover and read the part about his trips. *Mike Smith*

APPENDIX 11
Pullman dates to traffic, withdrawal and disposal

Note official allocations for the LMR sets were always to Derby even though there was one was at Reddish and the other similarly stabled. WR sets were all officially allocated to Old Oak Common but again would invariably out-station at Bristol (Dr Days), Wolverhampton (Cannock Road) and later at Swansea (Maliphant).

Although only officially withdrawn in May 1973 five vehicles were stored early. W60730 on 1/6/72 (robbed for spares) W60732 on 1/6/72 (tyre flats/rough riding then robbed for spares) W60095 on 1/10/72 (serviceable but due E exam) W60099 on 1/10/72 (No 2 Conrod thrown) W60091 post 12/72 (1.5in backlash in valve timing gears)

In May 1973 the three spare engines/Generators with defects at Swindon '9' shop: 307022/TST76/2 ex 60097 on 29/9/72 Main Gen Banding burst 307035/ DP51/1 ex 60093 on 20/11/72 No 12 piston/liner smashed/valves dropped 307042/ DP51/10 ex 60094 on 29/9/72 Main Gen Banding burst

Original Vehicle No. Subsequent renumbering	Original type. Subsequent reclassification	To Traffic	Withdrawn	Last Engine/Generator Fitted
M60090 W60090	DMBFL DMBSL	11/59	5/73	307037/DP51/6
M60091 W60091	DMBFL DMBSL	11/59	5/73	307041/DP51/9
M60092 W60092	DMBFL DMBSL	11/59	5/73	307040/DP51/3
M60093 W60093	DMBFL DMBSL	11/59	5/73	307036/DP51/4
W60094	DMBS	2/60	5/73	307072/DP51/11
W60095	DMBS	2/60	5/73	307038/DP51/7
W60096	DMBS	4/60	5/73	307039/DP51/2
W60097	DMBS	4/60	5/73	307033/DP51/8
W60098	DMBS	5/60	5/73	307034/DP51/5
W60099	DMBS	5/60	5/73	307699/TST76/1
W60644	MPSL	2/60	5/73	
W60645	MPSL	2/60	5/73	
W60646	MPSL	4/60	5/73	
W60647	MPSL	4/60	5/73	
W60648	MPSL	5/60	5/73	
W60649	MPSL	5/60	5/73	
M60730 W60739	MFLRK MSLRK	11/59	5/73	
M60731 W60731	MFLR MSLRK	11/59	5/73	
M60732 W60732	MFLRK MSLRK	11/59	5/73	
M60733/ W60733	MFLRK MSLRK	11/59	5/73	
W60734	TFLRK	2/60	5/73	
W60735	TFLRK	2/60	5/73	
W60736	TFLRK	4/60	5/73	
W60637	TFLRK	4/60	5/73	
W60738	TFLRK	5/60	5/73	
W60739	TFLRK	5/60	5/73	
M60740 W60740	TPFL	11/59	5/73	
M60741 W60741	TPFL	11/59	5/73	
M60742 W60742	TPFL	11/59	5/73	
M60743 W60743	TPFL	11/59	5/73	
W60744	TPFL	2/60	5/73	
W60745	TPFL	2/60	5/73	
W60746	TPFL	4/60	5/73	
W60747	TPFL	4/60	5/73	
W60748	TPFL	5/60	5/73	
W60749	TPFL	5/60	5/73	

Marsh Junction Bristol, BP and Class 31 D5530. *Gerry Nichols*

Nos W60096 and W60647 stabled n the Fish Dock at Bristol Temple Meads in March 1974 acting as standby emergency generators during the Miner's Strike.

Marsh Pond Sidings, Bristol. *Tommy Nurmela*

Forlorn and travel worn, a pair of power cars, one LMR one WR, await their fate at Old Oak Common sometime in 1973. *Rail Online ZF-5438-95371-1-009*

Old Oak Common 1973. No more jacketed stewards waiting … *David Mant*

Old Oak Common.

Old Oak Common, October 1973 – Nos W60095 and W6009 in profile not all that dissimilar to the original artists impression. *David Mant*

APPENDICES

Perhaps not the best advert for BR, out of use and visible alongside the main line.

Swindon, perhaps awaiting sale, preservation … or even consideration for future use on BR?

ABOVE Last run of the 'South Wales Pullman'. Back row, left to right: Winston Bendle, Jim Ace. Front row, left to right: Tommy Laughan, Gerry Hopkins, Mike Brooks.

BELOW Final days …

ABOVE Body shells torn from their bogies. *Peter James Morris*

BELOW The first two power cars built, ex Midland W60090 and W60091 sat in the sidings at Briton Ferry for some time and suffered from considerable vandalism. These were also the last two vehicle's to be scrapped and even after arriving at Messrs T. W. Ward's riverside scrapyard they survived well into 1976. *Gerald Williams*

377

APPENDIX 12
The official photo lists

As might be expected a number of 'Official' views were taken by the respective regions mainly at the time surrounding the train's introduction. Mostly these are within the Paddington 'C' and Euston 'DM' series of negatives. (There may be others in further lists of which the author is unaware.)

Below is what is believed to be a complete listing. Other than the very few already seen with these pages and which were not obtained from the NRM, it has not been possible to access these views so we can only imagine their content, that is if they even still exist as the entries for a large number were either struck-through or marked with an 'x'. Even so they afford an interesting perspective not just on the trains but for information on special workings the like which would otherwise not have been known of.

No doubt a similar large number of views were taken by the manufacturers themselves, but other than those rescued by former staff with many included within these pages, these too appear to have been lost to history unless they turn up in some of the as yet unsorted boxes of Metro-Cammell images that are now at the Kidderminster Railway Museum.

The entries shown in red are either marked as such within the official registers or have the annotation 'missing/destroyed/lost' against them.

Paddington 'C'			
28739-2874?	21/04/1960	Pullman Diesel. Copy of Colour Transparencies ('Midland Pullman' sets?)	
28979-86	02/05/1960	Pullman Diesel. Various views Copy of Colour Transparencies	
29878		Pullman Diesel poster	x
29981	Copy of 8/60	Pullman Diesel. Coffee served in 1st class saloon. Copy of transparency	
29982	Copy of 8/60	Pullman Diesel. Coffee served in 3rd class saloon. Copy of transparency	x
29983	Aug-60	Pullman Diesel. Woman operating seat first class	x
29984	Aug-60	Pullman Diesel. First class saloon	x
30110	23/08/1960	Pullman Diesel. Posters (letterpress)	x
30119-20	05/09/1960	Pullman Diesel. Leaving Paddington	
30201	05/09/1960	Pullman Diesel. At Ealing Broadway	
30247-6?	5-6-7/9/60	Pullman Diesel. Press run from Paddington, Bristol, Wolverhampton	x
30298	12/09/1960	Pullman Diesel. Bristol – at Subway Junction	x
30299	12/09/1960	Pullman Diesel. Birmingham – at Royal Oak	x
30300-2	12/09/1960	Pullman Diesel. Bristol and Birmingham entering Paddington	x
30303	12/09/1960	Pullman Diesel. At Paddington, Mayor of Paddington, Mr Hammond, and Driver	x
30304-5	12/09/1960	Pullman Diesel. Mayor of Paddington gives 'right away'.	x
30421-2	13/09/1960	Pullman Diesel. Arriving Paddington	x
30623	05/10/1960	Pullman Diesel and Station Master Paddington	
33593	02/06/1961	Display stand Pullman diesel	x
34581-2	06/09/1961	Pullman Services Posters (Diesel)	
34590-64	06/09/1961	Pullman demonstration run. South Wales	x
34602-4	06/09/1961	'South Wales Pullman' demonstration run	
36082		'South Wales Pullman' display stand	
38257	22/06/1962	'Bristol Pullman' at Didcot	x
38297	27/06/1962	Diesel Pullman at Saunderton	
38298	27/06/1962	Pullman Diesel at High Wycombe	x
38297	27/06/1952	Pullman Diesel at Saunderton	x
38314-5		Pullman Diesel up and down at Denham	x
38335	28/06/1962	Pullman Diesel at West Wycombe	x
38338	03/07/1962	Pullman Diesel at Maidenhead	x
38355	04/07/1962	Pullman Diesel at Iver.	x
38436-7	Jul-62	Pullman Diesel. First class saloon copy of transparency	x

34590-64	06/09/1961	Pullman demonstration run. South Wales	x
40091	03/01/1963	Pullman Diesel passing White Waltham. Copy neg.	
41609-11	31/05/1963	Pullman seat indicator board (posters)	
42023-5	30/07/1963	Pullman Diesel. Fry's Chocolate Filming	
45032	29/10/1964	Blue Pullman poster	
49883 1-22	06/03/1967	New 'Oxford Pullman'	
49886 1-4	03/03/1967	Last run 'Birmingham Pullman'	
50406/24	06/06/1967	Pullman passing Twyford	
50655		Pullman blue, in Sonning Cutting	
50660		Pullman blue near St Anne's Park Bristol	
51038 1-3	31/10/1967	Diesel Pullman new grey livery	
51058	10/11/1967	Diesel Pullman new livery Ruscombe	
51155 A & B	29/11/1967	Pullman blue, duplicate from C49516	
51597	21/03/1968	Pullman Bristol	
55159 1-9	19/12/1972	Pullman stewardess new uniforms	

Euston 'DM' series

6244	08/03/1960	Bedford Mid. Rd. 'Midland Pullman' approaching Bedford from North	
6245	08/03/1960	Bedford Mid. Rd. 'Midland Pullman' passing Bedford from North	
6246	08/03/1960	Bedford Mid. Rd. 'Midland Pullman' passing Bedford from North	
6247	08/03/1960	Bedford Mid. Rd. 'Midland Pullman passing Bedford from North	
6248	08/03/1960	Bedford Mid. Rd. 'Midland Pullman' approaching Bedford from North (rear view)	
6249	08/03/1960	Bedford Mid. Rd. 'Midland Pullman' passing Bedford from South (resr view)	
6250	08/03/1960	Bedford Mid. Rd. 'Midland Pullman' passing Bedford from South frontal	
6251	08/03/1960	Bedford Mid. Rd. 'Midland Pullman' M/S Driving Unit M60093	
6252	08/03/1960	Bedford Mid. Rd. 'Midland Pullman' Trailing unit M60092 coupling	
6253	08/03/1960	Bedford Mid. Rd. 'Midland Pullman'	
6344	08/03/1960	Bedford Midland Road 'Midland Pullman' approaching from the North	
6345	08/03/1960	Bedford Midland Road 'Midland Pullman' passing from the North	
6346	08/03/1960	Bedford Midland Road 'Midland Pullman' passing from the North	
6347	08/03/1960	Bedford Midland Road 'Midland Pullman' passing from the North	
6348	08/03/1960	Bedford Midland Road 'Midland Pullman' seen from the North, rear view	
6462	08/03/1960	Kettering 'Midland Pullman' on down fast line leaving Kettering	
6463	08/03/1960	Kettering 'Midland Pullman' on down fast line leaving Kettering low angle perspective	
6464	20/04/1960	'Midland Pullman'. Power car and low angle perspective	
6465	20/04/1960	'Midland Pullman'. Power car frontal	
6466	20/04/1960	'Midland Pullman'. Headlights and buffers	
6467	20/04/1960	'Midland Pullman'. Driver's controls	
6468	20/04/1960	'Midland Pullman'. General view driver's compartment	
6469	20/04/1960	'Midland Pullman'. Low angle, left hand perspective	
6470	20/04/1960	'Midland Pullman'. Low angle, left hand perspective	
6471	20/04/1960	Midland Pullman. Three-quarter, left hand perspective. High angle	
6472	20/04/1960	'Midland Pullman'. Three-quarter, left hand perspective	
6473	20/04/1960	'Midland Pullman'. Three-quarter, right hand perspective. Low angle	
6474	20/04/1960	'Midland Pullman' close-up, right side perspective, low angle	
6632	23/05/1960	'Midland Pullman' broadside view	
6633	23/05/1960	'Midland Pullman' broadside view	
6634	23/05/1960	'Midland Pullman' broadside view	

Euston 'DM' series (continued)			
6776	22/06/1960	Marylebone. 'Midland Pullman'. Attendants	
6777	22/06/1960	Marylebone. 'Midland Pullman'. Attendants	
6778	22/06/1960	Marylebone. 'Midland Pullman'. Interior of Parlour Car	
6779	22/06/1960	Marylebone. 'Midland Pullman'. Interior of Parlour Car	
6780	22/06/1960	Marylebone. 'Midland Pullman'. Seating and tables in Parlour Car	
6781	22/06/1960	Marylebone. 'Midland Pullman'. Guard pressing button	
6782	22/06/1960	Marylebone. 'Midland Pullman'. Chef in Kitchen preparing meals	
6633	23/05/1960	'Midland Pullman' broadside view	
6634	23/05/1960	'Midland Pullman' broadside view	
6776	22/06/1960	Marylebone. 'Midland Pullman'. Attendants	
6777	22/06/1960	Marylebone. 'Midland Pullman'. Attendants	
6778	22/06/1960	Marylebone. 'Midland Pullman'. Interior of Parlour Car	
6779	22/06/1960	Marylebone. 'Midland Pullman'. Interior of Parlour Car	
6780	22/06/1960	Marylebone. 'Midland Pullman'. Seating and tables in Parlour Car	
6781	22/06/1960	Marylebone. 'Midland Pullman'. Guard pressing button	
6782	22/06/1960	Marylebone. 'Midland Pullman'. Chef in Kitchen preparing meals	
6633	23/05/1960	'Midland Pullman' broadside view	
6634	23/05/1960	'Midland Pullman' broadside view	
6776	22/06/1960	Marylebone. 'Midland Pullman'. Attendants	
6777	22/06/1960	Marylebone. 'Midland Pullman'. Attendants	
6778	22/06/1960	Marylebone. 'Midland Pullman'. Interior of Parlour Car	
6779	22/06/1960	Marylebone. 'Midland Pullman'. Interior of Parlour Car	
6780	22/06/1960	Marylebone. 'Midland Pullman'. Seating and tables in Parlour Car	
6781	22/06/1960	Marylebone. 'Midland Pullman'. Guard pressing button	
6782	22/06/1960	Marylebone. 'Midland Pullman'. Chef in Kitchen preparing meals	
6783	22/06/1960	Marylebone. 'Midland Pullman'. Chef in Kitchen preparing meals	
6784	22/06/1960	Marylebone. 'Midland Pullman'. Chef and Attendants	
6785	22/06/1960	Marylebone. 'Midland Pullman'. Main and diner?	
6786	22/06/1960	Marylebone. 'Midland Pullman'. Passengers at lunch in Parlour	
6787	22/06/1960	Marylebone. 'Midland Pullman'. Passengers at lunch in Parlour	
6788	22/06/1960	Marylebone. 'Midland Pullman'. Passengers at lunch in Parlour	
6789	22/06/1960	Marylebone. 'Midland Pullman'. Passengers at lunch in Parlour	
6790	22/06/1960	Marylebone. 'Midland Pullman'. Passengers at lunch in Parlour	
6791	22/06/1960	Marylebone. 'Midland Pullman'. Passengers at lunch in Parlour	
6812	29/06/1960	Cricklewood. 'Midland Pullman'. General view of corridor connection	
6813	29/06/1960	Cricklewood. 'Midland Pullman'. General view of corridor connection	
6814	29/06/1960	Cricklewood. 'Midland Pullman'. Overlapping sections	
6815	29/06/1960	Cricklewood. 'Midland Pullman' Bulkhead end. M60091 power car	
6816	29/06/1960	Cricklewood. 'Midland Pullman' Bulkhead end. M60731 Kitchen	
6817	29/06/1960	Cricklewood. 'Midland Pullman' Bulkhead end. M60741 Parlour	
6818	29/06/1960	Cricklewood. 'Midland Pullman' Bulkhead end. M60740 Parlour	
6819	29/06/1960	Cricklewood. 'Midland Pullman' Bulkhead end. M60740 Parlour	
6820	29/06/1960	Cricklewood. 'Midland Pullman' Bulkhead end. M60741 Parlour	
6821	29/06/1960	Cricklewood. 'Midland Pullman' Bulkhead end. M60730 Kitchen	
6822	29/06/1960	Cricklewood. 'Midland Pullman' Bulkhead end. M60090 power car	
6823	29/06/1960	Cricklewood. 'Midland Pullman' Close up Driver's controls 60091	
6824	29/06/1960	Cricklewood.' Midland Pullman' Driving bogie on 60091	

Euston 'DM' series (continued)			
6825	29/06/1960	Cricklewood. 'Midland Pullman' Westinghouse (brake?) equipment	
6826	29/06/1960	Cricklewood. 'Midland Pullman' Driving bogie on 60091	
6827	29/06/1960	Cricklewood. 'Midland Pullman' Corridor connections and electrical linkages	
6828	29/06/1960	Cricklewood. 'Midland Pullman' Corridor connections and electrical linkages	
6829	29/06/1960	Cricklewood. 'Midland Pullman' Drawbar connections and electrical linkages	
6830	29/06/1960	Cricklewood. 'Midland Pullman' Pullman crest on side of 60731 Kitchen	
6831	29/06/1960	Cricklewood. 'Midland Pullman' Auxilliary motor under 60731 Kitchen	
6832	29/06/1960	Cricklewood. 'Midland Pullman' Propane gas compartments 60731 Kitchen	
6833	29/06/1960	Cricklewood. 'Midland Pullman' Bogies and connections	
6834	29/06/1960	Cricklewood. 'Midland Pullman' Stone-Kheops electrical connector switch	
6835	29/06/1960	Cricklewood. 'Midland Pullman' Air intake and filters	
6836	29/06/1960	Cricklewood. 'Midland Pullman' Part of Metro-Schlieren Bogie	
6837	29/06/1960	Cricklewood. 'Midland Pullman' Spares NP	
6839	04/07/1960	St Pancras Ticket Insp T. Hancock, Mr Handley SM	x
6840	04/07/1960	St Pancras 'Midland Pullman' arriving 11.57 Vertical	x
6841	04/07/1960	St Pancras 'Midland Pullman' arriving 11.57 Horizontal	x
6842	04/07/1960	St Pancras Handley, J. Royston, R. L. E. Lawrence, with letters	x
6843	04/07/1960	St Pancras Handley, J. Royston, R. L. E. Lawrence, with letters	x
6844	04/07/1960	St Pancras Arthur Garrett BBC 'Today', A. B. Rogers (M/C)	x
6845	04/07/1960	St Pancras. Train pulling out at 12.45 for Leicester	x
6846	04/07/1960	St Pancras Conductor R. Walton, F. D. M. Harding Conductor T. N. Peart	x
6847	04/07/1960	St Pancras Mr F. D. M. Harding with Pullman staff	x
6848	04/07/1960	St Pancras M. Upstone (Staff Superintendent) J. J. Morel (Catering Manager) Chef ... Harding	x
6849	04/07/1960	St Pancras Pullman cars on 12.45 to Leicester	x
6850	04/07/1960	St Pancras Passengers looking at Pullman display	x
6851	04/07/1960	St Pancras Passengers looking at Pullman display spare NP	x
6852	04/07/1960	St Pancras 4.00pm arrival from Leicester platform level	x
6853	04/07/1960	St Pancras 4.00pm arrival from Leicester passing gasholders	x
6854	04/07/1960	St Pancras 4.00pm arrival from Leicester entering station high angle	x
6855	04/07/1960	St Pancras 4.00pm arrival from Leicester D. Blee, and Major of St Pancras	x
6856	04/07/1960	St Pancras Mr Hardley (SM) Mr Blee, Mayoress and party	x
6857	04/07/1960	St Pancras Mayoress greeting Lord Mayor of London Sir Edmund Stockdale	x
6858	04/07/1960	St Pancras D. Blee, R. Dudson?, Mrs Arabin? Sir Edmund Stockdale	x
6859	04/07/1960	St Pancras D. Blee, Mrs Arabin? Sir Edmund Stockdale	x
6860	04/07/1960	St Pancras D. Blee, Mrs Arabin? Sir Edmund Stockdale	x
6861	04/07/1960	St Pancras Stella Murrell and Mrs Arabin	x
6862	04/07/1960	St Pancras Sir Edmund Stockdale and Driver W. Golding (Kentish Town)	x
6863	04/07/1960	St Pancras Sir Edmund Stockdale, Mrs Arabin and Chief Chef Thos Harding	x
6864	04/07/1960	St Pancras Sir Edmund Stockdale waving flag	x
6865	04/07/1960	St Pancras R. W. C.? D. Blee, Sir R. Wilson, R. L. E. Lawrence, R. G. Handley	x
6866	04/07/1960	St Pancras Dupes and spare (11)	X
6867	06/07/1960	St Pancras 'Midland Pullman' arriving passing Dock Junction	
6868	06/07/1960	St Pancras 'Midland Pullman' arriving passing Yacht Basin	
6869	06/07/1960	St Pancras 'Midland Pullman' 12.45pm departure leaving station from signal box	
6870	06/07/1960	St Pancras 'Midland Pullman' 12.45pm departure leaving station from signal box rear view	
6871	06/07/1960	St Pancras 'Midland Pullman' 12.45pm departure leaving station from signal box under gantry	
6872	06/07/1960	St Pancras 'Midland Pullman' 4.00pm arrival approaching	

Euston 'DM' series (*continued*)			
6873	06/07/1960	St Pancras 'Midland Pullman' 4.00pm arrival passing gas holder	
6874	06/07/1960	St Pancras 'Midland Pullman' 4.00pm arrival rear view entering station	
6890	07/07/1960	Silkstream Junction Up 'Midland Pullman' due 12.03pm passing through bridge	
6891	07/07/1960	Silkstream Junction Up 'Midland Pullman' due 12.03pm passing through bridge low angle	
6892	07/07/1960	Silkstream Junction Down 'Midland Pullman' 12.45pm to Leicester	
6893	07/07/1960	Silkstream Junction Down 'Midland Pullman' 12.45pm to Leicester low angle	
6894	07/07/1960	Mill Hill embankment Up 'Midland Pullman' due 4.00pm St Pancras	
6895	07/07/1960	Mill Hill embankment Up 'Midland Pullman' due 4.00pm St Pancras	
7019	26/07/1960	Up 'Midland Pullman' seen from overbridge	
7020	26/07/1960	Down 'Midland Pullman' seen from overbridge	
8542	26/09/1961	'Midland Pullman'	

A youthful Dominic Turner in the remains of the yesterday's train at Briton Ferry. *Jeremy Turner*

The end of the dream. *Gerald Williams*

INDEX

Adams, Stanley 2, 48, 51, 124
Aldridge 3, 55, 63
Associated Society of Locomotive Engineers and Firemen (ASLEF) 12, 23, 24, 25, 82, 269, 319
Aston .... 226, 366; *see also* depots and works
Aston Villa 283, 325, 368, 369
Automatic Train Control (ATC) 12, 63, 190–1, 247
ATC cancelling 14, 118, 190
ATC tests 191, 202–3
Automatic Warning System (AWS) 12, 176, 247, 273, 291, 339–40

Bakewell 156, 329, 332, 335
Barker, Hugh P. 17–20, 23–4, 27–8, 31, 39, 179, 253
Barman, Christian 48–52, 54, 60, 64, 82–3, 95, 132, 330, 331
Bedford 13, 19, 38, 64, 121, 136, 138, 152, 153, 184, 185, 318, 334, 335, 379
Beeching, Dr 16, 21, 28, 178, 184, 188, 272, 322
Birmingham 4, 12, 14, 16, 18, 20, 26, 34, 37, 38, 39, 44, 48, 50, 51, 52, 55, 63, 70, 71, 72, 83, 90, 93, 94, 101, 103, 104, 121, 126, 156, 180, 190, 193, 194, 195, 196, 198, 199, 200, 203, 207, 215, 218, 219, 220, 221, 223, 224, 225, 227, 228, 229, 230, 231, 242, 248, 249, 253, 254, 257, 262, 264, 300, 302, 303, 317, 318, 328, 336, 338, 358, 359, 360, 362, 365, 366, 378
Birmingham New Street 226, 262, 295, 303, 368, 370
Birmingham Snow Hill 28, 51, 192, 196, 198–9, 200, 220, 225, 231, 236, 262, 325, 328, 348, 352, 354, 368
'Birmingham Belle' 18, 20
'Birmingham Pullman' 8, 9, 49, 133, 197, 199, 203, 209, 217, 228, 229, 230, 234–5, 238, 240, 262, 295, 300, 326, 328, 352–8, 362, 370, 379

Blee, David 36, 39, 48, 50–1, 66, 82, 93, 142, 379
Board of Trade .... 190; *see also* Ministry of Transport
Bond, R. C. 30, 39, 48, 50
'Bournemouth Belle' 18, 20, 123, 124, 127, 162, 253, 254, 273, 282, 299
BR Research Department, Derby 19, 50, 68, 150
BR Works Committee 36, 37
'Brighton Belle' 18, 20, 23, 74, 123, 124, 127, 141, 145, 162, 254, 273, 320
Bristol 14, 16, 26, 32, 34, 35, 38, 39, 44, 50, 63, 93–4, 103, 121, 126, 180, 190, 192, 193, 194, 195, 196–8, 199–200, 201, 203, 204, 205, 209, 210, 213, 214, 215, 218, 222, 223, 224, 225, 227, 228, 230, 233, 234, 235, 236, 241, 247–9, 252, 253, 256, 257, 259, 261, 262, 265–6, 269, 270, 271, 272, 273, 274, 284, 285, 288, 289, 290, 293, 294, 295, 300, 301, 302, 304, 305, 317, 318, 332, 338, 348, 359, 360, 361, 362, 363, 364, 365, 366, 367, 371, 374, 375, 378–9
Bristol Parkway 294, 295
Bristol Temple Meads 28, 192, 196, 198, 209, 223, 268, 274, 277, 286, 289, 290, 295, 304, 311, 326, 337, 369, 370, 375
'Bristol Belle' 18
'Bristol Pullman' 8, 9, 38, 49, 133, 163, 198, 203, 210, 226, 230, 232, 234, 235, 239, 240, 252, 266, 271, 274, 277, 290, 295, 318, 319, 325, 326, 332, 333, 337, 352, 354, 356, 362, 365, 378
'Bristolian' 35, 93, 200, 289, 318, 366
British Railways (BR) 6, 7, 12, 14, 17, 20, 21, 22, 29, 30, 37, 38, 41, 42–3, 44, 46, 50, 52, 53, 60, 61, 77, 79, 81, 82, 84, 87, 90–1, 95, 103, 116–17, 119, 124, 125–6, 129, 135, 136, 157, 160, 162, 170, 173, 178, 188, 194, 196, 202, 247, 248, 249, 274, 285, 295, 305, 308, 317, 321, 323, 330, 332, 338, 343, 360

383

British Railways Board (BRB) 20, 37, 39, 42, 60, 70, 71, 146, 147, 153, 165, 175, 177, 185, 193, 250, 262–3, 284–5, 288, 290, 300, 323, 330, 359
British Railways Illustrated 7, 71
British Transport Commission 12, 17, 18–19, 28–31, 39, 54, 60, 71, 75, 77, 81, 84, 86, 113, 130, 157, 330
British Transport Films (BTF):
   'Blue Pullman' 8, 46, 47, 66, 73–4, 95, 124, 136, 321, 325, 326, 329
   'Let's Go to Birmingham' 8, 201, 231
British Transport Hotels & Catering Service (BTHCS) ... 12, 123–4, 126–33, 284, 317
BTC Technical Committee 26, 69

'Cambrian Coast Express' 94
'Capitals United Express' 366
Cardiff .... 23, 24, 126, 198, 226, 227, 228, 243, 246, 266, 273, 274, 277, 279, 285, 289, 290, 291, 295, 301, 302, 304, 306, 307, 308, 316, 317, 348, 370; *see also* depot and works: Cardiff Canton
Cardiff Central 289
Castle Bromwich 55, 63
Cheadle Heath 91, 122, 136, 140, 145, 148, 156, 174, 329, 334, 335
'Cheltenham Spa Express' 264, 366
Commonwealth bogie 48, 105, 183, 320
Cox, E. S. 55, 153, 199

Depots and works:
   Aston 68
   Austin Works, Longbridge 51
   Bedford 185
   Birmingham Railway & Carriage Works (BRCW) 12, 37, 40, 326, 329
   Bristol Bath Road 193, 194, 198, 223, 227, 258, 272, 274, 286, 293, 300, 301, 304, 368, 369
   Cardiff Canton 231, 286, 289, 301, 302
   Cricklewood 146, 163, 165, 173, 184, 380–81
   Dan-Y-Graig 312
   Derby 33, 63–4, 68, 72, 95, 136, 150, 152, 162, 167, 169, 173, 177–8, 179, 184, 185, 193–4, 226, 368, 374
   Kentish Town 87
   Laira, Plymouth 193, 194, 271
   Metropolitan-Cammell Carriage & Wagon Co Ltd 14, 103, 113
   Old Oak Common 146, 186, 192–3, 194, 196, 197, 198, 199, 202, 213, 227, 229, 231, 232, 233, 249, 256, 260, 262, 266, 269, 272, 273, 274, 275, 279, 290, 295, 300, 301, 302, 303, 309, 310, 311, 326, 336, 350, 352, 370, 374, 376
   Preston Park Works 162
   Reddish 87, 136, 139, 140, 141, 142, 143, 146, 155, 160, 165, 167, 173, 178, 184, 186, 249, 250, 251, 318, 374
   Swindon Works 18, 19, 20, 24, 30, 39, 51, 95, 101, 162, 163, 192, 193, 194, 198, 226, 227, 229, 230, 231, 233, 234, 247, 249, 260, 264, 265, 266, 268, 273, 274, 290, 301, 302, 303, 307, 310, 319, 323, 354, 357
   Tyseley 68, 192, 193, 194, 210, 231, 232, 249, 300
   Wolverton Carriage Works 36
Derby .... 27, 29, 33, 63–4, 68, 72, 77, 81, 82, 95, 105, 136, 146, 150, 151, 152, 153, 156, 167, 173, 175, 177, 180, 186, 329, 332; *see also* depots and works
Derby North Junction 177, 334, 335–6
Design Magazine 49, 54, 75, 78, 81, 95
Design Panel 16, 28, 37, 42–6, 48–60, 75–7, 86, 95, 132, 199, 291, 320–1, 330–1
Design Research Unit 60, 103
'Devon Belle' 18, 20, 22–3, 249, 253
Diesel-electric Pullman 14, 74, 77, 81, 84, 94, 103, 117, 118, 123, 332, 345, 346, 347
Diesel Multiple Unit (DMU) 6, 9, 16, 17, 18, 19, 20, 24, 25, 26, 27, 28, 31, 32, 35, 37, 39, 48, 60, 93, 97, 115, 130, 139, 155, 173, 180, 185, 194, 199, 224, 232, 247, 260, 264, 267, 272, 289, 290, 312, 318, 319, 331, 343, 352, 370
Cross Country DMU 232

WR set at Bristol Temple Meads awaiting departure for Paddington. In the 'six-foot' are the cables for the shore supply.

Diesel Multiple-Unit Mainline Express
  Services Committee 25–6, 35, 130
Dunbar, A. R. 129, 130–1

East Coast Main Line (ECML) 12, 29, 34, 217,
  319, 322
Eastern Region (ER) 139, 176, 185,
  227, 249–50, 251, 252, 290, 330, 357, 358
Edinburgh 18, 20, 107, 317, 332
Edinburgh Waverley 107
Electrification 17, 21, 23, 29,
  33, 34, 38, 140, 162, 167, 173, 175, 176,
  178, 179, 180, 183, 184–5, 248, 249,
  253, 258, 259, 320, 359, 366
Elliot, Sir John 32, 43, 45–6,
  48, 51–3, 55, 60, 64, 73, 79, 83, 97,
  121, 124, 162, 308, 318, 320, 330
Empty carriage stock (ecs) 12, 44, 140, 143,
  171, 173, 194, 198, 210, 231, 235, 244, 246, 250,
  269, 270, 271, 278, 286, 289, 293, 299, 367
Euston 17, 18, 19,
  20, 22, 27, 29, 38, 44, 48, 50, 71, 126, 136, 169, 175,
  176, 177, 179, 180, 184, 186, 248, 249, 262, 303,
  306, 319, 324, 377, 378, 379, 380, 381, 382
  Collector's Corner 324, 327

General Electric Company (Birmingham) 90, 113
Glasgow 18, 20, 27, 84, 107, 126,
  180, 305, 317, 332
Gloucester 101, 121, 264, 311,
  365, 366
'Golden Arrow' 123, 124, 127, 128,
  165, 318, 370
Grand, Kenneth Walter Chamberlain 48,
  50, 51, 83, 95, 194, 330
Grand National 171, 237, 367, 368
Grey Pullman 285, 288, 289, 307, 372

Harding, (Colonel) F. D. M. 32, 33–4,
  51, 53, 54, 90, 123, 124, 125, 129, 131,
  133, 135, 141, 143, 162, 230, 381
Harrison, J. F. 37, 39, 42, 46, 49, 50–3, 59,
  66, 70, 113, 147, 153, 199
Hole, Frank 33, 129, 317

'Holiday Inn Express' 370
Howe, Jack 6, 26, 28,
  32, 43–6, 49–55, 59, 60, 64–5, 70, 77, 79–81, 83,
  86, 95, 96, 97, 101, 109, 113, 127, 128, 130,
  132, 134, 172, 181, 199, 225, 234,
  241, 265, 272, 320–1, 323, 331
'Hull Pullman' 21

Inter-City 17, 19, 30, 37, 260, 273,
  319, 321, 322
InterCity 125 331
Ironside, Christopher 49, 51, 79, 103

Johnson, A. J. 180, 183
Johnson, George 198
Johnson, Norman 48, 51, 53, 130, 171
Johnson, Sir Henry Cecil 171, 175, 177, 188, 330

Kidderminster Railway Museum 11, 120, 208,
  366, 376
King's Cross 12, 20, 34, 127, 185,
  249–51, 262, 274, 317, 319, 373

Lade, Christopher 74, 124, 131, 141, 326
  Chris Lade Archive 74, 325
'Leeds Belle' 20
Leicester 2, 14, 15,
  18, 27, 36, 38, 63, 73, 79, 81, 82, 87, 90–1, 95, 103,
  105, 126, 130, 133, 136, 137, 142, 144, 145, 150,
  152–3, 155, 156–7, 160, 162, 163, 165, 167,
  170, 171–2, 176, 181, 182, 184, 188, 196,
  201, 277, 325, 332, 334, 335, 381–2
  Leicester London Road 126, 145
'Leicester Belle' 18
Liverpool 17, 20, 30, 126, 164–5,
  169, 171, 175–80, 183, 188, 229, 320, 370
Liverpool Lime Street 38, 171, 179, 325, 368
LMR Board 73, 169, 178–9
London Midland & Scottish Railway (LMS) 21,
  27, 60, 96
London Midland Region (LMR) 13, 14, 28,
  48, 60, 61, 81, 90, 91, 103, 113,
  119, 134–89, 317, 330, 359

London & North Eastern Railway (LNER) 21, 27, 29, 52, 63, 71, 96, 250, 330
London & North Western Railway (LNWR) 29, 163, 167, 175, 176, 183–5, 262, 295, 335

Manchester 2, 4, 14, 15, 16, 17, 21, 22, 23, 26, 28, 29, 33, 34, 35, 36, 38, 39, 48, 61, 62, 63–4, 70, 73, 74, 75, 81, 82, 86, 87, 90–1, 93, 94, 95, 116, 122, 124, 126, 127, 129, 131, 135–6, 138, 139, 140, 141, 143, 144–5, 147–50, 152, 155–7, 160–3, 165, 167, 169, 171–4, 178–80, 182, 184–6, 187, 188, 200, 249, 277, 317, 328, 332, 358
Manchester Central 14, 28, 29, 36, 48, 64, 73, 74, 81, 90, 91, 103, 122, 128, 135, 136, 140, 141, 143, 145, 148, 155, 156, 173, 179, 186, 196, 325, 328, 335
Manchester Piccadilly 4, 38, 320
Manchester Trafford Park 143
'Manchester Belle' 18, 20
'Manchester Pullman' 4, 90, 93, 152, 252
Marylebone 8, 10, 14, 20, 28, 44, 71–3, 74, 81, 82, 127, 149, 192, 193, 194, 262, 285, 321, 380
Marylebone Road, British Railways Headquarters ('The Kremlin') 12, 37, 48, 71, 72, 165, 184, 194–5, 321
Metropolitan-Cammell/Metro-Cammell............ 6, 11, 14, 28, 36, 37, 39, 41, 42–3, 46, 48, 49, 50–5, 59, 62–3, 64, 65, 68, 70, 74, 75, 77, 81, 84, 86, 90, 96, 103, 104, 113, 117, 118, 127, 152, 172, 193, 194, 231, 235, 290, 291, 305, 316, 319, 321, 325, 331, 354, 378
Factory at Saltley 41, 54, 55, 62, 63, 68, 103
Metro-Schlieren bogie 28, 46, 47, 48, 86, 105, 113, 117, 121, 151, 172, 286, 319–20, 381
'Midland Pullman'.......................... 2, 4, 8, 9, 19, 28, 29, 38, 45, 48, 55, 64, 65, 66, 73, 74, 86, 90–1, 94, 114, 116–17, 119, 122, 128, 135, 136, 138, 142–4, 147–9, 155–6, 157, 160, 162, 163, 166, 167, 172–3, 174, 180, 182, 186, 187, 227, 229, 256, 259, 264, 272, 274, 306, 318, 325–9, 334–5, 337, 352, 354, 357, 368, 373, 378, 379–81
Ministry of Supply 39

Ministry of Transport 190, 191, 197, 247
Ministry of Works 60
Modernisation Plan, The (1955) 5, 12, 15, 16–17, 27, 28, 29, 33, 34, 37, 43, 60, 96, 124, 319
Morris, E. J. (Ted) 129, 250, 317, 330
Motor Brake First (MBF) 12, 13, 291, 305
Motor Brake Second (MBS) 12, 13

Nanking Blue (livery) 8, 16, 37, 60, 82, 83, 103, 155, 199, 217, 235, 269, 272, 273, 274, 285, 305, 306, 312, 323, 324, 328, 329, 368–9
National Archives, The (Kew) 9, 23, 28, 34, 40, 47, 48, 59, 64, 70, 71, 81, 83, 105, 120, 133, 170, 185, 197, 299, 300, 321
National Railway Museum, The (NRM) 9, 74, 262, 325
National Union of Railwaymen (NUR) 23, 29, 37, 61, 64, 82, 123–4, 126, 127, 129–31, 133, 135, 157
Newcastle 34, 127, 180
Nock, O. S. 20, 155, 201, 332–7
North Eastern Region (NER).................... 20, 21, 24, 250, 251, 252, 345
Nottingham 2, 17, 19, 27, 29, 38, 79, 126, 130, 133, 140, 144, 146, 155–7, 160–4, 165, 170, 173, 180, 181–2, 184, 186, 188, 196, 201, 277, 317
Nottingham Midland 8, 140

Old Oak Common, see depots and works
Oxford 252, 257, 259, 261, 266, 285, 301, 358, 363, 364
'Oxford Pullman'................................ 252, 352, 357, 379

Paddington....................... 14, 16, 17, 22, 23, 24, 25, 27, 28, 34, 35, 36, 38, 39, 44, 48, 50, 51, 63, 71, 81, 93–4, 101, 103, 106, 127, 131, 181, 184, 190, 192, 194, 195, 196–9, 199–201, 203, 213, 215, 217, 218, 220, 223, 224, 225, 227, 228–32, 233, 234, 235, 236, 238, 239, 240, 242, 248, 249, 252, 253, 254, 257, 261, 262, 263, 264, 265, 266, 267, 269, 272, 273, 274, 277, 279, 282, 284–5, 286, 288–9, 290, 291, 293, 294, 295, 296, 297, 299, 300, 301, 302, 303, 307, 308, 317, 318–19, 325, 328, 332, 336, 354, 357, 358, 359, 360, 361, 366, 367, 369, 370, 378

Pearson, Arthur J. 39
Phillips Committee 29, 34–5, 39
Phillips, H. H. (Herbert) 25–7, 32, 36, 39, 130
Plymouth 257, 269, 270, 271, 278,
299, 366, 367, 370
Portman-Dixon, E. K. 32, 33, 39, 129
Pullman miscellaneous:
    Air-conditioning 30, 35, 46, 70, 73,
77, 81, 84, 87, 97, 100, 107, 112–13,
135, 146, 163, 176, 238, 267, 284
    Auxiliary engine 30, 40, 42, 53, 65,
68, 71, 90, 104, 107, 113, 115, 116, 117, 135, 151,
163, 176, 178, 231, 264, 275, 304, 343, 346, 365;
see also Rolls-Royce
    Auxiliary generator 111–12, 117, 177
    Coat of arms 6, 44, 51, 82, 86,
103, 262, 306
    Dining car 22, 61, 183, 290
    Heating and ventilation 6, 44, 66, 67,
104, 111
    Hot water supply 66, 67, 90
    Lapel badge 14, 156
    Lavatory compartments 47, 54, 67, 77,
111, 114, 122, 201, 272, 343, 349–51
    Luggage compartments 106, 109, 116
    Menus 32, 65, 125, 127, 225, 262,
305, 325, 328, 368
    Passenger saloon 106, 110, 218
    Restaurant Car Service 32, 33
    Signage and branding 31, 32, 101, 289,
325, 327
        Triang-Hornby 8, 304, 327
    Supplements 23, 257, 360, 362
    Table lamps 4, 45, 46, 52, 67,
79, 83, 104, 111, 123, 267, 286, 358
    Tickets 90, 91, 143, 149, 151,
161, 182, 272
    Timetables 29, 157, 163, 195, 200, 325
    Windscreen 231, 268, 312
    Wipers 2, 71, 114, 306
Pullman Car Company 23, 33, 42, 43,
45, 52, 54, 60, 90, 124, 128–31, 157,
230, 317, 328, 343, 352, 367
Pullman Society, The 11, 34, 123

'Queen of Scots' 20, 21, 34, 317
Railway Gazette 8, 14, 28, 42, 84,
100, 103, 135, 153, 162, 317
Railway Magazine 8, 155, 227,
304, 305, 306, 307, 311, 352, 354
Railway Observer 8, 73, 91, 95, 158,
217, 273, 290, 303, 309, 312, 357
Ratter, John 19, 39, 175, 176, 177, 182, 320
Robertson, Sir Brian 28–9, 59, 71, 124,
188, 322
Robertson, D. J. C. 118–19
Robson, A. E. 49, 60, 65, 66, 113, 194
Rolls-Royce 12, 90, 148, 198, 263, 279, 304
    Engine 65, 112, 113, 162, 176, 231, 291, 305;
see also Pullman miscellaneous: auxiliary engine
Royston, J. 61, 90, 91, 379

Schlieren bogie, see Metro-Schlieren bogie
Scottish Region (ScR) 12, 20, 21, 252
Scrapyards:
    Bird's, Cardiff 306, 307, 312, 316, 317
    G. Cohen, Morriston 306, 307, 309, 316, 317, 321
    T. W. Ward, Briton Ferry 306, 307,
311, 312, 316, 324, 377
Severn Tunnel Junction 197, 223, 295, 370
Sidings:
    Briton Ferry 311, 312, 377
    Cannock Road (Wolverhampton) 192, 194,
196, 197, 232, 234, 235, 372
    Dr Day's (Bristol) 35, 192, 193, 194,
196, 198, 218, 270, 293, 372
    Etches Park, Derby 165, 352
    Maliphant (Swansea) 192, 196, 266,
272, 273, 289, 370, 372
    Ninian Park (Cardiff) 306
Silkstream Junction, Hendon 139, 160, 380
'South Wales Pullman' 9, 23–5,
26, 31, 32, 81, 123, 124, 126, 127, 131, 133, 178,
194, 195, 223, 224, 227–32, 234, 235, 236, 240,
246, 254, 273–4, 289, 294, 295, 301, 319,
352, 354, 357, 362, 370, 377, 378;
see also 'Swansea Pullman'

Southern Region (SR) 18, 20, 27, 34, 113, 123–5, 165, 172, 228, 230, 252–3, 261, 279, 282, 319, 330, 331, 332, 354, 370
SS *Northern Star* 44
St Pancras 2, 14, 15, 16, 17, 27, 28, 29, 33, 34, 38, 48, 61, 63, 64, 70, 73, 74, 81, 82, 89, 90, 91, 93, 95, 103, 122, 124, 126, 127, 128, 135–6, 137, 139, 140, 143, 144, 145, 149–8, 160–74, 178, 180–6, 188, 196, 249, 263, 277, 317, 318, 319, 329, 332, 335, 381–2
Summerson, T. H. 46, 48, 50, 52–3, 82, 218
Swansea 18, 23, 63, 192, 196, 224, 227, 229, 232, 240, 246, 248, 259, 266, 273, 288–9, 291, 294–5, 301, 306, 307, 308, 312, 318, 319, 367, 368, 370, 372, 374
'Swansea Belle' 23
'Swansea Pullman' .... 10, 289, 295; see also 'South Wales Pullman'
Swindon .... 18, 19, 20, 24, 30, 39, 51, 81, 95, 1101, 162, 163, 169, 191, 192–3, 194, 195, 198, 202, 203, 210, 225, 226, 227, 229, 230, 231, 233, 234, 235, 239, 247, 249, 256, 260, 264–9, 273, 274, 285, 286, 290, 294, 295, 301–3, 307, 310, 319, 323, 324, 325, 333, 337, 352, 354, 357, 370, 371, 374, 377; see also depots and works: Swindon

'Thanet Belle' 18, 20
Traffic Survey Group (TSG) 34–5
Train ferry 231
Trains Illustrated 8, 38, 55, 59, 63, 79, 127, 209, 352, 357
'Trans European Express' 25, 31, 77, 84
Tunnels
    Dove Holes Tunnel 70, 334, 335
    Haverstock Tunnel 146, 163
    Severn Tunnel 273, 274, 294, 311
Tyseley Railway Museum 11

Upstone, Maurice 133, 381

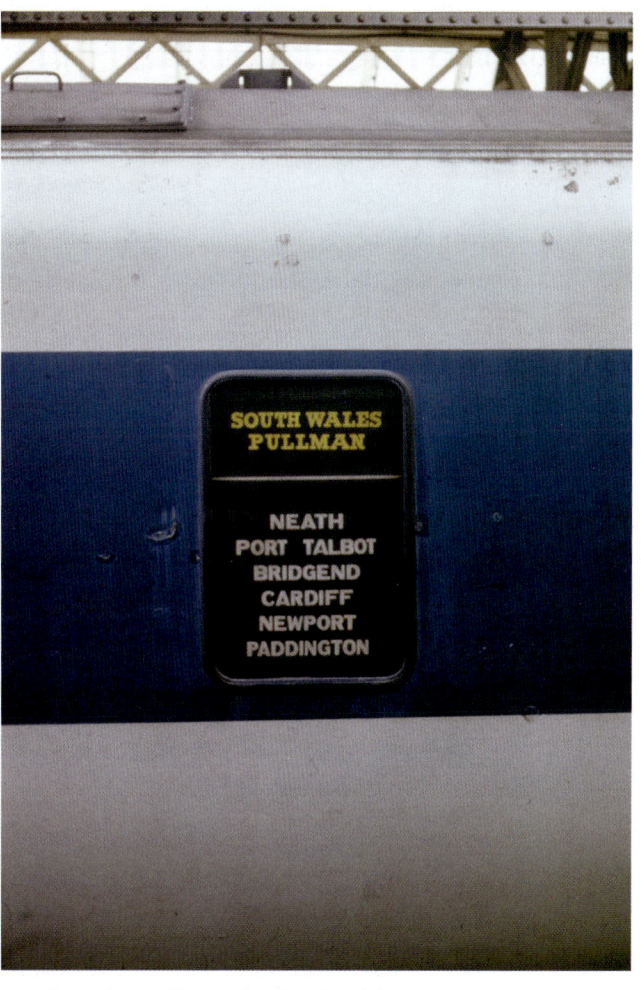

Viney, Bert 124, 131, 141

South Wales Pullman destination blind.

Wansbrough-Jones, Major General 48, 50, 131
West Coast 17, 34, 38, 126, 248
'Western Pullman' 8, 45
Western Queen 231, 354
Western Region (WR) 7, 8, 12, 13, 14, 23, 26, 28, 29, 32, 35, 36, 39, 48, 49–50, 51, 55, 59–60, 63, 67, 70, 81–4, 86, 87, 102, 103, 107, 108, 115, 118, 119, 130, 131, 132, 139, 160, 163–4, 170, 174, 175, 176, 190–247, 254, 257, 263, 265, 266, 267, 272, 277, 284, 286, 288, 289, 293, 300, 303, 305, 307, 317, 318, 325, 327–8, 330, 332, 333, 338, 352–8, 359–66, 367–8, 369, 370, 371, 374, 376
Williams, George 6, 26, 43, 45, 49, 50, 51, 52–3, 55, 59, 60, 65, 75, 79, 81, 87, 107, 120, 132, 185, 199, 321, 330, 331
'Wolverhampton Belle' 18

'Yorkshire Pullman' 21, 185

389

Blue Pullman in the 21st Century

Just as we were going to print, Locomotive Services Limited announced a new charter train many railway enthusiasts have dreamt of for years. An Inter City 125 HST set repainted into in the guise of the Blue Pullman.

Using ex EMT VP185 engined power cars and ex GWR first class Mk 3 coaches, the work is being carried out by Arlington Fleet Services at Eastleigh Works. Powerful new headlights will be fitted to avoid the need for a 'custard dipped' nose. The inaugural journey is intended to run in late 2020 and will follow as much of the route of the Midland Pullman as still exists from London St Pancras as far as Ambergate before necessarily then diverting via Edale to Manchester Piccadilly.

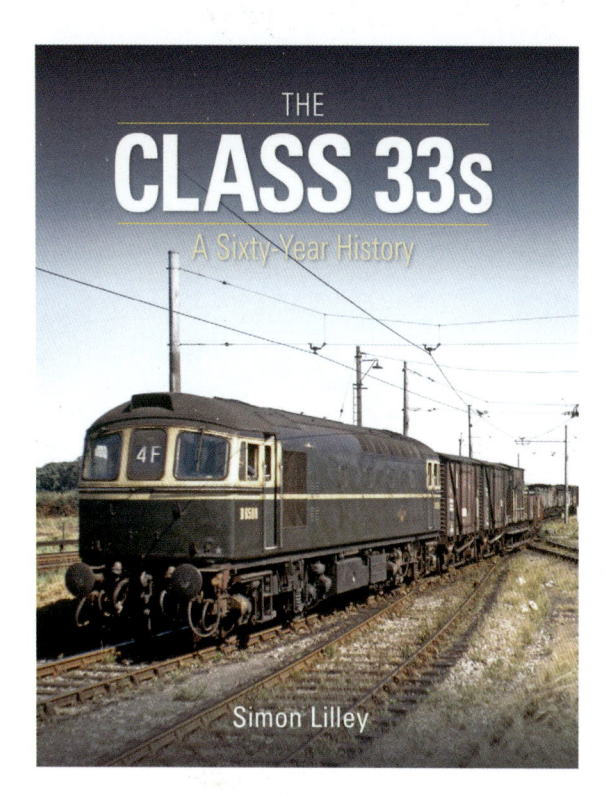

The Class 33s: A Sixty-Year History

Simon Lilley

1960 saw the first BRCW Ltd Type 3s, later TOPS Class 33, enter service on the Southern Region. The 98 locomotives were ordered as part of the Kent coast modernisation scheme. The final 12 locos had bodies 7 inches less wide than the rest of the class to allow them to work through the narrow tunnels between Tunbridge Wells and Hastings. For many years they were the mainstay of the Southern Region's locomotive fleet and were widely used across the south and west of England and beyond.

The Class 33s is the first detailed history of the class for 30 years, telling the story of these popular and successful locomotives from inception, through their design and operations to withdrawal from service. It draws on original source material from a number of archives and sheds new light on many aspects of these locomotives over their 60 years of service. This book is illustrated throughout with many photographs, almost all of which are published for the first time.

This is a welcome reappraisal of a long lived and respected class which will be of interest to modern traction enthusiasts and those modelling the post steam era on BR.

ISBN: 9781910809662
Hardcover, 224 pages, £25

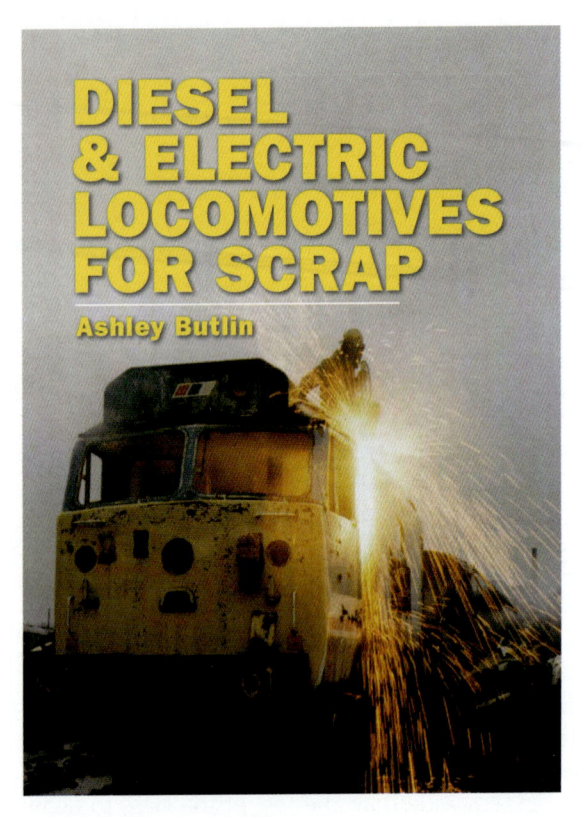

Diesel and Electric Locomotives for Scrap

Ashley Butlin

Diesel and Electric Locomotives for Scrap presents a detailed survey of all diesel and electric locomotives scrapped on Britain's railways since the start of British Railways in 1948 to the time of this book's original release in 2015. While it does not include DMUs and EMUs, the book lists each locomotive class separately, and within each class lists each locomotive built with details of every locomotive scrapped, i.e. when withdrawn and where sent for scrapping.

Comprehensively illustrated throughout in colour and black and white, showing examples of each class recorded when scrapped, the book also contains a separate section showing all preserved heritage diesel and electric locomotives on Britain's railways today.

Author Ashley Butlin has compiled this wealth of information intending this book to be as near a complete record of all diesel and electric locomotives scrapped in this period as possible. As such, it will be the ultimate work of reference for enthusiasts of modern traction.

ISBN: 9780860936701
Hardcover, 256 pages, £35